THE MODERN LIBRARY

OF THE WORLD'S BEST BOOKS

INTRODUCTION
TO ARISTOTLE

The publishers will be pleased to send, upon request, an illustrated folder setting forth the purpose and scope of THE MODERN LIBRARY, *and listing each volume in the series. Every reader of books will find titles he has been looking for, handsomely printed, in definitive editions, and at an unusually low price.*

INTRODUCTION
TO
ARISTOTLE

EDITED, WITH A GENERAL INTRODUCTION AND

INTRODUCTIONS TO THE PARTICULAR WORKS

BY RICHARD McKEON

Dean of the Division of the Humanities, University of Chicago

THE MODERN LIBRARY · NEW YORK

THE MODERN LIBRARY
is published by RANDOM HOUSE, INC.
BENNETT CERF · DONALD S. KLOPFER

Manufactured in the United States of America by H. Wolff

Contents

Preface

IT IS TRUE of Aristotle, as it is in the case of most philosophers, that the reading of his works is the only introduction to his philosophy. Yet some preliminaries to that
introduction are needed, since his works are not easily
accessible, and, when they are accessible, the place of any
one work in the complex system of his philosophy is not
discernible from reading it alone. The significance of what
Aristotle says in development or support of a theory is
usually clarified by the theories expounded in related sciences. This Introduction to Aristotle is a presentation in
which Aristotle is permitted to speak for himself in the
context of a sketched scheme of the relation of what he
says in one treatise to what he says elsewhere. Four treatises
are reproduced complete: the Posterior Analytics, On the
Soul, the Nicomachean Ethics, and the Poetics; they are
supplemented by complete books from three other treatises: one book from the Physics, two from the Metaphysics, and two from the Politics. The seven introductions
which precede these seven works place them in their contexts by describing their relations to other works or parts
of works, their place in the scheme of the Aristotelian sciences, and the fashion in which the subjects treated in the
sciences they expound may be considered in the approaches
proper to other sciences in the system. The General Introduction supplies the essential information concerning Aristotle, his times, and his influence, and fills in some of
the background and interrelations of the special introductions.

Grateful acknowledgment is hereby extended to the Oxford University Press for permission to reprint the translation of the works of Aristotle prepared under the editorship of W. D. Ross.

R. McK.

General Introduction

by RICHARD MCKEON

1. The Life and Times of Aristotle

ARISTOTLE was born in 384/3 B.C. in the little town of Stagira on the eastern coast of the peninsula of Chalcidice in Thrace. His father, Nicomachus, was court physician and, according to tradition, friend of Amyntas II, king of Macedon and father of Philip the Great. Nicomachus died while Aristotle was still a child, and he was raised by Proxenus of Atarneus, whose son Nicanor was later adopted, in turn, by Aristotle and was married to Aristotle's daughter. In 368/7, at the age of eighteen, Aristotle was sent to Athens, where he remained in close association with the Academy of Plato for twenty years, until the death of Plato in 348/7. After Plato's death he left Athens and, together with Xenocrates, visited the court of Hermias, a former member of the Academy who had become tyrant of Assos and Atarneus in Mysia in Asia Minor. Aristotle married Hermias' niece Pythias, and he probably taught at a kind of Academic center in Assos. Somewhat later he went to Mitylene in Lesbos, where he doubtless engaged in biological research. In 343/2, on the invitation of Philip of Macedon, he became tutor to Alexander. The instruction probably extended only to 340, when Alexander was appointed regent for his father, but his tutor did not return to Athens until 335/4, a year after the death of Philip.

The next twelve years Aristotle devoted with extraordinary industry to the establishment of a school, the Lyceum, to the institution and pursuit of a program of investigation, speculation, and teaching in almost every branch of knowledge, and to the composition of all, or most, or at least the more scientific portions, of those of his writings which are now extant. When Alexander died in 323, Aristotle's Macedonian connections brought him under suspicion and he fled Athens lest, as he is said to have remarked, the Athenians sin twice against philosophy. An accusation of impiety was brought against him, not unlike those which had been brought against Anaxagoras and Protagoras or that on which Socrates had been condemned. The specific charge was that he had instituted a private cult in the memory of his friend Hermias, since he had erected a statue to him at Delphi and had composed a poem, in what was alleged to be the manner of a paean, in his honor. He took refuge under the protection of Antipater, viceroy to Alexander, in Chalcis in Euboea, where he died in 322 a short time before the death of Demosthenes.

Most of the scant information that has come to us concerning the life of Aristotle is suggestive, but there is little positive evidence, in his works or in external sources, to support inferences concerning the formative forces that influenced his work. Since his father was a physician, he was a hereditary member of the guild of Asclepiads, and it is tempting to speculate on the youthful beginnings of his interest in biological investigations and his possible training in dissection, pharmacology, and medicine; but his father died when he was young, and there is no evidence in his works of an early training in medicine. He spent twenty years in the Academy; that period has been used as evidence of a close association with Plato which resulted in a deep impress on his thought, but it has also been argued, by scholars like Burnet and Taylor, that Plato was not in the Academy at the time of Aristotle's arrival, that he was away for repeated and lengthy periods during Aristotle's stay, and that Aristotle's knowledge of Platonism was acquired at second-hand and was never accurate. We do not know how he spent his time at the Academy: there is an ancient tradition that he undertook the teaching of rhetoric in opposition to the flourishing school of Isocrates; it seems probable that he participated in the biological research which was flourishing at the Academy; the fragments of his early dialogues suggest that he wrote works intended to popularize Platonism. His reasons for leaving Athens on the death of Plato can only be conjectured: he may have been dissatisfied with the prospects of the Academy under Plato's nephew and successor Speusippus, who seemed to Aristotle to have reduced metaphysics to mathematics, or Speusippus may have charged Aristotle and Xenocrates to open a branch of the Academy in Asia Minor. He probably taught in Assos; there is evidence in his biological writings that he collected specimens of animals and fish in Lesbos and in the waters adjacent to the island; he doubtless began the composition of some of the works that have survived during his travels.

In spite of the fact that the relation between Aristotle and Alexander has been a tempting subject for speculation since Plutarch and that the ambition to influence kings through philosophy was deeply implanted in the Academy, there is no evidence that Aristotle had any influence on the moral ideals or political ambitions of his royal pupil, and Aristotle in turn seems to have taken no account of the effects of the ideal of world empire on the forms of political association and on the possible survival of the Greek city state. There is good reason to doubt the accuracy of the legend that Alexander sent records of astronomical observations and biological specimens to his former master from the East. His writings contain interesting sidelights on the methods and adjuncts of teaching in the Lyceum, but the relation of his writings to the work of the Lyceum, and even the order of their composition, are far from clear. Since they are obviously not "published" works, it has been supposed that they are "lecture-notes," notes of students, or records of research and thought, brought periodically up to date, for consultation by advanced students. Since the structure of his doctrines is complex, and since he was long associated with the Academy and later a persistent critic of the doctrines of the Academy, his works have been chopped into pieces by critics seeking an evolution in them from Platonic idealism to scientific empiricism.

The period of Aristotle's manhood coincided with the reduction of the Greek city-states to the hegemony of Macedonia and the twelve or thirteen years of his work in the Lyceum with the campaigns of Alexander the Great. Hermias was doubtless a kind of advance-guard of Philip's projects against the Persians; Philip's choice of Aristotle as tutor to Alexander associated him closely with the political fortunes of Macedonia; and Alexander doubtless suspected him of complicity in the plot against his life for which Aristotle's nephew Callisthenes was executed; it is highly probable that the Lyceum received support and endowments from Callisthenes, Antipater, or even Alexander. In an important sense an epoch of Greek history was brought to a close when Alexander, Aristotle, and Demosthenes all died within somewhat more than a year.

The life of Aristotle was thus spent in a period which has seemed confused and dim to historians who have learned from Demosthenes to see it as the time of the loss of Greek liberties and the decline of Greek ideals; it has seemed a period of stirring action which came close to the fulfillment of an ambitious hope to those who see in the growth of panhellenism preached by Isocrates the beginnings of more stable political organizations and in the exploits of Alexander the spread of Greek ideals. Aristotle spent a large part of his life as an alien in Athens, and he seems to have been unsympathetic with, if not unmindful of, the ambitions of Alexander. Contemporary political events and social changes left few marks on his political and moral philosophy, and the search for effects of social conditions in his metaphysics and in his contributions to science has led only to speculative generalizations concerning the influence of environment on thought: to the conclusion that the existence of classes in society suggested hierarchies in his conception of the universe, that slave labor led him to neglect the mechanical arts and prefer the theoretic to the practical sciences, that his theories were therefore verbal rather than based on the resources of experience, and that his physical principles reflected his conception of political rule. Apart from such speculations, it is clear that the peace which was forced on Athens by Macedonian domination permitted Aristotle to organize a course of studies and to initiate a vast scheme of research into the history of political organizations, of science, and philosophy—the study of constitutions of Greek states, of the history of mathematics and medicine, and of the opinions of philosophers—as well as into the natural history of minerals, plants, and animals, and to lay the foundations thereby for one of the first attempts at an encyclopedic organization of human knowledge.

2. *Scientific Method in the Philosophy of Aristotle*

Aristotle's philosophy consists in his contributions to the sciences and his reflections on the interrelations among the sciences, for even metaphysics, which he called "first philosophy," was one of the theoretic sciences, and its subject matter included the study of the principles of the other sciences. The interest in the structure and system of the sciences leads Aristotle into frequent inquiries into the origins of the sciences, both in the historical sense of tracing the development of particular doctrines or the course of investigation of particular problems and in the formal sense of setting forth the requirements of scientific inquiry and proof.

In many of his important works, as in the *Physics, On the Soul,* and the *Metaphysics,* he discusses other men's theories and conjectures as introduction to his own formulation of the problems and his determination of the principles of a given science. Among other such histories he traces the development of logical theory and scientific method. The history is short, since Aristotle was convinced that he had himself originated most of what was sound and precise in logic, and it is schematic, since the brief development of logic led to an opposition of devices and concepts that are reconciled in his own inquiry into method.

Some progress had been made in the use of scientific method by the scientific investigations of the atomists, Leucippus and Democritus, the definitions of the Pythagoreans, the logical inquiries of Socrates into the nature of definition and inductive arguments, and the dialectical devices and theories of Plato. These developments, however, illustrated two extremes of method: the atomists reduced scientific explanation to the discovery of the material parts of the object to be explained and the dialecticians gave explanations which were inapplicable to the changing things of experience. In both approaches the true scientific method was distorted, and Aristotle's conception of scientific method is designed therefore to provide both the treatment of first principles which was inadequate in the practice of the atomists and the applications to motion and material things which were inaccurate in the theory of the dialecticians. Its novelties center about the treatment of causes, by which the application of principles to things is insured, and the analysis of terms and propositions, by which the accuracy of statement and inference is ascertained.

This contrast suggests an opposition of kinds of causal explanation, for the atomists had relied wholly on material causes for their investigations and the dialecticians had tended to an exclusive concern with formal causes. Yet to explain natural substances and motions, consideration of the efficient and final causes were of crucial importance, and Aristotle found only little and confused evidence of their use by his predecessors. He therefore used the four causes to isolate particular processes and problems from the continuum of nature, which he conceived to be unbroken from the functions of inorganic elements to the most complex functions of the human organism and from the center of the universe to the most distant heavenly body. Discovery of the causes supplies the first principles of the sciences and the connecting links of scientific demonstration, and the use of the causes therefore permitted him to differentiate a scheme of distinct sciences with distinguishable subject matters, principles, and methods, where Democritus and Plato had, according to Aristotle, only a single, unified science. Moreover, since scientific method depends on the discovery of principles which state causes, scientific proof could be distinguished from dialectic (which depends on the statement of opinions) and from eristic (which seeks only success in argument).

The peculiarities of words, thoughts, and things must therefore be separated in the interest of securing an adequate statement of causes in scientific proof, and once those distinctions have been made, the actual development of an argument can be stated formally, apart from consideration of the truth of the premisses on which it depends. Aristotle was consequently able to construct the elaborate analysis of syllogisms as a relation among terms, of propositions as kinds of predication of terms, and of immediate inference among propositions, and of the categories as simple terms, that has formed the traditional ground of what has been called the "Aristotelian logic." The logic of syllogisms, propositions, and terms, however, depends not merely on the formal relations that are exemplified in the statement of proof but on the possibility of discovering causes, which can be stated as connectives among terms only because they are links among the phenomena of nature. For knowledge and inquiry depend both on the prior knowledge of the inquirer or learner and on the existent state of things.

3. Experience, Art, and Science

Aristotle was convinced that all knowledge is derived from sensation and that the mind in its knowledge becomes in a sense all things, without however reducing knowledge to the motion of material particles reacting to stimuli, as Democritus did, or transforming things into changeless ideas, as Plato did. The psychological functions and intellectual habits of man introduce differentiations which are essential to the sciences as we know them, for science itself, as something known, is a habit of the mind, and Aristotle is therefore fond of tracing the steps of transition from sensation, to memory, to experience (which is developed from repeated memories), to art and science. So far as action is concerned, experience is not inferior to art, and men of experience succeed even better than those who have theory without experience, since experience is knowledge of individuals, art of universals, and actions and productions are concerned with the individual. But the man of experience knows only the fact, while art and science supply the causes, art for the processes of action and production, science for the understanding of being and natural change. The universal, which is first isolated in the recognition of the one in the many in experience, is thus the basis both of the skill of the artist and the knowledge of the scientist.

These distinctions are important since animals other than man live by appearances and memories and have but little of connected experience; but the human race lives also by art and reasoning. As possessions of the mind, art and practical wisdom, the virtues of making and doing, are distinguished by their concern with process and action from the other intellectual virtues—science, intuitive reason, and philosophic wisdom—which treat of the invariable. Psychological functions are likewise differentiated as they bear on practical or theoretic considerations: deliberation concerning actions to be taken is distinct from inquiry into the nature of things, and understanding of the affairs of men is distinct from opinion and scientific knowledge. But the possibility of knowledge of any kind, theoretic or practical, depends on the discovery of causes and on the transition from individual things perceived to universals understood. This is not a transition from things to constructs or inventions of the mind, but rather, as Aristotle likes to put it, from things prior and better known to us to things prior and better known in nature. Our reason is related to things best known in nature as the eyes of bats are to the blaze of day, and we therefore do not perceive first principles immediately, nor are they innate in our souls, but we proceed from the half-light of sensation to the principles of science which, once grasped, are better known than the conclusions which flow from them or the experiences from which they were derived. We get to know first principles, therefore, by induction, but they are apprehended as principles by intuition. In an inchoate sense they are present in sensation, for though the act of sense-perception is of the particular, its content is universal, as for example, "man" rather than any particular man; and they are isolated in the repetitions of experience—in induction, abstraction, and analogy—until they are perceived as principles in intuition. Moreover, as the universal is present and is fixed in the experience of individuals, so too particulars emerge at each point at which thought processes deal with ultimates—not only in sense-perception and imagination which treat of particulars of existence, but in judgment, understanding, and practical wisdom which treat of the particulars of practical decisions, and finally in intuitive reason which is concerned with the ultimates in both directions, with first terms and last, for the intuitive reason presupposed by demonstrations grasps the unchangeable and first terms, while the intuitive reason involved in practical reasoning grasps the last and variable fact.

4. The Theoretic Sciences

The differentiation among the sciences which have as their end simply to know depends on differences found in the things which constitute their subject matter. One large class of things exists "by nature," and such natural or physical things are distinguished from the products of art by the possession of an internal principle of motion and rest. They move and remain stationary in place according to fixed principles; some of them grow and decrease in size; some change in the qualities they possess and are generated and pass away. These natural things include compound inorganic bodies and their constitutive elements, plants and their parts, animals and their parts: all such objects are studied in the sciences of physics, which are in turn differentiated into the various subdivisions of physics strictly conceived, including astronomy, chemistry, and meteorology, as well as biology, and psychology, according to kinds of natures and motions. In general the concern of physics with "natures" signifies that its subject matter is never purely formal, but always includes matter and motion, and that the principles of the physical sciences are arrived at by induction from the changing things of experience. The surfaces and volumes, lines, points, and numbers, which are the subject matter of mathematics, are contained, like the properties studied by the physicist, in physical bodies, and indeed they are treated, as physical properties, in the various branches of physics. The mathematician, however, treats them differently from the physicist, for although they cannot exist apart from matter and motion in fact, they can be abstracted in thought and treated separately in science. The possibility of mathematics depends on this peculiarity which adapts quantity alone among the properties of things to abstract treatment. Finally, those forms which not only can be known apart but also exist apart from matter and motion are studied in First Philosophy or metaphysics. The concern of metaphysics with being as such, therefore, involves inquiry not only into the ultimate principles of knowledge and the ultimate causes of existence and change, but also into those principles of order which determine the interrelations of the universe, among these prime movers, God being the supreme and unmoved mover, exempt from the mutability of which he is the source. The general differentiation of forms according to their existence and intelligibility in matter or apart from matter determines the three theoretic sciences, Physics, Mathematics, and Metaphysics.

Aristotle's conception of substance is intimately interwoven in both his scheme of the sciences and his projection of the methods proper to the sciences. The objects which are studied in the physical sciences "have natures" or internal principles of motion which determine inorganic, organic, and psychological change. Chance and art are both distinguished from nature as external principles of change, one with and the other without intelligent planning. The inquiries of physics are limited to the connections of things with the processes and properties consequent on their natures as distinguished from the chance interconnections in which they may become involved or the artful contrivances which may supplement or modify what is natural. Metaphysics is concerned with being as such, and the necessity of differentiating being from what is contributed by the mind and by the manner of speech in inquiry into being and of separating what is essential to the conception and statement of truth from what conception and statement are true of, leads to the conclusion that that which is most truly is substance. Aristotle begins his investigation of substances with the natural things studied in physics—animals and plants and their parts, the elements and their compounds—and grants that if these were the only beings, or if indeed these did not imply beings of another kind, there would be no need for a separate science of metaphysics, since this inquiry would be a branch of physics. He finds evidence for a third kind of substance in addition to the two kinds of sensible substances—eternal and perishable—exemplified in that list, and the peculiar mark of both his metaphysics and his physics is therefore to be found in the central place occupied in each by a non-sensible substance. Mathematics, finally, is distinct from both physics and metaphysics. It is not, as it has been conceived in the Platonic tradition, the basic theory on which physics is built, but rather the study of that one property of sensible things, quantity, which yields an order and matter for scientific inquiry abstracted from the natural connections and motions of things. It is not, again in distinction from the Platonic tradition, dependent on the supposition of mathematical entities existent somehow apart from the things of experience, but derives its subject matter by abstraction from sense-experience.

All three of the theoretic sciences treat, despite differences in their subject matters, of that which can not be other than it is, that is, of the necessary rather than the contingent. It is by virtue of this characteristic in their subject matter that their propositions are necessary and not merely probable. Necessity, however, may be either "simple" or "hypothetical." Only those broad and universal considerations which are treated in metaphysics or those properties that are involved in the essence or definition of a thing follow by simple or absolute necessity. Necessity is hypothetical in both mathematics and physics, but the manner in which hypothetical reasoning yields necessity is precisely opposite in the two sciences. In mathematics if the premises are granted or are established, the argument can be shown to follow necessarily, but the premises are not necessarily true if the conclusion which is shown to follow from them is known to be true. In physics if a process or motion has been completed, it can be shown that the antecedent steps must necessarily have occurred, but it does not follow from the existence of the antecedent stages that the effect must necessarily follow. Necessity in metaphysics must be sought in the essence, in mathematics in the postulates, in physics in the matter; in all three the problem of discovering the necessary is a problem of definition and of the causes.

5. The Practical and Productive Sciences

The practical sciences are differentiated from the theoretic by their purposes or ends, but differences may be detected in their subject matters as a consequence of this difference of purposes and in the scientific methods appropriate to their study. The end of the theoretic sciences is knowledge, and the subject matters which are investigated and the truths which are sought in them do not depend on our action or our volition. The end of the practical sciences, on the other hand, is not merely to know, but rather to act in the light of knowledge: it is not the purpose of political science, for example, to know the good, but to make men good. Aristotle sometimes isolates the practical sciences in general by this contrast to the theoretic sciences, and some-times when his attention is turned to the differences among the ends of human purposes and operations, he differentiates the processes of making, which depend on an external matter, from those of doing, and thereby separates the arts from the virtues or the productive sciences from the practical sciences in the strict or narrow sense.

The differences between the subject matter and method of the practical sciences and those of the theoretic sciences may all be related to this difference of purpose. Since the end of the practical sciences is action, they have to do with potentialities, situations, and things which may be modified by human intelligence and volition. Their subject matter is things which may be other than they are, that is, contingent things as contrasted to necessary connections and to things which cannot be otherwise than they are found to be in the theoretic sciences. The inquirer in the practical sciences will therefore not seek the precision which is appropriate to mathematics or the other theoretic sciences. His definitions will be different, for his inquiries are not concerned with a "nature" or a "substance." The fashion in which a man grows, reproduces, nourishes himself, perceives or thinks may be studied as functions of his nature, but his virtues, the political and social institutions under which he lives, and the artificial objects he produces and appreciates depend on the habits induced by actions he has performed and influences he has suffered.

Yet each science is concerned with one class or genus of beings, and the practical and productive sciences may be related to their appropriate subject matter by contrasting their concern with action and production, or with doing and making, to the manner in which motion and change are investigated in physics. The physical sciences are confined to the study of substances which have the principles of their motion and rest present in themselves. The principle of action, on the other hand, is in the doer and the principle of production in the producer. Although the principles of the practical and productive sciences are both thus external as contrasted with the internal principles studied in physics, there is an important difference between them, for the principle of production is reason, or art, or some potency in the producer, while the principle of action is the will in the doer. Reason is therefore more important in art than in action, while the character of the agent is of crucial importance in the judgment of actions but irrelevant in art. The end of the practical sciences is to be found in the action itself and the state of character which produced it, while the end of the productive science is in the objects produced and the qualities discerned in those objects.

There are no sharp separations among the practical sciences. Ethics is a subdivision of Politics, and human conduct is studied in both, in ethics from the point of view of personal morality but with the recognition that the conduct of the individual is influenced by political institutions, in politics from the point of view of the associations and institutions of men but with the recognition that the character of communal institutions is determined by traits of the men who compose them. In both sciences, a natural foundation is sought for the ends of action and association. Ethics is concerned with the study of virtues, which are not natures or natural powers but habits; a natural basis is found for habits, however, in the potentialities of man which are influenced by repeated actions or passions. Politics is concerned with the study of constitutions or forms of human association, which likewise have no natural defi nitions or species, but a natural basis is found for habits in needs and interdependences of man for the ends of living and of living well, and in this sense the family, the village, and the state are natural and man is by nature a political animal.

The productive sciences are differentiated according to their products, and there are no sharply defined lines imposed by nature to separate the arts or to differentiate the kinds of artificial things. The Greeks did not differentiate the fine arts from the mechanical in the fashion that has been customary since the Renaissance, and they have therefore been criticized by humanists for confusing arts and trades, thereby degrading the artist, and by pragmatists for separating science and art, thereby reducing operations and mechanical contrivances to a servile level. The arts as conceived by Aristotle include not only such arts as painting, music, and poetry, but medicine, architecture, cobbling, and rhetoric. Since the arts imitate nature, they may be differentiated by consideration of the object, means, and manner of their imitation, and therefore, although he has no word for fine arts, Aristotle is able, in the opening chapter of the *Poetics*, to assemble the arts which we call fine by isolating their means of imitation and to differentiate tragedy from the other arts. Aristotle did, however, have a word by which to differentiate the liberal arts from the mechanical, and he sought their differentiation in educative influence of the arts in the formation of men for freedom.

The interrelations of the theoretic, practical, and productive sciences are thus far from simple: each group may be differentiated from the others by means of subject matter, end, and principle, yet each science is pertinent to all the others, and the subject matter of each may be treated incidentally from the point of view of the others and the principles of each may be employed incidentally in the others. The theoretic sciences are distinct from the practical and productive by their end or purpose. Yet the theoretic sciences appear among the subjects treated by the practical and productive sciences, since scientific knowledge is found among the intellectual virtues in ethics, the pursuit and teaching of science is a political problem, and the formulation of problems and presentation of conclusions is an artistic problem. Conversely the principles of the arts and of ethics and politics are studied in metaphysics; the proportions treated in mathematics supply a basis for the treatment of relations in the arts, virtues, and constitutions; and the psychological or intellectual processes involved in each are studied in psychology, which is a branch of physics. The practical sciences in like fashion are distinct from both the theoretic and the productive, yet the theoretic and productive sciences figure, not because of their proper problems but because of their practical implications, among the problems of ethics and politics, and the practical sciences derive basic distinctions from the theoretic sciences and are so involved in the problems of the arts that practical thinkers like the Sophists confused politics and rhetoric. The productive sciences, finally, are directed wholly to the artificial objects produced and they make their own materials, yet knowledge of the potentialities of materials, sensibilities of audiences, and formal interrelations may come from the theoretic and practical sciences, and the arts may in turn contribute to the construction of sciences, the formation of virtues, and the constitution of states.

The subtlety and clarity of the Aristotelian organization of the sciences depends on the discrimination of matter, purpose, and principle, which at once yields a sharp discrimination of artistic, moral, and theoretic considerations, and yet permits a single object or action, in its various circumstances or characteristics, to fall under the scrutiny of each mode of inquiry. The problem of the interrelations of the sciences has continued to be discussed in terms suggested by Aristotle, but without the functional variations he employed, with the result that the history of the discussion has been largely an alternation of efforts to reduce all sciences to theory or practice or art.

6. The Influence of Aristotle

The influence of Aristotle's writings on later philosophic speculation reflects in reverse the extremes between which he set his course: he has been reconciled with Democritus and reduced to a place among Plato's disciples, and he has been criticized for departing from the ideals set by the methods of both philosophers. The reputation which he has acquired and the turns which doctrines attributed to him have received in the context of other men's theories— and the influence of a philosopher is usually considered in some such manner—are difficult to explain by his works alone without consideration of the philosophic disputes which he sought to resolve and which served in turn as medium for the interpretation of his works. Aristotle's immediate influence seems to have bred scholars and specialists who seem quickly to have forgotten his scientific and philosophic principles and to have fixed philosophic terms and philosophic problems precisely but without holding to the meanings or solutions yielded by his philosophy. Theophrastus, his successor in the Lyceum, wrote on botany and on the history of the sciences of cosmology and physics; Eudemus of Rhodes, another of his disciples, wrote the first history of mathematics; Strato of Lampsacus, the third head of the Lyceum, undertook to reconcile the physics of Aristotle with the atomism of Democritus. During the Hellenistic period the discussion of problems of morals, logic, and physics reflects the impress of Aristotle's thought even in the far remove from Aristotle to which Stoics and Epicureans carried their discussions, but "peripatetic" apparently signified a scholar or a specialist in science rather than a philosopher, and Aristotle was thought of only as the most eminent of Plato's disciples.

This narrowly prescribed influence which Aristotle exercised in antiquity and continued to exercise in the early Middle Ages is explained in part by the slightness of the direct contact with his writings. According to an ancient legend, Aristotle's successor Theophrastus, fearful of the treatment and interpretation which Aristotle's works would receive in the Lyceum, presumably at the hands of his own successor, Strato, sold the manuscripts of Aristotle's works and his own to a pupil who took them to Asia Minor where his heirs protected them by concealing them in a cellar for 150 years. They were edited by Andronicus of Rhodes in the first century B.C., probably much as they are still edited. There is no evidence that these works, as distinguished from the "published" works and dialogues which are now lost, were known during this time, but there is no need to suppose that the hidden manuscripts were the only extant copies of the works. During the period in which Aristotle's labors seem to have resulted chiefly in the production, not of theoretic philosophers, but of experts, technicians, scholars, and pedagogues, the teachings of Plato, whose writings were never lost or concealed by the Academy, were professed by "Academics" who argued for varieties of skepticism and confined themselves to practical moral problems, and still later, with the beginnings of "Neoplatonism," they inspired philosophers to mysticism and theological speculations.

The acquaintance with Aristotle in the West, after the knowledge of Greek had become a rare accomplishment, was even more narrowly restricted, and early Christian philosophy took a practical imprint from Roman thought, modified by successive infiltrations of Greek influence which were Neoplatonic rather than Aristotelian. Two or more of the six treatises on logic in Aristotle's Organon were translated into Latin by Boethius in the sixth century A.D., and the first two of these short works, together with the commentaries of Boethius and his essays on related logical subjects constituted the chief source of information concerning Aristotle's philosophy in Western Europe from the sixth to the middle of the twelfth century. During the next century all of the writings of Aristotle were translated into Latin, and were made the subject of intense study and voluminous commentary.

The tradition of commentaries, written in a half dozen languages, in which Aristotle appears as an "authority" and as The Philosopher, is the source of the impression that Aristotle ruled men's minds with dogmatic sway for centuries. The Greek commentators wrote from about 125 A.D., when Aspasius flourished, to 550 A.D., the time of Olympiodorus, continuing sporadically until the fourteenth century, when Sophonias was at work: they included the excellent works of Alexander of Aphrodisias, who was known as The Exegete, and the learned repositories of Simplicius, which are the source of much of our information about the earlier tradition. The remains of the labors of these commentators, considerably thinned by the accidents of history, fill twenty-three substantial volumes in the excellent edition published in Berlin from 1882 to 1909. No similar editions are available of the Syriac commentaries which began to appear in the fifth and continued to be produced until the twelfth century, or of the Arabic commentaries, which include such distinguished and influential works as those of Algazeli, Avicenna, and Averroes, the last of whom earned the name The Commentator from the numerous commentaries (writen in Arabic, and soon translated or reported in Hebrew and Latin) which he prepared during the latter portion of the twelfth century. Hebrew philosophers continued the discussions initiated in these commentaries, and the long line of Latin commentaries which began to appear during the thirteenth century and continued into the seventeenth would, if all the manuscripts were assembled and published, probably exceed in bulk what survives of all the rest.

The commentaries on Aristotle assume a vast variety of forms and expound a vast variety of doctrines, exhibiting little tendency toward rigid adherence to the authority of a text or the dictate of a Master. Many of the Greek commentators were associated with the Academy or were avowed Neoplatonists or were, at least, in some manner imbued with Platonic doctrines, and their works contain ample indication of differences consequent on possible resolutions of the question, still agitated, whether Aristotle should be read as a systematic opponent to Plato or as one of his more or less inadequate and wrong-headed followers. Many of the problems discussed by the Greek commentators were early introduced into the Arabic and Latin traditions, or arose independently from similar considerations, and the Christian commentators were faced with the additional problem of reconciling Aristotle with Christianity and therefore of freeing him from interpretations attached to his doctrines by the Arabic philosophers. During the thirteenth century and increasingly during the later Middle Ages, commentaries on Aristotle became the major medium for philosophic disputation and independent scientific investigation. Albertus Magnus and Thomas Aquinas constructed their interpretations in explicit opposition to, and in less obvious dependence on, the Arabic interpretations, particularly those of the Averroists and the Avicennists. Even before the time of Petrarch and even after the time of Galileo, the discussion of the nature of the soul and its immortality was involved in a dispute between the Alexandrians and the Averroists, that is, between adherents of a third-century Greek commentator, The Exegete, and a twelfth-century Arab, The Commentator. Eventually commentaries were prepared to interpret Aristotle "according to the mind of" Aquinas, Scotus, Ockham, or Averroes. Disciples were won not so much to the philosophy of Aristotle as to interpretations of that philosophy, and the works of Aristotle have been no more rigid in determining a unique interpretation, nor less fertile in variety of intellectual inspiration, than the Bible or nature itself.

The revolt of philosophers during the sixteenth and

seventeenth centuries was as much against this scholastic mode of philosophic discussion as against Aristotle's doctrine, for much that was criticized as Aristotelian is found more easily in the commentaries than in Aristotle's works. The strictures against Aristotle which were part of the Renaissance reaction to him have been repeated since that time without adequate bases in Aristotle's doctrines or realization of how much of Aristotle was retained after the revolt. Yet during the period in which the direct influence of Aristotle has been slight in philosophy, the scholars have again been at work on the text of his writings. The great modern edition of his works, published by the Berlin Academy between 1831 and 1870, was the basis and beginning of a vast array of philological studies of the Aristotelian Corpus, its backgrounds, and tradition. His works are now available as they were never before and are accompanied by instruments and aids for their interpretation which make many of the old confusions even less plausible than they were. Moreover, Aristotle's name and doctrines are referred to increasingly in current philosophic discussions. In many cases the reference is only a reopening of old disputes and a repetition of old criticisms, but in some the citation of Aristotle is recognition that his terms and distinctions are embedded in our past intellectual traditions and our present habits of thought, and that an understanding of Aristotle may therefore shed light on the history of our problems and may suggest fruitful alternatives to the solutions that have become fashionable, or the subject of doubt. Such purposes—the understanding of strands of influence and discussion in Western civilization and the clarification of the basic problems of our philosophy—rather than the pursuit of historical or antiquarian curiosities, have led to new efforts to uncover the thought behind Aristotle's reputation and are reasons to return from what are alleged to have been his errors and his influences to an Introduction to Aristotle.

Logic

INTRODUCTION

The extant logical writings of Aristotle are six treatises, traditionally grouped under one name, the Organon. The Categories treats of simple terms and their peculiarities, differentiating ten most universal kinds or categories of terms as well as the simple relations—such as opposition, priority, simultaneity—which obtain between pairs of uncombined terms. On Interpretation treats of propositions, in which one term is asserted or denied of another and which therefore may be true or false, as well as the simple relations of immediate inference which obtain between pairs of propositions. The Prior Analytics treats of inferences and proofs or of syllogisms, which are combinations of three terms. Since all perfect inference may be reduced to a syllogism or a series of syllogisms, further logical differentiation of kinds of proofs is to be found in the premisses on which they are based. The Posterior Analytics treats of demonstration or scientific proof, which is reasoning based on true and primary premisses, that is, premisses which state the causes of the phenomena to be explained. The Topics treats of dialectical reasoning, which is based on opinions generally accepted, rather than on scientific premisses, which are believed on the strength not of something else but of themselves. On Sophistical Refutations, finally, treats of fallacious arguments which start from opinions that seem to be accepted generally, but are not really, or which seem to reason from opinions that are or seem to be accepted generally.

Aristotle's discussion of scientific knowledge in the Posterior Analytics is the source of many of the distinctions —and of most of the technical terms used in stating the distinctions—that have been important in the theories of scientific method developed by later logicians. Yet his formulation of the problems of scientific proof, although it involves the differentiation of induction and deduction, does not turn on the simple opposition of the inductive discovery of principles and their deductive use in demonstration. The problems of scientific proof, as he treated them, center about two processes, instruction and inquiry. All instruction by way of argument proceeds from preexistent knowledge, whether the argument be deductive or inductive, and the problems of scientific proof, so viewed, are concerned with the principles of the sciences and the conditions of inference from the principles. The analysis of principles and proofs, in this approach, turns on the terms in which arguments are stated, and Aristotle undertook to prove that each science had first principles proper to it and that an infinite regress of premisses is impossible. Therefore predication must terminate in both the upward and the downward direction, that is, in ascent to generality and descent to particularity, and there must be a finite number of steps between the most universal and the most particular. Inquiry, on the other hand, is into facts and causes, and the problems of scientific proof, so viewed, are concerned with the relation between definition and proof. The analysis of principles and proofs, in this approach, turns on the relation of knowledge to facts, and Aristotle undertook to differentiate kinds of definition, some indemonstrable, some susceptible of demonstration, and to prove that causes are the middle terms in scientific demonstration.

Aristotle's conception of scientific method depends, thus, on analysis of both the structure of knowledge and the connections of things. He was fond of saying that we have scientific knowledge of something demonstrable when we possess a demonstration of it; and he was no less fond of repeating that we have scientific knowledge when we know the cause. In both formulations the problem of scientific proof centers on the middle term, both in the sense of the term which justifies the conclusion of a proof and in the sense of the cause which accounts for the connections in a situation. The problem of finding a middle term depends for its solution in the one formulation, as instruction, on the quick wit requisite for the discernment of middle terms and in the other, as inquiry, on that inductive process by which universals and primary premisses are derived from sense-perception and experience. The primary premisses of scientific demonstration, however, are not themselves subject to scientific proof, although they may be tested in indirect dialectical examination. In like manner, the resolution of difficulties and the discovery of principles are dialectical problems so long as they turn on the establishment and defense of propositions, and they become scientific only when they are related to the statement of a basic cause. Although Aristotle first formulated the distinctions and technical terms in which much of the later discussion of scientific method was conducted, his own distinctions have been used in criticism of his logic. He has seemed to writers who stress the development of inductive logic to have given inadequate development to the methods of interpreting the facts of observation and experimentation, while his treatment of principles and inference has seemed to symbolic logicians, who stress the methods of mathematics, too little concerned with the forms of validation and proof. Yet many of the problems which became central to these later discussions of scientific method are found in other contexts, treated as metaphysics or dialectic or sophistic, rather than scientific method, as is appropriate in Aristotle's conception of the sciences. Thus, the dialectical inquiry into first principles is found in Book Gamma of the Metaphysics and the formulation of the devices by which possible solutions to problems may be assembled and tests of possible positions may be constructed are detailed in the Topics.

BOOK II

ANALYTICA POSTERIORA

CONTENTS

BOOK I

Analytica Posteriora

Posterior Analytics

Translated by G. R. G. Mure

⊔⊓⊔⊏

BOOK 1

1   All instruction given or received by way of argument 71ᵃ
proceeds from pre-existent knowledge. This becomes
evident upon a survey of all the species of such instruction. The mathematical sciences and all other speculative
disciplines are acquired in this way, and so are the two 5
forms of dialectical reasoning, syllogistic and inductive;
for each of these latter makes use of old knowledge to impart new, the syllogism assuming an audience that accepts
its premisses, induction exhibiting the universal as implicit
in the clearly known particular. Again, the persuasion ex-
erted by rhetorical arguments is in principle the same,
since they use either example, a kind of induction, or en- 10
thymeme, a form of syllogism.

The pre-existent knowledge required is of two kinds. In
some cases admission of the fact must be assumed, in others comprehension of the meaning of the term used, and
sometimes both assumptions are essential. Thus, we assume that every predicate can be either truly affirmed or
truly denied of any subject, and that 'triangle' means so
and so; as regards 'unit' we have to make the double assumption of the meaning of the word and the existence of 1ᵌ
the thing. The reason is that these several objects are not
equally obvious to us. Recognition of a truth may in some

cases contain as factors both previous knowledge and also
knowledge acquired simultaneously with that recognition
—knowledge, this latter, of the particulars actually falling
under the universal and therein already virtually known.
20 For example, the student knew beforehand that the angles
of every triangle are equal to two right angles; but it was
only at the actual moment at which he was being led on
to recognize this as true in the instance before him that he
came to know 'this figure inscribed in the semicircle' to
be a triangle. For some things (viz. the singulars finally
reached which are not predicable of anything else as subject) are only learnt in this way, i. e. there is here no recognition through a middle of a minor term as subject to a
major. Before he was led on to recognition or before he
actually drew a conclusion, we should perhaps say that in
25 a manner he knew, in a manner not.

If he did not in an unqualified sense of the term *know*
the existence of this triangle, how could he *know* without
qualification that its angles were equal to two right angles?
No: clearly he *knows* not without qualification but only
in the sense that he *knows* universally. If this distinction is
not drawn, we are faced with the dilemma in the *Meno*: [1]
either a man will learn nothing or what he already knows;
for we cannot accept the solution which some people of-
30 fer. A man is asked, 'Do you, or do you not, know that
every pair is even?' He says he does know it. The ques-
tioner then produces a particular pair, of the existence,
and so a *fortiori* of the evenness, of which he was unaware. The solution which some people offer is to assert
that they do not know that every pair is even, but only
that everything which they know to be a pair is even: yet
71ᵇ what they know to be even is that of which they have
demonstrated evenness, i. e. what they made the subject
of their premiss, viz. not merely every triangle or number
which they know to be such, but any and every number
or triangle without reservation. For no premiss is ever

[1] Plato, *Meno*, 80 E.

couched in the form 'every number which you know to be such', or 'every rectilinear figure which you know to be such': the predicate is always construed as applicable to any and every instance of the thing. On the other hand, I imagine there is nothing to prevent a man in one sense 5 knowing what he is learning, in another not knowing it. The strange thing would be, not if in some sense he knew what he was learning, but if he were to know it in that precise sense and manner in which he was learning it.[2]

2 We suppose ourselves to possess unqualified scientific knowledge of a thing, as opposed to knowing it in the accidental way in which the sophist knows, when we think that we know the cause on which the fact de- 10 pends, as the cause of that fact and of no other, and, further, that the fact could not be other than it is. Now that scientific knowing is something of this sort is evident—witness both those who falsely claim it and those who actually possess it, since the former merely imagine themselves to be, while the latter are also actually, in the condition described. Consequently the proper object of unqualified scientific knowledge is something which cannot be other than it is. 15

There may be another manner of knowing as well—that will be discussed later.[3] What I now assert is that at all events we do know by demonstration. By demonstration I mean a syllogism productive of scientific knowledge, a syllogism, that is, the grasp of which is *eo ipso* such knowledge. Assuming then that my thesis as to the nature of sci- 20 entific knowing is correct, the premises of demonstrated knowledge must be true, primary, immediate, better known than and prior to the conclusion, which is further related to them as effect to cause. Unless these conditions are satisfied, the basic truths will not be 'appropriate' to the conclusion. Syllogism there may indeed be without

[2] Cf. *An. Pr.* ii, ch. 21.
[3] Cf. the following chapter and more particularly ii, ch. 19.

these conditions, but such syllogism, not being productive
of scientific knowledge, will not be demonstration. The
25 premisses must be true: for that which is non-existent cannot be known—we cannot know, e. g., that the diagonal of a
square is commensurate with its side. The premisses must be
primary and indemonstrable; otherwise they will require
demonstration in order to be known, since to have knowledge, if it be not accidental knowledge, of things which are
demonstrable, means precisely to have a demonstration of
them. The premisses must be the causes of the conclusion,
30 better known than it, and prior to it; its causes, since we possess scientific knowledge of a thing only when we know its
cause; prior, in order to be causes; antecedently known,
this antecedent knowledge being not our mere understanding of the meaning, but knowledge of the fact as well.
Now 'prior' and 'better known' are ambiguous terms, for
there is a difference between what is prior and better known
72ª in the order of being and what is prior and better known
to man. I mean that objects nearer to sense are prior and
better known to man; objects without qualification prior
and better known are those further from sense. Now the
most universal causes are furthest from sense and particular
5 causes are nearest to sense, and they are thus exactly opposed to one another. In saying that the premisses of demonstrated knowledge must be primary, I mean that they
must be the 'appropriate' basic truths, for I identify primary
premiss and basic truth. A 'basic truth' in a demonstration
is an immediate proposition. An immediate proposition is
one which has no other proposition prior to it. A proposition is either part of an enunciation, i. e. it predicates a
single attribute of a single subject. If a proposition is dia-
10 lectical, it assumes either part indifferently; if it is demonstrative, it lays down one part to the definite exclusion of
the other because that part is true. The term 'enunciation'
denotes either part of a contradiction indifferently. A contradiction is an opposition which of its own nature excludes
a middle. The part of a contradiction which conjoins a

predicate with a subject is an affirmation; the part disjoin-
ing them is a negation. I call an immediate basic truth of 15
syllogism a 'thesis' when, though it is not susceptible of
proof by the teacher, yet ignorance of it does not constitute
a total bar to progress on the part of the pupil: one which
the pupil must know if he is to learn anything whatever
is an axiom. I call it an axiom because there are such truths
and we give them the name of axioms *par excellence*. If a
thesis assumes one part or the other of an enunciation, i. e.
asserts either the existence or the non-existence of a sub- 20
ject, it is a hypothesis; if it does not so assert, it is a definition. Definition *is* a 'thesis' or a 'laying something down',
since the arithmetician lays it down that to be a unit is to
be quantitatively indivisible; but it is not a hypothesis, for
to define what a unit is is not the same as to affirm its
existence.

Now since the required ground of our knowledge—i. e.
of our conviction—of a fact is the possession of such a syl- 25
logism as we call demonstration, and the ground of the
syllogism is the facts constituting its premisses, we must
not only know the primary premisses—some if not all of
them—beforehand, but know them better than the conclusion: for the cause of an attribute's inherence in a subject always itself inheres in the subject more firmly than
that attribute; e. g. the cause of our loving anything is dearer
to us than the object of our love. So since the primary
premisses are the cause of our knowledge—i. e. of our con- 30
viction—it follows that we know them better—that is, are
more convinced of them—than their consequences, precisely because our knowledge of the latter is the effect of
our knowledge of the premisses. Now a man cannot believe
in anything more than in the things he knows, unless he
has either actual knowledge of it or something better than
actual knowledge. But we are faced with this paradox if a
student whose belief rests on demonstration has not prior 33
knowledge; a man must believe in some, if not in all, of the
basic truths more than in the conclusion. Moreover, if a

man sets out to acquire the scientific knowledge that comes through demonstration, he must not only have a better knowledge of the basic truths and a firmer conviction of them than of the connexion which is being demonstrated: 72ᵇ more than this, nothing must be more certain or better known to him than these basic truths in their character as contradicting the fundamental premisses which lead to the opposed and erroneous conclusion. For indeed the conviction of pure science must be unshakable.

3   Some hold that, owing to the necessity of knowing the 5   primary premisses, there is no scientific knowledge. Others think there is, but that all truths are demonstrable. Neither doctrine is either true or a necessary deduction from the premisses. The first school, assuming that there is no way of knowing other than by demonstration, maintain that an infinite regress is involved, on the ground that if behind the prior stands no primary, we could not know the 10 posterior through the prior (wherein they are right, for one cannot traverse an infinite series): if on the other hand— they say—the series terminates and there are primary premisses, yet these are unknowable because incapable of demonstration, which according to them is the only form of knowledge. And since thus one cannot know the primary premisses, knowledge of the conclusions which follow from them is not pure scientific knowledge nor properly knowing at all, but rests on the mere supposition that the premisses 15 are true. The other party agree with them as regards knowing, holding that it is only possible by demonstration, but they see no difficulty in holding that all truths are demonstrated, on the ground that demonstration may be circular and reciprocal.

Our own doctrine is that not all knowledge is demonstrative: on the contrary, knowledge of the immediate prem-20 isses is independent of demonstration. (The necessity of this is obvious; for since we must know the prior premisses from

which the demonstration is drawn, and since the regress
must end in immediate truths, those truths must be indemonstrable.) Such, then, is our doctrine, and in addition
we maintain that besides scientific knowledge there is its
originative source which enables us to recognize the definitions.

Now demonstration must be based on premisses prior to 23
and better known than the conclusion; and the same
things cannot simultaneously be both prior and posterior to
one another: so circular demonstration is clearly not possible in the unqualified sense of 'demonstration', but only
possible if 'demonstration' be extended to include that
other method of argument which rests on a distinction between truths prior to us and truths without qualification
prior, i. e. the method by which induction produces knowl- 30
edge. But if we accept this extension of its meaning, our definition of unqualified knowledge will prove faulty; for there
seem to be two kinds of it. Perhaps, however, the second
form of demonstration, that which proceeds from truths
better known to us, is not demonstration in the unqualified
sense of the term.

The advocates of circular demonstration are not only
faced with the difficulty we have just stated: in addition
their theory reduces to the mere statement that if a thing
exists, then it does exist—an easy way of proving anything. 35
That this is so can be clearly shown by taking three terms,
for to constitute the circle it makes no difference whether
many terms or few or even only two are taken. Thus by direct proof, if A is, B must be; if B is, C must be; therefore
if A is, C must be. Since then—by the circular proof—if A
is, B must be, and if B is, A must be, A may be substituted 73ª
for C above. Then 'if B is, A must be' = 'if B is, C must be',
which above gave the conclusion 'if A is, C must be': but
C and A have been identified. Consequently the upholders
of circular demonstration are in the position of saying that
if A is, A must be—a simple way of proving anything. 5

Moreover, even such circular demonstration is impossible except in the case of attributes that imply one another, viz. 'peculiar' properties.

Now, it has been shown that the positing of one thing—be it one term or one premiss—never involves a necessary consequent: [4] two premisses constitute the first and small-
10 est foundation for drawing a conclusion at all and therefore a *fortiori* for the demonstrative syllogism of science. If, then, A is implied in B and C, and B and C are reciprocally implied in one another and in A, it is possible, as has been shown in my writings on the syllogism,[5] to prove all the assumptions on which the original conclusion rested, by circular demonstration in the first figure. But it has also
15 been shown that in the other figures either no conclusion is possible, or at least none which proves both the original premisses.[6] Propositions the terms of which are not convertible cannot be circularly demonstrated at all, and since convertible terms occur rarely in actual demonstrations, it is clearly frivolous and impossible to say that demonstration is reciprocal and that therefore everything can be dem-
20 onstrated.

4   Since the object of pure scientific knowledge cannot be other than it is, the truth obtained by demonstrative knowledge will be necessary. And since demonstrative knowledge is only present when we have a demonstration, it follows that demonstration is an inference from neces-sary premisses. So we must consider what are the premisses
25 of demonstration—i. e. what is their character: and as a pre-liminary, let us define what we mean by an attribute 'true in every instance of its subject', an 'essential' attribute, and a 'commensurate and universal' attribute. I call 'true in every instance' what is truly predicable of all instances—not of one to the exclusion of others—and at all times, not at

[4] *An. Pr.* i, ch. 25.
[5] *Ibid.* ii, ch. 5.
[6] *Ibid.* ii. cc. 5 and 6.

this or that time only; e. g. if animal is truly predicable of every instance of man, then if it be true to say 'this is a man', 'this is an animal' is also true, and if the one be true now the other is true now. A corresponding account holds if point is in every instance predicable as contained in line. There is evidence for this in the fact that the objection we raise against a proposition put to us as true in every instance is either an instance in which, or an occasion on which, it is not true. Essential attributes are (1) such as belong to their subject as elements in its essential nature (e. g. line thus belongs to triangle, point to line; for the very being or 'substance' of triangle and line is composed of these elements, which are contained in the formulae defining triangle and line): (2) such that, while they belong to certain subjects, the subjects to which they belong are contained in the attribute's own defining formula. Thus straight and curved belong to line, odd and even, prime and compound, square and oblong, to number; and also the formula defining any one of these attributes contains its subject—e. g. line or number as the case may be.

Extending this classification to all other attributes, I distinguish those that answer the above description as belonging essentially to their respective subjects; whereas attributes related in neither of these two ways to their subjects I call accidents or 'coincidents'; e. g. musical or white is a 'coincident' of animal.

Further (a) that is essential which is not predicated of a subject other than itself: e. g. 'the walking [thing]' walks and is white in virtue of being something else besides; whereas substance, in the sense of whatever signifies a 'this somewhat', is not what it is in virtue of being something else besides. Things, then, not predicated of a subject I call essential; things predicated of a subject I call accidental or 'coincidental'.

In another sense again (b) a thing consequentially connected with anything is essential; one not so connected is 'coincidental'. An example of the latter is 'While he was

walking it lightened': the lightning was not due to his walking; it was, we should say, a coincidence. If, on the other hand, there is a consequential connexion, the predication is essential; e. g. if a beast dies when its throat is being cut, then its death is also essentially connected with the
15 cutting, because the cutting was the cause of death, not death a 'coincident' of the cutting.

So far then as concerns the sphere of connexions scientifically known in the unqualified sense of that term, all attributes which (within that sphere) are essential either in the sense that their subjects are contained in them, or in the sense that they are contained in their subjects, are necessary as well as consequentially connected with their subjects. For it is impossible for them not to inhere in their subjects—either simply or in the qualified sense that
20 one or other of a pair of opposites must inhere in the subject; e. g. in line must be either straightness or curvature, in number either oddness or evenness. For within a single identical genus the contrary of a given attribute is either its privative or its contradictory; e. g. within number what is not odd is even, inasmuch as within this sphere even is a necessary consequent of not-odd. So, since any given predicate must be either affirmed or denied of any subject, essential attributes must inhere in their subjects of necessity.

Thus, then, we have established the distinction between
25 the attribute which is 'true in every instance' and the 'essential' attribute.

I term 'commensurately universal' an attribute which belongs to every instance of its subject, and to every instance essentially and as such; from which it clearly follows that all commensurate universals inhere necessarily in their subjects. The essential attribute, and the attribute that belongs to its subject as such, are identical. E. g. point and straight
30 belong to line essentially, for they belong to line as such: and triangle as such has two right angles, for it is essentially equal to two right angles.

An attribute belongs commensurately and universally to

a subject when it can be shown to belong to any random instance of that subject and when the subject is the first thing to which it can be shown to belong. Thus, e. g., (1) the equality of its angles to two right angles is not a commensurately universal attribute of figure. For though it is possible to show that a figure has its angles equal to two right angles, this attribute cannot be demonstrated of any 35 figure selected at haphazard, nor in demonstrating does one take a figure at random—a square is a figure but its angles are not equal to two right angles. On the other hand, any isosceles triangle has its angles equal to two right angles, yet isosceles triangle is not the primary subject of this attribute but triangle is prior. So whatever can be shown to have its angles equal to two right angles, or to possess any other attribute, in any random instance of itself and pri- 40 marily—that is the first subject to which the predicate in question belongs commensurately and universally, and the 74 demonstration, in the essential sense, of any predicate is the proof of it as belonging to this first subject commensurately and universally: while the proof of it as belonging to the other subjects to which it attaches is demonstration only in a secondary and unessential sense. Nor again (2) is equality to two right angles a commensurately universal attribute of isosceles; it is of wider application.

5   We must not fail to observe that we often fall into error because our conclusion is not in fact primary and commensurately universal in the sense in which we think 5 we prove it so. We make this mistake (1) when the subject is an individual or individuals above which there is no universal to be found: (2) when the subjects belong to different species and there is a higher universal, but it has no name: (3) when the subject which the demonstrator takes as a whole is really only a part of a larger whole; for then the demonstration will be true of the individual instances 10 within the part and will hold in every instance of it, yet the

demonstration will not be true of this subject primarily and
commensurately and universally. When a demonstration
is true of a subject primarily and commensurately and uni
versally, that is to be taken to mean that it is true of a given
subject primarily and as such. Case (3) may be thus exemplified. If a proof were given that perpendiculars to the
same line are parallel, it might be supposed that *lines thus
perpendicular* were the proper subject of the demonstration
15 because being parallel is true of every instance of them.
But it is not so, for the parallelism depends not on these
angles being equal to one another because each is a right
angle, but simply on their being equal to one another. An
example of (1) would be as follows: if isosceles were the
only triangle, it would be thought to have its angles equal
to two right angles qua isosceles. An instance of (2) would
be the law that proportionals alternate. Alternation used
to be demonstrated separately of numbers, lines, solids,
20 and durations, though it could have been proved of them
all by a single demonstration. Because there was no single
name to denote that in which numbers, lengths, durations,
and solids are identical, and because they differed specifically from one another, this property was proved of each
of them separately. To-day, however, the proof is commensurately universal, for they do not possess this attribute
qua lines or qua numbers, but qua manifesting this generic
25 character which they are postulated as possessing universally. Hence, even if one prove of each kind of triangle
that its angles are equal to two right angles, whether by
means of the same or different proofs; still, as long as one
treats separately equilateral, scalene, and isosceles, one does
not yet know, except sophistically, that triangle has its
angles equal to two right angles, nor does one yet know that
triangle has this property commensurately and universally,
30 even if there is no other species of triangle but these. For
one does not know that triangle as such has this property,
nor even that 'all' triangles have it—unless 'all' means 'each
taken singly': if 'all' means 'as a whole class', then, though

there be none in which one does not recognize this property, one does not know it of 'all triangles'.

When, then, does our knowledge fail of commensurate
universality, and when is it unqualified knowledge? If triangle be identical in essence with equilateral, i. e. with each
or all equilaterals, then clearly we have unqualified knowledge: if on the other hand it be not, and the attribute belongs to equilateral *qua* triangle; then our knowledge fails
of commensurate universality. 'But', it will be asked, 'does 35
this attribute belong to the subject of which it has been
demonstrated *qua* triangle or *qua* isosceles? What is the
point at which the subject to which it belongs is primary?
(i. e. to what subject can it be demonstrated as belonging
commensurately and universally?)' Clearly this point is the
first term in which it is found to inhere as the elimination
of inferior *differentiae* proceeds. Thus the angles of a brazen
isosceles triangle are equal to two right angles: but eliminate brazen and isosceles and the attribute remains. 'But'
—you may say—'eliminate figure or limit, and the attribute 74ᵇ
vanishes'. True, but figure and limit are not the first *differentiae* whose elimination destroys the attribute. 'Then
what is the first?' If it is triangle, it will be in virtue of
triangle that the attribute belongs to all the other subjects
of which it is predicable, and triangle is the subject to which
it can be demonstrated as belonging commensurately and
universally.

6   Demonstrative knowledge must rest on necessary basic
       truths; for the object of scientific knowledge cannot be 5
other than it is. Now attributes attaching essentially to their
subjects attach necessarily to them: for essential attributes
are either elements in the essential nature of their subjects
or contain their subjects as elements in their own essential
nature. (The pairs of opposites which the latter class includes are necessary because one member or the other necessarily inheres.) It follows from this that premisses of the
demonstrative syllogism must be connexions essential in 10

the sense explained: for all attributes must inhere essentially or else be accidental, and accidental attributes are not necessary to their subjects.

We must either state the case thus, or else premise that the conclusion of demonstration is necessary and that a demonstrated conclusion cannot be other than it is, and
15 then infer that the conclusion must be developed from necessary premisses. For though you may reason from true premisses without demonstrating, yet if your premisses are necessary you will assuredly demonstrate—in such necessity you have at once a distinctive character of demonstration. That demonstration proceeds from necessary premisses is also indicated by the fact that the objection we raise against a professed demonstration is that a premiss of it is not a
20 necessary truth—whether we think it altogether devoid of necessity, or at any rate so far as our opponent's previous argument goes. This shows how naïve it is to suppose one's basic truths rightly chosen if one starts with a proposition which is (1) popularly accepted and (2) true, such as the sophists' assumption that to know is the same as to possess knowledge.[7] For (1) popular acceptance or rejection is no criterion of a basic truth, which can only be the primary
25 law of the genus constituting the subject matter of the demonstration; and (2) not all truth is 'appropriate'.

A further proof that the conclusion must be the development of necessary premisses is as follows. Where demonstration is possible, one who can give no account which includes the cause has no scientific knowledge. If, then, we suppose a syllogism in which, though A necessarily inheres in C, yet B, the middle term of the demonstration, is not necessarily connected with A and C. then the man who
30 argues thus has no reasoned knowledge of the conclusion, since this conclusion does not owe its necessity to the middle term; for though the conclusion is necessary, the mediating link is a contingent fact. Or again, if a man is without knowledge now, though he still retains the steps of the ar-

7 Plato. Euthydemus, 277 B.

gument, though there is no change in himself or in the fact
and no lapse of memory on his part; then neither had he
knowledge previously. But the mediating link, not being
necessary, may have perished in the interval; and if so, 35
though there be no change in him nor in the fact, and
though he will still retain the steps of the argument, yet
he has not knowledge, and therefore had not knowledge
before. Even if the link has not actually perished but is
liable to perish, this situation is possible and might occur.
But such a condition cannot be knowledge.

When the conclusion is necessary, the middle through 75ᵇ
which it was proved may yet quite easily be non-necessary.
You can in fact infer the necessary even from a non-necessary premiss, just as you can infer the true from the not
true. On the other hand, when the middle is necessary the 5
conclusion must be necessary; just as true premisses always
give a true conclusion. Thus, if A is necessarily predicated
of B and B of C, then A is necessarily predicated of C. But
when the conclusion is non-necessary the middle cannot
be necessary either. Thus: let A be predicated non-neces- 10
sarily of C but necessarily of B, and let B be a necessary
predicate of C; then A too will be a necessary predicate of
C, which by hypothesis it is not.

To sum up, then: demonstrative knowledge must be
knowledge of a necessary nexus, and therefore must clearly
be obtained through a necessary middle term; otherwise its
possessor will know neither the cause nor the fact that his 15
conclusion is a necessary connexion. Either he will mistake
the non-necessary for the necessary and believe the necessity
of the conclusion without knowing it, or else he will not
even believe it—in which case he will be equally ignorant,
whether he actually infers the mere fact through middle
terms or the reasoned fact and from immediate premisses.

Of accidents that are not essential according to our definition of essential there is no demonstrative knowledge;
for since an accident, in the sense in which I here speak of
it, may also not inhere, it is impossible to prove its in- 20

herence as a necessary conclusion. A difficulty, however, might be raised as to why in dialectic, if the conclusion is not a necessary connexion, such and such determinate premises should be proposed in order to deal with such and such determinate problems. Would not the result be the same if one asked any questions whatever and then merely stated one's conclusion? The solution is that de-
25 terminate questions have to be put, not because the replies to them affirm facts which necessitate facts affirmed by the conclusion, but because these answers are propositions which if the answerer affirm, he must affirm the conclusion —and affirm it with truth if they are true

Since it is just those attributes within every genus which are essential and possessed by their respective subjects as such that are necessary, it is clear that both the conclusions and the premisses of demonstrations which produce scien-
30 tific knowledge are essential. For accidents are not neces-sary: and, further, since accidents are not necessary one does not necessarily have reasoned knowledge of a conclusion drawn from them (this is so even if the accidental prem-isses are invariable but not essential, as in proofs through signs; for though the conclusion be actually essential, one will not know it as essential nor know its reason); but to
35 have reasoned knowledge of a conclusion is to know it through its cause. We may conclude that the middle must be consequentially connected with the minor, and the major with the middle.

7   It follows that we cannot in demonstrating pass from one genus to another. We cannot, for instance, prove geometrical truths by arithmetic. For there are three ele-ments in demonstration: (1) what is proved, the conclu-
40 sion—an attribute inhering essentially in a genus; (2) the axioms, i. e. axioms which are premisses of demonstra-
75ᵇ tion; (3) the subject-genus whose attributes, i. e. essential properties, are revealed by the demonstration. The axioms which are premisses of demonstration may be identical in

two or more sciences: but in the case of two different genera such as arithmetic and geometry you cannot apply arithmetical demonstration to the properties of magnitudes 5 unless the magnitudes in question are numbers.[8] How in certain cases transference is possible I will explain later.[9]

Arithmetical demonstration and the other sciences likewise possess, each of them, their own genera; so that if the demonstration is to pass from one sphere to another, the genus must be either absolutely or to some extent the same. 10 If this is not so, transference is clearly impossible, because the extreme and the middle terms must be drawn from the same genus: otherwise, as predicated, they will not be essential and will thus be accidents. That is why it cannot be proved by geometry that opposites fall under one science, nor even that the product of two cubes is a cube. Nor can the theorem of any one science be demonstrated by 15 means of another science, unless these theorems are related as subordinate to superior (e. g. as optical theorems to geometry or harmonic theorems to arithmetic). Geometry again cannot prove of lines any property which they do not possess *qua* lines, i. e. in virtue of the fundamental truths of their peculiar genus: it cannot show, for example, that the straight line is the most beautiful of lines or the contrary of the circle; for these qualities do not belong to lines in virtue of their peculiar genus, but through some property 20 which it shares with other genera.

8 It is also clear that if the premisses from which the syllogism proceeds are commensurately universal, the conclusion of such demonstration—demonstration, i. e , in the unqualified sense—must also be eternal. Therefore no attribute can be demonstrated nor known by strictly scientific knowledge to inhere in perishable things. The proof can only be accidental, because the attribute's connexion 25 with its perishable subject is not commensurately universal

----

[8] Cf. *Met.* 1039[a] 9.
[9] Cf. i, cc. 9 and 13.

but temporary and special. If such a demonstration is made, one premiss must be perishable and not commensurately universal (perishable because only if it is perishable will the conclusion be perishable; not commensurately universal, because the predicate will be predicable of some instances of the subject and not of others); so that the conclusion can only be that a fact is true at the moment—not com-
30 mensurately and universally. The same is true of definitions, since a definition is either a primary premiss or a conclusion of a demonstration, or else only differs from a demonstration in the order of its terms. Demonstration and science of merely frequent occurrences—e. g. of eclipse as happening to the moon—are, as such, clearly eternal: whereas so far as they are not eternal they are not fully commensurate. Other subjects too have properties attaching to
35 them in the same way as eclipse attaches to the moon.

9   It is clear that if the conclusion is to show an attribute inhering as such, nothing can be demonstrated except from its 'appropriate' basic truths. Consequently a proof even from true, indemonstrable, and immediate premisses
40 does not constitute knowledge. Such proofs are like Bryson's method of squaring the circle; for they operate by taking as their middle a common character—a character, therefore, which the subject may share with another—and
76ᵇ consequently they apply equally to subjects different in kind. They therefore afford knowlege of an attribute only as inhering accidentally, not as belonging to its subject as such: otherwise they would not have been applicable to another genus.

Our knowledge of any attribute's connexion with a subject is accidental unless we know that connexion through the middle term in virtue of which it inheres, and as an
5 inference from basic premisses essential and 'appropriate' to the subject—unless we know, e. g., the property of possessing angles equal to two right angles as belonging to that

subject in which it inheres essentially, and as inferred from
basic premises essential and 'appropriate' to that subject:
so that if that middle term also belongs essentially to the
minor, the middle must belong to the same kind as the
major and minor terms. The only exceptions to this rule are
such cases as theorems in harmonics which are demonstrable by arithmetic. Such theorems are proved by the 10
same middle terms as arithmetical properties, but with a
qualification—the fact falls under a separate science (for
the subject genus is separate), but the reasoned fact concerns the superior science, to which the attributes essentially belong. Thus, even these apparent exceptions show
that no attribute is strictly demonstrable except from its
'appropriate' basic truths, which, however, in the case of
these sciences have the requisite identity of character. 15

It is no less evident that the peculiar basic truths of each
inhering attribute are indemonstrable; for basic truths from
which they might be deduced would be basic truths of all
that is, and the science to which they belonged would possess universal sovereignty. This is so because he knows
better whose knowledge is deduced from higher causes, for
his knowledge is from prior premises when it derives from 20
causes themselves uncaused: hence, if he knows better than
others or best of all, his knowledge would be science in a
higher or the highest degree. But, as things are, demonstration is not transferable to another genus, with such exceptions as we have mentioned of the application of geometrical demonstrations to theorems in mechanics or optics, or 25
of arithmetical demonstrations to those of harmonics.

It is hard to be sure whether one knows or not; for it is
hard to be sure whether one's knowledge is based on the
basic truths appropriate to each attribute—the differentia
of true knowledge. We think we have scientific knowledge
if we have reasoned from true and primary premises. But
that is not so: the conclusion must be homogeneous with 30
the basic facts of the science.

10   I call the basic truths of every genus those elements in
it the existence of which cannot be proved. As regards
both these primary truths and the attributes dependent on
them the meaning of the name is assumed. The fact of their
existence as regards the primary truths must be assumed;
but it has to be proved of the remainder, the attributes.
Thus we assume the meaning alike of unity, straight, and
35 triangular; but while as regards unity and magnitude we
assume also the fact of their existence, in the case of the
remainder proof is required.

Of the basic truths used in the demonstrative sciences
some are peculiar to each science, and some are common,
but common only in the sense of analogous, being of use
only in so far as they fall within the genus constituting the
province of the science in question.

40   Peculiar truths are, e. g., the definitions of line and
straight; common truths are such as 'take equals from
equals and equals remain'. Only so much of these common
76ᵇ truths is required as falls within the genus in question:
for a truth of this kind will have the same force even if
not used generally but applied by the geometer only to
magnitudes, or by the arithmetician only to numbers. Also
peculiar to a science are the subjects the existence as well
as the meaning of which it assumes, and the essential attri-
5 butes of which it investigates, e. g. in arithmetic units, in
geometry points and lines. Both the existence and the
meaning of the subjects are assumed by these sciences; but
of their essential attributes only the meaning is assumed.
For example arithmetic assumes the meaning of odd and
even, square and cube, geometry that of incommensurable,
or of deflection or verging of lines, whereas the existence of
10 these attributes is demonstrated by means of the axioms
and from previous conclusions as premisses. Astronomy too
proceeds in the same way. For indeed every demonstrative
science has three elements: (1) that which it posits, the
subject genus whose essential attributes it examines; (2)
15 the so-called axioms, which are primary premisses of its

demonstration; (3) the attributes, the meaning of which it assumes. Yet some sciences may very well pass over some of these elements; e. g. we might not expressly posit the existence of the genus if its existence were obvious (for instance, the existence of hot and cold is more evident than that of number); or we might omit to assume expressly the meaning of the attributes if it were well understood. In the same way the meaning of axioms, such as 'Take equals from 20 equals and equals remain', is well known and so not expressly assumed. Nevertheless in the nature of the case the essential elements of demonstration are three: the subject, the attributes, and the basic premisses.

That which expresses necessary self-grounded fact, and which we must necessarily believe,[10] is distinct both from the hypotheses of a science and from illegitimate postulate —I say 'must believe', because all syllogism, and therefore a fortiori demonstration, is addressed not to the spoken word, but to the discourse within the soul,[11] and though we can 25 always raise objections to the spoken word, to the inward discourse we cannot always object. That which is capable of proof but assumed by the teacher without proof is, if the pupil believes and accepts it, hypothesis, though only in a limited sense hypothesis—that is, relatively to the pupil; if the pupil has no opinion or a contrary opinion on the 30 matter, the same assumption is an illegitimate postulate. Therein lies the distinction between hypothesis and illegitimate postulate: the latter is the contrary of the pupil's opinion, demonstrable, but assumed and used without demonstration.

The definitions—viz. those which are not expressed as statements that anything is or is not—are not hypotheses: 35 but it is in the premisses of a science that its hypotheses are contained. Definitions require only to be understood, and this is not hypothesis—unless it be contended that the pupil's hearing is also an hypothesis required by the teacher.

[10] sc. axioms.
[11] Cf. Plato, *Theaetetus*, 189 E ff.

Hypotheses, on the contrary, postulate facts on the being of which depends the being of the fact inferred. Nor are the geometer's hypotheses false, as some have held, urging that
40 one must not employ falsehood and that the geometer is uttering falsehood in stating that the line which he draws is a foot long or straight, when it is actually neither. The
77ª truth is that the geometer does not draw any conclusion from the being of the particular line of which he speaks, but from what his diagrams symbolize. A further distinction is that all hypotheses and illegitimate postulates are either universal or particular, whereas a definition is neither.

11 So demonstration does not necessarily imply the be-
5   ing of Forms nor a One beside a Many, but it does necessarily imply the possibility of truly predicating one of many; since without this possibility we cannot save the universal, and if the universal goes, the middle term goes with it, and so demonstration becomes impossible. We conclude, then, that there must be a single identical term unequivocally predicable of a number of individuals.
10   The law that it is impossible to affirm and deny simultaneously the same predicate of the same subject is not expressly posited by any demonstration except when the conclusion also has to be expressed in that form; in which case the proof lays down as its major premiss that the major is truly affirmed of the middle but falsely denied. It makes no difference, however, if we add to the middle, or again to the minor term, the corresponding negative. For grant a
15 minor term of which it is true to predicate man—even if it be also true to predicate not-man of it—still grant simply that man is animal and not not-animal, and the conclusion follows: for it will still be true to say that Callias—even if it be also true to say that not-Callias—is animal and not not-animal. The reason is that the major term is predicable not only of the middle, but of something other than the
20 middle as well, being of wider application; so that the conclusion is not affected even if the middle is extended to

cover the original middle term and also what is not the original middle term.[12]

The law that every predicate can be either truly affirmed
or truly denied of every subject is posited by such demonstration as uses *reductio ad impossibile*, and then not always
universally, but so far as it is requisite; within the limits,
that is, of the genus—the genus, I mean (as I have already 25
explained [13]), to which the man of science applies his demonstrations. In virtue of the common elements of demonstration—I mean the common axioms which are used as
premisses of demonstration, not the subjects or the attributes demonstrated as belonging to them—all the sciences
have communion with one another, and in communion
with them all is dialectic and any science which might attempt a universal proof of axioms such as the law of ex- 30
cluded middle, the law that the subtraction of equals from
equals leaves equal remainders, or other axioms of the same
kind. Dialectic has no definite sphere of this kind, not being confined to a single genus. Otherwise its method would
not be interrogative; for the interrogative method is barred
to the demonstrator, who cannot use the opposite facts to
prove the same nexus. This was shown in my work on the
syllogism.[14]

                                                              35

12   If a syllogistic question [15] is equivalent to a proposition
        embodying one of the two sides of a contradiction, and
if each science has its peculiar propositions from which its
peculiar conclusion is developed, then there is such a thing
as a distinctively scientific question, and it is the interrogative form of the premisses from which the 'appropriate'

---

[12] Lit. 'even if the middle is itself and also what is not itself'; i. e.
you may pass from the middle term man to include not-man without
affecting the conclusion.

                        [13] Cf. 75^a 42 ff. and 76^b 13.

[14] *An. Pr.* i. 1. The 'opposite facts' are those which would be expressed in the alternatively possible answers to the dialectical question,
the dialectician's aim being to refute his interlocutor whether the
latter answers the question put to him affirmatively or in the negative.

        [15] i. e. a premiss put in the form of a question.

40 conclusion of each science is developed. Hence it is clear
that not every question will be relevant to geometry, nor to
medicine, nor to any other science: only those questions
will be geometrical which form premises for the proof of
77ᵇ the theorems of geometry or of any other science, such as
optics, which uses the same basic truths as geometry. Of the
other sciences the like is true. Of these questions the geometer is bound to give his account, using the basic truths of
geometry in conjunction with his previous conclusions; of
the basic truths the geometer, as such, is not bound to give
5 any account. The like is true of the other sciences. There
is a limit, then, to the questions which we may put to each
man of science; nor is each man of science bound to answer
all inquiries on each several subject, but only such as fall
within the defined field of his own science. If, then, in controversy with a geometer qua geometer the disputant confines himself to geometry and proves anything from geometrical premises, he is clearly to be applauded; if he goes
10 outside these he will be at fault, and obviously cannot even
refute the geometer except accidentally. One should therefore not discuss geometry among those who are not geometers, for in such a company an unsound argument will pass
15 unnoticed. This is correspondingly true in the other sciences.

Since there are 'geometrical' questions, does it follow
that there are also distinctively 'ungeometrical' questions?
Further, in each special science—geometry for instance—
what kind of error is it that may vitiate questions, and yet
not exclude them from that science? Again, is the erroneous
conclusion one constructed from premises opposite to the
20 true premises, or is it formal fallacy though drawn from
geometrical premises? Or, perhaps, the erroneous conclusion is due to the drawing of premises from another science; e. g. in a geometrical controversy a musical question is
distinctively ungeometrical, whereas the notion that paral-
lels meet is in one sense geometrical, being ungeometrical
in a different fashion: the reason being that 'ungeometri-

cal', like 'unrhythmical,' is equivocal, meaning in the one case not geometry at all, in the other bad geometry? It is 25 this error, i. e. error based on premisses of this kind—'of' the science but false—that is the contrary of science. In mathematics the formal fallacy is not so common, because it is the middle term in which the ambiguity lies, since the major is predicated of the whole of the middle and the middle of 30 the whole of the minor (the *predicate* of course never has the prefix 'all'); and in mathematics one can, so to speak, see these middle terms with an intellectual vision, while in dialectic the ambiguity may escape detection. E. g. 'Is every circle a figure?' A diagram shows that this is so, but the minor premiss 'Are epics circles?' is shown by the diagram to be false.

If a proof has an inductive minor premiss, one should not bring an 'objection' against it. For since every premiss must 35 be applicable to a number of cases (otherwise it will not be true in every instance, which, since the syllogism proceeds from universals, it must be), then assuredly the same is true of an 'objection'; since premisses and 'objections' are so far the same that anything which can be validly advanced as an 'objection' must be such that it could take the form of a 40 premiss, either demonstrative or dialectical. On the other hand arguments formally illogical do sometimes occur through taking as middles mere attributes of the major and minor terms. An instance of this is Caeneus' proof that fire 78ᵃ increases in geometrical proportion: 'Fire', he argues, 'increases rapidly, and so does geometrical proportion'. There is no syllogism so, but there is a syllogism if the most rapidly increasing proportion is geometrical and the most rapidly increasing proportion is attributable to fire in its 5 motion. Sometimes, no doubt, it is impossible to reason from premisses predicating mere attributes: but sometimes it is possible, though the possibility is overlooked. If false premisses could never give true conclusions 'resolution' would be easy, for premisses and conclusion would in that case inevitably reciprocate. I might then argue thus: let A be an existing fact; let the existence of A imply such and such facts actually known to me to exist, which we may call B. I can now, since they reciprocate, infer A from B.

10 Reciprocation of premisses and conclusion is more frequent in mathematics, because mathematics takes definitions, but never an accident, for its premisses—a second characteristic distinguishing mathematical reasoning from dialectical disputations.

A science expands not by the interposition of fresh middle terms, but by the apposition of fresh extreme terms. E. g. A is predicated of B, B of C, C of D, and so indefi-
15 nitely. Or the expansion may be lateral: e. g. one major, A, may be proved of two minors, C and E. Thus let A represent number—a number or number taken indeterminately; E determinate odd number; C any particular odd number. We can then predicate A of C. Next let D represent deter-
20 minate even number, and E even number. Then A is predicable of E.

13 Knowledge of the fact differs from knowledge of the reasoned fact. To begin with, they differ within the same science and in two ways: (1) when the premisses of the syllogism are not immediate (for then the proximate
25 cause is not contained in them—a necessary condition of knowledge of the reasoned fact): (2) when the premisses are immediate, but instead of the cause the better known of the two reciprocals is taken as the middle; for of two reciprocally predicable terms the one which is not the cause may quite easily be the better known and so become the middle term of the demonstration. Thus (2) (a) you might
30 prove as follows that the planets are near because they do not twinkle: let C be the planets, B not twinkling, A proximity. Then B is predicable of C; for the planets do not twinkle. But A is also predicable of B, since that which does not twinkle is near—we must take this truth as having been reached by induction or sense-perception. Therefore A is a
35 necessary predicate of C; so that we have demonstrated that

the planets are near. This syllogism, then, proves not the reasoned fact but only the fact; since they are not near because they do not twinkle, but, because they are near, do not twinkle. The major and middle of the proof, however, may be reversed, and then the demonstration will be of the reasoned fact. Thus: let C be the planets, B proximity, A 40 not twinkling. Then B is an attribute of C, and A—not 78ᵇ twinkling—of B. Consequently A is predicable of C, and the syllogism proves the reasoned fact, since its middle term is the proximate cause. Another example is the inference that the moon is spherical from its manner of waxing. Thus: since that which so waxes is spherical, and since the moon so waxes, clearly the moon is spherical. Put in this 5 form, the syllogism turns out to be proof of the fact, but if the middle and major be reversed it is proof of the reasoned fact; since the moon is not spherical because it waxes in a certain manner, but waxes in such a manner because it is spherical. (Let C be the moon, B spherical, and A waxing.) Again (b), in cases where the cause and the effect are not 10 reciprocal and the effect is the better known, the fact is demonstrated but not the reasoned fact. This also occurs (1) when the middle falls outside the major and minor, for here too the strict cause is not given, and so the demonstration is of the fact, not of the reasoned fact. For example, 15 the question 'Why does not a wall breathe?' might be answered, 'Because it is not an animal'; but that answer would not give the strict cause, because if not being an animal causes the absence of respiration, then being an animal should be the cause of respiration, according to the rule that if the negation of x causes the non-inherence of y, the 20 affirmation of x causes the inherence of y; e. g. if the disproportion of the hot and cold elements is the cause of ill health, their proportion is the cause of health; and conversely, if the assertion of x causes the inherence of y, the negation of x must cause y's non-inherence. But in the case given this consequence does not result; for not every animal breathes. A syllogism with this kind of cause takes place

in the second figure. Thus: let A be animal, B respiration,
C wall. Then A is predicable of all B (for all that breathes
is animal), but of no C; and consequently B is predicable
of no C; that is, the wall does not breathe. Such causes are
like far-fetched explanations, which precisely consist in
making the cause too remote, as in Anacharsis' account of
why the Scythians have no flute-players; namely because
they have no vines.

Thus, then, do the syllogism of the fact and the syllogism
of the reasoned fact differ within one science and according
to the position of the middle terms. But there is another
way too in which the fact and the reasoned fact differ, and
that is when they are investigated respectively by different
sciences. This occurs in the case of problems related to one
another as subordinate and superior, as when optical problems are subordinated to geometry, mechanical problems
to stereometry, harmonic problems to arithmetic, the data
of observation to astronomy. (Some of these sciences bear
almost the same name; e. g. mathematical and nautical
astronomy, mathematical and acoustical harmonics.) Here
it is the business of the empirical observers to know the
fact, of the mathematicians to know the reasoned fact; for
the latter are in possession of the demonstrations giving
the causes, and are often ignorant of the fact: just as we
have often a clear insight into a universal, but through lack
of observation are ignorant of some of its particular instances. These connexions [16] have a perceptible existence
though they are manifestations of forms. For the mathematical sciences concern forms: they do not demonstrate
properties of a substratum, since, even though the geometrical subjects are predicable as properties of a perceptible
substratum, it is not as thus predicable that the mathematician demonstrates properties of them. As optics is related
to geometry, so another science is related to optics, namely
the theory of the rainbow. Here knowledge of the fact is
within the province of the natural philosopher, knowledge

[16] sc. 'which require two sciences for their proof.' Cf. 78ᵇ 35.

of the reasoned fact within that of the optician, either qua optician or qua mathematical optician. Many sciences not standing in this mutual relation enter into it at points; e. g. medicine and geometry: it is the physician's business to know that circular wounds heal more slowly, the geometer's to know the reason why.

15

14 Of all the figures the most scientific is the first. Thus, it is the vehicle of the demonstrations of all the mathematical sciences, such as arithmetic, geometry, and optics, and practically of all sciences that investigate causes: for the 20 syllogism of the reasoned fact is either exclusively or generally speaking and in most cases in this figure—a second proof that this figure is the most scientific; for grasp of a reasoned conclusion is the primary condition of knowledge. Thirdly, the first is the only figure which enables us to pursue knowledge of the essence of a thing. In the second figure no affirmative conclusion is possible, and knowledge 25 of a thing's essence must be affirmative; while in the third figure the conclusion can be affirmative, but cannot be universal, and essence must have a universal character: e. g. man is not two-footed animal in any qualified sense, but universally. Finally, the first figure has no need of the others, while it is by means of the first that the other two 30 figures are developed, and have their intervals close-packed until immediate premisses are reached. Clearly, therefore, the first figure is the primary condition of knowledge.

15 Just as an attribute A may (as we saw) be atomically connected with a subject B, so its disconnexion may be atomic. I call 'atomic' connexions or disconnexions which involve no intermediate term; since in that case the connexion or disconnexion will not be mediated by something 35 other than the terms themselves. It follows that if either A or B, or both A and B, have a genus, their disconnexion cannot be primary. Thus: let C be the genus of A. Then, if C is not the genus of B—for A may well have a genus which is

40 not the genus of *B*—there will be a syllogism proving *A*'s
disconnexion from *B* thus:

79ᵇ

> all *A* is *C*,
> no *B* is *C*,
> ∴ no *B* is *A*.

Or if it is *B* which has a genus *D*, we have

> all *B* is *D*,
> no *D* is *A*,
> ∴ no *B* is *A*, by syllogism;

5 and the proof will be similar if both *A* and *B* have a genus.
That the genus of *A* need not be the genus of *B* and vice
versa, is shown by the existence of mutually exclusive co-
ordinate series of predication. If no term in the series *ACD*
. . . is predicable of any term in the series *BEF*. . . , and
10 if *G*—a term in the former series—is the genus of *A*, clearly
G will not be the genus of *B*; since, if it were, the series
would not be mutually exclusive. So also if *B* has a genus, it
will not be the genus of *A*. If, on the other hand, neither
A nor *B* has a genus and *A* does not inhere in *B*, this disconnexion must be atomic. If there be a middle term, one
15 or other of them is bound to have a genus, for the syllogism
will be either in the first or the second figure. If it is in the
first, *B* will have a genus—for the premiss containing it
must be affirmative; [17] if in the second, either *A* or *B* indifferently, since syllogism is possible if either is contained in
20 a negative premiss,[18] but not if both premisses are negative.

Hence it is clear that one thing may be atomically disconnected from another, and we have stated when and how
this is possible.

16 Ignorance—defined not as the negation of knowledge
but as a positive state of mind—is error produced by
inference.

---

[17] i.e. in Celarent.
[18] i.e. in Cesare or Camestres.

(1) Let us first consider propositions asserting a pred- 25
icate's immediate connexion with or disconnexion from
a subject. Here, it is true, positive error may befall one in
alternative ways; for it may arise where one directly believes
a connexion or disconnexion as well as where one's belief
is acquired by inference. The error, however, that consists
in a direct belief is without complication; but the error
resulting from inference—which here concerns us—takes
many forms. Thus, let A be atomically disconnected from
all B: then the conclusion inferred through a middle term 30
C, that all B is A, will be a case of error produced by syllogism. Now, two cases are possible. Either (*a*) both premisses, or (*b*) one premiss only, may be false. (*a*) If neither
A is an attribute of any C nor C of any B, whereas the
contrary was posited in both cases, both premisses will be
false. (C may quite well be so related to A and B that C is 35
neither subordinate to A nor a universal attribute of B: for
B, since A was said to be primarily disconnected from B,
cannot have a genus, and A need not necessarily be a universal attribute of all things. Consequently both premisses
may be false.) On the other hand, (*b*) one of the premisses 40
may be true, though not either indifferently but only the
major A–C; since, B having no genus, the premiss C–B
will always be false, while A–C may be true. This is the 80ᵇ
case if, for example, A is related atomically to both C and
B; because when the same term is related atomically to
more terms than one, neither of those terms will belong to
the other. It is, of course, equally the case if A–C is not
atomic.   5

Error of attribution, then, occurs through these causes
and in this form only—for we found that no syllogism of
universal attribution was possible in any figure but the first.
On the other hand, an error of non-attribution may occur
either in the first or in the second figure. Let us therefore
first explain the various forms it takes in the first figure and
the character of the premisses in each case.   10

(*c*) It may occur when both premisses are false; e. g.

supposing A atomically connected with both C and B, if it
be then assumed that no C is A, and all B is C, both premisses are false.

(d) It is also possible when one is false. This may be
either premiss indifferently. A-C may be true, C–B false
15 —A–C true because A is not an attribute of all things, C–B
false because C, which never has the attribute A, cannot be
an attribute of B; for if C–B were true, the premiss A–C
would no longer be true, and besides if both premisses were
true, the conclusion would be true. Or again, C–B may be
20 true and A–C false; e. g. both C and A contain B as genera,
one of them must be subordinate to the other, so that if the
premiss takes the form No C is A, it will be false. This
25 makes it clear that whether either or both premisses are
false, the conclusion will equally be false.

In the second figure the premisses cannot both be wholly
false; for if all B is A, no middle term can be with truth
universally affirmed of one extreme and universally denied
30 of the other: but premisses in which the middle is affirmed
of one extreme and denied of the other are the necessary
condition if one is to get a valid inference at all. Therefore
if, taken in this way, they are wholly false, their contraries
conversely should be wholly true. But this is impossible.
On the other hand, there is nothing to prevent both premisses being partially false; e. g. if actually some A is C and
35 some B is C, then if it is premised that all A is C and no
B is C, both premisses are false, yet partially, not wholly,
false. The same is true if the major is made negative instead
of the minor. Or one premiss may be wholly false, and it
may be either of them. Thus, supposing that actually an
40 attribute of all A must also be an attribute of all B,
80' then if C is yet taken to be a universal attribute of all A
but universally non-attributable to B, C–A will be true
but C–B false. Again, actually that which is an attribute
of no B will not be an attribute of all A either; for if
it be an attribute of all A, it will also be an attribute of
all B, which is contrary to supposition; but if C be never-

theless assumed to be a universal attribute of A, but 5
an attribute of no B, then the premiss C–B is true but the
major is false. The case is similar if the major is made the
negative premiss. For in fact what is an attribute of no A
will not be an attribute of any B either; and if it be yet
assumed that C is universally non-attributable to A, but a
universal attribute of B, the premiss C–A is true but the 10
minor wholly false. Again, in fact it is false to assume that
that which is an attribute of all B is an attribute of no A,
for if it be an attribute of all B, it must be an attribute
of some A. If then C is nevertheless assumed to be an attribute of all B but of no A, C–B will be true but C–A false.

It is thus clear that in the case of atomic propositions
erroneous inference will be possible not only when both 15
premisses are false but also when only one is false.

17 (2) In the case of attributes not atomically connected with or disconnected from their subjects, (a)
(i) as long as the false conclusion is inferred through the
'appropriate' middle, only the major and not both prem- 20
isses can be false. By 'appropriate middle' I mean the
middle term through which the contradictory—i. e. the
true—conclusion is inferrible. Thus, let A be attributable
to B through a middle term C: then, since to produce a
conclusion the premiss C–B must be taken affirmatively,
it is clear that this premiss must always be true, for its 25
quality is not changed. But the major A–C is false, for it is
by a change in the quality of A–C that the conclusion becomes its contradictory—i. e. true. Similarly (ii) if the middle is taken from another series of predication; e. g. suppose
D to be not only contained within A as a part within its whole
but also predicable of all B. Then the premiss D–B must remain unchanged, but the quality of A–D must be changed; 30
so that D–B is always true, A–D always false. Such error
is practically identical with that which is inferred through
the 'appropriate' middle. On the other hand, (b) if the
conclusion is not inferred through the 'appropriate' middle

—(i) when the middle is subordinate to A but is predicable
35 of no B, both premisses must be false, because if there is to
be a conclusion both must be posited as asserting the contrary of what is actually the fact, and so posited both
become false: e. g. suppose that actually all D is A
but no B is D; then if these premisses are changed in
quality, a conclusion will follow and both of the new
40 premisses will be false. When, however, (ii) the mid-
81ʳ dle D is not subordinate to A, A–D will be true, D–B
false––A–D true because A was not subordinate to D, D–B
false because if it had been true, the conclusion too would
have been true; but it is ex hypothesi false.

When the erroneous inference is in the second figure,
5 both premisses cannot be entirely false; since if B is subordinate to A, there can be no middle predicable of all of
one extreme and of none of the other as was stated before.[19]
One premiss, however, may be false, and it may be either
of them. Thus, if C is actually an attribute of both A and
10 B, but is assumed to be an attribute of A only and not of
B, C–A will be true, C–B false: or again if C be assumed
to be attributable to B but to no A, C–B will be true, C–A
false.

We have stated when and through what kinds of prem-
15 isses error will result in cases where the erroneous conclusion is negative. If the conclusion is affirmative, (a) (i)
it may be inferred through the 'appropriate' middle term.
In this case both premisses cannot be false since, as we
said before,[20] C–B must remain unchanged if there is to be
a conclusion, and consequently A–C, the quality of which
is changed, will always be false. This is equally true if (ii)
20 the middle is taken from another series of predication, as
was stated to be the case also with regard to negative
error; [21] for D–B must remain unchanged, while the quality

[19] Cf. 80ᵃ 29.
[20] Cf. 80ᵇ 17–26.
[21] Cf. 80ᵇ 26–32.

of A–D must be converted, and the type of error is the
same as before.

(b) The middle may be inappropriate. Then (i) if D is
subordinate to A, A–D will be true, but D–B false; since A 25
may quite well be predicable of several terms no one of
which can be subordinated to another. If, however, (ii)
D is not subordinate to A, obviously A–D, since it is
affirmed, will always be false, while D–B may be either
true or false; for A may very well be an attribute of no D, 30
whereas all B is D, e. g. no science is animal, all music is
science. Equally well A may be an attribute of no D, and D
of no B. It emerges, then, that if the middle term is not
subordinate to the major, not only both premisses but
either singly may be false.

Thus we have made it clear how many varieties of erroneous inference are liable to happen and through what 35
kinds of premisses they occur, in the case both of immediate and of demonstrable truths.

18 It is also clear that the loss of any one of the senses
entails the loss of a corresponding portion of knowledge, and that, since we learn either by induction or
by demonstration, this knowledge cannot be acquired. 40
Thus demonstation develops from universals, induction 81
from particulars; but since it is possible to familiarize the
pupil with even the so-called mathematical abstractions
only through induction—i. e. only because each subject
genus possesses, in virtue of a determinate mathematical
character, certain properties which can be treated as separate even though they do not exist in isolation—it is con- 5
sequently impossible to come to grasp universals except
through induction. But induction is impossible for those
who have not sense-perception. For it is sense-perception
alone which is adequate for grasping the particulars:
they cannot be objects of scientific knowledge, because
neither can universals give us knowledge of them without

induction, nor can we get it through induction without
sense-perception.

10 **19** Every syllogism is effected by means of three terms.
One kind of syllogism serves to prove that A inheres
in C by showing that A inheres in B and B in C; the other
is negative and one of its premisses asserts one term of another, while the other denies one term of another. It is
15 clear, then, that these are the fundamentals and so-called
hypotheses of syllogism. Assume them as they have been
stated, and proof is bound to follow—proof that A inheres
in C through B, and again that A inheres in B through some
other middle term, and similarly that B inheres in C. If
our reasoning aims at gaining credence and so is merely
dialectical, it is obvious that we have only to see that our
20 inference is based on premisses as credible as possible: so
that if a middle term between A and B is credible though
not real, one can reason through it and complete a dialectical syllogism. If, however, one is aiming at truth, one
must be guided by the real connexions of subjects and attributes. Thus: since there are attributes which are predi-
25 cated of a subject essentially or naturally and not coinci-
dentally—not, that is, in a sense in which we say 'That
white (thing) is a man', which is not the same mode of
predication as when we say 'The man is white': the man is
white not because he is something else but because he is
man, but the white is man because 'being white' coincides
with 'humanity' within one substratum—therefore there
30 are terms such as are naturally subjects of predicates. Suppose, then, C such a term not itself attributable to anything else as to a subject, but the proximate subject of the
attribute B—i. e. so that B–C is immediate; suppose further E related immediately to F, and F to B. The first
question is, must this series terminate, or can it proceed
to infinity? The second question is as follows: Suppose
nothing is essentially predicated of A, but A is predicated
35 primarily of H and of no intermediate prior term, and sup-

pose *H* similarly related to *G* and *G* to *B*; then must this series also terminate, or can it too proceed to infinity? There is this much difference between the questions: the first is, is it possible to start from that which is not itself attributable to anything else but is the subject of attributes, and ascend to infinity? The second is the problem whether 40 one can start from that which is a predicate but not itself a 82ᵛ subject of predicates, and descend to infinity? A third question is, if the extreme terms are fixed, can there be an infinity of middles? I mean this: suppose for example that *A* inheres in *C* and *B* is intermediate between them, but between *B* and *A* there are other middles, and between these 5 again fresh middles; can these proceed to infinity or can they not? This is the equivalent of inquiring, do demonstrations proceed to infinity, i. e. is everything demonstrable? Or do ultimate subject and primary attribute limit one another?

I hold that the same questions arise with regard to negative conclusions and premisses: viz. if *A* is attributable to no *B*, then either this predication will be primary, or there 10 will be an intermediate term prior to *B* to which *A* is not attributable—*G*, let us say, which is attributable to all *B*—and there may still be another term *H* prior to *G*, which is attributable to all *G*. The same questions arise, I say, because in these cases too either the series of prior terms to which *A* is not attributable is infinite or it terminates.

One cannot ask the same questions in the case of reciprocating terms, since when subject and predicate are con- 15 vertible there is neither primary nor ultimate subject, seeing that all the reciprocals qua subjects stand in the same relation to one another, whether we say that the subject has an infinity of attributes or that both subjects and attributes—and we raised the question in both cases—are infinite in number. These questions then cannot be asked—unless, indeed, the terms can reciprocate by two different modes, by accidental predication in one relation and natural predication in the other. 20

20 Now, it is clear that if the predications terminate in
both the upward and the downward direction (by
'upward' I mean the ascent to the more universal, by
'downward' the descent to the more particular), the middle terms cannot be infinite in number. For suppose that
25 A is predicated of F, and that the intermediates—call them
BB' B'' . . . —are infinite, then clearly you might descend
from A and find one term predicated of another ad infinitum, since you have an infinity of terms between you
and F; and equally, if you ascend from F, there are infinite terms between you and A. It follows that if these
processes are impossible there cannot be an infinity of inter-
30 mediates between A and F. Nor is it of any effect to urge
that some terms of the series AB . . . F are contiguous so
as to exclude intermediates, while others cannot be taken
into the argument at all: whichever terms of the series B
. . . I take, the number of intermediates in the direction
either of A or of F must be finite or infinite: where the
infinite series starts, whether from the first term or from a
35 later one, is of no moment, for the succeeding terms in any
case are infinite in number.

21 Further, if in affirmative demonstration the series
terminates in both directions, clearly it will terminate
too in negative demonstration. Let us assume that we cannot proceed to infinity either by ascending from the ulti-
82ᵇ mate term (by 'ultimate term' I mean a term such as F
was, not itself attributable to a subject but itself the subject of attributes), or by descending towards an ultimate
from the primary term (by 'primary term' I mean a term
predicable of a subject but not itself a subject [22]). If this
assumption is justified, the series will also terminate in the
5 case of negation. For a negative conclusion can be proved
in all three figures. In the first figure it is proved thus: no B
is A, all C is B. In packing the interval B–C we must reach

---

[22] sc. a predicate above which is no wider universal.

immediate propositions—as is always the case with the minor premiss—since B–C is affirmative. As regards the other premiss it is plain that if the major term is denied of a term D prior to B, D will have to be predicable of all B, 10 and if the major is denied of yet another term prior to D, this term must be predicable of all D. Consequently, since the ascending series is finite, the descent will also terminate and there will be a subject of which A is primarily non-predicable. In the second figure the syllogism is, all A is B, no C is B, ∴ no C is A. If proof of this [23] is required, plainly it may be shown either in the first figure as above, 15 in the second as here, or in the third. The first figure has been discussed, and we will proceed to display the second, proof by which will be as follows: all B is D, no C is D . . . , since it is required that B should be a subject of which a predicate is affirmed. Next, since D is to be proved not to belong to C, then D has a further predicate which is denied of C. Therefore, since the succession of predicates affirmed of an even higher universal terminates,[24] the suc- 20 cession of predicates denied terminates too.[25]

The third figure shows it as follows: all B is A, some B is not C, ∴ some A is not C. This premiss, i. e. C–B, will be proved either in the same figure or in one of the two figures discussed above. In the first and second figures the series 25 terminates. If we use the third figure, we shall take as premisses, all E is B, some E is not C, and this premiss

---

[23] *sc.* 'that no C is B'.

[24] i. e. each of the successive prosyllogisms required to prove the negative minors contains an affirmative major in which the middle is affirmed of a subject successively 'higher' or more universal than the subject of the first syllogism. Thus:

Syllogism:	Prosyllogisms:	
All B is D	All D is E	All E is F
No C is D	No C is E	No C is F
∴ No C is B	∴ No C is D	∴ No C is E

B, D, E, &c., are successively more universal subjects; and the series of affirmative majors containing them must *ex hypothesi* terminate.

[25] Since the series of affirmative majors terminates and since an affirmative major is required for each prosyllogism, we shall eventually reach a minor incapable of proof and therefore immediate.

again will be proved by a similar prosyllogism. But since it is assumed that the series of descending subjects also terminates, plainly the series of more universal non-predicables will terminate also. Even supposing that the proof is not confined to one method, but employs them all and is 30 now in the first figure, now in the second or third—even so the regress will terminate, for the methods are finite in number, and if finite things are combined in a finite number of ways, the result must be finite.

Thus it is plain that the regress of middles terminates in the case of negative demonstration, if it does so also in the case of affirmative demonstration. That in fact the regress terminates in both these cases may be made clear by the 35 following dialectical considerations.

22   In the case of predicates constituting the essential nature of a thing, it clearly terminates, seeing that if definition is possible, or in other words, if essential form is knowable, and an infinite series cannot be traversed, predicates constituting a thing's essential nature must be finite 83ª in number.[26] But as regards predicates generally we have the following prefatory remarks to make. (1) We can affirm without falsehood 'the white (thing) is walking', and 'that big (thing) is a log'; or again, 'the log is big', and 'the man walks'. But the affirmation differs in the two cases. When I 5 affirm 'the white is a log', I mean that something which happens to be white is a log—not that white is the substratum in which log inheres, for it was not qua white or qua a species of white that the white (thing) came to be a log, and the white (thing) is consequently not a log except incidentally. On the other hand, when I affirm 'the log is white', I do not mean that something else, which 10 happens also to be a log, is white (as I should if I said 'the musician is white', which would mean 'the man who hap-

---

[26] If the attributes in a series of predication such as we are discussing are substantial, they must be finite in number, because they are then the elements constituting the definition of a substance.

pens also to be a musician is white'); on the contrary, log is
here the substratum—the substratum which actually came
to be white, and did so qua wood or qua a species of wood
and qua nothing else.

If we must lay down a rule, let us entitle the latter kind
of statement predication, and the former not predication at 15
all, or not strict but accidental predication. 'White' and
'log' will thus serve as types respectively of predicate and
subject.

We shall assume, then, that the predicate is invariably
predicated strictly and not accidentally of the subject, for 20
on such predication demonstrations depend for their force.
It follows from this that when a single attribute is predicated of a single subject, the predicate must affirm of the
subject either some element constituting its essential nature, or that it is in some way qualified, quantified, essentially related, active, passive, placed, or dated.[27]

(2) Predicates which signify substance signify that the
subject is identical with the predicate or with a species of
the predicate. Predicates not signifying substance which 25
are predicated of a subject not identical with themselves or
with a species of themselves are accidental or coincidental;
e. g. white is a coincident of man, seeing that man is not
identical with white or a species of white, but rather with 30
animal, since man *is* identical with a species of animal.
These predicates which do not signify substance must be
predicates of some other subject, and nothing can be
white which is not also other than white. The Forms we
can dispense with, for they are mere sound without sense;
and even if there are such things, they are not relevant

---

[27] The first of three statements preliminary to a proof that predicates which are accidental—other than substantial—cannot be unlimited in number: Accidental is to be distinguished from essential or
natural predication [cf. i, ch. 4, 73ᵇ 5 ff. and *An. Pr.* i, ch. 25, 43ᵃ
25–6]. The former is alien to demonstration: hence, provided that a
single attribute is predicated of a single subject, all genuine predicates
fall either under the category of substance or under one of the adjectival categories.

to our discussion, since demonstrations are concerned with
35 predicates such as we have defined.[28]

(3) If A is a quality of B, B cannot be a quality of A—
a quality of a quality. Therefore A and B cannot be predicated reciprocally in strict predication: they
can be affirmed without falsehood of one another, but not
genuinely predicated of each other.[29] For one alternative
is that they should be substantially predicated of one another, i. e. B would become the genus or differentia of A—
83ᵇ the predicate now become subject. But it has been shown
that in these substantial predications neither the ascending predicates nor the descending subjects form an infinite
series; e. g. neither the series, man is biped, biped is animal, &c., nor the series predicating animal of man, man of
Callias, Callias of a further subject as an element of its essential nature, is infinite. For all such substance is definable,
5 and an infinite series cannot be traversed in thought: consequently neither the ascent nor the descent is infinite,
since a substance whose predicates were infinite would not
be definable. Hence they will not be predicated each as the
genus of the other; for this would equate a genus with one
10 of its own species. Nor (the other alternative) can a *quale*
be reciprocally predicated of a *quale*, nor any term belonging to an adjectival category of another such term, except
by accidental predication; for all such predicates are coincidents and are predicated of substances.[30] On the other

---

[28] Second preliminary statement: The precise distinction of sub-
stantive from adjectival predication makes clear (implicitly) the two
distinctions, (a) that between natural and accidental predication, (b)
that between substantival and adjectival predication, which falls
within natural predication. This enables us to reject the Platonic
Forms.

[29] Third preliminary statement merging into the beginning of the
proof proper: Reciprocal predication cannot produce an indefinite
regress because it is not natural predication.

[30] Expansion of third preliminary statement: Reciprocals A and B
might be predicated of one another (a) substantially; but it has been
proved already that because a definition cannot contain an infinity of
elements substantial predication cannot generate infinity; and it would
disturb the relation of genus and species: (b) as *qualia* or *quanta* &c.;
but this would be unnatural predication, because all such predicates
are adjectival, i.e. accidents, or coincidents, of substances.

hand—in proof of the impossibility of an infinite ascending series—every predication displays the subject as somehow qualified or quantified or as characterized under one
of the other adjectival categories, or else is an element in
its substantial nature: these latter are limited in number, 15
and the number of the widest kinds under which predications fall is also limited, for every predication must exhibit
its subject as somehow qualified, quantified, essentially related, acting or suffering, or in some place or at some time.[31]

I assume first that predication implies a single subject
and a single attribute, and secondly that predicates which
are not substantial are not predicated of one another. We
assume this because such predicates are all coincidents,
and though some are essential coincidents, others of a dif- 20
ferent type, yet we maintain that all of them alike are
predicated of some substratum and that a coincident is
never a substratum—since we do not class as a coincident
anything which does not owe its designation to its being
something other than itself, but always hold that any
coincident is predicated of some substratum other than
itself, and that another group of coincidents may have a
different substratum. Subject to these assumptions then,
neither the ascending nor the descending series of predica- 25
tion in which a single attribute is predicated of a single
subject is infinite.[32] For the subjects of which coincidents
are predicated are as many as the constitutive elements of

[31] The ascent of predicates is also finite; because all predicates fall
under one or other of the categories, and (a) the series of predicates
under each category terminates when the category is reached, and (b)
the number of the categories is limited. [(a) seems to mean that an
attribute as well as a substance is definable by genus and differentia,
and the elements in its definition must terminate in an upward direction at the category, and can therefore no more form an infinite series
than can the elements constituting the definition of a substance.]

[32] To reinforce this brief proof that descent and ascent are both
finite we may repeat the premisses on which it depends. These are (1)
the assumption that predication means the predication of one attribute
of one subject, and (2) our proof that accidents cannot be reciprocally
predicated of one another, because that would be unnatural predication. It follows from these premisses that both ascent and descent are
finite. [Actually (2) only reinforces the proof that the *descent* terminates.]

each individual substance, and these we have seen are not
infinite in number, while in the ascending series are contained those constitutive elements with their coincidents
—both of which are finite.[33] We conclude that there is a
given subject <D> of which some attribute <C> is
primarily predicable; that there must be an attribute <B>
30 primarily predicable of the first attribute, and that the
series must end with a term <A> not predicable of any
term prior to the last subject of which it was predicated
<B>, and of which no term prior to it is predicable.[34]

---

[33] To repeat again the proof that both ascent and descent are finite:
The subjects cannot be more in number than the constituents of a
definable form, and these, we know, are not infinite in number: hence
the descent is finite. The series regarded as an ascent contains subjects
and ever more universal accidents, and neither subjects nor accidents
are infinite in number.

[34] Formal restatement of the last conclusion. [This is obscure: apparently Aristotle here contemplates a hybrid series: category, accident,
further specified accident . . . substantial genus, subgenus . . .
infima species, individual substance.

If this interpretation of the first portion of the chapter is at all correct, Aristotle's first proof that the first two questions of ch. 19 must
be answered in the negative is roughly as follows: The ultimate subject
of all judgement is an individual substance, a concrete singular. Of
such concrete singulars you can predicate substantially only the elements constituting their infima species. These are limited in number
because they form an intelligible synthesis. So far, then, as substantial
predicates are concerned, the questions are answered. But these elements are also the subjects of which accidents, or coincidents, are
predicated, and therefore as regards accidental predicates, at any rate,
the descending series of subjects terminates. The ascending series of
attributes also terminates, (1) because each higher attribute in the
series can only be a higher genus of the accident predicated of the ultimate subject of its genus, and therefore an element in the accident's
definition; (2) because the number of the categories is limited.

We may note that the first argument seems to envisage a series
which, viewed as an ascent, starts with a concrete individual of which
the elements of its definition are predicated successively, specific differentia being followed by proximate genus, which latter is the starting-
point of a succession of ever more universal attributes terminating in a
category; and that the second argument extends the scope of the dispute to the sum total of all the trains of accidental predication which
one concrete singular substance can beget. It is, as so often in Aristotle, difficult to be sure whether he is regarding the infima species or
the concrete singular as the ultimate subject of judgement. I have assumed that he means the latter.]

The argument we have given is one of the so-called proofs; an alternative proof follows. Predicates so related to their subjects that there are other predicates prior to them predicable of those subjects are demonstrable; but of demonstrable propositions one cannot have something better than knowledge, nor can one know them without dem- 35 onstration. Secondly, if a consequent is only known through an antecedent (viz. premisses prior to it) and we neither know this antecedent nor have something better than knowledge of it, then we shall not have scientific knowledge of the consequent. Therefore, if it is possible through demonstration to know anything without quali-fication and not merely as dependent on the acceptance of certain premisses—i. e. hypothetically—the series of in-termediate predications must terminate. If it does not ter-minate, and beyond any predicate taken as higher than 84ᵃ another there remains another still higher, then every predi-cate is demonstrable. Consequently, since these demonstra-ble predicates are infinite in number and therefore cannot be traversed, we shall *not* know them by demonstration. If, therefore, we have not something better than knowl-edge of them, we cannot through demonstration have un- 5 qualified but only hypothetical science of anything.[35]

As dialectical proofs of our contention these may carry conviction, but an analytic process will show more briefly that neither the ascent nor the descent of predication can be infinite in the demonstrative sciences which are the ob- 10 ject of our investigation. Demonstration proves the inher-ence of essential attributes in things. Now attributes may be

---

[35] The former proof was dialectical. So is that which follows in this paragraph. If a predicate inheres in a subject but is subordinate to a higher predicate also predicable of that subject [i. e. not to a wider predicate but to a middle term giving logically prior premisses and in that sense higher], then the inherence can be known by demonstration and only by demonstration. But that means that it is known as the consequent of an antecedent. Therefore, if demonstration gives genu-ine knowledge, the series must terminate; i. e. every predicate is de-monstrable and known only as a consequent and therefore hypothet-ically, unless an antecedent known *per se* is reached.

essential for two reasons: either because they are elements
in the essential nature of their subjects, or because their
subjects are elements in their essential nature. An example
15 of the latter is odd as an attribute of number—though it
is number's attribute, yet number itself is an element in
the definition of odd; of the former, multiplicity or the
indivisible, which are elements in the definition of number. In neither kind of attribution can the terms be infinite. They are not infinite where each is related to the
term below it as odd is to number, for this would mean the
20 inherence in odd of another attribute of odd in whose nature odd was an essential element: but then number will
be an ultimate subject of the whole infinite chain of attributes, and be an element in the definition of each of
them. Hence, since an infinity of attributes such as contain their subject in their definition cannot inhere in a
single thing, the ascending series is equally finite.[36] Note,
moreover, that all such attributes must so inhere in the
ultimate subject—e. g. its attributes in number and number in them—as to be commensurate with the subject and
25 not of wider extent. Attributes which are essential elements
in the nature of their subjects are equally finite: otherwise definition would be impossible. Hence, if all the attributes predicated are essential and these cannot be
infinite, the ascending series will terminate, and consequently the descending series too.[37]

[36] As regards type (2) [the opening of the chapter has disposed of
type (1)]: in any series of such predicates any given term will contain
in its definition all the lower terms, and the series will therefore
terminate at the bottom in the ultimate subject. But since every term
down to and including the ultimate subject is contained in the definition of any given term, if the series ascend infinitely there must be a
term containing an infinity of terms in its definition. But this is impossible, and therefore the ascent terminates.

[37] Note too that either type of essential attribute must be commensurate with its subject, because the first defines, the second is
defined by, its subject; and consequently no subject can possess an
infinite number of essential predicates of either type, or definition
would be impossible. Hence if the attributes predicated are all essential, the series terminates in both directions. [This passage merely

If this is so, it follows that the intermediates between any two terms are also always limited in number.[38] An immediately obvious consequence of this is that demonstrations necessarily involve basic truths, and that the contention of some—referred to at the outset—that all truths are demonstrable is mistaken. For if there are basic truths, (a) not all truths are demonstrable, and (b) an infinite regress is impossible; since if either (a) or (b) were not a fact, it would mean that no interval was immediate and indivisible, but that all intervals were divisible. This is true because a conclusion is demonstrated by the interposition, not the apposition, of a fresh term. If such interposition could continue to infinity there might be an infinite number of terms between any two terms; but this is impossible if both the ascending and descending series of predication terminate; and of this fact, which before was shown dialectically, analytic proof has now been given.[39]

23 It is an evident corollary of these conclusions that if the same attribute A inheres in two terms C and D predicable either not at all, or not of all instances, of one another, it does not always belong to them in virtue of a common middle term. Isosceles and scalene possess the attribute of having their angles equal to two right angles in virtue of a common middle; for they possess it in so far as they are both a certain kind of figure, and not in so far as they differ from one another. But this is not always the case; for, were it so, if we take B as the common middle in

displays the ground underlying the previous argument that the ascent of attributes of type (2) is finite, and notes in passing its more obvious and already stated application to attributes of type (1).]

[38] It follows that the intermediates between a given subject and a given attribute must also be limited in number.

[39] Corollary: (a) demonstrations necessarily involve basic truths, and therefore (b) not all truths, as we saw [84[a] 32] that some maintain, are demonstrable [cf. 72[b] 6]. If either (a) or (b) were not a fact, since conclusions are demonstrated by the interposition of a middle and not by the apposition of an extreme term [cf. note on 78[a] 15], no premiss would be an immediate indivisible interval. This closes the analytic argument.

10 virtue of which A inheres in C and D, clearly B would inhere in C and D through a second common middle, and this in turn would inhere in C and D through a third, so that between two terms an infinity of intermediates would fall—an impossibility. Thus it need not always be in virtue of a common middle term that a single attribute inheres 15 in several subjects, since there must be immediate intervals. Yet if the attribute to be proved common to two subjects is to be one of their essential attributes, the middle terms involved must be within one subject genus and be derived from the same group of immediate premisses; for we have seen that processes of proof cannot pass from one genus to another.[40]

It is also clear that when A inheres in B, this can be dem-20 onstrated if there is a middle term. Further, the 'elements' of such a conclusion are the premisses containing the middle in question, and they are identical in number with the middle terms, seeing that the immediate propositions—or at least such immediate propositions as are universal—are the 'elements'. If, on the other hand, there is no middle term, demonstration ceases to be possible: we are on the way to the basic truths. Similarly if A does not inhere in 25 B, this can be demonstrated if there is a middle term or a term prior to B in which A does not inhere: otherwise there is no demonstration and a basic truth is reached. There are, moreover, as many 'elements' of the demonstrated conclusion as there are middle terms, since it is propositions containing these middle terms that are the basic premisses on which the demonstration rests; and as there are some indemonstrable basic truths asserting that 30 'this is that' or that 'this inheres in that', so there are others denying that 'this is that' or that 'this inheres in that'—in fact some basic truths will affirm and some will deny being.

When we are to prove a conclusion, we must take a primary essential predicate—suppose it C—of the subject B, and then suppose A similarly predicable of C. If we pro-

40 i, ch. 7.

ceed in this manner, no proposition or attribute which falls
beyond *A* is admitted in the proof: the interval is con-
stantly condensed until subject and predicate become in- 35
divisible, i. e. one. We have our unit when the premiss becomes immediate, since the immediate premiss alone is a
single premiss in the unqualified sense of 'single'. And as in
other spheres the basic element is simple but not identical
in all—in a system of weight it is the mina, in music the
quarter-tone, and so on—so in syllogism the unit is an im- 85ᵃ
mediate premiss, and in the knowledge that demonstration
gives it is an intuition. In syllogisms, then, which prove the
inherence of an attribute, nothing falls outside the major
term. In the case of negative syllogisms on the other hand,
(1) in the first figure nothing falls outside the major term
whose inherence is in question; e. g. to prove through a
middle *C* that *A* does not inhere in *B* the premisses required are, all *B* is *C*, no *C* is *A*. Then if it has to be proved 5
that no *C* is *A*, a middle must be found between *A* and *C*;
and this procedure will never vary.

(2) If we have to show that *E* is not *D* by means of the
premisses, all *D* is *C*; no *E*, or not all *E*,⁴¹ is *C*; then the
middle will never fall beyond *E*, and *E* is the subject of
which *D* is to be denied in the conclusion.

(3) In the third figure the middle will never fall beyond
the limits of the subject and the attribute denied of it.   10

24 Since demonstrations may be either commensurately
universal or particular,⁴² and either affirmative or negative; the question arises, which form is the better? And the
same question may be put in regard to so-called 'direct' 1ᵝ
demonstration and *reductio ad impossibile*. Let us first examine the commensurately universal and the particular
forms, and when we have cleared up this problem proceed
to discuss 'direct' demonstration and *reductio ad impossibile*.

⁴¹ Second figure, Camestres or Baroco.
⁴² The distinction is that of whole and part, genus and species; not
that of universal and singular.

The following considerations might lead some minds
20 to prefer particular demonstration.

(1) The superior demonstration is the demonstration
which gives us greater knowledge (for this is the ideal of
demonstration), and we have greater knowledge of a particular individual when we know it in itself than when we
know it through something else; e. g. we know Coriscus
25 the musician better when we know that Coriscus is musical
than when we know only that man is musical, and a like argument holds in all other cases. But commensurately universal demonstration, instead of proving that the subject
itself actually is x, proves only that something else is x—e. g.
in attempting to prove that isosceles is x, it proves not that
isosceles but only that triangle is x—whereas particular
demonstration proves that the subject itself is x. The demonstration, then, that a subject, as such, possesses an attribute is superior. If this is so, and if the particular rather
than the commensurately universal form so demonstrates,
30 particular demonstration is superior.

(2) The universal has not a separate being over against
groups of singulars. Demonstration nevertheless creates the
opinion that its function is conditioned by something like
this—some separate entity belonging to the real world;
35 that, for instance, of triangle or of figure or number, over
against particular triangles, figures, and numbers. But demonstration which touches the real and will not mislead is
superior to that which moves among unrealities and is delu-
sory. Now commensurately universal demonstration is of
the latter kind: if we engage in it we find ourselves reasoning after a fashion well illustrated by the argument that
the proportionate is what answers to the definition of some
85b entity which is neither line, number, solid, nor plane, but
a proportionate apart from all these. Since, then, such a
proof is characteristically commensurate and universal,
and less touches reality than does particular demonstration,
and creates a false opinion, it will follow that commensurate and universal is inferior to particular demonstration.

We may retort thus. (1) The first argument applies no more to commensurate and universal than to particular demonstration. If equality to two right angles is attributa- 5 ble to its subject not *qua* isosceles but *qua* triangle, he who knows that isosceles possesses that attribute knows the subject as *qua* itself possessing the attribute, to a less degree than he who knows that triangle has that attribute. To sum up the whole matter: if a subject is proved to possess *qua* triangle an attribute which it does not in fact possess *qua* triangle, that is not demonstration: but if it does possess it *qua* triangle, the rule applies that the greater knowledge is his who knows the subject as possessing its attribute *qua* that in virtue of which it actually does possess it. Since, 10 then, triangle is the wider term, and there is one identical definition of triangle—i. e. the term is not equivocal— and since equality to two right angles belongs to all tri- angles, it is isosceles *qua* triangle and not triangle *qua* isosceles which has its angles so related. It follows that he who knows a connexion universally has greater knowledge of it as it in fact is than he who knows the particular; and the inference is that commensurate and universal is superior 15 to particular demonstration. (2) If there is a single identi- cal definition—i. e. if the commensurate universal is un- equivocal—then the universal will possess being not less but more than some of the particulars, inasmuch as it is universals which comprise the imperishable, particulars that tend to perish.

(3) Because the universal has a single meaning, we are not therefore compelled to suppose that in these examples it has being as a substance apart from its particulars—any more than we need make a similar supposition in the other cases of unequivocal universal predication, viz. where the predicate signifies not substance but quality, essential re- latedness, or action. If such a supposition is entertained, 20 the blame rests not with the demonstration but with the hearer.

(4) Demonstration is syllogism that proves the cause,

i. e. the reasoned fact, and it is rather the commensurate universal than the particular which is causative (as may be shown thus: that which possesses an attribute through its own essential nature is itself the cause of the inherence, and the commensurate universal is primary;[43] hence the commensurate universal is the cause). Consequently commensurately universal demonstration is superior as more especially proving the cause, that is the reasoned fact.

(5) Our search for the reason ceases, and we think that we know, when the coming to be or existence of the fact before us is not due to the coming to be or existence of some other fact, for the last step of a search thus conducted is eo ipso the end and limit of the problem. Thus: 'Why did he come?' 'To get the money—wherewith to pay a debt—that he might thereby do what was right.' When in this regress we can no longer find an efficient or final cause, we regard the last step of it as the end of the coming—or being or coming to be—and we regard ourselves as then only having full knowledge of the reason why he came.

If, then, all causes and reasons are alike in this respect, and if this is the means to full knowledge in the case of final causes such as we have exemplified, it follows that in the case of the other causes also full knowledge is attained when an attribute no longer inheres because of something else. Thus, when we learn that exterior angles are equal to four right angles because they are the exterior angles of an isosceles, there still remains the question 'Why has isosceles this attribute?' and its answer 'Because it is a triangle, and a triangle has it because a triangle is a rectilinear figure.' If rectilinear figure possesses the property for no further reason,[44] at this point we have full knowledge—but at this point our knowledge has become commensurately universal, and so we conclude that commensurately universal demonstration is superior.

(6) The more demonstration becomes particular the

---

[43] And therefore also essential; cf. i, ch. 4, 73ᵇ 26 ff.
[44] i. e. for no reason other than its own nature.

more it sinks into an indeterminate manifold, while universal demonstration tends to the simple and determinate. But objects so far as they are an indeterminate manifold are unintelligible, so far as they are determinate, intelligible: they are therefore intelligible rather in so far as they are universal than in so far as they are particular. From this it follows that universals are more demonstrable: but since relative and correlative increase concomitantly, of the more demonstrable there will be fuller demonstration. Hence the commensurate and universal form, being more truly demonstration, is the superior.

(7) Demonstration which teaches two things is preferable to demonstration which teaches only one. He who possesses commensurately universal demonstration knows the particular as well, but he who possesses particular demonstration does not know the universal. So that this is an additional reason for preferring commensurately universal demonstration. And there is yet this further argument:

(8) Proof becomes more and more proof of the commensurate universal as its middle term approaches nearer to the basic truth, and nothing is so near as the immediate premiss which is itself the basic truth. If, then, proof from the basic truth is more accurate than proof not so derived, demonstration which depends more closely on it is more accurate than demonstration which is less closely dependent. But commensurately universal demonstration is characterized by this closer dependence, and is therefore superior. Thus, if A had to be proved to inhere in D, and the middles were B and C, B being the higher term would render the demonstration which it mediated the more universal.

Some of these arguments, however, are dialectical. The clearest indication of the precedence of commensurately universal demonstration is as follows: if of two propositions, a prior and a posterior, we have a grasp of the prior, we have a kind of knowledge—a potential grasp—of the posterior as well. For example, if one knows that the angles

of all triangles are equal to two right angles, one knows in a
sense—potentially—that the isosceles' angles also are equal
to two right angles, even if one does not know that the
isosceles is a triangle; but to grasp this posterior proposition is by no means to know the commensurate universal
either potentially or actually. Moreover, commensurately
30 universal demonstration is through and through intelligible; particular demonstration issues in sense-perception.

25 The preceding arguments constitute our defence of
      the superiority of commensurately universal to par-
ticular demonstration. That affirmative demonstration excels negative may be shown as follows.

(1) We may assume the superiority *ceteris paribus* of
the demonstration which derives from fewer postulates or
35 hypotheses—in short from fewer premises; for, given that
all these are equally well known, where they are fewer
knowledge will be more speedily acquired, and that is a
desideratum. The argument implied in our contention
that demonstration from fewer assumptions is superior may
be set out in universal form as follows. Assuming that in
both cases alike the middle terms are known, and that
middles which are prior are better known than such as are
posterior, we may suppose two demonstrations of the in-
36ᵇ herence of A in E, the one proving it through the middles
B, C and D, the other through F and G. Then A–D is
known to the same degree as A–E (in the second proof),
but A–D is better known than and prior to A–E (in the first
proof); since A–E is proved through A–D, and the ground
is more certain than the conclusion.

Hence demonstration by fewer premises is *ceteris paribus* superior. Now both affirmative and negative demonstration operate through three terms and two premises, but
whereas the former assumes only that something is, the
latter assumes both that something is and that something
else is not, and thus operating through more kinds of
premiss is inferior.

(2) It has been proved [45] that no conclusion follows if both premises are negative, but that one must be negative, the other affirmative. So we are compelled to lay down the following additional rule: as the demonstration expands, the affirmative premises must increase in number, but there cannot be more than one negative premiss in each complete proof.[46] Thus, suppose no *B* is *A*, and all *C* is *B*. Then, if both the premises are to be again expanded, a middle must be interposed. Let us interpose *D* between *A* and *B*, and *E* between *B* and *C*. Then clearly *E* is affirmatively related to *B* and *C*, while *D* is affirmatively related to *B* but negatively to *A*; for all *B* is *D*, but there must be no *D* which is *A*. Thus there proves to be a single negative premiss, *A–D*. In the further prosyllogisms too it is the same, because in the terms of an affirmative syllogism the middle is always related affirmatively to both extremes; in a negative syllogism it must be negatively related only to one of them, and so this negation comes to be a single negative premiss, the other premises being affirmative. If, then, that through which a truth is proved is a better known and more certain truth, and if the negative proposition is proved through the affirmative and not vice versa, affirmative demonstration, being prior and better known and more certain, will be superior.

(3) The basic truth of demonstrative syllogism is the universal immediate premiss, and the universal premiss asserts in affirmative demonstration and in negative denies: and the affirmative proposition is prior to and better known than the negative (since affirmation explains denial and is prior to denial, just as being is prior to not-being). It follows that the basic premiss of affirmative demonstration is superior to that of negative demonstration, and the demonstration which uses superior basic premises is superior.

(4) Affirmative demonstration is more of the nature of

---

[45] *An. Pr.* i, ch. 7.

[46] i. e. in one syllogism and two prosyllogisms proving its premises.

a basic form of proof, because it is a *sine qua non* of negative demonstration.

87ª **26**   Since affirmative demonstration is superior to negative, it is clearly superior also to *reductio ad impossibile*. We must first make certain what is the difference between negative demonstration and *reductio ad impossibile*. Let us
5 suppose that no B is A, and that all C is B: the conclusion necessarily follows that no C is A. If these premisses are assumed, therefore, the negative demonstration that no C is A is direct. *Reductio ad impossibile*, on the other hand, proceeds as follows: Supposing we are to prove that A does
· not inhere in B, we have to assume that it does inhere, and further that B inheres in C, with the resulting inference
10 that A inheres in C. This we have to suppose a known and admitted impossibility; and we then infer that A cannot inhere in B. Thus if the inherence of B in C is not questioned, A's inherence in B is impossible.

The order of the terms is the same in both proofs: they differ according to which of the negative propositions is the better known, the one denying A of B or the one denying
15 A of C. When the falsity of the conclusion [47] is the better known, we use *reductio ad impossibile*; when the major premiss of the syllogism is the more obvious, we use direct demonstration. All the same the proposition denying A of B is, in the order of being, prior to that denying A of C; for premisses are prior to the conclusion which follows from them, and 'no C is A' is the conclusion, 'no B is A' one of its
20 premisses. For the destructive result of *reductio ad impossibile* is not a proper conclusion, nor are its antecedents proper premisses. On the contrary: the constituents of syllogism are premisses related to one another as whole to part or part to whole, whereas the premisses A–C and A–B are
25 not thus related to one another. Now the superior demonstration is that which proceeds from better known and prior

---

[47] i.e. the impossibility of A–C, the conclusion of the hypothetical syllogism.

premisses, and while both these forms depend for credence on the not-being of something, yet the source of the one is prior to that of the other. Therefore negative demonstration will have an unqualified superiority to *reductio ad impossibile*, and affirmative demonstration, being superior to negative, will consequently be superior also to *reductio ad impossibile*. 30

27 The science which is knowledge at once of the fact and of the reasoned fact, not of the fact by itself without the reasoned fact, is the more exact and the prior science.

A science such as arithmetic, which is not a science of properties qua inhering in a substratum, is more exact than and prior to a science like harmonics, which is a science of properties inhering in a substratum; and similarly a science like arithmetic, which is constituted of fewer basic elements, is more exact than and prior to geometry, which requires additional elements. What I mean by 'additional elements' is this: a unit is substance without position, while 35 a point is substance with position; the latter contains an additional element.

28 A single science is one whose domain is a single genus, viz. all the subjects constituted out of the primary entities of the genus—i. e. the parts of this total subject—and their essential properties.

One science differs from another when their basic truths have neither a common source nor are derived those of the one science from those of the other. This is verified when we reach the indemonstrable premisses of a science, for 87ᵇ they must be within one genus with its conclusions: and this again is verified if the conclusions proved by means of them fall within one genus—i. e. are homogeneous.

29 One can have several demonstrations of the same connexion not only by taking from the same series of predication middles which are other than the immediately co- 5

hering term—e. g. by taking C, D, and F severally to prove
A–B—but also by taking a middle from another series.
Thus let A be change, D alteration of a property, B feeling
pleasure, and G relaxation. We can then without falsehood predicate D of B and A of D, for he who is pleased
10 suffers alteration of a property, and that which alters a
property changes. Again, we can predicate A of G without
falsehood, and G of B; for to feel pleasure is to relax, and to
relax is to change. So the conclusion can be drawn through
middles which are different, i. e. not in the same series—
yet not so that neither of these middles is predicable of the
other, for they must both be attributable to some one sub-
15 ject.

A further point worth investigating is how many ways of
proving the same conclusion can be obtained by varying
the figure.

30 There is no knowledge by demonstration of chance
conjunctions; for chance conjunctions exist neither
20 by necessity nor as general connexions but comprise what
comes to be as something distinct from these. Now demonstration is concerned only with one or other of these two;
for all reasoning proceeds from necessary or general premisses, the conclusion being necessary if the premisses are
25 necessary and general if the premisses are general. Consequently, if chance conjunctions are neither general nor
necessary, they are not demonstrable.

31 Scientific knowledge is not possible through the act
of perception. Even if perception as a faculty is of
'the such' and not merely of a 'this somewhat', yet one must
30 at any rate actually perceive a 'this somewhat', and at a
definite present place and time: but that which is commensurately universal and true in all cases one cannot perceive, since it is not 'this' and it is not 'now'; if it were, it
would not be commensurately universal—the term we ap-

ply to what is always and everywhere. Seeing, therefore, that demonstrations are commensurately universal and universals imperceptible, we clearly cannot obtain scientific knowledge by the act of perception: nay, it is obvious that 35 even if it were possible to perceive that a triangle has its angles equal to two right angles, we should still be looking for a demonstration—we should not (as some [48] say) possess knowledge of it; for perception must be of a particular, whereas scientific knowledge involves the recognition of the commensurate universal. So if we were on the moon, and saw the earth shutting out the sun's light, we 40 should not know the cause of the eclipse: we should perceive the present fact of the eclipse, but not the reasoned 88ª fact at all, since the act of perception is not of the commensurate universal. I do not, of course, deny that by watching the frequent recurrence of this event we might, after tracking the commensurate universal, possess a demonstration, for the commensurate universal is elicited from the several groups of singulars.

The commensurate universal is precious because it makes 5 clear the cause; so that in the case of facts like these which have a cause other than themselves universal knowledge [49] is more precious than sense-perceptions and than intuition. (As regards primary truths there is of course a different account to be given.[50]) Hence it is clear that knowledge of things demonstrable cannot be acquired by perception, un- 10 less the term perception is applied to the possession of scientific knowledge through demonstration. Nevertheless certain points do arise with regard to connexions to be proved which are referred for their explanation to a failure in sense-perception: there are cases when an act of vision would terminate our inquiry, not because in seeing we should be knowing, but because we should have elicited the universal from seeing; if, for example, we saw the pores

[48] Protagoras is perhaps referred to.
[49] i. e. demonstration through the commensurate universal.
[50] Cf. e. g. 100ᵇ 12.

in the glass and the light passing through, the reason of the
15 kindling would be clear to us [51] because we should at the
same time see it in each instance and intuit that it must be
so in all instances.

32   All syllogisms cannot have the same basic truths. This
may be shown first of all by the following dialectical
considerations. (1) Some syllogisms are true and some
20 false: for though a true inference is possible from false
premisses, yet this occurs once only—I mean if A, for instance, is truly predicable of C, but B, the middle, is false,
both A–B and B–C being false; nevertheless, if middles are
taken to prove these premisses, they will be false because
every conclusion which is a falsehood has false premisses,
25 while true conclusions have true premisses, and false and
true differ in kind. Then again, (2) falsehoods are not all
derived from a single identical set of principles: there are
falsehoods which are the contraries of one another and
cannot coexist, e. g. 'justice is injustice', and 'justice is cowardice'; 'man is horse', and 'man is ox'; 'the equal is greater',
and 'the equal is less'. From our established principles we
30 may argue the case as follows, confining ourselves therefore to true conclusions. Not even all these are inferred
from the same basic truths; many of them in fact have
basic truths which differ generically and are not transferable; units, for instance, which are without position,
cannot take the place of points, which have position. The
transferred terms could only fit in as middle terms or as
35 major or minor terms, or else have some of the other terms
between them, others outside them.

Nor can any of the common axioms—such, I mean, as
the law of excluded middle—serve as premisses for the
proof of all conclusions. For the kinds of being are dif-
88ᵇ ferent, and some attributes attach to *quanta* and some to
qualia only; and proof is achieved by means of the common

---

[51] A theory of the concentration of rays through a burning-glass
which was not Aristotle's.

axioms taken in conjunction with these several kinds and their attributes.

Again, it is not true that the basic truths are much fewer than the conclusions, for the basic truths are the premisses, and the premisses are formed by the apposition of a fresh extreme term or the interposition of a fresh middle. Moreover, the number of conclusions is indefinite, though the number of middle terms is finite; and lastly some of the basic truths are necessary, others variable.

Looking at it in this way we see that, since the number of conclusions is indefinite, the basic truth cannot be identical or limited in number. If, on the other hand, identity is used in another sense, and it is said, e. g., 'these and no other are the fundamental truths of geometry, these the fundamentals of calculation, these again of medicine'; would the statement mean anything except that the sciences have basic truths? To call them identical because they are self-identical is absurd, since everything can be identified with everything in that sense of identity. Nor again can the contention that all conclusions have the same basic truths mean that from the mass of all possible premisses any conclusion may be drawn. That would be exceedingly naïve, for it is not the case in the clearly evident mathematical sciences, nor is it possible in analysis, since it is the immediate premisses which are the basic truths, and a fresh conclusion is only formed by the addition of a new immediate premiss: but if it be admitted that it is these primary immediate premisses which are basic truths, each subject-genus will provide one basic truth. If, however, it is not argued that from the mass of all possible premisses any conclusion may be proved, nor yet admitted that basic truths differ so as to be generically different for each science, it remains to consider the possibility that, while the basic truths of all knowledge are within one genus, special premisses are required to prove special conclusions. But that this cannot be the case has been shown by our proof that the basic truths of things generically different

themselves differ generically. For fundamental truths are
of two kinds, those which are premisses of demonstration
and the subject-genus; and though the former are common,
the latter—number, for instance, and magnitude—are peculiar.

30 **33**   Scientific knowledge and its object differ from opinion
and the object of opinion in that scientific knowledge
is commensurately universal and proceeds by necessary
connexions, and that which is necessary cannot be otherwise. So though there are things which are true and real
and yet can be otherwise, *scientific knowledge* clearly does
not concern them: if it did, things which can be otherwise
35 would be incapable of being otherwise. Nor are they any
concern of *rational intuition*—by rational intuition I mean
an originative source of scientific knowledge—nor of in-
89ª demonstrable knowledge, which is the grasping of the immediate premiss. Since then rational intuition, science, and
opinion, and what is revealed by these terms, are the only
things that can be 'true', it follows that it is *opinion* that
is concerned with that which may be true or false, and can
be otherwise: opinion in fact is the grasp of a premiss which
is immediate but not necessary. This view also fits the ob-
5 served facts, for opinion is unstable, and so is the kind of
being we have described as its object. Besides, when a man
thinks a truth incapable of being otherwise he always thinks
that he knows it, never that he opines it. He thinks that
he opines when he thinks that a connexion, though actually
so, may quite easily be otherwise; for he believes that such
is the proper object of opinion, while the necessary is the
10 object of knowledge.

In what sense, then, can the same thing be the object of
both opinion and knowledge? And if any one chooses to
maintain that all that he knows he can also opine, why
should not opinion be knowledge? For he that knows and
he that opines will follow the same train of thought
through the same middle terms until the immediate premisses are reached; because it is possible to opine not only

the fact but also the reasoned fact, and the reason is the 15
middle term; so that, since the former knows, he that
opines also has knowledge.

The truth perhaps is that if a man grasp truths that cannot be other than they are, in the way in which he grasps
the definitions through which demonstrations take place,
he will have not opinion but knowledge: if on the other
hand he apprehends these attributes as inhering in their
subjects, but not in virtue of the subjects' substance and essential nature, he possesses opinion and not genuine knowl- 20
edge; and his opinion, if obtained through immediate
premisses, will be both of the fact and of the reasoned
fact; if not so obtained, of the fact alone. The object of
opinion and knowledge is not quite identical; it is only in a
sense identical, just as the object of true and false opinion
is in a sense identical. The sense in which some maintain 25
that true and false opinion can have the same object leads
them to embrace many strange doctrines, particularly the
doctrine that what a man opines falsely he does not opine
at all. There are really many senses of 'identical', and in one
sense the object of true and false opinion can be the same,
in another it cannot. Thus, to have a true opinion that the
diagonal is commensurate with the side would be absurd: 30
but because the diagonal with which they are both concerned is the same, the two opinions have objects so far the
same: on the other hand, as regards their essential definable
nature these objects differ. The identity of the objects of
knowledge and opinion is similar. Knowledge is the apprehension of, e. g. the attribute 'animal' as incapable of being
otherwise, opinion the apprehension of 'animal' as capable
of being otherwise—e. g. the apprehension that animal is 35
an element in the essential nature of man is knowledge; the
apprehension of animal as predicable of man but not as an
element in man's essential nature is opinion: man is the
subject in both judgments, but the mode of inherence
differs.

This also shows that one cannot opine and know the
same thing simultaneously; for then one would apprehend

the same ching as both capable and incapable of being
89ᵇ otherwise—an impossibility. Knowledge and opinion of
the same thing can coexist in two different people in the
sense we have explained, but not simultaneously in the
same person. That would involve a man's simultaneously
apprehending, e. g., (1) that man is essentially animal—
i. e. cannot be other than animal—and (2) that man is not
5 essentially animal, that is, we may assume, may be other
than animal.

Further consideration of modes of thinking and their distribution under the heads of discursive thought, intuition,
science, art, practical wisdom, and metaphysical thinking,
belongs rather partly to natural science, partly to moral phi-
ˀ ɔsophy.

10 **34** Quick wit is a faculty of hitting upon the middle term
instantaneously. It would be exemplified by a man
who saw that the moon has her bright side always turned
towards the sun, and quickly grasped the cause of this,
namely that she borrows her light from him; or observed
somebody in conversation with a man of wealth and
divined that he was borrowing money, or that the friendship of these people sprang from a common enmity. In all
15 these instances he has seen the major and minor terms and
then grasped the causes, the middle terms.

Let A represent 'bright side turned sunward', B 'lighted
from the sun', C the moon. Then B, 'lighted from the sun',
is predicable of C, the moon, and A, 'having her bright side
20 towards the source of her light', is predicable of B. So A is
predicable of C through B.

BOOK II

1   The kinds of question we ask are as many as the kinds
of things which we know. They are in fact four:—(1)
whether the connexion of an attribute with a thing is a fact,
25 (2) what is the reason of the connexion, (3) whether a

thing exists, (4) what is the nature of the thing. Thus,
when our question concerns a complex of thing and attribute and we ask whether the thing *is* thus or otherwise
qualified—whether, e. g., the sun suffers eclipse or not—
then we are asking as to the fact of a connexion. That our
inquiry ceases with the discovery that the sun does suffer
eclipse is an indication of this; and if we know from the
start that the sun suffers eclipse, we do not inquire whethei
it does so or not. On the other hand, when we know the
fact we ask the reason; as, for example, when we know that
the sun is being eclipsed and that an earthquake is in progress, it is the reason of eclipse or earthquake into which we 30
inquire.

Where a complex is concerned, then, those are the two
questions we ask; but for some objects of inquiry we have
a different kind of question to ask, such as whether there is
or is not a centaur or a God. (By 'is or is not' I mean 'is or
is not, without further qualification'; as opposed to 'is or
is not (e. g.) white'.) On the other hand, when we have
ascertained the thing's existence, we inquire as to its nature,
asking, for instance, 'what, then, is God?' or 'what is man?'. 35

2   These, then, are the four kinds of question we ask, and
it is in the answers to these questions that our knowledge consists.

Now when we ask whether a connexion is a fact, or
whether a thing without qualification *is*, we are really asking whether the connexion or the thing has a 'middle'; and
when we have ascertained either that the connexion is a
fact or that the thing *is*—i. e. ascertained either the partial
or the unqualified being of the thing—and are proceeding 90
to ask the reason of the connexion or the nature of the
thing, then we are asking what the 'middle' is.

(By distinguishing the fact of the connexion and the
existence of the thing as respectively the partial and the
unqualified being of the thing, I mean that if we ask 'does
the moon suffer eclipse?', or 'does the moon wax?', the

question concerns a part of the thing's being; for what we
are asking in such questions is whether a thing is this or
that, i. e. has or has not this or that attribute: whereas, if we
ask whether the moon or night exists, the question concerns the unqualified being of a thing.)

We conclude that in all our inquiries we are asking
5 either whether there is a 'middle' or what the 'middle' is:
for the 'middle' here is precisely the cause, and it is the
cause that we seek in all our inquiries. Thus, 'Does the
moon suffer eclipse?' means 'Is there or is there not a cause
producing eclipse of the moon?', and when we have learnt
that there is, our next question is, 'What, then, is this
cause?'; for the cause through which a thing *is*—not *is this*
or that, i. e. has this or that attribute, but without qualifica-
10 tion *is*—and the cause through which it is—not *is* without
qualification, but *is this* or *that* as having some essential
attribute or some accident—are both alike the 'middle'. By
that which *is* without qualification I mean the subject, e. g.
moon or earth or sun or triangle; by that which a subject
is (in the partial sense) I mean a property, e. g. eclipse,
equality or inequality, interposition or non-interposition.
15 For in all these examples it is clear that the nature of the
thing and the reason of the fact are identical: the question
'What is eclipse?' and its answer 'The privation of the
moon's light by the interposition of the earth' are identical
with the question 'What is the reason of eclipse?' or 'Why
does the moon suffer eclipse?' and the reply 'Because of the
failure of light through the earth's shutting it out'. Again,
for 'What is a concord? A commensurate numerical ratio
20 of a high and a low note', we may substitute 'What reason
makes a high and a low note concordant? Their relation
according to a commensurate numerical ratio.' 'Are the
high and the low note concordant?' is equivalent to 'Is their
ratio commensurate?'; and when we find that it is commensurate, we ask 'What, then, is their ratio?'.

Cases in which the 'middle' is sensible show that the ob-
25 ject of our inquiry is always the 'middle': we inquire, be-

cause we have not perceived it, whether there is or is not a 'middle' causing e. g. an eclipse. On the other hand, if we were on the moon we should not be inquiring either as to the fact or the reason, but both fact and reason would be obvious simultaneously. For the act of perception would have enabled us to know the universal too; since, the present fact of an eclipse being evident, perception would then at the same time give us the present fact of the earth's 30 screening the sun's light, and from this would arise the universal.

Thus, as we maintain, to know a thing's nature is to know the reason why it is; and this is equally true of things in so far as they are said without qualification to *be* as opposed to being possessed of some attribute, and in so far as they are said to be possessed of some attribute such as equal to two right angles, or greater or less.

3   It is clear, then, that all questions are a search for a 35 'middle'. Let us now state how essential nature is revealed, and in what way it can be reduced to demonstration;[1] what definition is, and what things are definable. And let us first discuss certain difficulties which these ques- 90 tions raise, beginning what we have to say with a point most intimately connected with our immediately preceding remarks, namely the doubt that might be felt as to whether or not it is possible to know the same thing in the same relation, both by definition and by demonstration. It might, I mean, be urged that definition is held to concern essential nature and is in every case universal and affirmative; where- 5 as, on the other hand, some conclusions are negative and some are not universal; e. g. all in the second figure are negative, none in the third are universal. And again, not even all affirmative conclusions in the first figure are definable, e. g. 'every triangle has its angles equal to two right angles'. An argument proving this difference between demonstration and definition is that to have scientific knowledge of

[1] Cf. 94ᵃ 11–14.

10 the demonstrable is identical with possessing a demonstration of it: hence if demonstration of such conclusions as
these is possible, there clearly cannot also be definition of
them. If there could, one might know such a conclusion
also in virtue of its definition without possessing the demonstration of it; for there is nothing to stop our having the
one without the other.

Induction too will sufficiently convince us of this difference; for never yet by defining anything—essential attribute
15 or accident—did we get knowledge of it. Again, if to define
is to acquire knowledge of a substance, at any rate such attributes are not substances.

It is evident, then, that not everything demonstrable can
be defined. What then? Can everything definable be demonstrated, or not? There is one of our previous arguments
20 which covers this too. Of a single thing qua single there is
a single scientific knowledge. Hence, since to know the demonstrable scientifically is to possess the demonstration of
it, an impossible consequence will follow:—possession of
its definition without its demonstration will give knowledge
of the demonstrable.

Moreover, the basic premisses of demonstrations are definitions, and it has already been shown [2] that these will be
found indemonstrable; either the basic premisses will be
25 demonstrable and will depend on prior premisses, and the
regress will be endless; or the primary truths will be indemonstrable definitions.

But if the definable and the demonstrable are not wholly
the same, may they yet be partially the same? Or is that
impossible, because there can be no demonstration of the
definable? There can be none, because definition is of the
30 essential nature or being of something, and all demonstrations evidently posit and assume the essential nature—
mathematical demonstrations, for example, the nature of
unity and the odd, and all the other sciences likewise. Moreover, every demonstration proves a predicate of a subject

2 Cf. 72[b] 18–25 and 84[a] 30–[b] 2.

as attaching or as not attaching to it, but in definition one
thing is not predicated of another; we do not, e. g., predi- 35
cate animal of biped nor biped of animal, nor yet figure of
plane—plane not being figure nor figure plane. Again, to
prove essential nature is not the same as to prove the fact
of a connexion. Now definition reveals essential nature,
demonstration reveals that a given attribute attaches or does **91**
not attach to a given subject; but different things require
different demonstrations—unless the one demonstration is
related to the other as part to whole. I add this because if
all triangles have been proved to possess angles equal to two
right angles, then this attribute has been proved to attach
to isosceles; for isosceles is a part of which all triangles constitute the whole. But in the case before us the fact and the 5
essential nature are not so related to one another, since the
one is not a part of the other.

So it emerges that not all the definable is demonstrable
nor all the demonstrable definable; and we may draw the
general conclusion that there is no identical object of which
it is possible to possess both a definition and a demonstra- 10
tion. It follows obviously that definition and demonstration
are neither identical nor contained either within the other:
if they were, their objects would be related either as identical or as whole and part.

4   So much, then, for the first stage of our problem. The
       next step is to raise the question whether syllogism—
i. e. demonstration—of the definable nature is possible or
as our recent argument assumed, impossible.

We might argue it impossible on the following grounds:
—(a) syllogism proves an attribute of a subject through
the middle term; on the other hand (b) its definable na- 15
ture is both 'peculiar' to a subject and predicated of it as
belonging to its essence. But in that case (1) the subject,
its definition, and the middle term connecting them must
be reciprocally predicable of one another; for if A is 'peculiar' to C, obviously A is 'peculiar' to B and B to C—in fact

all three terms are 'peculiar' to one another: and further (2) if A inheres in the essence of all B and B is predicated
20 universally of all C as belonging to C's essence, A also must be predicated of C as belonging to its essence.

If one does not take this relation as thus duplicated—if, that is, A is predicated as being of the essence of B, but B is not of the essence of the subjects of which it is predicated—A will not necessarily be predicated of C as belonging to its essence. So both premisses will predicate essence,
25 and consequently B also will be predicated of C as its essence. Since, therefore, both premisses do predicate essence —i. e. definable form—C's definable form will appear in the middle term before the conclusion is drawn.

We may generalize by supposing that it is possible to prove the essential nature of man. Let C be man, A man's essential nature—two-footed animal, or aught else it may be. Then, if we are to syllogize, A must be predicated of all B. But this premiss will be mediated by a fresh definition,
30 which consequently will also be the essential nature of man.[3] Therefore the argument assumes what it has to prove, since B too is the essential nature of man. It is, however, the case in which there are only the two premisses— i. e. in which the premisses are primary and immediate— which we ought to investigate, because it best illustrates the point under discussion.

Thus they who prove the essential nature of soul or man
35 or anything else through reciprocating terms beg the question. It would be begging the question, for example, to contend that the soul is that which causes its own life, and that what causes its own life is a self-moving number; for one would have to postulate that the soul is a self-moving
91ᵇ number in the sense of being identical with it. For if A is

[3] sc. 'and an indefinite regress occurs'. This argument is a corollary of the proof in 91ᵃ 15–26 that if the proposition predicating A—its definition—of C can be a conclusion, there must be a middle term, B, and since A, B, and C are reciprocally predicable, B too, as well as A, will be a definition of C.

predicable as a mere consequent of *B* and *B* of *C*, *A* will not on that account be the definable form of *C*: *A* will merely be what it was true to say of *C*. Even if *A* is predicated of all *B* inasmuch as *B* is identical with a species of *A*, still it will not follow: being an animal is predicated of being a man— since it is true that in all instances to be human is to be 5 animal, just as it is also true that every man is an animal— but not as identical with being man.

We conclude, then, that unless one takes both the prem- isses as predicating essence, one cannot infer that *A* is the definable form and essence of *C*: but if one does so take them, in assuming *B* one will have assumed, before drawing the conclusion, what the definable form of *C* is; so that there has been no inference, for one has begged the ques- 10 tion.

5 Nor, as was said in my formal logic, is the method of division a process of inference at all, since at no point does the characterization of the subject follow necessarily from the premising of certain other facts: division demon- strates as little as does induction. For in a genuine demon- 15 stration the conclusion must not be put as a question nor depend on a concession, but must follow necessarily from its premises, even if the respondent deny it. The definer asks 'Is man animal or inanimate?' and then assumes—he has not inferred—that man is animal. Next, when pre- sented with an exhaustive division of animal into terrestrial and aquatic, he assumes that man is terrestrial. Moreover, 20 that man is the complete formula, terrestrial-animal, does not follow necessarily from the premises: this too is an assumption, and equally an assumption whether the divi- sion comprises many differentiae or few. (Indeed as this method of division is used by those who proceed by it, even truths that can be inferred actually fail to appear as 25 such.) For why should not the whole of this formula be true of man, and yet not exhibit his essential nature or de-

finable form? Again, what guarantee is there against an unessential addition, or against the omission of the final or of
an intermediate determinant of the substantial being?

The champion of division might here urge that though
these lapses do occur, yet we can solve that difficulty if all
the attributes we assume are constituents of the definable
form, and if, postulating the genus, we produce by division
30 the requisite uninterrupted sequence of terms, and omit
nothing; and that indeed we cannot fail to fulfil these conditions if what is to be divided falls whole into the division
at each stage, and none of it is omitted; and that this—the
dividendum—must without further question be (ultimately) incapable of fresh specific division. Nevertheless,
we reply, division does not involve inference; if it gives
knowledge, it gives it in another way. Nor is there any absurdity in this: induction, perhaps, is not demonstration
any more than is division, yet it does make evident some
35 truth. Yet to state a definition reached by division is not
to state a conclusion: as, when conclusions are drawn without their appropriate middles, the alleged necessity by
which the inference follows from the premisses is open to
a question as to the reason for it, so definitions reached by
division invite the same question. Thus to the question
92ᵃ 'What is the essential nature of man?' the divider replies
'Animal, mortal, footed, biped, wingless'; and when at each
step he is asked 'Why?', he will say, and, as he thinks, prove
by division, that all animal is mortal or immortal: but such
a formula taken in its entirety is not definition; so that even
5 if division does demonstrate its formula, definition at any
rate does not turn out to be a conclusion of inference.

)   Can we nevertheless actually demonstrate what a thing
essentially and substantially is, but hypothetically,
i. e. by premising (1) that its definable form is constituted
by the 'peculiar' attributes of its essential nature; (2) that
such and such are the only attributes of its essential nature,
and that the complete synthesis of them is peculiar to the

thing; and thus—since in this synthesis consists the being of the thing—obtaining our conclusion? Or is the truth that, since proof must be through the middle term, the 10 definable form is once more assumed in this minor premiss too?

Further, just as in syllogizing we do not premise what syllogistic inference is (since the premisses from which we conclude must be related as whole and part),[4] so the definable form must not fall within the syllogism but remain outside the premisses posited. It is only against a doubt as to its having been a syllogistic inference at all that we have 15 to defend our argument as conforming to the definition of syllogism. It is only when some one doubts whether the conclusion proved is the definable form that we have to defend it as conforming to the definition of definable form which we assumed. Hence syllogistic inference must be possible even without the express statement of what syllogism is or what definable form is.

The following type of hypothetical proof also begs the question. If evil is definable as the divisible, and the defini- 20 tion of a thing's contrary—if it has one—is the contrary of the thing's definition; then, if good is the contrary of evil and the indivisible of the divisible, we conclude that to be good is essentially to be indivisible. The question is begged because definable form is assumed as a premiss, and as a premiss which is to prove definable form. 'But not the same definable form', you may object. That I admit, for in demonstrations also we premise that 'this' is predicable of 'that'; 25 but in this premiss the term we assert of the minor is neither the major itself nor a term identical in definition, or convertible, with the major.

Again, both proof by division and the syllogism just described are open to the question why man should be animal-biped-terrestrial and not merely animal and terrestrial, since

---

[4] A reminder of a necessary condition of syllogism. If the definition of syllogism is premised the conclusion would have to affirm some subject to be of the nature of syllogism.

30 what they premise does not ensure that the predicates shall
constitute a genuine unity and not merely belong to a single
subject as do musical and grammatical when predicated of
the same man.

7   How then by definition shall we prove substance or
    essential nature? We cannot show it as a fresh fact
35 necessarily following from the assumption of premises admitted to be facts—the method of demonstration: we may
not proceed as by induction to establish a universal on the
evidence of groups of particulars which offer no exception,
because induction proves not what the essential nature of
a thing is but that it has or has not some attribute. There-
92ᵇ fore, since presumably one cannot prove essential nature
by an appeal to sense perception or by pointing with the
finger, what other method remains?

   To put it another way: how shall we by definition prove
essential nature? He who knows what human—or any other
5 —nature is, must know also that man exists; for no one
knows the nature of what does not exist—one can know the
meaning of the phrase or name 'goat-stag' but not what the
essential nature of a goat-stag is. But further, if definition
can prove what is the essential nature of a thing, can it also
prove that it exists? And how will it prove them both by
the same process, since definition exhibits one single thing
10 and demonstration another single thing, and what human
nature is and the fact that man exists are not the same
thing? Then too we hold that it is by demonstration that
the being of everything must be proved—unless indeed to
be were its essence; and, since being is not a genus, it is not
the essence of anything. Hence the being of anything as
15 fact is matter for demonstration; and this is the actual procedure of the sciences, for the geometer assumes the meaning of the word triangle, but that it is possessed of some attribute he proves. What is it, then, that we shall prove in
defining essential nature? Triangle? In that case a man will

know by definition what a thing's nature is without knowing whether it exists. But that is impossible.

Moreover it is clear, if we consider the methods of defining actually in use, that definition does not prove that the thing defined exists: since even if there does actually exist something which is equidistant from a centre, yet why should the thing named in the definition exist? Why, in other words, should this be the formula defining circle? One might equally well call it the definition of mountain copper. For definitions do not carry a further guarantee that the thing defined can exist or that it is what they claim to define: one can always ask why.

Since, therefore, to define is to prove either a thing's essential nature or the meaning of its name, we may conclude that definition, if it in no sense proves essential nature, is a set of words signifying precisely what a name signifies. But that were a strange consequence; for (1) both what is not substance and what does not exist at all would be definable, since even non-existents can be signified by a name: (2) all sets of words or sentences would be definitions, since any kind of sentence could be given a name; so that we should all be talking in definitions, and even the *Iliad* would be a definition: (3) no demonstration can prove that any particular name means any particular thing: neither, therefore, do definitions, in addition to revealing the meaning of a name, also reveal that the name has this meaning. It appears then from these considerations that neither definition and syllogism nor their objects are identical, and further that definition neither demonstrates nor proves anything, and that knowledge of essential nature is not to be obtained either by definition or by demonstration.

3 We must now start afresh and consider which of these conclusions are sound and which are not, and what is the nature of definition, and whether essential nature is in any sense demonstrable and definable or in none.

Now to know its essential nature is, as we said, the same as to know the cause of a thing's existence, and the proof of this depends on the fact that a thing must have a cause. Moreover, this cause is either identical with the essential nature of the thing or distinct from it; [5] and if its cause is distinct from it, the essential nature of the thing is either demonstrable or indemonstrable. Consequently, if the cause is distinct from the thing's essential nature and demonstration is possible, the cause must be the middle term, and, the conclusion proved being universal and affirmative, the proof is in the first figure. So the method just examined of proving it through another essential nature would be one way of proving essential nature, because a conclusion containing essential nature must be inferred through a middle which is an essential nature just as a 'peculiar' property must be inferred through a middle which is a 'peculiar' property; so that of the two definable natures of a single thing this method will prove one and not the other.[6]

Now it was said before [7] that this method could not amount to demonstration of essential nature—it is actually a dialectical proof of it—so let us begin again and explain by what method it can be demonstrated. When we are aware of a fact we seek its reason, and though sometimes the fact and the reason dawn on us simultaneously, yet we cannot apprehend the reason a moment sooner than the fact; and clearly in just the same way we cannot apprehend a thing's definable form without apprehending that it exists, since while we are ignorant whether it exists we can-

---

[5] 'distinct from it'; i. e. in the case of *properties*, with the definition of which Aristotle is alone concerned in this chapter. The being of a property consists in its inherence in a substance through a middle which defines it. Cf. the following chapter.

[6] Aristotle speaks of two moments of the definable form as two essential natures. His argument amounts to this: that if the conclusion contains the whole definition, the question has been begged in the premisses (cf. ii, ch. 4). Hence syllogism—and even so merely dialectical syllogism—is only possible if premisses and conclusion each contain a part of the definition.

[7] ii, ch. 2.

not know its essential nature. Moreover we are aware 20
whether a thing exists or not sometimes through apprehending an element in its character, and sometimes accidentally,[8] as, for example, when we are aware of thunder as
a noise in the clouds, of eclipse as a privation of light, or
of man as some species of animal, or of the soul as a self-
moving thing. As often as we have accidental knowledge
that the thing exists, we must be in a wholly negative state 25
as regards awareness of its essential nature; for we have not
got genuine knowledge even of its existence, and to search
for a thing's essential nature when we are unaware that
it exists is to search for nothing. On the other hand, whenever we apprehend an element in the thing's character there
is less difficulty. Thus it follows that the degree of our
knowledge of a thing's essential nature is determined by
the sense in which we are aware that it exists. Let us then
take the following as our first instance of being aware of an
element in the essential nature. Let A be eclipse, C the 30
moon, B the earth's acting as a screen. Now to ask whether
the moon is eclipsed or not is to ask whether or not B has
occurred. But that is precisely the same as asking whether
A has a defining condition; and if this condition actually
exists, we assert that A also actually exists. Or again we may
ask which side of a contradiction the defining condition
necessitates: does it make the angles of a triangle equal or
not equal to two right angles? When we have found the
answer, if the premisses are immediate, we know fact and 35
reason together; if they are not immediate, we know the
fact without the reason, as in the following example: let C
be the moon, A eclipse, B the fact that the moon fails to
produce shadows [9] though she is full and though no visible
body intervenes between us and her. Then if B, failure to
produce shadows in spite of the absence of an intervening **93ᵛ**

---

[8] The distinction is that between genuine knowledge of a connexion
through its cause and accidental knowledge of it through a middle not
the cause.

[9] i.e. that there is no moonlight casting shadows on the earth on a
clear night at full moon

body, is attributable to C, and A, eclipse, is attributable to
B, it is clear that the moon is eclipsed, but the reason
why is not yet clear, and we know that eclipse exists, but we
do not know what its essential nature is. But when it is clear
5 that A is attributable to C and we proceed to ask the reason
of this fact, we are inquiring what is the nature of B: is it
the earth's acting as a screen, or the moon's rotation or her
extinction? But B is the definition of the other term, viz.,
in these examples, of the major term A; for eclipse is constituted by the earth acting as a screen. Thus, (1) 'What is
thunder?' 'The quenching of fire in cloud', and (2) 'Why
does it thunder?' 'Because fire is quenched in the cloud',
are equivalent. Let C be cloud, A thunder, B the quench-
10 ing of fire. Then B is attributable to C, cloud, since fire is
quenched in it; and A, noise, is attributable to B; and B is
assuredly the definition of the major term A. If there be a
further mediating cause of B, it will be one of the remaining partial definitions of A.

We have stated then how essential nature is discovered
15 and becomes known, and we see that, while there is no
syllogism—i. e. no demonstrative syllogism—of essential
nature, yet it is through syllogism, viz. demonstrative syllogism, that essential nature is exhibited. So we conclude
that neither can the essential nature of anything which has
a cause distinct from itself be known without demonstration, nor can it be demonstrated; and this is what we con-
20 tended in our preliminary discussions.[10]

9   Now while some things have a cause distinct from
themselves, others have not. Hence it is evident that
there are essential natures which are immediate, that is,
are basic premises; and of these not only *that* they are but
also *what* they are must be assumed or revealed in some
other way. This too is the actual procedure of the arithmetician, who assumes both the nature and the existence of

[10] ii, ch. 3.

unit. On the other hand, it is possible (in the manner ex- 25
plained) to exhibit through demonstration the essential
nature of things which have a 'middle',[11] i. e. a cause of
their substantial being other than that being itself; but we
do not thereby demonstrate it.

10 Since definition is said to be the statement of a thing's
nature, obviously one kind of definition will be a statement of the meaning of the name, or of an equivalent
nominal formula. A definition in this sense tells you, e. g. 30
the meaning of the phrase 'triangular character'.[12] When
we are aware that triangle exists, we inquire the reason why
it exists. But it is difficult thus to learn the definition of
things the existence of which we do not genuinely know—
the cause of this difficulty being, as we said before,[13] that we
only know accidentally whether or not the thing exists.
Moreover, a statement may be a unity in either of two ways, 35
by conjunction, like the *Iliad*, or because it exhibits a
single predicate as inhering not accidentally in a single
subject.[14]

That then is one way of defining definition. Another
kind of definition is a formula exhibiting the cause of a
thing's existence. Thus the former signifies without prov- 94ᵃ
ing, but the latter will clearly be a *quasi*-demonstration of
essential nature, differing from demonstration in the arrangement of its terms. For there is a difference between
stating why it thunders, and stating what is the essential
nature of thunder; since the first statement will be 'Because
fire is quenched in the clouds', while the statement of what
the nature of thunder is will be 'The noise of fire being 5
quenched in the clouds'. Thus the same statement takes a

[11] Cf., however, ii, ch. 2.
[12] i. e. as treated by geometry; that is, as abstracted a *materia* and
treated as a subject. Cf. 81ᵇ 25.
[13] Cf. 93ᵃ 16–27.
[14] Presumably a reason for there being a kind of definition other
than nominal. The reference is obviously to 92ᵇ 32.

different form: in one form it is continuous [15] demonstration, in the other definition. Again, thunder can be defined
as noise in the clouds, which is the conclusion of the dem-
10 onstration embodying essential nature. On the other hand
the definition of immediates is an indemonstrable positing
of essential nature. We conclude then that definition is (a)
an indemonstrable statement of essential nature, or (b) a
syllogism of essential nature differing from demonstration
in grammatical form, or (c) the conclusion of a demonstration giving essential nature.

Our discussion has therefore made plain (1) in what
sense and of what things the essential nature is demon-
15 strable, and in what sense and of what things it is not;
(2) what are the various meanings of the term definition,
and in what sense and of what things it proves the essential
nature, and in what sense and of what things it does not;
(3) what is the relation of definition to demonstration,
and how far the same thing is both definable and demonstrable and how far it is not.

20 **11** We think we have scientific knowledge when we know
the cause, and there are four causes: (1) the definable
form, (2) an antecedent which necessitates a consequent,[16]
(3) the efficient cause, (4) the final cause. Hence each of
these can be the middle term of a proof, for [17] (a) though
25 the inference from antecedent to necessary consequent
does not hold if only one premiss is assumed—two is the
minimum—still when there are two it holds on condition
that they have a single common middle term. So it is from
the assumption of this single middle term that the conclusion follows necessarily. The following example will also

[15] Demonstration, like a line, is continuous because its premisses are
parts which are conterminous (as linked by middle terms), and there
is a movement from premisses to conclusion. Definition resembles
rather the indivisible simplicity of a point.
[16] By this Aristotle appears to mean the material cause; cf. Physics
ii, 195ᵃ 18, 19, where the premisses of a syllogism are said to be the
material cause of the conclusion.
[17] sc. 'lest you should suppose that (2) could not be a middle'.

show this.[18] Why is the angle in a semicircle a right angle?
—or from what assumption does it follow that it is a right
angle? Thus, let A be right angle, B the half of two right
angles, C the angle in a semicircle. Then B is the cause in 30
virtue of which A, right angle, is attributable to C, the
angle in a semicircle, since $B = A$ and the other, viz. C,
$= B$, for C is half of two right angles. Therefore it is the
assumption of B, the half of two right angles, from which
it follows that A is attributable to C, i. e. that the angle in
a semicircle is a right angle. Moreover, B is identical with
(b) the defining form of A, since it is what A's definition [19]
signifies. Moreover, the formal cause has already been
shown to be the middle.[20] (c) 'Why did the Athenians 35
become involved in the Persian war?' means 'What cause
originated the waging of war against the Athenians?' and
the answer is, 'Because they raided Sardis with the Eretri-
ans', since this originated the war. Let A be war, B un- **94ᵇ**
provoked raiding, C the Athenians. Then B, unprovoked
raiding, is true of C, the Athenians, and A is true of B,
since men make war on the unjust aggressor. So A, having
war waged upon them, is true of B, the initial aggressors, 5
and B is true of C, the Athenians, who were the aggressors.
Hence here too the cause—in this case the efficient cause—
is the middle term. (d) This is no less true where the cause
is the final cause. E. g. why does one take a walk after
supper? For the sake of one's health. Why does a house
exist? For the preservation of one's goods. The end in view
is in the one case health, in the other preservation. To ask 10
the reason why one must walk after supper is precisely to
ask to what end one must do it. Let C be walking after
supper, B the non-regurgitation of food, A health. Then let

---

[18] sc. 'that (2) can appear as a middle'.
[19] Cf. Euclid, *Elem.* i, Def. x, but Aristotle may be referring to
some earlier definition. The proof here given that the angle in a semicircle is a right angle is not that of Euclid iii. 31; cf. Heath, *Greek
Mathematics*, i. pp. 339, 340.
[20] The reference is to 93ᵃ 3 ff., and other passages such as 94ᵃ 5 ff.,
where the middle is shown to define the major.

walking after supper possess the property of preventing
15 food from rising to the orifice of the stomach, and let
this condition be healthy; since it seems that B, the
non-regurgitation of food, is attributable to C, taking a
walk, and that A, health, is attributable to B. What, then,
is the cause through which A, the final cause, inheres in C?
It is B, the non-regurgitation of food; but B is a kind of
20 definition of A, for A will be explained by it. Why is B the
cause of A's belonging to C? Because to be in a condition
such as B is to be in health. The definitions must be trans-
posed, and then the detail will become clearer. Incidentally, here the order of coming to be is the reverse of what
it is in proof through the efficient cause: in the efficient
25 order the middle term must come to be first, whereas in the
teleological order the minor, C, must first take place, and
the end in view comes last in time.

The same thing may exist for an end and be necessitated
as well. For example, light shines through a lantern (1)
because that which consists of relatively small particles
30 necessarily passes through pores larger than those particles
—assuming that light does issue by penetration—and (2)
for an end, namely to save us from stumbling. If, then, a
thing can exist through two causes, can it come to be
through two causes—as for instance if thunder be a hiss and
a roar necessarily produced by the quenching of fire, and
also designed, as the Pythagoreans say, for a threat to terrify
35 those that lie in Tartarus? Indeed, there are very many such
cases, mostly among the processes and products of the
natural world; for nature, in different senses of the term
'nature', produces now for an end, now by necessity.

Necessity too is of two kinds. It may work in accordance
95ᵃ with a thing's natural tendency, or by constraint and in
opposition to it; as, for instance, by necessity a stone is
borne both upwards and downwards, but not by the same
necessity.

Of the products of man's intelligence some are never
due to chance or necessity but always to an end, as for

example a house or a statue; others, such as health or safety, 5 may result from chance as well.

It is mostly in cases where the issue is indeterminate (though only where the production does not originate in chance, and the end is consequently good), that a result is due to an end, and this is true alike in nature or in art. By chance, on the other hand, nothing comes to be for an end.

12 The effect may be still coming to be, or its occurrence 10 may be past or future, yet the cause will be the same as when it is actually existent—for it is the middle which is the cause—except that if the effect actually exists the cause is actually existent, if it is coming to be so is the cause, if its occurrence is past the cause is past, if future the cause is future. For example, the moon was eclipsed because the earth intervened, is becoming eclipsed because the earth is in process of intervening, will be eclipsed because the earth 15 will intervene, is eclipsed because the earth intervenes.

To take a second example: assuming that the definition of ice is solidified water, let C be water, A solidified, B the middle, which is the cause, namely total failure of heat. Then B is attributed to C, and A, solidification, to B: ice forms when B is occurring, has formed when B has oc- 20 curred, and will form when B shall occur.

This sort of cause, then, and its effect come to be simultaneously when they are in process of becoming, and exist simultaneously when they actually exist; and the same holds good when they are past and when they are future. But what of cases where they are not simultaneous? Can causes and effects different from one another form, as they seem to us to form, a continuous succession, a past effect resulting from a past cause different from itself, a future 25 effect from a future cause different from it, and an effect which is coming-to-be from a cause different from and prior to it? Now on this theory it is from the posterior event that we reason (and this though these later events actually have their source of origin in previous events—a fact which

shows that also when the effect is coming-to-be we still reason from the posterior event), and from the prior event we cannot reason (we cannot argue that because an event
30 A has occurred, therefore an event B has occurred subsequently to A but still in the past—and the same holds good if the occurrence is future)—cannot reason because, be the time interval definite or indefinite, it will never be possible to infer that because it is true to say that A occurred, therefore it is true to say that B, the subsequent event, occurred; for in the interval between the events, though A has already
35 occurred, the latter statement will be false. And the same argument applies also to future events; i. e. one cannot infer from an event which occurred in the past that a future event will occur. The reason of this is that the middle must be homogeneous, past when the extremes are past, future when they are future, coming to be when they are coming-to-be, actually existent when they are actually existent; and there cannot be a middle term homogeneous with extremes respectively past and future. And it is a further difficulty
40 in this theory that the time interval can be neither indefi-
95ᵇ nite nor definite, since during it the inference will be false. We have also to inquire what it is that holds events together so that the coming-to-be now occurring in actual things follows upon a past event. It is evident, we may suggest, that a past event and a present process cannot be 'contiguous', for not even two past events can be 'contigu-
5 ous'. For past events are limits and atomic; so just as points are not 'contiguous' neither are past events, since both are indivisible. For the same reason a past event and a present process cannot be 'contiguous', for the process is divisible, the event indivisible. Thus the relation of present process
10 to past event is analogous to that of line to point, since a process contains an infinity of past events. These questions, however, must receive a more explicit treatment in our general theory of change.[21]

The following must suffice as an account of the manner in which the middle would be identical with the cause

[21] Cf. *Physics* vi.

on the supposition that coming-to-be is a series of consecutive events: for *°* in the terms of such a series too the mid- 15
dle and major terms must form an immediate premiss; e. g.
we argue that, since *C* has occurred, therefore *A* occurred:
and *C*'s occurrence was posterior, *A*'s prior; but *C* is the
source of the inference because it is nearer to the present
moment, and the starting-point of time is the present. We
next argue that, since *D* has occurred, therefore *C* occurred.
Then we conclude that, since *D* has occurred, therefore 20
A must have occurred; and the cause is *C*, for since *D* has
occurred *C* must have occurred, and since *C* has occurred
A must previously have occurred.

If we get our middle term in this way, will the series
terminate in an immediate premiss, or since, as we said,
no two events are 'contiguous', will a fresh term always
intervene because there is an infinity of middles? No:
though no two events are 'contiguous' yet we must start
from a premiss consisting of a middle and the present event 25
as major. The like is true of future events too, since if it
is true to say that *D* will exist, it must be a prior truth to
say that *A* will exist, and the cause of this conclusion is *C*;
for if *D* will exist, *C* will exist prior to *D*, and if *C* will
exist, *A* will exist prior to it. And here too the same infinite
divisibility might be urged, since future events are not 'con- 30
tiguous'. But here too an immediate basic premiss must be
assumed. And in the world of fact this is so: if a house has
been built, then blocks must have been quarried and
shaped. The reason is that a house having been built necessitates a foundation having been laid, and if a foundation
has been laid blocks must have been shaped beforehand. 35
Again, if a house will be built, blocks will similarly be
shaped beforehand; and proof is through the middle in the

²² i. e. Aristotle has had in this chapter to explain (1) how syllogisms concerning a process of events can be brought into line with
other demonstrations equally derivable from immediate primary premisses, and (2) in what sense the middle term contains the cause. He
has in fact had (1) to show that in these syllogisms inference must
find its primary premiss in the effect, and (2) to imply that the
'cause' which appears as middle when cause and effect are not simultaneous is a *causa cognoscendi* and not *essendi*.

same way, for the foundation will exist before the house.

Now we observe in Nature a certain kind of circular process of coming-to-be; and this is possible only if the middle and extreme terms are reciprocal, since conversion is
40 conditioned by reciprocity in the terms of the proof. This
96ᵃ —the convertibility of conclusions and premises—has been proved in our early chapters,[23] and the circular process is an instance of this. In actual fact it is exemplified thus: when the earth had been moistened an exhalation was bound to rise, and when an exhalation had risen cloud was bound to form, and from the formation of cloud rain necessarily resulted, and by the fall of rain the earth was
5 necessarily moistened: but this was the starting-point, so that a circle is completed; for posit any one of the terms and another follows from it, and from that another, and from that again the first.

Some occurrences are universal (for they are, or come-to-be what they are, always and in every case); others again are not always what they are but only as a general rule: for
10 instance, not every man can grow a beard, but it is the general rule. In the case of such connexions the middle term too must be a general rule. For if A is predicted universally of B and B of C, A too must be predicted always and in every instance of C, since to hold in every instance and always is of the nature of the universal. But we have
15 assumed a connexion which is a general rule; consequently the middle term B must also be a general rule. So connexions which embody a general rule—i. e. which exist or come to be as a general rule—will also derive from immediate basic premises.

13 [24] We have already explained how essential nature is set
20   out in the terms of a demonstration, and the sense in which it is or is not demonstrable or definable; so let us now discuss the method to be adopted in tracing the elements predicated as constituting the definable form.

---

[23] i, ch. 3 and An. Pr. ii, cc. 3–5, 8–10.
[24] This chapter treats only the definition of substances.

Now of the attributes which inhere always in each several thing there are some which are wider in extent than it but not wider than its genus (by attributes of wider extent I mean all such as are universal attributes of each several subject, but in their application are not confined to that subject). I. e. while an attribute may inhere in every triad, yet also in a subject not a triad—as being inheres in triad but also in subjects not numbers at all—odd on the other hand is an attribute inhering in every triad and of wider application (inhering as it does also in pentad), but which does not extend beyond the genus of triad; for pentad is a number, but nothing outside number is odd. It is such attributes which we have to select, up to the exact point at which they are severally of wider extent than the subject but collectively coextensive with it; for this synthesis must be the substance of the thing. For example every triad possesses the attributes number, odd, and prime in both senses, i. e. not only as possessing no divisors, but also as not being a sum of numbers. This, then, is precisely what triad is, viz. a number, odd, and prime in the former and also the latter sense of the term: for these attributes taken severally apply, the first two to all odd numbers, the last to the dyad also as well as to the triad, but, taken collectively, to no other subject. Now since we have shown above [25] that attributes predicated as belonging to the essential nature are necessary and that universals are necessary, and since the attributes which we select as inhering in triad, or in any other subject whose attributes we select in this way, are predicated as belonging to its essential nature, triad will thus possess these attributes necessarily. Further, that the synthesis of them constitutes the substance of triad is shown by the following argument. If it is not identical with the being of triad, it must be related to triad as a genus named or nameless. It will then be of wider extent than triad—assuming that wider potential extent is the character of a genus. If on the other hand this synthesis is applicable to no subject other than the individual

[25] i, ch. 4.

triads, it will be identical with the being of triad, because
we make the further assumption that the substance of each
subject is the predication of elements in its essential nature
down to the last differentia characterizing the individuals. It
follows that any other synthesis thus exhibited will likewise
be identical with the being of the subject.

15   The author of a hand-book [26] on a subject that is a
generic whole should divide the genus into its first infimae
species—number e. g. into triad and dyad—and then endeavour to seize their definitions by the method we have
described—the definition, for example, of straight line or
circle or right angle. After that, having established what the
category is to which the subaltern genus belongs—quantity
20 or quality, for instance—he should examine the properties
'peculiar' to the species, working through the proximate
common differentiae. He should proceed thus because the
attributes of the genera compounded of the infimae species
will be clearly given by the definitions of the species; since
the basic element of them all [27] is the definition, i. e. the
simple infima species, and the attributes inhere essentially
in the simple infimae species, in the genera only in virtue
of these.

Divisions according to differentiae are a useful accessory
25 to this method. What force they have as proofs we did,
indeed, explain above,[28] but that merely towards collecting
the essential nature they may be of use we will proceed to
show. They might, indeed, seem to be of no use at all,
but rather to assume everything at the start and to be no
better than an initial assumption made without division.
30 But, in fact, the order in which the attributes are predicated
does make a difference—it matters whether we say animal
—tame—biped, or biped—animal—tame. For if every definable thing consists of two elements and 'animal-tame'
forms a unity, and again out of this and the further differ-

---

[26] With the remainder of the chapter compare An. Pr. i, ch. 25,
where the treatment covers all syllogism.
[27] sc. genera and species.
[28] ii. ch. 5 and An. Pr. i. ch. 31.

entia man (or whatever else is the unity under construction) is constituted, then the elements we assume have necessarily been reached by division. Again, division is the only possible method of avoiding the omission of any element of the essential nature. Thus, if the primary genus is assumed and we then take one of the lower divisions, the dividendum will not fall whole into this division: e. g. it is not all animal which is either whole-winged or split-winged but all winged animal, for it is winged animal to which this differentiation belongs. The primary differentiation of animal is that within which all animal falls. The like is true of every other genus, whether outside animal or a subaltern genus of animal; e. g. the primary differentiation of bird is that within which falls every bird, of fish that within which falls every fish. So, if we proceed in this way, we can be sure that nothing has been omitted: by any other method one is bound to omit something without knowing it.

To define and divide one need not know the whole of existence. Yet some hold it impossible to know the differentiae distinguishing each thing from every single other thing without knowing every single other thing; and one cannot, they say, know each thing without knowing its differentiae, since everything is identical with that from which it does not differ, and other than that from which it differs. Now first of all this is a fallacy: not every differentia precludes identity, since many differentiae inhere in things specifically identical, though not in the substance of these nor essentially. Secondly, when one has taken one's differing pair of opposites and assumed that the two sides exhaust the genus, and that the subject one seeks to define is present in one or other of them, and one has further verified its presence in one of them; then it does not matter whether or not one knows all the other subjects of which the differentiae are also predicated. For it is obvious that when by this process one reaches subjects incapable of further differentiation one will possess the for-

mula defining the substance. Moreover, to postulate that
20 the division exhausts the genus is not illegitimate if the
opposites exclude a middle; since if it is the differentia
of that genus, anything contained in the genus must lie on
one of the two sides.

In establishing a definition by division one should keep
three objects in view: (1) the admission only of elements
in the definable form, (2) the arrangement of these in the
25 right order, (3) the omission of no such elements. The first
is feasible because one can establish genus and differentia
through the topic of the genus,[29] just as one can conclude
the inherence of an accident through the topic of the accident.[30] The right order will be achieved if the right term
is assumed as primary, and this will be ensured if the term
30 selected is predicable of all the others but not all they of it;
since there must be one such term. Having assumed this
we at once proceed in the same way with the lower terms;
for our second term will be the first of the remainder, our
third the first of those which follow the second in a 'contiguous' series, since when the higher term is excluded, that
term of the remainder which is 'contiguous' to it will be
primary, and so on. Our procedure makes it clear that no
35 elements in the definable form have been omitted: we have
taken the differentia that comes first in the order of division, pointing out that animal e. g. is divisible exhaustively
into A and B, and that the subject accepts one of the two
as its predicate. Next we have taken the differentia of the
whole thus reached, and shown that the whole we finally
reach is not further divisible—i. e. that as soon as we have
taken the last differentia to form the concrete totality,
97ᵇ this totality admits of no division into species. For it is
clear that there is no superfluous addition, since all these
terms we have selected are elements in the definable form;
and nothing lacking, since any omission would have to be
a genus or a differentia. Now the primary term is a genus,

---

[29] Cf. *Topics* iv.
[30] Cf. *Topics* ii.

and this term taken in conjunction with its differentiae is a genus: moreover the differentiae are all included, because there is now no further differentia; if there were, the final concrete would admit of division into species, which, we said, is not the case.

To resume our account of the right method of investigation: We must start by observing a set of similar—i. e. specifically identical—individuals, and consider what element they have in common. We must then apply the same process to another set of individuals which belong to one species and are generically but not specifically identical with the former set. When we have established what the common element is in all members of this second species, and likewise in members of further species, we should again consider whether the results established possess any identity, and persevere until we reach a single formula, since this will be the definition of the thing. But if we reach not one formula but two or more, evidently the *definiendum* cannot be one thing but must be more than one. I may illustrate my meaning as follows. If we were inquiring what the essential nature of pride is, we should examine instances of proud men we know of to see what, as such, they have in common; e. g. if Alcibiades was proud, or Achilles and Ajax were proud, we should find, on inquiring what they all had in common, that it was intolerance of insult; it was this which drove Alcibiades to war, Achilles to wrath, and Ajax to suicide. We should next examine other cases, Lysander, for example, or Socrates, and then if these have in common indifference alike to good and ill fortune, I take these two results and inquire what common element have equanimity amid the vicissitudes of life and impatience of dishonour. If they have none, there will be two genera of pride. Besides, every definition is always universal and commensurate: the physician does not prescribe what is healthy for a single eye, but for all eyes or for a determinate species of eye. It is also easier by this method to define the single species than the universal,

and that is why our procedure should be from the several
species to the universal genera—this for the further reason
30 too that equivocation is less readily detected in genera than
in *infimae species*. Indeed, perspicuity is essential in definitions, just as inferential movement is the minimum required in demonstrations; and we shall attain perspicuity if
we can collect separately the definition of each species
through the group of singulars which we have established
—e. g. the definition of similarity not unqualified but re-
35 stricted to colours and to figures; the definition of acute-
ness, but only of sound—and so proceed to the common
universal with a careful avoidance of equivocation. We
may add that if dialectical disputation must not employ
metaphors, clearly metaphors and metaphorical expressions
are precluded in definition: otherwise dialectic would involve metaphors.

14   In order to formulate the connexions we wish to prove
98ᵃ   we have to select our analyses and divisions. The
method of selection consists in laying down the common
genus of all our subjects of investigation—if e. g. they are
animals, we lay down what the properties are which inhere
in every animal. These established, we next lay down the
properties essentially connected with the first of the re-
5 maining classes—e. g. if this first subgenus is bird, the essential properties of every bird—and so on, always characterizing the proximate subgenus. This will clearly at once
enable us to say in virtue of what character the subgenera
10 —man, e. g., or horse—possess their properties. Let A be
animal, B the properties of every animal, C, D, E, various
species of animal. Then it is clear in virtue of what character B inheres in D—namely A—and that it inheres in C
and E for the same reason: and throughout the remaining
subgenera always the same rule applies.

We are now taking our examples from the traditional
class-names, but we must not confine ourselves to con-
15 sidering these. We must collect any other common char-

acter which we observe, and then consider with what species it is connected and what properties belong to it. For
example, as the common properties of horned animals we
collect the possession of a third stomach and only one row
of teeth. Then since it is clear in virtue of what character
they possess these attributes—namely their horned character—the next question is, to what species does the
possession of horns attach?

Yet a further method of selection is by analogy: for we 20
cannot find a single identical name to give to a squid's
pounce, a fish's spine, and an animal's bone, although these
too possess common properties as if there were a single
osseous nature.

15 Some connexions that require proof are identical in
that they possess an identical 'middle'—e. g. a whole
group might be proved through 'reciprocal replacement' 25
—and of these one class are identical in genus, namely all
those whose difference consists in their concerning different subjects or in their mode of manifestation. This
latter class may be exemplified by the questions as to the
causes respectively of echo, of reflection, and of the rain
bow: the connexions to be proved which these questions
embody are identical generically, because all three are forms
of repercussion; but specifically they are different.

Other connexions that require proof only differ in that
the 'middle' of the one is subordinate to the 'middle' of 30
the other. For example: Why does the Nile rise towards the
end of the month? Because towards its close the month
is more stormy. Why is the month more stormy towards its
close? Because the moon is waning. Here the one cause is
subordinate to the other.

16 The question might be raised with regard to cause 35
and effect whether when the effect is present the
cause also is present; whether, for instance, if a plant sheds
its leaves or the moon is eclipsed, there is present also the

cause of the eclipse or of the fall of the leaves—the possession of broad leaves, let us say, in the latter case, in
98ᵇ the former the earth's interposition. For, one might argue,
if this cause is not present, these phenomena will have some
other cause: if it *is* present, its effect will be at once implied
by it—the eclipse by the earth's interposition, the fall of the
leaves by the possession of broad leaves; but if so, they will
be logically coincident and each capable of proof through
5 the other. Let me illustrate: Let A be deciduous character,
B the possession of broad leaves, C vine. Now if A inheres
in B (for every broad-leaved plant is deciduous), and B in
C (every vine possessing broad leaves); then A inheres in C
(every vine is deciduous), and the middle term B is the
10 cause. But we can also demonstrate that the vine has broad
leaves because it is deciduous. Thus, let D be broad-leaved,
E deciduous, F vine. Then E inheres in F (since every vine
is deciduous), and D in E (for every deciduous plant has
15 broad leaves): therefore every vine has broad leaves, and
the cause is its deciduous character. If,[31] however, they cannot each be the cause of the other (for cause is prior to effect, and the earth's interposition is the cause of the moon's
eclipse and not the eclipse of the interposition)—if, then,
demonstration through the cause is of the reasoned fact
20 and demonstration not through the cause is of the bare
fact, one who knows it through the eclipse knows the fact
of the earth's interposition but not the reasoned fact.
Moreover, that the eclipse is not the cause of the interposition, but the interposition of the eclipse, is obvious because the interposition is an element in the definition of
eclipse, which shows that the eclipse is known through the
interposition and not vice versa.

On the other hand, can a single effect have more than
25 one cause? One might argue as follows: if the same attribute is predicable of more than one thing as its primary
subject, let B be a primary subject in which A inheres, and
C another primary subject of A, and D and E primary sub-

[31] Here begins Aristotle's answer.

jects of B and C respectively. A will then inhere in D and E, and B will be the cause of A's inherence in D, C of A's inherence in E. The presence of the cause thus necessitates that of the effect, but the presence of the effect necessitates the presence not of all that may cause it but only of a 30 cause which yet need not be the whole cause. We may, however, suggest [32] that if the connexion to be proved is always universal and commensurate, not only will the cause be a whole but also the effect will be universal and commensurate. For instance, deciduous character will belong exclusively to a subject which is a whole, and, if this whole has species, universally and commensurately to those species—i. e. either to all species of plant or to a single 35 species. So in these universal and commensurate connexions the 'middle' and its effect must reciprocate, i. e. be convertible. Supposing, for example, that the reason why trees are deciduous is the coagulation of sap, then if a tree is deciduous, coagulation must be present, and if coagulation is present—not in any subject but in a tree— then that tree must be deciduous.

17   Can the cause of an identical effect be not identical 99ᵃ
in every instance of the effect but different? Or is that impossible? Perhaps it is impossible if the effect is demonstrated as essential and not as inhering in virtue of a symptom or an accident—because the middle is then the definition of the major term—though possible if the demonstration is not essential. Now it is possible to consider the effect and its subject as an accidental conjunction, though 5 such conjunctions would not be regarded as connexions demanding scientific proof. But if they are accepted as such, the middle will correspond to the extremes, and be equivocal if they are equivocal, generically one if they are generically one. Take the question why proportionals alternate. The cause when they are lines, and when they are numbers, is both different and identical; different in so far as lines are 30

[32] Here begins Aristotle's answer.

lines and not numbers, identical as involving a given deter
minate increment. In all proportionals this is so. Again, the
cause of likeness between colour and colour is other than
that between figure and figure; for likeness here is equivocal,
meaning perhaps in the latter case equality of the ratios of
the sides and equality of the angles, in the case of colours
15 identity of the act of perceiving them, or something else of
the sort. Again, connexions requiring proof which are
identical by analogy have middles also analogous.

The truth is that cause, effect, and subject are reciprocally predicable in the following way. If the species are
taken severally, the effect is wider than the subject (e. g.
the possession of external angles equal to four right angles
20 is an attribute wider than triangle or square), but it is coextensive with the species taken collectively (in this instance with all figures whose external angles are equal to
four right angles). And the middle likewise reciprocates,
for the middle is a definition of the major; which is incidentally the reason why all the sciences are built up through
definition.

We may illustrate as follows. Deciduous is a universal
attribute of vine, and is at the same time of wider extent
than vine; and of fig, and is of wider extent than fig: but it
25 is not wider than but coextensive with the totality of the
species. Then if you take the middle which is proximate, it
is a definition of deciduous. I say that, because you will
first reach a middle [33] next the subject,[34] and a premiss asserting it of the whole subject, and after that a middle—
the coagulation of sap or something of the sort—proving the
connexion of the first middle with the major:[35] but it is
the coagulation of sap at the junction of leaf-stalk and stem
which defines deciduous.[36]

[33] sc. broad-leaved.
[34] Vine, fig, &c.
[35] Broad-leaved with deciduous.
[36] Aristotle contemplates four terms: (1) deciduous, (2) coagulation, (3) broad-leaved. (4) vine, fig, &c.
If we get the middle proximate to (1) it is a definition of (1). But

If an explanation in formal terms of the inter-relation of cause and effect is demanded, we shall offer the follow- 30 ing. Let *A* be an attribute of all *B*, and *B* of every species of *D*, but so that both *A* and *B* are wider than their respective subjects. Then *B* will be a universal attribute of each species of *D* (since I call such an attribute universal even if it is not commensurate, and I call an attribute primary universal if it is commensurate,[37] not with each species severally but with their totality), and it extends beyond each of them taken separately. Thus, *B* is the cause of *A*'s inherence in the species of *D*: consequently *A* must 35 be of wider extent than *B*; otherwise why should *B* be the cause of *A*'s inherence in *D* any more than *A* the cause of *B*'s inherence in *D*? Now if *A* is an attribute of all the species of *E*, all the species of *E* will be united by possessing some common cause other than *B*: otherwise how shall we be able to say that *A* is predicable of all of which *E* is predicable, while *E* is not predicable of all of which *A* can 99ᵇ be predicated? I mean how can there fail to be some special cause of *A*'s inherence in *E*, as there was of *A*'s inherence in all the species of *D*? Then are the species of *E*, too, united by possessing some common cause? This cause we must look for. Let us call it *C*.[38]

in investigating vines, figs, &c. according to the method of chapter 13, we shall first find a common character of them in broad-leaved, and, taking this as a middle, we shall prove that vine, fig, &c., qua broad-leaved, are deciduous. But this proof is not demonstration, because broad-leaved is not a definition of deciduous. So our next step will be to find a middle—coagulation—mediating the major premiss of this proof, and demonstrate that broad-leaved plants, qua liable to coagulation, are deciduous. This is strict demonstration, because coagulation defines deciduous.

[37] But cf. i, ch. 4, 73ᵇ 21–74ᵃ 3.

[38] The schema of Aristotle's argument in this paragraph is:

We conclude, then, that the same effect may have more
than one cause, but not in subjects specifically identical.
5 For instance, the cause of longevity in quadrupeds is lack
of bile, in birds a dry constitution—or certainly something
different.

18 If immediate premises are not reached at once, and
there is not merely one middle but several middles, i. e.
several causes; is the cause of the property's inherence in
10 the several species the middle which is proximate to the
primary universal,[39] or the middle which is proximate to the
species? [40] Clearly the cause is that nearest to each species
severally in which it is manifested, for that is the cause of
the subject's falling under the universal. To illustrate formally: C is the cause of B's inherence in D; hence C is the
cause of A's inherence in D, B of A's inherence in C, while
the cause of A's inherence in B is B itself.

15 **19** As regards syllogism and demonstration, the definition of, and the conditions required to produce each
of them, are now clear, and with that also the definition
of, and the conditions required to produce, demonstrative knowledge, since it is the same as demonstration. As
to the basic premises, how they become known and what
is the developed state of knowledge of them is made clear
by raising some preliminary problems.
20   We have already said [41] that scientific knowledge through
demonstration is impossible unless a man knows the primary immediate premises. But there are questions which
might be raised in respect of the apprehension of these immediate premises: one might not only ask whether it is of
the same kind as the apprehension of the conclusions, but
also whether there is or is not scientific knowledge of both;
or scientific knowledge of the latter, and of the former a

[39] i. e. the property.
[40] the subject
[41] i, ch. 2.

different kind of knowledge; and, further, whether the developed states of knowledge are not innate but come 25 to be in us, or are innate but at first unnoticed. Now it is strange if we possess them from birth; for it means that we possess apprehensions more accurate than demonstration and fail to notice them. If on the other hand we acquire them and do not previously possess them, how could we apprehend and learn without a basis of pre-existent knowledge? For that is impossible, as we used to 30 find[42] in the case of demonstration. So it emerges that neither can we possess them from birth, nor can they come to be in us if we are without knowledge of them to the extent of having no such developed state at all. Therefore we must possess a capacity of some sort, but not such as to rank higher in accuracy than these developed states. And this at least is an obvious characteristic of all animals, for they possess a congenital discriminative capacity which 35 is called sense-perception. But though sense-perception is innate in all animals, in some the sense-impression comes to persist, in others it does not. So animals in which this persistence does not come to be have either no knowledge at all outside the act of perceiving, or no knowledge of objects of which no impression persists; animals in which it does come into being have perception and can continue to retain the sense-impression in the soul: and when such per- 100ᵇ sistence is frequently repeated a further distinction at once arises between those which out of the persistence of such sense-impressions develop a power of systematizing them and those which do not. So out of sense-perception comes to be what we call memory, and out of frequently repeated memories of the same thing develops experience; for a num- 5 ber of memories constitute a single experience.[43] From experience again—i. e. from the universal now stabilized in its entirety within the soul, the one beside the many which

[42] i, ch. 1.
[43] Cf. *Met* A 980ᵃ 28. *Met* A 1 should be compared with this chapter.

is a single identity within them all—originate the skill of
the craftsman and the knowledge of the man of science,
skill in the sphere of coming to be and science in the sphere
of being.

We conclude that these states of knowledge are neither
innate in a determinate form, nor developed from other
10 higher states of knowledge, but from sense-perception. It
is like a rout in battle stopped by first one man making a
stand and then another, until the original formation has
been restored. The soul is so constituted as to be capable
of this process.

Let us now restate the account given already, though
with insufficient clearness. When one of a number of
15 logically indiscriminable particulars has made a stand, the
earliest universal is present in the soul: for though the act
of sense-perception is of the particular, its content is uni-
100ᵇ versal—is man, for example, not the man Callias. A fresh
stand is made among these rudimentary universals, and
the process does not cease until the indivisible concepts,
the true universals, are established: e. g. such and such a
species of animal is a step towards the genus animal, which
by the same process is a step towards a further generaliza-
tion.

Thus it is clear that we must get to know the primary
premisses by induction; for the method by which even
5 sense-perception implants the universal is inductive. Now
of the thinking states by which we grasp truth, some are
unfailingly true, others admit of error—opinion, for instance, and calculation, whereas scientific knowing and intuition are always true: further, no other kind of thought
except intuition is more accurate than scientific knowledge,
whereas primary premisses are more knowable than dem-
10 onstrations, and all scientific knowledge is discursive.
From these considerations it follows that there will be no
scientific knowledge of the primary premisses, and since except intuition nothing can be truer than scientific knowledge, it will be intuition that apprehends the primary

premisses—a result which also follows from the fact that demonstration cannot be the originative source of demonstration, nor, consequently, scientific knowledge of scientific knowledge. If, therefore, it is the only other kind of true thinking except scientific knowing, intuition will be **19** the originative source of scientific knowledge. And the originative source of science grasps the original basic premiss, while science as a whole is similarly related as originative source to the whole body of fact.

Physics

INTRODUCTION

Aristotle conceived physics—the science of natures and of natural changes—broadly to include not only inorganic processes such as those studied in astronomy, physics, chemistry, and meteorology, but also biological and psychological phenomena. Four of his treatises on physics in the narrow sense have survived. In the Physics he treats of the principles of natural bodies and of natural motions, analyzes the concepts implied in motion (such as continuity, infinity, place, void, time), sets forth the kinds and causes of motion, and relates them all by tracing the causes of motion back to an unmoved mover. In On the Heavens he treats of the local motions of bodies, differentiating the motions of the sublunar elements from the motions of the "primary element" of which the heavenly bodies are formed. In On Generation and Corruption he treats of the causes of changes other than local motion which terrestrial bodies undergo, such as generation and corruption (or change in substance), alteration (or change in quality), and growth and diminution (or change in size). Finally in the Meteorology he treats of the interplay of natural elements and of mixtures and compounds, seeking the causes of comets, rain, snow, dew, winds, earthquakes, thunder, lightning, storms, rainbows, studying the processes which affect mixed bodies like water, metals, clays, oils, wines, and finally, effecting a transition to organic bodies by differentiating (1) elements, (2) "homogeneous bodies" (like the metals among inanimate things, or the wood and bark of plants, or the tissues and bones of animals), which possess different qualities than the elements of which they are compounded, and (3) "heterogeneous bodies" (like organs and parts, hands and faces), which possess functions and purposes distinct from those of the homogeneous bodies of which they are compounded.

Aristotle sometimes refers to the first two books of the Physics, in which the principles of natural change are treated explicitly, as the Physical Treatises. The number and nature of the principles of change and motion are determined in Book I from a dialectical examination of the opinions of earlier physicists and of the requirements of the phenomena. By "principles of motion" Aristotle means, not propositions in a science, but the irreducible terms of the process, which may serve in the formation of propositions. Any change or motion must have an initial and terminating point (the quality, place, or quantity at which the process began and the quality, place, or quantity at which it ended) and it must have a continuing subject which undergoes the motion: these three principles are privation, form, and matter. "Nature" is a cause of motion, to be distinguished from art in that nature is a cause of motion internal to the thing moved whereas art is an externally imposed cause of motion; nature is to be distinguished from chance and spontaneity in that nature is related essentially to the motions it causes (as in the specific operations and functions of an inorganic body or an organism) whereas chance and spontaneity are accidental or incidental causes of effects which might have been caused by art or nature (as when a man digging a well finds a buried pot of gold).

Aristotle's treatment of the principles of motion reflects his conception of the organization of the sciences, the requirements of proof, and the analysis of being. Physics is sharply distinguished by its concern with nature and motion from mathematics which abstracts from matter and motion and from metaphysics which treats of being as such and of the existence and essence of "separable" forms. The various branches of physics are likewise distinguishable by consideration of the kind of change studied (change of substance, or generation and corruption; change of quality or alteration; change of quantity, or growth and diminution; and change of place or locomotion), the kind of cause sought (formal, material, final, or efficient), and the kind of substance or nature in which the change occurs. These same distinctions, moreover, relate the materials of physics to the requirement of logical proof, for the examination of substances yields definitions and propositions, and the examination of causes yields the middle terms of scientific proof. They are, finally, translated into the terms of metaphysical problems which turn on the examination of the principles of all sciences and of the being and causes of things.

PHYSICA

CONTENTS

BOOK II

A.

Physica [1]

Physics

Translated by R. P. Hardie and R. K. Gaye

レレレレ

BOOK II

192ᵇ 1   Of things that exist, some exist by nature, some from
other causes. 'By nature' the animals and their parts
10 exist, and the plants and the simple bodies (earth, fire, air,
water)—for we say that these and the like exist 'by nature'.

All the things mentioned present a feature in which
they differ from things which are *not* constituted by nature.
15 Each of them has *within itself* a principle of motion and
of stationariness (in respect of place, or of growth and
decrease, or by way of alteration). On the other hand, a
bed and a coat and anything else of that sort, qua receiving
these designations—i. e. in so far as they are products of art
—have no innate impulse to change. But in so far as they
20 happen to be composed of stone or of earth or of a mixture of the two, they *do* have such an impulse, and just to
that extent—which seems to indicate that *nature is a source*

---

[1] The present treatise, usually called the *Physics*, deals with natural
body in general: the special kinds are discussed in Aristotle's other
physical works, the *De Caelo*, &c. The first book is concerned with
the elements of a natural body (matter and form): the second mainly
with the different types of cause studied by the physicist. Books III–
VII deal with movement, and the notions implied in it. The subject
of VIII is the prime mover, which, though not itself a natural body, is
the cause of movement in natural bodies.

or *cause of being moved and of being at rest in that to which it belongs primarily, in virtue of itself and not in virtue of a concomitant attribute.*

I say 'not in virtue of a concomitant attribute', because (for instance) a man who is a doctor might cure himself. Nevertheless it is not in so far as he is a patient that he 25 possesses the art of medicine: it merely has happened that the same man is doctor and patient—and that is why these attributes are not always found together. So it is with all other artificial products. None of them has in itself the source of its own production. But while in some cases (for instance houses and the other products of manual labour) that principle is in something else external to the thing, 30 in others—those which may cause a change in themselves in virtue of a concomitant attribute—it lies in the things themselves (but not in virtue of what they are).

'Nature' then is what has been stated. Things 'have a nature' which have a principle of this kind. Each of them is a substance; for it is a subject, and nature always implies a subject in which it inheres.

The term 'according to nature' is applied to all these 35 things and also to the attributes which belong to them in virtue of what they are, for instance the property of fire to be carried upwards—which is not a 'nature' nor 'has a nature' but is 'by nature' or 'according to nature'.

What nature is, then, and the meaning of the terms 'by nature' and 'according to nature', has been stated. That **193ᵃ** nature exists, it would be absurd to try to prove; for it is obvious that there are many things of this kind, and to prove what is obvious by what is not is the mark of a man 5 who is unable to distinguish what is self-evident from what is not. (This state of mind is clearly possible. A man blind from birth might reason about colours. Presumably therefore such persons must be talking about words without any thought to correspond.)

Some identify the nature or substance of a natural object with that immediate constituent of it which taken by

10 itself is without arrangement, e. g. the wood is the 'nature'
of the bed, and the bronze the 'nature' of the statue.

As an indication of this Antiphon points out that if you
planted a bed and the rotting wood acquired the power of
sending up a shoot, it would not be a bed that would
come up, but wood—which shows that the arrangement in
15 accordance with the rules of the art is merely an incidental
attribute, whereas the real nature is the other, which,
further, persists continuously through the process of making.

But if the material of each of these objects has itself the
same relation to something else, say bronze (or gold) to
water, bones (or wood) to earth and so on, that (they say)
20 would be their nature and essence. Consequently some assert earth, others fire or air or water or some or all of these,
to be the nature of the things that are. For whatever any
one of them supposed to have this character—whether one
thing or more than one thing—this or these he declared to
25 be the whole of substance, all else being its affections,
states, or dispositions. Every such thing they held to be
eternal (for it could not pass into anything else), but other
things to come into being and cease to be times without
number.

This then is one account of 'nature', namely that it is
the immediate material substratum of things which have in
themselves a principle of motion or change.

Another account is that 'nature' is the shape or form
30 which is specified in the definition of the thing.

For the word 'nature' is applied to what is according to
nature and the natural in the same way as 'art' is applied
to what is artistic or a work of art. We should not say in
the latter case that there is anything artistic about a thing,
35 if it is a bed only potentially, not yet having the form of a
bed; nor should we call it a work of art. The same is true of
natural compounds. What is potentially flesh or bone has
not yet its own 'nature', and does not exist 'by nature',
193ᵇ until it receives the form specified in the definition, which

we name in defining what flesh or bone is. Thus in the second sense of 'nature' it would be the shape or form (not separable except in statement) of things which have in themselves a source of motion. (The combination of the two, e. g. man, is not 'nature' but 'by nature' or 'natural'.)

The form indeed is 'nature' rather than the matter; for a thing is more properly said to be what it is when it has attained to fulfilment than when it exists potentially. Again man is born from man, but not bed from bed. That is why people say that the figure is not the nature of a bed, but the wood is—if the bed sprouted not a bed but wood would come up. But even if the figure is art, then on the same principle the shape of man is his nature. For man is born from man.

We also speak of a thing's nature as being exhibited in the process of growth by which its nature is attained. The 'nature' in this sense is not like 'doctoring', which leads not to the art of doctoring but to health. Doctoring must start from the art, not lead to it. But it is not in this way that nature (in the one sense) is related to nature (in the other). What grows qua growing grows from something into something. Into what then does it grow? Not into that from which it arose but into that to which it tends. The shape then is nature.

'Shape' and 'nature', it should be added, are used in two senses. For the privation too is in a way form. But whether in unqualified coming to be there is privation, i. e. a contrary to what comes to be, we must consider later.[2]

2   We have distinguished, then, the different ways in which the term 'nature' is used.

The next point to consider is how the mathematician differs from the physicist. Obviously physical bodies contain surfaces and volumes, lines and points, and these are the subject-matter of mathematics.

Further, is astronomy different from physics or a de-

[2] *De Gen. et Corr.* i. 3.

partment of it? It seems absurd that the physicist should be
supposed to know the nature of sun or moon, but not to
know any of their essential attributes, particularly as the
30 writers on physics obviously do discuss their shape also
and whether the earth and the world are spherical or not.

Now the mathematician, though he too treats of these
things, nevertheless does not treat of them as the limits of
a physical body; nor does he consider the attributes indicated as the attributes of such bodies. That is why he
separates them; for in thought they are separable from
motion, and it makes no difference, nor does any falsity result, if they are separated. The holders of the theory of
35 Forms do the same, though they are not aware of it; for
they separate the objects of physics, which are less separable
than those of mathematics. This becomes plain if one tries
194ᵃ to state in each of the two cases the definitions of the things
and of their attributes. 'Odd' and 'even', 'straight' and
'curved', and likewise 'number', 'line', and 'figure', do not
5 involve motion; not so 'flesh' and 'bone' and 'man'—these
are defined like 'snub nose', not like 'curved'.

Similar evidence is supplied by the more physical of the
branches of mathematics, such as optics, harmonics, and
astronomy. These are in a way the converse of geometry.
While geometry investigates physical lines but not qua
10 physical, optics investigates mathematical lines, but qua
physical, not qua mathematical.

Since 'nature' has two senses, the form and the matter,
we must investigate its objects as we would the essence
of snubness. That is, such things are neither independent
of matter nor can be defined in terms of matter only. Here
15 too indeed one might raise a difficulty. Since there are two
natures, with which is the physicist concerned? Or should
he investigate the combination of the two? But if the combination of the two, then also each severally. Does it belong
then to the same or to different sciences to know each
severally?

If we look at the ancients, physics would seem to be concerned with the *matter*. (It was only very slightly that Empedocles and Democritus touched on the forms and the essence.)

But if on the other hand art imitates nature, and it is the part of the same discipline to know the form and the matter up to a point (e. g. the doctor has a knowledge of health and also of bile and phlegm, in which health is realized, and the builder both of the form of the house and of the matter, namely that it is bricks and beams, and so forth): if this is so, it would be the part of physics also to know nature in both its senses.

Again, 'that for the sake of which', or the end, belongs to the same department of knowledge as the means. But the nature is the end or 'that for the sake of which'. For if a thing undergoes a continuous change and there is a stage which is last, this stage is the end or 'that for the sake of which'. (That is why the poet was carried away into making an absurd statement when he said 'he has the end [3] for the sake of which he was born'. For not every stage that is last claims to be an end, but only that which is best.)

For the arts make their material (some simply 'make' it, others make it serviceable), and we use everything as if it was there for our sake. (We also are in a sense an end. 'That for the sake of which' has two senses: the distinction is made in our work *On Philosophy*.[4]) The arts, therefore, which govern the matter and have knowledge are two, **194ᵇ** namely the art which uses the product and the art which directs the production of it. That is why the using art also is in a sense directive; but it differs in that it knows the form, whereas the art which is directive as being concerned with production knows the matter. For the helmsman knows and prescribes what sort of form a helm should have, the other from what wood it should be made and by means

[3] i. e. death.
[4] i. e. in the dialogue *De Philosophia*.

of what operations. In the products of art, however, we make the material with a view to the function, whereas in the products of nature the matter is there all along.

Again, matter is a relative term: to each form there cor-
10 responds a special matter. How far then must the physicist know the form or essence? Up to a point, perhaps, as the doctor must know sinew or the smith bronze (i. e. until he understands the purpose of each): and the physicist is concerned only with things whose forms are separable in-deed, but do not exist apart from matter. Man is begotten by man and by the sun as well. The mode of existence and
15 essence of the separable it is the business of the primary type of philosophy to define.

3 Now that we have established these distinctions, we must proceed to consider causes, their character and number. Knowledge is the object of our inquiry, and men do
20 not think they know a thing till they have grasped the 'why' of it (which is to grasp its primary cause). So clearly we too must do this as regards both coming to be and passing away and every kind of physical change, in order that, knowing their principles, we may try to refer to these principles each of our problems.

In one sense, then, (1) that out of which a thing comes to be and which persists, is called 'cause', e. g. the bronze
25 of the statue, the silver of the bowl, and the genera of which the bronze and the silver are species.

In another sense (2) the form or the archetype, i. e. the statement of the essence, and its genera, are called 'causes' (e. g. of the octave the relation of 2 : 1, and generally num-ber), and the parts in the definition.

Again (3) the primary source of the change or coming to rest; e. g. the man who gave advice is a cause, the father
30 is cause of the child, and generally what makes of what is made and what causes change of what is changed.

Again (4) in the sense of end or 'that for the sake of which' a thing is done, e. g. health is the cause of walking about. ('Why is he walking about?' we say. 'To be healthy', and, having said that, we think we have assigned the cause.) The same is true also of all the intermediate steps which are 35 brought about through the action of something else as means towards the end, e. g. reduction of flesh, purging, drugs, or surgical instruments are means towards health. All these things are 'for the sake of' the end, though they 195ᵇ differ from one another in that some are activities, others instruments.

This then perhaps exhausts the number of ways in which the term 'cause' is used.

As the word has several senses, it follows that there are several causes of the same thing (not merely in virtue of a concomitant attribute), e. g. both the art of the sculptor and the bronze are causes of the statue. These are causes 5 of the statue qua statue, not in virtue of anything else that it may be—only not in the same way, the one being the material cause, the other the cause whence the motion comes. Some things cause each other reciprocally, e. g. hard work causes fitness and *vice versa*, but again not in the same way, but the one as end, the other as the origin of change. 10 Further the same thing is the cause of contrary results. For that which by its presence brings about one result is sometimes blamed for bringing about the contrary by its absence. Thus we ascribe the wreck of a ship to the absence of the pilot whose presence was the cause of its safety.

All the causes now mentioned fall into four familiar divisions. The letters are the causes of syllables, the material 15 of artificial products, fire, &c., of bodies, the parts of the whole, and the premisses of the conclusion, in the sense of 'that from which'. Of these pairs the one set are causes in the sense of substratum, e. g. the parts, the other set in 20 the sense of essence—the whole and the combination and the form. But the seed and the doctor and the adviser, and generally the maker, are all sources whence the change or stationariness originates, while the others are causes in the sense of the end or the good of the rest; for 'that for the

sake of which' means what is best and the end of the things
25 that lead up to it. (Whether we say the 'good itself' or the
'apparent good' makes no difference.)

Such then is the number and nature of the kinds of
cause.

Now the modes of causation are many, though when
brought under heads they too can be reduced in number.
30 For 'cause' is used in many senses and even within the same
kind one may be prior to another (e. g. the doctor and the
expert are causes of health, the relation 2 : 1 and number of
the octave), and always what is inclusive to what is particular. Another mode of causation is the incidental and its
genera, e. g. in one way 'Polyclitus', in another 'sculptor'
35 is the cause of a statue, because 'being Polyclitus' and
'sculptor' are incidentally conjoined. Also the classes in
which the incidental attribute is included; thus 'a man'
195ᵇ could be said to be the cause of a statue or, generally, 'a
living creature'. An incidental attribute too may be more or
less remote, e. g. suppose that 'a pale man' or 'a musical
man' were said to be the cause of the statue.

All causes, both proper and incidental, may be spoken of
5 either as potential or as actual; e. g. the cause of a house
being built is either 'house-builder' or 'house-builder building'.

Similar distinctions can be made in the things of which
the causes are causes, e. g. of 'this statue' or of 'statue' or of
'image' generally, of 'this bronze' or of 'bronze' or of 'ma-
10 terial' generally. So too with the incidental attributes.
Again we may use a complex expression for either and say,
e. g., neither 'Polyclitus' nor 'sculptor' but 'Polyclitus,
sculptor'.

All these various uses, however, come to six in number,
under each of which again the usage is twofold. Cause
15 means either what is particular or a genus, or an incidental
attribute or a genus of that, and these either as a complex or
each by itself; and all six either as actual or as potential.
The difference is this much, that causes which are actually

at work and particular exist and cease to exist simultaneously with their effect, e. g. this healing person with this being-healed person and that housebuilding man with that being-built house; but this is not always true of potential 20 causes—the house and the housebuilder do not pass away simultaneously.

In investigating the cause of each thing it is always necessary to seek what is most precise (as also in other things): thus man builds because he is a builder, and a builder builds in virtue of his art of building. This last cause then is prior: and so generally.

Further, generic effects should be assigned to generic 25 causes, particular effects to particular causes, e. g. statue to sculptor, this statue to this sculptor; and powers are relative to possible effects, actually operating causes to things which are actually being effected.

This must suffice for our account of the number of causes and the modes of causation.   30

4   But chance also and spontaneity are reckoned among
      causes: many things are said both to be and to come to be as a result of chance and spontaneity. We must inquire therefore in what manner chance and spontaneity are present among the causes enumerated, and whether they are the same or different, and generally what chance and spontaneity are.   35

Some people [5] even question whether they are real or not. They say that nothing happens by chance, but that everything which we ascribe to chance or spontaneity has some 196ᵃ definite cause, e. g. coming 'by chance' into the market and finding there a man whom one wanted but did not expect to meet is due to one's wish to go and buy in the market. Similarly in other cases of chance it is always possible, they 5 maintain, to find something which is the cause; but not chance, for if chance were real, it would seem strange indeed, and the question might be raised, why on earth none

[5] Apparently Democritus is meant.

of the wise men of old in speaking of the causes of generation and decay took account of chance; whence it would
10 seem that they too did not believe that anything is by
chance. But there is a further circumstance that is surprising. Many things both come to be and are by chance
and spontaneity, and although all know that each of them
can be ascribed to some cause (as the old argument said
15 which denied chance), nevertheless they speak of some of
these things as happening by chance and others not. For
this reason also they ought to have at least referred to the
matter in some way or other.

Certainly the early physicists found no place for chance
among the causes which they recognized—love, strife,
mind, fire, or the like. This is strange, whether they supposed that there is no such thing as chance or whether they
20 thought there is but omitted to mention it—and that too
when they sometimes used it, as Empedocles does when he
says that the air is not always separated into the highest
region, but 'as it may chance'. At any rate he says in his
cosmogony that 'it happened to run that way at that time,
but it often ran otherwise.' He tells us also that most of the
parts of animals came to be by chance.

There are some [6] too who ascribe this heavenly sphere
25 and all the worlds to spontaneity. They say that the vortex
arose spontaneously, i. e. the motion that separated and arranged in its present order all that exists. This statement
might well cause surprise. For they are asserting that
chance is not responsible for the existence or generation
of animals and plants, nature or mind or something of the
30 kind being the cause of them (for it is not any chance thing
that comes from a given seed but an olive from one kind
and a man from another); and yet at the same time they
assert that the heavenly sphere and the divinest of visible
35 things arose spontaneously, having no such cause as is assigned to animals and plants. Yet if this is so, it is a fact
which deserves to be dwelt upon, and something might

[6] Apparently Democritus is meant.

well have been said about it. For besides the other absurdi-196ᵇ
ties of the statement, it is the more absurd that people
should make it when they see nothing coming to be spontaneously in the heavens, but much happening by chance
among the things which as they say are not due to chance;
whereas we should have expected exactly the opposite.

Others [7] there are who, indeed, believe that chance is a 5
cause, but that it is inscrutable to human intelligence, as
being a divine thing and full of mystery.

Thus we must inquire what chance and spontaneity are,
whether they are the same or different, and how they fit
into our division of causes.

5   First then we observe that some things always come 10
to pass in the same way, and others for the most part.
It is clearly of neither of these that chance is said to be the
cause, nor can the 'effect of chance' be identified with any
of the things that come to pass by necessity and always, or
for the most part. But as there is a third class of events besides these two—events which all say are 'by chance'—it is
plain that there is such a thing as chance and spontaneity;
for we know that things of this kind are due to chance and 15
that things due to chance are of this kind.

But, secondly, some events are for the sake of something,
others not. Again, some of the former class are in accordance with deliberate intention, others not, but both are in
the class of things which are for the sake of something. 20
Hence it is clear that even among the things which are
outside the necessary and the normal, there are some in
connexion with which the phrase 'for the sake of something' is applicable. (Events that are for the sake of something include whatever may be done as a result of thought
or of nature.) Things of this kind, then, when they come
to pass incidentally are said to be 'by chance'. For just as 25
a thing is something either in virtue of itself or incidentally,
so may it be a cause. For instance, the housebuilding faculty

[7] Democritus.

is in virtue of itself the cause of a house, whereas the pale or the musical [8] is the incidental cause. That which is *per se* cause of the effect is determinate, but the incidental cause is indeterminable, for the possible attributes of an individual are innumerable. To resume then; when a thing of this kind comes to pass among events which are for the sake of something, it is said to be spontaneous or by chance. (The distinction between the two must be made later [9]—for the present it is sufficient if it is plain that both are in the sphere of things done for the sake of something.)

Example: A man is engaged in collecting subscriptions for a feast. He would have gone to such and such a place for the purpose of getting the money, if he had known. He actually went there for another purpose, and it was only incidentally that he got his money by going there; and this was not due to the fact that he went there as a rule or necessarily, nor is the end effected (getting the money) a cause present in himself—it belongs to the class of things that are intentional and the result of intelligent deliberation. It is when these conditions are satisfied that the man is said to have gone 'by chance'. If he had gone of deliberate purpose and for the sake of this—if he always or normally went there when he was collecting payments—he would not be said to have gone 'by chance'.

It is clear then that chance is an incidental cause in the sphere of those actions for the sake of something which involve purpose. Intelligent reflection, then, and chance are in the same sphere, for purpose implies intelligent reflection.

It is necessary, no doubt, that the causes of what comes to pass by chance be indefinite; and that is why chance is supposed to belong to the class of the indefinite and to be inscrutable to man, and why it might be thought that, in a way, nothing occurs by chance. For all these statements

[8] Incidental attributes of the housebuilder.
[9] In ch. 6.

are correct, because they are well grounded. Things do, in a way, occur by chance, for they occur incidentally and chance is an *incidental* cause. But strictly it is not the cause —without qualification—of anything; for instance, a house-builder is the cause of a house; incidentally, a flute-player may be so.

And the causes of the man's coming and getting the money (when he did not come for the sake of that) are 15 innumerable. He may have wished to see somebody or been following somebody or avoiding somebody, or may have gone to see a spectacle. Thus to say that chance is a thing contrary to rule is correct. For 'rule' applies to what is always true or true for the most part, whereas chance belongs to a third type of event. Hence, to conclude, since causes of this kind are indefinite, chance too is indefinite. 20 (Yet in some cases one might raise the question whether any incidental fact might be the cause of the chance occurrence, e. g. of health the fresh air or the sun's heat may be the cause, but having had one's hair cut *cannot*; for some incidental causes are more relevant to the effect than others.)

Chance or fortune is called 'good' when the result is 25 good, 'evil' when it is evil. The terms 'good fortune' and 'ill fortune' are used when either result is of considerable magnitude. Thus one who comes within an ace of some great evil or great good is said to be fortunate or unfortunate. The mind affirms the presence of the attribute, ignoring the hair's breadth of difference. Further, it is with 30 reason that good fortune is regarded as unstable; for chance is unstable, as none of the things which result from it can be invariable or normal.

Both are then, as I have said, incidental causes—both chance and spontaneity—in the sphere of things which are capable of coming to pass not necessarily, nor normally, and with reference to such of these as might come to pass 35 for the sake of something.

6   They differ in that 'spontaneity' is the wider term. Every result of chance is from what is spontaneous, but not everything that is from what is spontaneous is from chance.

197ᵇ   Chance and what results from chance are appropriate to agents that are capable of good fortune and of moral action generally. Therefore necessarily chance is in the sphere of moral actions. This is indicated by the fact that good fortune is thought to be the same, or nearly the same, as happiness, and happiness to be a kind of moral action, 5 since it is well-doing. Hence what is not capable of moral action cannot do anything by chance. Thus an inanimate thing or a lower animal or a child cannot do anything by chance, because it is incapable of deliberate intention; nor can 'good fortune' or 'ill fortune' be ascribed to them, except metaphorically, as Protarchus, for example, said that the stones of which altars are made are fortunate because 10 they are held in honour, while their fellows are trodden under foot. Even these things, however, can in a way be affected by chance, when one who is dealing with them does something to them by chance, but not otherwise.

The spontaneous on the other hand is found both in the 15 lower animals and in many inanimate objects. We say, for example, that the horse came 'spontaneously', because, though his coming saved him, he did not come for the sake of safety. Again, the tripod fell 'of itself', because, though when it fell it stood on its feet so as to serve for a seat, it did not fall for the sake of that.

Hence it is clear that events which (1) belong to the general class of things that may come to pass for the sake of something, (2) do not come to pass for the sake of what actually results, and (3) have an external cause, may be 20 described by the phrase 'from spontaneity'. These 'spontaneous' events are said to be 'from chance' if they have the further characteristics of being the objects of deliberate intention and due to agents capable of that mode of action. This is indicated by the phrase 'in vain', which is used when

A, which is for the sake of B, does not result in B. For instance, taking a walk is for the sake of evacuation of the
bowels; if this does not follow after walking, we say that
we have walked 'in vain' and that the walking was 'vain'.
This implies that what is naturally the means to an end is 'in 23
vain', when it does not effect the end towards which it was
the natural means—for it would be absurd for a man to say
that he had bathed in vain because the sun was not eclipsed,
since the one was not done with a view to the other. Thus
the spontaneous is even according to its derivation the case
in which the thing itself happens in vain. The stone that
struck the man did not fall for the purpose of striking him; 30
therefore it fell spontaneously, because it might have fallen
by the action of an agent and for the purpose of striking.
The difference between spontaneity and what results by
chance is greatest in things that come to be by nature; for
when anything comes to be contrary to nature, we do not
say that it came to be by chance, but by spontaneity. Yet
strictly this too is different from the spontaneous proper; 35
for the cause of the latter is external, that of the former
internal.

We have now explained what chance is and what spontaneity is, and in what they differ from each other. Both 198ᵛ
belong to the mode of causation 'source of change', for
either some natural or some intelligent agent is always the
cause; but in this sort of causation the number of possible
causes is infinite.

Spontaneity and chance are causes of effects which,
though they might result from intelligence or nature, have 5
in fact been caused by something incidentally. Now since
nothing which is incidental is prior to what is per se, it is
clear that no incidental cause can be prior to a cause per se.
Spontaneity and chance, therefore, are posterior to intelligence and nature. Hence, however true it may be that the 10
heavens are due to spontaneity, it will still be true that intelligence and nature will be prior causes of this All and of
many things in it besides.

7   It is clear then that there are causes, and that the
number of them is what we have stated. The number
15 is the same as that of the things comprehended under the
question 'why'. The 'why' is referred ultimately either (1),
in things which do not involve motion, e. g. in mathematics,
to the 'what' (to the definition of 'straight line' or 'commensurable', &c.), or (2) to what initiated a motion, e. g.
'why did they go to war?—because there had been a raid';
20 or (3) we are inquiring 'for the sake of what?'—'that they
may rule'; or (4), in the case of things that come into being,
we are looking for the matter. The causes, therefore, are
these and so many in number.

Now, the causes being four, it is the business of the
physicist to know about them all, and if he refers his problems back to all of them, he will assign the 'why' in the way
25 proper to his science—the matter, the form, the mover,
'that for the sake of which'. The last three often coincide;
for the 'what' and 'that for the sake of which' are one,
while the primary source of motion is the same in species as
these (for man generates man), and so too, in general, are
all things which cause movement by being themselves
moved; and such as are not of this kind are no longer inside
the province of physics, for they cause motion not by possessing motion or a source of motion in themselves, but
being themselves incapable of motion. Hence there are
30 three branches of study, one of things which are incapable
of motion, the second of things in motion, but indestruct-
ible, the third of destructible things.

The question 'why', then, is answered by reference to the
matter, to the form, and to the primary moving cause. For
in respect of coming to be it is mostly in this last way that
causes are investigated—'what comes to be after what? what
was the primary agent or patient?' and so at each step of the
series.

35   Now the principles which cause motion in a physical way
are two, of which one is not physical, as it has no principle
198ᵇ of motion in itself. Of this kind is whatever causes move-

ment, not being itself moved, such as (1) that which is completely unchangeable, the primary reality, and (2) the essence of that which is coming to be, i. e. the form; for this is the end or 'that for the sake of which'. Hence since nature is for the sake of something, we must know this cause also. We must explain the 'why' in all the senses of the term, namely, (1) that from this that will necessarily result ('from this' either without qualification or in most cases); (2) that 'this must be so if that is to be so' (as the conclusion presupposes the premisses); (3) that this was the essence of the thing; and (4) because it is better thus (not without qualification, but with reference to the essential nature in each case).

8   We must explain then (1) that Nature belongs to the class of causes which act for the sake of something; (2) about the necessary and its place in physical problems, for all writers ascribe things to this cause, arguing that since the hot and the cold, &c., are of such and such a kind, therefore certain things *necessarily* are and come to be—and if they mention any other cause (one [10] his 'friendship and strife', another [11] his 'mind'), it is only to touch on it, and then good-bye to it.

A difficulty presents itself: why should not nature work, not for the sake of something, nor because it is better so, but just as the sky rains, not in order to make the corn grow, but of necessity? What is drawn up must cool, and what has been cooled must become water and descend, the result of this being that the corn grows. Similarly if a man's crop is spoiled on the threshing-floor, the rain did not fall for the sake of this—in order that the crop might be spoiled—but that result just followed. Why then should it not be the same with the parts in nature, e. g. that our teeth should come up *of necessity*—the front teeth sharp, fitted for tearing, the molars broad and useful for grinding down the food

[10] Empedocles.
[11] Anaxagoras.

—since they did not arise for this end, but it was merely a coincident result; and so with all other parts in which we suppose that there is purpose? Wherever then all the parts came about just what they would have been if they had 30 come to be for an end, such things survived, being organized spontaneously in a fitting way; whereas those which grew otherwise perished and continue to perish, as Empedocles says his 'man-faced ox-progeny' did.

Such are the arguments (and others of the kind) which may cause difficulty on this point. Yet it is impossible that this should be the true view. For teeth and all other natural 35 things either invariably or normally come about in a given way; but of not one of the results of chance or spontaneity is this true. We do not ascribe to chance or mere coincidence 199^a the frequency of rain in winter, but frequent rain in summer we do; nor heat in the dog-days, but only if we have it in winter. If then, it is agreed that things are either the result of coincidence or for an end, and these cannot be the result of coincidence or spontaneity, it follows that they 5 must be for an end; and that such things are all due to nature even the champions of the theory which is before us would agree. Therefore action for an end is present in things which come to be and are by nature.

Further, where a series has a completion, all the preceding steps are for the sake of that. Now surely as in intelli-10 gent action, so in nature; and as in nature, so it is in each action, if nothing interferes. Now intelligent action is for the sake of an end; therefore the nature of things also is so. Thus if a house, e. g., had been a thing made by nature, it would have been made in the same way as it is now by art; and if things made by nature were made also by art, they 15 would come to be in the same way as by nature. Each step then in the series is for the sake of the next; and generally art partly completes what nature cannot bring to a finish, and partly imitates her. If, therefore, artificial products are for the sake of an end, so clearly also are natural products.

The relation of the later to the earlier terms of the series is the same in both.

This is most obvious in the animals other than man: they make things neither by art nor after inquiry or deliberation. Wherefore people discuss whether it is by intelligence or by some other faculty that these creatures work,—spiders, ants, and the like. By gradual advance in this direction we come to see clearly that in plants too that is produced which is conducive to the end—leaves, e. g. grow to provide shade for the fruit. If then it is both by nature and for an end that the swallow makes its nest and the spider its web, and plants grow leaves for the sake of the fruit and send their roots down (not up) for the sake of nourishment, it is plain that this kind of cause is operative in things which come to be and are by nature. And since 'nature' means two things, the matter and the form, of which the latter is the end, and since all the rest is for the sake of the end, the form must be the cause in the sense of 'that for the sake of which'.

Now mistakes come to pass even in the operations of art: the grammarian makes a mistake in writing and the doctor pours out the wrong dose. Hence clearly mistakes are possible in the operations of nature also. If then in art there are cases in which what is rightly produced serves a purpose, and if where mistakes occur there was a purpose in what was attempted, only it was not attained, so must it be also in natural products, and monstrosities will be failures in the purposive effort. Thus in the original combinations the 'ox-progeny' if they failed to reach a determinate end must have arisen through the corruption of some principle corresponding to what is now the seed.

Further, seed must have come into being first, and not straightway the animals: the words 'whole-natured first . . .' [12] must have meant seed.

Again, in plants too we find the relation of means to end, though the degree of organization is less. Were there then

[12] Empedocles, Fr. 62. 4.

in plants also 'olive-headed vine-progeny', like the 'man-headed ox-progeny', or not? An absurd suggestion; yet there must have been, if there were such things among animals.

Moreover, among the seeds anything must have come to be at random. But the person who asserts this entirely does away with 'nature' and what exists 'by nature'. For those
15 things are natural which, by a continuous movement originated from an internal principle, arrive at some completion: the same completion is not reached from every principle; nor any chance completion, but always the tendency in each is towards the same end, if there is no impediment.

The end and the means towards it may come about by chance. We say, for instance, that a stranger has come by
20 chance, paid the ransom, and gone away, when he does so as if he had come for that purpose, though it was not for that that he came. This is incidental, for chance is an incidental cause, as I remarked before.[13] But when an event takes place always or for the most part, it is not incidental
25 or by chance. In natural products the sequence is invariable, if there is no impediment.

It is absurd to suppose that purpose is not present because we do not observe the agent deliberating. Art does not deliberate. If the ship-building art were in the wood, it would produce the same results by nature. If, therefore, purpose is present in art, it is present also in nature. The
30 best illustration is a doctor doctoring himself: nature is like that.

It is plain then that nature is a cause, a cause that operates for a purpose.

9   As regards what is 'of necessity', we must ask whether the necessity is 'hypothetical', or 'simple' as well. The
35 current view places what is of necessity in the process of
200ª production, just as if one were to suppose that the wall of a house necessarily comes to be because what is heavy is naturally carried downwards and what is light to the top,

[13] 196ᵇ 23–7.

wherefore the stones and foundations take the lowest place, with earth above because it is lighter, and wood at the top of all as being the lightest. Whereas, though the wall does not come to be *without* these, it is not *due* to these, except 5 as its material cause: it comes to be for the sake of sheltering and guarding certain things. Similarly in all other things which involve production for an end; the product cannot come to be without things which have a necessary nature, but it is not due to these (except as its material); it comes to be for an end. For instance, why is a saw such as it is? 10 To effect so-and-so and for the sake of so-and-so. This end, however, cannot be realized unless the saw is made of iron. It is, therefore, necessary for it to be of iron, *if* we are to have a saw and perform the operation of sawing. What is necessary then, is necessary *on a hypothesis*; it is not a result necessarily determined by antecedents. Necessity is in the matter, while 'that for the sake of which' is in the definition.

Necessity in mathematics is in a way similar to necessity 15 in things which come to be through the operation of nature. Since a straight line is what it is, it is necessary that the angles of a triangle should equal two right angles. But not conversely; though if the angles are *not* equal to two right angles, then the straight line is not what it is either. But in things which come to be for an end, the reverse is true. If the end is to exist or does exist, that also which pre- 20 cedes it will exist or does exist; otherwise just as there, if the conclusion is not true, the premiss will not be true, so here the end or 'that for the sake of which' will not exist. For this too is itself a starting-point, but of the reasoning, not of the action; while in mathematics the starting-point is the starting point of the reasoning only, as there is no action. If then there is to be a house, such-and-such things must be made 25 or be there already or exist, or generally the matter relative to the end, bricks and stones if it is a house. But the end is not due to these except as the matter, nor will it come to exist because of them. Yet if they do not exist at all, neither

will the house, or the saw—the former in the absence of
stones, the latter in the absence of iron—just as in the other
case the premisses will not be true, if the angles of the triangle are not equal to two right angles.

30   The necessary in nature, then, is plainly what we call by
the name of matter, and the changes in it. Both causes must
be stated by the physicist, but especially the end; for that is
the cause of the matter, not *vice versa*; and the end is 'that

35 for the sake of which', and the beginning starts from the
200ᵇ definition or essence; as in artificial products, since a house
is of such-and-such a kind, certain things must necessarily
come to be or be there already, or since health is this, these
things must necessarily come to be or be there already.
Similarly if man is this, then these; if these, then those.

5 Perhaps the necessary is present also in the definition. For
if one defines the operation of sawing as being a certain
kind of dividing, then this cannot come about unless the
saw has teeth of a certain kind; and these cannot be unless
it is of iron. For in the definition too there are some parts
that are, as it were, its matter.

Psychology and Biology

⎍⎍⎍⎍⎍⎍⎍⎍⎍⎍⎍⎍⎍⎍⎍⎍⎍⎍⎍⎍

INTRODUCTION

The study of the soul is a part of physics, as conceived by Aristotle, since the soul is the form of a natural body; and all branches of biological inquiry are dependent on the study of the soul, since the soul is the form of those natural bodies which have life potentially within them. The functions which the soul explains include, therefore, nutrition, growth, and reproduction (which animals share with plants), sensation, emotions, memory, and local motion (which man shares with other animals), and thought (which is peculiar to man among animals, although God in a sense shares in thinking). The soul is related to the organic body as actuality is related to potentiality. It is the "substance" of the organic body, that is, it corresponds to the definition of the organic body's essence, in such fashion according to Aristotle's example, that if an axe were a natural rather than an artificial body, its soul would be "cutting," and if the eye were an animal rather than an organ, its soul would be "seeing."

In the treatise On the Soul, the soul is presented as the formal, efficient, and final cause of living, and the processes of sensation and thought are elaborated at considerable length. This analysis of the higher activities of human living is supplemented by inquiry, in the Short Natural Treatises, into the common characteristics of animal bodies and into the similar objects of animal activity in sense and sensibles, memory and reminiscence, length and brevity of life, youth and old age, life and death, and respiration. The remaining activities of the soul, which are touched on briefly in On the Soul, are investigated in Aristotle's four biological treatises, and both bodily organs and psychic qualities are examined in the context of the study of human functions, partly because we are more familiar with man than with any other animal, partly because man is more rounded and complete than other animals and the qualities and capacities investigated in biology are found in their perfection in him (Cf. History of Animals i. 6. 491^a 19–23 and ix. 1. 608^b 4–8). The History of Animals is a lengthy classification of animals on the basis of similarities and differences in their parts, organs, and functions, including reproduction, heredity, the development of the embryo, diet, diseases, the effects of environment and the struggle for means of subsistence, psychological differences, and intelligence. On the Parts of Animals, which contains an excellent statement of method in the biological sciences, treats of biological phenomena that are explained by the material parts and organs of animals. On the Progression of Animals differentiates the modes of their locomotion. On the Generation of Animals treats of their reproduction as an instance of the operation of the efficient cause.

Aristotle is at pains to differentiate the properties investigated in physics from those treated in the arts (like the arts of carpentry and medicine) and those proper to the other theoretic sciences, mathematics and metaphysics. He also differentiates the method of the "true physicist," who investigates the functions of the soul by considering both matter and form, from the method of the "dialectician," who neglects the matter, and that of the materialistic "physicist," who reduces all explanation to the enumeration of material parts. The various psychological activities are therefore investigated functionally in relation to their proper objects, and the faculties of the soul—nutritive, sensitive, and intellective—are defined in terms of their activities. In that inquiry the consideration of universal knowledge and truth gives the intellectual processes a peculiar character, since mind is what it is in one sense by becoming all things, and in another sense by making all things, in knowledge of them. All the faculties of the soul, finally, are considered in terms of their mutual relations and their fitness for the conditions of life. Psychological inquiries occupy an extremely important position in

the philosophy of Aristotle, for the conception of the soul
lays the foundation for the continuity of functions in
nature, mounting continuously from the lifeless, to plants
and animals; it provides an analysis of intellectual processes
which would account for the character of the principles and
materials employed in scientific inquiries and proofs; it lays
the broad distinctions of potentialities in man which become by action and habituation the moral and intellectual
virtues.

DE ANIMA

CONTENTS

BOOK 1

De Anima

On the Soul

Translated by J. A. Smith

ЛЛЛ

BOOK I

1   Holding as we do that, while knowledge of any kind is
a thing to be honoured and prized, one kind of it may, **402ᵃ**
either by reason of its greater exactness or of a higher dignity and greater wonderfulness in its objects, be more honourable and precious than another, on both accounts we
should naturally be led to place in the front rank the study
of the soul. The knowledge of the soul admittedly contributes greatly to the advance of truth in general, and, above
all, to our understanding of Nature, for the soul is in some 5
sense the principle of animal life. Our aim is to grasp and
understand, first its essential nature, and secondly its properties; of these some are thought to be affections proper to
the soul itself, while others are considered to attach to the
animal ¹ owing to the presence within it of soul.

To attain any assured knowledge about the soul is one of
the most difficult things in the world. As the form of ques- 10
tion which here presents itself, viz. the question 'What is
it?', recurs in other fields, it might be supposed that there
was some single method of inquiry applicable to all objects
whose essential nature we are endeavouring to ascertain 15
(as there is for derived properties the single method of

---

¹ i. e. the complex of soul and body.

demonstration); in that case what we should have to seek
for would be this unique method. But if there is no such
single and general method for solving the question of essence, our task becomes still more difficult; in the case of
each different subject we shall have to determine the appropriate process of investigation. If to this there be a clear
answer, e. g. that the process is demonstration or division,
20 or some other known method, difficulties and hesitations
still beset us—with what facts shall we begin the inquiry?
For the facts which form the starting-points in different
subjects must be different, as e. g. in the case of numbers
and surfaces.

First, no doubt, it is necessary to determine in which
of the *summa genera* soul lies, what it is; is it 'a this-somewhat', a substance, or is it a quale or a quantum, or some
25 other of the remaining kinds of predicates which we have
distinguished? Further, does soul belong to the class of potential existents, or is it not rather an actuality? Our answer
to this question is of the greatest importance.

402ᵇ   We must consider also whether soul is divisible or is
without parts, and whether it is everywhere homogeneous
or not; and if not homogeneous, whether its various
forms are different specifically or generically: up to the
5 present time those who have discussed and investigated
soul seem to have confined themselves to the human soul.
We must be careful not to ignore the question whether
soul can be defined in a single unambiguous formula, as is
the case with animal, or whether we must not give a
separate formula for each sort of it, as we do for horse, dog,
man, god (in the latter case the 'universal' animal—and so
too every other 'common predicate'—being treated either
as nothing at all or as a later product²). Further, if what
exists is not a plurality of souls, but a plurality of parts of
10 one soul, which ought we to investigate first, the whole soul
or its parts? (It is also a difficult problem to decide which

² i. e. as presupposing the various sorts instead of being presupposed
by them.

of these parts are in nature distinct from one another.) Again, which ought we to investigate first, these parts or their functions, mind or thinking, the faculty or the act of sensation, and so on? If the investigation of the functions precedes that of the parts, the further question suggests itself: ought we not before either to consider the cor- 15 relative objects, e. g. of sense or thought? It seems not only useful for the discovery of the causes of the derived properties of substances to be acquainted with the essential nature of those substances (as in mathematics it is useful for the understanding of the property of the equality of the interior angles of a triangle to two right angles to know the 20 essential nature of the straight and the curved or of the line and the plane) but also conversely, for the knowledge of the essential nature of a substance is largely promoted by an acquaintance with its properties: for, when we are able to give an account conformable to experience of all or most of the properties of a substance, we shall be in the most favourable position to say something worth saying about the essential nature of that subject; in all demon- 25 stration a definition of the essence is required as a starting-point, so that definitions which do not enable us to dis- **403ᵃ** cover the derived properties, or which fail to facilitate even a conjecture about them, must obviously, one and all, be dialectical and futile.

A further problem presented by the affections of soul is this: are they all affections of the complex of body and soul, or is there any one among them peculiar to the soul by itself? To determine this is indispensable but difficult. If we consider the majority of them, there seems to be no 5 case in which the soul can act or be acted upon without involving the body; e. g. anger, courage, appetite, and sensation generally. Thinking seems the most probable exception; but if this too proves to be a form of imagination or to be impossible without imagination, it too requires a body as a condition of its existence. If there is any 10 way of acting or being acted upon proper to soul, soul will be capable of separate existence; if there is none, its separate existence is impossible. In the latter case, it will be like what is straight, which has many properties arising from the straightness in it, e. g. that of touching a bronze sphere at a point, though straightness divorced from the other constituents of the straight thing cannot touch it in this way; it cannot be so divorced at all, since it is always 15 found in a body. It therefore seems that all the affections of soul involve a body—passion, gentleness, fear, pity, courage, joy, loving, and hating; in all these there is a concurrent affection of the body. In support of this we may point to the fact that, while sometimes on the occasion of violent and striking occurrences there is no excitement or fear 20 felt, on others faint and feeble stimulations produce these emotions, viz. when the body is already in a state of tension resembling its condition when we are angry. Here is a still clearer case: in the absence of any external cause of terror we find ourselves experiencing the feelings of a man in terror. From all this it is obvious that the affections of soul are enmattered formulable essences.

Consequently their definitions ought to correspond, e. g. 25 anger should be defined as a certain mode of movement of such and such a body (or part or faculty of a body) by this or that cause and for this or that end. That is precisely why the study of the soul must fall within the science of Nature, at least so far as in its affections it manifests this double character. Hence a physicist would define an affection of soul differently from a dialectician; the latter 30 would define e. g. anger as the appetite for returning pain for pain, or something like that, while the former would define it as a boiling of the blood or warm substance surrounding the heart. The latter assigns the material conditions, the former the form or formulable essence; for what he states is the formulable essence of the fact, though for its actual existence there must be embodiment of it in a material such as is described by the other. Thus the essence of a house is assigned in such a formula as 'a shelter against

destruction by wind, rain, and heat'; the physicist would 5
describe it as 'stones, bricks, and timbers'; but there is a
third possible description which would say that it was that
form in that material with that purpose or end. Which,
then, among these is entitled to be regarded as the genuine
physicist? The one who confines himself to the material,
or the one who restricts himself to the formulable essence
alone? Is it not rather the one who combines both in a
single formula? If this is so, how are we to characterize the
other two? Must we not say that there is no type of thinker
who concerns himself with those qualities or attributes of
the material which are in fact inseparable from the material, and without attempting even in thought to sep- 10
arate them? The physicist is he who concerns himself with
all the properties active and passive of bodies or materials
thus or thus defined; attributes not considered as being of
this character he leaves to others, in certain cases it may
be to a specialist, e. g. a carpenter or a physician, in others
(a) where they are inseparable in fact, but are separable
from any particular kind of body by an effort of abstrac- 15
tion, to the mathematician, (b) where they are separate
both in fact and in thought from body altogether, to the
First Philosopher or metaphysician. But we must return
from this digression, and repeat that the affections of soul
are inseparable from the material substratum of animal
life, to which we have seen that such affections, e. g. passion and fear, attach, and have not the same mode of being
as a line or a plane.

2   For our study of soul it is necessary, while formulating 20
the problems of which in our further advance we are
to find the solutions, to call into council the views of those
of our predecessors who have declared any opinion on
this subject, in order that we may profit by whatever is
sound in their suggestions and avoid their errors.

The starting-point of our inquiry is an exposition of those
characteristics which have chiefly been held to belong to

25 soul in its very nature. Two characteristic marks have above all others been recognized as distinguishing that which has soul in it from that which has not—movement and sensation. It may be said that these two are what our predecessors have fixed upon as characteristic of soul.

Some say that what originates movement is both preeminently and primarily soul; believing that what is not 30 itself moved cannot originate movement in another, they arrived at the view that soul belongs to the class of things in 404ᵃ movement. This is what led Democritus to say that soul is a sort of fire or hot substance; his 'forms' or atoms are infinite in number; those which are spherical he calls fire and soul, and compares them to the motes in the air which we see in shafts of light coming through windows; the mixture of seeds of all sorts he calls the elements of the whole of Nature (Leucippus gives a similar account); the spher-5 ical atoms are identified with soul because atoms of that shape are most adapted to permeate everywhere, and to set all the others moving by being themselves in movement. This implies the view that soul is identical with what produces movement in animals. That is why, further, they regard respiration as the characteristic mark of life; as the 10 environment compresses the bodies of animals, and tends to extrude those atoms which impart movement to them, because they themselves are never at rest, there must be a reinforcement of these by similar atoms coming in from without in the act of respiration; for they prevent the extrusion of those which are already within by counteracting the compressing and consolidating force of the environ-15 ment; and animals continue to live only as long as they are able to maintain this resistance.

The doctrine of the Pythagoreans seems to rest upon the same ideas; some of them declared the motes in air, others what moved them, to be soul. These motes were referred to because they are seen always in movement, even in a complete calm.

The same tendency is shown by those who define soul as

that which moves itself; all seem to hold the view that 20
movement is what is closest to the nature of soul, and that
while all else is moved by soul, it alone moves itself. This
belief arises from their never seeing anything originating
movement which is not first itself moved.

Similarly also Anaxagoras (and whoever agrees with him
in saying that mind set the whole in movement) declares 25
the moving cause of things to be soul. His position must,
however, be distinguished from that of Democritus. Democritus
roundly identifies soul and mind, for he identifies
what appears with what is true—that is why he commends
Homer for the phrase 'Hector lay with thought distraught' [3];
he does not employ mind as a special faculty
dealing with truth, but identifies soul and mind. What 30
Anaxagoras says about them is more obscure; in many **404**
places he tells us that the cause of beauty and order is
mind, elsewhere that it is soul; it is found, he says, in all
animals, great and small, high and low, but mind (in the
sense of intelligence) appears not to belong alike to all 5
animals, and indeed not even to all human beings.

All those, then, who had special regard to the fact that
what has soul in it is moved, adopted the view that soul is
to be identified with what is eminently originative of movement.
All, on the other hand, who looked to the fact that
what has soul in it knows or perceives what is, identify
soul with the principle or principles of Nature, according 10
as they admit several such principles or one only. Thus
Empedocles declares that it is formed out of all his elements,
each of them also being soul; his words are:

> For 'tis by Earth we see Earth, by Water Water,
> By Ether Ether divine, by Fire destructive Fire,
> By Love Love, and Hate by cruel Hate.   15

In the same way Plato in the *Timaeus* [4] fashions the soul
out of his elements; for like, he holds, is known by like, and

[3] II. xxiii. 698.
[4] 35 A ff.

things are formed out of the principles or elements, so
that soul must be so too. Similarly also in his lectures 'On
Philosophy' it was set forth that the Animal-itself is compounded of the Idea itself of the One together with the
primary length, breadth, and depth, everything else, the
objects of its perception, being similarly constituted. Again
he puts his view in yet other terms: Mind is the monad,
science or knowledge the dyad (because [5] it goes undevi-
atingly from one point to another), opinion the number of
the plane,[6] sensation the number of the solid [7]; the numbers are by him expressly identified with the Forms themselves or principles, and are formed out of the elements;
now things are apprehended either by mind or science or
opinion or sensation, and these same numbers are the
Forms of things.

Some thinkers, accepting both premisses, viz. that the
soul is both originative of movement and cognitive, have
compounded it of both and declared the soul to be a self-
moving number.

As to the nature and number of the first principles
opinions differ. The difference is greatest between those
who regard them as corporeal and those who regard them
as incorporeal, and from both dissent those who make a
blend and draw their principles from both sources. The
number of principles is also in dispute; some admit one
only, others assert several. There is a consequent diversity
in their several accounts of soul; they assume, naturally
enough, that what is in its own nature originative of movement must be among what is primordial. That has led
some to regard it as fire, for fire is the subtlest of the elements and nearest to incorporeality; further, in the most
primary sense, fire both is moved and originates movement
in all the others.

Democritus has expressed himself more ingeniously than

---

[5] **Like** the straight line, whose number is the dyad.
[6] The triad.
[7] The tetrad.

the rest on the grounds for ascribing each of these two
characters to soul; soul and mind are, he says, one and the [10]
same thing, and this thing must be one of the primary and
indivisible bodies, and its power of originating movement
must be due to its fineness of grain and the shape of its
atoms; he says that of all the shapes the spherical is the
most mobile, and that this is the shape of the particles
of both fire and mind.

Anaxagoras, as we said above,[8] seems to distinguish between soul and mind, but in practice he treats them as a
single substance, except that it is mind that he specially
posits as the principle of all things; at any rate what he [15]
says is that mind alone of all that is is simple, unmixed,
and pure. He assigns both characteristics, knowing and
origination of movement, to the same principle, when he
says that it was mind that set the whole in movement.

Thales, too, to judge from what is recorded about him,
seems to have held soul to be a motive force, since he said [20]
that the magnet has a soul in it because it moves the iron.

Diogenes (and others) held the soul to be air because he
believed air to be finest in grain and a first principle; therein
lay the grounds of the soul's powers of knowing and originating movement. As the primordial principle from which
all other things are derived, it is cognitive; as finest in
grain, it has the power to originate movement.

Heraclitus too says that the first principle—the 'warm
exhalation' of which, according to him, everything else is [25]
composed—is soul; further, that this exhalation is most
incorporeal and in ceaseless flux; that what is in movement
requires that what knows it should be in movement; and
that all that is has its being essentially in movement (herein
agreeing with the majority).

Alcmaeon also seems to have held a similar view about
soul; he says that it is immortal because it resembles 'the
immortals', and that this immortality belongs to it in [30]
virtue of its ceaseless movement; for all the 'things divine',

[8] 404[b] 1–6.

moon, sun, the planets, and the whole heavens, are in perpetual movement.

Of more superficial writers, some, e. g. Hippo, have pro-
405ᵇ nounced it to be water; they seem to have argued from the
fact that the seed of all animals is fluid, for Hippo tries to
refute those who say that the soul is blood, on the ground
that the seed, which is the primordial soul, is not blood.

Another group (Critias, for example) did hold it to be
5 blood; they take perception to be the most characteristic
attribute of soul, and hold that perceptiveness is due to
the nature of blood.

Each of the elements has thus found its partisan, except
earth—earth has found no supporter unless we count as
such those who have declared soul to be, or to be com-
10 pounded of, *all* the elements. All, then, it may be said,
characterize the soul by three marks, Movement, Sensation, Incorporeality, and each of these is traced back to
the first principles. That is why (with one exception) all
those who define the soul by its power of knowing make it
either an element or constructed out of the elements. The
15 language they all use is similar; like, they say, is known by
like; as the soul knows everything, they construct it out of
all the principles. Hence all those who admit but one
cause or element, make the soul also one (e. g. fire or air),
while those who admit a multiplicity of principles make the
20 soul also multiple. The exception is Anaxagoras; he alone
says that mind is impassible and has nothing in common
with anything else. But, if this is so, how or in virtue of
what cause can it know? That Anaxagoras has not explained, nor can any answer be inferred from his words.
All who acknowledge pairs of opposites among their principles, construct the soul also out of these contraries, while
25 those who admit as principles only one contrary of each
pair, e. g. either hot or cold, likewise make the soul some
one of these. That is why, also, they allow themselves to be
guided by the names; those who identify soul with the hot
argue that zen (to live) is derived from zein (to boil),

while those who identify it with the cold say that soul (*psyche*) is so called from the process of respiration and refrigeration (*katapsyxis*).

Such are the traditional opinions concerning soul, to- 30 gether with the grounds on which they are maintained.

3 We must begin our examination with movement; for, doubtless, not only is it false that the essence of soul is correctly described by those who say that it is what moves **406ᵉ** (or is capable of moving) itself, but it is an impossibility that movement should be even an attribute of it.

We have already ⁹ pointed out that there is no necessity that what originates movement should itself be moved. There are two senses in which anything may be moved— either (a) indirectly, owing to something other than itself, 5 or (b) directly, owing to itself. Things are 'indirectly moved' which are moved as being contained in something which is moved, e. g. sailors in a ship, for they are moved in a different sense from that in which the ship is moved; the ship is 'directly moved', they are 'indirectly moved', because they are in a moving vessel. This is clear if we consider their limbs; the movement proper to the legs (and so to man) is walking, and in this case the sailors are not walking. Recog- 10 nizing the double sense of 'being moved', what we have to consider now is whether the soul is 'directly moved' and participates in such direct movement.

There are four species of movement—locomotion, altera- tion, diminution, growth; consequently if the soul is moved, it must be moved with one or several or all of these species of movement. Now if its movement is not inci- dental, there must be a movement natural to it, and, if so, 15 as all the species enumerated involve place, place must be natural to it. But if the essence of soul be to move itself, its being moved cannot be incidental to it, as it is to what is white or three cubits long; they too can be moved, but only incidentally—what is moved is that of which 'white'

⁹ *Phys.* viii. 5, esp. 257ᵃ 31–258ᵇ 9.

and 'three cubits long' are the attributes, the body in
20 which they inhere; hence they have no place: but if the
soul naturally partakes in movement, it follows that it
must have a place.

Further, if there be a movement natural to the soul,
there must be a counter-movement unnatural to it, and
conversely. The same applies to rest as well as to movement; for the *terminus ad quem* of a thing's natural move-
25 ment is the place of its natural rest, and similarly the
terminus ad quem of its enforced movement is the place of
its enforced rest. But what meaning can be attached to enforced movements or rests of the soul, it is difficult even to
imagine.

Further, if the natural movement of the soul be upward,
the soul must be fire; if downward, it must be earth; for upward and downward movements are the definitory characteristics of these bodies. The same reasoning applies to the
intermediate movements, *termini*, and bodies. Further,
30 since the soul is observed to originate movement in the
body, it is reasonable to suppose that it transmits to the
body the movements by which it itself is moved, and so,
reversing the order, we may infer from the movements of
the body back to similar movements of the soul. Now the
406ᵇ body is moved from place to place with movements of
locomotion. Hence it would follow that the soul too must
in accordance with the body change either its place as a
whole or the relative places of its parts. This carries with it
the possibility that the soul might even quit its body and re-
enter it, and with this would be involved the possibility of
a resurrection of animals from the dead. But, it may be con-
5 tended, the soul can be moved indirectly by something else;
for an animal can be pushed out of its course. Yes, but that
to whose *essence* belongs the power of being moved by
itself, cannot be moved by something else except incidentally,[10] just as what is good by or in itself cannot owe its

---

[10] i. e. so that what is moved is not it but something which 'goes
along with it', e.g. a vehicle in which it is contained.

goodness to something external to it or to some end to which it is a means.

If the soul *is* moved, the most probable view is that 10 what moves it is sensible things.[11]

We must note also that, if the soul moves itself, it must be the mover itself that is moved, so that it follows that if movement is in every case a displacement of that which is in movement, in that respect in which it is said to be moved, the movement of the soul must be a departure from its essential nature, at least if its self-movement is essential to it, not incidental.

Some go so far as to hold that the movements which 15 the soul imparts to the body in which it is are the same in kind as those with which it itself is moved. An example of this is Democritus, who uses language like that of the comic dramatist Philippus, who accounts for the movements that Daedalus imparted to his wooden Aphrodite by saying that he poured quicksilver into it; similarly Democritus says that the spherical atoms which according to him 20 constitute soul, owing to their own ceaseless movements draw the whole body after them and so produce its movements. We must urge the question whether it is these very same atoms which produce rest also—how they could do so, it is difficult and even impossible to say. And, in general, we may object that it is not in this way that the soul appears to originate movement in animals—it is through 25 intention or process of thinking.

It is in the same fashion that the *Timaeus*[12] also tries to give a physical account of how the soul moves its body; the soul, it is here said, is in movement, and so owing to their mutual implication moves the body also. After compounding the soul-substance out of the elements and dividing it in accordance with the harmonic numbers, in order that it may possess a connate sensibility for 'harmony' 30

---

[11] *sc.* in which case the movement can only be 'incidental'; for, as we shall see later, it is really the bodily organ of sensation that then is 'moved'.

[12] 35 A ff.

and that the whole may move in movements well attuned, the Demiurge bent the straight line into a circle; this single 407ª circle he divided into two circles united at two common points; one of these he subdivided into seven circles. All this implies that the movements of the soul are identified with the local movements of the heavens.

Now, in the first place, it is a mistake to say that the soul is a spatial magnitude. It is evident that Plato means 5 the soul of the whole to be like the sort of soul which is called mind—not like the sensitive or the desiderative soul, for the movements of neither of these are circular. Now mind is one and continuous in the sense in which the process of thinking is so, and thinking is identical with the thoughts which are its parts; these have a serial unity like that of number, not a unity like that of a spatial magnitude. Hence mind cannot have that kind of unity either; mind is either without parts or is continuous in some other way than that which characterizes a spatial magnitude. How, indeed, if it were a spatial magnitude, could mind 10 possibly think? Will it think with any one indifferently of its parts? In this case, the 'part' must be understood either in the sense of a spatial magnitude or in the sense of a point (if a point can be called a part of a spatial magnitude). If we accept the latter alternative, the points being infinite in number, obviously the mind can never exhaustively traverse them; if the former, the mind must think the same thing over and over again, indeed an infinite number of times (whereas it is manifestly possible to think 15 a thing once only). If contact of any part whatsoever of itself with the object is all that is required, why need mind move in a circle, or indeed possess magnitude at all? On the other hand, if contact with the whole circle is necessary, what meaning can be given to the contact of the parts? Further, how could what has no parts think what has parts, or what has parts think what has none? [13] We must identify the circle referred to with mind; for it is mind whose move-

[13] sc. but mind in fact thinks or cognizes both.

ment is thinking, and it is the circle whose movement is 20
revolution, so that if thinking is a movement of revolution,
the circle which has this characteristic movement must be
mind.

If the circular movement is eternal, there must be something which mind is always thinking—what can this be?
For all practical processes of thinking have limits—they
all go on for the sake of something outside the process,
and all theoretical processes come to a close in the same
way as the phrases in speech which express processes and
results of thinking. Every such linguistic phrase is either
definitory or demonstrative. Demonstration has both a 25
starting-point and may be said to end in a conclusion or
inferred result; even if the process never reaches final completion, at any rate it never returns upon itself again to its
starting-point, it goes on assuming a fresh middle term or
a fresh extreme, and moves straight forward, but circular
movement returns to its starting-point. Definitions, too,
are closed groups of terms.　　　　　　　　　　　　　30

Further, if the same revolution is repeated, mind must
repeatedly think the same object.

Further, thinking has more resemblance to a coming to
rest or arrest than to a movement; the same may be said of
inferring.

It might also be urged that what is difficult and enforced
is incompatible with blessedness; if the movement of the
soul is not of its essence, movement of the soul must be **407**ᵃ
contrary to its nature.[14] It must also be painful for the soul
to be inextricably bound up with the body; nay more, if, as
is frequently said and widely accepted, it is better for mind
not to be embodied, the union must be for it undesirable.

Further, the cause of the revolution of the heavens is 5
left obscure. It is not the essence of soul which is the cause
of this circular movement—that movement is only incidental to soul—nor is, *a fortiori*, the body its cause. Again,
it is not even asserted that it is better that soul should be so

[14] sc. 'and so a hindrance to its bliss'.

10 moved; and yet the reason for which God caused the soul to move in a circle can only have been that movement was better for it than rest, and movement of this kind better than any other. But since this sort of consideration is more appropriate to another field of speculation, let us dismiss it for the present.

The view we have just been examining, in company with most theories about the soul, involves the following 15 absurdity: they all join the soul to a body, or place it in a body, without adding any specification of the reason of their union, or of the bodily conditions required for it. Yet such explanation can scarcely be omitted; for some community of nature is presupposed by the fact that the one acts and the other is acted upon, the one moves and the other is moved; interaction always implies a *special* na- 20 ture in the two interagents. All, however, that these thinkers do is to describe the specific characteristics of the soul; they do not try to determine anything about the body which is to contain it, as if it were possible, as in the Pythagorean myths, that any soul could be clothed upon with any body—an absurd view, for each body seems to have a form and shape of its own. It is as absurd as to say 25 that the art of carpentry could embody itself in flutes; each art must use its tools, each soul its body.

4   There is yet another theory about soul, which has commended itself to many as no less probable than 30 any of those we have hitherto mentioned, and has ren- dered public account of itself in the court of popular discussion. Its supporters say that the soul is a kind of harmony, for (a) harmony is a blend or composition of contraries, and (b) the body is compounded out of con- traries. Harmony, however, is a certain proportion or com- position of the constituents blended, and soul can be neither the one nor the other of these. Further, the power of originating movement cannot belong to a harmony, while almost all concur in regarding this as a principal attribute of soul. It is more appropriate to call health (or 408ᵇ generally one of the good states of the body) a harmony than to predicate it of the soul. The absurdity becomes most apparent when we try to attribute the active and passive affections of the soul to a harmony; the necessary readjustment of their conceptions is difficult. Further, in using the word 'harmony' we have one or other of two 5 cases in our mind; the most proper sense is in relation to spatial magnitudes which have motion and position, where harmony means the disposition and cohesion of their parts in such a manner as to prevent the introduction into the whole of anything homogeneous with it, and the secondary sense, derived from the former, is that in which it means the ratio between the constituents so blended; in neither of these senses is it plausible to predicate it of 10 soul. That soul is a harmony in the sense of the mode of composition of the parts of the body is a view easily refutable; for there are many composite parts and those variously compounded; of what bodily part is mind or the sensitive or the appetitive faculty the mode of composition? And what *is* the mode of composition which constitutes each of them? It is equally absurd to identify the soul with the ratio of the mixture; for the mixture which makes flesh has a different ratio between the elements from that 15 which makes bone. The consequence of this view will therefore be that distributed throughout the whole body there will be many souls, since every one of the bodily parts is a different mixture of the elements, and the ratio of mixture is in each case a harmony, i. e. a soul.

From Empedocles at any rate we might demand an answer to the following question—for he says that each of the parts of the body is what it is in virtue of a ratio between the elements: is the soul identical with this ratio, 20 or is it not rather something over and above this which is formed in the parts? Is love the cause of any and every mixture, or only of those that are in the right ratio? Is love this ratio itself, or is love something over and above this?

Such are the problems raised by this account. But, on the other hand, if the soul is different from the mixture, why does it disappear at one and the same moment with that relation between the elements which constitutes flesh or the other parts of the animal body? Further, if the soul is not identical with the ratio of mixture, and it is consequently not the case that each of the parts has a soul, what is that which perishes when the soul quits the body?

That the soul cannot either be a harmony, or be moved in a circle, is clear from what we have said. Yet that it can be moved incidentally is, as we said above,[15] possible, and even that in a sense it can move itself, i. e. in the sense that *the vehicle* in which it is can be moved, and moved by it; in no other sense can the soul be moved in space. More legitimate doubts might remain as to its movement in view 408ᵇ of the following facts. We speak of the soul as being pained or pleased, being bold or fearful, being angry, perceiving, thinking. All these are regarded as modes of movement, and hence it might be inferred that the soul is moved. This, however, does not necessarily follow. We may admit to the full that being pained or pleased, or thinking, are movements (each of them a 'being moved'), and that the movement is originated by the soul. For example we may regard anger or fear as such and such movements of the heart, and thinking as such and such another movement of that organ, or of some other; these modifications may arise either from changes of place in certain parts or from qualitative alterations (the special nature of the parts and the special modes of their changes being for our present purpose irrelevant). Yet to say that it is *the soul* which is angry is as inexact as it would be to say that it is the soul that weaves webs or builds houses. It is doubtless better to avoid saying that the soul pities or learns or thinks, and rather to say that it is the man who does this with his soul. What we mean is not that the movement is in the soul, but that sometimes it terminates in the soul and sometimes

---

[15] 406ᵃ 30 ff., ᵇ5–8.

starts from it, sensation e. g. coming from without inwards, and reminiscence starting from the soul and terminating with the movements, actual or residual, in the sense
organs.

The case of mind is different; it seems to be an independent substance implanted within the soul and to be incapable of being destroyed. If it could be destroyed at all, it
would be under the blunting influence of old age. What 20
really happens in respect of mind in old age is, however.
exactly parallel to what happens in the case of the sense
organs; if the old man could recover the proper kind of eye,
he would see just as well as the young man. The incapacity
of old age is due to an affection not of the soul but of its
vehicle, as occurs in drunkenness or disease. Thus it is that
in old age the activity of mind or intellectual apprehension
declines only through the decay of some other inward 25
part; mind itself is impassible. Thinking, loving, and hating
are affections not of mind, but of that which has mind, so
far as it has it. That is why, when this vehicle decays,
memory and love cease; they were activities not of mind,
but of the composite which has perished; mind is, no doubt,
something more divine and impassible. That the soul can- 30
not be moved is therefore clear from what we have said,
and if it cannot be moved at all, manifestly it cannot be
moved by itself.

Of all the opinions we have enumerated, by far the most
unreasonable is that which declares the soul to be a self-
moving number; it involves in the first place all the impossibilities which follow from regarding the soul as moved, and
in the second special absurdities which follow from call- 409
ing it a number. How are we to imagine a unit being
moved? By what agency? What sort of movement can be
attributed to what is without parts or internal differences?
If the unit is both originative of movement and itself
capable of being moved, it must contain difference.[16]

Further, since they say a moving line generates a surface

[16] sc. 'and so, be no unit'.

and a moving point a line, the movements of the psychic
⁵ units must be lines (for a point is a unit having position,
and the number of the soul is, of course, somewhere and
has position).

Again, if from a number a number or a unit is subtracted,
the remainder is another number; but plants and many
animals when divided continue to live, and each segment
is thought to retain the same kind of soul.

It must be all the same whether we speak of units or
¹⁰ corpuscles; for if the spherical atoms of Democritus became
points, nothing being retained but their being a quantum,
there must remain in each a moving and a moved part,
just as there is in what is continuous; what happens has
nothing to do with the size of the atoms, it depends solely
upon their being a quantum. That is why there must
¹⁵ be something to originate movement in the units. If in the
animal what originates movement is the soul, so also must
it be in the case of the number, so that not the mover and
the moved together, but the mover only, will be the soul.
But how is it possible for one of the units to fulfil this
function of originating movement? There must be some
difference between such a unit and all the other units, and
²⁰ what difference can there be between one placed unit and
another except a difference of position? If then, on the
other hand, these psychic units within the body are different from the points of the body, there will be two sets of
units both occupying the same place; for each unit will
occupy a point. And yet, if there can be two, why cannot
there be an infinite number? For if things can occupy an indivisible place, they must themselves be indivisible. If, on
²⁵ the other hand, the points of the body are identical with
the units whose number is the soul, or if the number of the
points in the body is the soul, why have not all bodies
souls? For all bodies contain points or an infinity of points.

Further, how is it possible for these points to be isolated
or separated from their bodies, seeing that lines cannot be
³⁰ resolved into points?

5   The result is, as we have said,[17] that this view, while on the one side identical with that of those who maintain that soul is a subtle kind of body,[18] is on the other entangled in the absurdity peculiar to Democritus' way of describing **409** the manner in which movement is originated by soul. For if the soul is present throughout the whole percipient body, there must, if the soul be a kind of body, be two bodies in the same place; and for those who call it a number, there must be many points at one point, or every body **5** must have a soul, unless the soul be a different sort of number—other, that is, than the sum of the points existing in a body. Another consequence that follows is that the animal must be moved by its number precisely in the way that Democritus explained its being moved by his spherical psychic atoms. What difference does it make whether we speak of small spheres or of large [19] units, or, quite simply, of units in movement? One way or another, the move- **10** ments of the animal must be due to their movements. Hence those who combine movement and number in the same subject lay themselves open to these and many other similar absurdities. It is impossible not only that these characters should give the definition of soul—it is impossible that they should even be attributes of it. The point is clear if the attempt be made to start from this as the ac **15** count of soul and explain from it the affections and actions of the soul, e. g. reasoning, sensation, pleasure, pain, &c. For, to repeat what we have said earlier,[20] movement and number do not facilitate even conjecture about the derivative properties of soul.

Such are the three ways in which soul has traditionally been defined; one group of thinkers declared it to be that which is most originative of movement because it moves **20** itself, another group to be the subtlest and most nearly incorporeal of all kinds of body. We have now sufficiently

[17] 408[b] 33 ff.
[18] e. g. Heraclitus, and Diogenes of Apollonia.
[19] i. e. extended.
[20] 402[b] 25–403[a] 2.

set forth the difficulties and inconsistencies to which these theories are exposed. It remains now to examine the doctrine that soul is composed of the elements.

The reason assigned for this doctrine is that thus the soul may perceive or come to know everything that is, 25 but the theory necessarily involves itself in many impossibilities. Its upholders assume that like is known only by like, and imagine that by declaring the soul to be composed of the elements they succeed in identifying the soul with all the things it is capable of apprehending. But the elements are not the only things it knows; there are many others, or, more exactly, an infinite number of others, 30 formed out of the elements. Let us admit that the soul knows or perceives the elements out of which each of these composites is made up; but by what means will it know or perceive the composite whole, e. g. what God, man, flesh, bone (or any other compound) is? For each is, not 410ᵃ merely the elements of which it is composed, but those elements combined in a determinate mode or ratio, as Empedocles himself says of bone,

The kindly Earth in its broad-bosomed moulds
5   Won of clear Water two parts out of eight
And four of Fire; and so white bones were formed.

Nothing, therefore, will be gained by the presence of the elements in the soul, unless there be also present there the various formulae of proportion and the various compositions in accordance with them. Each element will indeed know its fellow outside, but there will be no knowledge of bone or man, unless they too are present in the constitution of the soul. The impossibility of this needs no pointing 10 out; for who would suggest that stone or man could enter into the constitution of the soul? The same applies to 'the good' and 'the not-good', and so on.

Further, the word 'is' has many meanings: it may be used of a 'this' or substance, or of a quantum, or of a quale, or of any other of the kinds of predicates we have distinguished. Does the soul consist of all of these or not? It does not appear that all have common elements. Is the soul formed 15 out of those elements alone which enter into substances? If so, how will it be able to know each of the other kinds of thing? Will it be said that each kind of thing has elements or principles of its own, and that the soul is formed out of the whole of these? In that case, the soul must be a quantum and a quale and a substance. But all that can be 20 made out of the elements of a quantum is a quantum, not a substance. These (and others like them) are the consequences of the view that the soul is composed of all the elements.

It is absurd, also, to say both (a) that like is not capable of being affected by like, and (b) that like is perceived or known by like, for perceiving, and also both thinking and knowing, are, on their own assumption, ways of being 25 affected or moved.

There are many puzzles and difficulties raised by saying, as Empedocles does, that each set of things is known by means of its corporeal elements and by reference to something in soul which is like them, and additional testimony is furnished by this new consideration; for all the parts of 30 the animal body which consist wholly of earth such as bones, sinews, and hair seem to be wholly insensitive and consequently not perceptive even of objects earthy like **410ᵇ** themselves, as they ought to have been.

Further, each of the principles will have far more ignorance than knowledge, for though each of them will know one thing, there will be many of which it will be ignorant. Empedocles at any rate must conclude that his God is the 5 least intelligent of all beings, for of him alone is it true that there is one thing, Strife, which he does not know, while there is nothing which mortal beings do not know, for there is nothing which does not enter into their composition.

In general, we may ask, Why has not everything a soul,

since everything either is an element, or is formed out of one or several or all of the elements? Each must certainly know one or several or all.

10   The problem might also be raised, What is that which unifies the elements into a soul? The elements correspond, it would appear, to the matter; what unites them, whatever it is, is the supremely important factor. But it is impossible that there should be something superior to, and dominant over, the soul (and a fortiori over the mind); it is reasonable 15 to hold that mind is by nature most primordial and domi- nant, while their statement is that it is the elements which are first of all that is.

All, both those who assert that the soul, because of its knowledge or perception of what is, is compounded out of the elements, and those who assert that it is of all things the most originative of movement, fail to take into consid- eration all kinds of soul. In fact (1) not all beings that per- 20 ceive can originate movement; there appear to be certain animals which are stationary, and yet local movement is the only one, so it seems, which the soul originates in animals. And (2) the same objection holds against all those who construct mind and the perceptive faculty out of the ele- ments; for it appears that plants live, and yet are not en- dowed with locomotion or perception, while a large number of animals are without discourse of reason. Even if these points were waived and mind admitted to be a part of the 25 soul (and so too the perceptive faculty), still, even so, there would be kinds and parts of soul of which they had failed to give any account.

The same objection lies against the view expressed in the 'Orphic' poems: there it is said that the soul comes in from 30 the whole when breathing takes place, being borne in upon the winds. Now this cannot take place in the case of plants, 411ᵃ nor indeed in the case of certain classes of animal, for not all classes of animal breathe. This fact has escaped the notice of the holders of this view.

If we must construct the soul out of the elements, there

is no necessity to suppose that *all* the elements enter into
its construction; one element in each pair of contraries will
suffice to enable it to know both that element itself and its
contrary. By means of the straight line we know both itself
and the curved—the carpenter's rule enables us to test 5
both—but what is curved does not enable us to distinguish
either itself or the straight.

Certain thinkers say that soul is intermingled in the
whole universe, and it is perhaps for that reason that Thales
came to the opinion that all things are full of gods. This
presents some difficulties: Why does the soul when it resides in air or fire not form an animal, while it does so 10
when it resides in mixtures of the elements, and that although it is held to be of higher quality when contained in
the former? (One might add the question, why the soul in
air is maintained to be higher and more immortal than that
in animals.) Both possible ways of replying to the former
question lead to absurdity or paradox; for it is beyond
paradox to say that fire or air is an animal, and it is absurd 15
to refuse the name of animal to what has soul in it. The
opinion that the elements have soul in them seems to have
arisen from the doctrine that a whole must be homogene
ous with its parts. If it is true that animals become animate
by drawing into themselves a portion of what surrounds
them, the partisans of this view are bound to say that the
soul of the Whole too is homogeneous with all its parts.
If the air sucked in is homogeneous, but soul heterogeneous, clearly while some part of soul will exist in the in- 20
breathed air, some other part will not. The soul must either
be homogeneous, or such that there are some parts of the
Whole in which it is not to be found.

From what has been said it is now clear that knowing
as an attribute of soul cannot be explained by soul's being
composed of the elements, and that it is neither sound nor
true to speak of soul as moved. But since (a) knowing 25
perceiving, opining, and further (b) desiring, wishing, and
generally all other modes of appetition, belong to soul, and

30 (c) the local movements of animals, and (d) growth, maturity, and decay are produced by the soul, we must ask
whether each of these is an attribute of the soul as a whole,
411ᵇ i. e. whether it is with the whole soul we think, perceive,
move ourselves, act or are acted upon, or whether each of
them requires a different part of the soul? So too with
regard to life. Does it depend on one of the parts of soul?
Or is it dependent on more than one? Or on all? Or has it
some quite other cause?

Some hold that the soul is divisible, and that one part
5 thinks, another desires. If, then, its nature admits of its
being divided, what can it be that holds the parts together?
Surely not the body; on the contrary it seems rather to be
the soul that holds the body together; at any rate when the
soul departs the body disintegrates and decays. If, then,
there is something else which makes the soul one, this uni-
10 fying agency would have the best right to the name of soul,
and we shall have to repeat for it the question: Is it one or
multipartite? If it is one, why not at once admit that 'the
soul' is one? If it has parts, once more the question must
be put: What holds its parts together, and so ad infinitum?

The question might also be raised about the parts of the
soul: What is the separate rôle of each in relation to the
15 body? For, if the whole soul holds together the whole body,
we should expect each part of the soul to hold together a
part of the body. But this seems an impossibility; it is
difficult even to imagine what sort of bodily part mind
will hold together, or how it will do this.

It is a fact of observation that plants and certain insects
20 go on living when divided into segments; this means that
each of the segments has a soul in it identical in species,
though not numerically identical in the different segments,
for both of the segments for a time possess the power of
sensation and local movement. That this does not last is
not surprising, for they no longer possess the organs necessary for self-maintenance. But, all the same, in each of the
25 bodily parts there are present all the parts of soul, and the

souls so present are homogeneous with one another and
with the whole; this means that the several parts of the soul
are indisseverable from one another, although the whole
soul is [21] divisible. It seems also that the principle found in
plants is also a kind of soul; for this is the only principle
which is common to both animals and plants; and this
exists in isolation from the principle of sensation, though 3ɔ
there is nothing which has the latter without the former.

BOOK II

1   Let the foregoing suffice as our account of the views **412ʳ**
        concerning the soul which have been handed on by our
predecessors; let us now dismiss them and make as it were
a completely fresh start, endeavouring to give a precise 5
answer to the question, What is soul? i. e. to formulate the
most general possible definition of it.

We are in the habit of recognizing, as one determinate
kind of what is, substance, and that in several senses, (a) in
the sense of matter or that which in itself is not 'a this', and
(b) in the sense of form or essence, which is that precisely
in virtue of which a thing is called 'a this', and thirdly (c)
in the sense of that which is compounded of both (a) and
(b). Now matter is potentiality, form actuality; of the latter 10
there are two grades related to one another as e. g. knowledge to the exercise of knowledge.

Among substances are by general consent reckoned
bodies and especially natural bodies; for they are the principles of all other bodies. Of natural bodies some have life
in them, others not; by life we mean self-nutrition and
growth (with its correlative decay). It follows that every 15
natural body which has life in it is a substance in the sense
of a composite.

But since it is also a *body* of such and such a kind, viz.
having life, the *body* cannot be soul; the body is the subject

---

[21] sc. 'in a sense, i. e. so as to preserve its homogeneity in even its
smallest part'.

or matter, not what is attributed to it. Hence the soul must
20 be a substance in the sense of the form of a natural body
having life potentially within it. But substance [1] is actuality,
and thus soul is the actuality of a body as above characterized. Now the word actuality has two senses corresponding
respectively to the possession of knowledge and the actual
exercise of knowledge. It is obvious that the soul is actuality
in the first sense, viz. that of knowledge as possessed, for
both sleeping and waking presuppose the existence of soul,
25 and of these waking corresponds to actual knowing, sleeping to knowledge possessed but not employed, and, in the
history of the individual, knowledge comes before its employment or exercise.

That is why the soul is the first grade of actuality of a
natural body having life potentially in it. The body so described is a body which is organized. The parts of plants in
412ᵇ spite of their extreme simplicity are 'organs'; e. g. the leaf
serves to shelter the pericarp, the pericarp to shelter the
fruit, while the roots of plants are analogous to the mouth
of animals, both serving for the absorption of food. If, then,
we have to give a general formula applicable to all kinds of
5 soul, we must describe it as the first grade of actuality of a
natural organized body. That is why we can wholly dismiss
as unnecessary the question whether the soul and the body
are one: it is as meaningless as to ask whether the wax and
the shape given to it by the stamp are one, or generally the
matter of a thing and that of which it is the matter.
Unity has many senses (as many as 'is' has), but the most
proper and fundamental sense of both is the relation of
an actuality to that of which it is the actuality.

We have now given an answer to the question, What is
10 soul?—an answer which applies to it in its full extent. It is
substance in the sense which corresponds to the definitive
formula of a thing's essence. That means that it is 'the essential whatness' of a body of the character just assigned.[2]

---

[1] sc. in the sense of form.
[2] viz. organized, or possessed potentially of life.

Suppose that what is literally an 'organ',[3] like an axe, were a *natural* body, its 'essential whatness', would have been its essence, and so its soul; if this disappeared from it, it would have ceased to be an axe, except in name. As it is,[4] it is just 15 an axe; it wants the character which is required to make its whatness or formulable essence a soul; for that, it would have had to be a *natural* body of a particular kind, viz. one having *in itself* the power of setting itself in movement and arresting itself. Next, apply this doctrine in the case of the 'parts' of the living body. Suppose that the eye were an animal—sight would have been its soul, for sight is the substance or essence of the eye which corresponds to the for- 20 mula,[5] the eye being merely the matter of seeing; when seeing is removed the eye is no longer an eye, except in name— it is no more a real eye than the eye of a statue or of a painted figure. We must now extend our consideration from the 'parts' to the whole living body; for what the departmental sense is to the bodily part which is its organ, that the whole faculty of sense is to the whole sensitive body as such.

We must not understand by that which is 'potentially 25 capable of living' what has lost the soul it had, but only what still retains it; but seeds and fruits are bodies which possess the qualification.[6] Consequently, while waking is actuality in a sense corresponding to the cutting and the 413ᵛ seeing,[7] the soul is actuality in the sense corresponding to the power of sight and the power in the tool;[8] the body corresponds to what exists in potentiality; as the pupil *plus* the power of sight constitutes the eye. so the soul *plus* the body constitutes the animal.

From this it indubitably follows that the soul is insepar-

---

[3] i. e. instrument.
[4] Being an artificial, not a natural, body.
[5] i. e. which states what it is to be an eye.
[6] Though only potentially, i. e. they are at a further remove from actuality than the fully formed and organized body.
[7] i. e. to the second grade of actuality.
[8] i. e. to the first grade of actuality.

able from its body, or at any rate that certain parts of it are
5 (if it has parts)—for the actuality of some of them is nothing but the actualities of their bodily parts. Yet some may
be separable because they are not the actualities of any body
at all. Further, we have no light on the problem whether
the soul may not be the actuality of its body in the sense
in which the sailor is the actuality [9] of the ship.

This must suffice as our sketch or outline determination
10 of the nature of soul.

2   Since what is clear or logically more evident emerges
from what in itself is confused but more observable by
us, we must reconsider our results from this point of view.
For it is not enough for a definitive formula to express as
15 most now do the mere fact; it must include and exhibit the
ground also. At present definitions are given in a form analogous to the conclusion of a syllogism; e. g. What is squaring? The construction of an equilateral rectangle equal to
a given oblong rectangle. Such a definition is in form
equivalent to a conclusion.[10] One that tells us that squaring
is the discovery of a line which is a mean proportional between the two unequal sides of the given rectangle discloses
the ground of what is defined.

We resume our inquiry from a fresh starting-point by
20 calling attention to the fact that what has soul in it differs
from what has not in that the former displays life. Now this
word has more than one sense, and provided any one alone
of these is found in a thing we say that thing is living.
Living, that is, may mean thinking or perception or local
movement and rest, or movement in the sense of nutrition,
25 decay and growth. Hence we think of plants also as living,
for they are observed to possess in themselves an originative
power through which they increase or decrease in all spatial
directions; they grow up and down, and everything that
grows increases its bulk alike in both directions or indeed

---

[9] i. e. actuator.
[10] i. e. it has nothing in it corresponding to a middle term.

in all, and continues to live so long as it can absorb nutriment.   30

This power of self-nutrition can be isolated from the
other powers mentioned, but not they from it—in mortal
beings at least. The fact is obvious in plants; for it is the
only psychic power they possess.

This is the originative power the possession of which
leads us to speak of things as living at all, but it is the pos- **413**
session of sensation that leads us for the first time to speak
of living things as animals; for even those beings which possess no power of local movement but do possess the power
of sensation we call animals and not merely living things.

The primary form of sense is touch, which belongs to
all animals. Just as the power of self-nutrition can be isolated from touch and sensation generally, so touch can be 5
isolated from all other forms of sense. (By the power of
self-nutrition we mean that departmental power of the soul
which is common to plants and animals: all animals whatsoever are observed to have the sense of touch.) What the
explanation of these two facts is, we must discuss later.[11]
At present we must confine ourselves to saying that soul is 10
the source of these phenomena and is characterized by
them, viz. by the powers of self-nutrition, sensation, thinking, and motivity.

Is each of these a soul or a part of a soul? And if a part,
a part in what sense? A part merely distinguishable by definition or a part distinct in local situation as well? In the case 15
of certain of these powers, the answers to these questions
are easy, in the case of others we are puzzled what to say.
Just as in the case of plants which when divided are observed to continue to live though removed to a distance
from one another (thus showing that in their case the soul
of each individual plant before division was actually one,
potentially many), so we notice a similar result in other
varieties of soul, i. e. in insects which have been cut in two; 20
each of the segments possesses both sensation and local

[11] iii. 12, esp. 434ᵃ 22–30, ᵇ10 ff.

movement; and if sensation, necessarily also imagination and appetition; for, where there is sensation, there is also pleasure and pain, and, where these, necessarily also desire.

25 We have no evidence as yet about mind or the power to think; it seems to be a widely different kind of soul, differing as what is eternal from what is perishable; it alone is capable of existence in isolation from all other psychic powers. All the other parts of soul, it is evident from what we have said, are, in spite of certain statements to the contrary, incapable of separate existence though, of course, distinguishable by definition. If opining is distinct from 30 perceiving, to be capable of opining and to be capable of perceiving must be distinct, and so with all the other forms of living above enumerated. Further, some animals possess all these parts of soul, some certain of them only, others one 414ª only (this is what enables us to classify animals); the cause must be considered later.[12] A similar arrangement is found also within the field of the senses; some classes of animals have all the senses, some only certain of them, others only one, the most indispensable, touch.

Since the expression 'that whereby we live and perceive' 5 has two meanings, just like the expression 'that whereby we know'—that may mean either (a) knowledge or (b) the soul, for we can speak of knowing by or with either, and similarly that whereby we are in health may be either (a) health or (b) the body or some part of the body; and since of the two terms thus contrasted knowledge or health is the name of a form, essence, or ratio, or if we so express it 10 an actuality of a recipient matter—knowledge of what is capable of knowing, health of what is capable of being made healthy (for the operation of that which is capable of originating change terminates and has its seat in what is changed or altered); further, since it is the soul by or with which primarily we live, perceive, and think:—it follows that the soul must be a ratio or formulable essence, not a

[12] iii. 12, 13.

matter or subject. For, as we said,[13] the word substance has
three meanings—form, matter, and the complex of both—
and of these three what is called matter is potentiality, what 15
is called form actuality. Since then the complex here is the
living thing, the body cannot be the actuality of the soul;
it is the soul which is the actuality of a certain kind of
body. Hence the rightness of the view that the soul cannot
be without a body, while it cannot be a body; it is not a 20
body but something relative to a body. That is why it is *in*
a body, and a body of a definite kind. It was a mistake,
therefore, to do as former thinkers did, merely to fit it into
a body without adding a definite specification of the kind or
character of that body. Reflection confirms the observed
fact; the actuality of any given thing can only be realized 25
in what is already potentially that thing, i. e. in a matter of
its own appropriate to it. From all this it follows that soul is
an actuality or formulable essence of something that possesses a potentiality of being besouled.

3　　Of the psychic powers above enumerated [14] some kinds
　　of living things, as we have said,[15] possess all, some less
than all, others one only. Those we have mentioned are the
nutritive, the appetitive, the sensory, the locomotive, and 30
the power of thinking. Plants have none but the first, the
nutritive, while another order of living things has this *plus*
the sensory. If any order of living things has the sensory, it **414ᵇ**
must also have the appetitive; for appetite is the genus of
which desire, passion, and wish are the species; now all animals have one sense at least, viz. touch, and whatever has a
sense has the capacity for pleasure and pain and therefore
has pleasant and painful objects present to it, and wherever
these are present, there is desire, for desire is just appetition
of what is pleasant. Further, all animals have the sense for 5

---

[13] 412ᵃ 7.
[14] 413ᵃ 23–5, ᵇ11–13, 21–4.
[15] 413ᵇ 32–414ᵃ 1.

food (for touch is the sense for food); the food of all living
things consists of what is dry, moist, hot, cold, and these are
the qualities apprehended by touch; all other sensible qualities are apprehended by touch only indirectly. Sounds,
colours, and odours contribute nothing to nutriment; flavours fall within the field of tangible qualities. Hunger and
thirst are forms of desire, hunger a desire for what is dry and
hot, thirst a desire for what is cold and moist; flavour is a
sort of seasoning added to both. We must later [16] clear up
these points, but at present it may be enough to say that all
animals that possess the sense of touch have also appetition.
The case of imagination is obscure; we must examine it
later.[17] Certain kinds of animals possess in addition the
power of locomotion, and still another order of animate beings, i. e. man and possibly another order like man or superior to him, the power of thinking, i. e. mind. It is now
evident that a single definition can be given of soul only in
the same sense as one can be given of figure. For, as in that
case there is no figure distinguishable and apart from triangle, &c., so here there is no soul apart from the forms of
soul just enumerated. It is true that a highly general definition can be given for figure which will fit all figures without
expressing the peculiar nature of any figure. So here in the
case of soul and its specific forms. Hence it is absurd in this
and similar cases to demand an absolutely general definition, which will fail to express the peculiar nature of anything that *is*, or again, omitting this, to look for separate
definitions corresponding to each *infima species*. The cases
of figure and soul are exactly parallel; for the particulars sub-
sumed under the common name in both cases—figures and
living beings—constitute a series, each successive term of
which potentially contains its predecessor, e. g. the square
the triangle, the sensory power the self-nutritive. Hence we
must ask in the case of each order of living things, What is
its soul, i. e. What is the soul of plant, animal, man? Why

[16] c. 11. iii. 12. 434[b] 18–21.
[17] iii. 3, 11. 433[b] 31–434[a] 7.

the terms are related in this serial way must form the sub- **415ᵃ**
ject of later examination.¹⁸ But the facts are that the power
of perception is never found apart from the power of self-
nutrition, while—in plants—the latter is found isolated
from the former. Again, no sense is found apart from that
of touch, while touch is found by itself; many animals have 5
neither sight, hearing, nor smell. Again, among living things
that possess sense some have the power of locomotion,
some not. Lastly, certain living beings—a small minority—
possess calculation and thought, for (among mortal beings)
those which possess calculation have all the other powers
above mentioned, while the converse does not hold—in- 10
deed some live by imagination alone, while others have not
even imagination. The mind that knows with immediate intuition presents a different problem.¹⁹

It is evident that the way to give the most adequate definition of soul is to seek in the case of each of its forms for
the most appropriate definition.

4   It is necessary for the student of these forms of soul
    first to find a definition of each, expressive of what it 15
is, and then to investigate its derivative properties, &c. But
if we are to express what each is, viz. what the thinking
power is, or the perceptive, or the nutritive, we must go
farther back and first give an account of thinking or perceiving, for in the order of investigation the question of
what an agent does precedes the question, what enables it
to do what it does. If this is correct, we must on the same
ground go yet another step farther back and have some clear 20
view of the objects of each; thus we must start with these
objects, e. g. with food, with what is perceptible, or with
what is intelligible.

It follows that first of all we must treat of nutrition and
reproduction,²⁰ for the nutritive soul is found along with all

---

¹⁸ iii. 12, 13.
¹⁹ Cf. iii. 4–8.
²⁰ sc. 'which we shall see to be inseparable from nutrition'.

the others and is the most primitive and widely distributed power of soul, being indeed that one in virtue of which all
25 are said to have life. The acts in which it manifests itself are reproduction and the use of food—reproduction, I say, because for any living thing that has reached its normal development and which is unmutilated, and whose mode of generation is not spontaneous, the most natural act is the production of another like itself, an animal producing an animal, a plant a plant, in order that, as far as its nature
415ᵇ allows, it may partake in the eternal and divine. That is the goal towards which all things strive, that for the sake of which they do whatsoever their nature renders possible. The phrase 'for the sake of which' is ambiguous; it may mean either (a) the end to achieve which, or (b) the being in whose interest, the act is done. Since then no living thing is able to partake in what is eternal and divine by un-interrupted continuance (for nothing perishable can for
5 ever remain one and the same), it tries to achieve that end in the only way possible to it, and success is possible in vary-ing degrees; so it remains not indeed as the self-same indi-vidual but continues its existence in something like itself—not numerically but specifically one.[21]

The soul is the cause or source of the living body. The terms cause and source have many senses. But the soul is the cause of its body alike in all three senses which we ex-
10 plicitly recognize. It is (a) the source or origin of move-ment, it is (b) the end, it is (c) the essence of the whole living body.

That it is the last, is clear; for in everything the essence is identical with the ground of its being, and here, in the case of living things, their being is to live, and of their being and their living the soul in them is the cause or source. Further, the actuality of whatever is potential is identical with its formulable essence.

[21] There is an unbroken current of the same specific life flowing through a discontinuous series of individual beings of the same species united by descent.

It is manifest that the soul is also the final cause of its 15
body. For Nature, like mind, always does whatever it does
for the sake of something, which something is its end. To
that something corresponds in the case of animals the soul
and in this it follows the order of nature; all natural bodies
are organs of the soul. This is true of those that enter into
the constitution of plants as well as of those which enter
into that of animals. This shows that that for the sake of 20
which they are is soul. We must here recall the two senses
of 'that for the sake of which', viz. (a) the end to achieve
which, and (b) the being in whose interest, anything is or
is done.

We must maintain, further, that the soul is also the
cause of the living body as the original source of local
movement. The power of locomotion is not found, however, in all living things. But change of quality and change
of quantity are also due to the soul. Sensation is held to
be a qualitative alteration, and nothing except what has
soul in it is capable of sensation. The same holds of the 25
quantitative changes which constitute growth and decay;
nothing grows or decays naturally [22] except what feeds
itself, and nothing feeds itself except what has a share of
soul in it.

Empedocles is wrong in adding that growth in plants is
to be explained, the downward rooting by the natural
tendency of earth to travel downwards, and the upward **416ᵉ**
branching by the similar natural tendency of fire to travel
upwards. For he misinterprets up and down; up and down
are not for all things what they are for the whole Cosmos:
if we are to distinguish and identify organs according to 5
their functions, the roots of plants are analogous to the
head in animals. Further, we must ask what is the force that
holds together the earth and the fire which tend to travel
in contrary directions; if there is no counteracting force,
they will be torn asunder; if there is, this must be the soul
and the cause of nutrition and growth. By some the ele-

[22] i. e. of itself.

10 ment of fire is held to be the cause of nutrition and growth, for it alone of the primary bodies or elements is observed to feed and increase itself. Hence the suggestion that in both plants and animals it is it which is the operative force. A concurrent cause in a sense it certainly is, but not
15 the principal cause; that is rather the soul; for while the growth of fire goes on without limit so long as there is a supply of fuel, in the case of all complex wholes formed in the course of nature there is a limit or ratio which determines their size and increase, and limit and ratio are marks of soul but not of fire, and belong to the side of formulable essence rather than that of matter.

Nutrition and reproduction are due to one and the same psychic power. It is necessary first to give precision to our account of food, for it is by this function of absorbing
20 food that this psychic power is distinguished from all the others. The current view is that what serves as food to a living thing is what is contrary to it—not that in every pair of contraries each is food to the other· to be food a contrary must not only be transformable into the other and vice versa, it must also in so doing increase the bulk of the other. Many a contrary is transformed into its other and vice versa, where neither is even a quantum and so cannot
25 increase in bulk, e. g. an invalid into a healthy subject. It is clear that not even those contraries which satisfy both the conditions mentioned above are food to one another in precisely the same sense; water may be said to feed fire, but not fire water. Where the members of the pair are elementary bodies only one of the contraries, it would appear, can be said to feed the other. But there is a difficulty
30 here. One set of thinkers assert that like is fed, as well as increased in amount, by like. Another set, as we have said, maintain the very reverse, viz. that what feeds and what is fed are contrary to one another; like, they argue, is incapable of being affected by like; but food is changed in the process of digestion, and change is always to what is opposite or to what is intermediate. Further, food is acted

upon by what is nourished by it, not the other way round, 35
as timber is worked by a carpenter and not conversely; **416ᵇ**
there is a change in the carpenter but it is merely a change
from not-working to working. In answering this problem
it makes all the difference whether we mean by 'the food'
the 'finished' or the 'raw' product. If we use the word food
of both, viz. of the completely undigested and the completely digested matter, we can justify both the rival accounts of it; taking food in the sense of undigested matter, 5
it is the contrary of what is fed by it, taking it as digested it
is like what is fed by it. Consequently it is clear that in a
certain sense we may say that both parties are right, both
wrong.

Since nothing except what is alive can be fed, what is fed
is the besouled body and just because it has soul in it.
Hence food is essentially related to what has soul in it. Food
has a power which is other than the power to increase the 10
bulk of what is fed by it; so far forth as what has soul in it
is a quantum, food may increase its quantity, but it is only
so far as what has soul in it is a 'this-somewhat' or substance
that food acts as food; in that case it maintains the being
of what is fed, and that continues to be what it is so long as
the process of nutrition continues. Further, it is the agent in
generation, i. e. not the generation of the individual fed 15
but the reproduction of another like it; the substance of the
individual fed is already in existence; the existence of no
substance is a self-generation but only a self-maintenance.

Hence the psychic power which we are now studying may *Def. 1*
be described as that which tends to maintain whatever has
this power in it of continuing such as it was, and food helps
it to do its work. That is why, if deprived of food, it must
cease to be.

The process of nutrition involves three factors, (a) what 20
is fed, (b) that wherewith it is fed, (c) what does the feeding; of these (c) is the first soul,[23] (a) the body which has
that soul in it, (b) the food. But since it is right to call

[23] i. e. the earliest and most indispensable kind of soul.

things after the ends they realize, and the end of this soul is
25 to generate another being like that in which it is, the first
soul ought to be named the reproductive soul. The expression (b) 'wherewith it is fed' is ambiguous just as is
the expression 'wherewith the ship is steered'; that may
mean either (i) the hand or (ii) the rudder, i. e. either (i)
what is moved and sets in movement, or (ii) what is merely
moved. We can apply this analogy here if we recall that all
food must be capable of being digested, and that what produces digestion is warmth; that is why everything that has
soul in it possesses warmth.

30   We have now given an outline account of the nature of
food; further details must be given in the appropriate place.

5   Having made these distinctions let us now speak of
sensation in the widest sense. Sensation depends, as
we have said,[24] on a process of movement or affection from
35 without, for it is held to be some sort of change of quality.
417ª Now some thinkers assert that like is affected only by like;
in what sense this is possible and in what sense impossible,
we have explained in our general discussion of acting and
being acted upon.[25]

Here arises a problem: why do we not perceive the senses
themselves as well as the external objects of sense, or why
without the stimulation of external objects do they not pro-
5 duce sensation, seeing that they contain in themselves fire,
earth, and all the other elements, which are the direct or
indirect objects of sense? It is clear that what is sensitive is
so only potentially, not actually. The power of sense is
parallel to what is combustible, for that never ignites itself
spontaneously, but requires an agent which has the power
of starting ignition; otherwise it could have set itself on
fire, and would not have needed actual fire to set it ablaze.

In reply we must recall that we use the word 'perceive'
in two ways, for we say (a) that what has the power to hear

---

[24] 415ᵇ 24, cf. 410ª 25.
[25] De Gen. et Corr. 323ᵇ 18 ff.

or see, 'sees' or 'hears', even though it is at the moment 10
asleep, and also (*b*) that what is actually seeing or hearing,
'sees' or 'hears'. Hence 'sense' too must have two meanings,
sense potential, and sense actual. Similarly 'to be a sentient'
means either (*a*) to have a certain power or (*b*) to manifest
a certain activity. To begin with, for a time, let us speak as
if there were no difference between (i) being moved or affected, and (ii) being active, for movement is a kind of 15
activity—an imperfect kind, as has elsewhere been explained.[26] Everything that is acted upon or moved is acted
upon by an agent which is actually at work. Hence it is
that in one sense, as has already been stated,[27] what acts
and what is acted upon are like, in another unlike, i. e. prior
to and during the change the two factors are unlike, after 20
it like.

But we must now distinguish not only *between* what is
potential and what is actual but also different senses in
which things can be said to be potential or actual; up to
now we have been speaking as if each of these phrases had
only one sense. We can speak of something as 'a knower'
either (*a*) as when we say that man is a knower, meaning
that man falls within the class of beings that know or have
knowledge, or (*b*) as when we are speaking of a man who
possesses a knowledge of grammar; each of these is so 25
called as having in him a certain potentiality, but there is
a difference between their respective potentialities, the one
(*a*) being a potential knower, because his kind or matter
is such and such, the other (*b*), because he can in the absence of any external counteracting cause realize his knowledge in actual knowing at will. This implies a third meaning of 'a knower' (*c*), one who is already realizing his
knowledge—he is a knower in actuality and in the most
proper sense is knowing, e. g. this A. Both the former are 30
potential knowers, who realize their respective potentialities, the one (*a*) by change of quality, i. e. repeated transi-

[26] *Phys.* 201ᵇ 31, 257ᵇ 8.
[27] 416ᵃ 29–ᵇ9.

tions from one state to its opposite [28] under instruction, the other (b) by the transition from the inactive possession of 417ᵇ sense or grammar to their active exercise. The two kinds of transition are distinct.

Also the expression 'to be acted upon' has more than one meaning; it may mean either (a) the extinction of one of two contraries by the other, or (b) the maintenance of what is potential by the agency of what is actual and already like what is acted upon, with such likeness as is compatible 5 with one's being actual and the other potential. For what possesses knowledge becomes an actual knower by a transition which is either not an alteration of it at all (being in reality a development into its true self or actuality) or at least an alteration in a quite different sense from the usual meaning.

Hence it is wrong to speak of a wise man as being 'altered' when he uses his wisdom, just as it would be absurd to speak of a builder as being altered when he is using his skill in building a house.

10   What in the case of knowing or understanding leads from potentiality to actuality ought not to be called teaching but something else. That which starting with the power to know learns or acquires knowledge through the agency of one who actually knows and has the power of teaching 15 either (a) ought not to be said 'to be acted upon' at all or (b) we must recognize two senses of alteration, viz. (i) the substitution of one quality for another, the first being the contrary of the second, or (ii) the development of an existent quality from potentiality in the direction of fixity or nature.

In the case of what is to possess sense, the first transition is due to the action of the male parent and takes place before birth so that at birth the living thing is, in respect of sensation, at the stage which corresponds to the *possession* of knowledge. Actual sensation corresponds to the stage of 20 the exercise of knowledge. But between the two cases com-

---

[28] viz. from ignorance or error to knowledge or truth.

pared there is a difference; the objects that excite the
sensory powers to activity, the seen, the heard, &c., are
outside. The ground of this difference is that what actual
sensation apprehends is individuals, while what knowledge
apprehends is universals, and these are in a sense within the
soul. That is why a man can exercise his knowledge when he
wishes, but his sensation does not depend upon himself— 25
a sensible object must be there. A similar statement must
be made about our *knowledge* of what is sensible—on the
same ground, viz. that the sensible objects are individual
and external.

A later more appropriate occasion may be found [29] thoroughly to clear up all this. At present it must be enough to 30
recognize the distinctions already drawn; a thing may be
said to be potential in either of two senses, (a) in the sense
in which we might say of a boy that he may become a general or (b) in the sense in which we might say the same of
an adult, and there are two corresponding senses of the 418ᵇ
term 'a potential sentient'. There are no separate names for
the two stages of potentiality; we have pointed out that they
are different and how they are different. We cannot help
using the incorrect terms 'being acted upon or altered' of
the two transitions involved. As we have said,[30] what has
the power of sensation is potentially like what the perceived object is actually; that is, while at the beginning of 5
the process of its being acted upon the two interacting
factors are dissimilar, at the end the one acted upon is assimilated to the other and is identical in quality with it.

6   In dealing with each of the senses we shall have first
to speak of the objects which are perceptible by each.
The term 'object of sense' covers three kinds of objects, two
kinds of which are, in our language, directly perceptible,
while the remaining one is only incidentally perceptible. Of
the first two kinds one (a) consists of what is perceptible

[29] iii. 4, 5.
[30] 417ᵃ 12–20.

by a single sense, the other (b) of what is perceptible by
10 any and all of the senses.[31] I call by the name of special
object of this or that sense that which cannot be perceived by any other sense than that one and in respect of
which no error is possible; in this sense colour is the special
object of sight, sound of hearing, flavour of taste. Touch,
indeed, discriminates more than one set of different qualities. Each sense has one kind of object which it discerns,
15 and never errs in reporting that what is before it is colour or
sound (though it may err as to what it is that is coloured
or where that is, or what it is that is sounding or where that
is). Such objects are what we propose to call the special
objects of this or that sense.

'Common sensibles' are movement, rest, number, figure,
magnitude; these are not peculiar to any one sense, but are
common to all. There are at any rate certain kinds of movement which are perceptible both by touch and by sight.

We speak of an incidental object of sense where e. g. the
20 white object which we see is the son of Diares; here because 'being the son of Diares' is incidental to the directly
visible white patch we speak of the son of Diares as being
(incidentally) perceived or seen by us. Because this is only
incidentally an object of sense, it in no way as such affects
the senses. Of the two former kinds, both of which are in
their own nature perceptible by sense, the first kind—that
of special objects of the several senses—constitute the
objects of sense in the strictest sense of the term and it is to
25 them that in the nature of things the structure of each
several sense is adapted.

7   The object of sight is the visible, and what is visible is
        (a) colour and (b) a certain kind of object which can
be described in words but which has no single name; what
we mean by (b) will be abundantly clear as we proceed.
Whatever is visible is colour and colour is what lies upon
30 what is in its own nature visible; 'in its own nature' here

---

[31] Really, it is enough if it is perceptible by more than one sense.

means not that visibility is involved in the definition of
what thus underlies colour, but that that substratum contains in itself the cause of visibility. Every colour has in it
the power to set in movement what is actually transparent; **418ᵇ**
that power constitutes its very nature. That is why it is not
visible except with the help of light; it is only in light that
the colour of a thing is seen. Hence our first task is to explain what light is.

Now there clearly is something which is transparent, and
by 'transparent' I mean what is visible, and yet not visible 5
in itself, but rather owing its visibility to the colour of *some-*
thing else; of this character are air, water, and many solid
bodies. Neither air nor water is transparent because it is
air or water; they are transparent because each of them has
contained in it a certain substance which is the same in both
and is also found in the eternal body which constitutes the
uppermost shell of the physical Cosmos. Of this substance
light is the activity—the activity of what is transparent so
far forth as it has in it the determinate power of becoming 10
transparent; where this power is present, there is also the
potentiality of the contrary, viz. darkness. Light is as it were
the proper colour of what is transparent, and exists whenever the potentially transparent is excited to actuality by
the influence of fire or something resembling 'the uppermost body'; for fire too contains something which is one
and the same with the substance in question.

We have now explained what the transparent is and
what light is; light is neither fire nor any kind whatsoever
of body nor an efflux from any kind of body (if it were, it 1
would again itself be a kind of body)—it is the presence of
fire or something resembling fire in what is transparent.
It is certainly not a body, for two bodies cannot be present
in the same place. The opposite of light is darkness; darkness is the absence from what is transparent of the corresponding positive state above characterized; clearly therefore, light is just the presence of that.

Empedocles (and with him all others who used the same 20

forms of expression) was wrong in speaking of light as
'travelling' or being at a given moment between the earth
and its envelope, its movement being unobservable by us;
that view is contrary both to the clear evidence of argu-
25 ment and to the observed facts; if the distance traversed
were short, the movement might have been unobservable,
but where the distance is from extreme East to extreme
West, the draught upon our powers of belief is too great.

What is capable of taking on colour is what in itself is
colourless, as what can take on sound is what is soundless;
what is colourless includes (a) what is transparent and (b)
30 what is invisible or scarcely visible, i. e. what is 'dark'.
The latter (b) is the same as what is transparent, when it is
potentially, not of course when it is actually transparent;
it is the same substance which is now darkness, now light.

Not everything that is visible depends upon light for its
419ª visibility. This is only true of the 'proper' colour of things.
Some objects of sight which in light are invisible, in darkness stimulate the sense; that is, things that appear fiery or
shining. This class of objects has no simple common name,
5 but instances of it are fungi, flesh, heads, scales, and eyes of
fish. In none of these is what is seen their own 'proper' colour. Why we see these at all is another question. At present
what is obvious is that what is seen in light is always colour.
That is why without the help of light colour remains invisible. Its being colour at all means precisely its having in it
10 the power to set in movement what is already actually
transparent, and, as we have seen, the actuality of what is
transparent is just light.

The following experiment makes the necessity of a
medium clear. If what has colour is placed in immediate
contact with the eye, it cannot be seen. Colour sets in
movement not the sense organ but what is transparent,
e. g. the air, and that, extending continuously from the ob-
15 ject of the organ, sets the latter in movement. Democritus
misrepresents the facts when he expresses the opinion that
if the interspace were empty one could distinctly see an ant

on the vault of the sky; that is an impossibility. Seeing is
due to an affection or change of what has the perceptive
faculty, and it cannot be affected by the seen colour itself;
it remains that it must be affected by what comes between.
Hence it is indispensable that there be *something* in between—if there were nothing, so far from seeing with 20
greater distinctness, we should see nothing at all.

We have now explained the cause why colour cannot be
seen otherwise than in light. Fire on the other hand is seen
both in darkness and in light; this double possibility follows
necessarily from our theory, for it is just fire that makes
what is potentially transparent actually transparent.

The same account holds also of sound and smell; if the
object of either of these senses is in immediate contact with 25
the organ no sensation is produced. In both cases the object
sets in movement only what lies between, and this in turn
sets the organ in movement: if what sounds or smells is
brought into immediate contact with the organ, no sensation will be produced. The same, in spite of all appear- 30
ances, applies also to touch and taste; why there is this apparent difference will be clear later.[32] What comes between
in the case of sounds is air; the corresponding medium in
the case of smell has no name. But, corresponding to what
is transparent in the case of colour, there is a quality found
both in air and water, which serves as a medium for what 35
has smell—I say 'in water' because animals that live in water
as well as those that live on land seem to possess the sense
of smell, and 'in air' because man and all other land animals **419**
that breathe, perceive smells only when they breathe air in.
The explanation of this too will be given later.[33]

8　　Now let us, to begin with, make certain distinctions
　　about sound and hearing.

Sound may mean either of two things—(a) actual, and 5
(b) potential, sound. There are certain things which, as we

---

[32] 422[b] 34 ff.
[33] 421[b] 13–422[a] 6.

say, 'have no sound', e. g. sponges or wool, others which have, e. g. bronze and in general all things which are smooth and solid—the latter are said to have a sound because they can make a sound, i. e. can generate actual sound between themselves and the organ of hearing.

Actual sound requires for its occurrence (i, ii) two such
10 bodies and (iii) a space between them; for it is generated by an impact. Hence it is impossible for one body only to generate a sound—there must be a body impinging and a body impinged upon; what sounds does so by striking against something else, and this is impossible without a movement from place to place.

As we have said, not all bodies can by impact on one another produce sound; impact on wool makes no sound,
15 while the impact on bronze or any body which is smooth and hollow does. Bronze gives out a sound when struck be-cause it is smooth; bodies which are hollow owing to re-flection repeat the original impact over and over again, the body originally set in movement being unable to escape from the concavity.

Further, we must remark that sound is heard both in air and in water, though less distinctly in the latter. Yet neither
20 air nor water is the principal cause of sound. What is re-quired for the production of sound is an impact of two solids against one another and against the air. The latter condition is satisfied when the air impinged upon does not retreat before the blow, i. e. is not dissipated by it.

That is why it must be struck with a sudden sharp blow, if it is to sound—the movement of the whip must outrun the dispersion of the air, just as one might get in a stroke at a heap or whirl of sand as it was travelling rapidly past.
25   An echo occurs, when, a mass of air having been unified, bounded, and prevented from dissipation by the containing walls of a vessel, the air originally struck by the impinging body and set in movement by it rebounds from this mass of air like a ball from a wall. It is probable that in all gen-eration of sound echo takes place, though it is frequently

only indistinctly heard. What happens here must be analogous to what happens in the case of light; light is always reflected—otherwise it would not be diffused and outside what was directly illuminated by the sun there would be 30 blank darkness; but this reflected light is not always strong enough, as it is when it is reflected from water, bronze, and other smooth bodies, to cast a shadow, which is the distinguishing mark by which we recognize light.

It is rightly said that an empty space plays the chief part in the production of hearing, for what people mean by 'the vacuum' is the air, which is what causes hearing, when that air is set in movement as one continuous mass; but owing to its friability it emits no sound, being dissipated by im- 35 pinging upon any surface which is not smooth. When the 420ᵇ surface on which it impinges is quite smooth, what is produced by the original impact is a united mass, a result due to the smoothness of the surface with which the air is in contact at the other end.

What has the power of producing sound is what has the power of setting in movement a single mass of air which is continuous from the impinging body up to the organ of hearing. The organ of hearing is physically united with air,[34] and because it is in air, the air inside is moved concurrently with the air outside. Hence animals do not hear 5 with all parts of their bodies, nor do all parts admit of the entrance of air; for even the part which can be moved and can sound has not air everywhere in it. Air in itself is, owing to its friability, quite soundless; only when its dissipation is prevented is its movement sound. The air in the ear is built into a chamber just to prevent this dissipating movement, in order that the animal may accurately apprehend 10 all varieties of the movements of the air outside. That is why we hear also in water, viz. because the water cannot get into the air chamber or even, owing to the spirals, into the outer ear. If this does happen, hearing ceases, as it also does if the tympanic membrane is damaged, just as sight

[34] i. e. it has air incorporated in its structure.

ceases if the membrane covering the pupil is damaged. It is
15 also a test of deafness whether the ear does or does not
reverberate like a horn; the air inside the ear has always a
movement of its own, but the sound we hear is always
the sounding of something else, not of the organ itself.
That is why we say that we hear with what is empty and
echoes, viz. because what we hear with is a chamber which
contains a bounded mass of air.

Which is it that 'sounds', the striking body or the struck?
Is not the answer 'it is both, but each in a different way'?
20 Sound is a movement of what can rebound from a smooth
surface when struck against it. As we have explained [35] not
everything sounds when it strikes or is struck, e. g. if one
25 needle is struck against another, neither emits any sound.
In order, therefore, that sound may be generated, what is
struck must be smooth, to enable the air to rebound and
be shaken off from it in one piece.

The distinctions between different sounding bodies show
themselves only in actual sound; [36] as without the help of
light colours remain invisible, so without the help of actual
sound the distinctions between acute and grave sounds remain inaudible. Acute and grave are here metaphors, trans-
30 ferred from their proper sphere, viz. that of touch, where
they mean respectively (a) what moves the sense much in
a short time, (b) what moves the sense little in a long time.
Not that what is sharp really moves fast, and what is grave,
slowly, but that the difference in the qualities of the one
420ᵇ and the other movement is due to their respective speeds.
There seems to be a sort of parallelism between what is
acute or grave to hearing and what is sharp or blunt to
touch; what is sharp as it were stabs, while what is blunt
pushes, the one producing its effect in a short, the other in
a long time, so that the one is quick, the other slow.

5   Let the foregoing suffice as an analysis of sound. Voice is

----

[35] 419ᵇ 6, 13.
[36] i. e. when these bodies, e. g. the strings of a lyre, are actually
sounding.

a kind of sound characteristic of what has soul in it; nothing
that is without soul utters voice, it being only by a metaphor that we speak of the voice of the flute or the lyre or
generally of what (being without soul) possesses the power
of producing a succession of notes which differ in length
and pitch and timbre. The metaphor is based on the fact
that all these differences are found also in voice. Many animals are voiceless, e. g. all non-sanguineous animals and
among sanguineous animals fish. This is just what we 1c
should expect, since voice is a certain movement of air. The
fish, like those in the Achelous, which are said to have voice,
really make the sounds with their gills or some similar organ. Voice is the sound made by an animal, and that with
a special organ. As we saw, everything that makes a sound
does so by the impact of something (*a*) against something
else, (*b*) across a space, (*c*) filled with air; hence it is only 15
to be expected that no animals utter voice except those
which take in air. Once air is inbreathed, Nature uses it
for two different purposes, as the tongue is used both for
tasting and for articulating; in that case of the two functions tasting is necessary for the animal's existence (hence
it is found more widely distributed), while articulate speech
is a luxury subserving its possessor's well-being; similarly in
the former case Nature employs the breath both as an in- 20
dispensable means to the regulation of the inner temperature of the living body and also as the matter of articulate
voice, in the interests of its possessor's well-being. Why its
former use is indispensable must be discussed elsewhere.[37]

The organ of respiration is the windpipe, and the organ
to which this is related as means to end is the lungs. The
latter is the part of the body by which the temperature of
land animals is raised above that of all others. But what
primarily requires the air drawn in by respiration is not 25
only this but the region surrounding the heart. That is
why when animals breathe the air must penetrate inwards.

Voice then is the impact of the inbreathed air against

[37] *De Resp.* 478ᵃ 28; P. A. 642ᵃ 31–ᵇ4.

the 'windpipe', and the agent that produces the impact is the soul resident in these parts of the body. Not every
30 sound, as we said, made by an animal is voice (even with the tongue we may merely make a sound which is not voice, or without the tongue as in coughing); what produces the impact must have soul in it and must be accompanied by an act of imagination, for voice is a sound with a meaning, and is not merely the result of any impact of the breath as in coughing; in voice the breath in the windpipe is used as an instrument to knock with against
421ᵃ the walls of the windpipe. This is confirmed by our inability to speak when we are breathing either out or in—we can only do so by holding our breath; we make the movements with the breath so checked. It is clear also why fish are voiceless; they have no windpipe. And they have no
5 windpipe because they do not breathe or take in air. Why they do not is a question belonging to another inquiry.[38]

9   Smell and its object are much less easy to determine than what we have hitherto discussed; the distinguishing characteristic of the object of smell is less obvious than those of sound or colour. The ground of this is that our power of smell is less discriminating and in general inferior
10 to that of many species of animals; men have a poor sense of smell and our apprehension of its proper objects is inseparably bound up with and so confused by pleasure and pain, which shows that in us the organ is inaccurate. It is probable that there is a parallel failure in the perception of colour by animals that have hard eyes: probably they discriminate differences of colour only by the presence or
15 absence of what excites fear, and that it is thus that human beings distinguish smells. It seems that there is an analogy between smell and taste, and that the species of tastes run parallel to those of smells—the only difference being that our sense of taste is more discriminating than our sense of smell, because the former is a modification of touch, which

[38] Cf. De Resp. 474ᵇ 25–9, 476ᵃ 6–15; P. A. 669ᵃ 2–5.

reaches in man the maximum of discriminative accuracy. 20
While in respect of all the other senses we fall below many
species of animals, in respect of touch we far excel all other
species in exactness of discrimination. That is why man is
the most intelligent of all animals. This is confirmed by
the fact that it is to differences in the organ of touch and to
nothing else that the differences between man and man in
respect of natural endowment are due; men whose flesh is 25
hard are ill-endowed by nature, men whose flesh is soft,
well-endowed.

As flavours may be divided into (a) sweet, (b) bitter, so
with smells. In some things the flavour and the smell
have the same quality, i. e. both are sweet or both bitter,
in others they diverge. Similarly a smell, like a flavour, may 30
be pungent, astringent, acid, or succulent. But, as we said,
because smells are much less easy to discriminate than
flavours, the names of these varieties are applied to smells
only metaphorically; for example 'sweet' is extended from **421**ᵇ
the taste to the smell of saffron or honey, 'pungent' to that
of thyme, and so on.³⁹

In the same sense in which hearing has for its object both
the audible and the inaudible, sight both the visible and 5
the invisible, smell has for its object both the odorous
and the inodorous. 'Inodorous' may be either (a) what has
no smell at all, or (b) what has a small or feeble smell. The
same ambiguity lurks in the word 'tasteless'.

Smelling, like the operation of the senses previously examined, takes place through a medium, i. e. through air or
water—I add water, because water-animals too (both 10
sanguineous and non-sanguineous) seem to smell just as
much as land-animals; at any rate some of them make directly for their food from a distance if it has any scent. That
is why the following facts constitute a problem for us. All
animals smell in the same way, but man smells only when
he inhales; if he exhales or holds his breath, he ceases to 15

---

³⁹ Because of the felt likeness between the respective smells and the
really sweet or pungent tastes of the same herbs, &c.

smell, no difference being made whether the odorous object is distant or near, or even placed inside the nose and actually on the wall of the nostril; it is a disability common to all the senses not to perceive what is in immediate contact with the organ of sense, but our failure to apprehend what is odorous without the help of inhalation is peculiar (the fact is obvious on making the experiment). Now since bloodless animals do not breathe, they must, it might be
20 argued, have some novel sense not reckoned among the usual five. Our reply must be that this is impossible, since it is scent that is perceived; a sense that apprehends what is odorous and what has a good or bad odour cannot be anything but smell. Further, they are observed to be deleteriously affected by the same strong odours as man is, e. g.
25 bitumen, sulphur, and the like. These animals must be able to smell without being able to breathe. The probable explanation is that in man the organ of smell has a certain superiority over that in all other animals just as his eyes have over those of hard-eyed animals. Man's eyes have in the eyelids a kind of shelter or envelope, which must be shifted or drawn back in order that we may see, while
30 hard-eyed animals have nothing of the kind, but at once see whatever presents itself in the transparent medium. Similarly in certain species of animals the organ of smell is like the eye of hard-eyed animals, uncurtained, while in others
422ᵃ which take in air it probably has a curtain over it, which is drawn back in inhalation, owing to the dilating of the veins or pores. That explains also why such animals cannot smell
5 under water; to smell they must first inhale, and that they cannot do under water.

Smells come from what is dry as flavours from what is moist. Consequently the organ of smell is potentially dry.

10   What can be tasted is always something that can be touched, and just for that reason it cannot be perceived *through* an interposed foreign body, for touch means the
10 absence of any intervening body. Further, the flavoured

and tasteable body is suspended in a liquid matter, and this is tangible. Hence, if we lived in water, we should perceive a sweet object introduced into the water, but the water would not be the medium through which we perceived; our perception would be due to the solution of the sweet substance in what we imbibed, just as if it were mixed with some drink. There is no parallel here to the perception of colour, which is due neither to any blending of anything with anything, nor to any efflux of anything from anything. In the case of taste, there is nothing corresponding to the medium in the case of the senses previously discussed; 15 but as the object of sight is colour, so the object of taste is flavour. But nothing excites a perception of flavour without the help of liquid; what acts upon the sense of taste must be either actually or potentially liquid like what is saline; it must be both (a) itself easily dissolved, and (b) capable of dissolving along with itself the tongue. Taste apprehends 20 both (a) what has taste and (b) what has no taste, if we mean by (b) what has only a slight or feeble flavour or what tends to destroy the sense of taste. In this it is exactly parallel to sight, which apprehends both what is visible and what is invisible (for darkness is invisible and yet is discriminated by sight; so is, in a different way, what is over-brilliant), and to hearing, which apprehends both sound and silence, of which the one is audible and the other 25 inaudible, and also over-loud sound. This corresponds in the case of hearing to over-bright light in the case of sight. As a faint sound is 'inaudible', so in a sense is a loud or violent sound. The word 'invisible' and similar privative terms cover not only (a) what is simply without some power, but also (b) what is adapted by nature to have it but has not it or has it only in a very low degree, as when we say that a species of swallow is 'footless' or that a variety of fruit is 'stoneless'. So too taste has as its object both what can be tasted and the tasteless—the latter in the sense of what has 30 little flavour or a bad flavour or one destructive of taste. The difference between what is tasteless and what is not

seems to rest ultimately on that between what is drinkable
and what is undrinkable—both are tasteable, but the latter
is bad and tends to destroy taste, while the former is the
normal stimulus of taste. What is drinkable is the common
object of both touch and taste.

422ᵇ   Since what can be tasted is liquid, the organ for its
perception cannot be either (a) actually liquid or (b) incapable of becoming liquid. Tasting means a being affected
by [40] what can be tasted as such; hence the organ of taste
must be liquefied, and so to start with must be non-liquid
5 but capable of liquefaction without loss of its distinctive nature. This is confirmed by the fact that the tongue cannot
taste either when it is too dry or when it is too moist; in the
latter case what occurs is due to a contact with the pre-
existent moisture in the tongue itself, when after a fore-
taste of some strong flavour we try to taste another flavour;
it is in this way that sick persons find everything they taste
bitter, viz. because, when they taste, their tongues are
overflowing with bitter moisture.

10   The species of flavour are, as in the case of colour, (a)
simple, i. e. the two contraries, the sweet and the bitter, (b)
secondary, viz. (i) on the side of the sweet, the succulent,
(ii) on the side of the bitter, the saline, (iii) between these
come the pungent, the harsh, the astringent, and the acid;
15 these pretty well exhaust the varieties of flavour. It follows
that what has the power of tasting is what is potentially of
that kind, and that what is tasteable is what has the power
of making it actually what it itself already is.

11   Whatever can be said of what is tangible, can be said
of touch, and vice versa; if touch is not a single sense
but a group of senses, there must be several kinds of what is
tangible. It is a problem whether touch is a single sense or
20 a group of senses. It is also a problem, what is the organ of
touch; is it or is it not the flesh (including what in certain
animals is homologous with flesh)? On the second view,

[40] sc. 'and so, as we have seen, a being assimilated to'.

flesh is 'the medium' of touch, the real organ being situated
farther inward. The problem arises because the field of each
sense is according to the accepted view determined as the
range between a single pair of contraries, white and black
for sight, acute and grave for hearing, bitter and sweet for
taste; but in the field of what is tangible we find several 25
such pairs, hot cold, dry moist, hard soft, &c. This problem
finds a partial solution, when it is recalled that in the case
of the other senses more than one pair of contraries are to
be met with, e. g. in sound not only acute and grave but
loud and soft, smooth and rough, &c.; there are similar con- 30
trasts in the field of colour. Nevertheless we are unable
clearly to detect in the case of touch what the single subject
is which underlies the contrasted qualities and corresponds
to sound in the case of hearing.

To the question whether the organ of touch lies inward
or not (i. e. whether we need look any farther than the
flesh), no indication in favour of the second answer can be
drawn from the fact that if the object comes into contact **423ª**
with the flesh it is at once perceived. For even under present
conditions if the experiment is made of making a web and
stretching it tight over the flesh, as soon as this web is
touched the sensation is reported in the same manner as
before, yet it is clear that the organ is not in this membrane.
If the membrane could be grown on to the flesh, the report
would travel still quicker. The flesh plays in touch very 5
much the same part as would be played in the other senses
by an air-envelope growing round our body; had we such an
envelope attached to us we should have supposed that it
was by a single organ that we perceived sounds, colours,
and smells, and we should have taken sight, hearing, and
smell to be a single sense. But as it is, because that
through which the different movements are transmitted is 10
not naturally attached to our bodies, the difference of the
various sense-organs is too plain to miss. But in the case of
touch the obscurity remains.

There must be such a naturally attached 'medium' as

flesh, for no living body could be constructed of air or
water; it must be something solid. Consequently it must
be composed of earth along with these, which is just what
15 flesh and its analogue in animals which have no true flesh
tend to be. Hence of necessity the medium through which
are transmitted the manifoldly contrasted tactual qualities must be a body naturally attached to the organism.
That they are manifold is clear when we consider touching
with the tongue; we apprehend at the tongue all tangible
qualities as well as flavour. Suppose all the rest of our flesh
20 was, like the tongue, sensitive to flavour, we should have
identified the sense of taste and the sense of touch; what
saves us from this identification is the fact that touch and
taste are not always found together in the same part of the
body. The following problem might be raised. Let us assume that every body has depth, i. e. has three dimensions,
and that if two bodies have a third body between them
25 they cannot be in contact with one another; let us remember that what is liquid is a body and must be or contain
water, and that if two bodies touch one another under
water, their touching surfaces cannot be dry, but must have
water between, viz. the water which wets their bounding
surfaces; from all this it follows that in water two bodies
cannot be in contact with one another. The same holds of
two bodies in air—air being to bodies in air precisely what
30 water is to bodies in water—but the facts are not so evident
to our observation, because we live in air, just as animals
423ᵇ that live in water would not notice that the things which
touch one another in water have wet surfaces. The problem,
then, is: does the perception of all objects of sense take
place in the same way, or does it not, e. g. taste and touch
requiring contact (as they are commonly thought to do),
while all other senses perceive over a distance? The distinc-
5 tion is unsound; we perceive what is hard or soft, as well
as the objects of hearing, sight, and smell, through a 'medium', only that the latter are perceived over a greater
distance than the former; that is why the facts escape our

notice. For we do perceive everything through a medium;
but in these cases the fact escapes us. Yet, to repeat what we
said before, if the medium for touch were a membrane
separating us from the object without our observing its
existence, we should be relatively to it in the same condi- 10
tion as we are now to air or water in which we are immersed;
in their case we fancy we can touch objects, nothing coming
in between us and them. But there remains this difference
between what can be touched and what can be seen or
can sound; in the latter two cases we perceive because the
medium produces a certain effect upon us, whereas in the
perception of objects of touch we are affected not by but 15
along with the medium; it is as if a man were struck through
his shield, where the shock is not first given to the shield
and passed on to the man, but the concussion of both is
simultaneous.

In general, flesh and the tongue are related to the real
organs of touch and taste, as air and water are to those of
sight, hearing, and smell. Hence in neither the one case
nor the other can there be any perception of an object 20
if it is placed immediately upon the organ, e. g. if a white
object is placed on the surface of the eye. This again shows
that what has the power of perceiving the tangible is seated
inside. Only so would there be a complete analogy with all
the other senses. In their case if you place the object on
the *organ* it is not perceived, here if you place it on the flesh
it *is* perceived; therefore flesh is not the organ but the 25
medium of touch.

What can be touched are distinctive qualities of body as
body; by such differences I mean those which characterize
the elements, viz. hot cold, dry moist, of which we have
spoken earlier in our treatise on the elements.[41] The organ
for the perception of these is that of touch—that part of the 30
body in which primarily the sense of touch resides. This is
that part which is potentially such as its object is actually:
for all sense-perception is a process of being so affected; so

[41] *De Gen. et Corr.* ii. 2, 3.

that that which makes something such as it itself actually is
424ª makes the other such because the other is already potentially such. That is why when an object of touch is equally
hot and cold or hard and soft we cannot perceive; what we
perceive must have a degree of the sensible quality lying
beyond the neutral point. This implies that the sense itself
is a 'mean' between any two opposite qualities which determine the field of that sense. It is to this that it owes
5 its power of discerning the objects in that field. What is
'in the middle' is fitted to discern; relatively to either extreme it can put itself in the place of the other. As what
is to perceive *both* white and black must, to begin with, be
actually neither but potentially either (and so with all the
other sense-organs), so the organ of touch must be neither
hot nor cold.

Further, as in a sense sight had [42] for its object both what
10 was visible and what was invisible (and there was a parallel
truth about all the other senses discussed),[43] so touch has
for its object both what is tangible and what is intangible.
Here by 'intangible' is meant (a) what like air possesses
some quality of tangible things in a very slight degree and
(b) what possesses it in an excessive degree, as destructive
things do.

We have now given an outline account of each of the
15 several senses.

12 The following results applying to any and every sense
may now be formulated.

(A) By a 'sense' is meant what has the power of receiving
into itself the sensible forms of things without the matter.
This must be conceived of as taking place in the way in
20 which a piece of wax takes on the impress of a signet-ring
without the iron or gold; we say that what produces the
impression is a signet of bronze or gold, but its particular
metallic constitution makes no difference: in a similar way

[42] 422ª 20 ff.
[43] 421ᵇ 3–6, 422ª 29.

the sense is affected by what is coloured or flavoured or sounding, but it is indifferent what in each case the *substance* is; what alone matters is what *quality* it has, i. e. in what *ratio* its constituents are combined.

(B) By 'an organ of sense' is meant that in which ultimately such a power is seated.

The sense and its organ are the same in fact, but their 25 essence is not the same. What perceives is, of course, a spatial magnitude, but we must not admit that either the having the power to perceive or the sense itself is a magnitude; what they are is a certain ratio or power *in* a magnitude. This enables us to explain why objects of sense which possess one of two opposite sensible qualities in a degree largely in excess of the other opposite destroy the organs of sense; if the movement set up by an object is too strong 30 for the organ, the equipoise of contrary qualities in the organ, which just *is* its sensory power, is disturbed; it is precisely as concord and tone are destroyed by too violently twanging the strings of a lyre. This explains also why plants cannot perceive, in spite of their having a portion of soul in them and obviously being affected by tangible objects themselves; for undoubtedly their temperature can be lowered or raised. The explanation is that they have no mean **424**ᵇ of contrary qualities, and so no principle in them capable of taking on the forms of sensible objects without their matter; in the case of plants the affection is an affection by form-and-matter together. The problem might be raised: Can what cannot smell be said to be affected by smells or what cannot see by colours, and so on? It might be said that 5 a smell is just what can be smelt, and if it produces any effect it can only be so as to make something smell it, and it might be argued that what cannot smell cannot be affected by smells and further that what can smell can be affected by it only in so far as it has in it the power to smell (similarly with the proper objects of all the other senses). Indeed that this *is* so is made quite evident as follows. Light or darkness, sounds and smells leave *bodies* quite un- 10

affected; what does affect bodies is not these but the bodies
which are their vehicles, e. g. what splits the trunk of a tree
is not the sound of the thunder but the air which accompanies thunder. Yes, but, it may be objected, bodies are
affected by what is tangible and by flavours. If not, by
what are things that are without soul affected, i. e. altered
in quality? Must we not, then, admit that the objects of the
other senses also may affect them? Is not the true account
this, that all bodies are capable of being affected by smells
15 and sounds, but that some on being acted upon, having no
boundaries of their own, disintegrate, as in the instance of
air, which does become odorous, showing that some effect
is produced on it by what is odorous? But smelling is more
than such an affection by what is odorous—what more?
Is not the answer that, while the air owing to the momen-
tary duration of the action upon it of what is odorous does
itself become perceptible to the sense of smell, smelling is
an observing of the result produced?

BOOK III

1   That there is no sixth sense in addition to the five
20   enumerated—sight, hearing, smell, taste, touch—may
be established by the following considerations·

If we have actually sensation of everything of which
touch can give us sensation (for all the qualities of the tan-
25 gible qua tangible are perceived by us through touch); and
if absence of a sense necessarily involves absence of a sense-
organ; and if (1) all objects that we perceive by immediate
contact with them are perceptible by touch, which sense we
actually possess, and (2) all objects that we perceive
through media, i. e. without immediate contact, are percep-
30 tible by or through the simple elements, e. g. air and water
(and this is so arranged that (a) if more than one kind of
sensible object is perceivable through a single medium, the
possessor of a sense-organ homogeneous with that medium
has the power of perceiving both kinds of objects; for ex-

ample, if the sense-organ is made of air, and air is a medium
both for sound and for colour; and that (b) if more than
one medium can transmit the same kind of sensible objects, as e. g. water as well as air can transmit colour, both **425ᵃ**
being transparent, then the possessor of either alone will be
able to perceive the kind of objects transmissible through
both); and if of the simple elements two only, air and
water, go to form sense-organs (for the pupil is made of
water, the organ of hearing is made of air, and the organ of
smell of one or other of these two, while fire is found
either in none or in all—warmth being an essential condition of all sensibility—and earth either in none or, if 5
anywhere, specially mingled with the components of the
organ of touch; wherefore it would remain that there can
be no sense-organ formed of anything except water and
air); and if these sense-organs are actually found in certain
animals;—then all the possible senses are possessed by those
animals that are not imperfect or mutilated (for even the 10
mole is observed to have eyes beneath its skin); so that,
if there is no fifth element and no property other than
those which belong to the four elements of our world, no
sense can be wanting to such animals.

Further, there cannot be a special sense-organ for the
common sensibles either, i. e. the objects which we per- 15
ceive incidentally through this or that special sense, e. g.
movement, rest, figure, magnitude, number, unity; for all
these we perceive by movement, e. g. magnitude by movement, and therefore also figure (for figure is a species of
magnitude), what is at rest by the absence of movement:
number is perceived by the negation of continuity, and by
the special sensibles; for each sense perceives one class of
sensible objects. So that it is clearly impossible that there 20
should be a special sense for any one of the common sensibles, e. g. movement; for, if that were so, our perception
of it would be exactly parallel to our present perception
of what is sweet by vision. *That* is so because we have a
sense for each of the two qualities, in virtue of which

when they happen to meet in one sensible object we are
25 aware of both contemporaneously. If it were not like this
our perception of the common qualities would always be
incidental, i. e. as is the perception of Cleon's son, where
we perceive him not as Cleon's son but as white, and the
white thing which we really perceive happens to be Cleon's
son.

But in the case of the common sensibles there is already
in us a general sensibility which enables us to perceive them
directly; there is therefore no special sense required for
their perception: if there were, our perception of them
would have been exactly like what has been above described.

30   The senses perceive each other's special objects incidentally; not because the percipient sense is this or that
special sense, but because all form a unity: this incidental
perception takes place whenever sense is directed at one
425ᵇ and the same moment to two disparate qualities in one
and the same object, e. g. to the bitterness and the yellow-
ness of bile; the assertion of the identity of both cannot
be the act of either of the senses; hence the illusion of
sense, e. g. the belief that if a thing is yellow it is bile.

It might be asked why we have more senses than one. Is
5 it to prevent a failure to apprehend the common sensibles,
e. g. movement, magnitude, and number, which go along
with the special sensibles? Had we no sense but sight, and
that sense no object but white, they would have tended
to escape our notice and everything would have merged for
us into an indistinguishable identity because of the concomitance of colour and magnitude. As it is, the fact that
the common sensibles are given in the objects of more than
one sense reveals their distinction from each and all of
10 the special sensibles.

2   Since it is through sense that we are aware that we
are seeing or hearing, it must be either by sight that we
are aware of seeing, or by some sense other than sight. But

the sense that gives us this new sensation must perceive both sight and its object, viz. colour: so that either (1) there will be two senses both percipient of the same sensible object, or (2) the sense must be percipient of itself. Further, even if the sense which perceives sight were dif- 15 ferent from sight, we must either fall into an infinite regress, or we must somewhere assume a sense which is aware of itself. If so, we ought to do this in the first case.

This presents a difficulty: if to perceive by sight is just to see, and what is seen is colour (or the coloured), then if we are to see that which sees, that which sees originally must be coloured. It is clear therefore that 'to perceive by sight' has more than one meaning; for even when we are 20 not *seeing*, it is by sight that we discriminate darkness from light, though not in the same way as we distinguish one colour from another. Further, in a sense even that which sees *is* coloured; for in each case the sense-organ is capable of receiving the sensible object without its matter. That is why even when the sensible objects are gone the sensings and imaginings continue to exist in the sense-organs.   25

The activity of the sensible object and that of the percipient sense is one and the same activity, and yet the distinction between their being remains. Take as illustration actual sound and actual hearing: a man may have hearing and yet not be hearing, and that which has a sound is not always sounding. But when that which can hear is actively hearing and that which can sound is sounding, then the 30 actual hearing and the actual sound are merged in one (these one might call respectively hearkening and sound- **426ᵃ** ing).

If it is true that the movement, both the acting and the being acted upon, is to be found in that which is acted upon,[1] both the sound and the hearing so far as it is actual must be found in that which has the faculty of hearing; for it is in the passive factor that the actuality of the active or motive factor is realized; that is why that which causes 5

[1] Cf. *Phys.* iii. 3.

movement may be at rest. Now the actuality of that which
can sound is just sound or sounding, and the actuality of
that which can hear is hearing or hearkening; 'sound' and
'hearing' are both ambiguous. The same account applies to
10 the other senses and their objects. For as the-acting-and-
being-acted-upon is to be found in the passive, not in the
active factor, so also the actuality of the sensible object and
that of the sensitive subject are both realized in the latter.
But while in some cases each aspect of the total actuality
has a distinct name, e. g. sounding and hearkening, in some
one or other is nameless, e. g. the actuality of sight is called
seeing, but the actuality of colour has no name: the actual-
15 ity of the faculty of taste is called tasting, but the actuality of flavour has no name. Since the actualities of the
sensible object and of the sensitive faculty are one actuality
in spite of the difference between their modes of being,
actual hearing and actual sounding appear and disappear
from existence at one and the same moment, and so actual
20 savour and actual tasting, &c., while as potentialities one of
them may exist without the other. The earlier students of
nature were mistaken in their view that without sight there
was no white or black, without taste no savour. This statement of theirs is partly true, partly false: 'sense' and 'the
sensible object' are ambiguous terms, i. e. may denote
25 either potentialities or actualities: the statement is true of
the latter, false of the former. This ambiguity they wholly
failed to notice.

   If voice always implies a concord, and if the voice and
the hearing of it are in one sense one and the same, and if
concord always implies a ratio, hearing as well as what is
30 heard must be a ratio. That is why the excess of either the
sharp or the flat destroys the hearing. (So also in the case of
426ᵇ savours excess destroys the sense of taste, and in the case
of colours excessive brightness or darkness destroys the
sight, and in the case of smell excess of strength whether
in the direction of sweetness or bitterness is destructive.)
This shows that the sense is a ratio.

That is also why the objects of sense are (1) pleasant when the sensible extremes such as acid or sweet or salt being pure and unmixed are brought into the proper ratio; [2] then they are pleasant: and in general what is blended is more pleasant than the sharp or the flat alone; or, to touch, that which is capable of being either warmed or chilled: the sense and the ratio are identical: while (2) in excess the sensible extremes are painful or destructive.

Each sense then is relative to its particular group of sensible qualities: it is found in a sense-organ as such [3] and discriminates the differences which exist within that group; e. g. sight discriminates white and black, taste sweet and bitter, and so in all cases. Since we also discriminate white from sweet, and indeed each sensible quality from every other, with what do we perceive that they are different? It must be by sense; for what is before us is sensible objects. (Hence it is also obvious that the flesh cannot be the ultimate sense-organ: if it were, the discriminating power could not do its work without immediate contact with the object.)

Therefore (1) discrimination between white and sweet cannot be effected by two agencies which remain separate; both the qualities discriminated must be present to something that is one and single. On any other supposition even if I perceived sweet and you perceived white, the difference between them would be apparent. What says that two things are different must be one; for sweet is different from white. Therefore what asserts this difference must be self-identical, and as what asserts, so also what thinks or perceives. That it is not possible by means of two agencies which remain separate to discriminate two objects which are separate is therefore obvious; and that (2) it is not possible to do this in separate moments of time may be seen if we look at it as follows. For as what asserts the dif-

[2] i. e. that which is involved in the structure of the sense-organ.

[3] The qualification appears to mean that the sense-organ may in other respects have other qualities. Thus the tongue can touch as well as taste.

ference between the good and the bad is one and the same,
25 so also the time at which it asserts the one to be different
and the other to be different is not accidental to the assertion (as it is for instance when I now assert a difference
but do not assert that there is now a difference); it asserts
thus—both now and that the objects are different now;
the objects therefore must be present at one and the same
moment. Both the discriminating power and the time of its
exercise must be one and undivided.

But, it may be objected, it is impossible that what is self-
identical should be moved at one and the same time with
30 contrary movements in so far as it is undivided, and in an
undivided moment of time. For if what is sweet be the quality perceived, it moves the sense or thought in this de-
427ᵃ terminate way, while what is bitter moves it in a contrary way, and what is white in a different way. Is it the
case then that what discriminates, though both numerically
one and indivisible, is at the same time divided in its being? In one sense, it is what is divided that perceives two
separate objects at once, but in another sense it does so
qua undivided; for it is divisible in its being, but spatially
and numerically undivided. ·

5   But is not this impossible? For while it is true that what
is self-identical and undivided may be both contraries at
once *potentially*, it cannot be self-identical in its being—it
must lose its unity by being put into activity. It is not
possible to be at once white and black, and therefore it
must also be impossible for a thing to be affected at one
and the same moment by the forms of both, assuming it to
be the case that sensation and thinking are properly so described.[4]

10   The answer is that just as what is called a 'point' is, as
being at once one and two, properly said to be divisible, so
here, that which discriminates is qua undivided one, and
active in a single moment of time, while so far forth as it is
divisible it twice over uses the same dot at one and the

⁴ i. e. as the being affected by the forms of sensible qualities.

same time. So far forth then as it takes the limit as two, it discriminates two separate objects with what in a sense is divided: while so far as it takes it as one, it does so with what is one and occupies in its activity a single moment of time.

About the principle in virtue of which we say that animals are percipient, let this discussion suffice.   15

3   There are two distinctive peculiarities by reference to which we characterize the soul—(1) local movement and (2) thinking, discriminating, and perceiving. Thinking, both speculative and practical, is regarded as akin to a form of perceiving; for in the one as well as the other the 20 soul discriminates and is cognizant of something which *is*. Indeed the ancients go so far as to identify thinking and perceiving; e. g. Empedocles says 'For 'tis in respect of what is present that man's wit is increased', and again 'whence it befalls them from time to time to think diverse thoughts', and Homer's phrase [5] 'For suchlike is man's 25 mind' means the same. They all look upon thinking as a bodily process like perceiving, and hold that like is *known* as well as *perceived* by like, as I explained at the beginning of our discussion.[6] Yet they ought at the same time to have accounted for error also; for it is more intimately 427ᵇ connected with animal existence and the soul continues longer in the state of error than in that of truth. They cannot escape the dilemma: either (1) whatever seems is true (and there are some who accept this) or (2) error is contact with the unlike; for that is the opposite of the knowing of like by like.

But it is a received principle that error as well as knowl- 5 edge in respect to contraries is one and the same.

That perceiving and practical thinking are not identical is therefore obvious; for the former is universal in the animal world, the latter is found in only a small division of

[5] *Od.* xviii. 136.
[6] 404ᵇ 8–18.

it. Further, speculative thinking is also distinct from perceiving—I mean that in which we find rightness and
10 wrongness—rightness in prudence, knowledge, true opinion, wrongness in their opposites; for perception of the
special objects of sense is always free from error, and is
found in all animals, while it is possible to think falsely as
well as truly, and thought is found only where there is
discourse of reason as well as sensibility. For imagination is
15 different from either perceiving or discursive thinking,
though it is not found without sensation, or judgement
without it. That this activity is not the same kind of
thinking as judgement is obvious. For imagining lies within
our own power whenever we wish (e. g. we can call up a
picture, as in the practice of mnemonics by the use of
20 mental images), but in forming opinions we are not free:
we cannot escape the alternative of falsehood or truth.
Further, when we think something to be fearful or threat-
ening, emotion is immediately produced, and so too with
what is encouraging; but when we merely imagine we remain as unaffected as persons who are looking at a painting
of some dreadful or encouraging scene. Again within the
field of judgement itself we find varieties—knowledge,
opinion, prudence, and their opposites; of the differences
between these I must speak elsewhere.[7]

Thinking is different from perceiving and is held to be
in part imagination, in part judgement: we must therefore
first mark off the sphere of imagination and then speak of
428ᵃ judgment. If then imagination is that in virtue of which an
image arises for us, excluding metaphorical uses of the term,
is it a single faculty or disposition relative to images, in
virtue of which we discriminate and are either in error or
not? The faculties in virtue of which we do this are sense,
opinion, science, intelligence.

That imagination is not sense is clear from the following
5 considerations: (1) Sense is either a faculty or an activity,
e. g. sight or seeing: imagination takes place in the ab-

[7] The reference is perhaps to E. N. 1139ᵇ 15 ff.

sence of both, as e. g. in dreams. (2) Again, sense is always present, imagination not. If actual imagination and actual sensation were the same, imagination would be found in all the brutes: this is held not to be the case; e. g. it is not found in ants or bees or grubs. (3) Again, sensations are always true, imaginations are for the most part false. (4) Once more, even in ordinary speech, we do not, when sense functions precisely with regard to its object, say that we imagine it to be a man, but rather when there is some failure of accuracy in its exercise. And (5), as we were saying before, visions appear to us even when our eyes are shut. Neither is imagination any of the things that are never in error: e. g. knowledge or intelligence; for imagination may be false.

It remains therefore to see if it is opinion, for opinion may be either true or false.

But opinion involves belief (for without belief in what we opine we cannot have an opinion), and in the brutes though we often find imagination we never find belief. Further, every opinion is accompanied by belief, belief by conviction, and conviction by discourse of reason: while there are some of the brutes in which we find imagination, without discourse of reason. It is clear then that imagination cannot, again, be (1) opinion *plus* sensation, or (2) opinion mediated by sensation, or (3) a blend of opinion and sensation;[8] this is impossible both for these reasons and because the content of the supposed opinion cannot be different from that of the sensation (I mean that imagination must be the blending of the perception of white with the opinion that it is white: it could scarcely be a blend of the opinion that it is good with the perception that it is white): to imagine is therefore (on this view) identical **428ᵛ** with the thinking of exactly the same as what one in the strictest sense perceives. But what we imagine is sometimes false though our contemporaneous judgement about it is true; e. g. we imagine the sun to be a foot in diameter

[8] For these three views Cf. Pl. *Tim.* 52 A, *Soph.* A, B, *Phil.* 39 B.

though we are convinced that it is larger than the in-
habited part of the earth, and the following dilemma presents itself. Either (a) while the fact has not changed and
5 the observer has neither forgotten nor lost belief in the
true opinion which he had, that opinion has disappeared,
or (b) if he retains it then his opinion is at once true and
false. A true opinion, however, becomes false only when
the fact alters without being noticed.

Imagination is therefore neither any one of the states
enumerated, nor compounded out of them.

10   But since when one thing has been set in motion another
thing may be moved by it, and imagination is held to be a
movement and to be impossible without sensation, i. e.
to occur in beings that are percipient and to have for its
content what can be perceived, and since movement may
be produced by actual sensation and that movement is
necessarily similar in character to the sensation itself, this
15 movement must be (1) necessarily (a) incapable of existing apart from sensation, (b) incapable of existing except
when we perceive, (2) such that in virtue of its possession
that in which it is found may present various phenomena
both active and passive, and (3) such that it may be either
true or false.

The reason of the last characteristic is as follows. Perception (1) of the special objects of sense is never in error
or admits the least possible amount of falsehood. (2)
That of the concomitance of the objects concomitant with
20 the sensible qualities comes next: in this case certainly we
may be deceived; for while the perception that there is
white before us cannot be false, the perception that what
is white is this or that may be false. (3) Third comes the
perception of the universal attributes which accompany
the concomitant objects to which the special sensibles attach (I mean e. g. of movement and magnitude); it is in
respect of these that the greatest amount of sense-illusion
is possible.

The motion which is due to the activity of sense in these

three modes of its exercise will differ from the activity of 25
sense; (1) the first kind of derived motion is free from error
while the sensation is present; (2) and (3) the others may
be erroneous whether it is present or absent, especially
when the object of perception is far off. If then imagina- 30
tion presents no other features than those enumerated
and is what we have described, then imagination must be a
movement resulting from an actual exercise of a power of **429ᵃ**
sense.

As sight is the most highly developed sense, the name
phantasia (imagination) has been formed from *phaos*
(light) because it is not possible to see without light.

And because imaginations remain in the organs of sense
and resemble sensations, animals in their actions are largely
guided by them, some (i. e. the brutes) because of the non- 5
existence in them of mind, others (i. e. men) because of
the temporary eclipse in them of mind by feeling or
disease or sleep.

About imagination, what it is and why it exists, let so
much suffice.

4   Turning now to the part of the soul with which the
soul knows and thinks (whether this is separable 10
from the others in definition only, or spatially as well) we
have to inquire (1) what differentiates this part, and (2)
how thinking can take place.

If thinking is like perceiving, it must be either a process
in which the soul is acted upon by what is capable of being
thought, or a process different from but analogous to that.
The thinking part of the soul must therefore be, while impassible, capable of receiving the form of an object; that is, 15
must be potentially identical in character with its object
without being the object. Mind must be related to what is
thinkable, as sense is to what is sensible.

Therefore, since everything is a possible object of
thought, mind in order, as Anaxagoras says, to dominate,
that is, to know, must be pure from all admixture; for the 20

co-presence of what is alien to its nature is a hindrance and a block: it follows that it too, like the sensitive part, can have no nature of its own, other than that of having a certain capacity. Thus that in the soul which is called mind (by mind I mean that whereby the soul thinks and judges) is, before it thinks, not actually any real thing. For this
25 reason it cannot reasonably be regarded as blended with the body: if so, it would acquire some quality, e. g. warmth or cold, or even have an organ like the sensitive faculty: as it is, it has none. It was a good idea to call the soul 'the place of forms', though (1) this description holds only of the intellective soul, and (2) even this is the forms only potentially, not actually.

Observation of the sense-organs and their employment
30 reveals a distinction between the impassibility of the sensitive and that of the intellective faculty. After strong
429ᵇ stimulation of a sense we are less able to exercise it than before, as e. g. in the case of a loud sound we cannot hear easily immediately after, or in the case of a bright colour or a powerful odour we cannot see or smell, but in the case of mind, thought about an object that is highly intelligible renders it more and not less able afterwards to think objects that are less intelligible: the reason is that while the faculty of sensation is dependent upon the body, mind is separable from it.

5   Once the mind has become each set of its possible objects, as a man of science has, when this phrase is used of one who is actually a man of science (this happens when he is now able to exercise the power on his own initiative), its condition is still one of potentiality, but in a different sense from the potentiality which preceded the acquisition of knowledge by learning or discovery: the mind too is then able to think itself.

10   Since we can distinguish between a spatial magnitude and what it is to be such, and between water and what it is to be water, and so in many other cases (though not in all; for in certain cases the thing and its form are identical),

flesh and what it is to be flesh are discriminated either by
different faculties, or by the same faculty in two different
states: for flesh necessarily involves matter and is like
what is snub-nosed, a *this* in a *this*.[9] Now it is by means of
the sensitive faculty that we discriminate the hot and the
cold, i. e. the factors which combined in a certain ratio 15
constitute flesh: the essential character of flesh is apprehended by something different either wholly separate
from the sensitive faculty or related to it as a bent line to
the same line when it has been straightened out.

Again in the case of abstract objects what is straight is
analogous to what is snub-nosed; for it necessarily implies a
continuum as its matter: its constitutive essence is different, if we may distinguish between straightness and what is
straight: let us take it to be two-ness. It must be appre- 20
hended, therefore, by a different power or by the same
power in a different state. To sum up, in so far as the realities it knows are capable of being separated from their
matter, so it is also with the powers of mind.

The problem might be suggested: if thinking is a passive
affection, then if mind is simple and impassible and has
nothing in common with anything else, as Anaxagoras says,
how can it come to think at all? For interaction between
two factors is held to require a precedent community of
nature between the factors. Again it might be asked, is
mind a possible object of thought to itself? For if mind is
thinkable *per se* and what is thinkable is in kind one and
the same, then either (a) mind will belong to everything, or
(b) mind will contain some element common to it with all
other realities which makes them all thinkable.

(1) Have not we already disposed of the difficulty about
interaction involving a common element, when we said [10]
that mind is in a sense potentially whatever is thinkable, 30
though actually it is nothing until it has thought? What it
thinks must be in it just as characters may be said to be on a

[9] i. e. a particular form in a particular matter.
[10] a15–24.

430ª writing-tablet on which as yet nothing actually stands written: this is exactly what happens with mind.

(2) Mind is itself thinkable in exactly the same way as its objects are. For (a) in the case of objects which involve no matter, what thinks and what is thought are identical; for speculative knowledge and its object are identical.
5 (Why mind is not always thinking we must consider later.) [11] (b) In the case of those which contain matter each of the objects of thought is only potentially present. It follows that while *they* will not have mind in them (for mind is a potentiality of them only in so far as they are capable of being disengaged from matter) mind may yet be thinkable.

5   Since in every class of things, as in nature as a whole,
10   we find two factors involved, (1) a matter which is potentially all the particulars included in the class, (2) a cause which is productive in the sense that it makes them all (the latter standing to the former, as e. g. an art to its material), these distinct elements must likewise be found within the soul.

And in fact mind as we have described it [12] is what it is
15 by virtue of becoming all things, while there is another which is what it is by virtue of making all things: this is a sort of positive state like light; for in a sense light makes potential colours into actual colours.

Mind in this sense of it is separable, impassible, unmixed, since it is in its essential nature activity (for always the active is superior to the passive factor, the originating force to the matter which it forms).

20   Actual knowledge is identical with its object: in the individual, potential knowledge is in time prior to actual knowledge, but in the universe as a whole it is not prior even in time. Mind is not at one time knowing and at another not. When mind is set free from its present con-

[11] Ch. 5.
[12] In ch. 4.

ditions it appears as just what it is and nothing more: this alone is immortal and eternal (we do not, however, remember its former activity because, while mind in this sense is impassible, mind as passive is destructible), and 25 without it nothing thinks.

6 The thinking then of the simple objects of thought is found in those cases where falsehood is impossible: where the alternative of true or false applies, there we always find a putting together of objects of thought in a quasi-unity. As Empedocles said that 'where heads of many a creature sprouted without necks' they afterwards by 30 Love's power were combined, so here too objects of thought which were given separate are combined, e. g. 'incommensurate' and 'diagonal': if the combination be of objects past or future the combination of thought includes in its content the date. For falsehood always involves a synthesis; for 430ᵇ even if you assert that what is white is not white you have included not-white in a synthesis. It is possible also to call all these cases division as well as combination. However that may be, there is not only the true or false assertion that Cleon is white but also the true or false assertion that he was or will be white. In each and every case that which 5 unifies is mind

Since the word 'simple' has two senses, i. e. may mean either (a) 'not capable of being divided' or (b) 'not actually divided', there is nothing to prevent mind from knowing what is undivided, e. g. when it apprehends a length (which is actually undivided) and that in an undivided time; for the time is divided or undivided in the same manner as the line. It is not possible, then, to tell 10 what part of the line it was apprehending in each half of the time: the object has no actual parts until it has been divided: if in thought you think each half separately, then by the same act you divide the time also, the half-lines becoming as it were new wholes of length. But if you think it as a whole consisting of these two possible parts, then also

you think it in a time which corresponds to both parts together. (But what is not quantitatively but qualitatively
15 simple is thought in a simple time and by a simple act of the soul.)

But that which mind thinks and the time in which it thinks are in this case divisible only incidentally and not as such. For in them too there is something indivisible (though, it may be, not isolable) which gives unity to the time and the whole of length; and this is found equally in every continuum whether temporal or spatial.

Points and similar instances of things that divide, them-
20 selves being indivisible, are realized in consciousness in the same manner as privations.

A similar account may be given of all other cases, e. g. how evil or black is cognized; they are cognized, in a sense, by means of their contraries. That which cognizes must have an element of potentiality in its being, and one of the contraries must be in it.[13] But if there is anything
25 that has no contrary, then it knows itself and is actually and possesses independent existence.

Assertion is the saying of something concerning something, e. g. affirmation, and is in every case either true or false: this is not always the case with mind: the thinking of the definition in the sense of the constitutive essence is never in error nor is it the assertion of something concerning something, but, just as while the seeing of the special object of sight can never be in error, the belief that the white object seen is a man may be mistaken, so too in the
30 case of objects which are without matter.

7   Actual knowledge is identical with its object: potential
431ᵃ   knowledge in the individual is in time prior to actual knowledge but in the universe it has no priority even in time; for all things that come into being arise from what

[13] i. e. it must be characterized actually by one and potentially by the other of the contraries.

actually is. In the case of sense clearly the sensitive faculty already was potentially what the object makes it to be actu- 5 ally; the faculty is not affected or altered. This must therefore be a different kind from movement; for movement is, as we saw,[14] an activity of what is imperfect, activity in the unqualified sense, i. e. that of what has been perfected, is different from movement.

To perceive then is like bare asserting or knowing; but when the object is pleasant or painful, the soul makes a quasi-affirmation or negation, and pursues or avoids the object. To feel pleasure or pain is to act with the sensitive 10 mean towards what is good or bad as such. Both avoidance and appetite when actual are identical with this: the faculty of appetite and avoidance are not different, either from one another or from the faculty of sense-perception; but their being is different.

To the thinking soul images serve as if they were contents of perception (and when it asserts or denies them to be 15 good or bad it avoids or pursues them). That is why the soul never thinks without an image. The process is like that in which the air modifies the pupil in this or that way and the pupil transmits the modification to some third thing (and similarly in hearing), while the ultimate point of arrival is one, a single mean, with different manners of being.

With what part of itself the soul discriminates sweet 20 from hot [15] I have explained before [16] and must now describe again as follows: That with which it does so is a sort of unity, but in the way just mentioned,[17] i. e. as a connecting term. And the two faculties it connects,[18] being one by analogy and numerically, are each to each as the qualities

---

[14] Cf. 417[b] 2–16.
[15] i. e. the sweetness and the heat in a sweet-hot object.
[16] 426[b] 12–427[a] 14.
[17] i. e. as one thing with two aspects; cf. l. 19.
[18] i. e. the faculty by which we discern sweet and that by which we discern hot.

discerned are to one another (for what difference does it
make whether we raise the problem of discrimination be-
25 tween disparates or between contraries, e. g. white and
black?). Let then C be to D as A is to B: [19] it follows *alter-*
nando that C:A::D:B. If then C and D belong to one subject, the case will be the same with them as with A and B;
431ᵇ A and B form a single identity with different modes of being; so too will the former pair. The same reasoning holds if
A be sweet and B white.

The faculty of thinking then thinks the forms in the
images, and as in the former case [20] what is to be pursued or
avoided is marked out for it, so where there is no sensation
5 and it is engaged upon the images it is moved to pursuit
or avoidance. E. g. perceiving by sense that the beacon is
fire, it recognizes in virtue of the general faculty of sense
that it signifies an enemy, because it sees it moving; but
sometimes by means of the images or thoughts which are
within the soul, just as if it were seeing, it calculates and
deliberates what is to come by reference to what is present;
and when it makes a pronouncement, as in the case of
sensation it pronounces the object to be pleasant or painful,
in this case it avoids or pursues; and so generally in cases of
action.

That too which involves no action, i. e. that which is true
10 or false, is in the same province with what is good or bad:
yet they differ in this, that the one set imply and the other
do not a reference to a particular person.

The so-called abstract objects the mind thinks just as, if
one had thought of the snub-nosed not as snub-nosed but
as hollow, one would have thought of an actuality without
15 the flesh in which it is embodied: it is thus that the mind
when it is thinking the objects of Mathematics thinks as
separate, elements which do not exist separate. In every
case the mind which is actively thinking is the objects

[19] i. e. let the faculty that discerns sweet be to that which discerns
not as sweet is to hot.

[20] i. e. that of sense-data.

which it thinks. Whether it is possible for it while not exist-ing separate from spatial conditions to think anything that is separate, or not, we must consider later.[21]

8   Let us now summarize our results about soul, and re-peat that the soul is in a way all existing things; for existing things are either sensible or thinkable, and knowl-edge is in a way what is knowable, and sensation is in a way what is sensible: in *what* way we must inquire.

Knowledge and sensation are divided to correspond with the realities, potential knowledge and sensation answering to potentialities, actual knowledge and sensation to actuali-ties. Within the soul the faculties of knowledge and sensa-tion are *potentially* these objects, the one what is knowable, the other what is sensible. They must be either the things themselves or their forms. The former alternative is of course impossible: it is not the stone which is present in the soul but its form.

It follows that the soul is analogous to the hand; for as the hand is a tool of tools,[22] so the mind is the form of **432ᵉ** forms and sense the form of sensible things.

Since according to common agreement there is nothing outside and separate in existence from sensible spatial mag-nitudes, the objects of thought are in the sensible forms, viz. both the abstract objects and all the states and affec-tions of sensible things. Hence (1) no one can learn or understand anything in the absence of sense, and (2) when the mind is actively aware of anything it is necessarily aware of it along with an image; for images are like sensu-ous contents except in that they contain no matter.

Imagination is different from assertion and denial; for what is true or false involves a synthesis of concepts. In what will the primary concepts differ from images? Must we not say that neither these nor even our other concepts are images, though they necessarily involve them?

---

[21] This promise does not seem to have been fulfilled.
[22] i. e. a tool for using tools.

15 **9**   The soul of animals is characterized by two faculties, (a) the faculty of discrimination which is the work of thought and sense, and (b) the faculty of originating local movement. Sense and mind we have now sufficiently examined. Let us next consider what it is in the soul which 20 originates movement. Is it a single part of the soul separate either spatially or in definition? Or is it the soul as a whole? If it is a part, is that part different from those usually distinguished or already mentioned by us, or is it one of them? The problem at once presents itself, in what sense we are to speak of parts of the soul, or how many we 25 should distinguish. For in a sense there is an infinity of parts: it is not enough to distinguish, with some thinkers,[23] the calculative, the passionate, and the desiderative, or with others [24] the rational and the irrational; for if we take the dividing lines followed by these thinkers we shall find parts far more distinctly separated from one another than these, namely those we have just mentioned: (1) the nu-30 tritive, which belongs both to plants and to all animals, and (2) the sensitive, which cannot easily be classed as either irrational or rational; further (3) the imaginative, which is, 432ᵇ in its being, different from all, while it is very hard to say with which of the others it is the same or not the same, supposing we determine to posit *separate* parts in the soul; and lastly (4) the appetitive, which would seem to be distinct both in definition and in power from all hitherto enumerated.

5   It is absurd to break up the last-mentioned faculty: as these thinkers do, for wish is found in the calculative part and desire and passion in the irrational; [25] and if the soul is tripartite appetite will be found in all three parts. Turning our attention to the present object of discussion, let us ask what that is which originates local movement of the animal.

The movement of growth and decay, being found in all

---

[23] Pl. *Rep.* 435–41.
[24] A popular view, Cf. *E. N.* 1102ᵃ 26–8.
[25] All three being forms of appetite.

living things, must be attributed to the faculty of repro- 10
duction and nutrition, which is common to all: inspiration
and expiration, sleep and waking, we must consider later: [26]
these too present much difficulty: at present we must consider local movement, asking what it is that originates forward movement in the animal.

That it is not the nutritive faculty is obvious; for this
kind of movement is always for an end and is accompanied 15
either by imagination or by appetite; for no animal moves
except by compulsion unless it has an impulse towards or
away from an object. Further, if it were the nutritive
faculty, even plants would have been capable of originating
such movement and would have possessed the organs
necessary to carry it out. Similarly it cannot be the
sensitive faculty either; for there are many animals which
have sensibility but remain fast and immovable throughout
their lives.   20

If then Nature never makes anything without a purpose
and never leaves out what is necessary (except in the case
of mutilated or imperfect growths; and that here we have
neither mutilation nor imperfection may be argued from
the facts that such animals (*a*) can reproduce their species
and (*b*) rise to completeness of nature and decay to an
end), it follows that, had they been capable of originating 25
forward movement, they would have possessed the organs
necessary for that purpose. Further, neither can the calculative faculty or what is called 'mind' be the cause of such
movement; for mind as speculative never thinks what is
practicable, it never says anything about an object to be
avoided or pursued, while this movement is always in something which is avoiding or pursuing an object. No, not even
when it is aware of such an object does it at once enjoin
pursuit or avoidance of it; e. g. the mind often thinks of 30
something terrifying or pleasant without enjoying the emotion of fear. It is the heart that is moved (or in the case of a
pleasant object some other part). Further, even when the 433

[26] Cf. *De Respiratione, De Somno*.

mind does command and thought bids us pursue or avoid
something, sometimes no movement is produced; we act
in accordance with desire, as in the case of moral weakness.
And, generally, we observe that the possessor of medical
knowledge is not necessarily healing, which shows that
something else is required to produce action in accordance
5 with knowledge; the knowledge alone is not the cause.
Lastly, appetite too is incompetent to account fully for
movement; for those who successfully resist temptation
have appetite and desire and yet follow mind and refuse to
enact that for which they have appetite.

10 These two at all events appear to be sources of movement: appetite and mind (if one may venture to re-
10 gard imagination as a kind of thinking; for many men
follow their imaginations contrary to knowledge, and in all
animals other than man there is no thinking or calculation
but only imagination).

Both of these then are capable of originating local movement, mind and appetite: (1) mind, that is, which calcu-
15 lates means to an end, i. e. mind practical (it differs from
mind speculative in the character of its end); while (2)
appetite is in every form of it relative to an end: for that
which is the object of appetite is the stimulant of mind
practical; and that which is last in the process of thinking
is the beginning of the action. It follows that there is a
justification for regarding these two as the sources of movement, i. e. appetite and practical thought; for the object of
appetite starts a movement and as a result of that thought
20 gives rise to movement, the object of appetite being to
it a source of stimulation. So too when imagination originates movement, it necessarily involves appetite.

That which moves therefore is a single faculty and the
faculty of appetite; for if there had been two sources of
movement—mind and appetite—they would have produced movement in virtue of some common character.
As it is, mind is never found producing movement without

appetite (for wish is a form of appetite; and when movement is produced according to calculation it is also according to wish), but appetite can originate movement con- 25
trary to calculation, for desire is a form of appetite. Now
mind is always right, but appetite and imagination may be
either right or wrong. That is why, though in any case it is
the object of appetite which originates movement, this object may be either the real or the apparent good. To produce movement the object must be more than this: it must
be good that can be brought into being by action; and only
what can be otherwise than as it is can thus be brought 30
into being. That then such a power in the soul as has been
described, i. e. that called appetite, originates movement 433ʳ
is clear. Those who distinguish parts in the soul, if they
distinguish and divide in accordance with differences of
power, find themselves with a very large number of parts,
a nutritive, a sensitive, an intellective, a deliberative, and
now an appetitive part; for these are more different from
one another than the faculties of desire and passion.

Since appetites run counter to one another, which happens when a principle of reason and a desire are contrary
and is possible only in beings with a sense of time (for
while mind bids us hold back because of what is future, desire is influenced by what is just at hand: a pleasant object
which is just at hand presents itself as both pleasant and
good, without condition in either case, because of want
of foresight into what is farther away in time), it follows 10
that while that which originates movement must be specifically one, viz. the faculty of appetite as such (or rather
farthest back of all the object of that faculty; for it is it
that itself remaining unmoved originates the movement by
being apprehended in thought or imagination), the things
that originate movement are numerically many.

All movement involves three factors, (1) that which
originates the movement, (2) that by means of which it
originates it, and (3) that which is moved. The expression
'that which originates the movement' is ambiguous: it may

mean either (a) something which itself is unmoved or (b)
15 that which at once moves and is moved. Here that which
moves without itself being moved is the realizable good,
that which at once moves and is moved is the faculty of
appetite (for that which is influenced by appetite so far
as it is actually so influenced is set in movement, and appetite in the sense of actual appetite is a kind of movement),
while that which is in motion is the animal. The instrument
which appetite employs to produce movement is no longer
20 psychical but bodily: hence the examination of it falls
within the province of the functions common to body and
soul.[27] To state the matter summarily at present, that which
is the instrument in the production of movement is to be
found where a beginning and an end coincide as e. g. in a
ball and socket joint; for there the convex and the concave
sides are respectively an end and a beginning (that is why
while the one remains at rest, the other is moved): they are
separate in definition but not separable spatially. For every-
25 thing is moved by pushing and pulling. Hence just as in the
case of a wheel, so here there must be a point which remains at rest, and from that point the movement must
originate.

To sum up, then, and repeat what I have said, inasmuch
as an animal is capable of appetite it is capable of self-
movement; it is not capable of appetite without possessing
imagination; and all imagination is either (1) calculative
30 or (2) sensitive. In the latter all animals, and not only man,
partake.

11 We must consider also in the case of imperfect animals, sc. those which have no sense but touch, what
it is that in them originates movement. Can they have
434ª imagination or not? or desire? Clearly they have feelings
of pleasure and pain, and if they have these they must have
desire. But how can they have imagination? Must not we
say that, as their movements are indefinite, they have
imagination and desire, but indefinitely?

[27] Cf. De Motu An. 702ª 21–703ª 22.

Sensitive imagination, as we have said,[28] is found in all animals, deliberative imagination only in those that are calculative: for whether this or that shall be enacted is already a task requiring calculation; and there must be a single standard to measure by, for that is pursued which is greater. It follows that what acts in this way must be able to make a unity out of several images.

This is the reason why imagination is held not to involve opinion, in that it does not involve opinion based on inference, though opinion involves imagination. Hence appetite contains no deliberative element. Sometimes it overpowers wish and sets it in movement: at times wish acts thus upon appetite, like one sphere imparting its movement to another, or appetite acts thus upon appetite, i. e. in the condition of moral weakness (though by nature the higher faculty is always more authoritative and gives rise to movement). Thus three modes of movement are possible.

The faculty of knowing is never moved but remains at rest. Since the one premiss or judgment is universal and the other deals with the particular (for the first tells us that such and such a kind of man should do such and such a kind of act, and the second that this is an act of the kind meant, and I a person of the type intended), it is the latter opinion that really originates movement, not the universal; or rather it is both, but the one does so while it remains in a state more like rest, while the other partakes in movement.

12   The nutritive soul then must be possessed by everything that is alive, and every such thing is endowed with soul from its birth to its death. For what has been born must grow, reach maturity, and decay—all of which are impossible without nutrition. Therefore the nutritive faculty must be found in everything that grows and decays.

But sensation need not be found in all things that live. For it is impossible for touch to belong either (1) to those whose body is uncompounded or (2) to those which are

[28] 433ᵇ 29.

incapable of taking in the forms without their matter.
30   But animals must be endowed with sensation, since
Nature does nothing in vain. For all things that exist by
Nature are means to an end, or will be concomitants of
means to an end. Every body capable of forward movement
434ᵇ would, if unendowed with sensation, perish and fail to
reach its end, which is the aim of Nature; for how could
it obtain nutriment? Stationary living things, it is true,
have as their nutriment that from which they have arisen;
but it is not possible that a body which is not stationary
but produced by generation should have a soul and a discerning mind without also having sensation. (Nor yet even
if it were not produced by generation. Why should it not
5 have sensation? Because it were better so either for the
body or for the soul? But clearly it would not be better for
either: the absence of sensation will not enable the one to
think better or the other to exist better.) Therefore no
body which is not stationary has soul without sensation.

But if a body has sensation, it must be either simple or
compound. And simple it cannot be; for then it could not
10 have touch, which is indispensable. This is clear from what
follows. An animal is a body with soul in it: every body is
tangible, i. e. perceptible by touch; hence necessarily, if an
animal is to survive, its body must have tactual sensation.
15 All the other senses, e. g. smell, sight, hearing, apprehend
through media; but where there is immediate contact the
animal, if it has no sensation, will be unable to avoid some
things and take others, and so will find it impossible to survive. That is why taste also is a sort of touch; it is relative
to nutriment, which is just tangible body; whereas sound,
colour, and odour are innutritious, and further neither grow
20 nor decay. Hence it is that taste also must be a sort of
touch, because it is the sense for what is tangible and nutri-
tious.

Both these senses, then, are indispensable to the animal,
and it is clear that without touch it is impossible for an
animal to be. All the other senses subserve well-being and

for that very reason belong not to any and every kind of animal, but only to some, e. g. those capable of forward 25 movement must have them; for, if they are to survive, they must perceive not only by immediate contact but also at a distance from the object. This will be possible if they can perceive through a medium, the medium being affected and moved by the perceptible object, and the animal by the medium. Just as that which produces local movement causes a change extending to a certain point, and that 30 which gave an impulse causes another to produce a new impulse so that the movement traverses a medium—the first mover impelling without being impelled, the last moved being impelled without impelling, while the medium (or media, for there are many) is both—so is it also in the case of alteration, except that the agent produces it 435ᵃ without the patient's changing its place. Thus if an object is dipped into wax, the movement goes on until submersion has taken place, and in stone it goes no distance at all, while in water the disturbance goes far beyond the object dipped: in air the disturbance is propagated farthest of all, the air acting and being acted upon, so long as it maintains an unbroken unity. That is why in the case of reflection it is 5 better, instead of saying that the sight issues from the eye and is reflected, to say that the air, so long as it remains one, is affected by the shape and colour. On a smooth surface the air possesses unity; hence it is that it in turn sets the sight in motion, just as if the impression on the wax 10 were transmitted as far as the wax extends.

13   It is clear that the body of an animal cannot be simple, i. e. consist of one element such as fire or air. For without touch it is impossible to have any other sense; for every body that has soul in it must, as we have said,[29] be capable of touch. All the other elements with the exception of earth 15 can constitute organs of sense, but all of them bring about perception only through something else, viz. through the

[29] 434ᵇ 10–24.

media. Touch takes place by direct contact with its objects, whence also its name. All the other organs of sense, no doubt, perceive by contact, only the contact is mediate: touch alone perceives by immediate contact. Consequently no animal body can consist of these other elements.

20 Nor can it consist solely of earth. For touch is as it were a mean between all tangible qualities, and its organ is capable of receiving not only all the specific qualities which characterize earth, but also the hot and the cold and all 25 other tangible qualities whatsoever. That is why we have no 435ᵇ sensation by means of bones, hair, &c., because they consist of earth. So too plants, because they consist of earth, have no sensation. Without touch there can be no other sense, and the organ of touch cannot consist of earth or of any other single element.

It is evident, therefore, that the loss of this one sense 5 alone must bring about the death of an animal. For as on the one hand nothing which is not an animal can have this sense, so on the other it is the only one which is indispensably necessary to what is an animal. This explains, further, the following difference between the other senses and touch. In the case of all the others excess of intensity in the qualities which they apprehend, i. e. excess of intensity in colour, sound, and smell, destroys not the animal but only 10 the organs of the sense (except incidentally, as when the sound is accompanied by an impact or shock, or where through the objects of sight or of smell certain other things are set in motion, which destroy by contact); flavour also destroys only in so far as it is at the same time tangible. But excess of intensity in tangible qualities, e. g. heat, cold, 15 or hardness, destroys the animal itself. As in the case of every sensible quality excess destroys the organ, so here what is tangible destroys touch, which is the essential mark of life; for it has been shown that without touch it is impossible for an animal to be. That is why excess in intensity of tangible qualities destroys not merely the organ, but the

animal itself, because this is the only sense which it must
have.

All the other senses are necessary to animals, as we have
said,[30] not for their being, but for their well-being. Such,
e. g., is sight, which, since it lives in air or water, or generally 20
in what is pellucid, it must have in order to see, and taste
because of what is pleasant or painful to it, in order that it
may perceive these qualities in its nutriment and so may
desire to be set in motion, and hearing that it may have
communication made to it, and a tongue that it may com- 25
municate with its fellows.

[30] 434^b 24.

Metaphysics

INTRODUCTION

The term "metaphysics" was invented by one of the early editors of Aristotle's works to serve as a title for a group of treatises which he placed "after the physics," a place which the Metaphysics still occupies in modern editions, separating the physical and biological sciences from the practical and productive sciences. The inquiries to which the term was applied constitute an independent science in the system of Aristotle, variously designated by him as "First Philosophy," "Theology," or "Wisdom." For in a philosophy in which sciences are distinguished by their proper principles and their proper subject matter, the examination of the first principles of the sciences or of the being shared by the diverse genera of things investigated in the various sciences does not fall within the province of any one of those sciences but constitutes the field of inquiry of a separate science.

As the investigation of problems of proof in logic led back to the problem of the discovery of causes in scientific demonstration, and as inquiry in physics had been found to consist in the search for causes, metaphysics is concerned with causes as such, and it is described as the science of first principles and causes. Aristotle found that his predecessors had tended first to limit their attention to material causes, that is, to explain things by the matter or the elements of which they are composed, and then had turned to the formal causes, that is, essences and definitions which they separated from matter and constituted into independent and self-subsistent Forms. The efficient cause and the final cause, that is, the source of the change and what it is to eventuate in, which Aristotle conceived to be his own peculiar contribution to the discussion of causes, were touched on only sporadically and vaguely by a few philosophers like Empedocles and Anaxagoras.

The problem of the metaphysician in treating of causes is, in a sense, the converse of that of the physicist, for whereas the investigation of nature consists in seeking to know causes and to state them in scientific formulae, the investigation of being requires the careful separation of traits of being from traits peculiar to certain kinds of being and from traits that might be attributed to things because of our ways of knowing them or because of our ways of formulating our knowledge. Aristotle therefore argues that truth and falsity are not in things, but only in thoughts, and that the differentiation of essential and accidental traits, which is necessary in scientific inquiry, is irrelevant to the conditions of being. In like fashion he investigates carefully the sense in which the parts of a true formula or statement may be said to correspond to the parts of the existent situation of which it is true. Once considerations of how things are differentiated, how we think about things, and how we state what we think, have been excluded, the study of being is seen to be primarily the study of substance, which in turn is analyzed into form and matter, actuality and potentiality. The conception of actuality and potentiality and the analysis of their relations to each other carries the inquiry beyond natural or sensible substances, that is, beyond elements and their compounds, plants and their parts, animals and their parts, and the heavenly bodies. In addition to the two kinds of substance—perishable sensible and eternal sensible—which are studied in physics, there is a third kind, immovable and nonsensible, whose existence is established in the famous proof of the necessity of an unmoved mover as cause of existence and motion, and whose nature therefore constitutes the peculiar subject-matter of metaphysics. For if there were no separated substances, all sciences would be reduced to physics, while if forms and numbers were conceived to be separated all philosophy would be reduced to mathematics.

Book I (or Alpha) sets forth the preliminary statement of the characteristics of first philosophy and the criticism of earlier conceptions of the causes. Book XII (or Lambda) investigates the existence and properties of the eternal mover. In both, the consequences of the metaphysical analysis in the conception of the relation of the sciences are apparent, for metaphysics must be differentiated by its subject-matter from physics and mathematics among the theoretic sciences, while the theoretic sciences, which have the acquisition of knowledge as their end must be differentiated by their purpose from the practical sciences, which have the performance of actions as their end, and from the productive sciences, which are directed to the making of artificial objects.

METAPHYSICA

CONTENTS

A. (I)

Λ. (XII)

mover, and one whose essence is actuality (actuality being prior to potency). To account for the uniform change in the universe, there must be one principle which acts always alike, and one whose action varies.

7. The eternal mover originates motion by being the primary object of desire (as it is of thought); being thoroughly actual, it cannot change or move; it is a living being, perfect, separate from sensible things, and without parts.

8. Besides the first mover there must be as many unmoved movers as there are simple motions involved in the motions of the planets. The number is probably either 55 or 47. As there is but one prime mover, there must be but one heaven.

9. The divine thought must be concerned with the most divine object, which is itself. Thought and the object of thought are never different when the object is immaterial.

10. How the good is present in the universe both as the order of the parts and (more primarily) as their ruler. Difficulties which attend the views of other philosophers.

Metaphysica

Metaphysics

Translated by W. D. Ross

⊔⌐⊔⌐

BOOK A (1)

1   All men by nature desire to know. An indication of
    this is the delight we take in our senses; for even apart **980ª**
from their usefulness they are loved for themselves; and
above all others the sense of sight. For not only with a view
to action, but even when we are not going to do anything, 25
we prefer seeing (one might say) to everything else. The
reason is that this, most of all the senses, makes us know
and brings to light many differences between things.

   By nature animals are born with the faculty of sensation,
and from sensation memory is produced in some of them,
though not in others. And therefore the former are more
intelligent and apt at learning than those which cannot **980ᵇ**
remember; those which are incapable of hearing sounds are
intelligent though they cannot be taught, e. g. the bee, and
any other race of animals that may be like it; and those
which besides memory have this sense of hearing can be
taught.

   The animals other than man live by appearances and
memories, and have but little of connected experience; 21
but the human race lives also by art and reasonings. Now
from memory experience is produced in men; for the several
memories of the same thing produce finally the capacity for

981ᵃ a single experience. And experience seems pretty much like science and art, but really science and art come to men *through* experience; for 'experience made art', as Polus says,[1] 'but inexperience luck'. Now art arises when from 5 many notions gained by experience one universal judgement about a class of objects is produced. For to have a judgement that when Callias was ill of this disease this did him good, and similarly in the case of Socrates and in many individual cases, is a matter of experience; but to judge that it has done good to all persons of a certain constitution, 10 marked off in one class, when they were ill of this disease, e. g. to phlegmatic or bilious people when burning with fever—this is a matter of art.

With a view to action experience seems in no respect inferior to art, and men of experience succeed even better 15 than those who have theory without experience. (The reason is that experience is knowledge of individuals, art of universals, and actions and productions are all concerned with the individual; for the physician does not cure man, except in an incidental way, but Callias or Socrates or some other called by some such individual name, who happens to 20 be a man. If, then, a man has the theory without the experience, and recognizes the universal but does not know the individual included in this, he will often fail to cure; for it is the individual that is to be cured.) But yet we think that 25 knowledge and understanding belong to art rather than to experience, and we suppose artists to be wiser than men of experience (which implies that Wisdom depends in all cases rather on knowledge); and this because the former know the cause, but the latter do not. For men of experi- 30 ence know that the thing is so, but do not know why, while the others know the 'why' and the cause. Hence we think also that the master-workers in each craft are more honour- 981ᵇ able and know in a truer sense and are wiser than the manual workers, because they know the causes of the things that are done (we think the manual workers are like certain

[1] Cf. Pl. *Gorg.* 448 c, 462 bc.

lifeless things which act indeed, but act without knowing
what they do, as fire burns—but while the lifeless things
perform each of their functions by a natural tendency, the 5
labourers perform them through habit); thus we view them
as being wiser not in virtue of being able to act, but of
having the theory for themselves and knowing the causes.
And in general it is a sign of the man who knows and of the
man who does not know, that the former can teach, and
therefore we think art more truly knowledge than experience is; for artists can teach, and men of mere experience
cannot.

Again, we do not regard any of the senses as Wisdom; 10
yet surely these give the most authoritative knowledge of
particulars. But they do not tell us the 'why' of anything—
e. g. why fire is hot; they only say *that* it is hot.

At first he who invented any art whatever that went beyond the common perceptions of man was naturally admired by men, not only because there was something useful 15
in the inventions, but because he was thought wise and
superior to the rest. But as more arts were invented, and
some were directed to the necessities of life, others to
recreation, the inventors of the latter were naturally always
regarded as wiser than the inventors of the former, because
their branches of knowledge did not aim at utility. Hence
when all such inventions were already established, the sci- 20
ences which do not aim at giving pleasure or at the necessities of life were discovered, and first in the places where
men first began to have leisure. This is why the mathematical arts were founded in Egypt; for there the priestly caste
was allowed to be at leisure.

We have said in the *Ethics* [2] what the difference is between art and science and the other kindred faculties; but 25
the point of our present discussion is this, that all men suppose what is called Wisdom to deal with the first causes
and the principles of things; so that, as has been said before,
the man of experience is thought to be wiser than the pos- 30

[2] 1139[b] 14–1141[b] 8

sessors of any sense-perception whatever, the artist wiser
than the men of experience, the master-worker than the
mechanic, and the theoretical kinds of knowledge to be
more of the nature of Wisdom than the productive. Clearly
982ᵃ then Wisdom is knowledge about certain principles and
causes.

2   Since we are seeking this knowledge, we must inquire
5   of what kind are the causes and the principles, the
knowledge of which is Wisdom. If one were to take the
notions we have about the wise man, this might perhaps
make the answer more evident. We suppose first, then, that
the wise man knows all things, as far as possible, although
10 he has not knowledge of each of them in detail; secondly,
that he who can learn things that are difficult, and not
easy for man to know, is wise (sense-perception is common
to all, and therefore easy and no mark of Wisdom); again,
that he who is more exact and more capable of teaching the
causes is wiser, in every branch of knowledge; and that of
15 the sciences, also, that which is desirable on its own account
and for the sake of knowing it is more of the nature of
Wisdom than that which is desirable on account of its results, and the superior science is more of the nature of Wisdom than the ancillary; for the wise man must not be
ordered but must order, and he must not obey another,
but the less wise must obey *him*.

Such and so many are the notions, then, which we have
20 about Wisdom and the wise. Now of these characteristics
that of knowing all things must belong to him who has in
the highest degree universal knowledge; for he knows in a
sense all the instances that fall under the universal. And
these things, the most universal, are on the whole the hard-
est for men to know; for they are farthest from the senses.
25 And the most exact of the sciences are those which deal
most with first principles; for those which involve fewer
principles are more exact than those which involve additional principles, e. g. arithmetic than geometry. But the

science which investigates causes is also *instructive*, in a higher degree, for the people who instruct us are those who tell the causes of each thing. And understanding and knowl- 30 edge pursued for their own sake are found most in the knowledge of that which is most knowable (for he who chooses to know for the sake of knowing will choose most readily that which is most truly knowledge, and such is the 982 knowledge of that which is most knowable); and the first principles and the causes are most knowable; for by reason of these, and from these, all other things come to be known, and not these by means of the things subordinate to them. And the science which knows to what end each thing must be done is the most authoritative of the sciences, and more 5 authoritative than any ancillary science; and this end is the good of that thing, and in general the supreme good in the whole of nature. Judged by all the tests we have mentioned, then, the name in question falls to the same science; this must be a science that investigates the first principles and 10 causes; for the good, i. e. the end, is one of the causes.

That it is not a science of production is clear even from the history of the earliest philosophers. For it is owing to their wonder that men both now begin and at first began to philosophize; they wondered originally at the obvious difficulties, then advanced little by little and stated diffi- 15 culties about the greater matters, e. g. about the phenomena of the moon and those of the sun and of the stars, and about the genesis of the universe. And a man who is puzzled and wonders thinks himself ignorant (whence even the lover of myth is in a sense a lover of Wisdom, for the myth is composed of wonders); therefore since they phi- 20 losophized in order to escape from ignorance, evidently they were pursuing science in order to know, and not for any utilitarian end. And this is confirmed by the facts; for it was when almost all the necessities of life and the things that make for comfort and recreation had been secured, that such knowledge began to be sought. Evidently then we do not seek it for the sake of any other advantage; but 25 as the man is free, we say, who exists for his own sake and not for another's, so we pursue this as the only free science, for it alone exists for its own sake.

Hence also the possession of it might be justly regarded as beyond human power, for in many ways human nature 30 is in bondage, so that according to Simonides 'God alone can have this privilege', and it is unfitting that man should not be content to seek the knowledge that is suited to him. 983ᵃ If, then, there is something in what the poets say, and jealousy is natural to the divine power, it would probably occur in this case above all, and all who excelled in this knowledge would be unfortunate. But the divine power cannot be jealous (nay, according to the proverb, 'bards 5 tell many a lie'), nor should any other science be thought more honourable than one of this sort. For the most divine science is also most honourable; and this science alone must be, in two ways, most divine. For the science which it would be most meet for God to have is a divine science, and so is any science that deals with divine objects; and this science alone has both these qualities; for (1) God is thought to be among the causes of all things and to be a first principle, and (2) such a science either God alone 10 can have, or God above all others. All the sciences, indeed, are more necessary than this, but none is better.

Yet the acquisition of it must in a sense end in something which is the opposite of our original inquiries. For all men begin, as we said, by wondering that things are as 15 they are, as they do about self-moving marionettes, or about the solstices or the incommensurability of the diagonal of a square with the side; for it seems wonderful to all who have not yet seen the reason, that there is a thing which cannot be measured even by the smallest unit. But we must end in the contrary and, according to the proverb, the better state, as is the case in these instances too when men learn the cause; for there is nothing which would surprise a geometer so much as if the diagonal 20 turned out to be commensurable.

We have stated, then, what is the nature of the science we are searching for, and what is the mark which our search and our whole investigation must reach.

3   Evidently we have to acquire knowledge of the original causes (for we say we know each thing only when we think we recognize its first cause), and causes are spoken of in four senses. In one of these we mean the substance, i. e. the essence (for the 'why' is reducible finally to the definition, and the ultimate 'why' is a cause and principle); in another the matter or substratum, in a third the source of the change, and in a fourth the cause opposed to this, the purpose and the good (for this is the end of all generation and change). We have studied these **983ᵇ** causes sufficiently in our work on nature,[3] but yet let us call to our aid those who have attacked the investigation of being and philosophized about reality before us. For obviously they too speak of certain principles and causes; to go over their views, then, will be of profit to the present inquiry, for we shall either find another kind of cause, or be more convinced of the correctness of those which we now maintain.

Of the first philosophers, then, most thought the principles which were of the nature of matter were the only principles of all things. That of which all things that are consist, the first from which they come to be, the last into which they are resolved (the substance remaining, but changing in its modifications), this they say is the element and this the principle of things, and therefore they think nothing is either generated or destroyed, since this sort of entity is always conserved, as we say Socrates neither comes to be absolutely when he comes to be beautiful or musical, nor ceases to be when he loses these characteristics, because the substratum, Socrates himself, remains. Just so they say nothing else comes to be or ceases to be; for there must be some entity—either one or more than

[3] *Phys.* ii. 3, 7.

one—from which all other things come to be, it being conserved.

Yet they do not all agree as to the number and the
20 nature of these principles. Thales, the founder of this type
of philosophy, says the principle is water (for which
reason he declared that the earth rests on water), getting
the notion perhaps from seeing that the nutriment of
all things is moist, and that heat itself is generated from
the moist and kept alive by it (and that from which
25 they come to be is a principle of all things). He got his
notion from this fact, and from the fact that the seeds of
all things have a moist nature, and that water is the origin
of the nature of moist things.

Some[4] think that even the ancients who lived long
before the present generation, and first framed accounts of
30 the gods, had a similar view of nature; for they made
Ocean and Tethys the parents of creation,[5] and described
the oath of the gods as being by water,[6] to which they give
the name of Styx; for what is oldest is most honourable,
and the most honourable thing is that by which one
984ᵃ swears. It may perhaps be uncertain whether this opinion
about nature is primitive and ancient, but Thales at any
rate is said to have declared himself thus about the first
cause. Hippo no one would think fit to include among these
thinkers, because of the paltriness of his thought.

5   Anaximenes and Diogenes make air prior to water, and
the most primary of the simple bodies, while Hippasus of
Metapontium and Heraclitus of Ephesus say this of fire,
and Empedocles says it of the four elements (adding a
fourth—earth—to those which have been named); for
10 these, he says, always remain and do not come to be, except
that they come to be more or fewer, being aggregated into
one and segregated out of one.

Anaxagoras of Clazomenae, who, though older than

[4] The reference is probably to Plato (*Crat.* 402 B, *Theaet.* 152 E,
162 D, 180 C).

[5] Hom. *Il.* xiv, 201, 246.
[6] *Ibid.* ii. 755, xiv. 271, xv. 37.

Empedocles, was later in his philosophical activity, says the principles are infinite in number; for he says almost all the things that are made of parts like themselves, in the manner of water or fire, are generated and destroyed in this way, only by aggregation and segregation, and are not in any other sense generated or destroyed, but remain eternally.

From these facts one might think that the only cause is the so-called material cause; but as men thus advanced, the very facts opened the way for them and joined in forcing them to investigate the subject. However true it may be that all generation and destruction proceed from some one or (for that matter) from more elements, why does this happen and what is the cause? For at least the substratum itself does not make itself change; e. g. neither the wood nor the bronze causes the change of either of them, nor does the wood manufacture a bed and the bronze a statue, but something else is the cause of the change. And to seek this is to seek the second cause, as we should say—that from which comes the beginning of the movement. Now those who at the very beginning set themselves to this kind of inquiry, and said the substratum was one,[7] were not at all dissatisfied with themselves; but some at least of those who maintained it to be one [8]—as though defeated by this search for the second cause—say the one and nature as a whole is unchangeable not only in respect of generation and destruction (for this is a primitive belief, and all agreed in it), but also of all other change; and this view is peculiar to them. Of those who said the universe was one, then, none succeeded in discovering a cause of **984ᵇ** this sort, except perhaps Parmenides, and he only inasmuch as he supposes that there is not only one but also in some sense two causes. But for those who make more elements [9] it is more possible to state the second cause, e. g. for those

---

[7] Thales, Anaximenes, and Heraclitus.
[8] The Eleatics.
[9] The reference is probably to Empedocles.

who make hot and cold, or fire and earth, the elements; for they treat fire as having a nature which fits it to move things, and water and earth and such things they treat in the contrary way.

When these men and the principles of this kind had had their day, as the latter were found inadequate to generate the nature of things men were again forced by the truth 10 itself, as we said,[10] to inquire into the next kind of cause. For it is not likely either that fire or earth or any such element should be the reason why things manifest goodness and beauty both in their being and in their coming to be, or that those thinkers should have supposed it was; nor again could it be right to entrust so great a matter to spontaneity and chance. When one man [11] said, then, that 15 reason was present—as in animals, so throughout nature—as the cause of order and of all arrangement, he seemed like a sober man in contrast with the random talk of his predecessors. We know that Anaxagoras certainly adopted these views, but Hermotimus of Clazomenae is credited 20 with expressing them earlier. Those who thought thus stated that there is a principle of things which is at the same time the cause of beauty, and that sort of cause from which things acquire movement.

4   One might suspect that Hesiod was the first to look for such a thing—or some one else who put love or 25 desire among existing things as a principle, as Parmenides, too, does; for he, in constructing the genesis of the universe, says:—

> Love first of all the Gods she planned.

And Hesiod says:—

> First of all things was chaos made, and then
> Broad-breasted earth, . . .
> And love, 'mid all the gods pre-eminent,

[10] a 18.
[11] Anaxagoras.

which implies that among existing things there must be 30
from the first a cause which will move things and bring
them together. How these thinkers should be arranged
with regard to priority of discovery let us be allowed to
decide later; [12] but since the contraries of the various forms
of good were also perceived to be present in nature—not
only order and the beautiful, but also disorder and the
ugly, and bad things in greater number than good, and 985
ignoble things than beautiful—therefore another thinker
introduced friendship and strife, each of the two the cause
of one of these two sets of qualities. For if we were to
follow out the view of Empedocles, and interpret it accord- 5
ing to its meaning and not to its lisping expression, we
should find that friendship is the cause of good things, and
strife of bad. Therefore, if we said that Empedocles in a
sense both mentions, and is the first to mention, the bad
and the good as principles, we should perhaps be right,
since the cause of all goods is the good itself.

These thinkers, as we say, evidently grasped, and to this 10
extent, two of the causes which we distinguished in our
work on nature [13]—the matter and the source of the movement—vaguely, however, and with no clearness, but as
untrained men behave in fights; for they go round their 15
opponents and often strike fine blows, but they do not fight
on scientific principles, and so too these thinkers do not
seem to know what they say; for it is evident that, as a rule,
they make no use of their causes except to a small extent.
For Anaxagoras uses reason as a *deus ex machina* for the
making of the world, and when he is at a loss to tell from
what cause something necessarily is, then he drags reason 2c
in, but in all other cases ascribes events to anything rather
than to reason.[14] And Empedocles, though he uses the
causes to a greater extent than this, neither does so sufficiently nor attains consistency in their use. At least, in

[12] The promise is not fulfilled.
[13] *Phys.* ii. 3, 7.
[14] Cf. Pl. *Phaedo*, 98 BC, *Laws*, 967 B–D.

many cases he makes love segregate things, and strife aggre-
25 gate them. For whenever the universe is dissolved into its
elements by strife, fire is aggregated into one, and so is each
of the other elements; but whenever again under the influence of love they come together into one, the parts must
again be segregated out of each element.

Empedocles, then, in contrast with his predecessors,
was the first to introduce the dividing of this cause, not
30 positing one source of movement, but different and contrary sources. Again, he was the first to speak of four
985ᵇ material elements; yet he does not use four, but treats them
as two only; he treats fire by itself, and its opposites—earth,
air, and water—as one kind of thing. We may learn this by
study of his verses.

This philosopher then, as we say, has spoken of the
principles in this way, and made them of this number.
Leucippus and his associate Democritus say that the full
5 and the empty are the elements, calling the one being and
the other non-being—the full and solid being being, the
empty non-being (whence they say being no more is than
non-being, because the solid no more is than the empty);
and they make these the material causes of things. And as
10 those who make the underlying substance one generate all
other things by its modifications, supposing the rare and
the dense to be the sources of the modifications, in the
same way these philosophers say the differences in the elements are the causes of all other qualities. These differences, they say, are three—shape and order and position.
15 For they say the real is differentiated only by 'rhythm'
and 'inter-contact' and 'turning'; and of these rhythm is
shape, inter-contact is order, and turning is position; for
A differs from N in shape, AN from NA in order, H from
H in position. The question of movement—whence or
how it is to belong to things—these thinkers, like the
others, lazily neglected.

Regarding the two causes, then, as we say, the inquiry

seems to have been pushed thus far by the early philos- 20
ophers.

5   Contemporaneously with these philosophers and before them, the so-called Pythagoreans, who were the
first to take up mathematics, not only advanced this study, 25
but also having been brought up in it they thought its
principles were the principles of all things. Since of these
principles numbers are by nature the first, and in numbers
they seemed to see many resemblances to the things that
exist and come into being—more than in fire and earth
and water (such and such a modification of numbers being
justice, another being soul and reason, another being op- 30
portunity—and similarly almost all other things being
numerically expressible); since, again, they saw that the
modifications and the ratios of the musical scales were ex
pressible in numbers;—since, then, all other things seemed
in their whole nature to be modelled on numbers, and
numbers seemed to be the first things in the whole of 986ᵇ
nature, they supposed the elements of numbers to be the
elements of all things, and the whole heaven to be a
musical scale and a number. And all the properties of numbers and scales which they could show to agree with the
attributes and parts and the whole arrangement of the 5
heavens, they collected and fitted into their scheme; and if
there was a gap anywhere, they readily made additions so
as to make their whole theory coherent. E. g. as the number
10 is thought to be perfect and to comprise the whole nature of numbers, they say that the bodies which move 10
through the heavens are ten, but as the visible bodies are
only nine, to meet this they invent a tenth—the 'counter-
earth'. We have discussed these matters more exactly elsewhere.[15]

But the object of our review is that we may learn from
these philosophers also what they suppose to be the principles and how these fall under the causes we have named. 15

[15] *De Caelo*, ii. 13.

Evidently, then, these thinkers also consider that number is the principle both as matter for things and as forming both their modifications and their permanent states, and hold that the elements of number are the even and the odd, and that of these the latter is limited, and the former unlimited; and that the One proceeds from both of these 20 (for it is both even and odd), and number from the One; and that the whole heaven, as has been said, is numbers.

Other members of this same school say there are ten principles, which they arrange in two columns of cognates 25 —limit and unlimited, odd and even, one and plurality, right and left, male and female, resting and moving, straight and curved, light and darkness, good and bad, square and oblong. In this way Alcmaeon of Croton seems also to have conceived the matter, and either he got this view from them or they got it from him; for he expressed 30 himself similarly to them. For he says most human affairs go in pairs, meaning not definite contrarieties such as the Pythagoreans speak of, but any chance contrarieties, e. g. white and black, sweet and bitter, good and bad, great and small. He threw out indefinite suggestions about the other contrarieties, but the Pythagoreans declared both how 986ᵇ many and which their contrarieties are.

From both these schools, then, we can learn this much, that the contraries are the principles of things; and how many these principles are and which they are, we can learn from one of the two schools. But how these principles can 5 be brought together under the causes we have named has not been clearly and articulately stated by them; they seem, however, to range the elements under the head of matter; for out of these as immanent parts they say substance is composed and moulded.

From these facts we may sufficiently perceive the meaning of the ancients who said the elements of nature were more than one; but there are some who spoke of the uni-10 verse as if it were one entity, though they were not all alike either in the excellence of their statement or in its conformity to the facts of nature. The discussion of them is in no way appropriate to our present investigation of causes, for they do not, like some of the natural philosophers, assume being to be one and yet generate it out of the one as out of matter, but they speak in another way; those others add change, since they generate the universe, but these thinkers say the universe is unchangeable. Yet *this* much is germane to the present inquiry: Parmenides seems to fasten on that which is one in definition, Melissus on that which is one in matter, for which reason the former says that it is limited, the latter that it is unlimited; while Xenophanes, the first of these partisans of the One (for Parmenides is said to have been his pupil), gave no clear statement, nor does he seem to have grasped the nature of either of these causes, but with reference to the whole material universe he says the One is God. Now these thinkers, as we said, must be neglected for the purposes of the present inquiry—two of them entirely, as being a little too naïve, viz. Xenophanes and Melissus; but Parmenides seems in places to speak with more insight. For, claiming that, besides the existent, nothing non-existent exists, he thinks that of necessity one thing exists, viz. the existent and nothing else (on this we have spoken more clearly in our work on nature),[16] but being forced to follow the observed facts, and supposing the existence of that which is one in definition, but more than one according to our sensations, he now posits two causes and two principles, calling them hot and cold, i. e. fire and earth; and of these he ranges the hot with the existent, and the other with the non-existent.

From what has been said, then, and from the wise men who have now sat in council with us, we have got thus much—on the one hand from the earliest philosophers, who regard the first principle as corporeal (for water and fire and such things are bodies), and of whom some suppose that there is one corporeal principle, others that there are

15

20

25

30

987ᵇ

5

---

[16] *Phys.* i. 3.

more than one, but both put these under the head of matter; and on the other hand from some who posit both this cause and besides this the source of movement, which we have got from some a single and from others as twofold.

Down to the Italian school, then, and apart from it,
10 philosophers have treated these subjects rather obscurely, except that, as we said, they have in fact used two kinds of cause, and one of these—the source of movement—some treat as one and others as two. But the Pythagoreans have
15 said in the same way that there are two principles, but added this much, which is peculiar to them, that they thought that finitude and infinity were not attributes of certain other things, e. g. of fire or earth or anything else of this kind, but that infinity itself and unity itself were the substance of the things of which they are predicated.
20 This is why number was the substance of all things. On this subject, then, they expressed themselves thus; and regarding the question of essence they began to make statements and definitions, but treated the matter too simply. For they both defined superficially and thought that the first subject of which a given definition was predicable was the substance of the thing defined, as if one supposed
25 that 'double' and '2' were the same, because 2 is the first thing of which 'double' is predicable. But surely to be double and to be 2 are not the same; if they are, one thing will be many [17]—a consequence which they actually drew.[18] From the earlier philosophers, then, and from their successors we can learn thus much.

6   After the systems we have named came the philos-
30   ophy of Plato, which in most respects followed these thinkers, but had peculiarities that distinguished it from the philosophy of the Italians. For, having in his youth first become familiar with Cratylus and with the Heraclitean doctrines (that all sensible things are ever in a state of flux

[17] i. e. 2 will be each of several things whose definition is predicable of it.

[18] e. g. 2 was identified both with opinion and with daring.

and there is no knowledge about them), these views he held even in later years. Socrates, however, was busying 987^b himself about ethical matters and neglecting the world of nature as a whole but seeking the universal in these ethical matters, and fixed thought for the first time on definitions; Plato accepted his teaching, but held that the problem applied not to sensible things but to entities of another kind 5 —for this reason, that the common definition could not be a definition of any sensible thing, as they were always changing. Things of this other sort, then, he called Ideas, and sensible things, he said, were all named after these, and in virtue of a relation to these; for the many existed by participation in the Ideas that have the same name as they. Only the name 'participation' was new; for the Pythago- 10 reans say that things exist by 'imitation' of numbers, and Plato says they exist by participation, changing the name. But what the participation or the imitation of the Forms could be they left an open question.

Further, besides sensible things and Forms he says there are the objects of mathematics, which occupy an intermediate position, differing from sensible things in being eternal 15 and unchangeable, from Forms in that there are many alike, while the Form itself is in each case unique.

Since the Forms were the causes of all other things, he thought their elements were the elements of all things. As matter, the great and the small were principles; as essential 20 reality, the One; for from the great and the small, by participation in the One, come the Numbers.

But he agreed with the Pythagoreans in saying that the One is substance and not a predicate of something else; and in saying that the Numbers are the causes of the reality of other things he agreed with them; but positing a dyad 25 and constructing the infinite out of great and small, instead of treating the infinite as one, is peculiar to him; and so is his view that the Numbers exist apart from sensible things, while they say that the things themselves are Numbers, and do not place the objects of mathematics

between Forms and sensible things. His divergence from
30 the Pythagoreans in making the One and the Numbers
separate from things, and his introduction of the Forms,
were due to his inquiries in the region of definitions (for
the earlier thinkers had no tincture of dialectic), and his
making the other entity besides the One a dyad was due to
the belief that the numbers, except those which were
prime, could be neatly produced out of the dyad as out of
some plastic material.

Yet what *happens* is the contrary; the theory is not a
988ª reasonable one. For they make many things out of the matter, and the form generates only once, but what we observe
is that one table is made from one matter, while the man
5 who applies the form, though he is one, makes many tables.
And the relation of the male to the female is similar; for
the latter is impregnated by one copulation, but the male
impregnates many females; yet these are analogues of those
first principles.

Plato, then, declared himself thus on the points in question; it is evident from what has been said that he has used
only two causes, that of the essence and the material cause
10 (for the Forms are the causes of the essence of all other
things, and the One is the cause of the essence of the
Forms); and it is evident what the underlying matter is,
of which the Forms are predicated in the case of sensible
things, and the One in the case of Forms, viz. that this is
a dyad, the great and the small. Further, he has assigned
the cause of good and that of evil to the elements, one to
15 each of the two, as we say [19] some of his predecessors sought
to do, e. g. Empedocles and Anaxagoras.

7   Our review of those who have spoken about first principles and reality and of the way in which they have
20 spoken, has been concise and summary; but yet we have
learnt *this* much from them, that of those who speak about
'principle' and 'cause' no one has mentioned any principle

[19] Cf. 984ᵇ 15–19, 32–ᵇ 10.

except those which have been distinguished in our work on nature,[20] but all evidently have some inkling of *them*, though only vaguely. For some speak of the first principle as matter, whether they suppose one or more first principles, and whether they suppose this to be a body or to 25 be incorporeal; e. g. Plato spoke of the great and the small, the Italians of the infinite, Empedocles of fire, earth, water, and air, Anaxagoras of the infinity of things composed of similar parts. These, then, have all had a notion of this kind of cause, and so have all who speak of air or fire or 30 water, or something denser than fire and rarer than air; for some have said the prime element is of this kind.

These thinkers grasped this cause only; but certain others have mentioned the source of movement, e. g. those who make friendship and strife, or reason, or love, a principle.

The essence, i. e. the substantial reality, no one has expressed distinctly. It is hinted at chiefly by those who be- 35 lieve in the Forms; for they do not suppose either that the 988ᵇ Forms are the matter of sensible things, and the One the matter of the Forms, or that they are the source of movement (for they say these are causes rather of immobility and of being at rest), but they furnish the Forms as the essence of every other thing, and the One as the essence of the Forms. 5

That for whose sake actions and changes and movements take place, they assert to be a cause in a way, but not in this way, i. e. not in the way in which it is its *nature* to be a cause. For those who speak of reason or friendship class these causes as goods; they do not speak, however, as if anything that exists either existed or came into being for the sake of these, but as if movements started from these. In the same way those who say the One or the existent is 10 the good, say that it is the cause of substance, but not that substance either is or comes to be for the sake of this. Therefore it turns out that in a sense they both say and do

[20] *Phys.* ii. 3, 7.

15 not say the good is a cause; for they do not call it a cause
qua good but only incidentally.

All these thinkers, then, as they cannot pitch on another
cause, seem to testify that we have determined rightly both
how many and of what sort the causes are. Besides this it
is plain that when the causes are being looked for, either
all four must be sought thus or they must be sought in one
20 of these four ways. Let us next discuss the possible difficulties with regard to the way in which each of these
thinkers has spoken, and with regard to his situation
relatively to the first principles.

8　　Those, then, who say the universe is one and posit one
kind of thing as matter, and as corporeal matter which
has spatial magnitude, evidently go astray in many ways.
For they posit the elements of bodies only, not of in-
25 corporeal things, though there are also incorporeal things.
And in trying to state the causes of generation and destruction, and in giving a physical account of all things, they do
away with the cause of movement. Further, they err in not
positing the substance, i. e. the essence, as the cause of
anything, and besides this in lightly calling any of the
30 simple bodies except earth the first principle, without inquiring how they are produced out of one another,—I
mean fire, water, earth, and air. For some things are produced out of each other by combination, others by separation, and this makes the greatest difference to their priority
and posteriority. For (1) in a way the property of being
35 most elementary of all would seem to belong to the first
thing from which they are produced by combination, and
989ᵃ this property would belong to the most fine-grained and
subtle of bodies. For this reason those who make fire the
principle would be most in agreement with this argument. But each of the other thinkers agrees that the ele-
5 ment of corporeal things is of this sort. At least none of
those who named one element claimed that earth was the
element, evidently because of the coarseness of its grain.

(Of the other three elements each has found some judge on its side; for some maintain that fire, others that water, others that air is the element. Yet why, after all, do they not name earth also, as most men do? For people say all things are earth. And Hesiod says earth was produced first 10 of corporeal things; so primitive and popular has the opinion been.) According to this argument, then, no one would be right who either says the first principle is any of the elements other than fire, or supposes it to be denser than air but rarer than water. But (2) if that which is 15 later in generation is prior in nature, and that which is concocted and compounded is later in generation, the contrary of what we have been saying must be true—water must be prior to air, and earth to water.

So much, then, for those who posit one cause such as we mentioned; but the same is true if one supposes more of 20 these, as Empedocles says the matter of things is four bodies. For he too is confronted by consequences some of which are the same as have been mentioned, while others are peculiar to him. For we see these bodies produced from one another, which implies that the same body does not always remain fire or earth (we have spoken about this in our works on nature [21]); and regarding the cause of movement 25 and the question whether we must posit one or two, he must be thought to have spoken neither correctly nor altogether plausibly. And in general, change of quality is necessarily done away with for those who speak thus, for on their view cold will not come from hot nor hot from cold. For if it did there would be something that accepted the contraries themselves, and there would be some one entity that became fire and water, which Empedocles denies.

As regards Anaxagoras, if one were to suppose that he 30 said there were two elements, the supposition would accord thoroughly with an argument which Anaxagoras himself did not state articulately, but which he must have ac-

[21] *De Caelo*, iii. 7.

cepted if any one had led him on to it. True, to say that
in the beginning all things were mixed is absurd both on
other grounds and because it follows that they must have
989ᵇ existed before in an unmixed form, and because nature
does not allow any chance thing to be mixed with any
chance thing, and also because on this view modifications
and accidents could be separated from substances (for the
same things which are mixed can be separated); yet if one
5 were to follow him up, piecing together what he means, he
would perhaps be seen to be somewhat modern in his
views. For when nothing was separated out, evidently nothing could be truly asserted of the substance that then existed. I mean, e. g., that it was neither white nor black,
nor grey nor any other colour, but of necessity colourless;
for if it had been coloured, it would have had one of these
10 colours. And similarly, by this same argument, it was fla-
vourless, nor had it any similar attribute; for it could not
be either of any quality or of any size, nor could it be any
definite kind of thing. For if it were, one of the particular
forms would have belonged to it, and this is impossible,
since all were mixed together; for the particular form would
necessarily have been already separated out, but he says
15 all were mixed except reason, and this alone was unmixed
and pure. From this it follows, then, that he must say the
principles are the One (for this is simple and unmixed)
and the Other, which is of such a nature as we suppose
the indefinite to be before it is defined and partakes of
some form. Therefore, while expressing himself neither
rightly nor clearly, he means something like what the
later thinkers say and what is now more clearly seen to be
20 the case.

But these thinkers are, after all, at home only in arguments about generation and destruction and movement;
for it is practically only of this sort of substance that they
seek the principles and the causes. But those who extend
25 their vision to all things that exist, and of existing things
suppose some to be perceptible and others not perceptible

evidently study both classes, which is all the more reason why one should devote some time to seeing what is good in their views and what bad from the standpoint of the inquiry we have now before us.

The 'Pythagoreans' treat of principles and elements stranger than those of the physical philosophers (the reason is that they got the principles from non-sensible 30 things, for the objects of mathematics, except those of astronomy, are of the class of things without movement); yet their discussions and investigations are all about nature; for they generate the heavens, and with regard to their parts and attributes and functions they observe the 990 phenomena, and use up the principles and the causes in explaining these, which implies that they agree with the others, the physical philosophers, that the *real* is just all that which is perceptible and contained by the so-called 'heavens'. But the causes and the principles which they 5 mention are, as we said, sufficient to act as steps even up to the higher realms of reality, and are more suited to these than to theories about nature. They do not tell us at all, however, how there can be movement if limit and unlimited and odd and even are the only things assumed, or how without movement and change there can be genera- 10 tion and destruction, or the bodies that move through the heavens can do what they do.

Further, if one either granted them that spatial magnitude consists of these elements, or this were proved, still how would some bodies be light and others have weight? To judge from what they assume and maintain they are 15 speaking no more of mathematical bodies than of perceptible; hence they have said nothing whatever about fire or earth or the other bodies of this sort, I suppose because they have nothing to say which applies *peculiarly* to perceptible things.

Further, how are we to combine the beliefs that the attributes of number, and number itself, are causes of what 20 exists and happens in the heavens both from the beginning

and now, and that there is no other number than this
number out of which the world is composed? When in
one particular region they place opinion and opportunity,
and, a little above or below, injustice and decision or
mixture, and allege, as proof, that each of these is a number,
25 and that there happens to be already in this place a plurality
of the extended bodies composed of numbers, because
these attributes of number attach to the various places—
this being so, is this number, which we must suppose each
of these abstractions to be, the same number which is
exhibited in the material universe, or is it another than
30 this? Plato says it is different; yet even he thinks that both
these bodies and their causes are numbers, but that the
intelligible numbers are causes, while the others are *sensible*.

9   Let us leave the Pythagoreans for the present; for it is
        enough to have touched on them as much as we have
990ᵇ done. But as for those who posit the Ideas as causes, firstly,
in seeking to grasp the causes of the things around us, they
introduced others equal in number to these, as if a man
who wanted to count things thought he would not be able
to do it while they were few, but tried to count them when
he had added to their number. For the Forms are prac-
5 tically equal to—or not fewer than—the things, in trying
to explain which these thinkers proceeded from them to
the Forms. For to each thing there answers an entity
which has the same name and exists apart from the substances, and so also in the case of all other groups there is a
one over many, whether the many are in this world or are
eternal.

Further, of the ways in which we prove that the Forms
10 exist, none is convincing; for from some no inference
necessarily follows, and from some arise Forms even of
things of which we think there are no Forms. For according to the arguments from the existence of the sciences
there will be Forms of all things of which there are sciences,

and according to the 'one over many' argument there will
be Forms even of negations, and according to the argument that there is an object for thought even when the
thing has perished, there will be Forms of perishable things;
for we have an image of these. Further, of the more ac- 15
curate arguments, some lead to Ideas of relations, of which
we say there is no independent class, and others introduce
the 'third man'.

And in general the arguments for the Forms destroy the
things for whose existence we are more zealous than for
the existence of the Ideas; for it follows that not the dyad
but number is first, i. e. that the relative is prior to the absolute—besides all the other points on which certain people 20
by following out the opinions held about the Ideas have
come into conflict with the principles of the theory.

Further, according to the assumption on which our belief in the Ideas rests, there will be Forms not only of
substances but also of many other things (for the concept
is single not only in the case of substances but also in the 25
other cases, and there are sciences not only of substance but
also of other things, and a thousand other such difficulties
confront them). But according to the necessities of the
case and the opinions held about the Forms, if Forms can
be shared in there must be Ideas of substances only. For
they are not shared in incidentally, but a thing must share
in its Form as in something not predicated of a subject 30
(by 'being shared in incidentally' I mean that e. g. if a
thing shares in 'double itself', it shares also in 'eternal', but
incidentally; for 'eternal' happens to be predicable of the
'double'). Therefore the Forms will be substance; but the
same terms indicate substance in this and in the ideal
world (or what will be the meaning of saying that there
is something apart from the particulars—the one over 991ᵃ
many?). And if the Ideas and the particulars that share
in them have the same form, there will be something common to these; for why should '2' be one and the same in
the perishable 2's or in those which are many but eternal,

and not the same in the '2 itself' as in the particular 2?
5 But if they have not the same form, they must have only
the name in common, and it is as if one were to call both
Callias and a wooden image a 'man', without observing
any community between them.[22]

Above all one might discuss the question what on earth
the Forms contribute to sensible things, either to those
that are eternal or to those that come into being and
10 cease to be. For they cause neither movement nor any
change in them. But again they help in no wise either
towards the knowledge of the other things (for they are
not even the substance of these, else they would have been
in them), or towards their being, if they are not in the particulars which share in them; though if they were, they
might be thought to be causes, as white causes whiteness
15 in a white object by entering into its composition. But
this argument, which first Anaxagoras and later Eudoxus
and certain others used, is very easily upset; for it is not
difficult to collect many insuperable objections to such a
view.

But, further, all other things cannot come from the
20 Forms in any of the usual senses of 'from'. And to say that
they are patterns and the other things share in them is to
use empty words and poetical metaphors. For what is it
that works, looking to the Ideas? And anything can either
be, or become, like another without being copied from it,
25 so that whether Socrates exists or not a man like Socrates
might come to be; and evidently this might be so even if
Socrates were eternal. And there will be several patterns of
the same thing, and therefore several Forms; e. g. 'animal'
and 'two-footed' and also 'man himself' will be Forms of
30 man. Again, the Forms are patterns not only of sensible
things, but of Forms themselves also; i. e. the genus, as
genus of various species, will be so; therefore the same
thing will be pattern and copy.

991ᵇ   Again, it would seem impossible that the substance and

22 With 990ᵇ 2–991ᵃ 8 Cf. xiii. 1078ᵇ 34–1079ᵇ 3.

that of which it is the substance should exist apart; how therefore, could the Ideas, being the substances of things, exist apart? In the *Phaedo* [23] the case is stated in this way—that the Forms are causes both of being and of becoming; yet when the Forms exist, still the things that 5 share in them do not come into being, unless there is something to originate movement; and many other things come into being (e. g. a house or a ring) of which we say there are no Forms. Clearly, therefore, even the other things can both be and come into being owing to such causes as produce the things just mentioned.[24]

Again, if the Forms are numbers, how can they be causes? Is it because existing things are other numbers, 10 e. g. one number is man, another is Socrates, another Callias? Why then are the one set of numbers causes of the other set? It will not make any difference even if the former are eternal and the latter are not. But if it is because things in this sensible world (e. g. harmony) are ratios of numbers, evidently the things between which they are ratios are some one class of things. If, then, this—the matter—is 15 some definite thing, evidently the numbers themselves too will be ratios of something to something else. E. g. if Callias is a numerical ratio between fire and earth and water and air, his Idea also will be a number of certain other underlying things; and man-himself, whether it is a number in a sense or not, will still be a numerical ratio of certain things and not a number proper, nor will it be a kind of number 20 merely because it is a numerical ratio.

Again, from many numbers one number is produced, but how can one Form come from many Forms? And if the number comes not from the many numbers themselves but from the units in them, e. g. in 10,000, how is it with the units? If they are specifically alike, numerous absurdities will follow, and also if they are not alike (neither the 25 units in one number being themselves like one another nor

---

[23] 100 c–e.
[24] With 991[a] 8–[b] 9 Cf. xiii. 1079[b] 12–1080[a] 8.

those in other numbers being all like to all); for in what will they differ, as they are without quality? This is not a plausible view, nor is it consistent with our thought on the matter.

Further, they must set up a second kind of number (with which arithmetic deals), and all the objects which are called 'intermediate' by some thinkers; and how do these exist or from what principles do they proceed? Or why 30 must they be intermediate between the things in this sensible world and the things-themselves?

Further, the units in 2 must each come from a prior 2; but this is impossible.

992ª   Further, why is a number, when taken all together, one?

Again, besides what has been said, if the units are diverse the Platonists should have spoken like those who say there are four, or two, elements; for each of these thinkers gives the name of element not to that which is common, e. g. 5 to body, but to fire and earth, whether there is something common to them, viz. body, or not. But in fact the Platonists speak as if the One were homogeneous like fire or water; and if this is so, the numbers will not be substances. Evidently, if there is a One-itself and this is a first principle, 'one' is being used in more than one sense; for otherwise the theory is impossible.

When we wish to reduce substances to their principles, 10 we state that lines come from the short and long (i. e. from a kind of small and great), and the plane from the broad and narrow, and body from the deep and shallow. Yet how then can either the plane contain a line, or the solid a line or a plane? For the broad and narrow is a different class 15 from the deep and shallow. Therefore, just as number is not present in these, because the many and few are different from these, evidently no other of the higher classes will be present in the lower. But again the broad is not a genus which includes the deep, for then the solid would have been a species of plane.[25] Further, from what principle will

[25] With 992ª 10–19 Cf. xiii. 1085ª 9–19.

the presence of the *points* in the line be derived? Plato even used to object to this class of things as being a geo-[20] metrical fiction. He gave the name of principle of the line —and this he often posited—to the indivisible lines. Yet these must have a limit; therefore the argument from which the existence of the line follows proves also the existence of the point.

In general, though philosophy seeks the cause of perceptible things, we have given this up (for we say nothing [25] of the cause from which change takes its start), but while we fancy we are stating the substance of perceptible things, we assert the existence of a second class of substances, while our account of the way in which they are the substances of perceptible things is empty talk; for 'sharing', as we said before,[26] means nothing.

Nor have the Forms any connexion with what we see to be the cause in the case of the arts, that for whose sake [30] both all mind and the whole of nature are operative [27]— with this cause which we assert to be one of the first principles; but mathematics has come to be identical with philosophy for modern thinkers, though they say that it should be studied for the sake of other things.[28]

Further, one might suppose that the substance which according to them underlies as matter is too mathematical, **992ᵇ** and is a predicate and differentia of the substance, i. e. of the matter, rather than the matter itself; i. e. the great and the small are like the rare and the dense which the [5] physical philosophers speak of, calling these the primary differentiae of the substratum; for these are a kind of excess and defect. And regarding movement, if the great and the small are to be movement, evidently the Forms will be moved; but if they are not to be movement, whence did movement come? The whole study of nature has been annihilated.

[26] 991ᵃ 20–22.
[27] *sc.* the final cause.
[28] Cf. Plato, Rep. vii. 531 D, 533 B–E.

And what is thought to be easy—to show that all things
10 are one—is not done; for what is proved by the method
of setting out instances [29] is not that all things are one but
that there is a One-itself,—if we grant all the assumptions.
And not even this follows, if we do not grant that the universal is a genus; and this in some cases it cannot be.

Nor can it be explained either how the lines and planes
and solids that come after the numbers exist or can exist,
15 or what significance they have; for these can neither be
Forms (for they are not numbers), nor the intermediates
(for those are the objects of mathematics), nor the perishable things. This is evidently a distinct fourth class.

In general, if we search for the elements of existing
things without distinguishing the many senses in which
things are said to exist, we cannot find them, especially if
the search for the elements of which things are made is
20 conducted in this manner. For it is surely impossible to
discover what 'acting' or 'being acted on', or 'the straight',
is made of, but if elements can be discovered at all, it is
only the elements of substances; therefore either to seek
the elements of all existing things or to think one has
them is incorrect.

And how could we *learn* the elements of all things? Evidently we cannot start by knowing anything before. For as
25 he who is learning geometry, though he may know other
things before, knows none of the things with which the
science deals and about which he is to learn, so is it in all
other cases. Therefore if there is a science of all things, such
as some assert to exist, he who is learning this will know
nothing before. Yet all learning is by means of premisses
30 which are (either all or some of them) known before—
whether the learning be by demonstration or by definitions; for the elements of the definition must be known before and be familiar; and learning by induction proceeds
993ª similarly. But again, if the science were actually innate, it

[29] For this Platonic method Cf. vii. 1031ᵇ 21, xiii. 1086ᵇ 9, xiv.
1090ª 17.

were strange that we are unaware of our possession of the greatest of sciences.

Again, how is one to come to know what all things are made of, and how is this to be made evident? This also affords a difficulty; for there might be a conflict of opinion, as there is about certain syllables; some say *za* is made out of *s* and *d* and *a*, while others say it is a distinct sound and none of those that are familiar.

Further, how could we know the objects of sense without having the sense in question? Yet we ought to, if the elements of which all things consist, as complex sounds consist of the elements proper to sound, are the same.

10   It is evident, then, even from what we have said before, that all men seem to seek the causes named in the *Physics*,[30] and that we cannot name any beyond these; but they seek these vaguely; and though in a sense they have all been described before, in a sense they have not been described at all. For the earliest philosophy is, on all subjects, like one who lisps, since it is young and in its beginnings. For even Empedocles says bone exists by virtue of the ratio in it. Now this is the essence and the substance of the thing. But it is similarly necessary that flesh and each of the other tissues should be the ratio of its elements, or that not one of them should; for it is on account of this that both flesh and bone and everything else will exist, and not on account of the matter, which *he* names—fire and earth and water and air. But while he would necessarily have agreed if another had said this, he has not said it clearly.

On these questions our views have been expressed before; but let us return to enumerate the difficulties that might be raised on these same points;[31] for perhaps we may get from them some help toward our later difficulties.

---

[30] ii. 3, 7.
[31] The reference is to Bk. iii.

BOOK Λ (XII)

1069ᵃ 1 The subject of our inquiry is substance; for the principles and the causes we are seeking are those of sub-
20 stances. For if the universe is of the nature of a whole,
substance is its first part; and if it coheres merely by virtue
of serial succession, on this view also substance is first,
and is succeeded by quality, and then by quantity. At the
same time these latter are not even being in the full sense,
but are qualities and movements of it—or else even the
not-white and the not-straight would be being; at least we
25 say even these are, e. g. 'there is a not-white'.[1] Further, none
of the categories other than substance can exist apart. And
the early philosophers also in practice testify to the pri-
macy of substance; for it was of substance that they
sought the principles and elements and causes. The thinkers of the present [2] day tend to rank universals as substances (for genera are universals, and these they tend to
describe as principles and substances, owing to the abstract nature of their inquiry); but the thinkers of old
ranked particular things as substances, e. g. fire and earth,
not what is common to both, body.

30   There are three kinds of substance—one that is sensible
(of which one subdivision is eternal and another is perishable; the latter is recognized by all men, and includes e. g.
plants and animals), of which we must grasp the elements,
whether one or many; and another that is immovable, and
35 this certain thinkers assert to be capable of existing apart,
some dividing it into two, others identifying the Forms and
the objects of mathematics, and others positing, of these
two, only the objects of mathematics.[3] The former two

[1] This is an implication of the ordinary type of judgement, 'x is
not white'.

[2] The Platonists.

[3] The three views appear to have been held respectively by Plato,
Xenocrates, and Speusippus.

kinds of substance are the subject of physics (for they 1069^b
imply movement); but the third kind belongs to another
science, if there is no principle common to it and to the
other kinds.

2   Sensible substance is changeable. Now if change proceeds from opposites or from intermediates, and not
from all opposites (for the voice is not-white [but it does 5
not therefore change to white]), but from the contrary,
there must be something underlying which changes into
the contrary state; for the *contraries* do not change.
Further, something persists, but the contrary does not
persist; there is, then, some third thing besides the contraries, viz. the matter. Now since changes are of four
kinds—either in respect of the 'what' or of the quality or
of the quantity or of the place, and change in respect of 10
'thisness' is simple generation and destruction, and change
in quantity is increase and diminution, and change in respect of an affection is alteration, and change of place is
motion, changes will be from given states into those contrary to them in these several respects. The matter, then,
which changes must be capable of both states. And since
that which 'is' has two senses, we must say that everything 15
changes from that which is potentially to that which is
actually, e. g. from potentially white to actually white,
and similarly in the case of increase and diminution. Therefore not only can a thing come to be, incidentally, out of
that which is not, but also all things come to be out of
that which is, but is potentially, and is not actually. And
this is the 'One' of Anaxagoras; for instead of 'all things 20
were together'—and the 'Mixture' of Empedocles and
Anaximander and the account given by Democritus—it is
better to say 'all things were together potentially but not
actually'. Therefore these thinkers seem to have had some
notion of matter. Now all things that change have matter,
but different matter; and of eternal things those which are 25

not generable but are movable in space have matter—not matter for generation, however, but for motion from one place to another.

One might raise the question from what sort of non-being generation proceeds; for 'non-being' has three senses. If, then, one form of non-being exists potentially, still it is not by virtue of a potentiality for any and every thing, but different things come from different things; nor is it satisfactory to say that 'all things were together'; for they differ in their matter, since otherwise why did an infinity of things come to be, and not one thing? For 'reason' is one, so that if matter also were one, that must have come to be in actuality which the matter was in potency.[4] The causes and the principles, then, are three, two being the pair of contraries of which one is definition and form and the other is privation, and the third being the matter.

3   Note, next, that neither the matter nor the form comes to be—and I mean the last matter and form. For everything that changes is something and is changed by something and into something. That by which it is changed is the immediate mover; that which is changed, the matter; that into which it is changed, the form. The process, then, will go on to infinity, if not only the bronze comes to be round but also the round or the bronze comes to be; therefore there must be a stop.

Note, next, that each substance comes into being out of something that shares its name. (Natural objects and other things both rank as substances.) For things come into being either by art or by nature or by luck or by spontaneity. Now art is a principle of movement in something other than the thing moved, nature is a principle in the thing itself (for man begets man), and the other causes are privations of these two.

There are three kinds of substance—the matter, which is a 'this' in appearance (for all things that are characterized

[4] sc. an undifferentiated unity.

by contact and not by organic unity are matter and sub- 19
stratum, e. g. fire, flesh, head; for these are all matter, and
the last matter is the matter of that which is in the full 11
sense substance); the nature, which is a 'this' or positive
state towards which movement takes place; and again,
thirdly, the particular substance which is composed of these
two, e. g. Socrates or Callias. Now in some cases the 'this'
does not exist apart from the composite substance, e. g. the
form of house does not so exist, unless the art of building 15
exists apart (nor is there generation and destruction of
these forms, but it is in another way that the house apart
from its matter, and health, and all ideals of art, exist and
do not exist); but if the 'this' exists apart from the concrete
thing, it is only in the case of natural objects. And so
Plato was not far wrong when he said that there are as
many Forms as there are kinds of natural object (if there
are Forms distinct from the things of this earth). The 21
moving causes exist as things preceding the effects, but
causes in the sense of definitions are simultaneous with
their effects. For when a man is healthy, then health also
exists; and the shape of a bronze sphere exists at the same
time as the bronze sphere. (But we must examine whether 2{
any form also survives afterwards. For in some cases there
is nothing to prevent this; e. g. the soul may be of this sort
—not all soul but the reason; for presumably it is impossible that all soul should survive.) Evidently then there is
no necessity, on this ground at least, for the existence of the
Ideas. For man is begotten by man, a given man by an
individual father; and similarly in the arts; for the medical 3»
art is the formal cause of health.

4　The causes and the principles of different things are
　　in a sense different, but in a sense, if one speaks
universally and analogically, they are the same for all. For
one might raise the question whether the principles and
elements are different or the same for substances and for 3{
relative terms, and similarly in the case of each of the cate-

gories. But it would be paradoxical if they were the same for all. For then from the same elements will proceed rela-1070ᵇ tive terms and substances. What then will this common element be? For (1) (a) there is nothing common to and distinct from substance and the other categories, viz. those which are predicated; but an element is prior to the things of which it is an element. But again (b) substance is not an element in relative terms, nor is any of these an element in substance. Further, (2) how can all things have the same elements? For none of the elements can be the same 5 as that which is composed of elements, e. g. b or a cannot be the same as ba. (None, therefore, of the intelligibles, e. g. being or unity, is an element; for these are predicable of each of the compounds as well.) None of the elements, then, will be either a substance or a relative term; but it must be one or other. All things, then, have not the same elements.

Or, as we are wont to put it, in a sense they have and 10 in a sense they have not; e. g. perhaps the elements of perceptible bodies are, as *form*, the hot, and in another sense the cold, which is the *privation*; and, as *matter*, that which directly and of itself potentially has these attributes; and substances comprise both these and the things composed of these, of which these are the principles, or any unity which is produced out of the hot and the cold, e. g. 15 flesh or bone; for the product must be different from the elements. These things then have the same elements and principles (though specifically different things have specifically different elements); but *all* things have not the same elements in this sense, but only analogically; i. e. one might say that there are three principles—the form, the privation, and the matter. But each of these is different 20 for each class; e. g. in colour they are white, black, and surface, and in day and night they are light, darkness, and air.

Since not only the elements present in a thing are causes, but also something external, i. e. the moving cause, clearly while 'principle' and 'element' are different both are causes, and 'principle' is divided into these two kinds [5] and that which acts as producing movement or rest is a principle and a substance. Therefore analogically there are three ele- 25 ments, and four causes and principles; but the elements are different in different things, and the proximate moving cause is different for different things. Health, disease, body; the moving cause is the medical art. Form, disorder of a particular kind, bricks; the moving cause is the building art. And since the moving cause in the case of natural 30 things is—for man, for instance, man, and in the products of thought the form or its contrary, there will be in a sense three causes, while in a sense there are four. For the medical art is in some sense health, and the building art is the form of the house, and man begets man; [6] further, besides these there is that which as first of all things moves all things. 35

5   Some things can exist apart and some cannot, and it is the former that are substances. And therefore all **1071ᵇ** things have the same causes,[7] because, without substances, modifications and movements do not exist. Further, these causes will probably be soul and body, or reason and desire and body.

And in yet another way, analogically identical things 5 are principles, i. e. actuality and potency; but these also are not only different for different things but also apply in different ways to them. For in some cases the same thing exists at one time actually and at another potentially, e. g. wine or flesh or man does so. (And these two fall under the above-named causes.[8] For the form exists actually, if it can exist apart, and so does the complex of form and 10 matter, and the privation, e. g. darkness or disease; but the matter exists potentially; for this is that which can become qualified either by the form or by the privation.) But the

---

[5] i. e. the principles which are elements and those which are not.
[6] i. e. the efficient cause is identical with the formal.
[7] i. e. the causes of substance are the causes of all things.
[8] i. e. the division into potency and actuality stands in a definite relation to the previous division into matter, form, and privation.

distinction of actuality and potentiality applies in another
way to cases where the matter of cause and of effect is not
the same, in some of which cases the form is not the same
but different; e. g. the cause of man is (1) the elements in
man (viz. fire and earth as matter, and the peculiar form),
and further (2) something else outside, i. e. the father, and
(3) besides these the sun and its oblique course, which are
neither matter nor form nor privation of man nor of the
same species with him, but moving causes.

Further, one must observe that some causes can be expressed in universal terms, and some cannot. The proximate principles of all things are the 'this' which is proximate in actuality, and another which is proximate in
potentiality.[9] The universal causes, then, of which we
spoke [10] do not exist. For it is the individual that is the
originative principle of the individuals. For while man is
the originative principle of man universally, there is no
universal man, but Peleus is the originative principle of
Achilles, and your father of you, and this particular *b* of
this particular *ba*, though *b* in general is the originative
principle of *ba* taken without qualification.

Further, if the causes of substances are the causes of all
things, yet different things have different causes and elements, as was said [11]; the causes of things that are not in
the same class, e. g. of colours and sounds, of substances
and quantities, are different except in an analogical sense;
and those of things in the same species are different, not in
species, but in the sense that the causes of different individuals are different, your matter and form and moving
cause being different from mine, while in their universal
definition they are the same. And if we inquire what are
the principles or elements of substances and relations and

---

[9] e. g. the proximate causes of a child are the individual father (who
on Aristotle's view is the efficient and contains the formal cause) and
the germ contained in the individual mother (which is the material
cause).

[10] In l. 17.
[11] In 1070[b] 17.

qualities—whether they are the same or different—clearly when the names of the causes are used in several senses the causes of each are the same, but when the senses are distinguished the causes are not the same but different, except that in the following senses the causes of all are the same. They are (1) the same or analogous in this sense, that matter, form, privation, and the moving cause are common to all things; and (2) the causes of substances may be treated as causes of all things in this sense, that when substances are removed all things are removed; further, (3) that which is first in respect of complete reality is the cause 35 of all things. But in another sense there are different first causes, viz. all the contraries which are neither generic nor ambiguous terms; and, further, the matters of different things are different. We have stated, then, what are the **1071ᵇ** principles of sensible things and how many they are, and in what sense they are the same and in what sense different.

6   Since there were [12] three kinds of substance, two of them physical and one unmovable, regarding the latter we must assert that it is necessary that there should be an eternal unmovable substance. For substances are the first of existing things, and if they are all destructible, 5 all things are destructible. But it is impossible that movement should either have come into being or cease to be (for it must always have existed), or that time should. For there could not be a before and an after if time did not exist. Movement also is continuous, then, in the sense in which time is; for time is either the same thing as movement or an attribute of movement. And there is no continuous movement except movement in place, and of 10 this only that which is circular is continuous.

But if there is something which is capable of moving things or acting on them, but is not actually doing so, there will not necessarily be movement; for that which

[12] Cf. 1069ᵃ 30.

has a potency need not exercise it. Nothing, then, is gained even if we suppose eternal substances, as the believers in the Forms do, unless there is to be in them
15 some principle which can cause change; nay, even this is not enough, nor is another substance besides the Forms enough; for if it is not to act, there will be no movement. Further, even if it acts, this will not be enough, if its essence is potency; for there will not be eternal movement, since that which is potentially may possibly not be. There
20 must, then, be such a principle, whose very essence is actuality. Further, then, these substances must be without matter; for they must be eternal, if anything is eternal. Therefore they must be actuality.

Yet there is a difficulty; for it is thought that everything that acts is able to act, but that not everything that is able
25 to act acts, so that the potency is prior. But if this is so, nothing that is need be; for it is possible for all things to be capable of existing but not yet to exist.

Yet if we follow the theologians who generate the world from night, or the natural philosophers who say that 'all things were together',[13] the same impossible result ensues. For how will there be movement, if there is no actually
30 existing cause? Wood will surely not move itself—the carpenter's art must act on it; nor will the menstrual blood nor the earth set themselves in motion, but the seeds must act on the earth and the semen on the menstrual blood.

This is why some suppose eternal actuality—e. g. Leucippus[14] and Plato[15]; for they say there is always movement. But why and what this movement is they do not say, nor, if the world moves in this way or that, do they tell us the cause of its doing so. Now nothing is moved at random, but there must always be something present to

---

[13] Anaxagoras.
[14] Cf. De Caelo, iii. 300[b] 8.
[15] Cf. Timaeus, 30 A.

move it; e. g. as a matter of fact a thing moves in one way 35
by nature, and in another by force or through the influence
of reason or something else. (Further, what sort of movement is primary? This makes a vast difference.) But again
for Plato, at least, it is not permissible to name here that **1072ᵃ**
which he sometimes supposes to be the source of movement—that which moves itself; [16] for the soul is later,
and coeval with the heavens, according to his account.[17]
To suppose potency prior to actuality, then, is in a sense
right, and in a sense not; and we have specified, these
senses.[18] That actuality is prior is testified by Anaxagoras 5
(for his 'reason' is actuality) and by Empedocles in his
doctrine of love and strife, and by those who say that there
is always movement, e. g. Leucippus. Therefore chaos or
night did not exist for an infinite time, but the same
things have always existed (either passing through a cycle
of changes or obeying some other law), since actuality is
prior to potency. If, then, there is a constant cycle, something must always remain,[19] acting in the same way. And 10
if there is to be generation and destruction, there must be
something else [20] which is always acting in different ways.
This must, then, act in one way in virtue of itself, and in
another in virtue of something else—either of a third agent,
therefore, or of the first. Now it must be in virtue of the
first. For otherwise this again causes the motion both of
the second agent and of the third. Therefore it is better
to say 'the first'. For it was the cause of eternal uni- 15
formity; and something else is the cause of variety, and
evidently both together are the cause of eternal variety.
This, accordingly, is the character which the motions
actually exhibit. What need then is there to seek for
other principles?

[16] Cf. *Phaedrus*, 245 c; *Laws*, 894 ε.
[17] Cf. *Timaeus*, 34 β.
[18] Cf. 1071ᵇ 22–26.
[19] i. e. the sphere of the fixed stars.
[20] i. e. the sun. Cf. *De Gen. et Corr.* ii. 336ᵃ 23 ff.

7   Since (1) this is a possible account of the matter, and
(2) if it were not true, the world would have proceeded out of night and 'all things together' and out of
20 non-being, these difficulties may be taken as solved. There
is, then, something which is always moved with an un-
ceasing motion, which is motion in a circle; and this is
plain not in theory only but in fact. Therefore the first
heaven [21] must be eternal. There is therefore also something which moves it. And since that which is moved and
moves is intermediate, there is something which moves
25 without being moved, being eternal, substance, and actuality. And the object of desire and the object of thought
move in this way; they move without being moved. The
primary objects of desire and of thought are the same. For
the apparent good is the object of appetite, and the real
good is the primary object of rational wish. But desire is
consequent on opinion rather than opinion on desire; for
30 the thinking is the starting-point. And thought is moved
by the object of thought, and one of the two columns of
opposites is in itself the object of thought; and in this,
substance is first, and in substance, that which is simple
and exists actually. (The one and the simple are not the
same; for 'one' means a measure, but 'simple' means that
the thing itself has a certain nature.) But the beautiful,
also, and that which is in itself desirable are in the same
35 column; and the first in any class is always best, or analogous to the best.

That a final cause may exist among unchangeable en-
1072ᵇ tities is shown by the distinction of its meanings. For the
final cause is (a) some being for whose good an action is
done, and (b) something at which the action aims; and of
these the latter exists among unchangeable entities though
the former does not. The final cause, then, produces motion as being loved, but all other things move by being
moved.

[21] i. e. the outer sphere of the universe, that in which the fixed stars
are set.

Now if something is moved it is capable of being otherwise than as it is. Therefore if its actuality is the primary 5
form of spatial motion, then in so far as it is subject to
change, in this respect it is capable of being otherwise—in
place, even if not in substance. But since there is something
which moves while itself unmoved, existing actually, this
can in no way be otherwise than as it is. For motion in
space is the first of the kinds of change, and motion in a
circle the first kind of spatial motion; and this the first 10
mover produces.[22] The first mover, then, exists of necessity; and in so far as it exists by necessity, its mode of being
is good, and it is in this sense a first principle. For the
necessary has all these senses—that which is necessary
perforce because it is contrary to the natural impulse, that
without which the good is impossible, and that which
cannot be otherwise but can exist only in a single way.

On such a principle, then, depend the heavens and the
world of nature. And it is a life such as the best which we
enjoy, and enjoy for but a short time (for it is ever in this 15
state, which we cannot be), since its actuality is also
pleasure. (And for this reason [23] are waking, perception,
and thinking most pleasant, and hopes and memories are
so on account of these.) And thinking in itself deals with
that which is best in itself, and that which is thinking in
the fullest sense with that which is best in the fullest
sense. And thought thinks on itself because it shares the 20
nature of the object of thought; for it becomes an object
of thought in coming into contact with and thinking its
objects, so that thought and object of thought are the
same. For that which is capable of receiving the object of
thought, i. e. the essence, is thought. But it is active when
it possesses this object. Therefore the possession rather
than the receptivity is the divine element which thought

---

[22] If it had any movement, it would have the first. But it produces
this and therefore cannot share in it; for if it did, we should have to
look for something that is prior to the first mover and imparts this
motion to it.

[23] sc. because they are activities or actualities.

seems to contain, and the act of contemplation is what
is most pleasant and best. If, then, God is always in that
good state in which we sometimes are, this compels our
⌐5 wonder; and if in a better this compels it yet more. And
God *is* in a better state. And life also belongs to God;
for the actuality of thought is life, and God is that actuality; and God's self-dependent actuality is life most good
and eternal. We say therefore that God is a living being,
eternal, most good, so that life and duration continuous
and eternal belong to God; for this *is* God.

Those who suppose, as the Pythagoreans [24] and Speusip-
30 pus [25] do, that supreme beauty and goodness are not present in the beginning, because the beginnings both of plants
and of animals are *causes*, but beauty and completeness
are in the *effects* of these,[26] are wrong in their opinion.
35 For the seed comes from other individuals which are prior
and complete, and the first thing is not seed but the complete being; e. g. we must say that before the seed there is
1073ᵃ a man—not the man produced from the seed, but another from whom the seed comes.

It is clear then from what has been said that there is a
substance which is eternal and unmovable and separate
from sensible things. It has been shown also that this
5 substance cannot have any magnitude, but is without part
and indivisible (for it produces movement through infinite
time, but nothing finite has infinite power; and, while every
magnitude is either infinite or finite, it cannot, for the
above reason, have finite magnitude, and it cannot have
10 infinite magnitude because there is no infinite magnitude
at all). But it has also been shown that it is impassive and
unalterable; for all the other changes are posterior to [27]
change of place.

---

[24] Cf. 1075ᵃ 36.
[25] Cf. vii. 1028ᵇ 21, xiv. 1091ᵃ 34, 1092ᵃ 11.
[26] i. e. the animal or plant is more beautiful and perfect than the seed.
[27] i. e. impossible without.

8   It is clear, then, why these things are as they are.

But we must not ignore the question whether we have to suppose one such substance or more than one, and if the latter, how many; we must also mention, regarding the opinions expressed by others, that they have said nothing about the number of the substances that can even be clearly stated. For the theory of Ideas has no special discussion of the subject; for those who speak of Ideas say the Ideas are numbers, and they speak of numbers now as unlimited, now [28] as limited by the number 10; but as for the reason why there should be just so many numbers, nothing is said with any demonstrative exactness. We however must discuss the subject, starting from the presuppositions and distinctions we have mentioned. The first principle or primary being is not movable either in itself or accidentally, but produces the primary eternal and single movement. But since that which is moved must be moved by something, and the first mover must be in itself unmovable, and eternal movement must be produced by something eternal and a single movement by a single thing, and since we see that besides the simple spatial movement of the universe, which we say the first and unmovable substance produces, there are other spatial movements—those of the planets—which are eternal (for a body which moves in a circle is eternal and unresting; we have proved these points in the physical treatises [29]), each of these movements also must be caused by a substance both unmovable in itself and eternal. For the nature of the stars [30] is eternal just because it is a certain kind of substance, and the mover is eternal and prior to the moved, and then which is prior to a substance must be a substance. Evidently, then, there must be substances which are of the

---

[28] The reference is to Plato (Cf. *Phys.* 206[b] 32).

[29] Cf. *Phys.* viii. 8, 9; *De Caelo*, i. 2, ii. 3–8.

[30] This is to be understood as a general term including both **fixed stars** and **planets**.

same number as the movements of the stars, and in their
nature eternal, and in themselves unmovable, and without
magnitude, for the reason before mentioned.[31]

1073ᵇ   That the movers are substances, then, and that one of
these is first and another second according to the same
order as the movements of the stars, is evident. But in the
number of the movements we reach a problem which must
be treated from the standpoint of that one of the mathematical sciences which is most akin to philosophy—viz. of
5 astronomy; for this science speculates about substance
which is perceptible but eternal, but the other mathematical sciences, i. e. arithmetic and geometry, treat of no
substance. That the movements are more numerous than
the bodies that are moved is evident to those who have
given even moderate attention to the matter; for each of
10 the planets has more than one movement. But as to the
actual number of these movements, we now—to give some
notion of the subject—quote what some of the mathematicians say, that our thought may have some definite num-
15 ber to grasp; but, for the rest, we must partly investigate for
ourselves, partly learn from other investigators, and if those
who study this subject form an opinion contrary to what
we have now stated, we must esteem both parties indeed,
but follow the more accurate.

Eudoxus supposed that the motion of the sun or of the
moon involves, in either case, three spheres, of which the
first is the sphere of the fixed stars, and the second moves
20 in the circle which runs along the middle of the zodiac,
and the third in the circle which is inclined across the
breadth of the zodiac; but the circle in which the moon
moves is inclined at a greater angle than that in which the
sun moves. And the motion of the planets involves, in each
case, four spheres, and of these also the first and second
25 are the same as the first two mentioned above (for the
sphere of the fixed stars is that which moves all the other
spheres, and that which is placed beneath this and has its

[31] Cf. ll. 5–11.

movement in the circle which bisects the zodiac is common to all), but the *poles* of the third sphere of each planet
are in the circle which bisects the zodiac, and the motion
of the fourth sphere is in the circle which is inclined at an
angle to the equator of the third sphere; and the poles of
the third sphere are different for each of the other planets, 30
but those of Venus and Mercury are the same.

Callippus made the position of the spheres the same as
Eudoxus did, but while he assigned the same number as
Eudoxus did to Jupiter and to Saturn, he thought two
more spheres should be added to the sun and two to the 35
moon, if one is to explain the observed facts; and one more
to each of the other planets.

But it is necessary, if all the spheres combined are to
explain the observed facts, that for each of the planets
there should be other spheres (one fewer than those hith- **1074ᵃ**
erto assigned) which counteract those already mentioned
and bring back to the same position the outermost sphere
of the star which in each case is situated below [32] the star
in question; for only thus can all the forces at work produce 5
the observed motion of the planets. Since, then, the spheres
involved in the movement of the planets themselves are—
eight for Saturn and Jupiter and twenty-five for the others,
and of these only those involved in the movement of
the lowest-situated planet need not be counteracted, the
spheres which counteract those of the outermost two
planets will be six in number, and the spheres which
counteract those of the next four planets will be sixteen;
therefore the number of all the spheres—both those which 10
move the planets and those which counteract these—will
be fifty-five. And if one were not to add to the moon
and to the sun the movements we mentioned,[33] the whole
set of spheres will be forty-seven in number.

Let this, then, be taken as the number of the spheres,

---

[32] i. e. inwards from, the universe being thought of as a system of
concentric spheres encircling the earth.

[33] In 1073ᵇ 35, 38–1074ᵃ 4

so that the unmovable substances and principles also may
15 probably be taken as just so many; the assertion of necessity
must be left to more powerful thinkers. But if there can
be no spatial movement which does not conduce to the
moving of a star, and if further every being and every substance which is immune from change and in virtue of
itself has attained to the best must be considered an end,
there can be no other being apart from these we have
20 named, but this must be the number of the substances.
For if there are others, they will cause change as being a
final cause of movement; but there cannot be other movements besides those mentioned. And it is reasonable to
25 infer this from a consideration of the bodies that are
moved; for if everything that moves is for the sake of that
which is moved, and every movement belongs to something that is moved, no movement can be for the sake
of itself or of another movement, but all the movements
must be for the sake of the stars. For if there is to be a
movement for the sake of a movement, this latter also will
30 have to be for the sake of something else; so that since
there cannot be an infinite regress, the end of every movement will be one of the divine bodies which move through
the heaven.

(Evidently there is but one heaven. For if there are
many heavens as there are many men, the moving principles, of which each heaven will have one, will be one in
form but in number many. But all things that are many in
35 number have matter; for one and the same definition, e. g.
that of man, applies to many things, while Socrates is one.
But the primary essence has not matter; for it is complete
reality. So the unmovable first mover is one both in definition and in number; so too, therefore, is that which is
moved always and continuously; therefore there is one
heaven alone.)

1074ᵇ Our forefathers in the most remote ages have handed
down to their posterity a tradition, in the form of a myth,

that these bodies are gods and that the divine encloses the whole of nature. The rest of the tradition has been added later in mythical form with a view to the persuasion of the 5 multitude and to its legal and utilitarian expediency; they say these gods are in the form of men or like some of the other animals, and they say other things consequent on and similar to these which we have mentioned. But if one were to separate the first point from these additions and take it alone—that they thought the first substances to be 10 gods, one must regard this as an inspired utterance, and reflect that, while probably each art and each science has often been developed as far as possible and has again perished, these opinions, with others, have been preserved until the present like relics of the ancient treasure. Only thus far, then, is the opinion of our ancestors and of our earliest predecessors clear to us.

9   The nature of the divine thought involves certain 15 problems; for while thought is held to be the most divine of things observed by us, the question how it must be situated in order to have that character involves difficulties. For if it thinks of nothing, what is there here of dignity? It is just like one who sleeps. And if it thinks, but this depends on something else, then (since that which is its substance is not the act of thinking, but a potency) it cannot be the best substance; for it is through thinking 20 that its value belongs to it. Further, whether its substance is the faculty of thought or the act of thinking, what does it think of? Either of itself or of something else; and if of something else, either of the same thing always or of something different. Does it matter, then, or not, whether it thinks of the good or of any chance thing? Are there not some things about which it is incredible that it should 25 think? Evidently, then, it thinks of that which is most divine and precious, and it does not change; for change would be change for the worse, and this would be already a movement. First, then, if 'thought' is not the act of thinking but a potency, it would be reasonable to suppose that the continuity of its thinking is wearisome to it. Secondly, there would evidently be something else more precious than thought, viz. that which is thought of. For 30 both thinking and the act of thought will belong even to one who thinks of the worst thing in the world, so that if this ought to be avoided (and it ought, for there are even some things which it is better not to see than to see), the act of thinking cannot be the best of things. Therefore it must be of itself that the divine thought thinks (since it is the most excellent of things), and its thinking is a thinking on thinking.

But evidently knowledge and perception and opinion 35 and understanding have always something else as their object, and themselves only by the way. Further, if thinking and being thought of are different, in respect of which does goodness belong to thought? For to be an act of thinking and to be an object of thought are not the same thing. We answer that in some cases the knowledge is the 1075ª object. In the productive sciences it is the substance or essence of the object, matter omitted, and in the theoretical sciences the definition or the act of thinking is the object. Since, then, thought and the object of thought are not different in the case of things that have not matter, the divine thought and its object will be the same, i. e. the thinking will be one with the object of its thought.

A further question is left—whether the object of the 5 divine thought is composite; for if it were, thought would change in passing from part to part of the whole. We answer that everything which has not matter is indivisible— as human thought, or rather the thought of composite beings, is in a certain period of time (for it does not possess the good at this moment or at that, but its best, being something *different* from it, is attained only in a whole 10 period of time), so throughout eternity is the thought which has *itself* for its object.

10 We must consider also in which of two ways the
    nature of the universe contains the good and the
highest good, whether as something separate and by itself,
or as the order of the parts. Probably in both ways, as an
army does; for its good is found both in its order and in its 15
leader, and more in the latter; for he does not depend on
the order but it depends on him. And all things are ordered
together somehow, but not all alike—both fishes and fowls
and plants; and the world is not such that one thing has
nothing to do with another, but they are connected. For all
are ordered together to one end, but it is as in a house, 20
where the freemen are least at liberty to act at random, but
all things or most things are already ordained for them,
while the slaves and the animals do little for the common
good, and for the most part live at random; for this is the
sort of principle that constitutes the nature of each. I mean,
for instance, that all must at least come to be dissolved into
their elements.[34] and there are other functions similarly
in which all share for the good of the whole.

We must not fail to observe how many impossible or 25
paradoxical results confront those who hold different views
from our own, and what are the views of the subtler thinkers, and which views are attended by fewest difficulties.
All make all things out of contraries. But neither 'all things'
nor 'out of contraries' is right; nor do these thinkers tell
us how all the things in which the contraries are present
can be made out of the contraries; for contraries are not 30
affected by one another. Now for us this difficulty is solved
naturally by the fact that there is a third element.[35] These
thinkers however make one of the two contraries matter;
this is done for instance by those who make the unequal
matter for the equal, or the many matter for the one.[36]
But this also is refuted in the same way; for the one matter

---

[34] sc. in order that higher forms of being may be produced by new
combinations of the elements.
[35] i. e. the substratum.
[36] The reference is to Platonists.

which underlies any pair of contraries is contrary to
nothing. Further, all things, except the one, will, on the
35 view we are criticizing, partake of evil; for the bad itself is
one of the two elements. But the other school [37] does not
treat the good and the bad even as principles; yet in all
things the good is in the highest degree a principle. The
school we first mentioned is right in saying that it is a
principle, but *how* the good is a principle they do not say—
whether as end or as mover or as form.

1075ᵇ   Empedocles [38] also has a paradoxical view; for he identifies the good with love, but this is a principle both as mover
(for it brings things together) and as matter (for it is part
5 of the mixture). Now even if it happens that the same
thing is a principle both as matter and as mover, still the
being, at least, of the two is not the same. In which
respect then is love a principle? It is paradoxical also that
strife should be imperishable; the nature of his 'evil' is
just strife.

Anaxagoras makes the good a motive principle; for his
'reason' moves things. But it moves them for an end, which
must be something other than it, except according to our
way of stating the case; for, on our view, the medical art is
10 in a sense health. It is paradoxical also not to suppose a
contrary to the good, i. e. to reason. But all who speak of
the contraries make no use of the contraries, unless we
bring their views into shape. And why some things are
perishable and others imperishable, no one tells us; for they
make all existing things out of the same principles. Further,
15 some make existing things out of the non-existent; and
others to avoid the necessity of this make all things one.

Further, why should there always be becoming, and
what is the cause of becoming?—this no one tells us.
And those who suppose two principles must suppose another, a superior principle, and so must those who believe

[37] The reference is to the Pythagoreans and Speusippus; Cf. xii.
1072ᵇ 31.

[38] Cf. i. 985ᵃ 4.

in the Forms; for why did things come to participate, or
why do they participate, in the Forms? And all other think- 20
ers [39] are confronted by the necessary consequence that
there is something contrary to Wisdom, i. e. to the highest
knowledge; but we are not. For there is nothing contrary to
that which is primary; for all contraries have matter, and
things that have matter exist only potentially; and the
ignorance which is contrary to any knowledge leads to an
object contrary to the object of the knowledge; but what
is primary has no contrary.

Again, if besides sensible things no others exist, there
will be no first principle, no order, no becoming, no 25
heavenly bodies, but each principle will have a principle
before it, as in the accounts of the theologians and all the
natural philosophers. But if the Forms or the numbers are
to exist, they will be causes of nothing; or if not that, at
least not of movement. Further, how is extension, i. e. a
continuum, to be produced out of unextended parts? For
number will not, either as mover or as form, produce a
continuum. But again there cannot be any *contrary* that is 30
also essentially a productive or moving principle; or it
would be possible not to be.[40] Or at least its action would
be posterior to its potency. The world, then, would not be
eternal. But it is; one of these premisses, then, must be
denied. And we have said how this must be done.[41] Further,
in virtue of what the numbers, or the soul and the body, or 35
in general the form and the thing, are one—of this no one
tells us anything; nor can any one tell, unless he says, as
we do, that the mover makes them one. And those who
say [42] mathematical number is first and go on to generate
one kind of substance after another and give different
principles for each, make the substance of the universe a 1076
mere series of episodes (for one substance has no influence

---

[39] The special reference is to Plato; Cf. *Rep.* 477.
[40] Since contraries must contain matter, and matter implies potentiality and contingency.
[41] Cf. 1071[b] 19, 20.
[42] Speusippus is meant; Cf. vii. 1028[b] 21, xiv. 1090[b] 13–20.

on another by its existence or non-existence), and they give us many governing principles; but the world refuses to be governed badly.

'The rule of many is not good; one ruler let there be.' [43]

[43] Cf. *Iliad*, ii. 204.

Ethics

INTRODUCTION

Since every art, inquiry, and action is directed to some good, the investigation of moral problems takes its peculiar turn in the philosophy of Aristotle from his undertaking to treat that end as a principle and a cause relative to the potentialities of man. For although there is some verbal agreement among men identifying the good with happiness, there is no agreement concerning what happiness is, and Aristotle concludes that happiness must be defined, not in terms of something else with which it is identical, but in terms of activity of the soul in accordance with perfect virtue.

The study of ethics is therefore in good part a study of virtues, that is, a study of values and actions not in terms of ends in which the action terminates but in terms of habits from which it originates, and the inquiry is in that sense functional and determined by the peculiarities and potentialities of individual men. "Habit" is a source of action distinct from "nature," which is not altered as a principle of motion by prior actions or by the influence of a rational principle, and from "art," which is more dependent than virtue on knowledge. There is no virtue proper to the vegetative faculty of the soul, since its functions are not affected by reason, but there are two varieties of virtues, moral virtues proper to the appetitive soul which shares in a rational principle, and intellectual virtues proper to the intellective soul. In addition to the virtues, however, Aristotle considers continence and superhuman virtue (which are also moral states), pleasure (which some men think a good and which is a mark of the good in the virtuous man), friendship (which either is a virtue or implies virtue), and the influence of the state in the inculcation of virtue. The relativity of the moral virtues to the potentialities of the individual man and the peculiarities of his environment does not lead to a moral relativism, however, for political justice is in part natural, and moral virtue is in accordance with the rule of right reason or of practical wisdom. Practical wisdom is in turn so closely dependent on philosophic wisdom, that wisdom may be said to be the formal cause of happiness, and happiness in the highest sense is found in the contemplative life.

The ethics of Aristotle reflects in many ways the place which it occupies in the system of the Aristotelian sciences. It is itself a science, although it does not employ the same method as the theoretic sciences and it does not aim at the same precision. It depends on the nature of man and borrows dialectical distinctions therefore from psychology to differentiate moral from intellectual virtues. Yet it treats, among the intellectual virtues, of those habits of mind which are the source of discursive scientific proof, intuition of first principles, and wisdom itself which combines scientific proof and principles. Moreover, among the practical sciences, it is not distinct, strictly, from political science, but it is rather the other aspect of the analysis of human action by which the study of the associations of men (which are affected by the character of their members) is supplemented by the study of the virtues of men (which are affected by political institutions). Political science, finally, which as a science makes use of first principles treated properly in metaphysics, is itself an "architectonic science," and as science of action determines what sciences will be studied in the state and in what manner.

ETHICA NICOMACHEA

CONTENTS

F. *Virtues of social intercourse.*

6. Friendliness, obsequiousness, churlishness.
7. Truthfulness, boastfulness, mock-modesty.
8. Ready wit, buffoonery, boorishness.

G. *A quasi-virtue.*

9. Shame, bashfulness, shamelessness.

H. *Justice.*

I. Its sphere and outer nature: in what sense it is a mean.

1. The just as the lawful (universal justice) and the just as the fair and equal (particular justice): the former considered.
2. The latter considered: divided into distributive and rectificatory justice.
3. Distributive justice, in accordance with geometrical proportion.
4. Rectificatory justice, in accordance with arithmetical progression.
5. Justice in exchange, reciprocity in accordance with proportion.
6. Political justice and analogous kinds of justice.
7. Natural and legal justice.

II. Its inner nature as involving choice.

8. The scale of degrees of wrongdoing.
9. Can a man be voluntarily treated unjustly? Is it the distributor or the recipient that is guilty of injustice in distribution? Justice not so easy as it might seem, because it is not a way of acting but an inner disposition.
10. Equity, a corrective of legal justice.
11. Can a man treat himself unjustly?

BOOK VI. INTELLECTUAL VIRTUE

A. *Introduction.*

1. Reasons for studying intellectual virtue: intellect divided into the contemplative and the calculative.

2. The object of the former is truth, that of the latter truth corresponding with right desire.

B. The chief intellectual virtues.

3. Science—demonstrative knowledge of the necessary and eternal.
4. Art—knowledge of how to make things.
5. Practical wisdom—knowledge of how to secure the ends of human life.
6. Intuitive reason—knowledge of the principles from which science proceeds.
7. Philosophic wisdom—the union of intuitive reason and science.
8. Relations between practical wisdom and political science.

C. Minor intellectual virtues concerned with conduct.

9. Goodness in deliberation, how related to practical wisdom.
10. Understanding—the critical quality answering to the imperative quality practical wisdom.
11. Judgment—right discrimination of the equitable: the place of intuition in morals.

D. Relation of philosophic to practical wisdom.

12. What is the use of philosophic and of practical wisdom? Philosophic wisdom is the formal cause of happiness; practical wisdom is what ensures the taking of proper means to the proper ends desired by moral virtue.
13. Relation of practical wisdom to natural virtue, moral virtue, and the right rule.

BOOK VII. CONTINENCE AND INCONTINENCE. PLEASURE

A. Continence and incontinence.

1. Six varieties of character: method of treatment: current opinions.

BOOK X. PLEASURE. HAPPINESS

A. *Pleasure.*

1. Two opposed views about pleasure.
2. Discussion of the view that pleasure is the good.
3. Discussion of the view that pleasure is wholly bad.
4. Definition of pleasure.
5. Pleasures differ with the activities which they accompany and complete: criterion of the value of pleasures.

B. *Happiness.*

6. Happiness is good activity, not amusement.
7. Happiness in the highest sense is the contemplative life.
8. Superiority of the contemplative life further considered.
9. Legislation is needed if the end is to be attained: transition to *Politics.*

Ethica Nicomachea

Nicomachean Ethics

Translated by W. D. Ross

⎍⎍⎍

BOOK I

1 Every art and every inquiry, and similarly every action
1094ᵃ   and pursuit, is thought to aim at some good; and for
this reason the good has rightly been declared [1] to be that
at which all things aim. But a certain difference is found
among ends; some are activities, others are products apart
5 from the activities that produce them. Where there are
ends apart from the actions, it is the nature of the products
to be better than the activities. Now, as there are many
actions, arts, and sciences, their ends also are many; the
end of the medical art is health, that of shipbuilding a
vessel, that of strategy victory, that of economics wealth.
10 But where such arts fall under a single capacity—as bridle-
making and the other arts concerned with the equipment
of horses fall under the art of riding, and this and every
military action under strategy, in the same way other arts
fall under yet others—in all of these the ends of the
master arts are to be preferred to all the subordinate ends;
15 for it is for the sake of the former that the latter are pursued. It makes no difference whether the activities themselves are the ends of the actions, or something else apart
from the activities, as in the case of the sciences just
mentioned.

[1] Perhaps by Eudoxus; Cf. 1172ᵇ 9.

2   If, then, there is some end of the things we do, which
we desire for its own sake (everything else being desired for the sake of this), and if we do not choose everything for the sake of something else (for at that rate the
process would go on to infinity, so that our desire would
be empty and vain), clearly this must be the good and the
chief good. Will not the knowledge of it, then, have a
great influence on life? Shall we not, like archers who have
a mark to aim at, be more likely to hit upon what is right?
If so, we must try, in outline at least to determine what
it is, and of which of the sciences or capacities it is the
object. It would seem to belong to the most authoritative
art and that which is most truly the master art. And politics appears to be of this nature; for it is this that ordains
which of the sciences should be studied in a state, and
which each class of citizens should learn and up to what
point they should learn them; and we see even the most
highly esteemed of capacities to fall under this, e. g.
strategy, economics, rhetoric; now, since politics uses the
rest of the sciences, and since, again, it legislates as to what
we are to do and what we are to abstain from, the end of
this science must include those of the others, so that this
end must be the good for man. For even if the end is the
same for a single man and for a state, that of the state
seems at all events something greater and more complete
whether to attain or to preserve; though it is worth while
to attain the end merely for one man, it is finer and more
godlike to attain it for a nation or for city-states. These,
then, are the ends at which our inquiry aims, since it is
political science, in one sense of that term.

3   Our discussion will be adequate if it has as much clearness as the subject-matter admits of, for precision is
not to be sought for alike in all discussions, any more than
in all the products of the crafts. Now fine and just actions,
which political science investigates, admit of much variety

and fluctuation of opinion, so that they may be thought to exist only by convention, and not by nature. And goods also give rise to a similar fluctuation because they bring harm to many people; for before now men have been un- done by reason of their wealth, and others by reason of 20 their courage. We must be content, then, in speaking of such subjects and with such premises to indicate the truth roughly and in outline, and in speaking about things which are only for the most part true and with premises of the same kind to reach conclusions that are no better. In the same spirit, therefore, should each type of statement be 25 received; for it is the mark of an educated man to look for precision in each class of things just so far as the nature of the subject admits; it is evidently equally foolish to ac- cept probable reasoning from a mathematician and to demand from a rhetorician scientific proofs.

Now each man judges well the things he knows, and of these he is a good judge. And so the man who has been 1095ª educated in a subject is a good judge of that subject, and the man who has received an all-round education is a good judge in general. Hence a young man is not a proper hearer of lectures on political science; for he is inexperienced in the actions that occur in life, but its discussions start from these and are about these; and, further, since he tends to follow his passions, his study will be vain and unprofitable, because the end aimed at is not knowledge but action. 5 And it makes no difference whether he is young in years or youthful in character; the defect does not depend on time, but on his living, and pursuing each successive ob- ject, as passion directs. For to such persons, as to the in- continent, knowledge brings no profit; but to those who 10 desire and act in accordance with a rational principle knowledge about such matters will be of great benefit.

These remarks about the student, the sort of treatment to be expected, and the purpose of the inquiry, may be taken as our preface.

4   Let us resume our inquiry and state, in view of the fact that all knowledge and every pursuit aims at some good, what it is that we say political science aims at and what is the highest of all goods achievable by action. 15 Verbally there is very general agreement; for both the general run of men and people of superior refinement say that it is happiness, and identify living well and doing well with being happy; but with regard to what happiness is they differ, and the many do not give the same account as the 20 wise. For the former think it is some plain and obvious thing, like pleasure, wealth, or honour; they differ, however, from one another—and often even the same man identifies it with different things, with health when he is ill, with wealth when he is poor; but, conscious of their ignorance, 25 they admire those who proclaim some great ideal that is above their comprehension. Now some [2] thought that apart from these many goods there is another which is self-subsistent and causes the goodness of all these as well. To examine all the opinions that have been held were perhaps somewhat fruitless; enough to examine those that are most prevalent or that seem to be arguable.

Let us not fail to notice, however, that there is a difference between arguments from and those to the first prin- 30 ciples. For Plato, too, was right in raising this question and asking, as he used to do, 'are we on the way from or to the first principles?' [3] There is a difference, as there is in a race-course between the course from the judges to the turning-point and the way back. For, while we must begin with what is known, things are objects of knowledge in **1095'** two senses—some to us, some without qualification. Presumably, then, we must begin with things known to us. Hence any one who is to listen intelligently to lectures about what is noble and just and, generally, about the subjects of political science must have been brought up 5

[2] The Platonic School; Cf. ch. 6.
[3] Cf. *Rep.* 511 в

in good habits. For the fact is the starting-point, and if this is sufficiently plain to him, he will not at the start need the reason as well; and the man who has been well brought up has or can easily get starting-points. And as for him who neither has nor can get them, let him hear the words of Hesiod:

10   Far best is he who knows all things himself;
        Good, he that hearkens when men counsel right;
        But he who neither knows, nor lays to heart
        Another's wisdom, is a useless wight.

5   Let us, however, resume our discussion from the point at which we digressed. To judge from the lives that 15 men lead, most men, and men of the most vulgar type, seem (not without some ground) to identify the good, or happiness, with pleasure; which is the reason why they love the life of enjoyment. For there are, we may say, three prominent types of life—that just mentioned, the political, and thirdly the contemplative life. Now the mass of mankind 20 are evidently quite slavish in their tastes, preferring a life suitable to beasts, but they get some ground for their view from the fact that many of those in high places share the tastes of Sardanapallus. A consideration of the prominent types of life shows that people of superior refinement and of active disposition identify happiness with honour; for this is, roughly speaking, the end of the political life. But it seems too superficial to be what we are looking for, 25 since it is thought to depend on those who bestow honour rather than on him who receives it, but the good we divine to be something proper to a man and not easily taken from him. Further, men seem to pursue honour in order that they may be assured of their goodness; at least it is by men of practical wisdom that they seek to be honoured, and among those who know them, and on the ground of their virtue; clearly, then, according to them, at any rate, virtue 30 is better. And perhaps one might even suppose this to be

rather than honour, the end of the political life. But even
this appears somewhat incomplete; for possession of virtue
seems actually compatible with being asleep, or with life-
long inactivity, and, further, with the greatest sufferings 1096ᵇ
and misfortunes; but a man who was living so no one would
call happy, unless he were maintaining a thesis at all costs.
But enough of this; for the subject has been sufficiently
treated even in the current discussions. Third comes the
contemplative life, which we shall consider later.[4]

The life of money-making is one undertaken under compulsion, and wealth is evidently not the good we are seek- 5
ing; for it is merely useful and for the sake of something
else. And so one might rather take the aforenamed ob
jects to be ends; for they are loved for themselves. But it is
evident that not even these are ends; yet many arguments
have been thrown away in support of them. Let us leave
this subject, then.   10

6   We had perhaps better consider the universal good
and discuss thoroughly what is meant by it, although
such an inquiry is made an uphill one by the fact that the
Forms have been introduced by friends of our own. Yet it
would perhaps be thought to be better, indeed to be our
duty, for the sake of maintaining the truth even to destroy
what touches us closely, especially as we are philosophers
or lovers of wisdom; for, while both are dear, piety requires 15
us to honour truth above our friends.

The men who introduced this doctrine did not posit
Ideas of classes within which they recognized priority and
posteriority (which is the reason why they did not maintain the existence of an Idea embracing all numbers);
but the term 'good' is used both in the category of substance and in that of quality and in that of relation, and
that which is per se, i. e. substance, is prior in nature to the 20
relative (for the latter is like an offshoot and accident of
being); so that there could not be a common Idea set over

4 1177ᵃ 12–1178ᵃ 8, 1178ᵃ 22–1179ᵃ 32.

all these goods. Further, since 'good' has as many senses as
'being' (for it is predicated both in the category of sub-
25 stance, as of God and of reason, and in quality, i. e. of the
virtues, and in quantity, i. e. of that which is moderate, and
in relation, i. e. of the useful, and in time, i. e. of the right
opportunity, and in place, i. e. of the right locality and
the like), clearly it cannot be something universally present
in all cases and single; for then it could not have been
predicated in all the categories but in one only. Further,
since of the things answering to one Idea there is one
30 science, there would have been one science of all the
goods; but as it is there are many sciences even of the things
that fall under one category, e. g. of opportunity, for opportunity in war is studied by strategics and in disease by
medicine, and the moderate in food is studied by medicine
and in exercise by the science of gymnastics. And one
might ask the question, what in the world they mean by 'a
thing itself', if (as is the case) in 'man himself' and in a
35 particular man the account of man is one and the same.
1096ᵇ For in so far as they are man, they will in no respect differ;
and if this is so, neither will 'good itself' and particular
goods, in so far as they are good. But again it will not be
good any the more for being eternal, since that which lasts
5 long is no whiter than that which perishes in a day. The
Pythagoreans seem to give a more plausible account of the
good, when they place the one in the column of goods; and
it is they that Speusippus seems to have followed.

But let us discuss these matters elsewhere [5]; an objection
to what we have said, however, may be discerned in the
10 fact that the Platonists have not been speaking about all
goods, and that the goods that are pursued and loved for
themselves are called good by reference to a single Form,
while those which tend to produce or to preserve these
somehow or to prevent their contraries are called so by
reference to these, and in a secondary sense. Clearly, then,

[5] Cf. *Met.* 986ᵃ 22–6, 1028ᵇ 21–4, 1072ᵇ 30–1073ᵃ 3, 1091ᵃ 29–ᵇ
3, ᵇ 13–1092ᵃ 17.

goods must be spoken of in two ways, and some must be good in themselves, the others by reason of these. Let us separate, then, things good in themselves from things use- 15 ful, and consider whether the former are called good by reference to a single Idea. What sort of goods would one call good in themselves? Is it those that are pursued even when isolated from others, such as intelligence, sight, and certain pleasures and honours? Certainly, if we pursue these also for the sake of something else, yet one would place them among things good in themselves. Or is nothing other 20 than the Idea of good good in itself? In that case the Form will be empty. But if the things we have named are also things good in themselves, the account of the good will have to appear as something identical in them all, as that of whiteness is identical in snow and in white lead. But of honour, wisdom, and pleasure, just in respect of their good- 25 ness, the accounts are distinct and diverse. The good, therefore, is not some common element answering to one Idea.

But what then do we mean by the good? It is surely not like the things that only chance to have the same name. Are goods one, then, by being derived from one good or by all contributing to one good, or are they rather one by analogy? Certainly as sight is in the body, so is 30 reason in the soul, and so on in other cases. But perhaps these subjects had better be dismissed for the present; for perfect precision about them would be more appropriate to another branch of philosophy.[6] And similarly with re-gard to the Idea; even if there is some one good which is universally predicable of goods or is capable of separate and independent existence, clearly it could not be achieved or attained by man; but we are now seeking something attainable. Perhaps, however, some one might think it 35 worth while to recognize this with a view to the goods that are attainable and achievable; for having this as a sort of pattern we shall know better the goods that are good for 1097

[6] Cf. Met. iv. 2.

us, and if we know them shall attain them. This argument
has some plausibility, but seems to clash with the procedure of the sciences; for all of these, though they aim at
5 some good and seek to supply the deficiency of it, leave on
one side the knowledge of the good. Yet that all the exponents of the arts should be ignorant of, and should not
even seek, so great an aid is not probable. It is hard, too,
to see how a weaver or a carpenter will be benefited in
regard to his own craft by knowing this 'good itself', or how
10 the man who has viewed the Idea itself will be a better
doctor or general thereby. For a doctor seems not even to
study health in this way, but the health of man, or perhaps rather the health of a particular man; it is individuals
that he is healing. But enough of these topics.

7   Let us again return to the good we are seeking, and ask
15   what it can be. It seems different in different actions
and arts; it is different in medicine, in strategy, and in the
other arts likewise. What then is the good of each? Surely
that for whose sake everything else is done. In medicine
20 this is health, in strategy victory, in architecture a house,
in any other sphere something else, and in every action
and pursuit the end; for it is for the sake of this that all
men do whatever else they do. Therefore, if there is an end
for all that we do, this will be the good achievable by
action, and if there are more than one, these will be the
goods achievable by action.

So the argument has by a different course reached the
same point; but we must try to state this even more clearly.
Since there are evidently more than one end, and we choose
25 some of these (e. g. wealth, flutes, and in general instruments) for the sake of something else, clearly not all ends
are final ends; but the chief good is evidently something
final. Therefore, if there is only one final end, this will be
what we are seeking, and if there are more than one, the
most final of these will be what we are seeking. Now we
30 call that which is in itself worthy of pursuit more final

than that which is worthy of pursuit for the sake of something else, and that which is never desirable for the sake of something else more final than the things that are desirable both in themselves and for the sake of that other thing, and <u>therefore we call final without qualification that which is always desirable in itself and never for the sake of something else.</u>

Now such a thing <u>happiness, above all else, is held to be;</u> for this we choose always for itself and never for the sake of something else, but honour, pleasure, reason, and every **1097ᵇ** virtue we choose indeed for themselves (for if nothing resulted from them we should still choose each of them), but we choose them also for the sake of happiness, judging 5 that by means of them we shall be happy. Happiness, on the other hand, no one chooses for the sake of these, nor, in general, for anything other than itself.

From the point of view of self-sufficiency the same result seems to follow; for the final good is thought to be self-sufficient. Now by self-sufficient we do not mean that which is sufficient for a man by himself, for one who lives 10 a solitary life, but also for parents, children, wife, and in general for his friends and fellow citizens, <u>since man is born for citizenship.</u> But some limit must be set to this; for if we extend our requirement to ancestors and descendants and friends' friends we are in for an infinite series. Let us examine this question, however, on another occasion; [7] the self-sufficient we now define as that which when iso- 15 lated makes life desirable and lacking in nothing; and such we think happiness to be; and further we think it most desirable of all things, without being counted as one good thing among others—if it were so counted it would clearly be made more desirable by the addition of even the least of goods; for that which is added becomes an 20 excess of goods, and of goods the greater is always more desirable. Happiness, then, is something final and self-sufficient, and is the end of action.

[7] i. 10, 11, ix. 10.

Presumably, however, to say that happiness is the chief good seems a platitude, and a clearer account of what it is is still desired. This might perhaps be given, if we could first ascertain the function of man. For just as for a flute-player, a sculptor, or any artist, and, in general, for all things that have a function or activity, the good and the 'well' is thought to reside in the function, so would it seem to be for man, if he has a function. Have the carpenter, then, and the tanner certain functions or activities, and has man none? Is he born without a function? Or as eye, hand, foot, and in general each of the parts evidently has a function, may one lay it down that man similarly has a function apart from all these? What then can this be? Life seems to be common even to plants, but we are seeking what is peculiar to man. Let us exclude, therefore, the life of nutrition and growth. Next there would be a life of perception, but it also seems to be common even to the horse, the ox, and every animal. There remains, then, an active life of the element that has a rational principle; of this, one part has such a principle in the sense of being obedient to one, the other in the sense of possessing one and exercising thought. And, as 'life of the rational element' also has two meanings, we must state that life in the sense of activity is what we mean; for this seems to be the more proper sense of the term. Now if the function of man is an activity of soul which follows or implies a rational principle, and if we say 'a so-and-so' and 'a good so-and-so' have a function which is the same in kind, e. g. a lyre-player and a good lyre-player, and so without qualification in all cases, eminence in respect of goodness being added to the name of the function (for the function of a lyre-player is to play the lyre, and that of a good lyre-player is to do so well): if this is the case, [and we state the function of man to be a certain kind of life, and this to be an activity or actions of the soul implying a rational principle, and the function of a good man to be the good and noble performance of these, and if any action is well performed when it

is performed in accordance with the appropriate excellence: 15
if this is the case,] human good turns out to be activity of
soul in accordance with virtue, and if there are more than
one virtue, in accordance with the best and most complete.

But we must add 'in a complete life'. For one swallow
does not make a summer, nor does one day; and so too one
day, or a short time, does not make a man blessed and
happy.

Let this serve as an outline of the good; for we must
presumably first sketch it roughly, and then later fill in the 20
details. But it would seem that any one is capable of carrying on and articulating what has once been well outlined,
and that time is a good discoverer or partner in such a work;
to which facts the advances of the arts are due; for any
one can add what is lacking. And we must also remember
what has been said before,[8] and not look for precision in 25
all things alike, but in each class of things such precision as
accords with the subject-matter, and so much as is appropriate to the inquiry. For a carpenter and a geometer investigate the right angle in different ways; the former does so
in so far as the right angle is useful for his work, while the 30
latter inquires what it is or what sort of thing it is; for he
is a spectator of the truth. We must act in the same way,
then, in all other matters as well, that our main task may
not be subordinated to minor questions. Nor must we demand the cause in all matters alike; it is enough in some
cases that the *fact* be well established, as in the case of the 1098
first principles; the fact is the primary thing or first principle. Now of first principles we see some by induction,
some by perception, some by a certain habituation, and
others too in other ways. But each set of principles we must
try to investigate in the natural way, and we must take
pains to state them definitely, since they have a great in- 5
fluence on what follows. For the beginning is thought to
be more than half of the whole, and many of the questions we ask are cleared up by it.

[8] 1094[b] 11–27.

8   We must consider it, however, in the light not only
of our conclusion and our premises, but also of what
is commonly said about it; for with a true view all the data
harmonize, but with a false one the facts soon clash. Now
goods have been divided into three classes,[9] and some are
described as external, others as relating to soul or to body;
we call those that relate to soul most properly and truly
goods, and psychical actions and activities we class as relating to soul. Therefore our account must be sound, at
least according to this view, which is an old one and agreed
on by philosophers. It is correct also in that we identify the
end with certain actions and activities; for thus it falls
among goods of the soul and not among external goods.
Another belief which harmonizes with our account is
that the happy man lives well and does well; for we have
practically defined happiness as a sort of good life and
good action. The characteristics that are looked for in happiness seem also, all of them, to belong to what we have
defined happiness as being. For some identify happiness
with virtue, some with practical wisdom, others with a kind
of philosophic wisdom, others with these, or one of these,
accompanied by pleasure or not without pleasure; while
others include also external prosperity. Now some of these
views have been held by many men and men of old, others
by a few eminent persons; and it is not probable that either
of these should be entirely mistaken, but rather that they
should be right in at least some one respect or even in most
respects.

With those who identify happiness with virtue or some
one virtue our account is in harmony; for to virtue belongs
virtuous activity. But it makes, perhaps, no small difference
whether we place the chief good in possession or in use, in
state of mind or in activity. For the state of mind may exist
without producing any good result, as in a man who is
asleep or in some other way quite inactive, but the activity
cannot; for one who has the activity will of necessity be

[9] Pl. *Euthyd.* 279 AB, *Phil.* 48 E, *Laws.* 743 E.

acting, and acting well. And as in the Olympic Games it is
not the most beautiful and the strongest that are crowned
but those who compete (for it is some of these that are 5
victorious), so those who act win, and rightly win, the
noble and good things in life.

Their life is also in itself pleasant. For pleasure is a state
of soul, and to each man that which he is said to be a lover
of is pleasant; e. g. not only is a horse pleasant to the lover
of horses, and a spectacle to the lover of sights, but also in 10
the same way just acts are pleasant to the lover of justice
and in general virtuous acts to the lover of virtue. Now for
most men their pleasures are in conflict with one another
because these are not by nature pleasant, but the lovers of
what is noble find pleasant the things that are by nature
pleasant; and virtuous actions are such, so that these are
pleasant for such men as well as in their own nature. Their
life, therefore, has no further need of pleasure as a sort of 15
adventitious charm, but has its pleasure in itself. For, besides what we have said, the man who does not rejoice in
noble actions is not even good; since no one would call a
man just who did not enjoy acting justly, nor any man
liberal who did not enjoy liberal actions; and similarly in all
other cases. If this is so, virtuous actions must be in them- 20
selves pleasant. But they are also good and noble, and have
each of these attributes in the highest degree, since the
good man judges well about these attributes; his judgement
is such as we have described.[10] Happiness then is the best,
noblest, and most pleasant thing in the world, and these
attributes are not severed as in the inscription at Delos— 25

> Most noble is that which is justest, and best is health;
> But pleasantest is it to win what we love.

For all these properties belong to the best activities; and
these, or one—the best—of these, we identify with happi-
ness.   3(

[10] i. e., he judges that virtuous actions are good and noble in the
highest degree.

Yet evidently, as we said,[11] it needs the external goods as well; for it is impossible, or not easy, to do noble acts 1099[b] without the proper equipment. In many actions we use friends and riches and political power as instruments; and there are some things the lack of which takes the lustre from happiness, as good birth, goodly children, beauty; for the man who is very ugly in appearance or ill-born or solitary and childless is not very likely to be happy, and perhaps 5 a man would be still less likely if he had thoroughly bad children or friends or had lost good children or friends by death. As we said,[11] then, happiness seems to need this sort of prosperity in addition; for which reason some identify happiness with good fortune, though others identify it with virtue.

Meno

9 (For this reason also the question is asked, whether happiness is to be acquired by learning or by habituation or some other sort of training, or comes in virtue of 10 some divine providence or again by chance.) Now if there is any gift of the gods to men, it is reasonable that happiness should be god-given, and most surely god-given of all human things inasmuch as it is the best. But this question would perhaps be more appropriate to another inquiry; hap-15 piness seems, however, even if it is not god-sent but comes as a result of virtue and some process of learning or training, to be among the most god-like things; for that which is the prize and end of virtue seems to be the best thing in the world, and something godlike and blessed.

It will also on this view be very generally shared; for all who are not maimed as regards their potentiality for 20 virtue may win it by a certain kind of study and care. But if it is better to be happy thus than by chance, it is reasonable that the facts should be so, since everything that depends on the action of nature is by nature as good as it can be, and similarly everything that depends on art or any rational cause, and especially if it depends on the best of

[11] 1098[b] 26–9.

all causes. To entrust to chance what is greatest and most
noble would be a very defective arrangement.

The answer to the question we are asking is plain also 25
from the definition of happiness; for it has been said [12] to
be a virtuous activity of soul, of a certain kind. Of the remaining goods, some must necessarily pre-exist as conditions of happiness, and others are naturally co-operative and
useful as instruments. And this will be found to agree with
what we said at the outset; [13] for we stated the end of
political science to the best end, and political science 30
spends most of its pains on making the citizens to be of a
certain character, viz. good and capable of noble acts.

It is natural, then, that we call neither ox nor horse nor
any other of the animals happy; for none of them is capable
of sharing in such activity. For this reason also a boy is not 1100ᵃ
happy; for he is not yet capable of such acts, owing to his
age; and boys who are called happy are being congratulated
by reason of the hopes we have for them. For there is required, as we said,[14] not only complete virtue but also a
complete life, since many changes occur in life, and all 5
manner of chances, and the most prosperous may fall into
great misfortunes in old age, as is told of Priam in the
Trojan Cycle; and one who has experienced such chances
and has ended wretchedly no one calls happy.

10 Must no one at all, then, be called happy while he 10
lives; must we, as Solon says, see the end? Even if we
are to lay down this doctrine, is it also the case that a man
is happy when he is *dead*? Or is not this quite absurd, especially for us who say that happiness is an activity? But if we 15
do not call the dead man happy, and if Solon does not
mean this, but that one can then safely *call* a man blessed
as being at last beyond evils and misfortunes, this also
affords matter for discussion; for both evil and good are

[12] 1098ᵃ 16.
[13] 1094ᵃ 27.
[14] 1098ᵃ 16–18.

thought to exist for a dead man, as much as for one who
20 is alive but not aware of them; e. g. honours and dishonours
and the good or bad fortunes of children and in general of
descendants. And this also presents a problem; for though
a man has lived happily up to old age and has had a death
worthy of his life, many reverses may befall his descendants
—some of them may be good and attain the life they de-
25 serve, while with others the opposite may be the case; and
clearly too the degrees of relationship between them and
their ancestors may vary indefinitely. It would be odd, then,
if the dead man were to share in these changes and become
at one time happy, at another wretched; while it would
also be odd if the fortunes of the descendants did not for
30 some time have some effect on the happiness of their ancestors.

But we must return to our first difficulty; for perhaps by
a consideration of it our present problem might be solved.
Now if we must see the end and only then call a man
happy, not as being happy but as having been so before,
35 surely this is a paradox, that when he is happy the attribute
that belongs to him is not to be truly predicated of him
because we do not wish to call living men happy, on ac-
1100ᵇ count of the changes that may befall them, and because
we have assumed happiness to be something permanent
and by no means easily changed, while a single man may
suffer many turns of fortune's wheel. For clearly if we were
5 to keep pace with his fortunes, we should often call the
same man happy and again wretched, making the happy
man out to be a 'chameleon and insecurely based'. Or is
this keeping pace with his fortunes quite wrong? Success or
failure in life does not depend on these, but human life,
as we said,[15] needs these as mere additions, while virtuous
activities or their opposites are what constitute happiness
10 or the reverse.

The question we have now discussed confirms our defini-

[15] 1099ᵃ 31–ᵇ 7.

tion. For no function of man has so much permanence as virtuous activities (these are thought to be more durable even than knowledge of the sciences), and of these themselves the most valuable are more durable because those who are happy spend their life most readily and most continuously in these; for this seems to be the reason why we do not forget them. The attribute in question,[16] then, will belong to the happy man, and he will be happy throughout his life; for always, or by preference to everything else, he will be engaged in virtuous action and contemplation, and he will bear the chances of life most nobly and altogether decorously, if he is 'truly good' and 'foursquare beyond reproach'.[17]

Now many events happen by chance, and events differing in importance; small pieces of good fortune or of its opposite clearly do not weigh down the scales of life one way or the other, but a multitude of great events if they turn out well will make life happier (for not only are they themselves such as to add beauty to life, but the way a man deals with them may be noble and good), while if they turn out ill they crush and maim happiness; for they both bring pain with them and hinder many activities. Yet even in these nobility shines through, when a man bears with resignation many great misfortunes, not through insensibility to pain but through nobility and greatness of soul.

If activities are, as we said,[18] what gives life its character, no happy man can become miserable; for he will never do the acts that are hateful and mean. For the man who is truly good and wise, we think, bears all the chances of life becomingly and always makes the best of circumstances, as a good general makes the best military use of the army at his command and a good shoemaker makes the best shoes out of the hides that are given him; and so with all

---

[16] Durability.
[17] Simonides.
[18] 1. 9.

other craftsmen. And if this is the case, the happy man can never become miserable—though he will not reach *blessedness*, if he meet with fortunes like those of Priam.

Nor, again, is he many-coloured and changeable; for neither will he be moved from his happy state easily or by any ordinary misadventures, but only by many great ones, nor, if he has had many great misadventures, will be recover his happiness in a short time, but if at all, only in a long and complete one in which he has attained many splendid successes.

Why then should we not say that he is happy who is active in accordance with complete virtue and is sufficiently equipped with external goods, not for some chance period but throughout a complete life? Or must we add 'and who is destined to live thus and die as befits his life'? Certainly the future is obscure to us, while happiness, we claim, is an end and something in every way final. If so, we shall call happy those among living men in whom these conditions are, and are to be, fulfilled—but happy men. So much for these questions.

11 [19]That the fortunes of descendants and of all a man's friends should not affect his happiness at all seems a very unfriendly doctrine, and one opposed to the opinions men hold; but since the events that happen are numerous and admit of all sorts of difference, and some come more near to us and others less so, it seems a long—nay, an infinite—task to discuss each in detail; a general outline will perhaps suffice. If, then, as some of a man's own misadventures have a certain weight and influence on life while others are, as it were, lighter, so too there are differences among the misadventures of our friends taken as a whole, and it makes a difference whether the various sufferings befall the living or the dead (much more even than whether lawless and terrible deeds are presupposed in a tragedy or done on the stage), this difference also must be taken into

[19] Aristotle now returns to the question stated in 1100[a] 18–30.

account; or rather, perhaps, the fact that doubt is felt
whether the dead share in any good or evil. For it seems, 35
from these considerations, that even if anything whether 1101ᵇ
good or evil penetrates to them, it must be something weak
and negligible, either in itself or for them, or if not, at least
it must be such in degree and kind as not to make happy
those who are not happy nor to take away their blessedness
from those who are. The good or bad fortunes of friends,
then, seem to have some effects on the dead, but effects 5
of such a kind and degree as neither to make the happy
unhappy nor to produce any other change of the kind.

12 These questions having been definitely answered, let
us consider whether happiness is among the things 10
that are praised or rather among the things that are prized;
for clearly it is not to be placed among *potentialities*.[20]
Everything that is praised seems to be praised because it
is of a certain kind and is related somehow to something
else; for we praise the just or brave man and in general both
the good man and virtue itself because of the actions and
functions involved, and we praise the strong man, the good 15
runner, and so on, because he is of a certain kind and is
related in a certain way to something good and important.
This is clear also from the praises of the gods; for it seems
absurd that the gods should be referred to our standard,
but this *is* done because praise involves a reference, as we
said, to something else. But if praise is for things such as 20
we have described, clearly what applies to the best things is
not praise, but something greater and better, as is indeed
obvious; for what we do to the gods and the most godlike
of men is to call them blessed and happy. And so too with
good *things*; no one praises happiness as he does justice, 25
but rather calls it blessed, as being something more divine
and better.

Eudoxus also seems to have been right in his method of
advocating the supremacy of pleasure; he thought that the

[20] Cf. *Top.* 126ᵇ 4; *M. M.* 1183ᵇ 20.

fact that, though a good, it is not praised indicated it to be better than the things that are praised, and that this is what 30 God and the good are; for by reference to these all other things are judged. *Praise* is appropriate to virtue, for as a result of virtue men tend to do noble deeds; but *encomia* are bestowed on acts, whether of the body or of the soul. 35 But perhaps nicety in these matters is more proper to those who have made a study of encomia; to us it is clear from 1102ª what has been said that happiness is among the things that are prized and perfect. It seems to be so also from the fact that it is a first principle; for it is for the sake of this that we all do all that we do, and the first principle and cause of goods is, we claim, something prized and divine.

encomia [margin note]

5 **13**   Since happiness is an activity of soul in accordance with perfect virtue, we must consider the nature of virtue; for perhaps we shall thus see better the nature of happiness. The true student of politics, too, is thought to have studied virtue above all things; for he wishes to make 10 his fellow citizens good and obedient to the laws. As an example of this we have the lawgivers of the Cretans and the Spartans, and any others of the kind that there may have been. And if this inquiry belongs to political science, clearly the pursuit of it will be in accordance with our original plan. But clearly the virtue we must study is human virtue; for the good we were seeking was human good and 15 the happiness human happiness. By human virtue we mean not that of the body but that of the soul; and happiness also we call an activity of soul. But if this is so, clearly the student of politics must know somehow the facts about soul, as the man who is to heal the eyes or the body as a whole must know about the eyes or the body; and all the 20 more since politics is more prized and better than medicine; but even among doctors the best educated spend much labour on acquiring knowledge of the body. The student of politics, then, must study the soul, and must study it with these objects in view, and do so just to the

extent which is sufficient for the questions we are discussing; for further precision is perhaps something more 25
laborious than our purposes require.

Some things are said about it, adequately enough, even
in the discussions outside our school, and we must use
these; e. g. that one element in the soul is irrational and
one has a rational principle. Whether these are separated 30
as the parts of the body or of anything divisible are, or are
distinct by definition but by nature inseparable, like convex and concave in the circumference of a circle, does not
affect the present question.

Of the irrational element one division seems to be widely
distributed, and vegetative in its nature, I mean that which
causes nutrition and growth; for it is this kind of power of
the soul that one must assign to all nurslings and to em- **1102ᵇ**
bryos, and this same power to full-grown creatures; this is
more reasonable than to assign some different power to
them. Now the excellence of this seems to be common to
all species and not specifically human; for this part or
faculty seems to function most in sleep, while goodness and 5
badness are least manifest in sleep (whence comes the saying that the happy are no better off than the wretched for
half their lives; and this happens naturally enough, since
sleep is an inactivity of the soul in that respect in which it
is called good or bad), unless perhaps to a small extent
some of the movements actually penetrate to the soul, and 10
in this respect the dreams of good men are better than
those of ordinary people. Enough of this subject, however;
let us leave the nutritive faculty alone, since it has by its
nature no share in human excellence.

There seems to be also another irrational element in the
soul—one which in a sense, however, shares in a rational
principle. For we praise the rational principle of the continent man and of the incontinent, and the part of their soul 15
that has such a principle, since it urges them aright and towards the best objects; but there is found in them also another element naturally opposed to the rational principle,

which fights against and resists that principle. For exactly
as paralysed limbs when we intend to move them to the
20 right turn on the contrary to the left, so is it with the soul;
the impulses of incontinent people move in contrary directions. But while in the body we see that which moves
astray, in the soul we do not. No doubt, however, we must
none the less suppose that in the soul too there is some-
25 thing contrary to the rational principle, resisting and opposing it. In what sense it is distinct from the other elements does not concern us. Now even this seems to have a
share in a rational principle, as we said; [21] at any rate in the
continent man it obeys the rational principle—and presumably in the temperate and brave man it is still more
obedient; for in him it speaks, on all matters, with the same
voice as the rational principle.

Therefore the irrational element also appears to be twofold. For the vegetative element in no way shares in a ra-
30 tional principle, but the appetitive, and in general the desiring element in a sense shares in it, in so far as it listens to
and obeys it; this is the sense in which we speak of 'taking
account' of one's father or one's friends, not that in which
we speak of 'accounting' for a mathematical property. That
the irrational element is in some sense persuaded by a rational principle is indicated also by the giving of advice and
1103ª by all reproof and exhortation. And if this element also
must be said to have a rational principle, that which has a
rational principle (as well as that which has not) will be
twofold, one subdivision having it in the strict sense and in
itself, and the other having a tendency to obey as one does
one's father.

Virtue too is distinguished into kinds in accordance with
this difference; for we say that some of the virtues are intel-
5 lectual and others moral, philosophic wisdom and understanding and practical wisdom being intellectual, liberality
and temperance moral. For in speaking about a man's character we do not say that he is wise or has understanding

[21] l. 13.

but that he is good-tempered or temperate; yet we praise the wise man also with respect to his state of mind; <u>and of states of mind we call those which merit praise virtues.</u> 10

BOOK II

1 Virtue, then, being of two kinds, intellectual and moral, intellectual virtue in the main owes both its 15 birth and its growth to teaching (for which reason it requires experience and time), <u>while moral virtue comes about as a result of habit,</u> (whence also its name *ethike* is <u>one that is formed by a slight variation from the word *ethos*</u> (habit). From this it is also plain that none of the moral virtues arises in us by nature; for nothing that exists by 20 nature can form a habit contrary to its nature. For instance the stone which by nature moves downwards cannot be habituated to move upwards, not even if one tries to train it by throwing it up ten thousand times; nor can fire be habituated to move downwards, nor can anything else that by nature behaves in one way be trained to behave in another. Neither by nature, then, nor contrary to nature do the virtues arise in us; rather we are adapted by nature to receive them, and are made perfect by habit. 25

Again, of all the things that come to us by nature we first acquire the potentiality and later exhibit the activity (this is plain in the case of the senses; for it was not by often 30 seeing or often hearing that we got these senses, but on the contrary we had them before we used them, and did not come to have them by using them); but the virtues we get by first exercising them, as also happens in the case of the arts as well. For the things we have to learn before we can do them, we learn by doing them, e. g. men become builders by building and lyre-players by playing the lyre; so too **1103ᵇ** <u>we become just by doing just acts, temperate by doing</u> temperate acts, brave by doing brave acts.

This is confirmed by what happens in states; <u>for legislators make the citizens good by forming habits in them,</u>

5 and this is the wish of every legislator, and those who do not effect it miss their mark, and it is in this that a good constitution differs from a bad one.

Again, it is from the same causes and by the same means that every virtue is both produced and destroyed, and similarly every art; for it is from playing the lyre that both good and bad lyre-players are produced. And the corresponding statement is true of builders and of all the rest; men will 10 be good or bad builders as a result of building well or badly. For if this were not so, there would have been no need of a teacher, but all men would have been born good or bad at their craft. This, then, is the case with the virtues also; by doing the acts that we do in our transactions with 15 other men we become just or unjust, and by doing the acts that we do in the presence of danger, and being habituated to feel fear or confidence, we become brave or cowardly. The same is true of appetites and feelings of anger; some men become temperate and good-tempered, others self-indulgent and irascible, by behaving in one way or the 20 other in the appropriate circumstances. Thus, in one word, states of character arise out of like activities. This is why the activities we exhibit must be of a certain kind; it is because the states of character correspond to the differences between these. It makes no small difference, then, whether we form habits of one kind or of another from our very 25 youth; it make a very great difference, or rather all the difference.

2   Since, then, the present inquiry does not aim at theoretical knowledge like the others (for we are inquiring not in order to know what virtue is, but in order to become good, since otherwise our inquiry would have been of no use), we must examine the nature of actions, namely how 30 we ought to do them; for these determine also the nature of the states of character that are produced, as we have said.[1] Now, that we must act according to the right rule

1 a 31–b 25.

is a common principle and must be assumed—it will be discussed later,[2] i. e. both what the right rule is, and how it is related to the other virtues. But this must be agreed upon **1104** beforehand, that the whole account of matters of conduct must be given in outline and not precisely, as we said at the very beginning [3] that the accounts we demand must be in accordance with the subject-matter; matters concerned with conduct and questions of what is good for us have no fixity, any more than matters of health. The general ac- 5 count being of this nature, the account of particular cases is yet more lacking in exactness; for they do not fall under any art or precept but the agents themselves must in each case consider what is appropriate to the occasion, as happens also in the art of medicine or of navigation.

But though our present account is of this nature we must give what help we can. First, then, let us consider 10 this, that it is the nature of such things to be destroyed by defect and excess, as we see in the case of strength and of health (for to gain light on things imperceptible we must use the evidence of sensible things); both excessive and defective exercise destroys the strength, and similarly drink 15 or food which is above or below a certain amount destroys the health, while that which is proportionate both produces and increases and preserves it. So too is it, then, in the case 20 of temperance and courage and the other virtues. For the man who flies from and fears everything and does not stand his ground against anything becomes a coward, and the man who fears nothing at all but goes to meet every danger becomes rash; and similarly the man who indulges in every pleasure and abstains from none becomes self-indulgent, while the man who shuns every pleasure, as boors do, be- 25 comes in a way insensible; temperance and courage, then, are destroyed by excess and defect, and preserved by the mean.

But not only are the sources and causes of their origina-

[2] vi. 13.
[3] 1094[b] 11–27.

tion and growth the same as those of their destruction, but also the sphere of their actualization will be the same; 30 for this is also true of the things which are more evident to sense, e. g. of strength; it is produced by taking much food and undergoing much exertion, and it is the strong man that will be most able to do these things. So too is it with the virtues; by abstaining from pleasures we become 35 temperate, and it is when we have become so that we are 1104ᵉ most able to abstain from them; and similarly too in the case of courage; for by being habituated to despise things that are terrible and to stand our ground against them we become brave, and it is when we have become so that we shall be most able to stand our ground against them.

3   We must take as a sign of states of character the 5   pleasure or pain that ensues on acts; for the man who abstains from bodily pleasures and delights in this very fact is temperate, while the man who is annoyed at it is self-indulgent, and he who stands his ground against things that are terrible and delights in this or at least is not pained is brave, while the man who is pained is a coward. For moral excellence is concerned with pleasures and pains; it 10 is on account of the pleasure that we do bad things, and on account of the pain that we abstain from noble ones. Hence we ought to have been brought up in a particular way from our very youth, as Plato says,[4] so as both to delight in and to be pained by the things that we ought; for this is the right education.

Again, if the virtues are concerned with actions and passions, and every passion and every action is accompanied 15 by pleasure and pain, for this reason also virtue will be concerned with pleasures and pains. This is indicated also by the fact that punishment is inflicted by these means; for it is a kind of cure, and it is the nature of cures to be effected by contraries.

[4] *Laws*, 653 A ff., *Rep.* 401 E–402 A.

Again, as we said but lately,[5] every state of soul has a nature relative to and concerned with the kind of things by which it tends to be made worse or better; but it is by reason of pleasures and pains that men become bad, by pursuing and avoiding these—either the pleasures and pains they ought not or when they ought not or as they ought not, or by going wrong in one of the other similar ways that may be distinguished. Hence men [6] even define the virtues as certain states of impassivity and rest; not well, however, because they speak absolutely, and do not say 'as one ought' and 'as one ought not' and 'when one ought or ought not', and the other things that may be added. We assume, then, that this kind of excellence tends to do what is best with regard to pleasures and pains, and vice does the contrary.

The following facts also may show us that virtue and vice are concerned with these same things. There being three objects of choice and three of avoidance, the noble, the advantageous, the pleasant, and their contraries, the base, the injurious, the painful, about all of these the good man tends to go right and the bad man to go wrong, and especially about pleasure; for this is common to the animals, and also it accompanies all objects of choice; for even the noble and the advantageous appear pleasant.

Again, it has grown up with us all from our infancy; this is why it is difficult to rub off this passion, engrained as it 1105ᵃ is in our life. And we measure even our actions, some of us more and others less, by the rule of pleasure and pain. For this reason, then, our whole inquiry must be about these; for to feel delight and pain rightly or wrongly has no small effect on our actions.

Again, it is harder to fight with pleasure than with anger, to use Heraclitus' phrase, but both art and virtue are always concerned with what is harder; for even the good is better

---

[5] ᵃ 27–ᵇ 3.
[6] Probably Speusippus is referred to.

10 when it is harder. Therefore for this reason also the whole concern both of virtue and of political science is with pleasures and pains; for the man who uses these well will be good, he who uses them badly bad.

That virtue, then, is concerned with pleasures and pains, and that by the acts from which it arises it is both increased and, if they are done differently, destroyed, and that the 15 acts from which it arose are those in which it actualizes itself—let this be taken as said.

4   The question might be asked, what we mean by saying [7] that we must become just by doing just acts, and temperate by doing temperate acts; for if men do just and 20 temperate acts, they are already just and temperate, exactly as, if they do what is in accordance with the laws of grammar and of music, they are grammarians and musicians.

Or is this not true even of the arts? It is possible to do something that is in accordance with the laws of grammar, either by chance or at the suggestion of another. A man 25 will be a grammarian, then, only when he has both done something grammatical and done it grammatically; and this means doing it in accordance with the grammatical knowledge in himself.

Again, the case of the arts and that of the virtues are not similar; for the products of the arts have their goodness in themselves, so that it is enough that they should have a certain character, but if the acts that are in accordance with 30 the virtues have themselves a certain character it does not follow that they are done justly or temperately. The agent also must be in a certain condition when he does them; in the first place he must have knowledge, secondly he must choose the acts, and choose them for their own sakes, and thirdly his action must proceed from a firm and unchangeable character. These are not reckoned in as condi-
1105[b] tions of the possession of the arts, except the bare knowledge; but as a condition of the possession of the virtues

[7] 1103[a] 31–[b] 25. 1104[a] 27–[b] 3.

knowledge has little or no weight, while the other conditions count not for a little but for everything, i. e. the very conditions which result from often doing just and temperate acts.

Actions, then, are called just and temperate when they are such as the just or the temperate man would do; but it is not the man who does these that is just and temperate, but the man who also does them as just and temperate men do them. It is well said, then, that it is by doing just acts that the just man is produced, and by doing temperate acts the temperate man; without doing these no one would have even a prospect of becoming good.

But most people do not do these, but take refuge in theory and think they are being philosophers and will become good in this way, behaving somewhat like patients who listen attentively to their doctors, but do none of the things they are ordered to do. As the latter will not be made well in body by such a course of treatment, the former will not be made well in soul by such a course of philosophy.

5 Next we must consider what virtue is. Since things that are found in the soul are of three kinds—passions, faculties, states of character, virtue must be one of these. By passions I mean appetite, anger, fear, confidence, envy, joy, friendly feeling, hatred, longing, emulation, pity, and in general the feelings that are accompanied by pleasure or pain; by faculties the things in virtue of which we are said to be capable of feeling these, e. g. of becoming angry or being pained or feeling pity; by states of character the things in virtue of which we stand well or badly with reference to the passions, e. g. with reference to anger we stand badly if we feel it violently or too weakly, and well if we feel it moderately; and similarly with reference to the other passions.

Now neither the virtues nor the vices are *passions*, because we are not called good or bad on the ground of our

30 passions, but are so called on the ground of our virtues and our vices, and because we are neither praised nor blamed for our passions (for the man who feels fear or anger is not praised, nor is the man who simply feels anger blamed, but the man who feels it in a certain way), but for our
1106ᵃ virtues and our vices we are praised or blamed.

Again, we feel anger and fear without choice, but the virtues are modes of choice or involve choice. Further, in respect of the passions we are said to be moved, but in
5 respect of the virtues and the vices we are said not to be moved but to be disposed in a particular way.

For these reasons also they are not *faculties*; for we are neither called good nor bad, nor praised nor blamed, for the simple capacity of feeling the passions; again, we have the faculties by nature, but we are not made good or bad by nature; we have spoken of this before.[8]

If, then, the virtues are neither passions nor faculties,
10 all that remains is that they should be *states of character*.

Thus we have stated what virtue is in respect of its genus.

6 We must, however, not only describe virtue as a state of character, but also say what sort of state it is. We
15 may remark, then, that every virtue or excellence both brings into good condition the thing of which it is the excellence and makes the work of that thing be done well; e. g. the excellence of the eye makes both the eye and its work good; for it is by the excellence of the eye that we see well. Similarly the excellence of the horse makes a horse
20 both good in itself and good at running and at carrying its rider and at awaiting the attack of the enemy. Therefore, if this is true in every case, the virtue of man also will be the state of character which makes a man good and which makes him do his own work well.

How this is to happen we have stated already,[9] but it will be made plain also by the following consideration of the

[8] 1103ᵃ 18–ᵇ 2.
[9] 1104ᵃ 11–27.

specific nature of virtue. In everything that is continuous 25
and divisible it is possible to take more, less, or an equal
amount, and that either in terms of the thing itself or
relatively to us; and the equal is an intermediate between
excess and defect. By the intermediate in the object I mean
that which is equidistant from each of the extremes, which 30
is one and the same for all men; by the intermediate relatively to us that which is neither too much nor too little—
and this is not one, nor the same for all. For instance, if
ten is many and two is few, six is the intermediate, taken
in terms of the object; for it exceeds and is exceeded by an
equal amount; this is intermediate according to arithmeti- 35
cal proportion. But the intermediate relatively to us is not
to be taken so; if ten pounds are too much for a particular **1106ᵇ**
person to eat and two too little, it does not follow that the
trainer will order six pounds; for this also is perhaps too
much for the person who is to take it, or too little—too
little for Milo,[10] too much for the beginner in athletic 5
exercises. The same is true of running and wrestling. Thus
a master of any art avoids excess and defect, but seeks the
intermediate and chooses this—the intermediate not in the
object but relatively to us.

If it is thus, then, that every art does its work well—by
looking to the intermediate and judging its works by this
standard (so that we often say of good works of art that it 10
is not possible either to take away or to add anything, implying that excess and defect destroy the goodness of works
of art, while the mean preserves it; and good artists, as we
say, look to this in their work), and if, further, virtue is
more exact and better than any art, as nature also is, then
virtue must have the quality of aiming at the intermediate. 15
I mean moral virtue; for it is this that is concerned with
passions and actions, and in these there is excess, defect,
and the intermediate. For instance, both fear and confidence and appetite and anger and pity and in general pleasure and pain may be felt both too much and too little, and

¹⁰ A famous wrestler.

20 in both cases not well; but to feel them at the right times, with reference to the right objects, towards the right people, with the right motive, and in the right way, is what is both intermediate and best, and this is characteristic of virtue. Similarly with regard to actions also there is excess, defect, and the intermediate. Now virtue is concerned with 25 passions and actions, in which excess is a form of failure, and so is defect, while the intermediate is praised and is a form of success; and being praised and being successful are both characteristics of virtue. Therefore virtue is a kind of mean, since, as we have seen, it aims at what is intermediate.

Again, it is possible to fail in many ways (for evil belongs to the class of the unlimited, as the Pythagoreans conjectured, and good to that of the limited), while to succeed 30 is possible only in one way (for which reason also one is easy and the other difficult—to miss the mark easy, to hit it difficult); for these reasons also, then, excess and defect are characteristic of vice, and the mean of virtue;

35   For men are good in but one way, but bad in many.

Virtue, then, is a state of character concerned with choice, lying in a mean, i. e. the mean relative to us, this 1107ᵃ being determined by a rational principle, and by that principle by which the man of practical wisdom would determine it. Now it is a mean between two vices, that which depends on excess and that which depends on defect; and again it is a mean because the vices respectively fall short of or exceed what is right in both passions and actions, 5 while virtue both finds and chooses that which is intermediate. Hence in respect of its substance and the definition which states its essence virtue is a mean, with regard to what is best and right an extreme.

But not every action nor every passion admits of a mean; for some have names that already imply badness, e. g. spite, 10 shamelessness, envy, and in the case of actions adultery, theft, murder; for all of these and suchlike things imply by their names that they are themselves bad, and not the excesses or deficiencies of them. It is not possible, then, ever to be right with regard to them; one must always be wrong. Nor does goodness or badness with regard to such things depend on committing adultery with the right woman, at the right time, and in the right way, but simply to do any of them is to go wrong. It would be equally absurd, then, to expect that in unjust, cowardly, and voluptuous action there should be a mean, an excess, and a deficiency; for at that rate there would be a mean of excess and of deficiency, an excess of excess, and a deficiency of deficiency. But as there is no excess and deficiency of temperance and courage because what is intermediate is in a sense an extreme, so too of the actions we have mentioned there is no mean nor any excess and deficiency, but however they are done they are wrong; for in general there is neither a mean of excess and deficiency, nor excess and deficiency of a mean.

7   We must, however, not only make this general statement, but also apply it to the individual facts. For among statements about conduct those which are general apply more widely, but those which are particular are more genuine, since conduct has to do with individual cases, and our statements must harmonize with the facts in these cases. We may take these cases from our table. With regard to feelings of fear and confidence courage is the mean; of the people who exceed, he who exceeds in fearlessness has 1107° no name (many of the states have no name), while the man who exceeds in confidence is rash, and he who exceeds in fear and falls short in confidence is a coward. With regard to pleasures and pains—not all of them, and not so much with regard to the pains—the mean is temperance, the excess self-indulgence. Persons deficient with regard to the pleasures are not often found; hence such persons also have received no name. But let us call them 'insensible'.

With regard to giving and taking of money the mean is
10 liberality, the excess and the defect prodigality and meanness. In these actions people exceed and fall short in contrary ways; the prodigal exceeds in spending and falls short
in taking, while the mean man exceeds in taking and falls
short in spending. (At present we are giving a mere outline
15 or summary, and are satisfied with this; later these states
will be more exactly determined.[11]) With regard to money
there are also other dispositions—a mean, magnificence
(for the magnificent man differs from the liberal man;
the former deals with large sums, the latter with small
ones), and excess, tastelessness and vulgarity, and a defi-
20 ciency, niggardliness; these differ from the states opposed
to liberality, and the mode of their difference will be
stated later.[12]

With regard to honour and dishonour the mean is
proper pride, the excess is known as a sort of 'empty
vanity', and the deficiency is undue humility; and as we
25 said [13] liberality was related to magnificence, differing from
it by dealing with small sums, so there is a state similarly
related to proper pride, being concerned with small honours while that is concerned with great. For it is possible
to desire honour as one ought, and more than one ought,
and less, and the man who exceeds in his desires is called
30 ambitious, the man who falls short unambitious, while the
intermediate person has no name. The dispositions also are
nameless, except that that of the ambitious man is called
ambition. Hence the people who are at the extremes lay
claim to the middle place; and we ourselves sometimes call
the intermediate person ambitious and sometimes unambi-
1108ᵃ tious, and sometimes praise the ambitious man and sometimes the unambitious. The reason of our doing this will
be stated in what follows; [14] but now let us speak of the

[11] iv. 1.
[12] 1122ᵃ 20–9, ᵇ 10–18.
[13] ll. 17–19.
[14] ᵇ 11–26, 1125ᵇ 14–18.

remaining states according to the method which has been indicated.

With regard to anger also there is an excess, a deficiency, and a mean. Although they can scarcely be said to have names, yet since we call the intermediate person good-tempered let us call the mean good temper; of the persons at the extremes let the one who exceeds be called irascible, and his vice irascibility, and the man who falls short an inirascible sort of person, and the deficiency inirascibility.

There are also three other means, which have a certain likeness to one another, but differ from one another: for they are all concerned with intercourse in words and actions, but differ in that one is concerned with truth in this sphere, the other two with pleasantness; and of this one kind is exhibited in giving amusement, the other in all the circumstances of life. We must therefore speak of these too, that we may the better see that in all things the mean is praiseworthy, and the extremes neither praiseworthy nor right, but worthy of blame. Now most of these states also have no names, but we must try, as in the other cases, to invent names ourselves so that we may be clear and easy to follow. With regard to truth, then, the intermediate is a truthful sort of person and the mean may be called truthfulness, while the pretence which exaggerates is boastfulness and the person characterized by it a boaster, and that which understates is mock modesty and the person characterized by it mock-modest. With regard to pleasantness in the giving of amusement the intermediate person is ready-witted and the disposition ready wit, the excess is buffoonery and the person characterized by it a buffoon, while the man who falls short is a sort of boor and his state is boorishness. With regard to the remaining kind of pleasantness, that which is exhibited in life in general, the man who is pleasant in the right way is friendly and the mean is friendliness, while the man who exceeds is an obsequious person if he has no end in view, a flatterer if he is aiming at his own advantage, and the man who falls short and is unpleasant in all circumstances is a quarrelsome and surly sort of person.

There are also means in the passions and concerned with
30 the passions; since shame is not a virtue, and yet praise is extended to the modest man. For even in these matters one man is said to be intermediate, and another to exceed, as for instance the bashful man who is ashamed of everything; while he who falls short or is not ashamed of anything at all is shameless, and the intermediate person is modest. Righteous indignation is a mean between envy
35 and spite, and these states are concerned with the pain and
1108ᵇ pleasures that are felt at the fortunes of our neighbours; the man who is characterized by righteous indignation is pained at undeserved good fortune, the envious man, going beyond him, is pained at all good fortune, and the
5 spiteful man falls so far short of being pained that he even rejoices. But these states there will be an opportunity of describing elsewhere; [15] with regard to justice, since it has not one simple meaning, we shall, after describing the other states, distinguish its two kinds and say how each of
10 them is a mean; [16] and similarly we shall treat also of the rational virtues.[17]

8 There are three kinds of disposition, then, two of them vices, involving excess and deficiency respectively, and one a virtue, viz. the mean, and all are in a sense opposed to all; for the extreme states are contrary both to the intermediate state and to each other, and the
15 intermediate to the extremes; as the equal is greater relatively to the less, less relatively to the greater, so the middle states are excessive relatively to the deficiencies, deficient

   [15] The reference may be to the whole treatment of the moral virtues in iii. 6–iv. 9, or to the discussion of shame in iv. 9 and an intended corresponding discussion of righteous indignation, or to the discussion of these two states in *Rhet.* ii. 6, 9, 10.
   [16] 1129ᵃ 26–ᵇ 1, 1130ᵃ 14–ᵇ 5, 1131ᵇ 9–15, 1132ᵃ 24–30, 1133ᵇ 30–1134ᵃ 1.
   [17] Bk. vi.

relatively to the excesses, both in passions and in actions.
For the brave man appears rash relatively to the coward,
and cowardly relatively to the rash man; and similarly the
temperate man appears self-indulgent relatively to the insensible man, insensible relatively to the self-indulgent, and
the liberal man prodigal relatively to the mean man, mean
relatively to the prodigal. Hence also the people at the
extremes push the intermediate man each over to the other,
and the brave man is called rash by the coward, cowardly by 25
the rash man, and correspondingly in the other cases.

These states being thus opposed to one another, the
greatest contrariety is that of the extremes to each other,
rather than to the intermediate; for these are further from
each other than from the intermediate, as the great is
further from the small and the small from the great than 30
both are from the equal. Again, to the intermediate some
extremes show a certain likeness, as that of rashness to
courage and that of prodigality to liberality; but the extremes show the greatest unlikeness to each other; now
contraries are defined as the things that are furthest from
each other, so that things that are further apart are more 35
contrary.

To the mean in some cases the deficiency, in some the **1109ᵃ**
excess is more opposed; e. g. it is not rashness, which is an
excess, but cowardice, which is a deficiency, that is more
opposed to courage, and not insensibility, which is a deficiency, but self-indulgence, which is an excess, that is 5
more opposed to temperance. This happens from two reasons, one being drawn from the thing itself; for because one
extreme is nearer and liker to the intermediate, we oppose
not this but rather its contrary to the intermediate. E. g.,
since rashness is thought liker and nearer to courage, and
cowardice more unlike, we oppose rather the latter to 10
courage; for things that are further from the intermediate
are thought more contrary to it. This, then, is one cause,
drawn from the thing itself; another is drawn from ourselves: for the things to which we ourselves more **naturally**

tend seem more contrary to the intermediate. For instance,
15 we ourselves tend more naturally to pleasures, and hence
are more easily carried away towards self-indulgence than
towards propriety. We describe as contrary to the mean,
then, rather the directions in which we more often go to
great lengths; and therefore self-indulgence, which is an
excess, is the more contrary to temperance.

9   That moral virtue is a mean, then, and in what sense
20   it is so, and that it is a mean between two vices, the
one involving excess, the other deficiency, and that it is
such because its character is to aim at what is intermediate
in passions and in actions, has been sufficiently stated.
Hence also it is no easy task to be good. For in everything
it is no easy task to find the middle, e. g. to find the
25 middle of a circle is not for every one but for him who
knows; so, too, any one can get angry—that is easy—or give
or spend money; but to do this to the right person, to the
right extent, at the right time, with the right motive, and in
the right way, *that* is not for every one, nor is it easy; wherefore goodness is both rare and laudable and noble.

Hence he who aims at the intermediate must first de-
30 part from what is the more contrary to it, as Calypso ad-
vises—

Hold the ship out beyond that surf and spray.[18]

For of the extremes one is more erroneous, one less so;
therefore, since to hit the mean is hard in the extreme, we
must as a second best, as people say, take the least of the
35 evils; and this will be done best in the way we describe.

But we must consider the things towards which we our-
1109[b] selves also are easily carried away; for some of us tend to
one thing, some to another; and this will be recognizable
from the pleasure and the pain we feel. We must drag

[18] *Od.* xii. 219 f. (Mackail's trans.). But it was Circe who gave the
advice (xii. 108), and the actual quotation is from Odysseus' orders
to his steersman.

ourselves away to the contrary extreme; for we shall get 5
into the intermediate state by drawing well away from error,
as people do in straightening sticks that are bent.

Now in everything the pleasant or pleasure is most to be
guarded against; for we do not judge it impartially. We
ought, then, to feel towards pleasure as the elders of the
people felt towards Helen, and in all circumstances repeat
their saying; [19] for if we dismiss pleasure thus we are less 10
likely to go astray. It is by doing this, then, (to sum the
matter up) that we shall best be able to hit the mean.

But this is no doubt difficult, and especially in individual
cases; for it is not easy to determine both how and with 15
whom and on what provocation and how long one should
be angry; for we too sometimes praise those who fall short
and call them good-tempered, but sometimes we praise
those who get angry and call them manly. The man, however, who deviates little from goodness is not blamed,
whether he do so in the direction of the more or of the
less, but only the man who deviates more widely; for *he*
does not fail to be noticed. But up to what point and to 20
what extent a man must deviate before he becomes blameworthy it is not easy to determine by reasoning, any more
than anything else that is perceived by the senses; such
things depend on particular facts, and the decision rests
with perception. So much, then, is plain, that the intermediate state is in all things to be praised, but that we must 25
incline sometimes towards the excess, sometimes towards
the deficiency; for so shall we most easily hit the mean and
what is right.

BOOK III

1   Since virtue is concerned with passions and actions, 30
     and on voluntary passions and actions praise and
blame are bestowed, on those that are involuntary pardon,
and sometimes also pity, to distinguish the voluntary and

[19] *Il.* iii. 156–60.

the involuntary is presumably necessary for those who are studying the nature of virtue, and useful also for legislators with a view to the assigning both of honours and of punishments.

35 Those things, then, are thought involuntary, which take 1110ᵃ place under compulsion or owing to ignorance; and that is compulsory of which the moving principle is outside, being a principle in which nothing is contributed by the person who is acting or is feeling the passion, e. g. if he were to be carried somewhere by a wind, or by men who had him in their power.

But with regard to the things that are done from fear of 5 greater evils or for some noble object (e. g. if a tyrant were to order one to do something base, having one's parents and children in his power, and if one did the action they were to be saved, but otherwise would be put to death), it may be debated whether such actions are involuntary or voluntary. Something of the sort happens also with regard to the throwing of goods overboard in a 10 storm; for in the abstract no one throws goods away voluntarily, but on condition of its securing the safety of himself and his crew any sensible man does so. Such actions, then, are mixed, but are more like voluntary actions; for they are worthy of choice at the time when they are done, and the end of an action is relative to the occasion. Both the terms, then, 'voluntary' and 'involuntary', must be used with reference to the moment of action. Now the man acts 15 voluntarily; for the principle that moves the instrumental parts of the body in such actions is in him, and the things of which the moving principle is in a man himself are in his power to do or not to do. Such actions, therefore, are voluntary, but in the abstract perhaps involuntary; for no one would choose any such act in itself.

For such actions men are sometimes even praised, when 20 they endure something base or painful in return for great and noble objects gained; in the opposite case they are blamed, since to endure the greatest indignities for no noble end or for a trifling end is the mark of an inferior person. On some actions praise indeed is not bestowed, but pardon is, when one does what he ought not under pressure which overstrains human nature and which no one 25 could withstand. But some acts, perhaps, we cannot be forced to do, but ought rather to face death after the most fearful sufferings; for the things that 'forced' Euripides' Alcmaeon to slay his mother seem absurd. It is difficult sometimes to determine what should be chosen at what cost, and what should be endured in return for what gain, and yet more difficult to abide by our decisions; for as a 30 rule what is expected is painful, and what we are forced to do is base, whence praise and blame are bestowed on those who have been compelled or have not.

What sort of acts, then, should be called compulsory? We answer that without qualification actions are so when **1110ᵇ** the cause is in the external circumstances and the agent contributes nothing. But the things that in themselves are involuntary, but now and in return for these gains are worthy of choice, and whose moving principle is in the agent, are in themselves involuntary, but now and in return 5 for these gains voluntary. They are more like voluntary acts; for actions are in the class of particulars, and the particular acts here are voluntary. What sort of things are to be chosen, and in return for what, it is not easy to state; for there are many differences in the particular cases.

But if some one were to say that pleasant and noble objects have a compelling power, forcing us from without, all acts would be for him compulsory; for it is for these objects that all men do everything they do. And those who 10 act under compulsion and unwillingly act with pain, but those who do acts for their pleasantness and nobility do them with pleasure; it is absurd to make external circumstances responsible, and not oneself, as being easily caught by such attractions, and to make oneself responsible for noble acts but the pleasant objects responsible for base acts. 15 The compulsory, then, seems to be that whose moving principle is outside, the person compelled contributing nothing.

Everything that is done by reason of ignorance is not voluntary; it is only what produces pain and repentance that is involuntary. For the man who has done something owing to ignorance, and feels not the least vexation at his action, has not acted voluntarily, since he did not know what he was doing, nor yet involuntarily, since he is not pained. Of people, then, who act by reason of ignorance he who repents is thought an involuntary agent, and the man who does not repent may, since he is different, be called a not voluntary agent; for, since he differs from the other, it is better that he should have a name of his own.

Acting by reason of ignorance seems also to be different from acting in ignorance; for the man who is drunk or in a rage is thought to act as a result not of ignorance but of one of the causes mentioned, yet not knowingly but in ignorance.

Now every wicked man is ignorant of what he ought to do and what he ought to abstain from, and it is by reason of error of this kind that men become unjust and in general bad; but the term 'involuntary' tends to be used not if a man is ignorant of what is to his advantage—for it is not mistaken purpose that causes involuntary action (it leads rather to wickedness), nor ignorance of the universal (for that men are blamed), but ignorance of particulars, i. e. of the circumstances of the action and the objects with which it is concerned. For it is on these that both pity and pardon depend, since the person who is ignorant of any of these acts involuntarily.

Perhaps it is just as well, therefore, to determine their nature and number. A man may be ignorant, then, of who he is, what he is doing, what or whom he is acting on, and sometimes also what (e. g. what instrument) he is doing it with, and to what end (e. g. he may think his act will conduce to some one's safety), and how he is doing it (e. g. whether gently or violently). Now of all of these no one could be ignorant unless he were mad, and evidently also he could not be ignorant of the agent; for how could he not know himself? But of what he is doing a man might be ignorant, as for instance people say 'it slipped out of their mouths as they were speaking', or 'they did not know it 10 was a secret', as Aeschylus said of the mysteries, or a man might say he 'let it go off when he merely wanted to show its working', as the man did with the catapult. Again, one might think one's son was an enemy, as Merope did, or that a pointed spear had a button on it, or that a stone was pumice-stone; or one might give a man a draught to save him, and really kill him; or one might want to touch a man, as people do in sparring, and really wound him. The 15 ignorance may relate, then, to any of these things, i. e. of the circumstances of the action, and the man who was ignorant of any of these is thought to have acted involuntarily, and especially if he was ignorant on the most important points; and these are thought to be the circumstances of the action and its end. Further, the doing of an act that is called involuntary in virtue of ignorance of this sort must be painful and involve repentance.   20

Since that which is done under compulsion or by reason of ignorance is involuntary, the voluntary would seem to be that of which the moving principle is in the agent himself, he being aware of the particular circumstances of the action. Presumably acts done by reason of anger or appetite are not rightly called involuntary.[1] For in the first place, on that showing none of the other animals 25 will act voluntarily, nor will children; and secondly, is it meant that we do not do voluntarily any of the acts that are due to appetite or anger, or that we do the noble acts voluntarily and the base acts involuntarily? Is not this absurd, when one and the same thing is the cause? But it would surely be odd to describe as involuntary the things one ought to desire; and we ought both to be angry at 30

[1] A reference to Pl. Laws 863 B, ff., where anger and appetite are coupled with ignorance as sources of wrong action.

certain things and to have an appetite for certain things,
e. g. for health and for learning. Also what is involuntary is
thought to be painful, but what is in accordance with appetite is thought to be pleasant. Again, what is the difference
in respect of involuntariness between errors committed
upon calculation and those committed in anger? Both are
1111ᵇ to be avoided, but the irrational passions are thought not
less human than reason is, and therefore also the actions
which proceed from anger or appetite are the man's actions.
It would be odd, then, to treat them as involuntary.

2   Both the voluntary and the involuntary having been
delimited, we must next discuss choice; for it is
5 thought to be most closely bound up with virtue and to
discriminate characters better than actions do.

Choice, then, seems to be voluntary, but not the same
thing as the voluntary; the latter extends more widely. For
both children and the lower animals share in voluntary
action, but not in choice, and acts done on the spur of the
moment we describe as voluntary, but not as chosen.

10   Those who say it is appetite or anger or wish or a kind of
opinion do not seem to be right. For choice is not common
to irrational creatures as well, but appetite and anger are.
Again, the incontinent man acts with appetite, but not
15 with choice; while the continent man on the contrary acts
with choice, but not with appetite. Again, appetite is contrary to choice, but not appetite to appetite. Again, appetite
relates to the pleasant and the painful, choice neither to
the painful nor to the pleasant.

Still less is it anger; for acts due to anger are thought to
be less than any others objects of choice.

20   But neither is it wish, though it seems near to it; for
choice cannot relate to impossibles, and if any one said he
chose them he would be thought silly; but there may be a
wish even for impossibles, e. g. for immortality. And wish
may relate to things that could in no way be brought about
25 by one's own efforts, e. g. that a particular actor or athlete

should win in a competition; but no one chooses such things, but only the things that he thinks could be brought about by his own efforts. Again, wish relates rather to the end, choice to the means; for instance, we wish to be healthy, but we choose the acts which will make us healthy, and we wish to be happy and say we do, but we cannot well say we choose to be so; for, in general, choice seems to relate to the things that are in our own power.

For this reason, too, it cannot be opinion; for opinion 30 is thought to relate to all kinds of things, no less to eternal things and impossible things than to things in our own power; and it is distinguished by its falsity or truth, not by its badness or goodness, while choice is distinguished rather by these.

Now with opinion in general perhaps no one even says it is identical. But it is not identical even with any kind of **1112ª** opinion; for by choosing what is good or bad we are men of a certain character, which we are not by holding certain opinions. And we choose to get or avoid something good or bad, but we have opinions about what a thing is or whom it is good for or how it is good for him; we can hardly be said to opine to get or avoid anything. And choice is 5 praised for being related to the right object rather than for being rightly related to it, opinion for being truly related to its object. And we choose what we best know to be good, but we opine what we do not quite know; and it is not the same people that are thought to make the best choices and to have the best opinions, but some are thought to have fairly good opinions, but by reason of vice to choose what they should not. If opinion precedes choice or accompanies 10 it, that makes no difference; for it is not this that we are considering, but whether it is *identical* with some kind of opinion.

What, then, or what kind of thing is it, since it is none of the things we have mentioned? It seems to be voluntary, but not all that is voluntary to be an object of choice. Is it, then, what has been decided on by previous deliberation? 15

At any rate choice involves a rational principle and thought. Even the name seems to suggest that it is what is chosen before other things.

3   Do we deliberate about everything, and is everything a possible subject of deliberation, or is deliberation 20 impossible about some things? We ought presumably to call not what a fool or a madman would deliberate about, but what a sensible man would deliberate about, a subject of deliberation. Now about eternal things no one deliberates, e. g. about the material universe or the incommensurability of the diagonal and the side of a square. But no more do we deliberate about the things that involve movement but always happen in the same way, whether of 25 necessity or by nature or from any other cause, e. g. the solstices and the risings of the stars; nor about things that happen now in one way, now in another, e. g. droughts and rains; nor about chance events, like the finding of treasure. But we do not deliberate even about all human affairs; for instance, no Spartan deliberates about the best constitution for the Scythians. For none of these things can be brought about by our own efforts.

We deliberate about things that are in our power and can 30 be done; and these are in fact what is left. For nature, necessity, and chance are thought to be causes, and also reason and everything that depends on man. Now every class of men deliberates about the things that can be done by their own efforts. And in the case of exact and self-contained sciences there is no deliberation, e. g. about the let-**1112ᵇ** ters of the alphabet (for we have no doubt how they should be written); but the things that are brought about by our own efforts, but not always in the same way, are the things about which we deliberate, e. g. questions of medical treatment or of money-making. And we do so more 5 in the case of the art of navigation than in that of gymnastics, inasmuch as it has been less exactly worked out, and again about other things in the same ratio, and more also in the case of the arts than in that of the sciences; for we have more doubt about the former. Deliberation is concerned with things that happen in a certain way for the most part, but in which the event is obscure, and with things in which it is indeterminate. We call in others to aid us in deliberation on important questions, distrusting ourselves as not being equal to deciding.

We deliberate not about ends but about means. For a doctor does not deliberate whether he shall heal, nor an orator whether he shall persuade, nor a statesman whether he shall produce law and order, nor does any one else deliberate about his end. They assume the end and consider how and by what means it is to be attained; and if it seems to be produced by several means they consider by which it is most easily and best produced, while if it is achieved by one only they consider how it will be achieved by this and by what means *this* will be achieved, till they come to the first cause, which in the order of discovery is last. For the person who deliberates seems to investigate and analyse in the way described as though he were analysing a geometrical construction [2] (not all investigation appears to be deliberation—for instance mathematical investigations —but all deliberation is investigation), and what is last in the order of analysis seems to be first in the order of becoming. And if we come on an impossibility, we give up the search, e. g. if we need money and this cannot be got; but if a thing appears possible we try to do it. By 'possible' things I mean things that might be brought about by our own efforts, and these in a sense include things that can be brought about by the efforts of our friends, since the moving principle is in ourselves. The subject of investigation is sometimes the instruments, sometimes the use of

---

[2] Aristotle has in mind the method of discovering the solution of a geometrical problem. The problem being to construct a figure of a certain kind, we suppose it constructed and then analyse it to see if there is some figure by constructing which we can construct the required figure, and so on till we come to a figure which our existing knowledge enables us to construct.

30 them; and similarly in the other cases—sometimes the means, sometimes the mode of using it or the means of bringing it about. It seems, then, as has been said, that man is a moving principle of actions; now deliberation is about the things to be done by the agent himself, and actions are for the sake of things other than themselves. For the end cannot be a subject of deliberation, but only the means; 1113ª nor indeed can the particular facts be a subject of it, as whether this is bread or has been baked as it should; for these are matters of perception. If we are to be always deliberating, we shall have to go on to infinity.

The same thing is deliberated upon and is chosen, except that the object of choice is already determinate, since 5 it is that which has been decided upon as a result of deliberation that is the object of choice. For every one ceases to inquire how he is to act when he has brought the moving principle back to himself and to the ruling part of himself; for this is what chooses. This is plain also from the ancient constitutions, which Homer represented; for the kings announced their choices to the people. The object of choice 10 being one of the things in our own power which is desired after deliberation, choice will be deliberate desire of things in our own power; for when we have decided as a result of deliberation, we desire in accordance with our deliberation.

We may take it, then, that we have described choice in outline, and stated the nature of its objects and the fact that it is concerned with means.

4   That wish is for the end has already been stated; ª 15   some think it is for the good, others for the apparent good. Now those who say that the good is the object of wish must admit in consequence that that which the man who does not choose aright wishes for is not an object of wish (for if it is to be so, it must also be good; but it was, if it so happened, bad); while those who say the apparent 20 good is the object of wish must admit that there is no

ª 1111ᵇ 26.

natural object of wish, but only what seems good to each man. Now different things appear good to different people, and, if it so happens, even contrary things.

If these consequences are unpleasing, are we to say that absolutely and in truth the good is the object of wish, but for each person the apparent good; that that which is in 25 truth an object of wish is an object of wish to the good man, while any chance thing may be so to the bad man, as in the case of bodies also the things that are in truth wholesome are wholesome for bodies which are in good condition, while for those that are diseased other things are wholesome—or bitter or sweet or hot or heavy, and so on; since the good man judges each class of things rightly, and in each the truth appears to him? For each state of char- 30 acter has its own ideas of the noble and the pleasant, and perhaps the good man differs from others most by seeing the truth in each class of things, being as it were the norm and measure of them. In most things the error seems to be due to pleasure; for it appears a good when it is not. We therefore choose the pleasant as a good, and avoid pain as 1113 an evil.

5 The end, then, being what we wish for, the means being what we deliberate about and choose, actions concerning means must be according to choice and voluntary. Now the exercise of the virtues is concerned with means. 5 Therefore virtue also is in our own power, and so too vice. For where it is in our power to act it is also in our power not to act, and vice versa; so that, if to act, where this is noble, is in our power, not to act, which will be base, will also be in our power, and if not to act, where this is noble, 10 is in our power, to act, which will be base, will also be in our power. Now if it is in our power to do noble or base acts, and likewise in our power not to do them, and this was what being good or bad meant,[4] then it is in our power to be virtuous or vicious.

[4] 1112ᵃ 1 f.

The saying that 'no one is voluntarily wicked nor in-
15 voluntarily happy' seems to be partly false and partly true;
for no one is involuntarily happy, but wickedness is voluntary. Or else we shall have to dispute what has just been
said, at any rate, and deny that man is a moving principle
or begetter of his actions as of children. But if these facts
are evident and we cannot refer actions to moving prin-
20 ciples other than those in ourselves, the acts whose moving
principles are in us must themselves also be in our power
and voluntary.

Witness seems to be borne to this both by individuals
in their private capacity and by legislators themselves; for
these punish and take vengeance on those who do wicked
acts (unless they have acted under compulsion or as a re-
25 sult of ignorance for which they are not themselves responsible), while they honour those who do noble acts, as
though they meant to encourage the latter and deter the
former. But no one is encouraged to do the things that are
neither in our power nor voluntary; it is assumed that
there is no gain in being persuaded not to be hot or in
30 pain or hungry or the like, since we shall experience these
feelings none the less. Indeed, we punish a man for his
very ignorance, if he is thought responsible for the ignorance, as when penalties are doubled in the case of
drunkenness; for the moving principle is in the man himself, since he had the power of not getting drunk and his
getting drunk was the cause of his ignorance. And we
punish those who are ignorant of anything in the laws that
1114ᵃ they ought to know and that is not difficult, and so too in
the case of anything else that they are thought to be ignorant of through carelessness; we assume that it is in
their power not to be ignorant, since they have the power
of taking care.

But perhaps a man is the kind of man not to take care.
Still they are themselves by their slack lives responsible for
5 becoming men of that kind, and men make themselves
responsible for being unjust or self-indulgent, in the one

case by cheating and in the other by spending their time
in drinking bouts and the like; for it is activities exercised
on particular objects that make the corresponding character. This is plain from the case of people training for
any contest or action; they practice the activity the whole
time. Now not to know that it is from the exercise of
activities on particular objects that states of character 10
are produced is the mark of a thoroughly senseless person.
Again, it is irrational to suppose that a man who acts unjustly does not wish to be unjust or a man who acts self-
indulgently to be self-indulgent. But if *without* being
ignorant a man does the things which will make him unjust, he will be unjust voluntarily. Yet it does not follow
that if he wishes he will cease to be unjust and will be just.
For neither does the man who is ill become well on those
terms. We may suppose a case in which he is ill volun- 15
tarily, through living incontinently and disobeying his
doctors. In that case it was *then* open to him not to be ill,
but not now, when he has thrown away his chance, just
as when you have let a stone go it is too late to recover it;
but yet it was in your power to throw it, since the moving
principle was in you. So, too, to the unjust and to the
self-indulgent man it was open at the beginning not to be- 20
come men of this kind, and so they are unjust and self-
indulgent voluntarily; but now that they have become so it
is not possible for them not to be so.

But not only are the vices of the soul voluntary, but
those of the body also for some men, whom we accordingly
blame; while no one blames those who are ugly by nature,
we blame those who are so owing to want of exercise and
care. So it is, too, with respect to weakness and infirmity; 25
no one would reproach a man blind from birth or by
disease or from a blow, but rather pity him, while every
one would blame a man who was blind from drunkenness
or some other form of self-indulgence. Of vices of the
body, then, those in our own power are blamed, those not
in our power are not. And if this be so, in the other cases 30

also the vices that are blamed must be in our own power.

Now some one may say that all men desire the apparent good, but have no control over the appearance, but the end appears to each man in a form answering to his
1114b character. We reply that if each man is somehow responsible for his state of mind, he will also be himself somehow responsible for the appearance; but if not, no one is responsible for his own evildoing, but every one does evil acts through ignorance of the end, thinking that by these
5 he will get what is best, and the aiming at the end is not self-chosen but one must be born with an eye, as it were, by which to judge rightly and choose what is truly good, and he is well endowed by nature who is well endowed with this. For it is what is greatest and most noble, and
10 what we cannot get or learn from another, but must have just such as it was when given us at birth, and to be well and nobly endowed with this will be perfect and true excellence of natural endowment. If this is true, then, how will virtue be more voluntary than vice? To both men
15 alike, the good and the bad, the end appears and is fixed by nature or however it may be, and it is by referring everything else to this that men do whatever they do.

Whether, then, it is not by nature that the end appears to each man such as it does appear, but something also depends on him, or the end is natural but because the good
20 man adopts the means voluntarily virtue is voluntary, vice also will be none the less voluntary; for in the case of the bad man there is equally present that which depends on himself in his actions even if not in his end. If, then, as is asserted, the virtues are voluntary (for we are ourselves somehow partly responsible for our states of character, and it is by being persons of a certain kind that we assume the end to be so and so), the vices also will be voluntary;
25 for the same is true of them.

With regard to the virtues in general we have stated their genus in outline, viz. that they are means and that they are states of character and that they tend, and by

their own nature, to the doing of the acts by which they
are produced, and that they are in our power and voluntary, and act as the right rule prescribes. But actions and
states of character are not voluntary in the same way; for
we are masters of our actions from the beginning right to
the end, if we know the particular facts, but though we
control the beginning of our states of character the gradual
progress is not obvious, any more than it is in illnesses; because it was in our power, however, to act in this way or
not in this way, therefore the states are voluntary.

Let us take up the several virtues, however, and say
which they are and what sort of things they are concerned
with and how they are concerned with them; at the same
time it will become plain how many they are. And first let
us speak of courage.

6 That it is a mean with regard to feelings of fear and
confidence has already been made evident; [5] and
plainly the things we fear are terrible things, and these
are, to speak without qualification, evils; for which reason
people even define fear as expectation of evil. Now we fear
all evils, e. g. disgrace, poverty, disease, friendliness, death,
but the brave man is not thought to be concerned with all;
for to fear some things is even right and noble, and it is
base not to fear them—e. g. disgrace; he who fears this is
good and modest, and he who does not is shameless. He
is, however, by some people called brave, by a transference
of the word to a new meaning; for he has in him something
which is like the brave man, since the brave man also is a
fearless person. Poverty and disease we perhaps ought not
to fear, nor in general the things that do not proceed from
vice and are not due to a man himself. But not even the
man who is fearless of these is brave. Yet we apply the
word to him also in virtue of a similarity; for some who in
the dangers of war are cowards are liberal and are confident in face of the loss of money. Nor is a man a coward if

[5] 1107[a] 33–[b] 4.

he fears insult to his wife and children or envy or anything of the kind; nor brave if he is confident when he is about to be flogged. With what sort of terrible things, then, is the brave man concerned? Surely with the greatest; for no
25 one is more likely than he to stand his ground against what is awe-inspiring. Now death is the most terrible of all things; for it is the end, and nothing is thought to be any longer either good or bad for the dead. But the brave man would not seem to be concerned even with death in all circumstances, e. g. at sea or in disease. In what circumstances, then? Surely in the noblest. Now such deaths are
30 those in battle; for these take place in the greatest and noblest danger. And these are correspondingly honoured in city-states and at the courts of monarchs. Properly, then, he will be called brave who is fearless in face of a noble death, and of all emergencies that involve death; and the emergencies of war are in the highest degree of this kind.
35 Yet at sea also, and in disease; the brave man is fearless,
1115ᵇ but not in the same way as the seamen; for he has given up hope of safety, and is disliking the thought of death in this shape, while they are hopeful because of their experience. At the same time, we show courage in situations where
5 there is the opportunity of showing prowess or where death is noble; but in these forms of death neither of these conditions is fulfilled.

7   What is terrible is not the same for all men; but we say there are things terrible even beyond human strength. These, then, are terrible to every one—at least to every sensible man; but the terrible things that are not beyond human strength differ in magnitude and degree, and so too do the things that inspire confidence. Now the
10 brave man is as dauntless as man may be. Therefore, while he will fear even the things that are not beyond human strength, he will face them as he ought and as the rule directs, for honour's sake; for this is the end of virtue. But it is possible to fear these more, or less, and again to fear
15 things that are not terrible as if they were. Of the faults

that are committed one consists in fearing what one should
not, another in fearing as we should not, another in fearing
when we should not, and so on; and so too with respect to
the things that inspire confidence. The man, then, who
faces and who fears the right things and from the right motive, in the right way and at the right time, and who feels
confidence under the corresponding conditions, is brave;
for the brave man feels and acts according to the merits of
the case and in whatever way the rule directs. Now the end ₂₀
of every activity is conformity to the corresponding state of
character. This is true, therefore, of the brave man as well
as of others. But courage is noble. Therefore the end also
is noble; for each thing is defined by its end. Therefore it
is for a noble end that the brave man endures and acts as
courage directs.

Of those who go to excess he who exceeds in fearlessness
has no name (we have said previously that many states of ₂₅
character have no names [6]), but he would be a sort of madman or insensible person if he feared nothing, neither
earthquakes nor the waves, as they say the Celts do not;
while the man who exceeds in confidence about what really
is terrible is rash. The rash man, however, is also thought
to be boastful and only a pretender to courage; at all events, ₃₀
as the brave man *is* with regard to what is terrible, so the
rash man wishes to *appear*; and so he imitates him in situations where he can. Hence also most of them are a mixture
of rashness and cowardice; for, while in these situations
they display confidence, they do not hold their ground
against what is really terrible. The man who exceeds in fear
is a coward; for he fears both what he ought not and as he ₃₅
ought not, and all the similar characterizations attach to **1116ᵃ**
him. He is lacking also in confidence; but he is more con-
spicuous for his excess of fear in painful situations. The
coward, then, is a despairing sort of person; for he fears
everything. The brave man, on the other hand, has the opposite disposition; for confidence is the mark of a hopeful
disposition. The coward, the rash man, and the brave man.

[6] 1107ᵇ 2, Cf. 1107ᵇ 29, 1108ᵃ 5.

5 then, are concerned with the same objects but are differently disposed towards them; for the first two exceed and fall short, while the third holds the middle, which is the right, position; and rash men are precipitate, and wish for dangers beforehand but draw back when they are in them, while brave men are keen in the moment of action, but quiet beforehand.

10   As we have said, then, courage is a mean with respect to things that inspire confidence or fear, in the circumstances that have been stated;[7] and it chooses or endures things because it is noble to do so, or because it is base not to do so.[8] But to die to escape from poverty or love or anything painful is not the mark of a brave man, but rather of a coward; for it is softness to fly from what is troublesome, and such a man endures death not because it is noble but to fly from evil.

8   Courage, then, is something of this sort, but the name
15   is also applied to five other kinds. (1) First comes the courage of the citizen-soldier; for this is most like true courage. Citizen-soldiers seem to face dangers because of the penalties imposed by the laws and the reproaches they would otherwise incur, and because of the honours they win by such action; and therefore those peoples seem to
20 be bravest among whom cowards are held in dishonour and brave men in honour. This is the kind of courage that Homer depicts, e. g. in Diomede and in Hector:

First will Polydamas be to heap reproach on me then;[9]

and

25   For Hector one day 'mid the Trojans shall utter his vaulting harangue:
     "Afraid was Tydeides, and fled from my face."[10]

[7] Ch. 6.
[8] 1115[b] 11–24.
[9] Il. xxii. 100.
[10] Il. viii. 148, 149.

This kind of courage is most like to that which we described earlier,[11] because it is due to virtue; for it is due to shame and to desire of a nobel object (i. e. honour) and avoidance of disgrace, which is ignoble. One might rank in the same class even those who are compelled by their 30 rulers; but they are inferior, inasmuch as they do what they do not from shame but from fear, and to avoid not what is disgraceful but what is painful; for their masters compel them, as Hector [12] does:

But if I shall spy any dastard that cowers far from the fight,
Vainly will such an one hope to escape from the dogs. 35

And those who give them their posts, and beat them if they retreat, do the same, and so do those who draw them up with trenches or something of the sort behind them; all 1116ᵇ of these apply compulsion. But one ought to be brave not under compulsion but because it is noble to be so.

(2) Experience with regard to particular facts is also thought to be courage; this is indeed the reason why Socrates thought courage was knowledge. Other people exhibit this quality in other dangers, and professional sol- 5 diers exhibit it in the dangers of war; for there seem to be many empty alarms in war, of which these have had the most comprehensive experience; therefore they seem brave, because the others do not know the nature of the facts. Again, their experience makes them most capable in attack 10 and in defence, since they can use their arms and have the kind that are likely to be best both for attack and for defence; therefore they fight like armed men against unarmed or like trained athletes against amateurs; for in such contests too it is not the bravest men that fight best, but those who are strongest and have their bodies in the best condi- 15 tion. Professional soldiers turn cowards, however, when the

---

[11] Chs. 6, 7.
[12] Aristotle's quotation is more like ïl. ii. 391–3, where Agamemnon speaks, than xv. 348–51, where Hector speaks.

danger puts too great a strain on them and they are inferior in numbers and equipment; for they are the first to fly, while citizen-forces die at their posts, as in fact happened at the temple of Hermes.[13] For to the latter flight is disgraceful and death is preferable to safety on those terms; while the former from the very beginning faced the danger on the assumption that they were stronger, and when they know the facts they fly, fearing death more than disgrace; but the brave man is not that sort of person.

(3) Passion also is sometimes reckoned as courage; those who act from passion, like wild beasts rushing at those who have wounded them, are thought to be brave, because brave men also are passionate; for passion above all things is eager to rush on danger, and hence Homer's 'put strength into his passion'[14] and 'aroused their spirit and passion'[15] and 'hard he breathed panting'[16] and 'his blood boiled'.[17] For all such expressions seem to indicate the stirring and onset of passion. Now brave men act for honour's sake, but passion aids them; while wild beasts act under the influence of pain; for they attack because they have been wounded or because they are afraid, since if they are in a forest they do not come near one. Thus they are not brave because, driven by pain and passion, they rush on danger without foreseeing any of the perils, since at that rate even asses would be brave when they are hungry; for blows will not drive them from their food; and lust also makes adulterers do many daring things. [Those creatures are not brave, then, which are driven on to danger by pain or passion.] The 'courage' that is due to passion seems to be the most natural, and to be courage if choice and motive be added.

Men, then, as well as beasts, suffer pain when they are

---

[13] The reference is to a battle at Coronea in the Sacred War, c. 353 B. C., in which the Phocians defeated the citizens of Coronea and some Boeotian regulars.
[14] This is a conflation of Il. xi. 11 or xiv. 151 and xvi. 529.
[15] Cf. Il. v. 470, xv. 232, 594.
[16] Cf. Od. xxiv. 318 f.
[17] The phrase does not occur in Homer; it is found in Theocr. xx. 15.

angry, and are pleased when they exact their revenge; those who fight for these reasons, however, are pugnacious but not brave; for they do not act for honour's sake nor as the rule directs, but from strength of feeling; they have, however, something akin to courage.

(4) Nor are sanguine people brave; for they are confident in danger only because they have conquered often and against many foes. Yet they closely resemble brave men, because both are confident; but brave men are confident for the reasons stated earlier,[18] while these are so because they think they are the strongest and can suffer nothing. (Drunken men also behave in this way; they become sanguine.) When their adventures do not succeed, however, they run away; but it was [18] the mark of a brave man to face things that are, and seem, terrible for a man, because it is noble to do so and disgraceful not to do so. Hence also it is thought the mark of a braver man to be fearless and undisturbed in sudden alarms than to be so in those that are foreseen; for it must have proceeded more from a state of character, because less from preparation; acts that are foreseen may be chosen by calculation and rule, but sudden actions must be in accordance with one's state of character.)

(5) People who are ignorant of the danger also appear brave, and they are not far removed from those of a sanguine temper, but are inferior inasmuch as they have no self-reliance while these have. Hence also the sanguine hold their ground for a time; but those who have been deceived about the facts fly if they know or suspect that these are different from what they supposed, as happened to the Argives when they fell in with the Spartans and took them for Sicyonians.[19]

9   We have, then, described the character both of brave men and of those who are thought to be brave.

Though courage is concerned with feelings of confidence

[18] 1115^b 11–24.
[19] At the Long Walls of Corinth, 392 B. C Cf. Xen. *Hell.* iv. 4. 10.

and of fear, it is not concerned with both alike, but more with the things that inspire fear; for he who is undisturbed 30 in face of these and bears himself as he should towards these is more truly brave than the man who does so towards the things that inspire confidence. It is for facing what is painful, then, as has been said,[20] that men are called brave. Hence also courage involves pain, and is justly praised; for it is harder to face what is painful than to abstain from what is pleasant. Yet the end which courage sets before it would 35 seem to be pleasant, but to be concealed by the attending 1117ᵇ circumstances, as happens also in athletic contests; for the end at which boxers aim is pleasant—the crown and the honours—but the blows they take are distressing to flesh 5 and blood, and painful, and so is their whole exertion; and because the blows and the exertions are many the end, which is but small, appears to have nothing pleasant in it. And so, if the case of courage is similar, death and wounds will be painful to the brave man and against his will, but he will face them because it is noble to do so or because it is base not to do so. And the more he is possessed of virtue 10 in its entirety and the happier he is, the more he will be pained at the thought of death; for life is best worth living for such a man, and he is knowingly losing the greatest goods, and this is painful. But he is none the less brave, and perhaps all the more so, because he chooses noble deeds of 15 war at that cost. It is not the case, then, with all the virtues that the exercise of them is pleasant, except in so far as it reaches its end. But it is quite possible that the best soldiers may be not men of this sort but those who are less brave but have no other good; for these are ready to face danger, and they sell their life for trifling gains.

20   So much, then, for courage; it is not difficult to grasp its nature in outline, at any rate, from what has been said.

After courage let us speak of temperance; for these seem to be the virtues of the irrational parts.

temperance

[20] 1115ᵇ 7–13.

10   We have said [21] that temperance is a mean with regard
to pleasures (for it is less, and not in the same way, [25]
concerned with pains); self-indulgence also is manifested
in the same sphere. Now, therefore, let us determine with
what sort of pleasures they are concerned. We may assume
the distinction between bodily pleasures and those of the
soul, such as love of honour and love of learning; for the
lover of each of these delights in that of which he is a lover, [30]
the body being in no way affected, but rather the mind; but
men who are concerned with such pleasures are called
neither temperate nor self-indulgent. Nor, again, are those
who are concerned with the other pleasures that are not
bodily; for those who are fond of hearing and telling stories
and who spend their days on anything that turns up are [35]
called gossips, but not self-indulgent, nor are those who are
pained at the loss of money or of friends.

Temperance must be concerned with bodily pleasures, **1118ᵃ**
but not all even of these; for those who delight in objects
of vision, such as colours and shapes and painting, are called [5]
neither temperate nor self-indulgent; yet it would seem
possible to delight even in these either as one should or to
excess or to a deficient degree.

And so too is it with objects of hearing; no one calls those
who delight extravagantly in music or acting self-indulgent,
nor those who do so as they ought temperate.

Nor do we apply these names to those who delight in
odour, unless it be incidentally; we do not call those self-
indulgent who delight in the odour of apples or roses or
incense, but rather those who delight in the odour of un- [10]
guents or of dainty dishes; for self-indulgent people delight
in these because these remind them of the objects of their
appetite. And one may see even other people, when they are
hungry, delighting in the smell of food; but to delight in
this kind of thing is the mark of the self-indulgent man; [15]
for these are objects of appetite to him.

[21] 1107ᵇ 4–6.

Nor is there in animals other than man any pleasure connected with these senses, except incidentally. For dogs do
not delight in the scent of hares, but in the eating of them,
20 but the scent told them the hares were there; nor does the
lion delight in the lowing of the ox, but in eating it; but he
perceived by the lowing that it was near, and therefore appears to delight in the lowing; and similarly he does not delight because he sees 'a stag or a wild goat',[22] but because
he is going to make a meal of it. Temperance and self-
indulgence, however, are concerned with the kind of pleas-
25 ures that the other animals share in, which therefore appear
slavish and brutish; these are touch and taste. But even of
taste they appear to make little or no use; for the business
of taste is the discriminating of flavours, which is done by
wine-tasters and people who season dishes; but they hardly
take pleasure in making these discriminations, or at least
30 self-indulgent people do not, but in the actual enjoyment,
which in all cases comes through touch, both in the case of
food and in that of drink and in that of sexual intercourse.
This is why a certain gourmand prayed that his throat
might become longer than a crane's, implying that it was
1118ᵇ the contact that he took pleasure in. Thus the sense with
which self-indulgence is connected is the most widely
shared of the senses; and self-indulgence would seem to be
justly a matter of reproach, because it attaches to us not as
men but as animals. To delight in such things, then, and to
love them above all others, is brutish. For even of the
pleasures of touch the most liberal have been eliminated,
e. g. those produced in the gymnasium by rubbing and by
5 the consequent heat; for the contact characteristic of the
self-indulgent man does not affect the whole body but only
certain parts.

11   Of the appetites some seem to be common, others to
be peculiar to individuals and acquired; e. g. the ap-
10 petite for food is natural, since every one who is without it

[22] Il. iii. 24.

craves for food or drink, and sometimes for both, and for love also (as Homer says) [23] if he is young and lusty; but not every one craves for this or that kind of nourishment or love, nor for the same things. Hence such craving appears to be our very own. Yet it has of course something natural about it; for different things are pleasant to different kinds of people, and some things are more pleasant to every one than chance objects. Now in the natural appetites few go wrong, and only in one direction, that of excess; for to eat or drink whatever offers itself till one is surfeited is to exceed the natural amount, since natural appetite is the replenishment of one's deficiency. Hence these people are called belly-gods, this implying that they fill their belly beyond what is right. It is people of entirely slavish character that become like this. But with regard to the pleasures peculiar to individuals many people go wrong and in many ways. For while the people who are 'fond of so and so' are so called because they delight either in the wrong things, or more than most people do, or in the wrong way, the self-indulgent exceed in all three ways; they both delight in some things that they ought not to delight in (since they are hateful), and if one ought to delight in some of the things they delight in, they do so more than one ought and than most men do.

Plainly, then, excess with regard to pleasures is self-indulgence and is culpable; with regard to pains one is not, as in the case of courage, called temperate for facing them or self-indulgent for not doing so, but the self-indulgent man is so called because he is pained more than he ought at not getting pleasant things (even his pain being caused by pleasure), and the temperate man is so called because he is not pained at the absence of what is pleasant and at his abstinence from it.

The self-indulgent man, then, craves for all pleasant things or those that are most pleasant, and is led by his appetite to choose these at the cost of everything else;

[23] *Il.* xxiv. 130.

hence he is pained both when he fails to get them and
when he is merely craving for them (for appetite involves
5 pain); but it seems absurd to be pained for the sake of
pleasure. People who fall short with regard to pleasures and
delight in them less than they should are hardly found; for
such insensibility is not human. Even the other animals
distinguish different kinds of food and enjoy some and not
others; and if there is any one who finds nothing pleasant
and nothing more attractive than anything else, he must be
10 something quite different from a man; this sort of person
has not received a name because he hardly occurs. The
temperate man occupies a middle position with regard to
these objects. For he neither enjoys the things that the self-
indulgent man enjoys most—but rather dislikes them—nor
in general the things that he should not, nor anything of
this sort to excess, nor does he feel pain or craving when
they are absent, or does so only to a moderate degree, and
15 not more than he should, nor when he should not, and so
on; but the things that, being pleasant, make for health or
for good condition, he will desire moderately and as he
should, and also other pleasant things if they are not hindrances to these ends, or contrary to what is noble, or beyond his means. For he who neglects these conditions loves
such pleasures more than they are worth, but the temperate
20 man is not that sort of person, but the sort of person that
the right rule prescribes

12 Self-indulgence is more like a voluntary state than
        cowardice. For the former is actuated by pleasure, the
latter by pain, of which the one is to be chosen and the
other to be avoided; and pain upsets and destroys the nature of the person who feels it, while pleasure does nothing
of the sort. Therefore self-indulgence is more voluntary.
25 Hence also it is more a matter of reproach; for it is easier
to become accustomed to its objects, since there are many
things of this sort in life, and the process of habituation to
them is free from danger, while with terrible objects the re-

verse is the case. But cowardice would seem to be voluntary in a different degree from its particular manifestations; for it is itself painless, but in these we are upset by pain, so that we even throw down our arms and disgrace ourselves in other ways; hence our acts are even thought to be done 31 under compulsion. For the self-indulgent man, on the other hand, the particular acts are voluntary (for he does them with craving and desire), but the whole state is less so; for no one craves to be self-indulgent.

The name self-indulgence is applied also to childish faults; for they bear a certain resemblance to what we have been considering. Which is called after which, makes no difference to our present purpose; plainly, however, the 1119 later is called after the earlier. The transference of the name seems not a bad one; for that which desires what is base and which develops quickly ought to be kept in a chastened condition, and these characteristics belong above all to appetite and to the child, since children in fact live at the beck and call of appetite, and it is in them that the desire 5 for what is pleasant is strongest. If, then, it is not going to be obedient and subject to the ruling principle, it will go to great lengths; for in an irrational being the desire for pleasure is insatiable even if it tries every source of gratification, and the exercise of appetite increases its innate force, and 10 if appetites are strong and violent they even expel the power of calculation. Hence they should be moderate and few, and should in no way oppose the rational principle—and this is what we call an obedient and chastened state—and as the child should live according to the direction of his tutor, so the appetitive element should live according to 15 rational principle. Hence the appetitive element in a temperate man should harmonize with the rational principle; for the noble is the mark at which both aim, and the temperate man craves for the things he ought, as he ought, and when he ought; and this is what rational principle directs.

Here we conclude our account of temperance.

1   Let us speak next of liberality. It seems to be the mean
with regard to wealth; for the liberal man is praised
not in respect of military matters, nor of those in respect
25 of which the temperate man is praised, nor of judicial decisions, but with regard to the giving and taking of wealth,
and especially in respect of giving. Now by 'wealth' we
mean all the things whose value is measured by money.
Further, prodigality and meanness are excesses and defects
30 with regard to wealth; and meanness we always impute to
those who care more than they ought for wealth, but we
sometimes apply the word 'prodigality' in a complex sense;
for we call those men prodigals who are incontinent and
spend money on self-indulgence. Hence also they are
thought the poorest characters; for they combine more
vices than one. Therefore the application of the word to
1120ᵃ them is not its proper use; for a 'prodigal' means a man
who has a single evil quality, that of wasting his substance;
since a prodigal is one who is being ruined by his own fault,
and the wasting of substance is thought to be a sort of ruin-
ing of oneself, life being held to depend on possession of
substance.

This, then, is the sense in which we take the word 'prod-
5 igality'. Now the things that have a use may be used either
well or badly; and riches is a useful thing; and everything
is used best by the man who has the virtue concerned with
it; riches, therefore, will be used best by the man who has
the virtue concerned with wealth; and this is the liberal
man. Now spending and giving seem to be the using of
wealth; taking and keeping rather the possession of it.
10 Hence it is more the mark of the liberal man to give to the
right people than to take from the right sources and not to
take from the wrong. For it is more characteristic of virtue
to do good than to have good done to one, and more characteristic to do what is noble than not to do what is base;

and it is not hard to see that giving implies doing good and doing what is noble, and taking implies having good done to one or not acting basely. And gratitude is felt towards 15 him who gives, not towards him who does not take, and praise also is bestowed more on him. It is easier, also, not to take than to give; for men are apter to give away their own too little than to take what is another's. Givers, too, are called liberal; but those who do not take are not praised for liberality but rather for justice; while those who take are 20 hardly praised at all. And the liberal are almost the most loved of all virtuous characters, since they are useful; and this depends on their giving.

Now virtuous actions are noble and done for the sake of the noble. Therefore the liberal man, like other virtuous men, will give for the sake of the noble, and rightly; for he will give to the right people, the right amounts, and at the 25 right time, with all the other qualifications that accompany right giving; and that too with pleasure or without pain; for that which is virtuous is pleasant or free from pain—least of all will it be painful. But he who gives to the wrong people or not for the sake of the noble but for some other cause, will be called not liberal but by some other name. Nor is he liberal who gives with pain; for he would prefer 30 the wealth to the noble act, and this is not characteristic of a liberal man. But no more will the liberal man take from wrong sources; for such taking is not characteristic of the man who sets no store by wealth. Nor will he be a ready asker; for it is not characteristic of a man who confers benefits to accept them lightly. But he will take from the right sources, e. g. from his own possessions, not as something 1120 noble but as a necessity, that he may have something to give. Nor will he neglect his own property, since he wishes by means of this to help others. And he will refrain from giving to anybody and everybody, that he may have something to give to the right people, at the right time, and where it is noble to do so. It is highly characteristic of a liberal man also to go to excess in giving, so that he leaves

5 too little for himself; for it is the nature of a liberal man not to look to himself. The term 'liberality' is used relatively to a man's substance; for liberality resides not in the multitude of the gifts but in the state of character of the giver, and this is relative to the giver's substance. There is therefore nothing to prevent the man who gives less from being the more liberal man, if he has less to give. Those are thought
10 to be more liberal who have not made their wealth but inherited it; for in the first place they have no experience of want, and secondly all men are fonder of their own produc-
15 tions, as are parents and poets. It is not easy for the liberal man to be rich, since he is not apt either at taking or at keeping, but at giving away, and does not value wealth for its own sake but as a means to giving. Hence comes the charge that is brought against fortune, that those who deserve riches most get it least. But it is not unreasonable that it should turn out so; for he cannot have wealth, any more
20 than anything else, if he does not take pains to have it. Yet he will not give to the wrong people nor at the wrong time, and so on; for he would no longer be acting in accordance with liberality, and if he spent on these objects he would have nothing to spend on the right objects. For, as has been said, he is liberal who spends according to his sub-
25 stance and on the right objects; and he who exceeds is prodigal. Hence we do not call despots prodigal; for it is thought not easy for them to give and spend beyond the amount of their possessions. Liberality, then, being a mean with regard to giving and taking of wealth, the liberal man will both give and spend the right amounts and on the right
30 objects, alike in small things and in great, and that with pleasure; he will also take the right amounts and from the right sources. For, the virtue being a mean with regard to both, he will do both as he ought; since this sort of taking accompanies proper giving, and that which is not of this sort is contrary to it, and accordingly the giving and taking that accompany each other are present together in the same
1121ᵃ man, while the contrary kinds evidently are not. But if

he happens to spend in a manner contrary to what is right and noble, he will be pained, but moderately and as he ought; for it is the mark of virtue both to be pleased and to be pained at the right objects and in the right way. Further, 5 the liberal man is easy to deal with in money matters; for he can be got the better of, since he sets no store by money, and is more annoyed if he has not spent something that he ought than pained if he has spent something that he ought not, and does not agree with the saying of Simonides.

The prodigal errs in these respects also; for he is neither pleased nor pained at the right things or in the right way; this will be more evident as we go on. We have said [1] that 10 prodigality and meanness are excesses and deficiencies, and in two things, in giving and in taking; for we include spending under giving. Now prodigality exceeds in giving and not taking, and falls short in taking, while meanness falls short in giving, and exceeds in taking, except in small 15 things.

The characteristics of prodigality are not often combined; for it is not easy to give to all if you take from none; private persons soon exhaust their substance with giving, and it is to these that the name of prodigals is applied—though a man of this sort would seem to be in no small degree better than a mean man. For he is easily cured both 20 by age and by poverty, and thus he may move towards the middle state. For he has the characteristics of the liberal man, since he both gives and refrains from taking, though he does neither of these in the right manner or well. Therefore if he were brought to do so by habituation or in some other way, he would be liberal; for he will then give to the right people, and will not take from the wrong sources. This is why he is thought to have not a bad character; it is 25 not the mark of a wicked or ignoble man to go to excess in giving and not taking, but only of a foolish one. The man who is prodigal in this way is thought much better than the mean man both for the aforesaid reasons and because he

[1] 1119ᵇ 27.

benefits many while the other benefits no one, not even himself.

But most prodigal people, as has been said,[2] also take from the wrong sources, and are in this respect mean. They become apt to take because they wish to spend and cannot do this easily; for their possessions soon run short. Thus they are forced to provide means from some other source. At the same time, because they care nothing for honour, they take recklessly and from any source; for they have an appetite for giving, and they do not mind how or from what source. Hence also their giving is not liberal; for it is not noble, nor does it aim at nobility, nor is it done in the right way; sometimes they make rich those who should be poor, and will give nothing to people of respectable character, and much to flatterers or those who provide them with some other pleasure. Hence also most of them are self-indulgent; for they spend lightly and waste money on their indulgences, and incline towards pleasures because they do not live with a view to what is noble.

The prodigal man, then, turns into what we have described if he is left untutored, but if he is treated with care he will arrive at the intermediate and right state. But meanness is both incurable (for old age and every disability is thought to make men mean) and more innate in men than prodigality; for most men are fonder of getting money than of giving. It also extends widely, and is multiform, since there seem to be many kinds of meanness.

For it consists in two things, deficiency in giving and excess is taking, and is not found complete in all men but is sometimes divided; some men go to excess in taking, others fall short in giving. Those who are called by such names as 'miserly', 'close', 'stingy', all fall short in giving, but do not covet the possessions of others nor wish to get them. In some this is due to a sort of honesty and avoidance of what is disgraceful (for some seem, or at least profess, to hoard their money for this reason, that they may not

[2] ll. 16–19.

some day be forced to do something disgraceful; to this class belong the cheeseparer and every one of the sort; he is so called from his excess of unwillingness to give anything); while others again keep their hands off the property of others from fear, on the ground that it is not easy, if one takes the property of others oneself, to avoid having one's own taken by them; they are therefore content neither to take nor to give.

Others again exceed in respect of taking by taking any- 30 thing and from any source, e. g. those who ply sordid trades, pimps and all such people, and those who lend small sums and at high rates. For all of these take more than they 1122ᵉ ought and from wrong sources. What is common to them is evidently sordid love of gain; they all put up with a bad name for the sake of gain, and little gain at that. For those who make great gains but from wrong sources, and not the right gains, e. g. despots when they sack cities and spoil 5 temples, we do not call mean but rather wicked, impious, and unjust. But the gamester and the footpad [and the highwayman] belong to the class of the mean, since they have a sordid love of gain. For it is for gain that both of them ply their craft and endure the disgrace of it, and the one faces the greatest dangers for the sake of the booty, while the other makes gain from his friends, to whom he 10 ought to be giving. Both, then, since they are willing to make gain from wrong sources, are sordid lovers of gain; therefore all such forms of taking are mean.

And it is natural that meanness is described as the contrary of liberality; for not only is it a greater evil than prodigality, but men err more often in this direction than 15 in the way of prodigality as we have described it.

So much, then, for liberality and the opposed vices.

2   It would seem proper to discuss magnificence next.
For this also seems to be a virtue concerned with 20 wealth; but it does not like liberality extend to all the actions that are concerned with wealth, but only to those

that involve expenditure; and in these it surpasses liberality
in scale. For, as the name itself suggests, it is a fitting
expenditure involving largeness of scale. But the scale is
relative; for the expense of equipping a trireme is not the
25 same as that of heading a sacred embassy. It is what is
fitting, then, in relation to the agent, and to the circumstances and the object. The man who in small or middling
things spends according to the merits of the case is not
called magnificent (e g. the man who can say 'many a
gift I gave the wanderer'),[3] but only the man who does so
in great things. For the magnificent man is liberal, but the
30 liberal man is not necessarily magnificent. The deficiency
of this state of character is called niggardliness, the excess
vulgarity, lack of taste, and the like, which do not go to
excess in the amount spent on right objects, but by showy
expenditure in the wrong circumstances and the wrong
manner; we shall speak of these vices later.[4]

The magnificent man is like an artist; for he can see what
is fitting and spend large sums tastefully. For, as we said
35 at the beginning,[5] a state of character is determined by its
1122ᵇ activities and by its objects. Now the expenses of the
magnificent man are large and fitting. Such, therefore, are
also his results; for thus there will be a great expenditure
and one that is fitting to its result. Therefore the result
should be worthy of the expense, and the expense should
5 be worthy of the result, or should even exceed it. And the
magnificent man will spend such sums for honour's sake;
for this is common to the virtues. And further he will do so
gladly and lavishly; for nice calculation is a niggardly thing.
And he will consider how the result can be made most
beautiful and most becoming rather than for how much it
can be produced and how it can be produced most cheaply.
10 It is necessary, then, that the magnificent man be also
liberal. For the liberal man also will spend what he ought

---

[3] *Od.* xvii. 420.
[4] 1123ᵃ 19–33.
[5] Not in so many words, but Cf. 1103ᵇ 21–23, 1104ᵃ 27–29.

and as he ought; and it is in these matters that the greatness implied in the name of the magnificent man—his
bigness, as it were—is manifested, since liberality is concerned with these matters; and at an equal expense he will
produce a more magnificent work of art. For a possession
and a work of art have not the same excellence. The most
valuable possession is that which is worth most, e. g. gold, 15
but the most valuable work of art is that which is great and
beautiful (for the contemplation of such a work inspires
admiration, and so does magnificence); and a work has an
excellence—viz. magnificence—which involves magnitude.
Magnificence is an attribute of expenditures of the kind
which we call honourable, e. g. those connected with the
gods—votive offerings, buildings, and sacrifices—and similarly with any form of religious worship, and all those that
are proper objects of public-spirited ambition, as when 20
people think they ought to equip a chorus or a trireme,
or entertain the city, in a brilliant way. But in all cases,
as has been said,[6] we have regard to the agent as well and
ask who he is and what means he has; for the expenditure 25
should be worthy of his means, and suit not only the
result but also the producer. Hence a poor man cannot be
magnificent, since he has not the means with which to
spend large sums fittingly; and he who tries is a fool, since
he spends beyond what can be expected of him and what 's
proper, but it is *right* expenditure that is virtuous. But great
expenditure is becoming to those who have suitable means 30
to start with, acquired by their own efforts or from ancestors or connexions, and to people of high birth or reputation, and so on; for all these things bring with them greatness and prestige. Primarily, then, the magnificent man is 35
of this sort, and magnificence is shown in expenditures of
this sort, as has been said;[7] for these are the greatest and
most honourable. Of *private* occasions of expenditure the
most suitable are those that take place once for all. e. g. a

[6] a 24-26.
[7] ll. 19-23.

1123ᵃ wedding or anything of the kind, or anything that interests the whole city or the people of position in it, and also the receiving of foreign guests and the sending of them on their
5 way, and gifts and counter-gifts; for the magnificent man spends not on himself but on public objects, and gifts bear some resemblance to votive offerings. A magnificent man will also furnish his house suitably to his wealth (for even a house is a sort of public ornament), and will spend by pref-erence on those works that are lasting (for these are the most beautiful), and on every class of things he will spend what
10 is becoming; for the same things are not suitable for gods and for men, nor in a temple and in a tomb. And since each expenditure may be great of its kind, and what is most magnificent absolutely is great expenditure on a great object, but what is magnificent *here* is what is great in *these* circumstances, and greatness in the work differs from
15 greatness in the expense (for the most beautiful ball or bottle is magnificent as a gift to a child, but the price of it is small and mean)—therefore it is characteristic of the magnificent man, whatever kind of result he is producing, to produce it magnificently (for such a result is not easily surpassed) and to make it worthy of the expenditure.

Such, then, is the magnificent man; the man who goes to excess and is vulgar exceeds, as has been said,[8] by spend-
20 ing beyond what is right. For on small objects of expendi-ture he spends much and displays a tasteless showiness; e. g. he gives a club dinner on the scale of a wedding banquet, and when he provides the chorus for a comedy he brings them on to the stage in purple, as they do at Megara.
25 And all such things he will do not for honour's sake but to show off his wealth, and because he thinks he is admired for these things, and where he ought to spend much he spends little and where little, much. The niggardly man on the other hand will fall short in everything, and after spend-ing the greatest sums will spoil the beauty of the result for a trifle, and whatever he is doing he will hesitate and con-

[8] 1122ᵃ 31-33.

ider how he may spend least, and lament even that, and 30
ink he is doing everything on a bigger scale than he
ught.

These states of character, then, are vices; yet they do not
bring *disgrace* because they are neither harmful to one's
neighbour nor very unseemly.

3   Pride seems even from its name [9] to be concerned with
      great things; what sort of great things, is the first ques-
tion we must try to answer. It makes no difference whether
we consider the state of character or the man characterized 35
by it. Now the man is thought to be proud who thinks
himself worthy of great things, being worthy of them; for 1123
he who does so beyond his deserts is a fool, but no virtuous
man is foolish or silly. The proud man, then, is the man
we have described. For he who is worthy of little and thinks
himself worthy of little is temperate, but not proud; for 5
pride implies greatness, as beauty implies a good-sized
body, and little people may be neat and well-proportioned
but cannot be beautiful. On the other hand, he who thinks
himself worthy of great things, being unworthy of them, is
vain; though not every one who thinks himself worthy of
more than he really is worthy of is vain. The man who
thinks himself worthy of less than he is really worthy of is
unduly humble, whether his deserts be great or moderate,
or his deserts be small but his claims yet smaller. And the 10
man whose deserts are great would seem *most* unduly
humble; for what would he have done if they had been
less? The proud man, then, is an extreme in respect of the
greatness of his claims, but a mean in respect of the rightness of them; for he claims what is in accordance with his
merits, while the others go to excess or fall short.

If, then, he deserves and claims great things, and above
all the greatest things, he will be concerned with one thing
in particular. Desert is relative to external goods; and the

[9] 'Pride' of course has not the etymological associations of *megalo-
psychia*, but seems in other respects the best translation.

proud man's object — honour

greatest of these, we should say, is that which we render
to the gods, and which people of position most aim at, and
which is the prize appointed for the noblest deeds; and this
is honour; that is surely the greatest of external goods. Honours and dishonours, therefore, are the objects with respect
to which the proud man is as he should be. And even apart
from argument it is with honour that proud men appear
to be concerned; for it is honour that they chiefly claim,
but in accordance with their deserts. The unduly humble
man falls short both in comparison with his own merits and
in comparison with the proud man's claims. The vain man
goes to excess in comparison with his own merits, but does
not exceed the proud man's claims.

Now the proud man, since he deserves most, must be
good in the highest degree; for the better man always
deserves more, and the best man most. Therefore the truly
proud man must be good. And greatness in every virtue
would seem to be characteristic of a proud man. And it
would be most unbecoming for a proud man to fly from
danger, swinging his arms by his sides, or to wrong another; for to what end should he do disgraceful acts, he to
whom nothing is great? If we consider him point by point,
we shall see the utter absurdity of a proud man who is not
good. Nor, again, would he be worthy of honour if he were
bad; for honour is the prize of virtue, and it is to the good
that it is rendered. Pride, then, seems to be a sort of crown
of the virtues; for it makes them greater, and it is not found
without them. Therefore it is hard to be truly proud; for it
is impossible without nobility and goodness of character.
It is chiefly with honours and dishonours, then, that the
proud man is concerned; and at honours that are great and
conferred by good men he will be moderately pleased,
thinking that he is coming by his own or even less than
his own; for there can be no honour that is worthy of perfect virtue, yet he will at any rate accept it since they have
nothing greater to bestow on him; but honour from casual
people and on trifling grounds he will utterly despise, since

it is not this that he deserves, and dishonour too, since in his case it cannot be just. In the first place, then, as has been said,[10] the proud man is concerned with honours; yet he will also bear himself with moderation towards wealth and power and all good or evil fortune, whatever may befall him, and will be neither over-joyed by good fortune nor over-pained by evil. For not even towards honour does he bear himself as if it were a very great thing. Power and wealth are desirable for the sake of honour (at least those who have them wish to get honour by means of them); and for him to whom even honour is a little thing the others must be so too. Hence proud men are thought to be disdainful.

The goods of fortune also are thought to contribute towards pride. For men who are well-born are thought worthy of honour, and so are those who enjoy power or wealth; for they are in a superior position, and everything that has a superiority in something good is held in greater honour. Hence even such things make men prouder; for they are honoured by some for having them; but in truth the good man alone is to be honoured; he, however, who has both advantages is thought the more worthy of honour. But those who without virtue have such goods are neither justified in making great claims nor entitled to the name of 'proud'; for these things imply perfect virtue. Disdainful and insolent, however, even those who have such goods become. For without virtue it is not easy to bear gracefully the goods of fortune; and, being unable to bear them, and thinking themselves superior to others, they despise others and themselves do what they please. They imitate the proud man without being like him, and this they do where they can; so they do not act virtuously, but they do despise others. For the proud man despises justly (since he thinks truly), but the many do so at random.

He does not run into trifling dangers, nor is he fond of danger, because he honours few things; but he will face

10 1123ᵇ 15–22.

great dangers, and when he is in danger he is unsparing of his life, knowing that there are conditions on which life is not worth having. And he is the sort of man to confer benefits, but he is ashamed of receiving them; for the one is the mark of a superior, the other of an inferior. And he is apt to confer greater benefits in return; for thus the original benefactor besides being paid will incur a debt to him, and will be the gainer by the transaction. They seem also to remember any service they have done, but not those they have received (for he who receives a service is inferior to him who has done it, but the proud man wishes to be superior), and to hear of the former with pleasure, of the latter with displeasure; this, it seems, is why Thetis did not mention to Zeus the services she had done him,[11] and why the Spartans did not recount their services to the Athenians, but those they had received. It is a mark of the proud man also to ask for nothing or scarcely anything, but to give help readily, and to be dignified towards people who enjoy high position and good fortune, but unassuming towards those of the middle class; for it is a difficult and lofty thing to be superior to the former, but easy to be so to the latter, and a lofty bearing over the former is no mark of ill-breeding, but among humble people it is as vulgar as a display of strength against the weak. Again, it is characteristic of the proud man not to aim at the things commonly held in honour, or the things in which others excel; to be sluggish and to hold back except where great honour or a great work is at stake, and to be a man of few deeds, but of great and notable ones. He must also be open in his hate and in his love (for to conceal one's feelings, i. e. to care less for truth than for what people will think, is a coward's part), and must speak and act openly; for he is free of speech because he is contemptuous, and he is given to telling the truth, except when he speaks in irony to the vulgar. He must be 1125ᵃ unable to make his life revolve round another, unless it be a friend; for this is slavish, and for this reason all flatterers are

[11] In fact she did, *Il.* i. 503.

servile and people lacking in self-respect are flatterers. Nor
is he given to admiration; for nothing to him is great. Nor
is he mindful of wrongs; for it is not the part of a proud man
to have a long memory, especially for wrongs, but rather to 5
overlook them. Nor is he a gossip; for he will speak neither
about himself nor about another, since he cares not to be
praised nor for others to be blamed; nor again is he given to
praise; and for the same reason he is not an evil-speaker,
even about his enemies, except from haughtiness. With
regard to necessary or small matters he is least of all men 10
given to lamentation or the asking of favours; for it is the
part of one who takes such matters seriously to behave
so with respect to them. He is one who will possess beautiful and profitless things rather than profitable and useful
ones; for this is more proper to a character that suffices to
itself.

Further, a slow step is thought proper to the proud
man, a deep voice, and a level utterance; for the man who
takes few things seriously is not likely to be hurried, nor the
man who thinks nothing great to be excited, while a shrill 15
voice and a rapid gait are the results of hurry and excitement.

Such, then, is the proud man; the man who falls short
of him is unduly humble, and the man who goes beyond
him is vain. Now even these are not thought to be bad (for
they are not malicious), but only mistaken. For the unduly humble man, being worthy of good things, robs him- 20
self of what he deserves, and seems to have something bad
about him from the fact that he does not think himself
worthy of good things, and seems also not to know himself;
else he would have desired the things he was worthy of,
since these were good. Yet such people are not thought to
be fools, but rather unduly retiring. Such a reputation, 25
however, seems actually to make them worse; for each class
of people aims at what corresponds to its worth, and these
people stand back even from noble actions and undertak-
ings, deeming themselves unworthy, and from external

goods no less. Vain people, on the other hand, are fools and ignorant of themselves, and that manifestly; for, not being worthy of them, they attempt honourable undertak-
30 ings, and then are found out; and they adorn themselves with clothing and outward show and such things, and wish their strokes of good fortune to be made public, and speak about them as if they would be honoured for them. But undue humility is more opposed to pride than vanity is; for it is both commoner and worse.

Pride, then, is concerned with honour on the grand scale,
35 as has been said.[12]

4   There seems to be in the sphere of honour also, as
1125ᵇ   was said in our first remarks on the subject,[13] a virtue which would appear to be related to pride as liberality is to magnificence. For neither of these has anything to do with
5 the grand scale, but both dispose us as is right with regard to middling and unimportant objects; as in getting and giving of wealth there is a mean and an excess and defect, so too honour may be desired more than is right, or less, or from the right sources and in the right way. We blame both the ambitious man as aiming at honour more than is
10 right and from wrong sources, and the unambitious man as not willing to be honoured even for noble reasons. But sometimes we praise the ambitious man as being manly and a lover of what is noble, and the unambitious man as being moderate and self-controlled, as we said in our first treatment of the subject.[14] Evidently, since 'fond of such and such an object' has more than one meaning, we do not assign the term 'ambition' or 'love of honour' always to the same thing, but when we praise the quality we think of the
15 man who loves honour more than most people, and when we blame it we think of him who loves it more than is right. The mean being without a name, the extremes seem

¹² 1107ᵇ 26, 1123ᵃ 34–ᵇ 22.
¹³ Ib. 24–27.
¹⁴ 1107ᵇ 33.

to dispute for its place as though that were vacant by default. But where there is excess and defect, there is also an intermediate; now men desire honour both more than they should and less; therefore it is possible also to do so as one should; at all events this is the state of character that is ²⁰ praised, being an unnamed mean in respect of honour. Relatively to ambition it seems to be unambitiousness, and relatively to unambitiousness it seems to be ambition, while relatively to both severally it seems in a sense to be both together. This appears to be true of the other virtues also. But in this case the extremes seem to be contradictories because the mean has not received a name. ²³

5 Good temper is a mean with respect to anger; the middle state being unnamed, and the extremes almost without a name as well, we place good temper in the middle position, though it inclines towards the deficiency, which is without a name. The excess might be called a sort ³⁰ of 'irascibility'. For the passion is anger, while its causes are many and diverse.

The man who is angry at the right things and with the right people, and, further, as he ought, when he ought, and as long as he ought, is praised. This will be the good-tempered man, since good temper is praised. For the good-tempered man tends to be unperturbed and not to be led by ³⁵ passion, but to be angry in the manner, at the things, and **1126** for the length of time, that the rule dictates; but he is thought to err rather in the direction of deficiency; for the good-tempered man is not revengeful, but rather tends to make allowances.

The deficiency, whether it is a sort of 'inirascibility' or whatever it is, is blamed. For those who are not angry at the things they should be angry at are thought to be fools, ⁵ and so are those who are not angry in the right way, at the right time, or with the right persons; for such a man is thought not to feel things nor to be pained by them, and, since he does not get angry, he is thought unlikely to

defend himself; and to endure being insulted and put up
with insult to one's friends is slavish.

The excess can be manifested in all the points that have
been named (for one can be angry with the wrong persons,
10 at the wrong things, more than is right, too quickly, or too
long); yet all are not found in the same person. Indeed
they could not; for evil destroys even itself, and if it is complete becomes unbearable. Now hot-tempered people get
angry quickly and with the wrong persons and at the wrong
things and more than is right, but their anger ceases quickly
15 —which is the best point about them. This happens to
them because they do not restrain their anger but retaliate
openly owing to their quickness of temper, and then their
anger ceases. By reason of excess choleric people are quick-
tempered and ready to be angry with everything and on
every occasion; whence their name. Sulky people are hard
20 to appease, and retain their anger long; for they repress
their passion. But it ceases when they retaliate; for revenge
relieves them of their anger, producing in them pleasure
instead of pain. If this does not happen they retain their
burden; for owing to its not being obvious no one even rea-
25 sons with them, and to digest one's anger in oneself takes
time. Such people are most troublesome to themselves and
to their dearest friends. We call bad-tempered those who
are angry at the wrong things, more than is right, and
longer, and cannot be appeased until they inflict vengeance
or punishment.

To good temper we oppose the excess rather than the
defect; for not only is it commoner (since revenge is the
30 more human), but bad-tempered people are worse to live
with.

What we have said in our earlier treatment of the subject [15] is plain also from what we are now saying; viz. that
it is not easy to define how, with whom, at what, and how
long one should be angry, and at what point right action
35 ceases and wrong begins. For the man who strays a little

[15] 1109ᵇ 14–26.

from the path, either towards the more or towards the less,
is not blamed; since sometimes we praise those who exhibit
the deficiency, and call them good-tempered, and sometimes we call angry people manly, as being capable of rul- 1126ᵇ
ing. How far, therefore, and how a man must stray before
he becomes blameworthy, it is not easy to state in words;
for the decision depends on the particular facts and on
perception. But so much at least is plain, that the middle
state is praiseworthy—that in virtue of which we are angry 5
with the right people, at the right things, in the right way,
and so on, while the excesses and defects are blameworthy
—slightly so if they are present in a low degree, more if in
a higher degree, and very much if in a high degree. Evidently, then, we must cling to the middle state.—Enough
of the states relative to anger. 10

6   In gatherings of men, in social life and the interchange
     of words and deeds, some men are thought to be obse-
quious, viz. those who to give pleasure praise everything
and never oppose, but think it their duty 'to give no pain
to the people they meet'; while those who, on the contrary, 15
oppose everything and care not a whit about giving pain
are called churlish and contentious. That the states we have
named are culpable is plain enough, and that the middle
state is laudable—that in virtue of which a man will put up
with, and will resent, the right things and in the right way;
but no name has been assigned to it, though it most resembles friendship. For the man who corresponds to this 20
middle state is very much what, with affection added, we
call a good friend. But the state in question differs from
friendship in that it implies no passion or affection for one's
associates; since it is not by reason of loving or hating that
such a man takes everything in the right way, but by being
a man of a certain kind. For he will behave so alike towards 25
those he knows and those he does not know, towards intimates and those who are not so, except that in each of
these cases he will behave as is befitting; for it is not proper

to have the same care for intimates and for strangers, nor again is it the same conditions that make it right to give pain to them. Now we have said generally that he will associate with people in the right way; but it is by reference to what is honourable and expedient that he will aim at not
30 giving pain or at contributing pleasure. For he seems to be concerned with the pleasures and pains of social life; and wherever it is not honourable, or is harmful, for him to contribute pleasure, he will refuse, and will choose rather to give pain; also if his acquiescence in another's action would bring disgrace, and that in a high degree, or injury,
35 on that other, while his opposition brings a little pain, he will not acquiesce but will decline. He will associate
1127ᵃ differently with people in high station and with ordinary people, with closer and more distant acquaintances, and so too with regard to all other differences, rendering to each class what is befitting, and while for its own sake he chooses to contribute pleasure, and avoids the giving of
5 pain, he will be guided by the consequences, if these are greater, i. e. honour and expediency. For the sake of a great future pleasure, too, he will inflict small pains.

The man who attains the mean, then, is such as we have described, but has not received a name; of those who contribute pleasure, the man who aims at being pleasant with no ulterior object is obsequious, but the man who does so
10 in order that he may get some advantage in the direction of money or the things that money buys is a flatterer; while the man who quarrels with everything is, as has been said,¹⁶ churlish and contentious. And the extremes seem to be contradictory to each other because the mean is without a name.

7   The mean opposed to boastfulness is found in almost the same sphere; and this also is without a name. It
15 will be no bad plan to describe these states as well; for we shall both know the facts about character better if we go through them in detail, and we shall be convinced that the

¹⁶ 1125ᵇ 14–16.

virtues are means if we see this to be so in all cases. In the field of social life those who make the giving of pleasure or pain their object in associating with others have been described; [17] let us now describe those who pursue truth or falsehood alike in words and deeds and in the claims they put forward. The boastful man, then, is thought to be apt to claim the things that bring glory, when he has not got them, or to claim more of them than he has, and the mock-modest man on the other hand to disclaim what he has or belittle it, while the man who observes the mean is one who calls a thing by its own name, being truthful both in life and in word, owning to what he has, and neither more nor less. Now each of these courses may be adopted either with or without an object. But each man speaks and acts and lives in accordance with his character, if he is not acting for some ulterior object. And falsehood is *in itself* [18] mean and culpable, and truth noble and worthy of praise. Thus the truthful man is another case of a man who, being in the mean, is worthy of praise, and both forms of untruthful man are culpable, and particularly the boastful man.

Let us discuss them both, but first of all the truthful man. We are not speaking of the man who keeps faith in his agreements, i. e. in the things that pertain to justice or injustice (for this would belong to another virtue), but the man who in the matters in which nothing of this sort is at **1127**ᵇ stake is true both in word and in life because his character is such. But such a man would seem to be as a matter of fact equitable. For the man who loves truth, and is truthful where nothing is at stake, will still more be truthful where something is at stake; he will avoid falsehood as something base, seeing that he avoided it even for its own sake; and such a man is worthy of praise. He inclines rather to understate the truth; for this seems in better taste because exaggerations are wearisome.

He who claims more than he has with no ulterior object

---

[17] Ch. 6.
[18] i. e. apart from any ulterior object it may serve.

is a contemptible sort of fellow (otherwise he would not
10 have delighted in falsehood), but seems futile rather than
bad; but if he does it for an object, he who does it for the
sake of reputation or honour is (for a boaster) not very
much to be blamed, but he who does it for money, or the
things that lead to money, is an uglier character (it is not
the capacity that makes the boaster, but the purpose; for
it is in virtue of his state of character and by being a man
of a certain kind that he is a boaster); as one man is a liar
15 because he enjoys the lie itself, and another because he
desires reputation or gain. Now those who boast for the
sake of reputation claim such qualities as win praise or
congratulation, but those whose object is gain claim qualities which are of value to one's neighbours and one's lack
of which is not easily detected, e. g. the powers of a seer,
20 a sage, or a physician. For this reason it is such things as
these that most people claim and boast about; for in them
the above-mentioned qualities are found.

Mock-modest people, who understate things, seem more
attractive in character; for they are thought to speak not
for gain but to avoid parade; and here too it is qualities
25 which bring reputation that they disclaim, as Socrates used
to do. Those who disclaim trifling and obvious qualities
are called humbugs and are more contemptible; and sometimes this seems to be boastfulness, like the Spartan dress;
for both excess and great deficiency are boastful. But
30 those who use understatement with moderation and understate about matters that do not very much force themselves
on our notice seem attractive. And it is the boaster that
seems to be opposed to the truthful man; for he is the worse
character.

8   Since life includes rest as well as activity, and in this
     is included leisure and amusement, there seems here
1128ᵃ also to be a kind of intercourse which is tasteful; there is
such a thing as saying—and again listening to—what one
should and as one should. The kind of people one is speak-

ing or listening to will also make a difference. Evidently
here also there is both an excess and a deficiency as compared with the mean. Those who carry humour to excess 5
are thought to be vulgar buffoons, striving after humour at
all costs, and aiming rather at raising a laugh than at saying
what is becoming and at avoiding pain to the object of their
fun; while those who can neither make a joke themselves
nor put up with those who do are thought to be boorish
and unpolished. But those who joke in a tasteful way are
called ready-witted, which implies a sort of readiness to 10
turn this way and that; for such sallies are thought to be
movements of the character, and as bodies are discriminated by their movements, so too are characters. The
ridiculous side of things is not far to seek, however, and
most people delight more than they should in amusement
and in jesting, and so even buffoons are called ready-witted 15
because they are found attractive; but that they differ from
the ready-witted man, and to no small extent, is clear from
what has been said.

To the middle state belongs also tact; it is the mark of a
tactful man to say and listen to such things as befit a good
and well-bred man; for there are some things that it befits 20
such a man to say and to hear by way of jest, and the well-
bred man's jesting differs from that of a vulgar man, and
the joking of an educated man from that of an uneducated.
One may see this even from the old and the new comedies;
to the authors of the former indecency of language was
amusing, to those of the latter innuendo is more so; and
these differ in no small degree in respect of propriety. Now 25
should we define the man who jokes well by his saying
what is not unbecoming to a well-bred man, or by his not
giving pain, or even giving delight, to the hearer? Or is the
latter definition, at any rate, itself indefinite, since different
things are hateful or pleasant to different people? The kind
of jokes he will listen to will be the same; for the kind he
can put up with are also the kind he seems to make. There
are, then, jokes he will not make; for the jest is a sort of

30 abuse, and there are things that lawgivers forbid us to abuse; and they should, perhaps, have forbidden us even to make a jest of such. The refined and well-bred man, therefore, will be as we have described, being as it were a law to himself.

Such, then, is the man who observes the mean, whether he be called tactful or ready-witted. The buffoon, on the other hand, is the slave of his sense of humour, and spares
35 neither himself nor others if he can raise a laugh, and says things none of which a man of refinement would say, and
1128ᵇ to some of which he would not even listen. The boor, again, is useless for such social intercourse; for he contributes nothing and finds fault with everything. But relaxation and amusement are thought to be a necessary element in life.

The means in life that have been described, then, are three in number, and are all concerned with an interchange
5 of words and deeds of some kind. They differ, however, in that one is concerned with truth, and the other two with pleasantness. Of those concerned with pleasure, one is displayed in jests, the other in the general social intercourse of life.

9   Shame should not be described as a virtue; for it is
10   more like a feeling than a state of character. It is defined, at any rate, as a kind of fear of dishonour, and produces an effect similar to that produced by fear of danger; for people who feel disgraced blush, and those who fear death turn pale. Both, therefore, seem to be in a sense bodily conditions, which is thought to be characteristic of feeling rather than of a state of character.

The feeling is not becoming to every age, but only to
15 youth. For we think young people should be prone to the feeling of shame because they live by feeling and therefore commit many errors, but are restrained by shame; and we praise young people who are prone to this feeling, but an older person no one would praise for being prone to the

sense of disgrace, since we think he should not do anything
that need cause this sense. For the sense of disgrace is not 20
even characteristic of a good man,[19] since it is consequent
on bad actions (for such actions should not be done; and
if some actions are disgraceful in very truth and others
only according to common opinion, this makes no difference; for neither class of actions should be done, so that no
disgrace should be felt); and it is a mark of a bad man 25
even to be such as to do any disgraceful action. To be so
constituted as to feel disgraced if one does such an action,
and for this reason to think oneself good, is absurd; for it is
for voluntary actions that shame is felt, and the good man
will never voluntarily do bad actions. But shame may be 30
said to be conditionally a good thing; if a good man does
such actions, he will feel disgraced; but the virtues are not
subject to such a qualification. And if shamelessness—not
to be ashamed of doing base actions—is bad, that does not
make it good to be ashamed of doing such actions. Continence too is not virtue, but a mixed sort of state; this will 35
be shown later.[20] Now, however, let us discuss justice.

BOOK V *1 - 7*

1   With regard to justice and injustice we must consider **1129ᵃ**
(1) what kind of actions they are concerned with, (2)
what sort of mean justice is, and (3) between what ex- 5
tremes the just act is intermediate. Our investigation
shall follow the same course as the preceding discussions.

We see that all men mean by justice that kind of state of
character which makes people disposed to do what is just
and makes them act justly and wish for what is just; and
similarly by injustice that state which makes them act un- 10
justly and wish for what is unjust. Let us too, then, lay this
down as a general basis. For the same is not true of the
sciences and the faculties as of states of character. A

---

[19] sc. still less is it itself a virtue.
[20] vii. 1–10.

faculty or a science which is one and the same is held to relate to contrary objects, but a state of character which is
15 one of two contraries does *not* produce the contrary results;
e. g. as a result of health we do not do what is the opposite
of healthy, but only what is healthy; for we say a man walks
healthily, when he walks as a healthy man would.

Now often one contrary state is recognized from its contrary, and often states are recognized from the subjects that
20 exhibit them; for (A) if good condition is known, bad condition also becomes known, and (B) good condition is
known from the things that are in good condition, and
they from it. If good condition is firmness of flesh, it is
necessary both that bad condition should be flabbiness of
flesh and that the wholesome should be that which causes
firmness in flesh. And it follows for the most part that if
25 one contrary is ambiguous the other also will be ambiguous; e. g. if 'just' is so, that 'unjust' will be so too.

Now 'justice' and 'injustice' seem to be ambiguous, but
because their different meanings approach near to one another the ambiguity escapes notice and is not obvious as
it is, comparatively, when the meanings are far apart, e. g.
(for here the difference in outward form is great) as the
30 ambiguity in the use of *kleis* for the collar-bone of an animal and for that with which we lock a door. Let us take
as a starting-point, then, the various meanings of 'an unjust man'. Both the lawless man and the grasping and unfair man are thought to be unjust, so that evidently both
the law-abiding and the fair man will be just. The just,
then, is the lawful and the fair, the unjust the unlawful and
the unfair.

Since the unjust man is grasping, he must be concerned
1129ᵇ with goods—not all goods, but those with which prosperity and adversity have to do, which taken absolutely are
always good, but for a particular person are not always
5 good. Now men pray for and pursue these things; but they
should not, but should pray that the things that are good
absolutely may also be good for them, and should choose

the things that are good for them. The unjust man does not always choose the greater, but also the less—in the case of things bad absolutely; but because the lesser evil is itself thought to be in a sense good, and graspingness is directed at the good, therefore he is thought to be grasping. And he is unfair; for this contains and is common to both.

Since the lawless man was seen to be unjust and the law-abiding man just, evidently all lawful acts are in a sense just acts; for the acts laid down by the legislative art are lawful, and each of these, we say, is just. Now the laws in their enactments on all subjects aim at the common advantage either of all or of the best or of those who hold power, or something of the sort; so that in one sense we call those acts just that tend to produce and preserve happiness and its components for the political society. And the law bids us do both the acts of a brave man (e. g. not to desert our post nor take to flight nor throw away our arms), and those of a temperate man (e. g. not to commit adultery nor to gratify one's lust), and those of a good-tempered man (e. g. not to strike another nor to speak evil), and similarly with regard to the other virtues and forms of wickedness, commanding some acts and forbidding others; and the rightly-framed law does this rightly, and the hastily conceived one less well.

This form of justice, then, is complete virtue, but not absolutely, but in relation to our neighbour. And therefore justice is often thought to be the greatest of virtues, and 'neither evening nor morning star' is so wonderful; and proverbially 'in justice is every virtue comprehended'. And it is complete virtue in its fullest sense, because it is the actual exercise of complete virtue. It is complete because he who possesses it can exercise his virtue not only in himself but towards his neighbour also; for many men can exercise virtue in their own affairs, but not in their relations to their neighbour. This is why the saying of Bias is thought to be true, that 'rule will show the man'; for a ruler is necessarily in relation to other men and a member

of a society. For this same reason justice, alone of the virtues, is thought to be 'another's good',[1] because it is re-
5 lated to our neighbour; for it does what is advantageous to another, either a ruler or a copartner. Now the worst man is he who exercises his wickedness both towards himself and towards his friends, and the best man is not he who exercises his virtue towards himself but he who exercises it towards another; for this is a difficult task. Justice in this
10 sense, then, is not part of virtue but virtue entire, nor is the contrary injustice a part of vice but vice entire. What the difference is between virtue and justice in this sense is plain from what we have said; they are the same but their essence is not the same; what, as a relation to one's neighbour, is justice is, as a certain kind of state without qualification, virtue.

2   But at all events what we are investigating is the justice which is a *part* of virtue; for there is a justice
15 of this kind, as we maintain. Similarly it is with injustice in the particular sense that we are concerned.

That there is such a thing is indicated by the fact that while the man who exhibits in action the other forms of wickedness acts wrongly indeed, but not graspingly (e. g. the man who throws away his shield through cowardice or speaks harshly through bad temper or fails to help a friend with money through meanness), when a man acts grasp-
20 ingly he often exhibits none of these vices—no, nor all together, but certainly wickedness of some kind (for we blame him) and injustice. There is, then, another kind of injustice which is a part of injustice in the wide sense, and a use of the word 'unjust' which answers to a part of what is unjust in the wide sense of 'contrary to the law'. Again, if one man commits adultery for the sake of gain and
25 makes money by it, while another does so at the bidding of appetite though he loses money and is penalized for it, the latter would be held to be self-indulgent rather than grasp-

[1] Pl. *Rep.* 343 c.

ing, but the former is unjust, but not self-indulgent; evidently, therefore, he is unjust by reason of his making gain
by his act. Again, all other unjust acts are ascribed invariably to some particular kind of wickedness, e. g. adul- 30
tery to self-indulgence, the desertion of a comrade in battle
to cowardice, physical violence to anger; but if a man makes
gain, his action is ascribed to no form of wickedness but injustice. Evidently, therefore, there is apart from injustice in
the wide sense another, 'particular', injustice which shares
the name and nature of the first, because its definition falls
within the same genus: for the significance of both consists
in a relation to one's neighbour, but the one is concerned **1130ᵇ**
with honour or money or safety—or that which includes all
these, if we had a single name for it—and its motive is the
pleasure that arises from gain; while the other is concerned
with all the objects with which the good man is concerned. 5

It is clear, then, that there is more than one kind of
justice, and that there is one which is distinct from virtue
entire; we must try to grasp its genus and differentia.

The unjust has been divided into the unlawful and the
unfair, and the just into the lawful and the fair. To the
unlawful answers the afore-mentioned sense of injustice.
But since the unfair and the unlawful are not the same, but
are different as a part is from its whole (for all that is unfair 10
is unlawful, but not all that is unlawful is unfair), the unjust and injustice in the sense of the unfair are not the same
as but different from the former kind, as part from whole;
for injustice in this sense is a part of injustice in the wide
sense, and similarly justice in the one sense of justice in
the other. Therefore we must speak also about particular 15
justice and particular injustice, and similarly about the just
and the unjust. The justice, then, which answers to the
whole of virtue, and the corresponding injustice, one being
the exercise of virtue as a whole, and the other that of vice
as a whole, towards one's neighbour, we may leave on one
side. And how the meanings of 'just' and 'unjust' which an- 20
swer to these are to be distinguished is evident; for prac-

tically the majority of the acts commanded by the law are those which are prescribed from the point of view of virtue taken as a whole; for the law bids us practise every virtue and forbids us to practise any vice. And the things that tend
25 to produce virtue taken as a whole are those of the acts prescribed by the law which have been prescribed with a view to education for the common good. But with regard to the education of the individual as such, which makes him without qualification a good man, we must determine later [2] whether this is the function of the political art or of another; for perhaps it is not the same to be a good man and a good citizen of any state taken at random.

Of particular justice and that which is just in the cor-
30 responding sense, (A) one kind is that which is manifested in distributions of honour or money or the other things that fall to be divided among those who have a share in the constitution (for in these it is possible for one man to have a share either unequal or equal to that of another); and (B) one is that which plays a rectifying part in trans-
1131ᵃactions between man and man. Of this there are two divisions; of transactions (1) some are voluntary and (2) others involuntary—voluntary such transactions as sale, purchase, loan for consumption, pledging, loan for use, depositing, letting (they are called voluntary because the
5 origin of these transactions is voluntary), while of the involuntary (a) some are clandestine, such as theft, adultery, poisoning, procuring, enticement of slaves, assassination, false witness, and (b) others are violent, such as assault, imprisonment, murder, robbery with violence, mutilation, abuse, insult.

10 **3**   (A) We have shown that both the unjust man and the unjust act are unfair or unequal; now it is clear that there is also an intermediate between the two unequals involved in either case. And this is the equal; for

    [2] 1179ᵇ 20–1181ᵇ 12. Pol. 1276ᵇ 16–1277ᵇ 32, 1278ᵃ 40–ᵇ5, 1288ᵃ 32–ᵇ2, 1333ᵃ 11–16, 1337ᵃ 11–14.

in any kind of action in which there is a more and a less there is also what is equal. If, then, the unjust is unequal, the just is equal, as all men suppose it to be, even apart from argument. And since the equal is intermediate, the just will be an intermediate. Now equality implies at least 15 two things. The just, then, must be both intermediate and equal and relative (i. e. for certain persons). And qua intermediate it must be between certain things (which are respectively greater and less); qua equal, it involves two things; qua just, it is for certain people. The just, therefore, involves at least four terms; for the persons for whom it is in fact just are two, and the things in which it is mani- 20 fested, the objects distributed, are two. And the same equality will exist between the persons and between the things concerned; for as the latter—the things concerned— are related, so are the former; if they are not equal, they will not have what is equal, but this is the origin of quarrels and complaints—when either equals have and are awarded unequal shares, or unequals equal shares. Further, this is plain from the fact that awards should be 'according to 25 merit'; for all men agree that what is just in distribution must be according to merit in some sense, though they do not all specify the same sort of merit, but democrats identify it with the status of freeman, supporters of oligarchy with wealth (or with noble birth), and supporters of aristocracy with excellence.

The just, then, is a species of the proportionate (propor- 30 tion being not a property only of the kind of number which consists of abstract units, but of number in general). For proportion is equality of ratios, and involves four terms at least (that discrete proportion involves four terms is plain, but so does continuous proportion, for it uses one term as two and mentions it twice; e. g. 'as the line A is to the line B, so is the line B to the line C'; the line B, then, has been **1131** mentioned twice, so that if the line B be assumed twice, the proportional terms will be four); and the just, too, involves at least four terms, and the ratio between one pair is

the same as that between the other pair; for there is a similar distinction between the persons and between the
5 things. As the term A, then, is to B, so will C be to D, and therefore, *alternando*, as A is to C, B will be to D. Therefore also the whole is in the same ratio to the whole; [3] and this coupling the distribution effects, and, if the terms are so combined, effects justly. The conjunction, then, of the term A with C and of B with D is what is just in distribution,[4] and this species of the just is intermediate, and the
10 unjust is what violates the proportion; for the proportional is intermediate, and the just is proportional. (Mathematicians call this kind of proportion geometrical; for it is in geometrical proportion that it follows that the whole is to
15 the whole as either part is to the corresponding part.) This proportion is not continuous; for we cannot get a single term standing for a person and a thing.

This, then, is what the just is—the proportional; the unjust is what violates the proportion. Hence one term becomes too great, the other too small, as indeed happens in practice; for the man who acts unjustly has too much, and the man who is unjustly treated too little, of what is good.
20 In the case of evil the reverse is true; for the lesser evil is reckoned a good in comparison with the greater evil, since the lesser evil is rather to be chosen than the greater, and what is worthy of choice is good, and what is worthier of choice a greater good.

This, then, is one species of the just.

4   (b) The remaining one is the rectificatory, which
15   arises in connexion with transactions both voluntary

---

[3] Person A + thing C to person B + thing D.

[4] The problem of distributive justice is to divide the distributable honour or reward into parts which are to one another as are the merits of the persons who are to participate. If
A (first person) : B (second person) :: C (first portion) : D (second portion), then (*alternando*) A : C :: B : D,
and therefore (*componendo*) A + C : B + D :: A : B.
In other words the position established answers to the relative merits of the parties.

and involuntary. This form of the just has a different specific character from the former. For the justice which
distributes common possessions is always in accordance
with the kind of proportion mentioned above [5] (for in the
case also in which the distribution is made from the common funds of a partnership it will be according to the 30
same ratio which the funds put into the business by the
partners bear to one another); and the injustice opposed
to this kind of justice is that which violates the proportion.
But the justice in transactions between man and man is a 1132
sort of equality indeed, and the injustice a sort of inequality; not according to that kind of proportion, however,
but according to arithmetical proportion.[6] For it makes no
difference whether a good man has defrauded a bad man or
a bad man a good one, nor whether it is a good or a bad man
that has committed adultery; the law looks only to the
distinctive character of the injury, and treats the parties as 5
equal, if one is in the wrong and the other is being wronged,
and if one inflicted injury and the other has received it.
Therefore, this kind of injustice being an inequality, the
judge tries to equalize it; for in the case also in which one
has received and the other has inflicted a wound, or one
has slain and the other been slain, the suffering and the
action have been unequally distributed; but the judge tries
to equalize things by means of the penalty, taking away 10
from the gain of the assailant. For the term 'gain' is applied generally to such cases, even if it be not a term ap-

---

[5] l. 12 f.

[6] The problem of 'rectificatory justice' has nothing to do with punishment proper but is only that of rectifying a wrong that has been
done, by awarding damages; i. e. rectificatory justice is that of
the civil, not that of the criminal courts. The parties are treated by the
court as equal (since a law court is not a court of morals), and the
wrongful act is reckoned as having brought equal gain to the wrongdoer and loss to his victim; it brings A to the position $A + C$, and B
to the position $B - C$. The judge's task is to find the arithmetical
mean between these, and this he does by transferring C from A to B.
Thus (A being treated as $= B$) we get the arithmetical 'proportion'
$$(A + C) - (A + C - C) = (A + C - C) - (B - C)$$
or $$(A + C) - (B - C + C) = (B - C + C) - (B - C).$$

propriate to certain cases, e. g. to the person who inflicts a
wound—and 'loss' to the sufferer; at all events when the
suffering has been estimated, the one is called loss and the
15 other gain. Therefore the equal is intermediate between
the greater and the less, but the gain and the loss are respectively greater and less in contrary ways; more of the
good and less of the evil are gain, and the contrary is loss;
intermediate between them is, as we saw,[7] the equal, which
we say is just; therefore corrective justice will be the inter-
20 mediate between loss and gain. This is why, when people
dispute, they take refuge in the judge; and to go to the
judge is to go to justice; for the nature of the judge is to be
a sort of animate justice; and they seek the judge as an
intermediate, and in some states they call judges mediators,
on the assumption that if they get what is intermediate
they will get what is just. The just, then, is an intermediate, since the judge is so. Now the judge restores equality;
it is as though there were a line divided into unequal
25 parts, and he took away that by which the greater segment
exceeds the half, and added it to the smaller segment. And
when the whole has been equally divided, then they say
they have 'their own'—i. e. when they have got what is
equal. The equal is intermediate between the greater and
the lesser line according to arithmetical proportion. It is
30 for this reason also that it is called just (dikaion), because
it is a division into two equal parts (dicha), just as if one
were to call it (dichaion); and the judge (dicastes) is one
who bisects (dichastes). For when something is subtracted
from one of two equals and added to the other, the other is
in excess by these two; since if what was taken from the
one had not been added to the other, the latter would have
been in excess by one only. It therefore exceeds the inter-
1132[b] mediate by one, and the intermediate exceeds by one that
from which something was taken. By this, then, we shall
recognize both what we must subtract from that which has
more, and what we must add to that which has less; we

must add to the latter that by which the intermediate exceeds it, and subtract from the greatest that by which it 5 exceeds the intermediate. Let the lines AA', BB', CC' be equal to one another; from the line AA' let the segment AE have been subtracted, and to the line CC' let the segment CD [8] have been added, so that the whole line DCC' exceeds the line EA' by the segment CD and the segment CF; therefore it exceeds the line BB' by the segment CD.

A   E   A'
_____   _____

B   B'
_____

D   C   F   C'
_____●_____●_____

These names, both loss and gain, have come from voluntary exchange; for to have more than one's own is called gain- 11 ing, and to have less than one's original share is called losing, e. g. in buying and selling and in all other matters 15 in which the law has left people free to make their own terms; but when they get neither more nor less but just what belongs to themselves, they say that they have their own and that they neither lose nor gain.

Therefore the just is intermediate between a sort of gain and a sort of loss, viz. those which are involuntary; [9] it consists in having an equal amount before and after the trans- 20 action.

5   Some think that *reciprocity* is without qualification just, as the Pythagoreans said; for they defined justice without qualification as reciprocity. Now 'reciprocity' fits neither distributive nor rectificatory justice—yet people 25 want even the justice of Rhadamanthus to mean this:

[8] sc. equal to AE.
[9] i. e. for the loser.

Should a man suffer what he did, right justice would be done

- -for in many cases reciprocity and rectificatory justice are not in accord, e. g. (1) if an official has inflicted a wound, he should not be wounded in return, and if some one has 30 wounded an official, he ought not to be wounded only but punished in addition. Further (2) there is a great difference between a voluntary and an involuntary act. But in associations for exchange this sort of justice does hold men together—reciprocity in accordance with a proportion and not on the basis of precisely equal return. For it is by proportionate requital that the city holds together. Men 1133ª seek to return either evil for evil—and if they cannot do so, think their position mere slavery—or good for good—and if they cannot do so there is no exchange, but it is by exchange that they hold together. This is why they give a prominent place to the temple of the Graces—to promote the requital of services; for this is characteristic of grace— we should serve in return one who has shown grace to us, and should another time take the initiative in showing it.

5   Now proportionate return is secured by cross-conjunction. Let A be a builder, B a shoemaker, C a house, D a shoe. The builder, then, must get from the shoemaker the 10 latter's work, and must himself give him in return his own. If, then, first there is proportionate equality of goods, and then reciprocal action takes place, the result we mention will be effected. If not, the bargain is not equal, and does not hold; for there is nothing to prevent the work of the one being better than that of the other; they must 15 therefore be equated. (And this is true of the other arts also; for they would have been destroyed if what the patient suffered had not been just what the agent did, and of the same amount and kind.) For it is not two doctors that associate for exchange, but a doctor and a farmer, or in general people who are different and unequal; but these must be equated. This is why all things that are exchanged

must be somehow comparable. It is for this end that
money has been introduced, and it becomes in a sense an
intermediate; for it measures all things, and therefore the
excess and the defect—how many shoes are equal to a 20
house or to a given amount of food. The number of shoes
exchanged for a house [or for a given amount of food]
must therefore correspond to the ratio of builder to shoemaker. For if this be not so, there will be no exchange and
no intercourse. And this proportion will not be effected
unless the goods are somehow equal. All goods must 25
therefore be measured by some one thing, as we said before.
Now this unit is in truth demand, which holds all things
together (for if men did not need one another's goods at
all, or did not need them equally, there would be either no
exchange or not the same exchange); but money has become by convention a sort of representative of demand; 30
and this is why it has the name 'money' (*nomisma*)—because it exists not by nature but by law (*nomos*) and it is
in our power to change it and make it useless. There will,
then, be reciprocity when the terms have been equated so
that as farmer is to shoemaker, the amount of the shoemaker's work is to that of the farmer's work for which it
exchanges. But we must not bring them into a figure of **1133ᵇ**
proportion when they have already exchanged (otherwise
one extreme will have both excesses), but when they still
have their own goods. Thus they are equals and associates
just because this equality can be effected in their case. Let
A be a farmer, C food, B a shoemaker, D his product 5
equated to C. If it had not been possible for reciprocity to
be thus effected, there would have been no association of
the parties. That demand holds things together as a single
unit is shown by the fact that when men do not need one
another, i. e. when neither needs the other or one does not
need the other, they do not exchange, as we do when some
one wants what one has oneself, e. g. when people permit
the exportation of corn in exchange for wine. This equation
therefore must be established. And for the future exchange 10

—that if we do not need a thing now we shall have it if ever we do need it—money is as it were our surety; for it must be possible for us to get what we want by bringing the money. Now the same thing happens to money itself as to goods—it is not always worth the same; yet it tends to be steadier. This is why all goods must have a price set on them; for then there will always be exchange, and if so, association of man with man. Money, then, acting as a measure, makes goods commensurate and equates them; for neither would there have been association if there were not exchange, nor exchange if there were not equality, nor equality if there were not commensurability. Now in truth it is impossible that things differing so much should become commensurate, but with reference to demand they may become so sufficiently. There must, then, be a unit, and that fixed by agreement (for which reason it is called money); for it is this that makes all things commensurate, since all things are measured by money. Let A be a house, B ten minae, C a bed. A is half of B, if the house is worth five minae or equal to them; the bed, C, is a tenth of B; it is plain, then, how many beds are equal to a house, viz. five. That exchange took place thus before there was money is plain; for it makes no difference whether it is five beds that exchange for a house, or the money value of five beds.

We have now defined the unjust and the just. These having been marked off from each other, it is plain that just action is intermediate between acting unjustly and being unjustly treated; for the one is to have too much and the other to have too little. Justice is a kind of mean, but not in the same way as the other virtues, but because it relates to an intermediate amount, while injustice relates to the extremes. And justice is that in virtue of which the just man is said to be a doer, by choice, of that which is just, and one who will distribute either between himself and another or between two others not so as to give more of what is desirable to himself and less to his neighbour (and conversely with what is harmful), but so as to give what is equal in accordance with proportion; and similarly in distributing between two other persons. Injustice on the other hand is similarly related to the unjust, which is excess and defect, contrary to proportion, of the useful or hurtful. For which reason injustice is excess and defect, viz. because it is productive of excess and defect—in one's own case excess of what is in its own nature useful and defect of what is [10] hurtful, while in the case of others it is as a whole like what it is in one's own case, but proportion may be violated in either direction. In the unjust act to have too little is to be unjustly treated; to have too much is to act unjustly.

Let this be taken as our account of the nature of justice and injustice, and similarly of the just and the unjust in [15] general.

6   Since acting unjustly does not necessarily imply being unjust, we must ask what sort of unjust acts imply that the doer is unjust with respect to each type of injustice, e. g. a thief, an adulterer, or a brigand. Surely the answer does not turn on the difference between these types. For a man might even lie with a woman knowing who she was, but the origin of his act might be not deliberate choice but passion. He acts unjustly, then, but is not unjust; e. g. a man is not [20] a thief, yet he stole, nor an adulterer, yet he committed adultery; and similarly in all other cases.

Now we have previously stated how the reciprocal is related to the just; [10] but we must not forget that what we are looking for is not only what is just without qualification [25] but also political justice. This is found among men who share their life with a view to self-sufficiency, men who are free and either proportionately or arithmetically equal, so that between those who do not fulfil this condition there is no political justice but justice in a special sense and by analogy. For justice exists only between men whose mutual relations are governed by law; and law exists for [30] men between whom there is injustice; for legal justice is

[10] 1132ᵇ 21–1133ᵇ 28.

the discrimination of the just and the unjust. And between men between whom there is injustice there is also unjust action (though there is not injustice between all between whom there is unjust action), and this is assigning too much to oneself of things good in themselves and too little of things evil in themselves. This is why we do not 35 allow a *man* to rule, but *rational principle*, because a man behaves thus in his own interests and becomes a tyrant. **1134ᵇ** The magistrate on the other hand is the guardian of justice, and, if of justice, then of equality also. And since he is assumed to have no more than his share, if he is just (for he does not assign to himself more of what is good in itself, unless such a share is proportional to his merits—so that it is for others that he labours, and it is for this reason that 5 men, as we stated previously,[11] say that justice is 'another's good'), therefore a reward must be given him, and this is honour and privilege; but those for whom such things are not enough become tyrants.

The justice of a master and that of a father are not the same as the justice of citizens, though they are like it; for there can be no injustice in the unqualified sense towards things that are one's own, but a man's chattel,[12] and his 10 child until it reaches a certain age and sets up for itself, are as it were part of himself, and no one chooses to hurt himself (for which reason there can be no injustice towards oneself). Therefore the justice or injustice of citizens is not manifested in these relations; for it was as we saw [13] according to law, and between people naturally subject to law, and these as we saw [14] are people who have an equal 15 share in ruling and being ruled. Hence justice can more truly be manifested towards a wife than towards children and chattels, for the former is household justice; but even this is different from political justice.

[11] 1130ᵃ 3.
[12] i. e. his slave.
[13] ᵃ 30.
[14] ᵃ 26–8.

7   Of political justice part is natural, part legal—natural, that which everywhere has the same force and does not exist by people's thinking this or that; legal, that which is originally indifferent, but when it has been laid down is not indifferent, e. g. that a prisoner's ransom shall be a mina, or that a goat and not two sheep shall be sacrificed, and again all the laws that are passed for particular cases, e. g. that sacrifice shall be made in honour of Brasidas, and the provisions of decrees. Now some think that all justice is of this sort, because that which is by nature is unchangeable and has everywhere the same force (as fire burns both here and in Persia), while they see change in the things recognized as just. This, however, is not true in this unqualified way, but is true in a sense; or rather, with the gods it is perhaps not true at all, while with us there is something that is just even by nature, yet all of it is changeable; but still some is by nature, some not by nature. It is evident which sort of thing, among things capable of being otherwise, is by nature; and which is not but is legal and conventional, assuming that both are equally changeable. And in all other things the same distinction will apply; by nature the right hand is stronger, yet it is possible that all men should come to be ambidextrous. The things which **1135ᵃ** are just by virtue of convention and expediency are like measures; for wine and corn measures are not everywhere equal, but larger in wholesale and smaller in retail markets. Similarly, the things which are just not by nature but by human enactment are not everywhere the same, since constitutions also are not the same, though there is but one which is everywhere by nature the best.

Of things just and lawful each is related as the universal to its particulars; for the things that are done are many, but of them each is one, since it is universal.

There is a difference between the act of injustice and what is unjust, and between the act of justice and what is just; for a thing is unjust by nature or by enactment; and this very thing, when it has been done, is an act of injustice, but before it is done is not yet that but is unjust. So, too, with an act of justice (though the general term is rather 'just action', and 'act of justice' is applied to the correction of the act of injustice).

Each of these must later [15] be examined separately with regard to the nature and number of its species and the nature of the things with which it is concerned.

8 Acts just and unjust being as we have described them, a man acts unjustly or justly whenever he does such acts voluntarily; when involuntarily, he acts neither unjustly nor justly except in an incidental way; for he does things which happen to be just or unjust. Whether an act is or is not one of injustice (or of justice) is determined by its voluntariness or involuntariness; for when it is voluntary it is blamed, and at the same time is then an act of injustice; so that there will be things that are unjust but not yet acts of injustice, if voluntariness be not present as well. By the voluntary I mean, as has been said before, [16] any of the things in a man's own power which he does with knowledge, i. e. not in ignorance either of the person acted on or of the instrument used or of the end that will be attained (e. g. whom he is striking, with what and to what end), each such act being done not incidentally nor under compulsion (e. g. if A takes B's hand and therewith strikes C, B does not act voluntarily; for the act was not in his own power). The person struck may be the striker's father, and the striker may know that it is a man or one of the persons present, but not know that it is his father; a similar distinction may be made in the case of the end, and with regard to the whole action. Therefore that which is done in ignorance, or though not done in ignorance is not in the agent's power, or is done under compulsion, is involuntary (for many natural processes, even,

[15] Possibly a reference to an intended (or now lost) book of the *Politics* on laws.

[16] 1109^{b}35–1111^{a}24.

we knowingly both perform and experience, none of which
is either voluntary or involuntary; e. g. growing old or 1135ᵃ
dying). But in the case of unjust and just acts alike the
injustice or justice may be only incidental; for a man might
return a deposit unwillingly and from fear, and then he
must not be said either to do what is just or to act justly, 5
except in an incidental way. Similarly the man who under
compulsion and unwillingly fails to return the deposit must
be said to act unjustly, and to do what is unjust, only
incidentally. Of voluntary acts we do some by choice,
others not by choice; by choice those which we do after 10
deliberation, not by choice those which we do without
previous deliberation. Thus there are three kinds of injury
in transactions between man and man; those done in ignorance are *mistakes* when the person acted on, the act, the
instrument, or the end that will be attained is other than
the agent supposed; the agent thought either that he was
not hitting any one or that he was not hitting with this
missile or not hitting this person or to this end, but a result followed other than that which he thought likely (e. g. 15
he threw not with intent to wound but only to prick), or
the person hit or the missile was other than he supposed.
Now when (1) the injury takes place contrary to reasonable expectation, it is a *misadventure*. When (2) it is not
contrary to reasonable expectation, but does not imply vice,
it is a *mistake* (for a man makes a mistake when the fault
originates in him, but is the victim of accident when the
origin lies outside him). When (3) he acts with knowledge
but not after deliberation, it is an *act of injustice*—e. g. the 20
acts due to anger or to other passions necessary or natural to
man; for when men do such harmful and mistaken acts
they act unjustly, and the acts are acts of injustice, but this
does not imply that the doers are unjust or wicked; for the
injury is not due to vice. But when (4) a man acts from 25
choice, he is an *unjust man* and a vicious man.

Hence acts proceeding from anger are rightly judged not
to be done of malice aforethought; for it is not the man

who acts in anger but he who enraged him that starts the mischief. Again, the matter in dispute is not whether the thing happened or not, but its justice; for it is apparent injustice that occasions rage. For they do not dispute about 30 the occurrence of the act—as in commercial transactions where one of the two parties *must* be vicious [17]—unless they do so owing to forgetfulness; but, agreeing about the fact, they dispute on which side justice lies (whereas a man who has deliberately injured another cannot help knowing that he has done so), so that the one thinks he is being treated unjustly and the other disagrees.

1136ᵃ   But if a man harms another by choice, he acts unjustly; and *these* are the acts of injustice which imply that the doer is an unjust man, provided that the act violates proportion or equality. Similarly, a man *is just* when he acts justly by choice; but he *acts justly* if he merely acts voluntarily.

5   Of involuntary acts some are excusable, others not. For the mistakes which men make not only in ignorance but also from ignorance are excusable, while those which men do not from ignorance but (though they do them *in* ignorance) owing to a passion which is neither natural nor such as man is liable to, are not excusable.

10 **9**   Assuming that we have sufficiently defined the suffering and doing of injustice, it may be asked (1) whether the truth is expressed in Euripides' paradoxical words:

'I slew my mother, that's my tale in brief.'
'Were you both willing, or unwilling both?'

Is it truly possible to be willingly treated unjustly, or is all 15 suffering of injustice on the contrary involuntary, as all unjust action is voluntary? And is all suffering of injustice of the latter kind or else all of the former, or is it sometimes

---

[17] The plaintiff, if he brings a false accusation; the defendant, if he denies a true one.

voluntary, sometimes involuntary? So, too, with the case
of being justly treated; all just action is voluntary, so that
it is reasonable that there should be a similar opposition
in either case—that both being unjustly and being justly
treated should be either alike voluntary or alike involun- 20
tary. But it would be thought paradoxical even in the case
of being justly treated, if it were always voluntary; for some
are unwillingly treated justly. (2) One might raise this
question also, whether every one who has suffered what is
unjust is being unjustly treated, or on the other hand it is
with suffering as with acting. In action and in passivity 25
alike it is possible to partake of justice incidentally, and
similarly (it is plain) of injustice; for to do what is unjust
is not the same as to act unjustly, nor to suffer what is unjust as to be treated unjustly, and similarly in the case of
acting justly and being justly treated; for it is impossible
to be unjustly treated if the other does not act unjustly,
or justly treated unless he acts justly. Now if to act un- 30
justly is simply to harm some one voluntarily, and 'voluntarily' means 'knowing the person acted on, the instrument,
and the manner of one's acting', and the incontinent man
voluntarily harms himself, not only will he voluntarily be
unjustly treated but it will be possible to treat oneself
unjustly. (This also is one of the questions in doubt,
whether a man can treat himself unjustly.) Again, a man
may voluntarily, owing to incontinence, be harmed by 1136
another who acts voluntarily, so that it would be possible
to be voluntarily treated unjustly. Or is our definition incorrect; must we to 'harming another, with knowledge both
of the person acted on, of the instrument, and of the manner' add 'contrary to the wish of the person acted on'? Then
a man may be voluntarily harmed and voluntarily suffer 5
what is unjust, but no one is voluntarily treated unjustly;
for no one wishes to be unjustly treated, not even the incontinent man. He acts contrary to his wish; for no one
wishes for what he does not think to be good, but the incontinent man does do things that he does not think he

ought to do. Again, one who gives what is his own, as
Homer says Glaucus gave Diomede

Armour of gold for brazen, the price of a hundred beeves
10 for nine,[18] is not unjustly treated; for though to give is in
his power, to be unjustly treated is not, but there must be
some one to treat him unjustly. It is plain, then, that being
unjustly treated is not voluntary.

15   Of the questions we intended to discuss two still remain for discussion; (3) whether it is the man who has
assigned to another more than his share that acts unjustly,
or he who has the excessive share, and (4) whether it is
possible to treat oneself unjustly. The questions are connected; for if the former alternative is possible and the
distributor acts unjustly and not the man who has the excessive share, then if a man assigns more to another than
20 to himself, knowingly and voluntarily, he treats himself
unjustly; which is what modest people seem to do, since
the virtuous man tends to take less than his share. Or does
this statement too need qualification? For (a) he perhaps
gets more than his share of some other good, e. g. of
honour or of intrinsic nobility. (b) The question is solved
by applying the distinction we applied to unjust action; [19]
for he suffers nothing contrary to his own wish, so that he is
not unjustly treated as far as this goes, but at most only
suffers harm.

25   It is plain too that the distributor acts unjustly, but not
always the man who has the excessive share; for it is not
he to whom what is unjust appertains that acts unjustly,
but he to whom it appertains to do the unjust act voluntarily, i. e. the person in whom lies the origin of the action,
and this lies in the distributor, not in the receiver. Again,
30 since the word 'do' is ambiguous, and there is a sense in
which lifeless things, or a hand, or a servant who obeys an
order, may be said to slay, he who gets an excessive share
does not act unjustly, though he 'does' what is unjust.

18 Il. vi. 236.
19 ll. 3–5.

Again, if the distributor gave his judgment in ignorance, he does not act unjustly in respect of legal justice, and his judgment is not unjust in this sense, but in a sense it *is* unjust (for legal justice and primordial justice are differ- **1137** ent); but if with knowledge he judged unjustly, he is him- self aiming at an excessive share either of gratitude or of revenge. As much, then, as if he were to share in the plunder, the man who has judged unjustly for these reasons has got too much; the fact that what he gets is different from what he distributes makes no difference, for even if he awards land with a view to sharing in the plunder he gets not land but money.

Men think that acting unjustly is in their power, and 5 therefore that being just is easy. But it is not; to lie with one's neighbour's wife, to wound another, to deliver a bribe, is easy and in our power, but to do these things as a result of a certain state of character is neither easy nor in our power. Similarly to know what is just and what is unjust requires, men think, no great wisdom, because it is not hard to understand the matters dealt with by the laws 10 (though these are not the things that are just, except inci- dentally); but how actions must be done and distributions effected in order to be just, to know *this* is a greater achieve- ment than knowing what is good for the health; though even there, while it is easy to know that honey, wine, hellebore, cautery, and the use of the knife are so, to know how, to whom, and when these should be applied with a 15 view to producing health, is no less an achievement than that of being a physician. Again, for this very reason [20] men think that acting unjustly is characteristic of the just man no less than of the unjust, because he would be not less but even more capable of doing each of these unjust acts; [21] for he could lie with a woman or wound a neigh- bour; and the brave man could throw away his shield and turn to flight in this direction or in that. But to play the 20

[20] i. e. that stated in l. 4 f., that acting unjustly is in our own power.
[21] Cf. ll. 6–8.

coward or to act unjustly consists not in doing these things, except incidentally, but in doing them as the result of a certain state of character, just as to practise medicine and healing consists not in applying or not applying the knife, in using or not using medicines, but in doing so in a certain
25 way.

Just acts occur between people who participate in things good in themselves and can have too much or too little of them; for some beings (e. g. presumably the gods) cannot have too much of them, and to others, those who are incurably bad, not even the smallest share in them is beneficial but all such goods are harmful, while to others they are beneficial up to a point; therefore justice is essentially
30 something human.

10 Our next subject is equity and the equitable (to epieikes), and their respective relations to justice and the just. For on examination they appear to be neither absolutely the same nor generically different; and while we
35 sometimes praise what is equitable and the equitable man (so that we apply the name by way of praise even to instances of the other virtues, instead of 'good,' meaning by
1137ᵇ epieikesteron that a thing is better), at other times, when we reason it out, it seems strange if the equitable, being something different from the just, is yet praiseworthy; for either the just or the equitable is not good, if they are different; or, if both are good, they are the same.
5   These, then, are pretty much the considerations that give rise to the problem about the equitable; they are all in a sense correct and not opposed to one another; for the equitable, though it is better than one kind of justice, yet is just, and it is not as being a different class of thing that it is better than the just. The same thing, then, is just and
10 equitable, and while both are good the equitable is superior. What creates the problem is that the equitable is just, but not the legally just but a correction of legal justice. The reason is that all law is universal but about some things it is not possible to make a universal statement which shall be

correct. In those cases, then, in which it is necessary to 15
speak universally, but not possible to do so correctly,
the law takes the usual case, though it is not ignorant of the
possibility of error. And it is none the less correct; for the
error is not in the law nor in the legislator but in the nature
of the thing, since the matter of practical affairs is of this
kind from the start. When the law speaks universally, then, 20
and a case arises on it which is not covered by the universal
statement, then it is right, where the legislator fails us and
has erred by over-simplicity, to correct the omission—to say
what the legislator himself would have said had he been
present, and would have put into his law if he had known.
Hence the equitable is just, and better than one kind of 25
justice—not better than absolute justice but better than the
error that arises from the absoluteness of the statement.
And this is the nature of the equitable, a correction of law
where it is defective owing to its universality. In fact this is
the reason why all things are not determined by law, viz.
that about some things it is impossible to lay down a law,
so that a decree is needed. For when the thing is indefinite
the rule also is indefinite, like the leaden rule used in mak- 30
ing the Lesbian moulding; the rule adapts itself to the
shape of the stone and is not rigid, and so too the decree is
adapted to the facts.

It is plain, then, what the equitable is, and that it is just
and is better than one kind of justice. It is evident also from
this who the equitable man is; the man who chooses and 35
does such acts, and is no stickler for his rights in a bad sense **1138ᵃ**
but tends to take less than his share though he has the law
on his side, is equitable, and this state of character is equity,
which is a sort of justice and not a different state of character.

11 Whether a man can treat himself unjustly or not, is
evident from what has been said.[22] For (a) one class 5
of just acts are those acts in accordance with any virtue
which are prescribed by the law; e. g. the law does not ex-

[22] Cf. 1129ᵃ 32–ᵇ 1, 1136ᵃ 10–1137ᵃ 4.

pressly permit suicide, and what it does not expressly permit it forbids. Again, when a man in violation of the law harms another (otherwise than in retaliation) voluntarily, he acts unjustly, and a voluntary agent is one who knows both the person he is affecting by his action and the instrument he is using; and he who through anger voluntarily stabs him-10 self does this contrary to the right rule of life, and this the law does not allow; therefore he is acting unjustly. But towards whom? Surely towards the state, not towards himself. For he suffers voluntarily, but no one is voluntarily treated unjustly. This is also the reason why the state punishes; a certain loss of civil rights attaches to the man who destroys himself, on the ground that he is treating the state unjustly.

Further (b) in that sense of 'acting unjustly' in which the man who 'acts unjustly' is unjust only and not bad all round, it is not possible to treat oneself unjustly (this is 15 different from the former sense; the unjust man in one sense of the term is wicked in a particularized way just as the coward is, not in the sense of being wicked all round, so that his 'unjust act' does not manifest wickedness in general). For (i) that would imply the possibility of the same thing's having been subtracted from and added to the same thing at the same time; but this is impossible—the just and the unjust always involve more than one person. 20 Further, (ii) unjust action is voluntary and done by choice, and takes the initiative (for the man who because he has suffered does the same in return is not thought to act unjustly); but if a man harms himself he suffers and does the same things at the same time. Further, (iii) if a man could treat himself unjustly, he could be voluntarily treated unjustly. Besides, (iv) no one acts unjustly without committing particular acts of injustice; but no one can commit 25 adultery with his own wife or housebreaking on his own house or theft on his own property.

In general, the question 'can a man treat himself unjustly?' is solved also by the distinction we applied to the question 'can a man be voluntarily treated unjustly?' [23]

[23] Cf. 1136^a 31–^{b} 5.

(It is evident too that both are bad, being unjustly treated and acting unjustly; for the one means having less and the other having more than the intermediate amount, which plays the part here that the healthy does in the 30 medical art, and that good condition does in the art of bodily training. But still acting unjustly is the worse, for it involves vice and is blameworthy—involves vice which is either of the complete and unqualified kind or almost so (we must admit the latter alternative, because not all voluntary unjust action implies injustice as a state of character), while being unjustly treated does not involve vice 35 and injustice in oneself. In itself, then, being unjustly treated is less bad, but there is nothing to prevent its being **1138** incidentally a greater evil. But theory cares nothing for this; it calls pleurisy a more serious mischief than a stumble; yet the latter may become incidentally the more serious, if the fall due to it leads to your being taken prisoner or put to death by the enemy.)

Metaphorically and in virtue of a certain resemblance 5 there is a justice, not indeed between a man and himself, but between certain parts of him; yet not every kind of justice but that of master and servant or that of husband and wife.[24] For these are the ratios in which the part of the soul that has a rational principle stands to the irrational part; and it is with a view to these parts that people also think a man can be unjust to himself, viz. because these 10 parts are liable to suffer something contrary to their respective desires; there is therefore thought to be a mutual justice between them as between ruler and ruled.

Let this be taken as our account of justice and the other, i. e. the other moral, virtues.

BOOK VI

1   Since we have previously said that one ought to choose that which is intermediate, not the excess nor the defect,[1] and that the intermediate is determined by the dic-

[24] Cf. 1134[b] 15–17.
[1] 1104[a] 11–27, 1106[a] 26–1107[a] 27.

20 tates of the right rule,[2] let us discuss the nature of these dictates. In all the states of character we have mentioned,[3] as in all other matters, there is a mark to which the man who has the rule looks, and heightens or relaxes his activity accordingly, and there is a standard which determines the mean states which we say are intermediate between excess 25 and defect, being in accordance with the right rule. But such a statement, though true, is by no means clear; for not only here but in all other pursuits which are objects of knowledge it is indeed true to say that we must not exert ourselves nor relax our efforts too much nor too little, but to an intermediate extent and as the right rule dictates; but if a man had only this knowledge he would be none the 30 wiser—e. g. we should not know what sort of medicines to apply to our body if some one were to say 'all those which the medical art prescribes, and which agree with the prac-tice of one who possesses the art.' Hence it is necessary with regard to the states of the soul also not only that this true statement should be made, but also that it should be deter-mined what is the right rule and what is the standard that fixes it.

We divided the virtues of the soul and said that some are 35 virtues of character and others of intellect.[4] Now we have 1139ᵃ discussed in detail the moral virtues;[3] with regard to the others let us express our view as follows, beginning with some remarks about the soul. We said before[5] that there are two parts of the soul—that which grasps a rule or ra-5 tional principle, and the irrational; let us now draw a similar distinction within the part which grasps a rational principle. And let it be assumed that there are two parts which grasp a rational principle—one by which we contemplate the kind of things whose originative causes are invariable, and one by which we contemplate variable things; for where objects differ in kind the part of the soul answering to each

[2] 1107ᵃ 1, Cf. 1103ᵇ 31, 1114ᵇ 29.
[3] In iii. 6–v. 11.
[4] 1103ᵃ 3–7.
[5] 1102ᵃ 26–8.

of the two is different in kind, since it is in virtue of a
certain likeness and kinship with their objects that they 10
have the knowledge they have. Let one of these parts be
called the scientific and the other the calculative; for to deliberate and to calculate are the same thing, but no one
deliberates about the invariable. Therefore the calculative
is one part of the faculty which grasps a rational principle.
We must, then, learn what is the best state of each of these
two parts; for this is the virtue of each. 15

2 The virtue of a thing is relative to its proper work.
Now there are three things in the soul which control
action and truth—sensation, reason, desire.
Of these sensation originates no action; this is plain from
the fact that the lower animals have sensation but no share
in action. 20
What affirmation and negation are in thinking, pursuit
and avoidance are in desire; so that since moral virtue is a
state of character concerned with choice, and choice is deliberate desire, therefore both the reasoning must be true
and the desire right, if the choice is to be good, and the 25
latter must pursue just what the former asserts. Now this
kind of intellect and of truth is practical; of the intellect
which is contemplative, not practical nor productive, the
good and the bad state are truth and falsity respectively
(for this is the work of everything intellectual); while of 30
the part which is practical and intellectual the good state is
truth in agreement with right desire.
The origin of action—its efficient, not its final cause—
is choice, and that of choice is desire and reasoning with a
view to an end. This is why choice cannot exist either without reason and intellect or without a moral state; for good
action and its opposite cannot exist without a combination 35
of intellect and character. Intellect itself, however, moves
nothing, but only the intellect which aims at an end and is
practical; for this rules the productive intellect as well, since **1139**ᵇ
every one who makes makes for an end, and that which is

made is not an end in the unqualified sense (but only an
end in a particular relation, and the end of a particular
operation)—only that which is *done* is that; for good action is an end, and desire aims at this. Hence choice is
either desiderative reason or ratiocinative desire, and such
5 an origin of action is a man. (It is to be noted that nothing
that is past is an object of choice, e. g. no one chooses to
have sacked Troy; for no one *deliberates* about the past, but
about what is future and capable of being otherwise, while
what is past is not capable of not having taken place; hence
Agathon is right in saying

10   For this alone is lacking even to God,
    To make undone things that have once been done.)

The work of both the intellectual parts, then, is truth.
Therefore the states that are most strictly those in respect
of which each of these parts will reach truth are the virtues
of the two parts.

3   Let us begin, then, from the beginning, and discuss
15   these states once more. Let it be assumed that the
states by virtue of which the soul possesses truth by way
of affirmation or denial are five in number, i. e. art, scientific
knowledge, practical wisdom, philosophic wisdom, intuitive
reason; we do not include judgement and opinion because
in these we may be mistaken.

Now what *scientific knowledge* is, if we are to speak exactly and not follow mere similarities, is plain from what
20 follows. We all suppose that what we know is not even
capable of being otherwise; of things capable of being
otherwise we do not know, when they have passed outside
our observation, whether they exist or not. Therefore the
object of scientific knowledge is of necessity. Therefore it is
eternal; for things that are of necessity in the unqualified
sense are all eternal; and things that are eternal are ungen-
erated and imperishable. Again, every science is thought to
25 be capable of being taught, and its object of being learned.

And all teaching starts from what is already known, as we maintain in the *Analytics* [6] also; for it proceeds sometimes through induction and sometimes by syllogism. Now induction is the starting-point which knowledge even of the universal presupposes, while syllogism proceeds *from* universals. There are therefore starting-points from which syllogism proceeds, which are not reached by syllogism; it is therefore by induction that they are acquired. Scientific 30 knowledge is, then, a state of capacity to demonstrate, and has the other limiting characteristics which we specify in the *Analytics*; [7] for it is when a man believes in a certain way and the starting-points are known to him that he has scientific knowledge, since if they are not better known to him than the conclusion, he will have his knowledge only incidentally.

Let this, then, be taken as our account of scientific knowledge. 35

4 In the variable are included both things made and things done; making and acting are different (for their **1140ª** nature we treat even the discussions outside our school as reliable); so that the reasoned state of capacity to act is different from the reasoned state of capacity to make. 5 Hence too they are not included one in the other; for neither is acting making nor is making acting. Now since architecture is an art and is essentially a reasoned state of capacity to make, and there is neither any art that is not such a state nor any such state that is not an art, *art* is identical with a state of capacity to make, involving a true course of reasoning. All art is concerned with coming into 10 being, i. e. with contriving and considering how something may come into being which is capable of either being or not being, and whose origin is in the maker and not in the thing made; for art is concerned neither with things that are, or come into being, by necessity, nor with things that

---

[6] *An. Post.* 71ª 1.
[7] Ib. ᵇ 9–23.

do so in accordance with nature (since these have their
15 origin in themselves). Making and acting being different,
art must be a matter of making, not of acting. And in a
sense chance and art are concerned with the same objects;
as Agathon says, 'art loves chance and chance loves art'.
Art, then, as has been said,[8] is a state concerned with mak-
20 ing, involving a true course of reasoning, and lack of art on
the contrary is a state concerned with making, involving a
false course of reasoning; both are concerned with the variable.

5　　Regarding *practical wisdom* we shall get at the truth
25　　by considering who are the persons we credit with it.
Now it is thought to be the mark of a man of practical
wisdom to be able to deliberate well about what is good
and expedient for himself, not in some particular respect,
e. g. about what sorts of thing conduce to health or to
strength, but about what sorts of thing conduce to the
good life in general. This is shown by the fact that we credit
men with practical wisdom in some particular respect when
30 they have calculated well with a view to some good end
which is one of those that are not the object of any art.
It follows that in the general sense also the man who is
capable of deliberating has practical wisdom. Now no one
deliberates about things that are invariable, nor about
things that it is impossible for him to do. Therefore,
since scientific knowledge involves demonstration, but
there is no demonstration of things whose first principles
35 are variable (for all such things might actually be otherwise), and since it is impossible to deliberate about things
1140ᵇ that are of necessity, practical wisdom cannot be scientific
knowledge nor art; not science because that which can be
done is capable of being otherwise, not art because action
and making are different kinds of thing. The remaining
5 alternative, then, is that it is a true and reasoned state of
capacity to act with regard to the things that are good or
bad for man. For while making has an end other than itself,

[8] l. 9.

action cannot; for good action itself is its end. It is for this reason that we think Pericles and men like him have practical wisdom, viz. because they can see what is good for themselves and what is good for men in general; we con- 10 sider that those can do this who are good at managing households or states. (This is why we call temperance (*sophrosyne*) by this name; we imply that it preserves one's practical wisdom (*sodsousa ten phronesin*). Now what it preserves is a judgement of the kind we have described. For it it not any and every judgement that pleasant and painful objects destroy and pervert, e. g. the judgement that the triangle has or has not its angles equal to two right 15 angles, but only judgements about what is to be done. For the originating causes of the things that are done consist in the end at which they are aimed; but the man who has been ruined by pleasure or pain forthwith fails to see any such originating cause—to see that for the sake of this or because of this he ought to choose and do whatever he chooses and does; for vice is destructive of the originating cause of action.)

Practical wisdoₙ, then, must be a reasoned and true state of capacity to act with regard to human goods. But 20 further, while there is such a thing as excellence in art, there is no such thing as excellence in practical wisdom; and in art he who errs willingly is preferable, but in practical wisdom, as in the virtues, he is the reverse. Plainly, then, practical wisdom is a virtue and not an art. There being two parts of the soul that can follow a course of 25 reasoning, it must be the virtue of one of the two, i. e. of that part which forms opinions; for opinion is about the variable and so is practical wisdom. But yet it is not only a reasoned state; this is shown by the fact that a state of that sort may be forgotten but practical wisdom cannot. 30

6 Scientific knowledge is judgement about things that are universal and necessary, and the conclusions of demonstration, and all scientific knowledge, follow from first principles (for scientific knowledge involves apprehen-

sion of a rational ground). This being so, the first principle
from which what is scientifically known follows cannot be
an object of scientific knowledge, of art, or of practical
35 wisdom; for that which can be scientifically known can be
demonstrated, and art and practical wisdom deal with
1141ᵃ things that are variable. Nor are these first principles the
objects of philosophic wisdom, for it is a mark of the
philosopher to have demonstration about some things. If,
then, the states of mind by which we have truth and are
never deceived about things invariable or even variable are
scientific knowledge, practical wisdom, philosophic wis-
5 dom, and intuitive reason, and it cannot be any of the
three (i. e. practical wisdom, scientific knowledge, or philosophic wisdom), the remaining alternative is that it is
intuitive reason that grasps the first principles.

7   Wisdom (1) in the arts we ascribe to their most finished exponents, e. g. to Phidias as a sculptor and to
10 Polyclitus as a maker of portrait-statues, and here we mean
nothing by wisdom except excellence in art; but (2) we
think that some people are wise in general, not in some
particular field or in any other limited respect, as Homer
says in the *Margites*,

Him did the gods make neither a digger nor yet a
15   ploughman
Nor wise in anything else.

Therefore wisdom must plainly be the most finished of
the forms of knowledge. It follows that the wise man must
not only know what follows from the first principles, but
must also possess truth about the first principles. Therefore
wisdom must be intuitive reason combined with scientific
knowledge—scientific knowledge of the highest objects
which has received as it were its proper completion.
20   Of the highest objects, we say; for it would be strange
to think that the art of politics, or practical wisdom, is the
best knowledge, since man is not the best thing in the

world. Now if what is healthy or good is different for men
and for fishes, but what is white or straight is always the 25
same, any one would say that what is wise is the same but
what is practically wise is different; for it is to that which
observes well the various matters concerning itself that one
ascribes practical wisdom, and it is to this that one will
entrust such matters. This is why we say that some even
of the lower animals have practical wisdom, viz. those
which are found to have a power of foresight with regard to
their own life. It is evident also that philosophic wisdom
and the art of politics cannot be the same; for if the state
of mind concerned with a man's own interests is to be 30
called philosophic wisdom, there will be many philosophic
wisdoms; there will not be one concerned with the good of
all animals (any more than there is one art of medicine for
all existing things), but a different philosophic wisdom
about the good of each species.

But if the argument be that man is the best of the animals, this makes no difference; for there are other things 1141ᵉ
much more divine in their nature even than man, e. g.,
most conspicuously, the bodies of which the heavens are
framed. From what has been said it is plain, then, that
philosophic wisdom is scientific knowledge, combined with
intuitive reason, of the things that are highest by nature.
This is why we say Anaxagoras, Thales, and men like them
have philosophic but not practical wisdom, when we see 5
them ignorant of what is to their own advantage, and why
we say that they know things that are remarkable, admirable, difficult, and divine, but useless; viz. because it is not
human goods that they seek.

Practical wisdom on the other hand is concerned with
things human and things about which it is possible to
deliberate; for we say this is above all the work of the man 10
of practical wisdom, to deliberate well, but no one deliberates about things invariable, nor about things which have
not an end, and that a good that can be brought about by
action. The man who is without qualification good at delib-

erating is the man who is capable of aiming in accordance
with calculation at the best for man of things attainable by
15 action. Nor is practical wisdom concerned with universals
only—it must also recognize the particulars; for it is practical, and practice is concerned with particulars. This is why
some who do not know, and especially those who have
experience, are more practical than others who know; for
if a man knew that light meats are digestible and wholesome, but did not know which sorts of meat are light, he
20 would not produce health, but the man who knows that
chicken is wholesome is more likely to produce health.

Now practical wisdom is concerned with action; therefore one should have both forms of it, or the latter in preference to the former. But of practical as of philosophic
wisdom there must be a controlling kind.

8 Political wisdom and practical wisdom are the same
state of mind, but their essence is not the same. Of the
wisdom concerned with the city, the practical wisdom
which plays a controlling part is legislative wisdom, while
25 that which is related to this as particulars to their universal
is known by the general name 'political wisdom'; this has to
do with action and deliberation, for a decree is a thing to
be carried out in the form of an individual act. This is why
the exponents of this art are alone said to 'take part in
politics'; for these alone 'do things' as manual labourers 'do
things'.

Practical wisdom also is identified especially with that
form of it which is concerned with a man himself—with
the individual; and this is known by the general name
30 'practical wisdom'; of the other kinds one is called household management, another legislation, the third politics,
and of the latter one part is called deliberative and the other
judicial. Now knowing what is good for oneself will be one
kind of knowledge, but it is very different from the other
1142ª kinds; and the man who knows and concerns himself with
his own interests is thought to have practical wisdom,

while politicians are thought to be busybodies; hence the words of Euripides,

> But how could I be wise, who might at ease,
> Numbered among the army's multitude,
> Have had an equal share? . . .
> For those who aim too high and do too much 5

Those who think thus seek their own good, and consider that one ought to do so. From this opinion, then, has come the view that such men have practical wisdom; yet perhaps one's own good cannot exist without household manage- ment, nor without a form of government. Further, how 10 one should order one's own affairs is not clear and needs inquiry.

What has been said is confirmed by the fact that while young men become geometricians and mathematicians and wise in matters like these, it is thought that a young man of practical wisdom cannot be found. The cause is that such wisdom is concerned not only with universals but with particulars, which become familiar from experience, but a 15 young man has no experience, for it is length of time that gives experience; indeed one might ask this question too, why a boy may become a mathematician, but not a philos- opher or a physicist. Is it because the objects of mathe- matics exist by abstraction, while the first principles of these other subjects come from experience, and because young men have no conviction about the latter but merely use the proper language, while the essence of mathematical objects is plain enough to them?

Further, error in deliberation may be either about the 20 universal or about the particular; we may fail to know either that all water that weighs heavy is bad, or that this particu- lar water weighs heavy.

That practical wisdom is not scientific knowledge is evident; for it is, as has been said,[9] concerned with the ultimate particular fact, since the thing to be done is of this 25

[9] 1141ᵇ 14–22.

nature. It is opposed, then, to intuitive reason; for intuitive reason is of the limiting premisses, for which no reason can be given, while practical wisdom is concerned with the ultimate particular, which is the object not of scientific knowledge but of perception—not the perception of qualities peculiar to one sense but a perception akin to that by which we perceive that the particular figure before us is a triangle; for in that direction as well as in that of the major premiss there will be a limit. But this is rather perception
30 than practical wisdom, though it is another kind of perception than that of the qualities peculiar to each sense.

9 There is a difference between inquiry and deliberation; for deliberation is inquiry into a particular kind of thing. We must grasp the nature of excellence in deliberation as well—whether it is a form of scientific knowledge, or opinion, or skill in conjecture, or some other kind of thing. Scientific knowledge it is not; for men do not
1142ᵇ inquire about the things they know about, but good deliberation is a kind of deliberation, and he who deliberates inquires and calculates. Nor is it skill in conjecture; for this both involves no reasoning and is something that is quick in its operation, while men deliberate a long time, and they say that one should carry out quickly the con-
5 clusions of one's deliberation, but should deliberate slowly. Again, readiness of mind is different from excellence in deliberation; it is a sort of skill in conjecture. Nor again is excellence in deliberation opinion of any sort. But since the man who deliberates badly makes a mistake, while he who deliberates well does so correctly, excellence in deliberation is clearly a kind of correctness, but neither of knowledge nor of opinion; for there is no such thing as
10 correctness of knowledge (since there is no such thing as error of knowledge), and correctness of opinion is truth; and at the same time everything that is an object of opinion is already determined. But again excellence in deliberation involves reasoning. The remaining alternative, then, is that

it is correctness of thinking; for this is not yet assertion, since, while even opinion is not inquiry but has reached the stage of assertion, the man who is deliberating, whether he does so well or ill, is searching for something and calcu- 15 lating.

But excellence in deliberation is a certain correctness of deliberation; hence we must first inquire what deliberation is and what it is about. And, there being more than one kind of correctness, plainly excellence in deliberation is not any and every kind; for (1) the incontinent man and the bad man, if he is clever, will reach as a result of his calculation what he sets before himself, so that he will have deliberated correctly, but he will have got for himself a great evil. Now to have deliberated well is thought to be a good thing; for it is this kind of correctness of deliberation 20 that is excellence in deliberation, viz. that which tends to attain what is good. But (2) it is possible to attain even good by a false syllogism, and to attain what one ought to do but not by the right means, the middle term being false; so that this too is not yet excellence in deliberation —this state in virtue of which one attains what one ought 25 but not by the right means. Again (3) it is possible to attain it by long deliberation while another man attains it quickly. Therefore in the former case we have not yet got excellence in deliberation, which is rightness with regard to the expedient—rightness in respect both of the end, the manner, and the time. (4) Further it is possible to have deliberated well either in the unqualified sense or with reference to a particular end. Excellence in deliberation in the unqualified sense, then, is that which succeeds with reference to what is the end in the unqualified sense, and excellence in deliberation in a particular sense is that which 30 succeeds relatively to a particular end. If, then, it is characteristic of men of practical wisdom to have deliberated well, excellence in deliberation will be correctness with regard to what conduces to the end of which practical wisdom is the true apprehension.

10 Understanding, also, and goodness of understanding, in virtue of which men are said to be men of under-143ᵃstanding or of good understanding, are neither entirely the same as opinion or scientific knowledge (for at that rate all men would have been men of understanding), nor are they one of the particular sciences, such as medicine, the science of things connected with health, or geometry, 5 the science of spatial magnitudes. For understanding is neither about things that are always and are unchangeable, nor about any and every one of the things that come into being, but about things which may become subjects of questioning and deliberation. Hence it is about the same objects as practical wisdom; but understanding and practical wisdom are not the same. For practical wisdom issues commands, since its end is what ought to be done or not to be done; but understanding only judges. (Un-10 derstanding is identical with goodness of understanding, men of understanding with men of good understanding.) Now understanding is neither the having nor the acquiring of practical wisdom; but as learning is called understanding when it means the exercise of the faculty of knowledge, so 'understanding' is applicable to the exercise of the faculty of opinion for the purpose of judging of what some one else says about matters with which practical wis-15 dom is concerned—and of judging soundly; for 'well' and 'soundly' are the same thing. And from this has come the use of the name 'understanding' in virtue of which men are said to be 'of good understanding', viz. from the application of the word to the grasping of scientific truth; for we often call such grasping understanding.

11 What is called judgement, in virtue of which men are 20 said to 'be sympathetic judges' and to 'have judgement', is the right discrimination of the equitable. This is shown by the fact that we say the equitable man is above all others a man of sympathetic judgement, and identify equity with sympathetic judgement about certain facts.

And sympathetic judgement is judgement which discriminates what is equitable and does so correctly; and correct
judgement is that which judges what is true.

Now all the states we have considered converge, as might 25
be expected, to the same point; for when we speak of
judgement and understanding and practical wisdom and
intuitive reason we credit the same people with possessing
judgement and having reached years of reason and with
having practical wisdom and understanding. For all these
faculties deal with ultimates, i. e. with particulars; and
being a man of understanding and of good or sympathetic
judgement consists in being able to judge about the things 30
with which practical wisdom is concerned; for the equities
are common to all good men in relation to other men. Now
all things which have to be done are included among
particulars or ultimates; for not only must the man of
practical wisdom know particular facts, but understanding
and judgement are also concerned with things to be done,
and these are ultimates. And intuitive reason is concerned
with the ultimates in both directions; for both the first 35
terms and the last are objects of intuitive reason and not
of argument, and the intuitive reason which is presupposed 1143ᵃ
by demonstrations grasps the unchangeable and first terms,
while the intuitive reason involved in practical reasonings
grasps the last and variable fact, i. e. the minor premiss.
For these variable facts are the starting-points for the
apprehension of the end, since the universals are reached
from the particulars; of these therefore we must have per- 5
ception, and this perception is intuitive reason.

This is why these states are thought to be natural endowments—why, while no one is thought to be a philosopher
by nature, people are thought to have by nature judgement,
understanding, and intuitive reason. This is shown by the
fact that we think our powers correspond to our time of
life, and that a particular age brings with it intuitive reason
and judgement; this implies that nature is the cause.
[Hence intuitive reason is both beginning and end; for

10 demonstrations are from these and about these.] Therefore we ought to attend to the undemonstrated sayings and opinions of experienced and older people or of people of practical wisdom not less than to demonstrations; for because experience has given them an eye they see aright.

We have stated, then, what practical and philosophic wisdom are, and with what each of them is concerned, and 15 we have said that each is the virtue of a different part of the soul.

12 Difficulties might be raised as to the utility of these qualities of mind. For (1) philosophic wisdom will contemplate none of the things that will make a man happy (for it is not concerned with any coming into be- 20 ing), and though practical wisdom has *this* merit, for what purpose do we need it? Practical wisdom is the quality of mind concerned with things just and noble and good for man, but these are the things which it is the mark of a good man to do, and we are none the more able to act for *knowing* them if the virtues are states of *character*, just 25 as we are none the better able to act for knowing the things that are healthy and sound, in the sense not of producing but of issuing from the state of health; for we are none the more able to act for having the art of medicine or of gymnastics. But (2) if we are to say that a man should have practical wisdom not for the sake of knowing moral truths 30 but for the sake of becoming good, practical wisdom will be of no use to those who are good; but again it is of no use to those who have *not* virtue; for it will make no difference whether they have practical wisdom themselves or obey others who have it, and it would be enough for us to do what we do in the case of health; though we wish to become healthy, yet we do not learn the art of medicine. (3) Besides this, it would be thought strange if practical wisdom, being inferior to philosophic wisdom, is to be put in authority over it, as seems to be implied by the fact that

the art which produces anything rules and issues commands
about that thing.

These, then, are the questions we must discuss; so far we 35
have only stated the difficulties.

(1) Now first let us say that in themselves these states 1144ª
must be worthy of choice because they are the virtues of
the two parts of the soul respectively, even if neither of
them produce anything.

(2) Secondly, they do produce something, not as the art
of medicine produces health, however, but as health produces health;[10] so does philosophic wisdom produce happiness; for, being a part of virtue entire, by being possessed 5
and by actualizing itself it makes a man happy.

(3) Again, the work of man is achieved only in accordance with practical wisdom as well as with moral virtue; for
virtue makes us aim at the right mark, and practical wisdom makes us take the right means. (Of the fourth part of
the soul—the nutritive [11]—there is no such virtue; for 10
there is nothing which it is in its power to do or not to do.)

(4) With regard to our being none the more able to do
because of our practical wisdom what is noble and just, let
us begin a little further back, starting with the following
principle. As we say that some people who do just acts are
not necessarily just, i. e. those who do the acts ordained 15
by the laws either unwillingly or owing to ignorance or for
some other reason and not for the sake of the acts themselves (though, to be sure, they do what they should and
all the things that the good man ought), so is it, it seems,
that in order to be good one must be in a certain state when
one does the several acts, i. e. one must do them as a result 20
of choice and for the sake of the acts themselves. Now
virtue makes the choice right, but the question of the
things which should naturally be done to carry out our

[10] i. e. as health, as an inner state, produces the activities which we
know as constituting health.

[11] The other three being the scientific, the calculative, and the desiderative.

choice belongs not to virtue but to another faculty. We
must devote our attention to these matters and give a
clearer statement about them. There is a faculty which is
25 called cleverness; and this is such as to be able to do the
things that tend towards the mark we have set before ourselves, and to hit it. Now if the mark be noble, the cleverness is laudable, but if the mark be bad, the cleverness is
mere smartness; hence we call even men of practical wisdom clever or smart. Practical wisdom is not the faculty,
but it does not exist without this faculty. And this eye of
30 the soul acquires its formed state not without the aid of
virtue, as has been said [12] and is plain; for the syllogisms
which deal with acts to be done are things which involve a
starting-point, viz. 'since the end, i. e. what is best, is of
such and such a nature', whatever it may be (let it for the
sake of argument be what we please); and this is not evident except to the good man; for wickedness perverts us
35 and causes us to be deceived about the starting-points of
action. Therefore it is evident that it is impossible to be
practically wise without being good.

13 We must therefore consider virtue also once more;
1144ᵇ   for virtue too is similarly related; as practical wisdom
is to cleverness—not the same, but like it—so is natural
virtue to virtue in the strict sense. For all men think that
each type of character belongs to its possessors in some
sense by nature; for from the very moment of birth we are
5 just or fitted for self-control or brave or have the other
moral qualities; but yet we seek something else as that
which is good in the strict sense—we seek for the presence
of such qualities in another way. For both children and
brutes have the natural dispositions to these qualities, but
without reason these are evidently hurtful. Only we seem
10 to see this much, that, while one may be led astray by them,
as a strong body which moves without sight may stumble
badly because of its lack of sight, still, if a man once ac-

[12] ll. 6–26.

quires reason, that makes a difference in action; and his
state, while still like what it was, will then be virtue in the
strict sense. Therefore, as in the part of us which forms
opinions there are two types, cleverness and practical wisdom, so too in the moral part there are two types, natural 15
virtue and virtue in the strict sense, and of these the latter
involves practical wisdom. This is why some say that all the
virtues are forms of practical wisdom, and why Socrates in
one respect was on the right track while in another he went
astray; in thinking that all the virtues were forms of practical wisdom he was wrong, but in saying they implied practical wisdom he was right. This is confirmed by the fact 20
that even now all men, when they define virtue, after nam-
ing the state of character and its objects add 'that (state)
which is in accordance with the right rule'; now the right
rule is that which is in accordance with practical wisdom.
All men, then, seem somehow to divine that this kind of
state is virtue, viz. that which is in accordance with practical 25
wisdom. But we must go a little further. For it is not
merely the state in accordance with the right rule, but the
state that implies the presence of the right rule, that is
virtue; and practical wisdom is a right rule about such
matters. Socrates, then, thought the virtues were rules or
rational principles (for he thought they were, all of them,
forms of scientific knowledge), while we think they *involve*
a rational principle.

It is clear, then, from what has been said, that it is not 30
possible to be good in the strict sense without practical
wisdom, nor practically wise without moral virtue. But in
this way we may also refute the dialectical argument whereby it might be contended that the virtues exist in separation
from each other; the same man, it might be said, is not
best equipped by nature for all the virtues, so that he will
have already acquired one when he has not yet acquired 35
another. This is possible in respect of the natural virtues,
but not in respect of those in respect of which a man is 1145ᵃ
called without qualification good; for with the presence of

the one quality, practical wisdom, will be given all the virtues. And it is plain that, even if it were of no practical value, we should have needed it because it is the virtue of the part of us in question; plain too that the choice will
5 not be right without practical wisdom any more than without virtue; for the one determines the end and the other makes us do the things that lead to the end.

But again it is not *supreme* over philosophic wisdom, i. e. over the superior part of us, any more than the art of medicine is over health; for it does not use it but provides
10 for its coming into being; it issues orders, then, for its sake, but not to it. Further, to maintain its supremacy would be like saying that the art of politics rules the gods because it issues orders about all the affairs of the state.

BOOK VII

15 **1**   Let us now make a fresh beginning and point out that of moral states to be avoided there are three kinds— vice, incontinence, brutishness. The contraries of two of these are evident—one we call virtue, the other continence;
20 to brutishness it would be most fitting to oppose super-human virtue, a heroic and divine kind of nature, as Homer has represented Priam saying of Hector that he was very good,

> For he seemed not, he,
> The child of a mortal man, but as one that of God's
>   seed came.[1]

Therefore if, as they say, men become gods by excess of virtue, of this kind must evidently be the state opposed to the brutish state; for as a brute has no vice or virtue, so
25 neither has a god; his state is higher than virtue, and that of a brute is a different kind of state from vice.

Now, since it is rarely that a godlike man is found—to use the epithet of the Spartans, who when they admire any one highly call him a 'godlike man'—so too the brutish

[1] *Il.* xxiv. 258 f.

type is rarely found among men; it is found chiefly among
barbarians, but some brutish qualities are also produced 30
by disease or deformity; and we also call by this evil name
those men who go beyond all ordinary standards by
reason of vice. Of this kind of disposition, however, we
must later make some mention,[2] while we have discussed
vice before;[3] we must now discuss incontinence and softness (or effeminacy), and continence and endurance; for 35
we must treat each of the two neither as identical with
virtue or wickedness, nor as a different genus. We must, as **1145ᵇ**
in all other cases, set the observed facts before us and, after
first discussing the difficulties, go on to prove, if possible,
the truth of all the common opinions about these affections
of the mind, or, failing this, of the greater number and the
most authoritative; for if we both refute the objections 5
and leave the common opinions undisturbed, we shall
have proved the case sufficiently.

Now (1) both continence and endurance are thought
to be included among things good and praiseworthy, and
both incontinence and softness among things bad and
blameworthy; and the same man is thought to be continent 10
and ready to abide by the result of his calculations, or incontinent and ready to abandon them. And (2) the incontinent man, knowing that what he does is bad, does it
as a result of passion, while the continent man, knowing
that his appetites are bad, refuses on account of his rational principle to follow them. (3) The temperate man
all men call continent and disposed to endurance, while 15
the continent man some maintain to be always temperate
but others do not; and some call the self-indulgent man
incontinent and the incontinent man self-indulgent indiscriminately while others distinguish them. (4) The man
of practical wisdom, they sometimes say, cannot be incontinent, while sometimes they say that some who are
practically wise and clever are incontinent. Again (5) men

[2] Ch. 5.
[3] Bks. II–V.

are said to be incontinent even with respect to anger,
20 honour, and gain.—These, then, are the things that are
said.

2 Now we may ask (1) how a man who judges rightly can
behave incontinently. That he should behave so when
he has knowledge, some say is impossible; for it would be
strange—so Socrates [4] thought—if when knowledge was in
25 a man something else could master it and drag it about
like a slave. For *Socrates* was entirely opposed to the view
in question, holding that there is no such thing as incontinence; no one, he said, when he judges acts against
what he judges best—people act so only by reason of
ignorance. Now this view plainly contradicts the observed facts, and we must inquire about what happens to
such a man; if he acts by reason of ignorance, what is the
30 manner of his ignorance? For that the man who behaves
incontinently does not, before he gets into this state, *think*
he ought to act so, is evident. But there are some who con-
cede certain of Socrates' contentions but not others; that
nothing is stronger than knowledge they admit, but not
that no one acts contrary to what has seemed to him the
better course, and therefore they say that the incontinent
man has not knowledge when he is mastered by his
35 pleasures, but opinion. But *if* it is opinion and not knowl-
1146ᵃ edge, if it is not a strong conviction that resists but a weak
one, as in men who hesitate, we sympathize with their
failure to stand by such convictions against strong appetites; but we do not sympathize with wickedness, nor
with any of the other blameworthy states. Is it then
5 *practical wisdom* whose resistance is mastered? That is the
strongest of all states. But this is absurd; the same man will
be at once practically wise and incontinent, but no one
would say that it is the part of a practically wise man to do
willingly the basest acts. Besides, it has been shown before
that the man of practical wisdom is one who will act [5] (for

---

4 *Ti. Prot.* 352 b, c
5 1140ᵇ 4-6.

he is a man concerned with the individual facts) [6] and who has the other virtues.[7]

(2) Further, if continence involves having strong and bad appetites, the temperate man will not be continent nor the continent man temperate; for a temperate man will have neither excessive nor bad appetites. But the continent man must; for if the appetites are good, the state of character that restrains us from following them is bad, so that not all continence will be good; while if they are weak and not bad, there is nothing admirable in resisting them, and if they are weak and bad, there is nothing great in resisting these either.

(3) Further, if continence makes a man ready to stand by any and every opinion, it is bad, i. e. if it makes him stand even by a false opinion; and if incontinence makes a man apt to abandon any and every opinion, there will be a good incontinence, of which Sophocles' Neoptolemus in the *Philoctetes* [8] will be an instance; for he is to be praised for not standing by what Odysseus persuaded him to do, because he is pained at telling a lie.

(4) Further, the sophistic argument presents a difficulty; the syllogism arising from men's wish to expose paradoxical results arising from an opponent's view, in order that they may be admired when they succeed, is one that puts us in a difficulty (for thought is bound fast when it will not rest because the conclusion does not satisfy it, and cannot advance because it cannot refute the argument). There is an argument from which it follows that folly coupled with incontinence is virtue; for a man does the opposite of what he judges, owing to incontinence, but judges what is good to be evil and something that he should not do, and in consequence he will do what is good and not what is evil.

(5) Further, he who on conviction does and pursues and chooses what is pleasant would be thought to be better than one who does so as a result not of calculation but of

---

[6] 1141[b] 16, 1142[a] 24.
[7] 1144[b] 30–1145[a] 2.
[8] ll. 895–916.

incontinence; for he is easier to cure since he may be persuaded to change his mind. But to the incontinent man may be applied the proverb 'when water chokes, what is one to wash it down with?' If he had been persuaded of
35 the rightness of what he does, he would have desisted when
1146ᵇ he was persuaded to change his mind; but now he acts in spite of his being persuaded of something quite different.

(6) Further, if incontinence and continence are concerned with any and every kind of object, who is it that is incontinent in the unqualified sense? No one has all the forms of incontinence, but we say some people are in-
5 continent without qualification.

3   Of some such kind are the difficulties that arise; some of these points must be refuted and the others left in possession of the field; for the solution of the difficulty is the discovery of the truth. (1) We must consider first, then, whether incontinent people act knowingly or not, and in what sense knowingly; then (2) with what sorts of object the incontinent and the continent man may be said to be concerned (i. e. whether with any and every
10 pleasure and pain or with certain determinate kinds), and whether the continent man and the man of endurance are the same or different; and similarly with regard to the other matters germane to this inquiry. The starting-point of our investigation is (a) the question whether the continent man and the incontinent are differentiated by their objects
15 or by their attitude, i. e. whether the incontinent man is incontinent simply by being concerned with such and such objects, or, instead, by his attitude, or, instead of that, by both these things; (b) the second question is whether incontinence and continence are concerned with any and every object or not. The man who is incontinent in the unqualified sense is neither concerned with any and every
20 object, but with precisely those with which the self-indulgent man is concerned, nor is he characterized by being simply related to these (for then his state would be the same as self-indulgence), but by being related to them in a

certain way. For the one is led on in accordance with his own choice, thinking that he ought always to pursue the present pleasure; while the other does not think so, but yet pursues it.

(1) As for the suggestion that it is true opinion and not knowledge against which we act incontinently, that makes no difference to the argument; for some people when in a state of opinion do not hesitate, but think they know exactly. If, then, the notion is that owing to their weak conviction those who have opinion are more likely to act against their judgement than those who know, we answer that there need be no difference between knowledge and opinion in this respect; for some men are no less convinced of what they think than others of what they know; as is shown by the case of Heraclitus. But (a), since we use the word 'know' in two senses (for both the man who has knowledge but is not using it and he who is using it are said to know), it will make a difference whether, when a man does what he should not, he has the knowledge but is not exercising it, or is exercising it; for the latter seems strange, but not the former.

(b) Further, since there are two kinds of premisses, there is nothing to prevent a man's having both premisses and acting against his knowledge, provided that he is using only the universal premiss and not the particular; for it is particular acts that have to be done. And there are also two kinds of universal term; one is predicable of the agent, the other of the object; e. g. 'dry food is good for every man', and 'I am a man', or 'such and such food is dry'; but whether 'this food is such and such', of this the incontinent man either has not or is not exercising the knowledge.[9] There will, then, be, firstly, an enormous difference between these manners of knowing, so that to know

---

[9] i. e., if I am to be able to deduce from (a) 'dry food is good for all men' that 'this food is good for me', I must have (b) the premiss 'I am a man' and (c) the premisses (i) 'x food is dry', (ii) 'this food is x'. I cannot fail to know (b), and I may know (c i); but if I do not know (c ii), or know it only 'at the back of my mind', I shall not draw the conclusion.

in one way when we act incontinently would not seem anything strange, while to know in the other way would be extraordinary.

And further (c) the possession of knowledge in another sense than those just named is something that happens to men; for within the case of having knowledge but not using it we see a difference of state, admitting of the possibility of having knowledge in a sense and yet not having it, as in the instance of a man asleep, mad, or drunk. But now this is just the condition of men under the influence of passion; for outbursts of anger and sexual appetites and some other such passions, it is evident, actually alter our bodily condition, and in some men even produce fits of madness. It is plain, then, that incontinent people must be said to be in a similar condition to men asleep, mad, or drunk. The fact that men use the language that flows from knowledge proves nothing; for even men under the influence of these passions utter scientific proofs and verses of Empedocles, and those who have just begun to learn a science can string together its phrases, but do not yet know it; for it has to become part of themselves, and that takes time; so that we must suppose that the use of language by men in an incontinent state means no more than its utterance by actors on the stage.

(d) Again, we may also view the cause as follows with reference to the facts of human nature. The one opinion is universal, the other is concerned with the particular facts, and here we come to something within the sphere of perception; when a single opinion results from the two, the soul must in one type of case [10] affirm the conclusion, while in the case of opinions concerned with production it must immediately act (e. g. if 'everything sweet ought to be tasted', and 'this is sweet', in the sense of being one of the particular sweet things, the man who can act and is not prevented must at the same time actually act accordingly). When, then, the universal opinion is present in us for

[10] i. e. in scientific reasoning.

bidding us to taste, and there is also the opinion that 'everything sweet is pleasant', and that 'this is sweet' (now this is the opinion that is active),[11] and when appetite happens to be present in us, the one opinion bids us avoid the object, but appetite leads us towards it (for it can move 35 each of our bodily parts); so that it turns out that a man behaves incontinently under the influence (in a sense) of a rule and an opinion, and of one not contrary in itself, but only incidentally—for the appetite is contrary, not the 1147 opinion—to the right rule. It also follows that this is the reason why the lower animals are not incontinent, viz. because they have no universal judgment but only imagina- 5 tion and memory of particulars.

The explanation of how the ignorance is dissolved and the incontinent man regains his knowledge, is the same as in the case of the man drunk or asleep and is not particular to this condition; we must go to the students of natural science for it. Now, the last premiss both being an opinion about a perceptible object, and being what determines our 10 actions, this a man either has not when he is in the state of passion, or has it in the sense in which having knowledge did not mean knowing but only talking, as a drunken man may mutter the verses of Empedocles.[12] And because the last term is not universal nor equally an object of scientific knowledge with the universal term, the position that 15 Socrates sought to establish [13] actually seems to result; for it is not in the presence of what is thought to be knowledge proper that the affection of incontinence arises (nor is it this that is dragged about' as a result of the state of passion), but in that of perceptual knowledge.[14]

This must suffice as our answer to the question of action

---

[11] i. e. determines action (Cf. [b]10).
[12] Cf. [a]10–24.
[13] 1145[b] 22–24.
[14] Even before the minor premiss of the practical syllogism has been obscured by passion, the incontinent man has not scientific knowledge in the strict sense, since his minor premiss is not universal but has for its subject a sensible particular, e. g. 'this glass of wine'.

with and without knowledge, and how it is possible to behave incontinently with knowledge.

20 **4**   (2) We must next discuss whether there is any one
who is incontinent without qualification, or all men
who are incontinent are so in a particular sense, and if there
is, with what sort of objects he is concerned. That both
continent persons and persons of endurance, and incontinent and soft persons, are concerned with pleasures and
pains, is evident.

Now of the things that produce pleasure some are necessary, while others are worthy of choice in themselves
25 but admit of excess, the bodily causes of pleasure being
necessary (by such I mean both those concerned with food
and those concerned with sexual intercourse, i. e. the bodily
matters with which we defined [15] self-indulgence and temperance as being concerned), while the others are not
necessary but worthy of choice in themselves (e. g. victory,
30 honour, wealth, and good and pleasant things of this sort).
This being so, (a) those who go to excess with reference to
the latter, contrary to the right rule which is in themselves, are not called incontinent simply, but incontinent
with the qualification 'in respect of money, gain, honour,
or anger',—not simply incontinent, on the ground that they
are different from incontinent people and are called incontinent by reason of a resemblance. (Compare the case
35 of Anthropos (Man), who won a contest at the Olympic
1148ᵃ games; in his case the general definition of man differed
little from the definition peculiar to *him*, but yet it was
different.) [16] This is shown by the fact that incontinence
either without qualification or in respect of some particular
bodily pleasure is blamed not only as a fault but as a kind of
vice, while none of the people who are incontinent in these
other respects is so blamed.

[15] III. 10.
[16] i. e. the definition appropriate to him was not 'rational animal'
but 'rational animal who won the boxing contest at Olympia in 456
B. C.'

But (*b*) of the people who are incontinent with respect to bodily enjoyments, with which we say the temperate and the self-indulgent man are concerned, he who pursues the excesses of things pleasant—and shuns those of things painful, of hunger and thirst and heat and cold and all the objects of touch and taste—not by choice but contrary to his choice and his judgment, is called incontinent, not with the qualification 'in respect of this or that', e. g. of anger, but just simply. This is confirmed by the fact that men are called 'soft' with regard to these pleasures, but not with regard to any of the others. And for this reason we group together the incontinent and the self-indulgent, the continent and the temperate man—but not any of these other types—because they are concerned somehow with the same pleasures and pains; but though these are concerned with the same objects, they are not similarly related to them, but some of them make a deliberate choice while the others do not.[17]

This is why we should describe as self-indulgent rather the man who without appetite or with but a slight appetite pursues the excesses of pleasure and avoids moderate pains, than the man who does so because of his strong appetites; for what would the former do, if he had in addition a vigorous appetite, and a violent pain at the lack of the 'necessary' objects?

Now of appetites and pleasures some belong to the class of things generically noble and good—for some pleasant things are by nature worthy of choice, while others are contrary to these, and others are intermediate, to adopt our previous distinction [18]—e. g. wealth, gain, victory, honour. And with reference to all objects whether of this or of the intermediate kind men are not blamed for being affected by them, for desiring and loving them, but for doing so in a certain way, i. e. for going to excess. (This is why all those

---

[17] i. e. the temperate and the self-indulgent, not the continent and the incontinent.

[18] 1147ᵇ 23–31, where, however, the 'contraries' are not mentioned.

who contrary to the rule either are mastered by or pursue
30 one of the objects which are naturally noble and good, e. g.
those who busy themselves more than they ought about
honour or about children and parents, [are not wicked]; for
these too are goods, and those who busy themselves about
them are praised; but yet there is an excess even in them—
if like Niobe one were to fight even against the gods, or
1148ᵇ were to be as much devoted to one's father as Satyrus
nicknamed 'the filial', who was thought to be very silly on
this point.[19]) There is no wickedness, then, with regard to
these objects, for the reason named, viz. because each of
them is by nature a thing worthy of choice for its own sake;
yet excesses in respect of them are bad and to be avoided.
5 Similarly there is no incontinence with regard to them; for
incontinence is not only to be avoided but is also a thing
worthy of blame; but owing to a similarity in the state of
feeling people apply the name incontinence, adding in
each case what it is in respect of, as we may describe as a
bad doctor or a bad actor one whom we should not call
bad, simply. As, then, in this case we do not apply the term
without qualification because each of these conditions is
10 not badness but only analogous to it, so it is clear that in
the other case also that alone must be taken to be incontinence and continence which is concerned with the same
objects as temperance and self-indulgence, but we apply
the term to anger by virtue of a resemblance; and this is
why we say with a qualification 'incontinent in respect of
anger' as we say 'incontinent in respect of honour, or of
gain'.

15 **5**   (1) Some things are pleasant by nature, and of these
(a) some are so without qualification, and (b) others
are so with reference to particular classes either of animals
or of men; while (2) others are not pleasant by nature,

---

[19] Nothing is really known about the Satyrus referred to, but Prof.
Burnet's suggestion that he was a king of Bosporus who deified his father seems probable.

but (a) some of them become so by reason of injuries to the system, and (b) others by reason of acquired habits, and (c) others by reason of originally bad natures. This being so, it is possible with regard to each of the latter kinds to discover similar states of character to those recognized with regard to the former; I mean (A) the brutish states,[20] 2c as in the case of the female who, they say, rips open pregnant women and devours the infants, or of the things in which some of the tribes about the Black Sea that have gone savage are said to delight—in raw meat or in human flesh, or in lending their children to one another to feast upon—or of the story told of Phalaris.[21]

These states are brutish, but (B) others arise as a result of disease [22] (or, in some cases, of madness, as with the man who sacrificed and ate his mother, or with the slave 23 who ate the liver of his fellow), and others are morbid states (C) resulting from custom,[23] e. g. the habit of plucking out the hair or of gnawing the nails, or even coals or earth, and in addition to these paederasty; for these arise in some by nature and in others, as in those who have been the victims of lust from childhood, from habit. 30

Now those in whom nature is the cause of such a state no one would call incontinent, any more than one would apply the epithet to women because of the passive part they play in copulation; nor would one apply it to those who are in a morbid condition as a result of habit. To have these various types of habit is beyond the limits of vice, as brutishness is too; for a man who has them to master or be 1149ᵇ mastered by them is not simple [continence or] incontinence but that which is so by analogy, as the man who is in this condition in respect of fits of anger is to be called incontinent in respect of that feeling, but not incontinent simply.

For every excessive state whether of folly, of cowardice,

---

[20] Answering to (2 c).
[21] sc. and the bull. But Cf. 1149ᵃ 14.
[22] Answering to (2 a).
[23] Answering to (2 b).

5 of self-indulgence, or of bad temper, is either brutish or morbid; the man who is by nature apt to fear everything, even the squeak of a mouse, is cowardly with a brutish cowardice, while the man who feared a weasel did so in consequence of disease; and of foolish people those who by nature are thoughtless and live by their senses alone are brutish, like some races of the distant barbarians, while 10 those who are so as a result of disease (e. g. of epilepsy) or of madness are morbid. Of these characteristics it is possible to have some only at times, and not to be mastered by them, e. g. Phalaris may have restrained a desire to eat the flesh of a child or an appetite for unnatural sexual pleasure; but it is also possible to be mastered, not merely 15 to have the feelings. Thus, as the wickedness which is on the human level is called wickedness simply, while that which is not is called wickedness not simply but with the qualification 'brutish' or 'morbid', in the same way it is plain that some incontinence is brutish and some morbid, 20 while only that which corresponds to human self-indulgence is incontinence simply.

That incontinence and continence, then, are concerned only with the same objects as self-indulgence and temperance and that what is concerned with other objects is a type distinct from incontinence, and called incontinence by a metaphor and not simply, is plain.

6   That incontinence in respect of anger is less disgraceful than that in respect of the appetites is what we 25 will now proceed to see. (1) Anger seems to listen to argument to some extent, but to mishear it, as do hasty servants who run out before they have heard the whole of what one says, and then muddle the order, or as dogs bark if there is but a knock at the door, before looking to see if it is a 30 friend; so anger by reason of the warmth and hastiness of its nature, though it hears, does not hear an order, and springs to take revenge. For argument or imagination informs us that we have been insulted or slighted, and anger, reasoning as it were that anything like this must be fought against, boils up straightway; while appetite, if argument or perception merely says that an object is pleasant, springs 35 to the enjoyment of it. Therefore anger obeys the argu- **1149** ment in a sense, but appetite does not. It is therefore more disgraceful; for the man who is incontinent in respect of anger is in a sense conquered by argument, while the other is conquered by appetite and not by argument.

(2) Further, we pardon people more easily for following natural desires, since we pardon them more easily for 5 following such appetites as are common to all men, and in so far as they are common; now anger and bad temper are more natural than the appetites for excess, i. e. for unnecessary objects. Take for instance the man who defended himself on the charge of striking his father by saying 'yes, but he struck his father, and he struck his,' and' 10 (pointing to his child) 'this boy will strike me when he is a man; it runs in the family'; or the man who when he was being dragged along by his son bade him stop at the doorway, since he himself had dragged his father only as far as that.

(3) Further, those who are more given to plotting against others are more criminal. Now a passionate man is not given to plotting, nor is anger itself—it is open; but 15 the nature of appetite is illustrated by what the poets call Aphrodite, 'guile-weaving daughter of Cyprus', and by Homer's words about her 'embroidered girdle':

> And the whisper of wooing is there,
> Whose subtlety stealeth the wits of the wise, how
>   prudent soe'er.[24]

Therefore if this form of incontinence is more criminal and disgraceful than that in respect of anger, it is both incontinence without qualification and in a sense vice.

(4) Further, no one commits wanton outrage with a feeling of pain, but every one who acts in anger acts with 20

[24] *Il.* xiv. 214, 217.

pain, while the man who commits outrage acts with pleasure. If, then, those acts at which it is most just to be angry are more criminal than others, the incontinence which is due to appetite is the more criminal; for there is no wanton outrage involved in anger.

Plainly, then, the incontinence concerned with appetite is more disgraceful than that concerned with anger,
25 and continence and incontinence are concerned with bodily appetites and pleasures; but we must grasp the differences among the latter themselves. For, as has been said at the beginning,[25] some are human and natural both in kind and in magnitude, others are brutish, and others are due to organic injuries and diseases. Only with the first
30 of these are temperance and self-indulgence concerned; this is why we call the lower animals neither temperate nor self-indulgent except by a metaphor, and only if some one race of animals exceeds another as a whole in wantonness, destructiveness, and omnivorous greed; these have no power of choice or calculation, but they are departures
35 from the natural norm,[26] as, among men, madmen are. Now
1150ᵃ brutishness is a less evil than vice, though more alarming; for it is not that the better part has been perverted, as in man—they have no better part. Thus it is like comparing a lifeless thing with a living in respect of badness; for the badness of that which has no originative source of movement is always less hurtful, and reason is an originative
5 source. Thus it is like comparing injustice in the abstract with an unjust man. Each is in some sense worse; for a bad man will do ten thousand times as much evil as a brute.

7   With regard to the pleasures and pains and appetites and aversions arising through touch and taste, to which
10 both self-indulgence and temperance were formerly narrowed down,[27] it is possible to be in such a state as to be

[25] 1148ᵇ 15–31.
[26] And therefore cannot be called self-indulgent properly, but can be so called by a metaphor.
[27] III. 10.

defeated even by those of them which most people master,
or to master even those by which most people are defeated;
among these possibilities, those relating to pleasures are
incontinence and continence, those relating to pains softness and endurance. The state of most people is intermediate, even if they lean more towards the worse states. 15

Now, since some pleasures are necessary while others are
not, and are necessary up to a point while the excesses of
them are not, nor the deficiencies, and this is equally true
of appetites and pains, the man who pursues the excesses
of things pleasant, or pursues to excess necessary objects, 20
and does so by choice, for their own sake and not at all for
the sake of any result distinct from them, is self-indulgent;
for such a man is of necessity unlikely to repent, and therefore incurable, since a man who cannot repent cannot be
cured. The man who is deficient in his pursuit of them is
the opposite of self-indulgent; the man who is intermediate
is temperate. Similarly, there is the man who avoids bodily
pains not because he is defeated by them but by choice.
(Of those who do not choose such acts, one kind of man is 25
led to them as a result of the pleasure involved, another
because he avoids the pain arising from the appetite, so
that these types differ from one another. Now any one
would think worse of a man if with no appetite or with
weak appetite he were to do something disgraceful, than if
he did it under the influence of powerful appetite, and
worse of him if he struck a blow not in anger than if he
did it in anger; for what would he have done if he had been 30
strongly affected? This is why the self-indulgent man is
worse than the incontinent.) Of the states named, then,[28]
the latter is rather a kind of softness;[29] the former is self-
indulgence. While to the incontinent man is opposed
the continent, to the soft is opposed the man of endurance;
for endurance consists in resisting, while continence con- 35

[28] In ll. 19–25.
[29] Not softness proper, which is non-deliberate avoidance of pain
(ll. 13–15).

sists in conquering, and resisting and conquering are different, as not being beaten is different from winning; this is
1150^b why continence is also more worthy of choice than endurance. Now the man who is defective in respect of resistance
to the things which most men both resist and resist successfully is soft and effeminate; for effeminacy too is a kind
of softness; such a man trails his cloak to avoid the pain of
lifting it, and plays the invalid without thinking himself
wretched, though the man he imitates is a wretched man.

5   The case is similar with regard to continence and incontinence. For if a man is defeated by violent and excessive pleasures or pains, there is nothing wonderful in
that; indeed we are ready to pardon him if he has resisted,
as Theodectes' Philoctetes does when bitten by the snake,
10 or Carcinus' Cercyon in the *Alope*, and as people who try
to restrain their laughter burst out in a guffaw, as happened
to Xenophantus. But it is surprising if a man is defeated by
and cannot resist pleasures or pains which most men can
hold out against, when this is not due to heredity or disease, like the softness that is hereditary with the kings of
the Scythians, or that which distinguishes the female sex
15 from the male.

The lover of amusement, too, is thought to be self-indulgent, but is really soft. For amusement is a relaxation, since it is a rest from work; and the lover of amusement is one of the people who go to excess in this.

Of incontinence one kind is impetuosity, another weakness. For some men after deliberating fail, owing to their
20 emotion, to stand by the conclusions of their deliberation,
others because they have not deliberated are led by their
emotion; since some men (just as people who first tickle
others are not tickled themselves), if they have first perceived and seen what is coming and have first roused
themselves and their calculative faculty, are not defeated
by their emotion, whether it be pleasant or painful. It is
25 keen and excitable people that suffer especially from the
impetuous form of incontinence; for the former by reason

of their quickness and the latter by reason of the violence of their passions do not await the argument, because they are apt to follow their imagination.

8   The self-indulgent man, as was said,[30] is not apt to repent; for he stands by his choice; but any incontinent man is likely to repent. This is why the position is not as it was expressed in the formulation of the problem,[31] but the self-indulgent man is incurable and the incontinent man curable; for wickedness is like a disease such as dropsy or consumption, while incontinence is like epilepsy; the former is a permanent, the latter an intermittent badness. And generally incontinence and vice are different in kind; vice is unconscious of itself, incontinence is not (of incontinent men themselves, those who become temporarily beside themselves are better than those who have the rational principle but do not abide by it, since the latter are defeated by a weaker passion, and do not act without previous deliberation like the others); for the incontinent man is like the people who get drunk quickly and on little wine, i. e. on less than most people.

Evidently, then, incontinence is not vice (though perhaps it is so in a qualified sense); for incontinence is contrary to choice while vice is in accordance with choice; not but what they are similar in respect of the actions they lead to; as in the saying of Demodocus about the Milesians, 'the Milesians are not without sense, but they do the things that senseless people do', so too incontinent people are not criminal, but they will do criminal acts.

Now, since the incontinent man is apt to pursue, not on conviction, bodily pleasures that are excessive and contrary to the right rule, while the self-indulgent man is convinced because he is the sort of man to pursue them, it is on the contrary the former that is easily persuaded to change his mind, while the latter is not. For virtue and vice respec-

---

[30] a 21.
[31] 1146ᵃ 31–ᵇ 2.

tively preserve and destroy the first principle, and in actions the final cause is the first principle, as the hypotheses [32] are in mathematics; neither in that case is it argument that teaches the first principles, nor is it so here—virtue either natural or produced by habituation is what teaches right opinion about the first principle. Such a man as this, then, is temperate; his contrary is the self-indulgent.

20 But there is a sort of man who is carried away as a result of passion and contrary to the right rule—a man whom passion masters so that he does not act according to the right rule, but does not master to the extent of making him ready to believe that he ought to pursue such pleasures without reserve; this is the incontinent man, who is better 25 than the self-indulgent man, and not bad without qualification; for the best thing in him, the first principle, is preserved. And contrary to him is another kind of man, he who abides by his convictions and is not carried away, at least as a result of passion. It is evident from these considerations that the latter is a good state and the former a bad one.

9 Is the man continent who abides by any and every rule and any and every choice, or the man who abides 30 by the right choice, and is he incontinent who abandons any and every choice and any and every rule, or he who abandons the rule that is not false and the choice that is right; this is how we put it before in our statement of the problem.[33] Or is it incidentally any and every choice but 35 per se the true rule and the right choice by which the one 1151[b] abides and the other does not? If any one chooses or pursues this for the sake of that, per se he pursues and chooses the latter, but incidentally the former. But when we speak without qualification we mean what is per se. Therefore in

[32] i. e. the assumptions of the existence of the primary objects of mathematics, such as the straight line or the unit.
[33] 1146[a] 16–31.

a sense the one abides by, and the other abandons, any and
every opinion; but without qualification, the true opinion.

There are some who are apt to abide by their opinion,
who are called strong-headed, viz. those who are hard to 5
persuade in the first instance and are not easily persuaded to
change; these have in them something like the continent
man, as the prodigal is in a way like the liberal man and
the rash man like the confident man; but they are different
in many respects. For it is to passion and appetite that
the one will not yield, since on occasion the continent man
will be easy to persuade; but it is to argument that the
others refuse to yield, for they do form appetites and many 10
of them are led by their pleasures. Now the people who are
strong-headed are the opinionated, the ignorant, and the
boorish—the opinionated being influenced by pleasure and
pain; for they delight in the victory they gain if they are
not persuaded to change, and are pained if their decisions
become null and void as decrees sometimes do; so that they 15
are liker the incontinent than the continent man.

But there are some who fail to abide by their resolutions,
not as a result of incontinence, e. g. Neoptolemus in Sophocles' *Philoctetes*; yet it was for the sake of pleasure that he
did not stand fast—but a noble pleasure; for telling the
truth was noble to him, but he had been persuaded by 20
Odysseus to tell the lie. For not every one who does anything for the sake of pleasure is either self-indulgent or bad
or incontinent, but he who does it for a disgraceful pleasure.

Since there is also a sort of man who takes less delight
than he should in bodily things, and does not abide by the
rule, he who is intermediate between him and the incontinent man is the continent man; for the incontinent man 25
fails to abide by the rule because he delights too much in
them, and this man because he delights in them too little;
while the continent man abides by the rule and does not
change on either account. Now if continence is good, both
the contrary states must be bad, as they actually appear to

30 be; but because the other extreme is seen in few people and seldom, as temperance is thought to be contrary only to self-indulgence, so is continence to incontinence.

Since many names are applied analogically, it is by analogy that we have come to speak of the 'continence' of the temperate man; for both the continent man and the 35 temperate man are such as to do nothing contrary to the 1152ᵃ rule for the sake of the bodily pleasures, but the former has and the latter has not bad appetites, and the latter is such as not to feel pleasure contrary to the rule, while the former is such as to feel pleasure but not to be led by it. And the incontinent and the self-indulgent man are also like an- 5 other; they are different, but both pursue bodily pleasures —the latter, however, also thinking that he ought to do so, while the former does not think this.

10 Nor can the same man have practical wisdom and be incontinent; for it has been shown [34] that a man is at the same time practically wise, and good in respect of character. Further, a man has practical wisdom not by knowing only but by being able to act; but the incontinent man is unable to act—there is, however, nothing to prevent a 10 clever man from being incontinent; this is why it is some-times actually thought that some people have practical wisdom but are incontinent, viz. because cleverness and practical wisdom differ in the way we have described in our first discussions,[35] and are near together in respect of their reasoning, but differ in respect of their purpose—nor yet is the incontinent man like the man who knows and is con- 15 templating a truth, but like the man who is asleep or drunk. And he acts willingly (for he acts in a sense with knowledge both of what he does and of the end to which he does it), but is not wicked, since his purpose is good; so that he is half-wicked. And he is not a criminal; for he does not act of malice aforethought; of the two types of in-

[34] 1144ᵃ 11–ᵇ 32.
[35] 1144ᵃ 23–ᵇ4.

continent man the one does not abide by the conclusions of his deliberation, while the excitable man does not de- 20 liberate at all. And thus the incontinent man is like a city which passes all the right decrees and has good laws, but makes no use of them, as in Anaxandrides' jesting remark,

'The city willed it, that cares nought for laws';

but the wicked man is like a city that uses its laws, but has wicked laws to use.

Now incontinence and continence are concerned with 25 that which is in excess of the state characteristic of most men; for the continent man abides by his resolutions more and the incontinent man less than most men can.

Of the forms of incontinence, that of excitable people is more curable than that of those who deliberate but do not abide by their decisions, and those who are incontinent through habituation are more curable than those in whom incontinence is innate; for it is easier to change a habit 30 than to change one's nature; even habit is hard to change just because it is like nature, as Evenus says:

I say that habit's but long practice, friend,
And this becomes men's nature in the end.

We have now stated what continence, incontinence, endurance, and softness are, and how these states are related 35 to each other.

11   The study of pleasure and pain belongs to the province **1152ᵇ** of the political philosopher; for he is the architect of the end, with a view to which we call one thing bad and another good without qualification. Further, it is one of our necessary tasks to consider them; for not only did we lay it down that moral virtue and vice are concerned with 5 pains and pleasures,[36] but most people say that happiness

---

[36] 1104ᵇ 8–1105ᵃ 13.

involves pleasure; this is why the blessed man is called by a name derived from a word meaning enjoyment.[37]

Now (1) some people think that no pleasure is a good, either in itself or incidentally, since the good and pleasure are not the same; (2) others think that some pleasures are good but that most are bad. (3) Again there is a third view, that even if all pleasures are goods, yet the best thing in the world cannot be pleasure. (1) The reasons given for the view that pleasure is not a good at all are (a) that every pleasure is a perceptible process to a natural state, and that no process is of the same kind as its end, e. g. no process of building of the same kind as a house. (b) A temperate man avoids pleasures. (c) A man of practical wisdom pursues what is free from pain, not what is pleasant. (d) The pleasures are a hindrance to thought, and the more so the more one delights in them, e. g. in sexual pleasure; for no one could think of anything while absorbed in this. (e) There is no art of pleasure; but every good is the product of some art. (f) Children and the brutes pursue pleasures. (2) The reasons for the view that not all pleasures are good are that (a) there are pleasures that are actually base and objects of reproach, and (b) there are harmful pleasures; for some pleasant things are unhealthy. (3) The reason for the view that the best thing in the world is not pleasure is that pleasure is not an end but a process.

12   These are pretty much the things that are said. That it does not follow from these grounds that pleasure is not a good, or even the chief good, is plain from the following considerations. (A) [38] (a) First, since that which is good may be so in either of two senses (one thing good simply and another good for a particular person), natural constitutions and states of being, and therefore also the corresponding movements and processes, will be correspondingly divisible. Of those which are thought to be bad

[37] makarios from mala chairein!
[38] (A) is the answer to (1 a) and (3).

some will be bad if taken without qualification but not bad
for a particular person, but worthy of his choice, and
some will not be worthy of choice even for a particular 30
person, but only at a particular time and for a short period,
though not without qualification; while others are not even
pleasures, but seem to be so, viz. all those which involve
pain and whose end is curative, e. g. the processes that go
on in sick persons.

(b) Further, one kind of good being activity and another being state, the processes that restore us to our natural
state are only incidentally pleasant; for that matter the 35
activity at work in the appetites for them is the activity of
so much of our state and nature as has remained unim-
paired; for there are actually pleasures that involve no pain **1153ᵃ**
or appetite (e. g. those of contemplation), the nature in
such a case not being defective at all. That the others are
incidental is indicated by the fact that men do not enjoy
the same pleasant objects when their nature is in its settled
state as they do when it is being replenished, but in the
former case they enjoy the things that are pleasant without
qualification, in the latter the contraries of these as well; for
then they enjoy even sharp and bitter things, none of 5
which is pleasant either by nature or without qualification.
The states they produce, therefore, are not pleasures
naturally or without qualification; for as pleasant things
differ, so do the pleasures arising from them.

(c) Again, it is not necessary that there should be something else better than pleasure, as some say the end is better
than the process; for pleasures are not processes nor do 10
they all involve process—they are activities and ends;
nor do they arise when we are becoming something, but
when we are exercising some faculty; and not all pleasures
have an end different from themselves, but only the
pleasures of persons who are being led to the perfecting of
their nature. This is why it is not right to say that pleasure
is perceptible process, but it should rather be called activity 15
of the natural state, and instead of 'perceptible' 'unim-

peded'. It is thought by some people to be process just because they think it is in the strict sense good; for they think that activity is process, which it is not.

(B) [39] The view that pleasures are bad because some pleasant things are unhealthy is like saying that healthy things are bad because some healthy things are bad for
20 money-making; both are bad in the respect mentioned, but they are not bad for that reason—indeed, thinking itself is sometimes injurious to health.

Neither practical wisdom nor any state of being is impeded by the pleasure arising from it; it is foreign pleasures that impede, for the pleasures arising from thinking and learning will make us think and learn all the more.

(C) [40] The fact that no pleasure is the product of any
25 art arises naturally enough; there is no art of any other activity either, but only of the corresponding faculty; though for that matter the arts of the perfumer and the cook are thought to be arts of pleasure.

(D) [41] The arguments based on the grounds that the temperate man avoids pleasure and that the man of practical wisdom pursues the painless life, and that children and the brutes pursue pleasure, are all refuted by the same consideration. We have pointed out [42] in what sense pleasures are good without qualification and in what sense some are not good; now both the brutes and children pur-
30 sue pleasures of the latter kind (and the man of practical wisdom pursues tranquil freedom from that kind), viz. those which imply appetite and pain, i. e. the bodily pleasures (for it is these that are of this nature) and the excesses of them, in respect of which the self-indulgent man is self-indulgent. This is why the temperate man
35 avoids these pleasures; for even he has pleasures of his own.

[39] Answer to (2 b) and (1 d).
[40] Answer to (1 e).
[41] Answer to (1 b), (1 c), (1 f).
[42] 1152ᵇ 26–1153ᵃ 7.

13 But further (E) it is agreed that pain is bad and to
be avoided; for some pain is without qualification 1153ᵇ
bad, and other pain is bad because it is in some respect an
impediment to us. Now the contrary of that which is to
be avoided, qua something to be avoided and bad, is
good. Pleasure, then, is necessarily a good. For the answer
of Speusippus, that pleasure is contrary both to pain and
to good, as the greater is contrary both to the less and to the 5
equal, is not successful; since he would not say that
pleasure is essentially just a species of evil.

  And (F) [48] if certain pleasures are bad, that does not
prevent the chief good from being some pleasure, just as
the chief good may be some form of knowledge though
certain kinds of knowledge are bad. Perhaps it is even
necessary, if each disposition has unimpeded activities, that, 10
whether the activity (if unimpeded) of all our dispositions
or that of some one of them is happiness, this should be the
thing most worthy of our choice; and this activity is
pleasure. Thus the chief good would be some pleasure,
though most pleasures might perhaps be bad without
qualification. And for this reason all men think that the
happy life is pleasant and weave pleasure into their ideal
of happiness—and reasonably too; for no activity is perfect 15
when it is impeded, and happiness is a perfect thing; this is
why the happy man needs the goods of the body and external goods, i. e. those of fortune, viz. in order that he
may not be impeded in these ways. Those who say that the
victim on the rack or the man who falls into great misfortunes is happy if he is good, are, whether they mean to
or not, talking nonsense. Now because we need fortune as 20
well as other things, some people think good fortune the
same thing as happiness; but it is not that, for even good
fortune itself when in excess is an impediment, and perhaps should then be no longer called good fortune; for its
limit is fixed by reference to happiness.

<hr>

[48] Answer to (2 a).

25 And indeed the fact that all things, both brutes and men, pursue pleasure is an indication of its being somehow the chief good:

No voice is wholly lost that many peoples . . .

But since no one nature or state either is or is thought the 30 best for all, neither do all pursue the same pleasure; yet all pursue pleasure. And perhaps they actually pursue not the pleasure they think they pursue nor that which they would say they pursue, but the same pleasure; for all things have by nature something divine in them. But the bodily pleasures have appropriated the name both because we oftenest steer our course for them and because all men 35 share in them; thus because they alone are familiar, men think there are no others.

1154ᵃ It is evident also that if pleasure, i. e. the activity of our faculties, is not a good, it will not be the case that the happy man lives a pleasant life; for to what end should he need pleasure, if it is not a good but the happy man may even 5 live a painful life? For pain is neither an evil nor a good, if pleasure is not; why then should he avoid it? Therefore, too, the life of the good man will not be pleasanter than that of any one else, if his activities are not more pleasant.

14 (G) [44] With regard to the bodily pleasures, those who say that some pleasures are very much to be 10 chosen, viz. the noble pleasures, but not the bodily pleasures, i. e. those with which the self-indulgent man is concerned, must consider why, then, the contrary things are bad. For the contrary of bad is good. Are the necessary pleasures good in the sense in which even that which is not bad is good? Or are they good up to a point? Is it that where you have states and processes of which there cannot be too much, there cannot be too much of the corresponding pleasure, and that where there can be too much of the 15 one there can be too much of the other also? Now there can be too much of bodily goods, and the bad man is bad

[44] Answer to (2).

by virtue of pursuing the excess, not by virtue of pursuing the necessary pleasures (for *all* men enjoy in some way or other both dainty foods and wines and sexual intercourse, but not all men do so as they ought). The contrary is the case with pain; for he does not avoid the excess of it, he avoids it altogether; and this is peculiar to him, for the 20 alternative to excess of pleasure is not pain, except to the man who pursues this excess.

Since we should state not only the truth, but also the cause of error—for this contributes towards producing conviction, since when a reasonable explanation is given of why the false view appears true, this tends to produce belief in the true view—therefore we must state why the 25 bodily pleasures appear the more worthy of choice. (a) Firstly, then, it is because they expel pain; owing to the excesses of pain that men experience, they pursue excessive and in general bodily pleasure as being a cure for the pain. Now curative agencies produce intense feeling— 30 which is the reason why they are pursued—because they show up against the contrary pain. (Indeed pleasure is thought not to be good for these two reasons, as has been said,[45] viz. that (α) some of them are activities belonging to a bad nature—either congenital, as in the case of a brute, or due to habit, i. e. those of bad men; while (β) others are meant to cure a defective nature, and it is better to be in a healthy state than to be getting into it, but these arise during the process of being made perfect and are **1154**[1] therefore only incidentally good.) (b) Further, they are pursued because of their violence by those who cannot enjoy other pleasures. (At all events they go out of their way to manufacture thirsts somehow for themselves. When these are harmless, the practice is irreproachable; when they are hurtful, it is bad.) For they have nothing else to enjoy, and, besides, a neutral state is painful to many 5 people because of their nature. For the animal nature is always in travail, as the students of natural science also

[45] 1152[b] 26–33.

testify, saying that sight and hearing are painful; but we have become used to this, as they maintain. Similarly, while, in youth, people are, owing to the growth that is going on, in a situation like that of drunken men, and
10 youth is pleasant,[46] on the other hand people of excitable nature [47] always need relief; for even their body is ever in torment owing to its special composition, and they are always under the influence of violent desire; but pain is driven out both by the contrary pleasure, and by any chance pleasure if it be strong; and for these reasons they become
15 self-indulgent and bad. But the pleasures that do not involve pains do not admit of excess; and these are among the things pleasant by nature and not incidentally. By things pleasant incidentally I mean those that act as cures (for because as a result people are cured, through some action of the part that remains healthy, for this reason the process is thought pleasant); by things naturally pleasant I mean those that stimulate the action of the healthy nature.
20   There is no one thing that is always pleasant, because our nature is not simple but there is another element in us as well, inasmuch as we are perishable creatures, so that if the one element does something, this is unnatural to the other nature, and when the two elements are evenly balanced, what is done seems neither painful nor pleasant; for
25 if the nature of anything were simple, the same action would always be most pleasant to it. This is why God always enjoys a single and simple pleasure; for there is not only an activity of movement but an activity of immobility, and pleasure is found more in rest than in movement. But 'change in all things is sweet', as the poet says, because of some vice; for as it is the vicious man that is changeable, 30 so the nature that needs change is vicious; for it is not simple nor good.

[46] i. e. the growth or replenishment that is going on produces exhilaration and pleasure.

[47] Lit., melancholic people, those characterized by an excess of black bile.

We have now discussed continence and incontinence, and pleasure and pain, both what each is and in what sense some of them are good and others bad; it remains to speak of friendship.

BOOK VIII

1   After what we have said, a discussion of friendship **1155ᵉ** would naturally follow, since it is a virtue or implies virtue, and is besides most necessary with a view to living. 5 For without friends no one would choose to live, though he had all other goods; even rich men and those in possession of office and of dominating power are thought to need friends most of all; for what is the use of such prosperity without the opportunity of beneficence, which is exercised chiefly and in its most laudable form towards friends? Or how can prosperity be guarded and preserved 10 without friends? The greater it is, the more exposed is it to risk. And in poverty and in other misfortunes men think friends are the only refuge. It helps the young, too, to keep from error; it aids older people by ministering to their needs and supplementing the activities that are failing from weakness; those in the prime of life it stimulates to noble 15 actions—'two going together' [1]—for with friends men are more able both to think and to act. Again, parent seems by nature to feel it for offspring and offspring for parent, not only among men but among birds and among most animals; it is felt mutually by members of the same race, 20 and especially by men, whence we praise lovers of their fellowmen. We may see even in our travels how near and dear every man is to every other. Friendship seems too to hold states together, and lawgivers to care more for it than for justice; for unanimity seems to be something like friendship, and this they aim at most of all, and expel faction as their worst enemy; and when men are friends they have 25 no need of justice, while when they are just they need

[1] *Il.* x. 224.

friendship as well, and the truest form of justice is thought to be a friendly quality.

But it is not only necessary but also noble; for we praise those who love their friends, and it is thought to be a fine 30 thing to have many friends; and again we think it is the same people that are good men and are friends.

Not a few things about friendship are matters of debate. Some define it as a kind of likeness and say like people are friends, whence come the sayings 'like to like', 'birds of a 35 feather flock together', and so on; others on the contrary 1155ᵇ say 'two of a trade never agree'. On this very question they inquire for deeper and more physical causes, Euripides saying that 'parched earth loves the rain, and stately heaven when filled with rain loves to fall to earth', and Heraclitus that 'it is what opposes that helps' and 'from different tones 5 comes the fairest tune' and 'all things are produced through strife'; while Empedocles, as well as others, expresses the opposite view that like aims at like. The physical problems we may leave alone (for they do not belong to the present inquiry); let us examine those which are human and in-volve character and feeling, e. g. whether friendship can 10 arise between any two people or people cannot be friends if they are wicked, and whether there is one species of friendship or more than one. Those who think there is only one because it admits of degrees have relied on an in-adequate indication; for even things different in species 15 admit of degree. We have discussed this matter previously.

2   The kinds of friendship may perhaps be cleared up if we first come to know the object of love. For not everything seems to be loved but only the lovable, and this is good, pleasant, or useful; but it would seem to be that by which some good or pleasure is produced that is useful, so that it is the good and the useful that are lovable as ends. 20 Do men love, then, the good, or what is good for them? These sometimes clash. So too with regard to the pleasant.

Now it is thought that each loves what is good for himself,
and that the good is without qualification lovable, and what
is good for each man is lovable for him; but each man loves
not what is good for him but what seems good. This how- 25
ever will make no difference; we shall just have to say that
this is 'that which seems lovable'. Now there are three
grounds on which people love; of the love of lifeless objects
we do not use the word 'friendship'; for it is not mutual
love, nor is there a wishing of good to the other (for it
would surely be ridiculous to wish wine well; if one wishes 30
anything for it, it is that it may keep, so that one may have
it oneself); but to a friend we say we ought to wish what
is good for his sake. But to those who thus wish good we
ascribe only goodwill, if the wish is not reciprocated; goodwill when it is reciprocal being friendship. Or must we add
'when it is recognized'? For many people have goodwill to 35
those whom they have not seen but judge to be good or 1156
useful; and one of these might return this feeling. These
people seem to bear goodwill to each other; but how could
one call them friends when they do not know their mutual
feelings? To be friends, then, they must be mutually recognized as bearing goodwill and wishing well to each other 5
for one of the aforesaid reasons.

3 Now these reasons differ from each other in kind; so,
therefore, do the corresponding forms of love and
friendship. There are therefore three kinds of friendship,
equal in number to the things that are lovable; for with
respect to each there is a mutual and recognized love, and
those who love each other wish well to each other in that
respect in which they love one another. Now those who 10
love each other for their utility do not love each other
for themselves but in virtue of some good which they get
from each other. So too with those who love for the sake
of pleasure; it is not for their character that men love ready-
witted people, but because they find them pleasant. There·

15 fore those who love for the sake of utility love for the
sake of what is good for *themselves*, and those who love
for the sake of pleasure do so for the sake of what is pleasant
to *themselves*, and not in so far as the other is the person
loved but in so far as he is useful or pleasant. And thus
these friendships are only incidental; for it is not as being
the man he is that the loved person is loved, but as provid-
20 ing some good or pleasure. Such friendships, then, are
easily dissolved, if the parties do not remain like themselves; for if the one party is no longer pleasant or useful
the other ceases to love him.

Now the useful is not permanent but is always changing.
Thus when the motive of the friendship is done away, the
friendship is dissolved, inasmuch as it existed only for the
25 ends in question. This kind of friendship seems to exist
chiefly between old people (for at that age people pursue
not the pleasant but the useful) and, of those who are in
their prime or young, between those who pursue utility.
And such people do not live much with each other either;
for sometimes they do not even find each other pleasant;
therefore they do not need such companionship unless
they are useful to each other; for they are pleasant to each
other only in so far as they rouse in each other hopes of
30 something good to come. Among such friendships people
also class the friendship of host and guest. On the other
hand the friendship of young people seems to aim at
pleasure; for they live under the guidance of emotion,
and pursue above all what is pleasant to themselves and
what is immediately before them; but with increasing age
their pleasures become different. This is why they quickly
35 become friends and quickly cease to be so; their friendship
changes with the object that is found pleasant, and such
pleasure alters quickly.

1156ᵇ Young people are amorous too; for the greater part of the
friendship of love depends on emotion and aims at pleasure; this is why they fall in love and quickly fall out of love,
changing often within a single day. But these people do

wish to spend their days and lives together; for it is thus
that they attain the purpose of their friendship.   5

Perfect friendship is the friendship of men who are good,
and alike in virtue; for these wish well alike to each other
qua good, and they are good in themselves. Now those
who wish well to their friends for their sake are most
truly friends; for they do this by reason of their own nature 10
and not incidentally; therefore their friendship lasts as long
as they are good—and goodness is an enduring thing.
And each is good without qualification and to his friend,
for the good are both good without qualification and useful to each other. So too they are pleasant; for the good are 15
pleasant both without qualification and to each other, since
to each his own activities and others like them are pleasurable, and the actions of the good are the same or like.
And such a friendship is as might be expected permanent,
since there meet in it all the qualities that friends should
have. For all friendship is for the sake of good or of pleasure
—good or pleasure either in the abstract or such as will be 20
enjoyed by him who has the friendly feeling—and is based
on a certain resemblance; and to a friendship of good
men all the qualities we have named belong in virtue of the
nature of the friends themselves; for in the case of this kind
of friendship the other qualities also [2] are alike in both
friends, and that which is good without qualification is
also without qualification pleasant, and these are the most
lovable qualities. Love and friendship therefore are found
most and in their best form between such men.

But it is natural that such friendships should be infre-
quent; for such men are rare. Further, such friendship
requires time and familiarity; as the proverb says, men can- 25
not know each other till they have 'eaten salt together';
nor can they admit each other to friendship or be friends
till each has been found lovable and been trusted by each.
Those who quickly show the marks of friendship to each

[2] i. e. absolute pleasantness, relative goodness, and relative pleasantness, as well as absolute goodness.

30 other wish to be friends, but are not friends unless they
both are lovable and know the fact; for a wish for friendship may arise quickly, but friendship does not.

4 This kind of friendship, then, is perfect both in respect of duration and in all other respects, and in it
each gets from each in all respects the same as, or some-
35 thing like what, he gives; which is what ought to happen
1157ᵃ between friends. Friendship for the sake of pleasure bears
a resemblance to this kind; for good people too are pleasant
to each other. So too does friendship for the sake of utility;
for the good are also useful to each other. Among men of
these inferior sorts too, friendships are most permanent
5 when the friends get the same thing from each other (e. g.
pleasure), and not only that but also from the same source,
as happens between ready-witted people, not as happens
between lover and beloved. For these do not take pleasure
in the same things, but the one in seeing the beloved and
the other in receiving attentions from his lover; and when
the bloom of youth is passing the friendship sometimes
passes too (for the one finds no pleasure in the sight of the
10 other, and the other gets no attentions from the first); but
many lovers on the other hand are constant, if familiarity
has led them to love each other's characters, these being
alike. But those who exchange not pleasure but utility in
their amour are both less truly friends and less constant.
15 Those who are friends for the sake of utility part when the
advantage is at an end; for they were lovers not of each
other but of profit.

For the sake of pleasure or utility, then, even bad men
may be friends of each other, or good men of bad, or one
who is neither good nor bad may be a friend to any sort of
person, but for their own sake clearly only good men can
be friends; for bad men do not delight in each other unless
some advantage come of the relation.

20 The friendship of the good too and this alone is proof

against slander; for it is not easy to trust any one's talk about a man who has long been tested by oneself; and it is among good men that trust and the feeling that 'he would never wrong me' and all the other things that are demanded in true friendship are found. In the other kinds of friendship, however, there is nothing to prevent these evils arising.

For men apply the name of friends even to those whose motive is utility, in which sense states are said to be friendly (for the alliances of states seem to aim at advantage), and to those who love each other for the sake of pleasure, in which sense children are called friends. Therefore we too ought perhaps to call such people friends, and say that there are several kinds of friendship—firstly and in the proper sense that of good men qua good, and by analogy the other kinds; for it is in virtue of something good and something akin to what is found in true friendship that they are friends, since even the pleasant is good for the lovers of pleasure. But these two kinds of friendship are not often united, nor do the same people become friends for the sake of utility and of pleasure; for things that are only incidentally connected are not often coupled together.

Friendship being divided into these kinds, bad men will be friends for the sake of pleasure or of utility, being in this **1157ᵃ** respect like each other, but good men will be friends for their own sake, i. e. in virtue of their goodness. These, then, are friends without qualification; the others are friends incidentally and through a resemblance to these.

5   As in regard to the virtues some men are called good in respect of a state of character, others in respect of an activity, so too in the case of friendship; for those who live together delight in each other and confer benefits on each other, but those who are asleep or locally separated are not performing, but are disposed to perform, the activi-

ties of friendship; distance does not break off the friend-
10 ship absolutely, but only the activity of it. But if the absence is lasting, it seems actually to make men forget their
friendship; hence the saying 'out of sight, out of mind'.
Neither old people nor sour people seem to make friends
easily; for there is little that is pleasant in them, and no
15 one can spend his days with one whose company is painful, or not pleasant, since nature seems above all to avoid
the painful and to aim at the pleasant. Those, however,
who approve of each other but do not live together seem to
be well-disposed rather than actual friends. For there is
nothing so characteristic of friends as living together (since
20 while it is people who are in need that desire benefits, even
those who are supremely happy desire to spend their days
together; for solitude suits such people least of all); but
people cannot live together if they are not pleasant and do
not enjoy the same things, as friends who are companions
seem to do.

The truest friendship, then, is that of the good, as we
25 have frequently said; [3] for that which is without qualification good or pleasant seems to be lovable and desirable,
and for each person that which is good or pleasant to him;
and the good man is lovable and desirable to the good man
for both these reasons. Now it looks as if love were a feel-
30 ing, friendship a state of character; for love may be felt just
as much towards lifeless things, but mutual love involves
choice and choice springs from a state of character; and
men wish well to those whom they love, for their sake, not
as a result of feeling but as a result of a state of character.
And in loving a friend men love what is good for themselves; for the good man in becoming a friend becomes a
35 good to his friend. Each, then, both loves what is good for
himself, and makes an equal return in goodwill and in
pleasantness; for friendship is said to be equality, and both
of these are found most in the friendship of the good.

[3] 1156[b] 7, 23, 33, 1157[a] 30, [b]4.

6   Between sour and elderly people friendship arises less 1158
readily, inasmuch as they are less good-tempered and
enjoy companionship less; for these are thought to be the
greatest marks of friendship and most productive of it.
This is why, while young men become friends quickly, old 5
men do not; it is because men do not become friends with
those in whom they do not delight; and similarly sour
people do not quickly make friends either. But such men
may bear goodwill to each other; for they wish one another
well and aid one another in need; but they are hardly
friends because they do not spend their days together nor
delight in each other, and these are thought the greatest
marks of friendship.

One cannot be a friend to many people in the sense of 10
having friendship of the perfect type with them, just as one
cannot be in love with many people at once (for love is a
sort of excess of feeling, and it is the nature of such only
to be felt towards one person); and it is not easy for
many people at the same time to please the same person
very greatly, or perhaps even to be good in his eyes. One
must, too, acquire some experience of the other person and
become familiar with him, and that is very hard. But with a 15
view to utility or pleasure it is possible that many people
should please one; for many people are useful or pleasant,
and these services take little time.

Of these two kinds that which is for the sake of pleasure
is the more like friendship, when both parties get the
same things from each other and delight in each other or
in the same things, as in the friendships of the young; for 20
generosity is more found in such friendships. Friendship
based on utility is for the commercially minded. People
who are supremely happy, too, have no need of useful
friends, but do need pleasant friends: for they wish to live
with some one and, though they can endure for a short
time what is painful, no one could put up with it continuously, nor even with the Good itself if it were painful

to him; this is why they look out for friends who are
35 pleasant. Perhaps they should look out for friends who,
being pleasant, are also good, and good for them, too; for
so they will have all the characteristics that friends should
have.

People in positions of authority seem to have friends
who fall into distinct classes; some people are useful to
them and others are pleasant, but the same people are rarely
both; for they seek neither those whose pleasantness is ac-
30 companied by virtue nor those whose utility is with a view
to noble objects, but in their desire for pleasure they seek
for ready-witted people, and their other friends they
choose as being clever at doing what they are told, and
these characteristics are rarely combined. Now we have
said that the good man is at the same time pleasant and
useful; [4] but such a man does not become the friend of one
who surpasses him in station, unless he is surpassed also
35 in virtue; if this is not so, he does not establish equality
by being proportionally exceeded in both respects. But
people who surpass him in both respects are not so easy
to find.

However that may be, the aforesaid friendships involve
1158ᵇ equality; for the friends get the same things from one another and wish the same things for one another,
or exchange one thing for another, e. g. pleasure for
utility; we have said,[5] however, that they are both less truly
friendships and less permanent. But it is from their like-
5 ness and their unlikeness to the same thing that they are
thought both to be and not to be friendships. It is by their
likeness to the friendship of virtue that they seem to be
friendships (for one of them involves pleasure and the
other utility, and these characteristics belong to the friendship of virtue as well); while it is because the friendship
of virtue is proof against slander and permanent, while
these quickly change (besides differing from the former

⁴ 1156ᵇ 13–15, 1157ᵃ 1–3.
ᶠ 1156ᵃ 16–24, 1157ᵃ 20–33.

in many other respects), that they appear *not* to be friendships; i. e. it is because of their unlikeness to the friendship of virtue.

7 But there is another kind of friendship, viz. that which involves an inequality between the parties, e. g. that of father to son and in general of elder to younger, that of man to wife and in general that of ruler to subject. And these friendships differ also from each other; for it is not the same that exists between parents and children and between rulers and subjects, nor is even that of father to son the same as that of son to father, nor that of husband to wife the same as that of wife to husband. For the virtue and the function of each of these is different, and so are the reasons for which they love; the love and the friendship are therefore different also. Each party, then, neither gets the same from the other, nor ought to seek it; but when children render to parents what they ought to render to those who brought them into the world, and parents render what they should to their children, the friendship of such persons will be abiding and excellent. In all friendships implying inequality the love also should be proportional, i. e. the better should be more loved than he loves, and so should the more useful, and similarly in each of the other cases; for when the love is in proportion to the merit of the parties, then in a sense arises equality, which is certainly held to be characteristic of friendship.

But equality does not seem to take the same form in acts of justice and in friendship; for in acts of justice what is equal in the primary sense is that which is in proportion to merit, while quantitative equality is secondary, but in friendship quantitative equality is primary and proportion to merit secondary. This becomes clear if there is a great interval in respect of virtue or vice or wealth or anything else between the parties; for then they are no longer friends, and do not even expect to be so. And this is most manifest in the case of the gods; for they surpass us most

1159ᵃ decisively in all good things. But it is clear also in the case of kings; for with them, too, men who are much their inferiors do not expect to be friends; nor do men of no account expect to be friends with the best or wisest men. In such cases it is not possible to define exactly up to what point friends can remain friends; for much can be taken away and friendship remain, but when one party is re-
5 moved to a great distance, as God is, the possibility of friendship ceases. This is in fact the origin of the question whether friends really wish for their friends the greatest goods, e. g. that of being gods; since in that case their friends will no longer be friends to them, and therefore will not be good things for them (for friends are good things). The answer is that if we were right in saying that friend wishes good to friend for his sake,⁶ his friend must
10 remain the sort of being he is, whatever that may be; therefore it is for him only so long as he remains a man that he will wish the greatest goods. But perhaps not all the greatest goods; for it is for himself most of all that each man wishes what is good.

8   Most people seem, owing to ambition, to wish to be loved rather than to love; which is why most men love flattery; for the flatterer is a friend in an inferior position, or pretends to be such and to love more than he is loved;
15 and being loved seems to be akin to being honoured, and this is what most people aim at. But it seems to be not for its own sake that people choose honour, but incidentally. For most people enjoy being honoured by those in positions of authority because of their hopes (for they think
20 that if they want anything they will get it from them; and therefore they delight in honour as a token of favour to come); while those who desire honour from good men, and men who know, are aiming at confirming their own opinion of themselves; they delight in honour, therefore, because they believe in their own goodness on the strength of the

⁶ 1155ᵇ 31.

judgement of those who speak about them. In being loved, on the other hand, people delight for its own sake; whence it would seem to be better than being honoured, and 25 friendship to be desirable in itself. But it seems to lie in loving rather than in being loved, as is indicated by the delight mothers take in loving; for some mothers hand over their children to be brought up, and so long as they know their fate they love them and do not seek to be loved 30 in return (if they cannot have both), but seem to be satisfied if they see them prospering; and they themselves love their children even if these owing to their ignorance give them nothing of a mother's due. Now since friendship depends more on loving, and it is those who love their friends that are praised, loving seems to be the characteristic virtue of friends, so that it is only those in whom this is 35 found in due measure that are lasting friends, and only their friendship that endures.

It is in this way more than any other that even unequals can be friends; they can be equalized. Now equality and **1159**[t] likeness are friendship, and especially the likeness of those who are like in virtue; for being steadfast in themselves they hold fast to each other, and neither ask nor give base serv- 5 ices, but (one may say) even prevent them; for it is characteristic of good men neither to go wrong themselves nor to let their friends do so. But wicked men have no steadfastness (for they do not remain even like to themselves), but become friends for a short time because they delight in each other's wickedness. Friends who are useful 10 or pleasant last longer; i. e. as long as they provide each other with enjoyments or advantages. Friendship for utility's sake seems to be that which most easily exists between contraries, e. g. between poor and rich, between ignorant and learned; for what a man actually lacks he aims at, and one gives something else in return. But under this head, 15 too, we might bring lover and beloved, beautiful and ugly. This is why lovers sometimes seem ridiculous, when they demand to be loved as they love; if they are equally lovable

their claim can perhaps be justified, but when they have nothing lovable about them it is ridiculous. Perhaps, how-
20 ever, contrary does not even aim at contrary by its own nature, but only incidentally, the desire being for what is intermediate; for that is what is good, e. g. it is good for the dry not to become wet [7] but to come to the intermediate state, and similarly with the hot and in all other cases. These subjects we may dismiss; for they are indeed somewhat foreign to our inquiry.

25 **9**   Friendship and justice seem, as we have said at the outset of our discussion,[8] to be concerned with the same objects and exhibited between the same persons. For in every community there is thought to be some form of justice, and friendship too; at least men address as friends their fellow-voyagers and fellow-soldiers, and so too those associated with them in any other kind of community. And the extent of their association is the extent of their friend-
30 ship, as it is the extent to which justice exists between them. And the proverb 'what friends have is common property' expresses the truth; for friendship depends on community. Now brothers and comrades have all things in common, but the others to whom we have referred have definite things in common—some more things, others
35 fewer; for of friendships, too, some are more and others less
1160ᵃ truly friendships. And the claims of justice differ too; the duties of parents to children and those of brothers to each other are not the same nor those of comrades and those of fellow-citizens, and so, too, with the other kinds of friendship. There is a difference, therefore, also between the acts that are unjust towards each of these classes of associates, and the injustice increases by being exhibited towards those who are friends in a fuller sense; e. g. it is a more terrible thing to defraud a comrade than a fellow-citizen,
5 more terrible not to help a brother than a stranger, and

[7] Cf. 1155ᵇ 3.
[8] 1155ᵃ 22–28.

more terrible to wound a father than any one else. And the demands of justice also seem to increase with the intensity of the friendship, which implies that friendship and justice exist between the same persons and have an equal extension.

Now all forms of community are like parts of the political community; for men journey together with a view to some particular advantage, and to provide something that they need for the purposes of life; and it is for the sake of advantage that the political community too seems both to have come together originally and to endure, for this is what legislators aim at, and they call just that which is to the common advantage. Now the other communities aim at advantage bit by bit, e. g. sailors at what is advantageous on a voyage with a view to making money or something of the kind, fellow-soldiers at what is advantageous in war, whether it is wealth or victory or the taking of a city that they seek, and members of tribes and demes act similarly [Some communities seem to arise for the sake of pleasure, viz. religious guilds and social clubs; for these exist respectively for the sake of offering sacrifice and of companionship. But all these seem to fall under the political community; for it aims not at present advantage but at what is advantageous for life as a whole], offering sacrifices and arranging gatherings for the purpose, and assigning honours to the gods, and providing pleasant relaxations for themselves. For the ancient sacrifices and gatherings seem to take place after the harvest as a sort of firstfruits, because it was at these seasons that people had most leisure. All the communities, then, seem to be parts of the political community; and the particular kinds of friendship will correspond to the particular kinds of community.

10   There are three kinds of constitution, and an equal number of deviation-forms—perversions, as it were, of them. The constitutions are monarchy, aristocracy, and thirdly that which is based on a property qualification,

which it seems appropriate to call timocratic, though most
people are wont to call it polity. The best of these is
35 monarchy, the worst timocracy. The deviation from monarchy is tyranny; for both are forms of one-man rule, but
1160ᵇ there is the greatest difference between them; the tyrant
looks to his own advantage, the king to that of his subjects.
For a man is not a king unless he is sufficient to himself
and excels his subjects in all good things; and such a man
needs nothing further; therefore he will not look to his own
5 interests but to those of his subjects; for a king who is not
like that would be a mere titular king. Now tyranny is the
very contrary of this; the tyrant pursues his own good.
And it is clearer in the case of tyranny that it is the worst
deviation-form; ⁀ but it is the contrary of the best that is
worst.[10] Monarchy passes over into tyranny; for tyranny is
10 the evil form of one-man rule and the bad king becomes
a tyrant. Aristocracy passes over into oligarchy by the badness of the rulers, who distribute contrary to equity what
belongs to the city—all or most of the good things to
15 themselves, and office always to the same people, paying
most regard to wealth; thus the rulers are few and are bad
men instead of the most worthy. Timocracy passes over
into democracy; for these are coterminous, since it is the
ideal even of timocracy to be the rule of the majority, and
all who have the property qualification count as equal.
20 Democracy is the least bad of the deviations; for in its case
the form of constitution is but a slight deviation. These
then are the changes to which constitutions are most subject; for these are the smallest and easiest transitions.

One may find resemblances to the constitutions and,
as it were, patterns of them even in households. For the as-
25 sociation of a father with his sons bears the form of
monarchy, since the father cares for his children; and this
is why Homer calls Zeus 'father'; it is the ideal of monarchy
to be paternal rule. But among the Persians the rule of the
father is tyrannical; they use their sons as slaves. Tyrannical

---

⁹ Than it is that monarchy is the best genuine form (ᵃ 35).
¹⁰ Therefore monarchy must be the best.

too is the rule of a master over slaves; for it is the advantage of the master that is brought about in it. Now this seems to 30 be a correct form of government, but the Persian type is perverted; for the modes of rule appropriate to different relations are diverse. The association of man and wife seems to be aristocratic; for the man rules in accordance with his worth, and in those matters in which a man should rule, but the matters that befit a woman he hands over to her. 35 If the man rules in everything the relation passes over into oligarchy; for in doing so he is not acting in accordance with their respective worth, and not ruling in virtue of his superiority. Sometimes, however, women rule, because **1161ᵃ** they are heiresses; so their rule is not in virtue of excellence but due to wealth and power, as in oligarchies. The association of brothers is like timocracy; for they are equal, except 5 in so far as they differ in age; hence if they differ much in age, the friendship is no longer of the fraternal type. Democracy is found chiefly in masterless dwellings (for here every one is on an equality), and in those in which the ruler is weak and every one has license to do as he pleases.

11   Each of the constitutions may be seen to involve 10 friendship just in so far as it involves justice. The friendship between a king and his subjects depends on an excess of benefits conferred; for he confers benefits on his subjects if being a good man he cares for them with a view to their well-being, as a shepherd does for his sheep (whence Homer called Agamemnon 'shepherd of the peo- 15 ples'). Such too is the friendship of a father, though this exceeds the other in the greatness of the benefits conferred; for he is responsible for the existence of his children, which is thought the greatest good, and for their nurture and upbringing. These things are ascribed to ancestors as well. Further, by nature a father tends to rule over his sons, ancestors over descendants, a king over his subjects. These friendships imply superiority of one party over the other, which is why ancestors are honoured. The justice there- 20 fore that exists between persons so related is not the same

on both sides but is in every case proportioned to merit; for that is true of the friendship as well. The friendship of man and wife, again, is the same that is found in an aristocracy; for it is in accordance with virtue—the better gets more of what is good, and each gets what befits him; and so, too, with the justice in these relations. The friendship of brothers is like that of comrades; for they are 25 equal and of like age, and such persons are for the most part like in their feelings and their character. Like this, too, is the friendship appropriate to timocratic government; for in such a constitution the ideal is for the citizens to be equal and fair; therefore rule is taken in turn, and on equal terms; and the friendship appropriate here will correspond.

But in the deviation-forms, as justice hardly exists, so 30 too does friendship. It exists least in the worst form; in tyranny there is little or no friendship. For where there is nothing common to ruler and ruled, there is not friendship either, since there is not justice; e. g. between craftsman and 35 tool, soul and body, master and slave; the latter in each 1161^b case is benefited by that which uses it, but there is no friendship nor justice towards lifeless things. But neither is there friendship towards a horse or an ox, nor to a slave qua slave. For there is nothing common to the two parties; the slave is a living tool and the tool a lifeless slave. Qua 5 slave then, one cannot be friends with him. But qua man one can; for there seems to be some justice between any man and any other who can share in a system of law or be a party to an agreement; therefore there can also be friendship with him in so far as he is a man. Therefore while in tyrannies friendship and justice hardly exist, in democracies they exist more fully; for where the citizens are equal 10 they have much in common.

12   Every form of friendship, then, involves association, as has been said.[11] One might, however, mark off from the rest both the friendship of kindred and that of comrades. Those of fellow-citizens, fellow-tribesmen, fellow-

[11] 1159^b 29–32.

voyagers, and the like are more like mere friendships of association; for they seem to rest on a sort of compact. With them we might class the friendship of host and guest.

The friendship of kinsmen itself, while it seems to be of many kinds, appears to depend in every case on parental friendship; for parents love their children as being a part of themselves, and children their parents as being something originating from them. Now (1) parents know their offspring better than their children know that they are their children, and (2) the originator feels his offspring to be his own more than the offspring do their begetter; for the product belongs to the producer (e. g. a tooth or hair or anything else to him whose it is), but the producer does not belong to the product, or belongs in a less degree. And (3) the length of time produces the same result; parents love their children as soon as these are born, but children love their parents only after time has elapsed and they have acquired understanding or the power of discrimination by the senses. From these considerations it is also plain why mothers love more than fathers do. Parents, then, love their children as themselves (for their issue are by virtue of their separate existence a sort of other selves), while children love their parents as being born of them, and brothers love each other as being born of the same parents; for their identity with them makes them identical with each other (which is the reason why people talk of 'the same blood', 'the same stock', and so on). They are, therefore, in a sense the same thing, though in separate individuals. Two things that contribute greatly to friendship are a common upbringing and similarity of age; for 'two of an age take to each other', and people brought up together tend to be comrades; whence the friendship of brothers is akin to **1162^a** that of comrades. And cousins and other kinsmen are bound up together by derivation from brothers, viz. by being derived from the same parents. They come to be closer together or farther apart by virtue of the nearness or distance of the original ancestor.

The friendship of children to parents, and of men to

5 gods, is a relation to them as to something good and superior; for they have conferred the greatest benefits, since they are the causes of their being and of their nourishment, and of their education from their birth; and this kind of friendship possesses pleasantness and utility also, more than that of strangers, inasmuch as their life is lived more in common. The friendship of brothers has the character-
10 istics found in that of comrades (and especially when these are good), and in general between people who are like each other, inasmuch as they belong more to each other and start with a love for each other from their very birth, and inasmuch as those born of the same parents and brought up together and similarly educated are more akin in character; and the test of time has been applied most fully and convincingly in their case.

Between other kinsmen friendly relations are found in
15 due proportion. Between man and wife friendship seems to exist by nature; for man is naturally inclined to form couples—even more than to form cities, inasmuch as the household is earlier and more necessary than the city, and reproduction is more common to man with the animals. With the other animals the union extends only to this point, but human beings live together not only for
20 the sake of reproduction but also for the various purposes of life; for from the start the functions are divided, and those of man and woman are different; so they help each other by throwing their peculiar gifts into the common
25 stock. It is for these reasons that both utility and pleasure seem to be found in this kind of friendship. But this friendship may be based also on virtue, if the parties are good; for each has its own virtue and they will delight in the fact. And children seem to be a bond of union (which is the reason why childless people part more easily); for children are a good common to both and what is common holds them together.

How man and wife and in general friend and friend ought mutually to behave seems to be the same question as how it is just for them to behave; for a man does not 30 seem to have the same duties to a friend, a stranger, a comrade, and a schoolfellow.

13 There are three kinds of friendship, as we said at the outset of our inquiry,[12] and in respect of each some are friends on an equality and others by virtue of a superior- 35 ity (for not only can equally good men become friends but 'a better man can make friends with a worse, and similarly **1162ᵇ** in friendships of pleasure or utility the friends may be equal or unequal in the benefits they confer). This being so, equals must effect the required equalization on a basis of equality in love and in all other respects, while unequals must render what is in proportion to their superiority or inferiority.

Complaints and reproaches arise either only or chiefly in the friendship of utility, and this is only to be expected. 5 For those who are friends on the ground of virtue are anxious to do well by each other (since that is a mark of virtue and of friendship), and between men who are emulating each other in this there cannot be complaints or quarrels; no one is offended by a man who loves him and does well by him—if he is a person of nice feeling he takes his revenge by doing well by the other. And the man 10 who excels the other in the services he renders will not complain of his friend, since he gets what he aims at; for each man desires what is good. Nor do complaints arise much even in friendships of pleasure; for both get at the same time what they desire, if they enjoy spending their time together; and even a man who complained of an- 15 other for not affording him pleasure would seem ridiculous, since it is in his power not to spend his days with him.

But the friendship of utility is full of complaints; for as they use each other for their own interests they always want to get the better of the bargain, and think they have got less than they should, and blame their partners be-

¹² 1156ᵃ 7.

20 cause they do not get all they 'want and deserve'; and those who do well by others cannot help them as much as those whom they benefit want.

Now it seems that, as justice is of two kinds, one unwritten and the other legal, one kind of friendship of utility is moral and the other legal. And so complaints arise most of all when men do not dissolve the relation in the 25 spirit of the same type of friendship in which they contracted it. The *legal* type is that which is on fixed terms; its purely commercial variety is on the basis of immediate payment, while the more liberal variety allows time but stipulates for a definite *quid pro quo*. In this variety the debt is clear and not ambiguous, but in the postponement it con-30 tains an element of friendliness; and so some states do not allow suits arising out of such agreements, but think men who have bargained on a basis of credit ought to accept the consequences. The *moral* type is not on fixed terms; it makes a gift, or does whatever it does, as to a friend; but one expects to receive as much or more, as having not given but lent; and if a man is worse off when the relation 35 is dissolved than he was when it was contracted he will complain. This happens because all or most men, while they wish for what is noble, choose what is advantageous; now it is noble to do well by another without a view to repayment, but it is the receiving of benefits that is advantageous.

1163ᵃ   Therefore if we can we should return the equivalent of what we have received (for we must not make a man our friend against his will; we must recognize that we were mistaken at the first and took a benefit from a person we should not have taken it from—since it was not from a friend, nor from one who did it just for the sake of acting 5 so—and we must settle up just as if we had been benefited on fixed terms). Indeed, one would agree to repay if one could (if one could not, even the giver would not have expected one to do so); therefore if it is possible we must repay. But at the outset we must consider the man by

whom we are being benefited and on what terms he is acting, in order that we may accept the benefit on these terms,
or else decline it.

It is disputable whether we ought to measure a service
by its utility to the receiver and make the return with a 10
view to that, or by the benevolence of the giver. For those
who have received say they have received from their benefactors what meant little to the latter and what they might
have got from others—minimizing the service; while the
givers, on the contrary, say it was the biggest thing they
had, and what could not have been got from others, and
that it was given in times of danger or similar need. Now if 15
the friendship is one that aims at *utility*, surely the advantage to the receiver is the measure. For it is he that asks
for the service, and the other man helps him on the assumption that he will receive the equivalent; so the assistance has been precisely as great as the advantage to the
receiver, and therefore he must return as much as he has
received, or even more (for that would be nobler). In 20
friendships based on *virtue* on the other hand, complaints
do not arise, but the purpose of the doer is a sort of measure; for in purpose lies the essential element of virtue
and character.

14 Differences arise also in friendships based on superiority; for each expects to get more out of them, but
when this happens the friendship is dissolved. Not only 25
does the better man think he ought to get more, since more
should be assigned to a good man, but the more useful
similarly expects this; they say a useless man should not get
as much as they should, since it becomes an act of public
service and not a friendship if the proceeds of the friendship do not answer to the worth of the benefits conferred.
For they think that, as in a commercial partnership those 30
who put more in get more out, so it should be in friendship.
But the man who is in a state of need and inferiority makes
the opposite claim; they think it is the part of a good friend

to help those who are in need; what, they say, is the use of
being the friend of a good man or a powerful man, if one is
35 to get nothing out of it?

At all events it seems that each party is justified in his
1163ᵇ claim, and that each should get more out of the friendship
than the other—not more of the same thing, however, but
the superior more honour and the inferior more gain; for
honour is the prize of virtue and of beneficence, while gain
is the assistance required by inferiority.

It seems to be so in constitutional arrangements also; the
5 man who contributes nothing good to the common stock
is not honoured; for what belongs to the public is given to
the man who benefits the public, and honour does belong
to the public. It is not possible to get wealth from the
10 common stock and at the same time honour. For no one
puts up with the smaller share in *all* things; therefore to the
man who loses in wealth they assign honour and to the man
who is willing to be paid, wealth, since the proportion to
merit equalizes the parties and preserves the friendship, as
we have said.[13]

This then is also the way in which we should associate
with unequals; the man who is benefited in respect of
wealth or virtue must give honour in return, repaying what
he can. For friendship asks a man to do what he can, not
15 what is proportional to the merits of the case; since that
cannot always be done, e. g. in honours paid to the gods or
to parents; for no one could ever return to them the equivalent of what he gets, but the man who serves them to the
utmost of his power is thought to be a good man.

This is why it would not seem open to a man to disown
20 his father (though a father may disown his son; being in
debt, he should repay, but there is nothing by doing which
a son will have done the equivalent of what he has received,
so that he is always in debt. But creditors can remit a debt;
and a father can therefore do so too. At the same time it is
thought that presumably no one would repudiate a son

[13] 1162ᵃ 34–ᵇ 4. Cf. 1158ᵇ 27. 1159ᵃ 35–ᵇ 3.

who was not far gone in wickedness; for apart from the
natural friendship of father and son it is human nature not
to reject a son's assistance. But the son, if he *is* wicked, will 25
naturally avoid aiding his father, or not be zealous about
it; for most people wish to get benefits, but avoid doing
them, as a thing unprofitable.—So much for these questions.

BOOK IX

1 In all friendships between dissimilars it is, as we have
said,[1] proportion that equalizes the parties and preserves the friendship; e. g. in the political form of friendship the shoemaker gets a return for his shoes in proportion 35
to his worth, and the weaver and all other craftsmen do the 1164ᵃ
same. Now here a common measure has been provided in
the form of money, and therefore everything is referred
to this and measured by this; but in the friendship of lovers
sometimes the lover complains that his excess of love is not
met by love in return (though perhaps there is nothing 5
lovable about him), while often the beloved complains
that the lover who formerly promised everything now per-
forms nothing. Such incidents happen when the lover loves
the beloved for the sake of pleasure while the beloved loves
the lover for the sake of utility, and they do not both
possess the qualities expected of them. If these be the objects of the friendship it is dissolved when they do not
get the things that formed the motives of their love; for 10
each did not love the other person himself but the qualities he had, and these were not enduring; that is why the
friendships also are transient. But the love of characters,
as has been said, endures because it is self-dependent.[2] Differences arise when what they get is something different
and not what they desire; for it is like getting nothing at all

[1] This has not been said precisely of friendship between dissimilars,
but Cf. 1132ᵇ 31–33, 1158ᵇ 27, 1159ᵃ 35–ᵇ 3, 1162ᵃ 34–ᵇ 4, 1163ᵇ
11.

[2] 1156ᵇ 9–12.

15 when we do not get what we aim at; compare the story of the person who made promises to a lyre-player, promising him the more, the better he sang, but in the morning, when the other demanded the fulfilment of his promises, said that he had given pleasure [3] for pleasure. Now if this had been what each wanted, all would have been well; but if the one wanted enjoyment but the other gain, and the one has what he wants while the other has not, the terms of the association will not have been properly fulfilled; for 20 what each in fact wants is what he attends to, and it is for the sake of that that he will give what he has.

But who is to fix the worth of the service; he who makes the sacrifice or he who has got the advantage? At any rate the other seems to leave it to him. This is what they say 25 Protagoras used to do; [4] whenever he taught anything whatsoever, he bade the learner assess the value of the knowledge, and accepted the amount so fixed. But in such matters some men approve of the saying 'let a man have his fixed reward'.

Those who get the money first and then do none of the things they said they would, owing to the extravagance of their promises, naturally find themselves the objects of complaint; for they do not fulfil what they agreed to. The 30 sophists are perhaps compelled to do this because no one would give money for the things they *do* know. These people then, if they do not do what they have been paid for, are naturally made the objects of complaint.

But where there is no contract of service, those who give up something for the sake of the other party cannot (as we have said [5]) be complained of (for that is the nature of the 35 friendship of virtue), and the return to them must be made 1164ᵇ on the basis of their purpose (for it is purpose that is the characteristic thing in a friend and in virtue). And so too, it seems, should one make a return to those with whom one

---

[3] i. e. the pleasure of expectation.
[4] Cf. Pl. *Prot.* 328 B, C.
[5] 1162ᵇ 6–13.

has studied philosophy; for their worth cannot be measured against money, and they can get no honour which will balance their services, but still it is perhaps enough, 5 as it is with the gods and with one's parents, to give them what one can.

If the gift was not of this sort, but was made with a view to a return, it is no doubt preferable that the return made should be one that seems fair to both parties, but if this cannot be achieved, it would seem not only necessary that the person who gets the first service should fix the reward, 10 but also just; for if the other gets in return the equivalent of the advantage the beneficiary has received, or the price he would have paid for the pleasure, he will have got what is fair as from the other.

We see this happening too with things put up for sale, and in some places there are laws providing that no actions shall arise out of voluntary contracts, on the assumption that one should settle with a person to whom one has given 15 credit, in the spirit in which one bargained with him. The law holds that it is more just that the person to whom credit was given should fix the terms than that the person who gave a credit should do so. For most things are not assessed at the same value by those who have them and those who want them; each class values highly what is its own and what it is offering; yet the return is made on the 20 terms fixed by the receiver. But no doubt the receiver should assess a thing not at what it seems worth when he has it, but at what he assessed it at before he had it.

2   A further problem is set by such questions as, whether one should in all things give the preference to one's father and obey him, or whether when one is ill one should trust a doctor, and when one has to elect a general should 25 elect a man of military skill; and similarly whether one should render a service by preference to a friend or to a good man, and should show gratitude to a benefactor or oblige a friend, if one cannot do both.

All such questions are hard, are they not, to decide with precision? For they admit of many variations of all sorts in
30 respect both of the magnitude of the service and of its nobility and necessity. But that we should not give the preference in all things to the same person is plain enough; and we must for the most part return benefits rather than oblige friends, as we must pay back a loan to a creditor rather than make one to a friend. But perhaps even this is not always true; e. g. should a man who has been ransomed
35 out of the hands of brigands ransom his ransomer in re-
1165ª turn, whoever he may be (or pay him if he has not been captured but demands payment), or should he ransom his father? It would seem that he should ransom his father in preference even to himself. As we have said,[6] then, generally the debt should be paid, but if the gift is exceedingly noble or exceedingly necessary, one should defer to these
5 considerations. For sometimes it is not even fair to return the equivalent of what one has received, when the one man has done a service to one whom he knows to be good, while the other makes a return to one whom he believes to be bad. For that matter, one should sometimes not lend in return to one who has lent to oneself; for the one person lent to a good man, expecting to recover his loan, while the other has no hope of recovering from one who is believed
10 to be bad. Therefore if the facts really are so, the demand is not fair; and if they are not, but people think they are, they would be held to be doing nothing strange in refusing. As we have often pointed out,[7] then, discussions about feelings and actions have just as much definiteness as their subject-matter.

That we should not make the same return to everyone, nor give a father the preference in everything, as one does
15 not sacrifice everything to Zeus,[8] is plain enough; but since we ought to render different things to parents, brothers,

[6] 1164ᵇ 31–1165ª 2.
[7] 1094ᵇ 11–27, 1098ª 26–29, 1103ᵇ 34–1104ª 5.
[8] Cf. 1134ᵇ 18–24.

comrades, and benefactors, we ought to render to each class what is appropriate and becoming. And this is what people seem in fact to do; to marriages they invite their kinsfolk; for these have a part in the family and therefore in the doings that affect the family; and at funerals also they think that kinsfolk, before all others, should meet, 20 for the same reason. And it would be thought that in the matter of food we should help our parents before all others, since we owe our own nourishment to them, and it is more honourable to help in this respect the authors of our being even before ourselves; and honour too one should give to one's parents as one does to the gods, but not any and every honour; for that matter one should not give the 25 same honour to one's father and one's mother, nor again should one give them the honour due to a philosopher or to a general, but the honour due to a father, or again to a mother. To all older persons, too, one should give honour appropriate to their age, by rising to receive them and finding seats for them and so on; while to comrades and brothers one should allow freedom of speech and common use 30 of all things. To kinsmen, too, and fellow-tribesmen and fellow-citizens and to every other class one should always try to assign what is appropriate, and to compare the claims of each class with respect to nearness of relation and to virtue or usefulness. The comparison is easier when the persons belong to the same class, and more laborious when they are different. Yet we must not on *that* account 35 shrink from the task, but decide the question as best we can.

3   Another question that arises is whether friendships should or should not be broken off when the other party does not remain the same. Perhaps we may say that 1165ᵇ there is nothing strange in breaking off a friendship based on utility or pleasure, when our friends no longer have these attributes. For it was of these attributes that we were the friends; and when these have failed it is reasonable to

⁵ love no longer. But one might complain of another if, when he loved us for our usefulness or pleasantness, he pretended to love us for our character. For, as we said at the outset,⁹ most differences arise between friends when they are not friends in the spirit in which they think they are. So when a man has deceived himself and has thought he was being loved for his character, when the other person ¹⁰ was doing nothing of the kind, he must blame himself; but when he has been deceived by the pretences of the other person, it is just that he should complain against his deceiver; he will complain with more justice than one does against people who counterfeit the currency, inasmuch as the wrongdoing is concerned with something more valuable.

But if one accepts another man as good, and he turns out badly and is seen to do so, must one still love him? Surely it is impossible, since not everything can be loved, ¹⁵ but only what is good. What is evil neither can nor should be loved; for it is not one's duty to be a lover of evil, nor to become like what is bad; and we have said ¹⁰ that like is dear to like. Must the friendship, then, be forthwith broken off? Or is this not so in all cases, but only when one's friends are incurable in their wickedness? If they are capable of being reformed one should rather come to the ²⁰ assistance of their character or their property, inasmuch as this is better and more characteristic of friendship. But a man who breaks off such a friendship would seem to be doing nothing strange; for it was not to a man of this sort that he was a friend; when his friend has changed, therefore, and he is unable to save him, he gives him up.

But if one friend remained the same while the other became better and far outstripped him in virtue, should ²⁵ the latter treat the former as a friend? Surely he cannot. When the interval is great this becomes most plain, e. g. in the case of childish friendships; if one friend remained a

⁹ 1162ᵇ 23–25.
¹⁰ 1156ᵇ 19–21, 1159ᵇ 1.

child in intellect while the other became a fully developed
man, how could they be friends when they neither approved of the same things nor delighted in and were pained
by the same things? For not even with regard to each other
will their tastes agree, and without this (as we saw [11]) they
cannot be friends; for they cannot live together. But we
have discussed these matters.[12]

Should he, then, behave no otherwise towards him than
he would if he had never been his friend? Surely he should
keep a remembrance of their former intimacy, and as we
think we ought to oblige friends rather than strangers, so
to those who have been our friends we ought to make
some allowance for our former friendship, when the
breach has not been due to excess of wickedness.

4 Friendly relations with one's neighbours, and the
marks by which friendships are defined, seem to have **1166ᵃ**
proceeded from a man's relations to himself. For (1) we define a friend as one who wishes and does what is good, or
seems so, for the sake of his friend, or (2) as one who
wishes his friend to exist and live, for his sake; which
mothers do to their children, and friends do who have
come into conflict. And (3) others define him as one who
lives with and (4) has the same tastes as another, or (5)
one who grieves and rejoices with his friend; and this too
is found in mothers most of all. It is by some one of these
characteristics that friendship too is defined.

Now each of these is true of the good man's relation to
himself (and of all other men in so far as they think themselves good; virtue and the good man seem, as has been
said,[13] to be the measure of every class of things). For [14]
his opinions are harmonious, and he desires the same things
with all his soul; and therefore [15] he wishes for himself what

---

[11] 1157ᵇ 22–24.
[12] ib. 17–24, 1158ᵇ 33–35.
[13] 1113ᵃ 22–33, Cf. 1099ᵃ 13.
[14] (4) above.
[15] (1) above.

is good and what seems so, and does it (for it is character-
15 istic of the good man to work out the good), and does so
for his own sake (for he does it for the sake of the intellectual element in him, which is thought to be the man
himself); and [16] he wishes himself to live and be preserved,
and especially the element by virtue of which he thinks.
For existence is good to the virtuous man, and each man
wishes himself what is good, while no one chooses to
20 possess the whole world if he has first to become some one
else (for that matter, even now God possesses the good [17]);
he wishes for this only on condition of being whatever he is;
and the element that thinks would seem to be the individual man, or to be so more than any other element in
him. And [18] such a man wishes to live with himself; for he
does so with pleasure, since the memories of his past acts
25 are delightful and his hopes for the future are good, and
therefore pleasant. His mind is well stored too with subjects of contemplation. And [19] he grieves and rejoices, more
than any other, with himself; for the same thing is always
painful, and the same thing always pleasant, and not one
thing at one time and another at another; he has, so to
speak, nothing to repent of.

Therefore, since each of these characteristics belongs
30 to the good man in relation to himself, and he is related to
his friend as to himself (for his friend is another self),
friendship too is thought to be one of these attributes,
and those who have these attributes to be friends. Whether
there is or is not friendship between a man and himself
is a question we may dismiss for the present; [20] there would
35 seem to be friendship in so far as he is two or more, to
1166b judge from the aforementioned attributes of friendship,

---

[17] sc. but as no one gains by God's now having the good, he would
not gain if a new person which was no longer himself were to possess
it. Cf. 1159[a] 5–11.

[18] (3) above.
[19] (5) above.
[20] Cf. 1168[a] 28–1169[b] 2.

and from the fact that the extreme of friendship is likened to one's love for oneself.

But the attributes named seem to belong even to the majority of men, poor creatures though they may be. Are we to say then that in so far as they are satisfied with themselves and think they are good, they share in these attributes? Certainly no one who is thoroughly bad and impious has these attributes, or even seems to do so. They hardly belong even to inferior people; for they [21] are at variance with themselves, and have appetites for some things and rational desires for others. This is true, for instance, of incontinent people; for they choose, instead of the things they themselves think good, things that are pleasant but hurtful; while others again, through cowardice and laziness, shrink from doing what they think best for themselves. And [22] those who have done many terrible deeds and are hated for their wickedness even shrink from life and destroy themselves. And [23] wicked men seek for people with whom to spend their days, and shun themselves; for they remember many a grievous deed, and anticipate others like them, when they are by themselves, but when they are with others they forget. And [24] having nothing lovable in them they have no feeling of love to themselves. Therefore [25] also such men do not rejoice or grieve with themselves; for their soul is rent by faction, and one element in it by reason of its wickedness grieves when it abstains from certain acts, while the other part is pleased, and one draws them this way and the other that, as if they were pulling them in pieces. If a man cannot at the same time be pained and pleased, at all events after a short time he is pained because he was pleased, and he could have wished that these things had not been pleasant to him; for bad men are laden with repentance.

---

[21] (4) above.
[22] (2) above.
[23] (3) above.
[24] (1) above.
[25] (5) above.

Therefore the bad man does not seem to be amicably
25 disposed even to himself, because there is nothing in him
to love; so that if to be thus is the height of wretchedness,
we should strain every nerve to avoid wickedness and
should endeavour to be good; for so and only so can one
be either friendly to oneself or a friend to another.

5   Goodwill is a friendly sort of relation, but is not
30   *identical* with friendship; for one may have goodwill
both towards people whom one does not know, and without their knowing it, but not friendship. This has indeed
been said already.[26] But goodwill is not even friendly feeling. For it does not involve intensity or desire, whereas
these accompany friendly feeling; and friendly feeling implies intimacy while goodwill may arise of a sudden, as it
35 does towards competitors in a contest; we come to feel
1167a goodwill for them and to share in their wishes, but we
would not *do* anything with them; for, as we said, we feel
goodwill suddenly and love them only superficially.

Goodwill seems, then, to be a beginning of friendship,
as the pleasure of the eye is the beginning of love. For no
one loves if he has not first been delighted by the form
5 of the beloved, but he who delights in the form of another
does not, for all that, love him, but only does so when he
also longs for him when absent and craves for his presence;
so too it is not possible for people to be friends if they
have not come to feel goodwill for each other, but those
who feel goodwill are not for all that friends; for they only
wish well to those for whom they feel goodwill, and would
not do anything with them nor take trouble for them. And
10 so one might by an extension of the term friendship say
that goodwill is inactive friendship, though when it is pro-
longed and reaches the point of intimacy it becomes friendship—not the friendship based on utility nor that based on
pleasure; for goodwill too does not arise on those terms.
The man who has received a benefit bestows goodwill in

[26] 1155b 32–1156a 5.

return for what has been done to him, but in doing so is only doing what is just; while he who wishes some one to prosper because he hopes for enrichment through him 15 seems to have goodwill not to him but rather to himself, just as a man is not a friend to another if he cherishes him for the sake of some use to be made of him. In general, goodwill arises on account of some excellence and worth, when one man seems to another beautiful or brave or something of the sort, as we pointed out in the case of competitors in a contest. 20

6 Unanimity also seems to be a friendly relation. For this reason it is not identity of opinion; for that might occur even with people who do not know each other; nor do we say that people who have the same views on any and every subject are unanimous, e. g. those who agree about 25 the heavenly bodies (for unanimity about these is not a friendly relation), but we do say that a city is unanimous when men have the same opinion about what is to their interest, and choose the same actions, and do what they have resolved in common. It is about things to be done, therefore, that people are said to be unanimous, and, among these, about matters of consequence and in which it is possible for both or all parties to get what they want; e. g. a city is unanimous when all its citizens think that 30 the offices in it should be elective, or that they should form an alliance with Sparta, or that Pittacus should be their ruler—at a time when he himself was also willing to rule. But when each of two people wishes himself to have the thing in question, like the captains in the *Phoenissae*,²⁷ they are in a state of faction; for it is not 35 unanimity when each of two parties thinks of the same thing, whatever that may be, but only when they think of the same thing in the same hands, e. g. when both the common people and those of the better class wish the best **1167ᵉ** men to rule; for thus and thus alone do all get what they

²⁷ Eteocles and Polynices (Eur. *Phoen.* 588 ff.).

aim at. Unanimity seems, then, to be political friendship, as indeed it is commonly said to be; for it is concerned with things that are to our interest and have an influence on our life.

5   Now such unanimity is found among good men; for they are unanimous both in themselves and with one another, being, so to say, of one mind (for the wishes of such men are constant and not at the mercy of opposing currents like a strait of the sea), and they wish for what is just and what is advantageous, and these are the objects of their common endeavour as well. But bad men cannot be unanimous except to a small extent, any more than they 10 can be friends, since they aim at getting more than their share of advantages, while in labour and public service they fall short of their share; and each man wishing for advantage to himself criticizes his neighbour and stands in his way; for if people do not watch it carefully the common weal is soon destroyed. The result is that they are in a state 15 of faction, putting compulsion on each other but unwilling themselves to do what is just.

7   Benefactors are thought to love those they have benefited, more than those who have been well treated love those that have treated them well, and this is discussed as though it were paradoxical. Most people think it is because the latter are in the position of debtors and the former of creditors; and therefore as, in the case of loans, 20 debtors wish their creditors did not exist, while creditors actually take care of the safety of their debtors, so it is thought that benefactors wish the objects of their action to exist since they will then get their gratitude, while the 25 beneficiaries take no interest in making this return. Epicharmus would perhaps declare that they say this because they 'look at things on their bad side', but it is quite like human nature; for most people are forgetful, and are more anxious to be well treated than to treat others well. But the

cause would seem to be more deeply rooted in the nature
of things; the case of those who have lent money is not
even analogous. For they have no friendly feeling to their
debtors, but only a wish that they may be kept safe with 30
a view to what is to be got from them; while those who have
done a service to others feel friendship and love for those
they have served even if these are not of any use to them
and never will be. This is what happens with craftsmen
too; every man loves his own handiwork better than he 35
would be loved by it if it came alive; and this happens perhaps most of all with poets; for they have an excessive love 1168
for their own poems, doting on them as if they were their
children. This is what the position of benefactors is like;
for that which they have treated well is their handiwork,
and therefore they love this more than the handiwork does
its maker. The cause of this is that existence is to all men a 5
thing to be chosen and loved, and that we exist by virtue
of activity (i. e. by living and acting), and that the handiwork is in a sense, the producer in activity; he loves his
handiwork, therefore, because he loves existence. And this
is rooted in the nature of things; for what he is in potentiality, his handiwork manifests in activity.

At the same time to the benefactor that is noble which
depends on his action, so that he delights in the object of
his action, whereas to the patient there is nothing noble 10
in the agent, but at most something advantageous, and this
is less pleasant and lovable. What is pleasant is the activity
of the present, the hope of the future, the memory of the
past; but most pleasant is that which depends on activity,
and similarly this is most lovable. Now for a man who has
made something his work remains (for the noble is last- 15
ing), but for the person acted on the utility passes away.
And the memory of noble things is pleasant, but that of
useful things is not likely to be pleasant, or is less so; though
the reverse seems true of expectation.

Further, love is like activity, being loved like passivity;

and loving and its concomitants are attributes of those who
20 are the more active.[28]

Again, all men love more what they have won by labour;
e. g. those who have made their money love it more than
those who have inherited it; and to be well treated seems
to involve no labour, while to treat others well is a laborious
25 task. These are the reasons, too, why mothers are fonder
of their children than fathers; bringing them into the world
costs them more pains, and they know better that the children are their own. This last point, too, would seem to
apply to benefactors.

8 The question is also debated, whether a man should
love himself most, or some one else. People criticize
those who love themselves most, and call them self-lovers,
30 using this as an epithet of disgrace, and a bad man seems
to do everything for his own sake, and the more so the more
wicked he is—and so men reproach him, for instance, with
doing nothing of his own accord—while the good man acts
for honour's sake, and the more so the better he is, and acts
for his friend's sake, and sacrifices his own interest.
35   But the facts clash with these arguments, and this is not
1168ᵇ surprising. For men say that one ought to love best one's
best friend, and a man's best friend is one who wishes well
to the object of his wish for his sake, even if no one is to
know of it; and these attributes are found most of all in a
man's attitude towards himself, and so are all the other
5 attributes by which a friend is defined; for, as we have
said,[29] it is from this relation that all the characteristics of
friendship have extended to our neighbours. All the prov-
erbs, too, agree with this, e. g. 'a single soul', and 'what
friends have is common property', and 'friendship is equality', and 'charity begins at home'; for all these marks will
be found most in a man's relation to himself; he is his own
best friend and therefore ought to love himself best. It is

[28] i. e. benefactors.
[29] Ch. 4.

therefore a reasonable question, which of the two views 10 we should follow; for both are plausible.

Perhaps we ought to mark off such arguments from each other and determine how far and in what respects each view is right. Now if we grasp the sense in which each school uses the phrase 'lover of self', the truth may become 15 evident. Those who use the term as one of reproach ascribe self-love to people who assign to themselves the greater share of wealth, honours, and bodily pleasures; for these are what most people desire, and busy themselves about as though they were the best of all things, which is the reason, too, why they become objects of competition. So those who are grasping with regard to these things gratify their ap- 20 petites and in general their feelings and the irrational element of the soul; and most men are of this nature (which is the reason why the epithet has come to be used as it is—it takes its meaning from the prevailing type of self-love, which is a bad one); it is just, therefore, that men who are lovers of self in this way are reproached for being so. That it is those who give themselves the preference in regard to objects of this sort that most people usually call lovers of self is plain; for if a man were always anxious that he him- 25 self, above all things, should act justly, temperately, or in accordance with any other of the virtues, and in general were always to try to secure for himself the honourable course, no one will call such a man a lover of self or blame him.

But such a man would seem more than the other a lover of self; at all events he assigns to himself the things that are noblest and best, and gratifies the most authoritative element in himself and in all things obeys this; and just as a 30 city or any other systematic whole is most properly identified with the most authoritative element in it, so is a man; and therefore the man who loves this and gratifies it is most of all a lover of self. Besides, a man is said to have or not to have self-control according as his reason has or has not the control, on the assumption that this is the man himself;

35 and the things men have done on a rational principle are
1169ᵉ thought most properly their own acts and voluntary acts.
That this is the man himself, then, or is so more than anything else, is plain, and also that the good man loves most
this part of him. Whence it follows that he is most truly a
lover of self, of another type than that which is a matter
of reproach, and as different from that as living according
to a rational principle is from living as passion dictates, and
desiring what is noble from desiring what seems advantageous. Those, then, who busy themselves in an exceptional
degree with noble actions all men approve and praise; and if
all were to strive towards what is noble and strain every
nerve to do the noblest deeds, everything would be as it
should be for the common weal, and every one would
10 secure for himself the goods that are greatest, since virtue is
the greatest of goods.

Therefore the good man should be a lover of self (for he
will both himself profit by doing noble acts, and will
benefit his fellows), but the wicked man should not; for he
will hurt both himself and his neighbours, following as he
15 does evil passions. For the wicked man, what he does
clashes with what he ought to do, but what the good man
ought to do he does; for reason in each of its possessors
chooses what is best for itself, and the good man obeys his
reason. It is true of the good man too that he does many
acts for the sake of his friends and his country, and if neces-
20 sary dies for them; for he will throw away both wealth and
honours and in general the goods that are objects of competition, gaining for himself nobility; since he would prefer
a short period of intense pleasure to a long one of mild enjoyment, a twelve-month of noble life to many years of
25 humdrum existence, and one great and noble action to
many trivial ones. Now those who die for others doubtless
attain this result; it is therefore a great prize that they
choose for themselves. They will throw away wealth too on
condition that their friends will gain more; for while a
man's friend gains wealth he himself achieves nobility; he

is therefore assigning the greater good to himself. The same 30
too is true of honour and office; all these things he will
sacrifice to his friend; for this is noble and laudable for himself. Rightly then is he thought to be good, since he chooses
nobility before all else. But he may even give up actions to
his friend; it may be nobler to become the cause of his
friend's acting than to act himself. In all the actions, there- 35
fore, that men are praised for, the good man is seen to
assign to himself the greater share in what is noble. In this
sense, then, as has been said, a man should be a lover of 1169^1
self; but in the sense in which most men are so, he ought
not.

9 It is also disputed whether the happy man will need
friends or not. It is said that those who are supremely
happy and self-sufficient have no need of friends; for they 5
have the things that are good, and therefore being self-
sufficient they need nothing further, while a friend, being
another self, furnishes what a man cannot provide by his
own effort; whence the saying 'when fortune is kind, what
need of friends?' But it seems strange, when one assigns all
good things to the happy man, not to assign friends, who 10
are thought the greatest of external goods. And if it is more
characteristic of a friend to do well by another than to be
well done by, and to confer benefits is characteristic of the
good man and of virtue, and it is nobler to do well by
friends than by strangers, the good man will need people
to do well by. This is why the question is asked whether we 15
need friends more in prosperity or in adversity, on the assumption that not only does a man in adversity need people
to confer benefits on him, but also those who are prospering need people to do well by. Surely it is strange, too, to
make the supremely happy man a solitary; for no one would
choose the whole world on condition of being alone, since
man is a political creature and one whose nature is to live
with others. Therefore even the happy man lives with
others; for he has the things that are by nature good. And

20 plainly it is better to spend his days with friends and good men than with strangers or any chance persons. Therefore the happy man needs friends.

What then is it that the first school means, and in what respect is it right? Is it that most men identify friends with useful people? Of such friends indeed the supremely happy man will have no need, since he already has the things that 25 are good; nor will he need those whom one makes one's friends because of their pleasantness, or he will need them only to a small extent (for his life, being pleasant, has no need of adventitious pleasure); and because he does not need such friends he is thought not to need friends.

But that is surely not true. For we have said at the outset [30] that happiness is an activity; and activity plainly comes into being and is not present at the start like a piece 30 of property. If (1) happiness lies in living and being active, and the good man's activity is virtuous and pleasant in itself, as we have said at the outset,[31] and (2) a thing's being one's own is one of the attributes that make it pleasant, and (3) we can contemplate our neighbours better than ourselves and their actions better than our own, and if the 35 actions of virtuous men who are their friends are pleasant to 1170ᵃ good men (since these have both the attributes that are naturally pleasant [32])—if this be so, the supremely happy man will need friends of this sort, since his purpose is to contemplate worthy actions and actions that are his own, and the actions of a good man who is his friend have both these qualities.

Further, men think that the happy man ought to live pleasantly. Now if he were a solitary, life would be hard for 5 him; for by oneself it is not easy to be continuously active; but with others and towards others it is easier. With others therefore his activity will be more continuous, and it is in itself pleasant, as it ought to be for the man who is su-

[30] 1098ᵃ 16ᵇ, 31–1099ᵃ 7.
[31] 1099ᵃ 14, 21.
[32] i. e. the attribute of goodness and that of being their own.

premely happy; for a good man qua good delights in virtuous actions and is vexed at vicious ones, as a musical man enjoys beautiful tunes but is pained at bad ones. A certain 10 training in virtue arises also from the company of the good, as Theognis has said before us.

If we look deeper into the nature of things, a virtuous friend seems to be naturally desirable for a virtuous man. For that which is good by nature, we have said,[33] is for the virtuous man good and pleasant in itself. Now life is de- 15 fined in the case of animals by the power of perception, in that of man by the power of perception or thought; and a power is defined by reference to the corresponding activity, which is the essential thing; therefore life seems to be essentially the act of perceiving or thinking. And life is among the things that are good and pleasant in themselves, 20 since it is determinate and the determinate is of the nature of the good; and that which is good by nature is also good for the virtuous man (which is the reason why life seems pleasant to all men); but we must not apply this to a wicked and corrupt life nor to a life spent in pain; for such a life is indeterminate, as are its attributes. The nature of 25 pain will become plainer in what follows.[34] But if life itself is good and pleasant (which it seems to be, from the very fact that all men desire it, and particularly those who are good and supremely happy; for to such men life is most desirable, and their existence is the most supremely happy); and if he who sees perceives that he sees, and he who hears, that he hears, and he who walks, that he walks, and in the 30 case of all other activities similarly there is something which perceives that we are active, so that if we perceive, we perceive that we perceive, and if we think, that we think; and if to perceive that we perceive or think is to perceive that we exist (for existence was defined as perceiv- 1170 ing or thinking); and if perceiving that one lives is in itself one of the things that are pleasant (for life is by nature

[33] 1099[a] 7–11, 1113[a] 25–33.
[34] x. 1–5.

good, and to perceive what is good present in oneself is pleasant); and if life is desirable, and particularly so for good men, because to them existence is good and pleasant 5 (for they are pleased at the consciousness of the presence in them of what is in itself good); and if as the virtuous man is to himself, he is to his friend also (for his friend is another self):—if all this be true, as his own being is desirable for each man, so, or almost so, is that of his friend. Now his being was seen to be desirable because he per- 10 ceived his own goodness, and such perception is pleasant in itself. He needs, therefore, to be conscious of the existence of his friend as well, and this will be realized in their living together and sharing in discussion and thought; for this is what living together would seem to mean in the case of man, and not, as in the case of cattle, feeding in the same place.

If, then, being is in itself desirable for the supremely 15 happy man (since it is by its nature good and pleasant), and that of his friend is very much the same, a friend will be one of the things that are desirable. Now that which is desirable for him he must have, or he will be deficient in this respect. The man who is to be happy will therefore need virtuous friends.

20 **10**   Should we, then, make as many friends as possible, or—as in the case of hospitality it is thought to be suitable advice, that one should be 'neither a man of many guests nor a man with none'—will that apply to friendship as well; should a man neither be friendless nor have an excessive number of friends?

To friends made with a view to utility this saying would seem thoroughly applicable; for to do services to many people in return is a laborious task and life is not long 25 enough for its performance. Therefore friends in excess of those who are sufficient for our own life are superfluous, and hindrances to the noble life; so that we have no need of them. Of friends made with a view to *pleasure*, also, few are enough, as a little seasoning in food is enough.

But as regards *good* friends, should we have as many as possible, or is there a limit to the number of one's friends, as there is to the size of a city? You cannot make a city of ten men, and if there are a hundred thousand it is a city no longer. But the proper number is presumably not a single number, but anything that falls between certain fixed points. So for friends too there is a fixed number—perhaps **1171ᶜ** the largest number with whom one can live together (for that, we found,[35] is thought to be very characteristic of friendship); and that one cannot live with many people and divide oneself up among them is plain. Further, they too must be friends of one another, if they are all to spend their days together; and it is a hard business for this condition to be fulfilled with a large number. It is found difficult, too, to rejoice and to grieve in an intimate way with many people, for it may likely happen that one has at once to be happy with one friend and to mourn with another. Presumably, then, it is well not to seek to have as many friends as possible, but as many as are enough for the purpose of living together; for it would seem actually impossible to be a great friend to many people. This is why one cannot love several people; love is ideally a sort of excess of friendship, and that can only be felt towards one person; therefore great friendship too can only be felt towards a few people. This seems to be confirmed in practice; for we do not find many people who are friends in the comradely way of friendship, and the famous friendships of this sort are always between two people. Those who have many friends and mix intimately with them all are thought to be no one's friend, except in the way proper to fellow-citizens, and such people are also called obsequious. In the way proper to fellow-citizens, indeed, it is possible to be the friend of many and yet not be obsequious but a genuinely good man;

[35] 1157ᵇ 19, 1158ᵃ 3, 10.

but one cannot have with many people the friendship based
20 on virtue and on the character of our friends themselves,
and we must be content if we find even a few such.

11 Do we need friends more in good fortune or in bad?
They are sought after in both; for while men in adversity need help, in prosperity they need people to live with
and to make the objects of their beneficence; for they wish
to do well by others. Friendship, then, is more necessary in
25 bad fortune, and so it is useful friends that one wants in
this case; but it is more noble in good fortune, and so we
also seek for good men as our friends, since it is more desirable to confer benefits on these and to live with these.
For the very presence of friends is pleasant both in good
30 fortune and also in bad, since grief is lightened when
friends sorrow with us. Hence one might ask whether they
share as it were our burden, or—without that happening—
their presence by its pleasantness, and the thought of their
grieving with us, make our pain less. Whether it is for these
reasons or for some other that our grief is lightened, is a
question that may be dismissed; at all events what we have
described appears to take place.
But their presence seems to contain a mixture of various
35 factors. The very seeing of one's friends is pleasant, espe-
1171ᵇ cially if one is in adversity, and becomes a safeguard against
grief (for a friend tends to comfort us both by the sight of
him and by his words, if he is tactful, since he knows our
5 character and the things that please or pain us); but to see
him pained at our misfortunes is painful; for every one
shuns being a cause of pain to his friends. For this reason
people of a manly nature guard against making their friends
grieve with them, and, unless he be exceptionally insensible
to pain, such a man cannot stand the pain that ensues for
his friends, and in general does not admit fellow-mourners
10 because he is not himself given to mourning; but women
and womanly men enjoy sympathisers in their grief, and
love them as friends and companions in sorrow. But in all

things one obviously ought to imitate the better type of person.

On the other hand, the presence of friends in our *prosperity* implies both a pleasant passing of our time and the pleasant thought of their pleasure at our own good fortune. For this cause it would seem that we ought to summon our friends readily to share our good fortunes (for the beneficent character is a noble one), but summon them to our bad fortunes with hesitation; for we ought to give them as little a share as possible in our evils—whence the saying 'enough is my misfortune'. We should summon friends to us most of all when they are likely by suffering a few inconveniences to do us a great service.

Conversely, it is fitting to go unasked and readily to the aid of those in adversity (for it is characteristic of a friend to render services, and especially to those who are in need and have not demanded them; such action is nobler and pleasanter for both persons); but when our friends are prosperous we should join readily in their activities (for they need friends for these too), but be tardy in coming forward to be the objects of their kindness; for it is not noble to be keen to receive benefits. Still, we must no doubt avoid getting the reputation of kill-joys by repulsing them; for that sometimes happens.

The presence of friends, then, seems desirable in all circumstances.

12 Does it not follow, then, that, as for lovers the sight of the beloved is the thing they love most, and they prefer this sense to the others because on it love depends most for its being and for its origin, so for friends the most desirable thing is living together? For friendship is a partnership, and as a man is to himself, so is he to his friend; now in his own case the consciousness of his being is desirable, and so therefore is the consciousness of his friend's being, and the activity of this consciousness is produced when they live together, so that it is natural that they aim 1172ᵃ

at this. And whatever existence means for each class of
men, whatever it is for whose sake they value life, in that
they wish to occupy themselves with their friends; and so
some drink together, others dice together, others join in
athletic exercises and hunting, or in the study of philoso-
5 phy, each class spending their days together in whatever
they love most in life; for since they wish to live with their
friends, they do and share in those things which give them
the sense of living together. Thus the friendship of bad
men turns out an evil thing (for because of their instability
10 they unite in bad pursuits, and besides they become evil by
becoming like each other), while the friendship of good
men is good, being augmented by their companionship;
and they are thought to become better too by their activities and by improving each other; for from each other they
take the mould of the characteristics they approve—whence
the saying 'noble deeds from noble men'.—So much, then,
15 for friendship; our next task must be to discuss pleasure.

BOOK X

1   After these matters we ought perhaps next to discuss
      pleasure. For it is thought to be most intimately con-
nected with our human nature, which is the reason why
20 in educating the young we steer them by the rudders of
pleasure and pain; it is thought, too, that to enjoy the
things we ought and to hate the things we ought has the
greatest bearing on virtue of character. For these things
extend right through life, with a weight and power of their
25 own in respect both to virtue and to the happy life, since
men choose what is pleasant and avoid what is painful;
and such things, it will be thought, we should least of all
omit to discuss, especially since they admit of much dispute. For some [1] say pleasure is the good, while others,[2] on

---

[1] The school of Eudoxus, Cf. [b]9. Aristippus is perhaps also referred
to.

[2] The school of Speusippus, Cf. 1153[b] 5.

the contrary, say it is thoroughly bad—some no doubt being persuaded that the facts are so, and others thinking it
has a better effect on our life to exhibit pleasure as a bad 30
thing even if it is not; for most people (they think) incline
towards it and are the slaves of their pleasures, for which
reason they ought to lead them in the opposite direction,
since thus they will reach the middle state. But surely this
is not correct. For arguments about matters concerned with
feelings and actions are less reliable than facts: and so when 35
they clash with the facts of perception they are despised,
and discredit the truth as well; if a man who runs down **1172ᵇ**
pleasure is once seen to be aiming at it, his inclining towards it is thought to imply that it is all worthy of being
aimed at; for most people are not good at drawing distinctions. True arguments seem, then, most useful, not only
with a view to knowledge, but with a view to life also; 5
for since they harmonize with the facts they are believed,
and so they stimulate those who understand them to live
according to them.—Enough of such questions; let us proceed to review the opinions that have been expressed about
pleasure.

2 Eudoxus thought pleasure was the good because he
     saw all things, both rational and irrational, aiming at 10
it, and because in all things that which is the object of
choice is what is excellent, and that which is most the object of choice the greatest good; thus the fact that all things
moved towards the same object indicated that this was for
all things the chief good (for each thing, he argued, finds
its own good, as it finds its own nourishment); and that
which is good for all things and at which all aim was *the* 15
good. His arguments were credited more because of the
excellence of his character than for their own sake; he was
thought to be remarkably self-controlled, and therefore it
was thought that he was not saying what he did say as a
friend of pleasure, but that the facts really were so. He
believed that the same conclusion followed no less plainly

from a study of the contrary of pleasure; pain was in itself
an object of aversion to all things, and therefore its contrary
20 must be similarly an object of choice. And again that is
most an object of choice which we choose not because or
for the sake of something else, and pleasure is admittedly of
this nature; for no one asks to what end he is pleased, thus
implying that pleasure is in itself an object of choice. Further, he argued that pleasure when added to any good, e. g.
to just or temperate action, makes it more worthy of choice,
25 and that it is only by itself that the good can be increased.

This argument seems to show it to be one of the goods,
and no more a good than any other; for every good is more
worthy of choice along with another good than taken alone.
And so it is by an argument of this kind that Plato [3] proves
the good not to be pleasure; he argues that the pleasant life
30 is more desirable with wisdom than without, and that if the
mixture is better, pleasure is not the good; for the good cannot become more desirable by the addition of anything to
it. Now it is clear that nothing else, any more than pleasure,
can be the good if it is made more desirable by the addition
of any of the things that are good in themselves. What,
then, is there that satisfies this criterion, which at the same
time we can participate in? It is something of this sort that
we are looking for.

Those who object that that at which all things aim is not
35 necessarily good are, we may surmise, talking nonsense.
For we say that that which every one thinks really is so;
1173ᵃ and the man who attacks this belief will hardly have anything more credible to maintain instead. If it is senseless
creatures that desire the things in question, there might be
something in what they say; but if intelligent creatures do
so as well, what sense can there be in this view? But perhaps even in inferior creatures there is some natural good
stronger than themselves which aims at their proper good.

Nor does the argument about the contrary of pleasure
5 seem to be correct. They say that if pain is an evil it does

[3] Phil. 60 B–F

not follow that pleasure is a good; for evil is opposed to evil
and at the same time both are opposed to the neutral state
—which is correct enough but does not apply to the things
in question. For if both pleasure and pain belonged to the 10
class of evils they ought both to be objects of aversion,
while if they belonged to the class of neutrals neither
should be an object of aversion or they should both be
equally so; but in fact people evidently avoid the one as
evil and choose the other as good; that then must be the
nature of the opposition between them.

3   Nor again, if pleasure is not a quality, does it follow
    that it is not a good; for the activities of virtue are not
qualities either, nor is happiness.

They say,[4] however, that the good is determinate, while 15
pleasure is indeterminate, because it admits of degrees.
Now if it is from the feeling of pleasure that they judge
thus, the same will be true of justice and the other virtues,
in respect of which we plainly say that people of a certain
character are so more or less, and act more or less in accord- 20
ance with these virtues; for people may be more just or
brave, and it is possible also to act justly or temperately
more or less. But if their judgement is based on the various
pleasures, surely they are not stating the real cause,[5] if in
fact some pleasures are unmixed and others mixed. Again,
just as health admits of degrees without being indetermi- 25
nate, why should not pleasure? The same proportion is not
found in all things, nor a single proportion always in the
same thing, but it may be relaxed and yet persist up to a
point, and it may differ in degree. The case of pleasure also
may therefore be of this kind.

Again, they assume [6] that the good is perfect while movements and comings into being are imperfect, and try to 30
exhibit pleasure as being a movement and a coming into

    [4] Ib. 24 E–25 A, 31 A.
        [5] sc., of the badness of (some) pleasures.
            [6] Pl. *Phil.* 53 C–54 D.

being. But they do not seem to be right even in saying that
it is a movement. For speed and slowness are thought to
be proper to every movement, and if a movement, e. g.
that of the heavens, has not speed or slowness in itself, it
has it in relation to something else; but of pleasure neither
of these things is true. For while we may become pleased
1173^b quickly as we may become angry quickly, we cannot be
pleased quickly, not even in relation to some one else, while
we can walk, or grow, or the like, quickly. While, then,
we can change quickly or slowly into a state of pleasure, we
cannot quickly exhibit the activity of pleasure, i. e. be
pleased. Again, how can it be a coming into being? It is not
thought that any chance thing can come out of any chance
5 thing, but that a thing is dissolved into that out of which
it comes into being; and pain would be the destruction of
that of which pleasure is the coming into being.

They say, too,[7] that pain is the lack of that which is according to nature, and pleasure is replenishment. But these
experiences are bodily. If then pleasure is replenishment
with that which is according to nature, that which feels
pleasure will be that in which the replenishment takes
10 place, i. e. the body; but that is not thought to be the case;
therefore the replenishment is not pleasure, though one
would be pleased when replenishment was taking place,
just as one would be pained if one was being operated on.[8]
This opinion seems to be based on the pains and pleasures
connected with nutrition; on the fact that when people
have been short of food and have felt pain beforehand they
are pleased by the replenishment. But this does not happen
15 with all pleasures; for the pleasures of learning and, among
the sensuous pleasures, those of smell, and also many
sounds and sights, and memories and hopes, do not pre-

---

[7] Ib. 31 E–32 B, 42 C, D.
[8] The point being that the being replenished no more *is* pleasure
than the being operated on *is* pain. For the instance, Cf. Pl. *Tim.*
65 B.

suppose pain. Of what then will these be the coming into being? There has not been lack of anything of which they could be the supplying anew.

In reply to those who bring forward the disgraceful pleasures one may say that these are not pleasant; if things 20 are pleasant to people of vicious constitution, we must not suppose that they are also pleasant to others than these, just as we do not reason so about the things that are wholesome or sweet or bitter to sick people, or ascribe whiteness to the things that seem white to those suffering from a disease of the eye. Or one might answer thus—that the pleasures are desirable, but not from *these* sources, as 25 wealth is desirable, but not as the reward of betrayal, and health, but not at the cost of eating anything and everything. Or perhaps pleasures differ in kind; for those derived from noble sources are different from those derived from base sources, and one cannot get the pleasure of the just man without being just, nor that of the musical man without being musical, and so on. 30

The fact, too, that a friend is different from a flatterer seems to make it plain that pleasure is not a good or that pleasures are different in kind; for the one is thought to consort with us with a view to the good, the other with a view to our pleasure, and the one is reproached for his conduct while the other is praised on the ground that he consorts with us for different ends. And no one would choose to live with the intellect of a child throughout his **1174ᵉ** life, however much he were to be pleased at the things that children are pleased at, nor to get enjoyment by doing some most disgraceful deed, though he were never to feel any pain in consequence. And there are many things we should be keen about even if they brought no pleasure, e. g. 5 seeing, remembering, knowing, possessing the virtues. If pleasures necessarily do accompany these, that makes no odds; we should choose these even if no pleasure resulted. It seems to be clear, then, that neither is pleasure the good

10 nor is all pleasure desirable, and that some pleasures are desirable in themselves being different in kind or in their sources from the others. So much for the things that are said about pleasure and pain.

4   What pleasure is, or what kind of thing it is, will become plainer if we take up the question again from 15 the beginning. Seeing seems to be at any moment complete, for it does not lack anything which coming into being later will complete its form; and pleasure also seems to be of this nature. For it is a whole, and at no time can one find a pleasure whose form will be completed if the pleasure lasts longer. For this reason, too, it is not a movement. For every movement (e. g. that of building) takes 20 time and is for the sake of an end, and is complete when it has made what it aims at. It is complete, therefore, only in the whole time or at that final moment. In their parts and during the time they occupy, all movements are incomplete, and are different in kind from the whole movement and from each other. For the fitting together of the stones is different from the fluting of the column, and 25 these are both different from the making of the temple; and the making of the temple is complete (for it lacks nothing with a view to the end proposed), but the making of the base or of the triglyph is incomplete; for each is the making of only a part. They differ in kind, then, and it is not possible to find at any and every time a movement complete in form, but if at all, only in the whole time. So, too, in the case of walking and all other movements. 30 For if locomotion is a movement from here to there, it, too, has differences in kind—flying, walking, leaping, and so on. And not only so, but in walking itself there are such differences; for the whence and whither are not the same in the whole racecourse and in a part of it, nor in one part 1174ᵇ and in another, nor is it the same thing to traverse this line and that; for one traverses not only a line but one which is in a place, and this one is in a different place from that. We have discussed movement with precision in another work,[9] but it seems that it is not complete at any and every time, but that the many movements are incomplete and different in kind, since the whence and whither give them 5 their form. But of pleasure the form is complete at any and every time. Plainly, then, pleasure and movement must be different from each other, and pleasure must be one of the things that are whole and complete. This would seem to be the case, too, from the fact that it is not possible to move otherwise than in time, but it is possible to be pleased; for that which takes place in a moment is a whole.

From these considerations it is clear, too, that these thinkers are not right in saying there is a movement or a coming into being of pleasure. For these cannot be ascribed to all things, but only to those that are divisible and not 10 wholes; there is no coming into being of seeing nor of a point nor of a unit, nor is any of these a movement or coming into being; therefore there is no movement or coming into being of pleasure either; for it is a whole.

Since every sense is active in relation to its object, and a sense which is in good condition acts perfectly in relation 15 to the most beautiful of its objects (for perfect activity seems to be ideally of this nature; whether we say that it is active, or the organ in which it resides, may be assumed to be immaterial), it follows that in the case of each sense the best activity is that of the best-conditioned organ in relation to the finest of its objects. And this activity will be the most complete and pleasant. For, while there is pleasure in respect of any sense, and in respect of thought 20 and contemplation no less, the most complete is pleasantest, and that of a well-conditioned organ in relation to the worthiest of its objects is the most complete; and the pleasure completes the activity. But the pleasure does not complete it in the same way as the combination of object and sense, both good, just as health and the doctor are not 25 in the same way the cause of a man's being healthy. (That pleasure is produced in respect to each sense is plain; for we speak of sights and sounds as pleasant. It is also plain that it arises most of all when both the sense is at its best and it is active in reference to an object which corresponds; when both object and perceiver are of the best there will

30 always be pleasure, since the requisite agent and patient are both present.) Pleasure completes the activity not as the corresponding permanent state does, by its immanence, but as an end which supervenes as the bloom of youth does on those in the flower of their age. So long, then, as both the intelligible or sensible object and the discriminating or contemplative faculty are as they should be, the pleasure will be involved in the activity; for when both the

1175ª passive and the active factor are unchanged and are related to each other in the same way, the same result naturally follows.

How, then, is it that no one is continuously pleased? Is it that we grow weary? Certainly all human things are incapable of continuous activity. Therefore pleasure also is

5 not continuous; for it accompanies activity. Some things delight us when they are new, but later do so less, for the same reason; for at first the mind is in a state of stimulation and intensely active about them, as people are with respect to their vision when they look hard at a thing, but afterwards our activity is not of this kind, but has grown relaxed; for which reason the pleasure also is dulled.

10   One might think that all men desire pleasure because they all aim at life; life is an activity, and each man is active about those things and with those faculties that he loves most; e. g. the musician is active with his hearing in ref-

15 erence to tunes, the student with his mind in reference to theoretical questions, and so on in each case; now pleasure completes the activities, and therefore life, which they desire. It is with good reason, then, that they aim at pleasure too, since for every one it completes life, which is desirable. But whether we choose life for the sake of pleasure or pleasure for the sake of life is a question we may dismiss

20 for the present. For they seem to be bound up together and

not to admit of separation, since without activity pleasure does not arise, and every activity is completed by the attendant pleasure.

5 For this reason pleasures seem, too, to differ in kind.

For things different in kind are, we think, completed by different things (we see this to be true both of natural objects and of things produced by art, e. g. animals, trees, 25 a painting, a sculpture, a house, an implement); and, similarly, we think that activities differing in kind are completed by things differing in kind. Now the activities of thought differ from those of the senses, and both differ among themselves, in kind; so, therefore, do the pleasures that complete them.

This may be seen, too, from the fact that each of the pleasures is bound up with the activity it completes. For an activity is intensified by its proper pleasure, since each 30 class of things is better judged of and brought to precision by those who engage in the activity with pleasure; e. g. it is those who enjoy geometrical thinking that become geometers and grasp the various propositions better, and, similarly, those who are fond of music or of building, and so on, make progress in their proper function by enjoying it; so 35 the pleasures intensify the activities, and what intensifies a thing is proper to it, but things different in kind have properties different in kind.

This will be even more apparent from the fact that ac-1175ᵇ tivities are hindered by pleasures arising from other sources. For people who are fond of playing the flute are incapable of attending to arguments if they overhear some one playing the flute, since they enjoy flute-playing more than the 5 activity in hand; so the pleasure connected with flute-playing destroys the activity concerned with argument. This happens, similarly, in all other cases, when one is active about two things at once; the more pleasant activity drives out the other, and if it is much more pleasant does so all the more, so that one even ceases from the other. This is

10 why when we enjoy anything very much we do not throw
ourselves into anything else, and do one thing only when
we are not much pleased by another; e. g. in the theatre the
people who eat sweets do so most when the actors are poor.
Now since activities are made precise and more enduring
and better by their proper pleasure, and injured by alien
15 pleasures, evidently the two kinds of pleasure are far apart.
For alien pleasures do pretty much what proper pains do,
since activities are destroyed by their proper pains; e. g. if
a man finds writing or doing sums unpleasant and painful,
he does not write, or does not do sums, because the activity
20 is painful. So an activity suffers contrary effects from its
proper pleasures and pains, i. e. from those that supervene
on it in virtue of its own nature. And alien pleasures have
been stated to do much the same as pain; they destroy
the activity, only not to the same degree.

Now since activities differ in respect of goodness and
badness, and some are worthy to be chosen, others to be
25 avoided, and others neutral, so, too, are the pleasures; for to
each activity there is a proper pleasure. The pleasure proper
to a worthy activity is good and that proper to an unworthy
activity bad; just as the appetites for noble objects are
laudable, those for base objects culpable. But the pleasures
30 involved in activities are more proper to them than the
desires; for the latter are separated both in time and in
nature, while the former are close to the activities, and so
hard to distinguish from them that it admits of dispute
whether the activity is not the same as the pleasure. (Still
pleasure does not seem to be thought or perception—that
would be strange; but because they are not found apart they
35 appear to some people the same.) As activities are different,
then, so are the corresponding pleasures. Now sight is su-
1176ª perior to touch in purity, and hearing and smell to taste;
the pleasures, therefore, are similarly superior, and those
of thought superior to these, and within each of the two
kinds some are superior to others.

Each animal is thought to have a proper pleasure, as it

has a proper function; viz. that which corresponds to its activity. If we survey them species by species, too, this will be evident; horse, dog, and man have different pleasures, as Heraclitus says 'asses would prefer sweepings to gold'; for food is pleasanter than gold to asses. So the pleasures of creatures different in kind differ in kind, and it is plausible to suppose that those of a single species do not differ. But they vary to no small extent, in the case of men at least; the same things delight some people and pain others, and are painful and odious to some, and pleasant to and liked by others. This happens, too, in the case of sweet things; the same things do not seem sweet to a man in a fever and a healthy man—nor hot to a weak man and one in good condition. The same happens in other cases. But in all such matters that which appears to the good man is thought to be really so. If this is correct, as it seems to be, and virtue and the good man as such are the measure of each thing, those also will be pleasures which appear so to him, and those things pleasant which he enjoys. If the things he finds tiresome seem pleasant to some one, that is nothing surprising; for men may be ruined and spoilt in many ways; but the things are not pleasant, but only pleasant to these people and to people in this condition. Those which are admittedly disgraceful plainly should not be said to be pleasures, except to a perverted taste; but of those that are thought to be good what kind of pleasure or what pleasure should be said to be that proper to man? Is it not plain from the corresponding activities? The pleasures follow these. Whether, then, the perfect and supremely happy man has one or more activities, the pleasures that perfect these will be said in the strict sense to be pleasures proper to man, and the rest will be so in a secondary and fractional way, as are the activities.

6 Now that we have spoken of the virtues, the forms of friendship, and the varieties of pleasure, what remains is to discuss in outline the nature of happiness, since this

is what we state the end of human nature to be. Our discussion will be the more concise if we first sum up what we
have said already. We said,[10] then, that it is not a disposition; for if it were it might belong to some one who was
35 asleep throughout his life, living the life of a plant, or,
1176ᵇ again, to some one who was suffering the greatest misfortunes. If these implications are unacceptable, and we must
rather class happiness as an activity, as we have said before,[11] and if some activities are necessary, and desirable
for the sake of something else, while others are so in themselves, evidently happiness must be placed among those
5 desirable in themselves, not among those desirable for
the sake of something else; for happiness does not lack
anything, but is self-sufficient. Now those activities are
desirable in themselves from which nothing is sought beyond the activity. And of this nature virtuous actions are
thought to be; for to do noble and good deeds is a thing
desirable for its own sake.

Pleasant amusements also are thought to be of this nature; we choose them not for the sake of other things; for
we are injured rather than benefited by them, since we are
10 led to neglect our bodies and our property. But most of the
people who are deemed happy take refuge in such pastimes,
which is the reason why those who are ready-witted at them
are highly esteemed at the courts of tyrants; they make
themselves pleasant companions in the tyrants' favourite
15 pursuits, and that is the sort of man they want. Now these
things are thought to be of the nature of happiness because
people in despotic positions spend their leisure in them,
but perhaps such people prove nothing; for virtue and reason, from which good activities flow, do not depend on
despotic position; nor, if these people, who have never
tasted pure and generous pleasure, take refuge in the bodily
20 pleasures, should these for that reason be thought more

[10] 1095ᵇ 31–1096ᵃ 2, 1098ᵇ 31–1099ᵃ 7.
[11] 1098ᵃ 5–7.

desirable; for boys, too, think the things that are valued
among themselves are the best. It is to be expected, then,
that, as different things seem valuable to boys and to men,
so they should to bad men and to good. Now, as we have
often maintained,[12] those things are both valuable and 25
pleasant which are such to the good man; and to each man
the activity in accordance with his own disposition is most
desirable, and, therefore, to the good man that which is in
accordance with virtue. Happiness, therefore, does not lie
in amusement; it would, indeed, be strange if the end were
amusement, and one were to take trouble and suffer hard-
ship all one's life in order to amuse oneself. For, in a word, 30
everything that we choose we choose for the sake of something else—except happiness, which is an end. Now to
exert oneself and work for the sake of amusement seems
silly and utterly childish. But to amuse oneself in order
that one may exert oneself, as Anacharsis puts it, seems
right; for amusement is a sort of relaxation, and we need
relaxation because we cannot work continuously. Relaxa- 35
tion, then, is not an end; for it is taken for the sake of
activity.

The happy life is thought to be virtuous; now a virtuous
life requires exertion, and does not consist in amusement. 1177ᵃ
And we say that serious things are better than laughable
things and those connected with amusement, and that the
activity of the better of any two things—whether it be two
elements of our being or two men—is the more serious; but
the activity of the better is *ipso facto* superior and more of 5
the nature of happiness. And any chance person—even a
slave—can enjoy the bodily pleasures no less than the best
man; but no one assigns to a slave a share in happiness—
unless he assigns to him also a share in human life. For 10
happiness does not lie in such occupations, but, as we have
said before,[13] in virtuous activities.

[12] 1099ᵃ 13, 1113ᵃ 22–33, 1166ᵃ 12, 1170ᵃ 14–16, 1176ᵃ 15–22.
[13] 1098ᵃ 16, 1176ᵃ 35–ᵇ9.

7   If happiness is activity in accordance with virtue, it is
reasonable that it should be in accordance with the
highest virtue; and this will be that of the best thing in us.
Whether it be reason or something else that is this element
15 which is thought to be our natural ruler and guide and to
take thought of things noble and divine, whether it be itself
also divine or only the most divine element in us, the activity of this in accordance with its proper virtue will be
perfect happiness. That this activity is contemplative we
have already said.[14]

Now this would seem to be in agreement both with what
20 we said before [15] and with the truth. For, firstly, this activity is the best (since not only is reason the best thing
in us, but the objects of reason are the best of knowable
objects); and, secondly, it is the most continuous, since we
can contemplate truth more continuously than we can *do*
anything. And we think happiness has pleasure mingled
with it, but the activity of philosophic wisdom is admit-
25 tedly the pleasantest of virtuous activities; at all events the
pursuit of it is thought to offer pleasures marvellous for
their purity and their enduringness, and it is to be expected
that those who know will pass their time more pleasantly
than those who inquire. And the self-sufficiency that is
spoken of must belong most to the contemplative activity.
For while a philosopher, as well as a just man or one pos-
30 sessing any other virtue, needs the necessaries of life, when
they are sufficiently equipped with things of that sort the
just man needs people towards whom and with whom he
shall act justly, and the temperate man, the brave man,
and each of the others is in the same case, but the philosopher, even when by himself, can contemplate truth, and
the better the wiser he is; he can perhaps do so better if
1177ᵇ he has fellow-workers, but still he is the most self-sufficient.
And this activity alone would seem to be loved for its own

[14] This has not been said, but Cf. 1095ᵇ 14–1096ª 5, 1141ª 18–ᵇ 3,
1143ᵇ 33–1144ª 6, 1145ª 6–11.

[15] 1097ª 25–ᵇ 21, 1099ª 7–21, 1173ᵇ 15–19, 1174ᵇ 20–23, 1175ᵇ
36–1176ª 3.

sake; for nothing arises from it apart from the contemplating, while from practical activities we gain more or less
apart from the action. And happiness is thought to depend 5
on leisure; for we are busy that we may have leisure, and
make war that we may live in peace. Now the activity of
the practical virtues is exhibited in political or military
affairs, but the actions concerned with these seem to be unleisurely. Warlike actions are completely so (for no one
chooses to be at war, or provokes war, for the sake of being
at war; any one would seem absolutely murderous if he 10
were to make enemies of his friends in order to bring about
battle and slaughter); but the action of the statesman is
also unleisurely, and—apart from the political action itself
—aims at despotic power and honours, or at all events
happiness, for him and his fellow citizens—a happiness
different from political action, and evidently sought as be- 15
ing different. So if among virtuous actions political and
military actions are distinguished by nobility and greatness,
and these are unleisurely and aim at an end and are not
desirable for their own sake, but the activity of reason,
which is contemplative, seems both to be superior in serious worth and to aim at no end beyond itself, and to have
its pleasure proper to itself (and this augments the 20
activity), and the self-sufficiency, leisureliness, unwearied-
ness (so far as this is possible for man), and all the other
attributes ascribed to the supremely happy man are evidently those connected with this activity, it follows that
this will be the complete happiness of man, if it be allowed
a complete term of life (for none of the attributes of happiness is incomplete).   25

But such a life would be too high for man; for it is
not in so far as he is man that he will live so, but in so
far as something divine is present in him; and by so much
as this is superior to our composite nature is its activity superior to that which is the exercise of the other kind of
virtue. If reason is divine, then, in comparison with man,
the life according to it is divine in comparison with human 30

life. But we must not follow those who advise us, being men, to think of human things, and, being mortal, of mortal things, but must, so far as we can, make ourselves immortal, and strain every nerve to live in accordance with 1178ᵃ the best thing in us; for even if it be small in bulk, much more does it in power and worth surpass everything. This would seem, too, to be each man himself, since it is the authoritative and better part of him. It would be strange, then, if he were to choose not the life of his self but that of something else. And what we said before [16] will apply now; 5 that which is proper to each thing is by nature best and most pleasant for each thing; for man, therefore, the life according to reason is best and pleasantest, since reason more than anything else *is* man. This life therefore is also the happiest.

8   But in a secondary degree the life in accordance with the other kind of virtue is happy; for the activities in 10 accordance with this befit our human estate. Just and brave acts, and other virtuous acts, we do in relation to each other, observing our respective duties with regard to contracts and services and all manner of actions and with regard to passions; and all of these seem to be typically human. 15 Some of them seem even to arise from the body, and virtue of character to be in many ways bound up with the passions. Practical wisdom, too, is linked to virtue of character, and this to practical wisdom, since the principles of practical wisdom are in accordance with the moral virtues and rightness in morals is in accordance with practical wisdom. Being connected with the passions also, the moral virtues must belong to our composite nature; and the virtues of 20 our composite nature are human; so, therefore, are the life and the happiness which correspond to these. The excellence of the reason is a thing apart; we must be content to say this much about it, for to describe it precisely is a task greater than our purpose requires. It would seem,

[16] 1169ᵇ 33, 1176ᵇ 26.

however, also to need external equipment but little, or less 25
than moral virtue does. Grant that both need the necessaries, and do so equally, even if the statesman's work is
the more concerned with the body and things of that sort;
for there will be little difference there; but in what they
need for the exercise of their activities there will be much
difference. The liberal man will need money for the doing
of his liberal deeds, and the just man too will need it for 30
the returning of services (for wishes are hard to discern, and
even people who are not just pretend to wish to act justly);
and the brave man will need power if he is to accomplish
any of the acts that correspond to his virtue, and the temperate man will need opportunity; for how else is either
he or any of the others to be recognized? It is debated, too,
whether the will or the deed is more essential to virtue, 35
which is assumed to involve both; it is surely clear that its **1178ᵇ**
perfection involves both; but for deeds many things are
needed, and more, the greater and nobler the deeds are. But
the man who is contemplating the truth needs no such
thing, at least with a view to the exercise of his activity;
indeed they are, one may say, even hindrances, at all events 5
to his contemplation; but in so far as he is a man and lives
with a number of people, he chooses to do virtuous acts;
he will therefore need such aids to living a human life.

But that perfect happiness is a contemplative activity
will appear from the following consideration as well. We
assume the gods to be above all other beings blessed and
happy; but what sort of actions must we assign to them?
Acts of justice? Will not the gods seem absurd if they make 10
contracts and return deposits, and so on? Acts of a brave
man, then, confronting dangers and running risks because
it is noble to do so? Or liberal acts? To whom will they
give? It will be strange if they are really to have money or
anything of the kind. And what would their temperate
acts be? Is not such praise tasteless, since they have no bad 15
appetites? If we were to run through them all, the circumstances of action would be found trivial and unworthy of

gods. Still, every one supposes that they *live* and therefore that they are active; we cannot suppose them to sleep like
20 Endymion. Now if you take away from a living being action, and still more production, what is left but contemplation? Therefore the activity of God, which surpasses all others in blessedness, must be contemplative; and of human activities, therefore, that which is most akin to this must be most of the nature of happiness.

This is indicated, too, by the fact that the other animals have no share in happiness, being completely deprived of such activity. For while the whole life of the gods is
25 blessed, and that of men too in so far as some likeness of such activity belongs to them, none of the other animals is happy, since they in no way share in contemplation. Happiness extends, then, just so far as contemplation does, and those to whom contemplation more fully belongs are more truly happy, not as a mere concomitant but in virtue
30 of the contemplation; for this is in itself precious. Happiness, therefore, must be some form of contemplation.

But, being a man, one will also need external prosperity; for our nature is not self-sufficient for the purpose of contemplation, but our body also must be healthy and must
35 have food and other attention. Still, we must not think
1179ᵃ that the man who is to be happy will need many things or great things, merely because he cannot be supremely happy without external goods; for self-sufficiency and action do not involve excess, and we can do noble acts without ruling
5 earth and sea; for even with moderate advantages one can act virtuously (this is manifest enough; for private persons are thought to do worthy acts no less than despots—indeed even more); and it is enough that we should have so much as that; for the life of the man who is active in accordance with virtue will be happy. Solon, too, was perhaps
10 sketching well the happy man when he described him as moderately furnished with externals but as having done (as Solon thought) the noblest acts, and lived temperately; for one can with but moderate possessions do what one

ought. Anaxagoras also seems to have supposed the happy man not to be rich nor a despot, when he said that he would not be surprised if the happy man were to seem to most people a strange person; for they judge by externals, 15 since these are all they perceive. The opinions of the wise seem, then, to harmonize with our arguments. But while even such things carry some conviction, the truth in practical matters is discerned from the facts of life; for these are 20 the decisive factor. We must therefore survey what we have already said, bringing it to the test of the facts of life, and if it harmonizes with the facts we must accept it, but if it clashes with them we must suppose it to be mere theory. Now he who exercises his reason and cultivates it seems to be both in the best state of mind and most dear to the gods. For if the gods have any care for human affairs, as 25 they are thought to have, it would be reasonable both that they should delight in that which was best and most akin to them (i. e. reason) and that they should reward those who love and honour this most, as caring for the things that are dear to them and acting both rightly and nobly. And that all these attributes belong most of all to the 30 philosopher is manifest. He, therefore, is the dearest to the gods. And he who is that will presumably be also the happiest; so that in this way too the philosopher will more than any other be happy.

9 If these matters and the virtues, and also friendship and pleasure, have been dealt with sufficiently in outline, are we to suppose that our programme has reached 35 its end? Surely, as the saying goes, where there are things to be done the end is not to survey and recognize the vari- 1179ᵃ ous things, but rather to do them; with regard to virtue, then, it is not enough to know, but we must try to have and use it, or try any other way there may be of becoming good. Now if arguments were in themselves enough to make men good, they would justly, as Theognis says, have ᵣ won very great rewards, and such rewards should have been

provided; but as things are, while they seem to have power
to encourage and stimulate the generous-minded among
our youth, and to make a character which is gently born,
10 and a true lover of what is noble, ready to be possessed by
virtue, they are not able to encourage the many to nobility
and goodness. For these do not by nature obey the sense of
shame, but only fear, and do not abstain from bad acts
because of their baseness but through fear of punishment;
living by passion they pursue their own pleasures and the
15 means to them, and avoid the opposite pains, and have not
even a conception of what is noble and truly pleasant,
since they have never tasted it. What argument would re-
mould such people? It is hard, if not impossible, to remove
by argument the traits that have long since been incorporated in the character; and perhaps we must be content
if, when all the influences by which we are thought to become good are present, we get some tincture of virtue.

Now some think that we are made good by nature, others
20 by habituation, others by teaching. Nature's part evidently
does not depend on us, but as a result of some divine causes
is present in those who are truly fortunate; while argument
and teaching, we may suspect, are not powerful with all
men, but the soul of the student must first have been
25 cultivated by means of habits for noble joy and noble hatred, like earth which is to nourish the seed. For he who
lives as passion directs will not hear argument that dis-
suades him, nor understand it if he does; and how can we
persuade one in such a state to change his ways? And in
general passion seems to yield not to argument but to
force. The character, then, must somehow be there already
30 with a kinship to virtue, loving what is noble and hating
what is base.

But it is difficult to get from youth up a right training
for virtue if one has not been brought up under right laws;
for to live temperately and hardily is not pleasant to most
people, especially when they are young. For this reason
35 their nurture and occupations should be fixed by law; for

they will not be painful when they have become customary. But it is surely not enough that when they are young **1180ᵉ** they should get the right nurture and attention; since they must, even when they are grown up, practise and be habituated to them, we shall need laws for this as well, and generally speaking to cover the whole of life; for most people obey necessity rather then argument, and punishments rather than the sense of what is noble.

This is why some think [17] that legislators ought to stimulate men to virtue and urge them forward by the motive 5 of the noble, on the assumption that those who have been well advanced by the formation of habits will attend to such influences; and that punishments and penalties should be imposed on those who disobey and are of inferior nature, while the incurably bad should be completely banished.[18] A good man (they think), since he lives with his mind fixed on what is noble, will submit to argument, while a bad man, whose desire is for pleasure, is corrected 10 by pain like a beast of burden. This is, too, why they say the pains inflicted should be those that are most opposed to the pleasures such men love.

However that may be, if (as we have said) [19] the man who is to be good must be well trained and habituated, 15 and go on to spend his time in worthy occupations and neither willingly nor unwillingly do bad actions, and if this can be brought about if men live in accordance with a sort of reason and right order, provided this has force—if this be so, the paternal command indeed has not the required force or compulsive power (nor in general has the 20 command of one man, unless he be a king or something similar), but the law has compulsive power, while it is at the same time a rule proceeding from a sort of practical wisdom and reason. And while people hate men who oppose their impulses, even if they oppose them rightly, the

[17] Pl. *Laws* 722 D ff.
[18] Pl. *Prot.* 325 A.
[19] 1179ᵇ 31–1180ᵃ 5.

law in its ordaining of what is good is not burdensome.
25   In the Spartan state alone, or almost alone, the legislator
seems to have paid attention to questions of nurture and
occupations; in most states such matters have been neglected, and each man lives as he pleases, Cyclops-fashion,
'to his own wife and children dealing law'.[20] Now it is
30 best that there should be a public and proper care for such
matters; but if they are neglected by the community it
would seem right for each man to help his children and
friends towards virtue, and that they should have the
power, or at least the will, to do this.

It would seem from what has been said that he can do
this better if he makes himself capable of legislating. For
public control is plainly effected by laws, and good con-
35 trol by good laws; whether written or unwritten would
1180ᵇ seem to make no difference, nor whether they are laws
providing for the education of individuals or of groups—
any more than it does in the case of music or gymnastics
and other such pursuits. For as in cities laws and prevailing
types of character have force, so in households do the in-
5 junctions and the habits of the father, and these have even
more because of the tie of blood and the benefits he confers; for the children start with a natural affection and
disposition to obey. Further, private education has an advantage over public, as private medical treatment has; for
while in general rest and abstinence from food are good
10 for a man in a fever, for a particular man they may not be;
and a boxer presumably does not prescribe the same style
of fighting to all his pupils. It would seem, then, that the
detail is worked out with more precision if the control is
private; for each person is more likely to get what suits his
case.

But the details can be best looked after, one by one, by
a doctor or gymnastic instructor or any one else who has
the general knowledge of what is good for every one or
for people of a certain kind (for the sciences both are

[20] *Od.* ix. 114 f.

said to be, and are, concerned with what is universal); not 15 but what some particular detail may perhaps be well looked after by an unscientific person, if he has studied accurately in the light of experience what happens in each case, just as some people seem to be their own best doctors, though they could give no help to any one else. None the less, it will perhaps be agreed that if a man does wish to become 20 master of an art or science he must go to the universal, and come to know it as well as possible; for, as we have said, it is with this that the sciences are concerned.

And surely he who wants to make men, whether many or few, better by his care must try to become capable of legislating, if it is through laws that we can become good. For to get any one whatever—any one who is put before 25 us—into the right condition is not for the first chance comer; if any one can do it, it is the man who knows, just as in medicine and all other matters which give scope for care and prudence.

Must we not, then, next examine whence or how one can learn how to legislate? Is it, as in all other cases, from statesmen? Certainly it was thought to be a part of states-manship.[21] Or is a difference apparent between states- 30 manship and the other sciences and arts? In the others the same people are found offering to teach the arts and practising them, e. g. doctors or painters; but while the sophists profess to teach politics, it is practised not by any 35 of them but by the politicians, who would seem to do so 1181ᵃ by dint of a certain skill and experience rather than of thought; for they are not found either writing or speaking about such matters (though it were a nobler occupation perhaps than composing speeches for the law-courts and the assembly), nor again are they found to have made statesmen of their own sons or any other of their friends. 5 But it was to be expected that they should if they could; for there is nothing better than such a skill that they could have left to their cities, or could prefer to have for them-

[21] 1141ᵇ 24.

selves, or, therefore, for those dearest to them. Still, experience seems to contribute not a little; else they could
10 not have become politicians by familiarity with politics; and so it seems that those who aim at knowing about the art of politics need experience as well.

But those of the sophists who profess the art seem to be very far from teaching it. For, to put the matter generally, they do not even know what kind of thing it is nor what kinds of things it is about; otherwise they would not have
15 classed it as identical with rhetoric or even inferior to it,[22] nor have thought it easy to legislate by collecting the laws that are thought well of;[23] they say it is possible to select the best laws, as though even the selection did not demand intelligence and as though right judgement were not the greatest thing, as in matters of music. For while people
20 experienced in any department judge rightly the works produced in it, and understand by what means or how they are achieved, and what harmonizes with what, the inexperienced must be content if they do not fail to see whether the work has been well or ill made—as in the case of painting. Now laws are as it were the 'works' of the political art;
1181[b] how then can one learn from them to be a legislator, or judge which are best? Even medical men do not seem to be made by a study of text-books. Yet people try, at any rate, to state not only the treatments, but also how particular
5 classes of people can be cured and should be treated—distinguishing the various habits of body; but while this seems useful to experienced people, to the inexperienced it is valueless. Surely, then, while collections of laws, and of constitutions also, may be serviceable to those who can study them and judge what is good or bad and what enact-
10 ments suit what circumstances, those who go through such collections without a practised faculty will not have right judgement (unless it be as a spontaneous gift of nature),

[22] Isoc. *Antid.* § 80.
[23] Ib. §§ 82, 83.

though they may perhaps become more intelligent in such matters.

Now our predecessors have left the subject of legislation to us unexamined; it is perhaps best, therefore, that we should ourselves study it, and in general study the question of the constitution, in order to complete to the best of our 15 ability our philosophy of human nature. First, then, if anything has been said well in detail by earlier thinkers, let us try to review it; then in the light of the constitutions we have collected let us study what sorts of influence preserve and destroy states, and what sorts preserve or destroy the particular kinds of constitution, and to what causes it is due that some are well and others ill administered. When 20 these have been studied we shall perhaps be more likely to see with a comprehensive view, which constitution is best, and how each must be ordered, and what laws and customs it must use, if it is to be at its best.[24] Let us make a beginning of our discussion.

[24] 1181ᵇ 12–23 is a programme for the *Politics*, agreeing to a large extent with the existing contents of that work.

Politics

ⴊⴊⴊⴊⴊⴊⴊⴊⴊⴊⴊⴊⴊⴊⴊⴊⴊⴊⴊⴊⴊⴊⴊⴊⴊⴊⴊⴊⴊⴊⴊⴊⴊⴊⴊⴊⴊⴊ

INTRODUCTION

Since every community is established with a view to some good, the investigation of political problems takes its peculiar turn in the philosophy of Aristotle from his undertaking to treat the communities of men in terms of the natural bases of human association and the varieties of ends obtainable by association. He stresses the differences that distinguish the qualifications of statesman, king, householder, and master, which Plato had argued were the same, and his demonstration that the state is "natural," since it is essential to living well, is based on analysis of its parts—the family, the household, and village—which are likewise "natural," since they are essential to mere living.

There is therefore a basic pluralism and dynamism in the political analyses of Aristotle, for there are as many kinds of states as there are characteristics in men and their situations affecting human relations or the purposes that may be sought in association. They may be classified under three main heads, since a "constitution," as Aristotle uses the term, is an arrangement of magistracies and is therefore identical with governments, which are of three main kinds—monarchy, aristocracy, and polity—dependent on whether the supreme authority is exercised by one, or the few, or the many. These three forms of government may be differentiated in turn into many subspecies, or they may be distinguished from three perversions—tyranny, oligarchy, and extreme democracy—dependent on whether their aim is the common welfare or private interest. When the kinds of states treated under these six heads are compared, the criteria of what is "best" may be sought in four different senses: (1) the best in the abstract (and then political problems are conceived largely in terms of the education and improvement of citizens as a means of improving political institutions and their functioning), (2) the best under particular circumstances (and then political problems are conceived in terms of fitting political institutions and their operations to the limitations and predicaments of a state), (3) the best in general (and then political problems are conceived in terms of balances of powers and functions for the resolution of problems and the conduct of political affairs), and (4) the best in the modification or preservation of the original forms of government (and then political problems are conceived in terms of the prevention or furtherance of revolutions).

In Book I of the Politics, the natural foundation of the state is sought in the analysis of its parts. In Book III, the basic principles and fundamental distinctions of political science are set up. In those two books the chief possibilities of political action are determined and prefigured. For the state is defined in terms of the citizen and the citizen in terms of his participation in the functions of government. This definition, Aristotle recognizes, is best adapted to a democracy, and he therefore uses the generic term "polity" (which is also translated "constitution") to designate the good form of democratic government. The functions of citizenship, however, require abilities and virtues in the citizen, and the proper exercise of those functions depends on equality and justice in the state, and Aristotle is therefore fond of repeating his observation that the good citizen will be the same as the good man only in the perfect state. The constitution of a state depends on who the citizens are and on what they may be educated to become, but it may also be formulated in terms of the general interplay of functions of government (and modern constitutional thinking has profited by the tradition of thought in which Aristotle's differentiation of the legislative, executive, and judicial functions has been elaborated) or in terms of the revolutions by which real or alleged inequalities and injustices are to be remedied (and Machiavelli found many of his devices in Aristotle's treatment of power and persuasion).

There is no simple relation between ethics, which is part of political science, and political science conceived as the study of the state, for the state influences the education and formation of its citizens and the character of its citizens determines the constitution of the state. Nor is there a simple relation between politics and the theoretic sciences, for knowledge affects the conditions of citizens and states, and states influence the development of science; nor indeed between politics and the arts, since the same interdependence is found there. But politics is itself a "science," in need of a scientific method, which some men, notably the sophists, have confused with rhetoric; and legislation is an "art," which sophists have separated from its subject matter by studying collections of laws as if a physician could be made by the study of medical textbooks. The controlling consideration in all these variabilities of political determination is that all states are established on a kind of equality and justice, and that politics is a practical, not a theoretic, science, whose end is not to acquire knowledge of what virtue is but to make men good.

POLITICA

CONTENTS

BOOK I

Chapters 1, 2. Definition and structure of the State.

Chapters 3–13. Household economy. The Slave. Property. Children and Wives.

men but calls for no detailed description; any one who is a natural master can acquire it for himself.

8. As to property and the modes of acquiring it. This subject concerns us in so far as property is an indispensable substratum to the household.

9. But we do not need that form of finance which accumulates wealth for its own sake. This is unnatural finance. It has been made possible by the invention of coined money. It accumulates money by means of exchange. Natural and unnatural finance are often treated as though they were the same, but differ in their aims;

10. Also in their subject-matter; for natural finance is only concerned with the fruits of the earth and animals.

11. Natural finance is necessary to the householder; he must therefore know about live stock, agriculture, possibly about the exchange of the products of the earth, such as wood and minerals, for money. Special treatises on finance exist, and the subject should be specially studied by statesmen.

12. Lastly, we must discuss and distinguish the relations of husband to wife, of father to child.

13. In household management persons call for more attention than things; free persons for more than slaves. Slaves are only capable of an inferior kind of virtue. Socrates was wrong in denying that there are several kinds of virtue. Still the slave must be trained in virtue. The education of the free man will be subsequently discussed.

BOOK III

Chapters 1–5. The Citizen, civic virtue, and the civic body.

1. How are we to define a citizen? He is more than a mere denizen; private rights do not make a citizen. He is ordinarily one who possesses political power; who sits on juries and in the assembly. But it is hard to find a definition which applies to all so-called citizens. To define him as the son of citizen parents is futile.

2. Some say that his civic rights must have been justly acquired. But he is a citizen who has political power, however acquired.

3. Similarly the state is defined by reference to the distribu-

tion of political power; when the mode of distribution is changed a new state comes into existence.

4. The good citizen may not be a good man; the good citizen is one who does good service to his state, and this state may be bad in principle. In a constitutional state the good citizen knows both how to rule and how to obey. The good man is one who is fitted to rule. But the citizen in a constitutional state learns to rule by obeying orders. Therefore citizenship in such a state is a moral training.

5. Mechanics will not be citizens in the best state. Extreme democracies, and some oligarchies, neglect this rule. But circumstances oblige them to do this. They have no choice.

Chapters 6–13. The Classification of Constitutions; Democracy and Oligarchy; Kingship.

6. The aims of the state are two: to satisfy man's social instinct, and to fit him for the good life. Political rule differs from that over slaves in aiming primarily at the good of those who are ruled.

7. Constitutions are bad or good according as the common welfare is, or is not, their aim. Of good Constitutions there are three: Monarchy, Aristocracy, and Polity. Of bad there are also three: Tyranny, Oligarchy, Extreme Democracy. The bad are perversions of the good.

8. Democracies and Oligarchies are not made by the numerical proportion of the rulers to the ruled. Democracy is the rule of the poor; oligarchy is that of the rich.

9. Democrats take Equality for their motto; oligarchs believe that political rights should be unequal and proportionate to wealth. But both sides miss the true object of the state, which is virtue. Those who do most to promote virtue deserve the greatest share of power.

10. On the same principle, Justice is not the will of the majority or of the wealthier, but that course of action which the moral aim of the state requires.

11. But are the Many or the Few likely to be the better rulers? It would be unreasonable to give the highest offices to the Many. But they have a faculty of criticism which fits them for deliberative and judicial power. The good critic need not be an expert; experts are sometimes bad

judges. Moreover, the Many have a greater stake in the city than the Few. But the governing body, whether Few or Many, must be held in check by the laws.

12. On what principle should political power be distributed? Granted that equals deserve equal shares; who are these equals? Obviously those who are equally able to be of service to the state.

13. Hence there is something in the claims advanced by the wealthy, the free born, the noble, the highly gifted. But no one of these classes should be allowed to rule the rest. A state should consist of men who are equal, or nearly so, in wealth, in birth, in moral and intellectual excellence. The principle which underlies Ostracism is plausible. But in the ideal state, if a pre-eminent individual be found, he should be made a king.

Chapters 14–18. The Forms of Monarchy.

14. Of Monarchy there are five kinds, (1) the Spartan, (2) the Barbarian, (3) the elective dictatorship, (4) the Heroic, (5) Absolute Kingship.

15. The last of these forms might appear the best polity to some; that is, if the king acts as the embodiment of law. For he will dispense from the law in the spirit of the law. But this power would be less abused if reserved for the Many. Monarchy arose to meet the needs of primitive society; it is now obsolete and on various grounds objectionable.

6. It tends to become hereditary; it subjects equals to the rule of an equal. The individual monarch may be misled by his passions, and no single man can attend to all the duties of government.

17. One case alone can be imagined in which Absolute Kingship would be just.

18. Let us consider the origin and nature of the best polity, now that we have agreed not to call Absolute Kingship the best.

Politica

Politics

Translated by Benjamin Jowett

⊔⊔⊔

BOOK I

Every state is a community of some kind, and every
community is established with a view to some good; **1252ᵃ**
for mankind always act in order to obtain that which they
think good. But, if all communities aim at some good,
the state or political community, which is the highest of
all, and which embraces all the rest, aims at good in a 5
greater degree than any other, and at the highest good.

Some people think[1] that the qualifications of a statesman, king, householder, and master are the same, and that
they differ, not in kind, but only in the number of their
subjects. For example, the ruler over a few is called a mas- 10
ter; over more, the manager of a household; over a still
larger number, a statesman or king, as if there were no
difference between a great household and a small state. The
distinction which is made between the king and the statesman is as follows: When the government is personal, the
ruler is a king; when, according to the rules of the political 15
science, the citizens rule and are ruled in turn, then he is
called a statesman.

But all this is a mistake; for governments differ in kind,
as will be evident to any one who considers the matter ac-

[1] Cp. Plato, *Politicus*, 258 ᴇ–259 ᴅ

cording to the method [2] which has hitherto guided us. As
20 in other departments of science, so in politics, the compound should always be resolved into the simple elements
or least parts of the whole. We must therefore look at the
elements of which the state is composed, in order that we
may see in what the different kinds of rule differ from one
another, and whether any scientific result can be attained
about each one of them.

2   He who thus considers things in their first growth and
origin, whether a state or anything else, will obtain the
25 clearest view of them. In the first place there must be a
union of those who cannot exist without each other;
namely, of male and female, that the race may continue
(and this is a union which is formed, not of deliberate
purpose, but because, in common with other animals and
30 with plants, mankind have a natural desire to leave behind
them an image of themselves), and of natural ruler and
subject, that both may be preserved. For that which can
foresee by the exercise of mind is by nature intended to be
lord and master, and that which can with its body give
effect to such foresight is a subject, and by nature a slave;
1252ᵇ hence master and slave have the same interest. Now nature
has distinguished between the female and the slave. For
she is not niggardly, like the smith who fashions the
Delphian knife for many uses; she makes each thing for a
single use, and every instrument is best made when in-
5 tended for one and not for many uses. But among barbarians no distinction is made between women and slaves, because there is no natural ruler among them: they are a
community of slaves, male and female. Wherefore the
poets say—

'It is meet that Hellenes should rule over barbarians';

as if they thought that the barbarian and the slave were by
nature one.

[2] Cp. 1256ᵃ2.

Out of these two relationships between man and woman, master and slave, the first thing to arise is the 10 family, and Hesiod is right when he says—

'First house and wife and an ox for the plough',

for the ox is the poor man's slave. The family is the association established by nature for the supply of men's everyday wants, and the members of it are called by Charondas 'companions of the cupboard', and by Epimenides the Cretan, 'companions of the manger.' But when several families are united, and the association aims at 15 something more than the supply of daily needs, the first society to be formed is the village. And the most natural form of the village appears to be that of a colony from the family, composed of the children and grandchildren, who are said to be 'suckled with the same milk'. And this is the 20 reason why Hellenic states were originally governed by kings; because the Hellenes were under royal rule before they came together, as the barbarians still are. Every family is ruled by the eldest, and therefore in the colonies of the family the kingly form of government prevailed because they were of the same blood. As Homer says: [3]

'Each one gives law to his children and to his wives.'

For they lived dispersedly, as was the manner in ancient times. Wherefore men say that the Gods have a king, because they themselves either are or were in ancient times under the rule of a king. For they imagine, not only the 25 forms of the Gods, but their ways of life to be like their own.

When several villages are united in a single complete community, large enough to be nearly or quite self-sufficing, the state comes into existence, originating in the bare needs of life, and continuing in existence for the sake of a good life. And therefore, if the earlier forms of society are 30

[3] *Od.* ix. 114, quoted by Plato, *Laws*, iii. 680 B, and in *N. Eth.* x. 1180ᵃ 28.

on nature

natural, so is the state. for it is the end of them, and the
nature of a thing is its end. For what each thing is when
fully developed, we call its nature, whether we are speaking of a man, a horse, or a family. Besides, the final cause
and end of a thing is the best, and to be self-sufficing is the
1253ᵃ end and the best.

Hence it is evident that the state is a creation of nature,
and that man is by nature a political animal. And he who by
nature and not by mere accident is without a state, is either
a bad man or above humanity; he is like the

> 'Tribeless, lawless, heartless one,'

whom Homer [4] denounces—the natural outcast is forthwith a lover of war; he may be compared to an isolated
piece at draughts.

Now, that man is more of a political animal than bees or
any other gregarious animals is evident. Nature, as we
often say, makes nothing in vain,[5] and man is the only
animal whom she has endowed with the gift of speech.[6]
10 And whereas mere voice is but an indication of pleasure or
pain, and is therefore found in other animals (for their
nature attains to the perception of pleasure and pain and
the intimation of them to one another, and no further),
the power of speech is intended to set forth the expedient
and inexpedient, and therefore likewise the just and the un-
15 just. And it is a characteristic of man that he alone has any
sense of good and evil, of just and unjust, and the like, and
the association of living beings who have this sense makes a
family and a state.

Further, the state is by nature clearly prior to the family
and to the individual, since the whole is of necessity prior
20 to the part; for example, if the whole body be destroyed,
there will be no foot or hand, except in an equivocal

---

[4] *Il.* ix. 63.
[5] Cp. 1256ᵇ 20.
[6] Cp. vii. 1332ᵇ 5.

sense, as we might speak of a stone hand; for when destroyed the hand will be no better than that. But things are defined by their working and power; and we ought not to say that they are the same when they no longer have their proper quality, but only that they have the same 25 name. The proof that the state is a creation of nature and prior to the individual is that the individual, when isolated, is not self-sufficing; and therefore he is like a part in relation to the whole. But he who is unable to live in society, or who has no need because he is sufficient for himself, must be either a beast or a god: he is no part of a state. A social instinct is implanted in all men by nature, and yet he 30 who first founded the state was the greatest of benefactors. For man, when perfected, is the best of animals, but, when separated from law and justice, he is the worst of all; since armed injustice is the more dangerous, and he is equipped at birth with arms, meant to be used by intelligence and virtue, which he may use for the worst ends. Wherefore, if 35 he have not virtue, he is the most unholy and the most savage of animals, and the most full of lust and gluttony. But justice is the bond of men in states, for the administration of justice, which is the determination of what is just,[7] is the principle of order in political society.

3   Seeing then that the state is made up of households, before speaking of the state we must speak of the management of the household. The parts of household **1253** management correspond to the persons who compose the household, and a complete household consists of slaves and freemen. Now we should begin by examining everything in its fewest possible elements; and the first and fewest possi- 5 ble parts of a family are master and slave, husband and wife, father and children. We have therefore to consider what each of these three relations is and ought to be:—I mean the relation of master and servant, the marriage relation 10

[7] Cp. N. Eth. v. 1134ᵃ 31.

(the conjunction of man and wife has no name of its own),
and thirdly, the procreative relation (this also has no proper
name). And there is another element of a household, the
so-called art of getting wealth, which, according to some, is
identical with household management, according to others,
a principal part of it; the nature of this art will also have to
be considered by us.

15   Let us first speak of master and slave, looking to the
needs of practical life and also seeking to attain some better
theory of their relation than exists at present. For some are
of opinion that the rule of a master is a science, and that
the management of a household, and the mastership of
20 slaves, and the political and royal rule, as I was saying at
the outset,[8] are all the same. Others affirm that the rule of
a master over slaves is contrary to nature, and that the distinction between slave and freeman exists by law only, and
not by nature; and being an interference with nature is
therefore unjust.

4   Property is a part of the household, and the art of
       acquiring property is a part of the art of managing the
household; for no man can live well, or indeed live at all,
25 unless he be provided with necessaries. And as in the arts
which have a definite sphere the workers must have their
own proper instruments for the accomplishment of their
work, so it is in the management of a household. Now
instruments are of various sorts; some are living, others
lifeless; in the rudder, the pilot of a ship has a lifeless, in
the look-out man, a living instrument; for in the arts the
servant is a kind of instrument. Thus, too, a possession
30 is an instrument for maintaining life. And so, in the arrangement of the family, a slave is a living possession, and
property a number of such instruments; and the servant is
himself an instrument which takes precedence of all other
instruments. For if every instrument could accomplish its
own work, obeying or anticipating the will of others, like

[8] Plato in *Pol.* 258 E–259 D, referred to already in 1252ª 7–16.

the statues of Daedalus, or the tripods of Hephaestus, 35
which, says the poet,[9]

'of their own accord entered the assembly of the Gods';

if, in like manner, the shuttle would weave and the plectrum
touch the lyre without a hand to guide them, chief workmen would not want servants, nor masters slaves. Here,
however, another distinction must be drawn; the instru- 1254
ments commonly so called are instruments of production,
whilst a possession is an instrument of action. The shuttle,
for example, is not only of use; but something else is made
by it, whereas of a garment or of a bed there is only the
use. Further, as production and action are different in
kind, and both require instruments, the instruments which 5
they employ must likewise differ in kind. But life is action
and not production, and therefore the slave is the minister
of action. Again, a possession is spoken of as a part is spoken
of; for the part is not only a part of something else, but
wholly belongs to it; and this is also true of a possession. 10
The master is only the master of the slave; he does not belong to him, whereas the slave is not only the slave of his
master, but wholly belongs to him. Hence we see what is
the nature and office of a slave; he who is by nature not
his own but another's man, is by nature a slave; and he 15
may be said to be another's man who, being a human being,
is also a possession. And a possession may be defined as an
instrument of action, separable from the possessor.

5   But is there any one thus intended by nature to be a
      slave, and for whom such a condition is expedient and
right, or rather is not all slavery a violation of nature?

There is no difficulty in answering this question, on 20
grounds both of reason and of fact. For that some should
rule and others be ruled is a thing not only necessary, but
expedient; from the hour of their birth, some are marked
out for subjection, others for rule.

[9] Hom. *Il.* xviii. 376.

And there are many kinds both of rulers and subjects
25 (and that rule is the better which is exercised over better
subjects—for example, to rule over men is better than to
rule over wild beasts; for the work is better which is executed by better workmen, and where one man rules and
another is ruled, they may be said to have a work); for in
all things which form a composite whole and which are
30 made up of parts, whether continuous or discrete, a distinction between the ruling and the subject element comes to
light. Such a duality exists in living creatures, but not in
them only; it originates in the constitution of the universe;
even in things which have no life there is a ruling principle,
as in a musical mode. But we are wandering from the subject. We will therefore restrict ourselves to the living crea-
35 ture, which, in the first place, consists of soul and body: and
of these two, the one is by nature the ruler, and the other
the subject. But then we must look for the intentions of
nature in things which retain their nature, and not in
things which are corrupted. And therefore we must study
the man who is in the most perfect state both of body and
soul, for in him we shall see the true relation of the two;
1254^b although in bad or corrupted natures the body will often
appear to rule over the soul, because they are in an evil
and unnatural condition. At all events we may firstly observe in living creatures both a despotical and a constitutional rule; for the soul rules the body with a despotical
rule, whereas the intellect rules the appetites with a
5 constitutional and royal rule. And it is clear that the rule of
the soul over the body, and of the mind and the rational
element over the passionate, is natural and expedient;
whereas the equality of the two or the rule of the inferior
is always hurtful. The same holds good of animals in rela-
10 tion to men; for tame animals have a better nature than
wild, and all tame animals are better off when they are
ruled by man; for then they are preserved. Again, the male
is by nature superior, and the female inferior; and the
one rules, and the other is ruled; this principle, of neces-

sity, extends to all mankind. Where then there is such a 15
difference as that between soul and body, or between men
and animals (as in the case of those whose business is to
use their body, and who can do nothing better), the lower
sort are by nature slaves, and it is better for them as for all
inferiors that they should be under the rule of a master.
For he who can be, and therefore is, another's, and he who
participates in rational principle enough to apprehend, but 20
not to have, such a principle, is a slave by nature. Whereas
the lower animals cannot even apprehend a principle; they
obey their instincts. And indeed the use made of slaves
and of tame animals is not very different; for both with
their bodies minister to the needs of life. Nature would
like to distinguish between the bodies of freemen and 25
slaves, making the one strong for servile labour, the other
upright, and although useless for such services, useful for
political life in the arts both of war and peace. But the op- 30
posite often happens—that some have the souls and others
have the bodies of freemen. And doubtless if men differed
from one another in the mere forms of their bodies as
much as the statues of the Gods do from men, all would
acknowledge that the inferior class should be slaves of the 35
superior. And if this is true of the body, how much more
just that a similar distinction should exist in the soul? but
the beauty of the body is seen, whereas the beauty of the
soul is not seen. It is clear, then, that some men are by **1255**ᵃ
nature free, and others slaves, and that for these latter
slavery is both expedient and right.

6   But that those who take the opposite view have in a
     certain way right on their side, may be easily seen. For
the words slavery and slave are used in two senses. There
is a slave or slavery by law as well as by nature. The law of 5
which I speak is a sort of convention—the law by which
whatever is taken in war is supposed to belong to the vic-
tors. But this right many jurists impeach, as they would
an orator who brought forward an unconstitutional meas-

ure: they detest the notion that, because one man has the power of doing violence and is superior in brute strength,
10 another shall be his slave and subject. Even among philosophers there is a difference of opinion. The origin of the dispute, and what makes the views invade each other's territory, is as follows: in some sense virtue, when furnished with means, has actually the greatest power of exercising force: and as superior power is only found where there is superior excellence of some kind, power seems to imply virtue, and the dispute to be simply one about justice (for
15 it is due to one party identifying justice with goodwill,[10] while the other identifies it with the mere rule of the stronger). If these views are thus set out separately, the
20 other views [11] have no force or plausibility against the view that the superior in virtue ought to rule, or be master. Others, clinging, as they think, simply to a principle of justice (for law and custom are a sort of justice), assume that slavery in accordance with the custom of war is justified by law, but at the same moment they deny this. For
25 what if the cause of the war be unjust? And again, no one would ever say that he is a slave who is unworthy to be a slave. Were this the case, men of the highest rank would be slaves and the children of slaves if they or their parents chance to have been taken captive and sold. Wherefore Hellenes do not like to call Hellenes slaves, but confine the
30 term to barbarians. Yet, in using this language, they really mean the natural slave of whom we spoke at first; [12] for it must be admitted that some are slaves everywhere, others nowhere. The same principle applies to nobility. Hellenes regard themselves as noble everywhere, and not only in
35 their own country, but they deem the barbarians noble

[10] i. e. mutual goodwill, which is held to be incompatible with the relation of master and slave.

[11] i. e. those stated in ll. 5–12, that the stronger always has, and that he never has, a right to enslave the weaker. Aristotle finds that these views cannot maintain themselves against his intermediate view, that the superior in *virtue* should rule.

[12] Chap. 5.

only when at home, thereby implying that there are two sorts of nobility and freedom, the one absolute, the other relative. The Helen of Theodectes says:

'Who would presume to call me servant who am on both sides sprung from the stem of the Gods?'

What does this mean but that they distinguish freedom and slavery, noble and humble birth, by the two principles 40 of good and evil? They think that as men and animals beget **1255** men and animals, so from good men a good man springs. But this is what nature, though she may intend it, cannot always accomplish.

We see then that there is some foundation for this difference of opinion, and that all are not either slaves by 5 nature or freemen by nature, and also that there is in some cases a marked distinction between the two classes, rendering it expedient and right for the one to be slaves and the others to be masters: the one practising obedience, the others exercising the authority and lordship which nature intended them to have. The abuse of this authority is injurious to both; for the interests of part and whole,[13] of 10 body and soul, are the same, and the slave is a part of the master, a living but separated part of his bodily frame. Hence, where the relation of master and slave between them is natural they are friends and have a common interest, but where it rests merely on law and force the reverse is true.   15

7   The previous remarks are quite enough to show that the rule of a master is not a constitutional rule, and that all the different kinds of rule are not, as some affirm, the same with each other.[14] For there is one rule exercised over subjects who are by nature free, another over subjects who are by nature slaves. The rule of a household is a mon-

---

[13] Cp. 1254[a] 8.
[14] Plato. *Polit.* 258 E–259 D, referred to already in 1252[a] 7–16, 1253[b] 18–20.

archy, for every house is under one head: whereas constitutional rule is a government of freemen and equals. The
20 master is not called a master because he has science,[15] but
because he is of a certain character, and the same remark
applies to the slave and the freeman. Still there may be a
science for the master and a science for the slave. The
science of the slave would be such as the man of Syracuse
taught, who made money by instructing slaves in their
25 ordinary duties. And such a knowledge may be carried
further, so as to include cookery and similar menial arts.
For some duties are of the more necessary, others of the
more honourable sort; as the proverb says, 'slave before
slave, master before master'. But all such branches of
30 knowledge are servile. There is likewise a science of the
master, which teaches the use of slaves; for the master as
such is concerned, not with the acquisition, but with the
use of them. Yet this so-called science is not anything great
or wonderful; for the master need only know how to order
that which the slave must know how to execute. Hence
35 those who are in a position which places them above toil
have stewards who attend to their households while they
occupy themselves with philosophy or with politics. But
the art of acquiring slaves, I mean of justly acquiring them,
differs both from the art of the master and the art of the
slave, being a species of hunting or war.[16] Enough of the
40 distinction between master and slave.

8   Let us now inquire into property generally, and into
1256ª   the art of getting wealth, in accordance with our usual
method,[17] for a slave has been shown [18] to be a part of
property. The first question is whether the art of getting
wealth is the same with the art of managing a household
or a part of it, or instrumental to it; and if the last, whether
in the way that the art of making shuttles is instrumental

[15] *Polit.* 259 c, 293 c.
[16] Cp. vii. 1333ᵇ 38.
[17] Of understanding the whole by the part, Cp. 1252ª 17.
[18] Chap. 4.

to the art of weaving, or in the way that the casting of
bronze is instrumental to the art of the statuary, for they
are not instrumental in the same way, but the one provides
tools and the other material; and by material I mean the
substratum out of which any work is made; thus wool is
the material of the weaver, bronze of the statuary. Now it is
easy to see that the art of household management is not
identical with the art of getting wealth, for the one uses
the material which the other provides. For the art which
uses household stores can be no other than the art of household management. There is, however, a doubt whether the
art of getting wealth is a part of household management or
a distinct art. If the getter of wealth has to consider whence
wealth and property can be procured, but there are many
sorts of property and riches, then are husbandry, and the
care and provision of food in general, parts of the wealth-
getting art or distinct arts? Again, there are many sorts of
food, and therefore there are many kinds of lives both of
animals and men; they must all have food, and the differences in their food have made differences in their ways of
life. For of beasts, some are gregarious, others are solitary;
they live in the way which is best adapted to sustain them,
accordingly as they are carnivorous or herbivorous or omnivorous: and their habits are determined for them by nature in such a manner that they may obtain with greater
facility the food of their choice. But, as different species
have different tastes, the same things are not naturally
pleasant to all of them; and therefore the lives of carnivorous or herbivorous animals further differ among themselves. In the lives of men too there is a great difference.
The laziest are shepherds, who lead an idle life, and get
their subsistence without trouble from tame animals; their
flocks having to wander from place to place in search of
pasture, they are compelled to follow them, cultivating a
sort of living farm. Others support themselves by hunting,
which is of different kinds. Some, for example, are brigands,
others, who dwell near lakes or marshes or rivers or a sea in

which there are fish, are fishermen, and others live by the
pursuit of birds or wild beasts. The greater number obtain
40 a living from the cultivated fruits of the soil. Such are the
modes of subsistence which prevail among those whose
1256ᵇ industry springs up of itself, and whose food is not acquired
by exchange and retail trade—there is the shepherd, the
husbandman, the brigand, the fisherman, the hunter. Some
gain a comfortable maintenance out of two employments,
eking out the deficiencies of one of them by another: thus
5 the life of a shepherd may be combined with that of a
brigand, the life of a farmer with that of a hunter. Other
modes of life are similarly combined in any way which the
needs of men may require. Property, in the sense of a bare
livelihood, seems to be given by nature herself to all, both
when they are first born, and when they are grown up. For
10 some animals bring forth, together with their offspring, so
much food as will last until they are able to supply themselves; of this the vermiparous or oviparous animals are
an instance; and the viviparous animals have up to a certain time a supply of food for their young in themselves,
which is called milk. In like manner we may infer that, after
15 the birth of animals, plants exist for their sake, and that
the other animals exist for the sake of man, the tame for
use and food, the wild, if not all, at least the greater part
of them, for food, and for the provision of clothing and
various instruments. Now if nature makes nothing incom-
20 plete, and nothing in vain, the inference must be that she
has made all animals for the sake of man. And so, in one
point of view, the art of war is a natural art of acquisition,
for the art of acquisition includes hunting, an art which we
ought to practise against wild beasts, and against men who,
25 though intended by nature to be governed, will not submit;
for war of such a kind is naturally just.[19]

Of the art of acquisition then there is one kind which by
nature is a part of the management of a household, in so
far as the art of household management must either find

[19] Cp. 1255ᵇ 38, 1333ᵇ 38.

ready to hand, or itself provide, such things necessary to
life, and useful for the community of the family or state, 30
as can be stored. They are the elements of true riches; for
the amount of property which is needed for a good life is   *limited*
not unlimited, although Solon in one of his poems says that   *property*

'No bound to riches has been fixed for man'.

But there is a boundary fixed, just as there is in the other
arts; for the instruments of any art are never unlimited,
either in number or size, and riches may be defined as a 35
number of instruments to be used in a household or in a   *natural*
state. And so we see that there is a natural art of acquisition   *art of*
which is practised by managers of households and by states-   *riches*
men, and what is the reason of this.

9   There is another variety of the art of acquisition which
    is commonly and rightly called an art of wealth-getting, 40
and has in fact suggested the notion that riches and property have no limit. Being nearly connected with the pre-**1257ᵃ**
ceding, it is often identified with it. But though they are
not very different, neither are they the same. The kind al-   *&*
ready described is given by nature, the other is gained by   *unnatural*
experience and art.   *art of wealth*
    Let us begin our discussion of the question with the
following considerations: 5
    Of everything which we possess there are two uses: both
belong to the thing as such, but not in the same manner,
for one is the proper, and the other the improper or   *barter,*
secondary use of it. For example, a shoe is used for wear,   *not*
and is used for exchange; both are uses of the shoe. He who 10 *natural*
gives a shoe in exchange for money or food to him who
wants one, does indeed use the shoe as a shoe, but this is
not its proper or primary purpose, for a shoe is not made to
be an object of barter. The same may be said of all possessions, for the art of exchange extends to all of them, and 15
it arises at first from what is natural, from the circumstance

that some have too little, others too much. Hence we may infer that retail trade is not a natural part of the art of getting wealth; had it been so, men would have ceased to exchange when they had enough. In the first community, 20 indeed, which is the family, this art is obviously of no use, but it begins to be useful when the society increases. For the members of the family originally had all things in common; later, when the family divided into parts, the parts shared in many things, and different parts in different things, which they had to give in exchange for what they 25 wanted, a kind of barter which is still practised among barbarous nations who exchange with one another the necessaries of life and nothing more; giving and receiving wine, for example, in exchange for corn, and the like. This sort of barter is not part of the wealth-getting art and 30 is not contrary to nature, but is needed for the satisfaction of men's natural wants. The other or more complex form of exchange grew, as might have been inferred, out of the simpler. When the inhabitants of one country became more dependent on those of another, and they imported what they needed, and exported what they had too much 35 of, money necessarily came into use. For the various necessaries of life are not easily carried about, and hence men agreed to employ in their dealings with each other something which was intrinsically useful and easily applicable to the purposes of life, for example, iron, silver, and the like. Of this the value was at first measured simply by size and 40 weight, but in process of time they put a stamp upon it, to save the trouble of weighing and to mark the value.

1257ᵇ   When the use of coin had once been discovered, out of the barter of necessary articles arose the other art of wealth-getting, namely, retail trade; which was at first probably a simple matter, but became more complicated as soon as men learned by experience whence and by what exchanges 5 the greatest profit might be made. Originating in the use of coin, the art of getting wealth is generally thought to be

chiefly concerned with it, and to be the art which produces riches and wealth; having to consider how they may
be accumulated. Indeed, riches is assumed by many to be
only a quantity of coin, because the arts of getting wealth
and retail trade are concerned with coin. Others maintain
that coined money is a mere sham, a thing not natural, but
conventional only, because, if the users substitute another
commodity for it, it is worthless, and because it is not useful
as a means to any of the necessities of life, and, indeed, he
who is rich in coin may often be in want of necessary food.
But how can that be wealth of which a man may have a
great abundance and yet perish with hunger, like Midas in
the fable, whose insatiable prayer turned everything that
was set before him into gold?

Hence men seek after a better notion of riches and of
the art of getting wealth than the mere acquisition of coin,
and they are right. For natural riches and the natural art of
wealth-getting are a different thing; in their true form they
are part of the management of a household; whereas retail
trade is the art of producing wealth, not in every way, but
by exchange. And it is thought to be concerned with coin;
for coin is the unit of exchange and the measure or limit of
it. And there is no bound to the riches which spring from
this art of wealth-getting.[20] As in the art of medicine there
is no limit to the pursuit of health, and as in the other arts
there is no limit to the pursuit of their several ends, for they
aim at accomplishing their ends to the uttermost (but of
the means there is a limit, for the end is always the limit),
so, too, in this art of wealth-getting there is no limit of the
end, which is riches of the spurious kind, and the acquisition of wealth. But the art of wealth-getting which consists
in household management, on the other hand, has a limit;
the unlimited acquisition of wealth is not its business.
And, therefore, in one point of view, all riches must have a
limit; nevertheless, as a matter of fact, we find the opposite

[20] Cp. 1256^b 32.

to be the case; for all getters of wealth increase their hoard
of coin without limit. The source of the confusion is the
near connexion between the two kinds of wealth-getting;
35 in either, the instrument is the same, although the use is
different, and so they pass into one another; for each is a
use of the same property, but with a difference: accumula-
tion is the end in the one case, but there is a further end in
the other. Hence some persons are led to believe that getting wealth is the object of household management, and
the whole idea of their lives is that they ought either to in-
40 crease their money without limit, or at any rate not to lose
it. The origin of this disposition in men is that they are intent upon living only, and not upon living well; and, as
1258ᵃ their desires are unlimited, they also desire that the means
of gratifying them should be without limit. Those who do
5 aim at a good life seek the means of obtaining bodily
pleasures; and, since the enjoyment of these appears to depend on property, they are absorbed in getting wealth:
and so there arises the second species of wealth-getting. For,
as their enjoyment is in excess, they seek an art which produces the excess of enjoyment; and, if they are not able to
supply their pleasures by the art of getting wealth, they try
10 other arts, using in turn every faculty in a manner contrary
to nature. The quality of courage, for example, is not intended to make wealth, but to inspire confidence; neither is
this the aim of the general's or of the physician's art; but the
one aims at victory and the other at health. Nevertheless,
some men turn every quality or art into a means of getting
wealth; this they conceive to be the end, and to the promo-
tion of the end they think all things must contribute.

Thus, then, we have considered the art of wealth-getting
15 which is unnecessary, and why men want it; and also the
necessary art of wealth-getting, which we have seen to be
different from the other, and to be a natural part of the art
of managing a household, concerned with the provision
of food, not, however, like the former kind, unlimited, but
having a limit.

10   And we have found the answer to our original question,[21] Whether the art of getting wealth is the business of the manager of a household and of the statesman 20
or not their business?—viz. that wealth is presupposed by
them. For as political science does not make men, but
takes them from nature and uses them, so too nature provides them with earth or sea or the like as a source of food.
At this stage begins the duty of the manager of a household, who has to order the things which nature supplies;— 25
he may be compared to the weaver who has not to make
but to use wool, and to know, too, what sort of wool is
good and serviceable or bad and unserviceable. Were this
otherwise, it would be difficult to see why the art of getting
wealth is a part of the management of a household and the
art of medicine not; for surely the members of a household
must have health just as they must have life or any other 30
necessary. The answer is that as from one point of view the
master of the house and the ruler of the state have to consider about health, from another point of view not they but
the physician; so in one way the art of household management, in another way the subordinate art, has to consider
about wealth. But, strictly speaking, as I have already said,
the means of life must be provided beforehand by nature;   *Means of*
for the business of nature is to furnish food to that which is 35   *life,*
born, and the food of the offspring is always what remains   *mature,*
over of that from which it is produced.[22] Wherefore the   *food*
art of getting wealth out of fruits and animals is always
natural.

There are two sorts of wealth-getting, as I have said [23];
one is a part of household management, the other is retail
trade: the former necessary and honourable, while that
which consists in exchange is justly censured; for it is un- 40
natural, and a mode by which men gain from one another. **1258**^b
The most hated sort, and with the greatest reason, is usury,

[21] 1256^a 3.
[22] Cp. 1256^b 10.
[23] 1256^a 15–1258^a 18.

which makes a gain out of money itself, and not from the natural object of it. For money was intended to be used in exchange, but not to increase at interest. And this term interest,[24] which means the birth of money from money, is applied to the breeding of money because the offspring resembles the parent. Wherefore of all modes of getting wealth this is the most unnatural.

11 Enough has been said about the theory of wealth-getting; we will now proceed to the practical part. The discussion of such matters is not unworthy of philosophy, but to be engaged in them practically is illiberal and irksome. The useful parts of wealth-getting are, first, the knowledge of live-stock—which are most profitable, and where, and how—as, for example, what sort of horses or sheep or oxen or any other animals are most likely to give a return. A man ought to know which of these pay better than others, and which pay best in particular places, for some do better in one place and some in another. Secondly, husbandry, which may be either tillage or planting, and the keeping of bees and of fish, or fowl, or of any animals which may be useful to man. These are the divisions of the true or proper art of wealth-getting and come first. Of the other, which consists in exchange, the first and most important division is commerce (of which there are three kinds—the provision of a ship, the conveyance of goods, exposure for sale—these again differing as they are safer or more profitable), the second is usury, the third, service for hire—of this, one kind is employed in the mechanical arts, the other in unskilled and bodily labour. There is still a third sort of wealth-getting intermediate between this and the first or natural mode which is partly natural, but is also concerned with exchange, viz. the industries that make their profit from the earth, and from things growing from the earth which, although they bear no fruit, are nevertheless profitable; for example, the cutting of timber and

[24] *tokos*, lit. 'offspring'.

all mining. The art of mining, by which minerals are obtained, itself has many branches, for there are various kinds of things dug out of the earth. Of the several divisions of wealth-getting I now speak generally; a minute consideration of them might be useful in practice, but it would be tiresome to dwell upon them at greater length now.

Those occupations are most truly arts in which there is 35 the least element of chance; they are the meanest in which the body is most deteriorated, the most servile in which there is the greatest use of the body, and the most illiberal in which there is the least need of excellence.

Works have been written upon these subjects by various persons; for example, by Chares the Parian, and Apol- 40 lodorus the Lemnian, who have treated of Tillage and 1259ᵃ Planting, while others have treated of other branches; any one who cares for such matters may refer to their writings. It would be well also to collect the scattered stories of the ways in which individuals have succeeded in amassing a fortune; for all this is useful to persons who value the art of 5 getting wealth. There is the anecdote of Thales the Milesian and his financial device, which involves a principle of universal application, but is attributed to him on account of his reputation for wisdom. He was reproached for his poverty, which was supposed to show that philosophy was 10 of no use. According to the story, he knew by his skill in the stars while it was yet winter that there would be a great harvest of olives in the coming year; so, having a little money, he gave deposits for the use of all the olive-presses in Chios and Miletus, which he hired at a low price because no one bid against him. When the harvest-time came, and many were wanted all at once and of a sudden, he let them 15 out at any rate which he pleased, and made a quantity of money. Thus he showed the world that philosophers can easily be rich if they like, but that their ambition is of another sort. He is supposed to have given a striking proof of his wisdom, but, as I was saying, his device for getting 20 wealth is of universal application, and is nothing but the

Thales

creation of a monopoly. It is an art often practised by cities when they are in want of money; they make a monopoly of provisions.

There was a man of Sicily, who, having money deposited with him, bought up all the iron from the iron mines; afterwards, when the merchants from their various markets came to buy, he was the only seller, and without much increasing the price he gained 200 per cent. Which when Dionysius heard, he told him that he might take away his money, but that he must not remain at Syracuse, for he thought that the man had discovered a way of making money which was injurious to his own interests. He made the same discovery as Thales; they both contrived to create a monopoly for themselves. And statesmen as well ought to know these things; for a state is often as much in want of money and of such devices for obtaining it as a household, or even more so; hence some public men devote themselves entirely to finance.

12 Of household management we have seen [25] that there are three parts—one is the rule of a master over slaves, which has been discussed already,[26] another of a father, and the third of a husband. A husband and father, we saw, rules over wife and children, both free, but the rule differs, the rule over his children being a royal, over his wife a constitutional rule. For although there may be exceptions to the order of nature, the male is by nature fitter for command than the female, just as the elder and full-grown is superior to the younger and more immature. But in most constitutional states the citizens rule and are ruled by turns, for the idea of a constitutional state implies that the natures of the citizens are equal, and do not differ at all.[27] Nevertheless, when one rules and the other is ruled we endeavour to create a difference of outward forms and names

[25] 1253ᵇ 3–11.
[26] 1253ᵇ 14–1255ᵇ 39.
[27] Cp. ii. 1261ᵃ 39, iii. 1288ᵃ 12.

and titles of respect, which may be illustrated by the saying
of Amasis about his foot-pan.[28] The relation of the male to
the female is of this kind, but there the inequality is permanent. The rule of a father over his children is royal, for
he rules by virtue both of love and of the respect due to
age, exercising a kind of royal power. And therefore Homer
has appropriately called Zeus 'father of Gods and men', because he is the king of them all. For a king is the natural
superior of his subjects, but he should be of the same kin
or kind with them, and such is the relation of elder and
younger, of father and son.

13 Thus it is clear that household management attends
more to men than to the acquisition of inanimate
things, and to human excellence more than to the excellence of property which we call wealth, and to the virtue
of freemen more than to the virtue of slaves. A question
may indeed be raised, whether there is any excellence at
all in a slave beyond and higher than merely instrumental
and ministerial qualities—whether he can have the virtues
of temperance, courage, justice, and the like; or whether
slaves possess only bodily and ministerial qualities. And,
whichever way we answer the question, a difficulty arises;
for, if they have virtue, in what will they differ from freemen? On the other hand, since they are men and share in
rational principle, it seems absurd to say that they have no
virtue. A similar question may be raised about women and
children, whether they too have virtues: ought a woman to
be temperate and brave and just, and is a child to be called
temperate, and intemperate, or not? So in general we may
ask about the natural ruler, and the natural subject, whether
they have the same or different virtues. For if a noble
nature is equally required in both, why should one of them
always rule, and the other always be ruled? Nor can we say
that this is a question of degree, for the difference between
ruler and subject is a difference of kind, which the differ-

[28] Herod. ii. 172.

ence of more and less never is. Yet how strange is the supposition that the one ought, and that the other ought not,
40 to have virtue! For if the ruler is intemperate and unjust,
1260ª how can he rule well? if the subject, how can he obey well?
If he be licentious and cowardly, he will certainly not do his
duty. It is evident, therefore, that both of them must have a
share of virtue, but varying as natural subjects also vary
5 among themselves. Here the very constitution of the soul
has shown us the way; in it one part naturally rules, and
the other is subject, and the virtue of the ruler we maintain to be different from that of the subject;—the one being the virtue of the rational, and the other of the irrational part. Now, it is obvious that the same principle
applies generally, and therefore almost all things rule and
are ruled according to nature. But the kind of rule differs;—
the freeman rules over the slave after another manner from
10 that in which the male rules over the female, or the man
over the child; although the parts of the soul are present in
all of them, they are present in different degrees. For the
slave has no deliberative faculty at all; the woman has, but it
15 is without authority, and the child has, but it is immature.
So it must necessarily be supposed to be with the moral virtues also; all should partake of them, but only in such manner and degree as is required by each for the fulfillment of
his duty. Hence the ruler ought to have moral virtue in perfection, for his function, taken absolutely, demands a master
artificer, and rational principle is such an artificer; the sub-
20 jects, on the other hand, require only that measure of virtue
which is proper to each of them. Clearly, then, moral virtue belongs to all of them; but the temperance of a man and
of a woman, or the courage and justice of a man and of a
woman, are not, as Socrates maintained,[29] the same; the
courage of a man is shown in commanding, of a woman in
25 obeying. And this holds of all other virtues, as will be more
clearly seen if we look at them in detail, for those who say
generally that virtue consists in a good disposition of the

[29] Plato, Meno, 72 A–73 C.

soul, or in doing rightly, or the like, only deceive themselves. Far better than such definitions is their mode of
speaking, who, like Gorgias,[30] enumerate the virtues. All
classes must be deemed to have their special attributes; as
the poet says of women,

'Silence is a woman's glory', 30

but this is not equally the glory of man. The child is imperfect, and therefore obviously his virtue is not relative to
himself alone, but to the perfect man and to his teacher,
and in like manner the virtue of the slave is relative to a
master. Now we determined [31] that a slave is useful for the
wants of life, and therefore he will obviously require only
so much virtue as will prevent him from failing in his duty 35
through cowardice or lack of self-control. Some one will
ask whether, if what we are saying is true, virtue will not
be required also in the artisans, for they often fail in their
work through the lack of self-control? But is there not a
great difference in the two cases? For the slave shares in his
master's life; the artisan is less closely connected with him, 40
and only attains excellence in proportion as he becomes a
slave. The meaner sort of mechanic has a special and
separate slavery; and whereas the slave exists by nature, not 1260ᵇ
so the shoemaker or other artisan. It is manifest, then,
that the master ought to be the source of such excellence in
the slave, and not a mere possessor of the art of mastership
which trains the slave in his duties.[32] Wherefore they are 5
mistaken who forbid us to converse with slaves and say
that we should employ command only,[33] for slaves stand
even more in need of admonition than children.

So much for this subject; the relations of husband and
wife, parent and child, their several virtues, what in their
intercourse with one another is good, and what is evil,
and how we may pursue the good and escape the evil, 10

[30] Meno, 71 E, 72 A.
[31] 1254ᵇ 16–39. Cf. 1259ᵇ 25 sq.
[32] Cp. 1255ᵇ 23, 31–35.
[33] Plato, Laws, vi. 777 E.

will have to be discussed when we speak of the different forms of government.[34] For, inasmuch as every family is a part of a state, and these relationships are the parts of a family, and the virtue of the part must have regard to the virtue of the whole, women and children must be trained
15 by education with an eye to the constitution,[35] if the virtues of either of them are supposed to make any difference in the virtues of the state. And they must make a difference: for the children grow up to be citizens, and half the free persons in a state are women.[36]

Of these matters, enough has been said; of what remains,
20 let us speak at another time. Regarding, then, our present inquiry as complete, we will make a new beginning. And, first, let us examine the various theories of a perfect state.

BOOK III

1274ᵇ 1 He who would inquire into the essence and attributes of various kinds of governments must first of all determine 'What is a state?' At present this is a disputed ques-
35 tion. Some say that the state has done a certain act; others, no, not the state,[1] but the oligarchy or the tyrant. And the legislator or statesman is concerned entirely with the state; a constitution or government being an arrangement of the inhabitants of a state. But a state is composite, like any
40 other whole made up of many parts;—these are the citizens,
1275ᵃ who compose it. It is evident, therefore, that we must begin by asking, Who is the citizen, and what is the meaning of the term? For here again there may be a difference of opinion. He who is a citizen in a democracy will often not
5 be a citizen in an oligarchy. Leaving out of consideration those who have been made citizens, or who have obtained the name of citizen in any other accidental manner, we may say, first, that a citizen is not a citizen because he lives in

---

[34] The question is not actually discussed in the *Politics*.
[35] Cp. v. 1310ᵃ 12–36, viii. 1337ᵃ 11–18.
[36] Plato, *Laws*, vi. 781 A.
[1] Cp. 1276ᵃ 8.

a certain place, for resident aliens and slaves share in the place; nor is he a citizen who has no legal right except that of suing and being sued; for this right may be enjoyed 10 under the provisions of a treaty. Nay, resident aliens in many places do not possess even such rights completely, for they are obliged to have a patron, so that they do but imperfectly participate in citizenship, and we call them citizens only in a qualified sense, as we might apply the term to children who are too young to be on the register, 15 or to old men who have been relieved from state duties. Of these we do not say quite simply that they are citizens, but add in the one case that they are not of age, and in the other, that they are past the age, or something of that sort; 20 the precise expression is immaterial, for our meaning is clear. Similar difficulties to those which I have mentioned may be raised and answered about deprived citizens and about exiles. But the citizen whom we are seeking to define is a citizen in the strictest sense, against whom no such exception can be taken, and his special characteristic is that he shares in the administration of justice, and in offices. Now of offices some are discontinuous, and the same persons are not allowed to hold them twice, or can only hold them after a fixed interval; others have no limit of time— 25 for example, the office of dicast or ecclesiast.[2] It may, indeed, be argued that these are not magistrates at all, and that their functions give them no share in the government. But surely it is ridiculous to say that those who have the supreme power do not govern. Let us not dwell further upon this, which is a purely verbal question; what we want is a common term including both dicast and ecclesiast. Let 30 us, for the sake of distinction, call it 'indefinite office', and we will assume that those who share in such office are citizens. This is the most comprehensive definition of a citizen, and best suits all those who are generally so called.

But we must not forget that things of which the under-

---

[2] 'Dicast' = juryman and judge in one: 'ecclesiast' = member of the ecclesia or assembly of the citizens.

35 lying principles differ in kind, one of them being first,
another second, another third, have, when regarded in this
relation, nothing, or hardly anything, worth mentioning in
common. Now we see that governments differ in kind,
and that some of them are prior and that others are posterior; those which are faulty or perverted are necessarily
1275ᵇ posterior to those which are perfect. (What we mean by
perversion will be hereafter explained.[3]) The citizen then
of necessity differs under each form of government; and our
5 definition is best adapted to the citizen of a democracy;
but not necessarily to other states. For in some states the
people are not acknowledged, nor have they any regular
assembly, but only extraordinary ones; and suits are distributed by sections among the magistrates. At Lacedaemon, for instance, the Ephors determine suits about con-
10 tracts, which they distribute among themselves, while the
elders are judges of homicide, and other causes are decided
by other magistrates. A similar principle prevails at Car-
thage; [4] there certain magistrates decide all causes. We may,
indeed, modify our definition of the citizen so as to include
these states. In them it is the holder of a definite, not of
15 an indefinite office, who legislates and judges, and to some
or all such holders of definite offices is reserved the right of
deliberating or judging about some things or about all
things. The conception of the citizen now begins to clear
up.

He who has the power to take part in the deliberative or
judicial administration of any state is said by us to be a
20 citizen of that state; and, speaking generally, a state is a
body of citizens sufficing for the purposes of life.

2   But in practice a citizen is defined to be one of whom
both the parents are citizens; other insist on going
25 further back; say to two or three or more ancestors. This
is a short and practical definition; but there are some who

[3] Cp. 1279ᵃ 19.
[4] Cp. ii. 1273ᵃ 19.

raise the further question: How this third or fourth ancestor came to be a citizen? Gorgias of Leontini, partly because he was in a difficulty, partly in irony, said—'Mortars
are what is made by the mortar-makers, and the citizens of
Larissa are those who are made by the magistrates; [5] for it is
their trade to make Larissaeans.' Yet the question is really 30
simple, for, if according to the definition just given they
shared in the government, they were citizens. This is a
better definition than the other. For the words, 'born of a
father or mother who is a citizen', cannot possibly apply to
the first inhabitants or founders of a state.

There is a greater difficulty in the case of those who have
been made citizens after a revolution, as by Cleisthenes at 35
Athens after the expulsion of the tyrants, for he enrolled
in tribes many metics, both strangers and slaves. The doubt
in these cases is, not who is, but whether he who is ought 1276ᵃ
to be a citizen; and there will still be a further doubt,
whether he who ought not to be a citizen, is one in fact, for
what ought not to be is what is false. Now, there are some
who hold office, and yet ought not to hold office, whom we
describe as ruling, but ruling unjustly. And the citizen was
defined [6] by the fact of his holding some kind of rule or
office—he who holds a judicial or legislative office fulfils 5
our definition of a citizen. It is evident, therefore, that the
citizens about whom the doubt has arisen must be called
citizens.

3 Whether they ought to be so or not is a question
which is bound up with the previous inquiry.[7] For a
parallel question is raised respecting the state, whether a
certain act is or is not an act of the state; for example,
in the transition from an oligarchy or a tyranny to a democracy. In such cases persons refuse to fulfil their contracts 10

---

[5] An untranslatable play upon the word *demiourgos*, which means
either 'a magistrate' or 'an artisan'.
[6] 1275ᵃ 22 sqq.
[7] Cp. 1274ᵇ 34.

or any other obligations, on the ground that the tyrant, and
not the state, contracted them; they argue that some constitutions are established by force, and not for the sake of
the common good. But this would apply equally to democ-
15 racies, for they too may be founded on violence, and then
the acts of the democracy will be neither more nor less acts
of the state in question than those of an oligarchy or of a
tyranny. This question runs up into another:—on what
principle shall we ever say that the state is the same, or
different? It would be a very superficial view which considered only the place and the inhabitants (for the soil and
the population may be separated, and some of the inhabit-
20 ants may live in one place and some in another). This,
however, is not a very serious difficulty; we need only remark that the word 'state' is ambiguous.[8]

It is further asked: When are men, living in the same
25 place, to be regarded as a single city—what is the limit?
Certainly not the wall of the city, for you might surround
all Peloponnesus with a wall. Like this, we may say, is
Babylon,[9] and every city that has the compass of a nation
rather than a city; Babylon, they say, had been taken for
three days before some part of the inhabitants became
30 aware of the fact. This difficulty may, however, with advantage be deferred [10] to another occasion; the statesman has
to consider the size of the state, and whether it should consist of more than one nation or not.

Again, shall we say that while the race of inhabitants,
35 as well as their place of abode, remain the same, the city
is also the same, although the citizens are always dying and
being born, as we call rivers and fountains the same, although the water is always flowing away and coming again?
Or shall we say that the generations of men, like the rivers,
40 are the same, but that the state changes? For since the state

---

[8] i. e. Polis means both 'state' and 'city'.

[9] Cp. ii. 1265ᵃ 14.

[10] The size of the state is discussed in vii. 1326ᵃ 8–1327ᵃ 3; the
question whether it should consist of more than one nation is barely
touched upon. in v. 1303ᵃ 25–ᵇ 3.

is a partnership, and is a partnership of citizens in a consti- **1276ᵇ**
tution, when the form of the government changes, and becomes different, then it may be supposed that the state is
no longer the same, just as a tragic differs from a comic
chorus, although the members of both may be identical. 5
And in this manner we speak of every union or composition
of elements as different when the form of their composition
alters; for example, a scale containing the same sounds is
said to be different, accordingly as the Dorian or the Phryg-
ian mode is employed. And if this is true it is evident that 10
the sameness of the state consists chiefly in the sameness of
the constitution, and it may be called or not called by the
same name, whether the inhabitants are the same or entirely different. It is quite another question, whether a state
ought or ought not to fulfil engagements when the form of 15
government changes.

4 There is a point nearly allied to the preceding:
Whether the virtue of a good man and a good citizen
is the same or not.[11] But, before entering on this discussion, we must certainly first obtain some general notion of 20
the virtue of the citizen. Like the sailor, the citizen is a
member of a community. Now, sailors have different functions, for one of them is a rower, another a pilot, and a
third a look-out man, a fourth is described by some similar
term; and while the precise definition of each individual's 25
virtue applies exclusively to him, there is, at the same time,
a common definition applicable to them all. For they have
all of them a common object, which is safety in navigation.
Similarly, one citizen differs from another, but the salvation
of the community is the common business of them all. This
community is the constitution; the virtue of the citizen 30
must therefore be relative to the constitution of which he
is a member. If, then, there are many forms of government,
it is evident that there is not one single virtue of the good
citizen which is perfect virtue. But we say that the good

[11] Cp. N. Eth. v. 1130ᵇ 28.

man is he who has one single virtue which is perfect virtue.
Hence it is evident that the good citizen need not of neces-
35 sity possess the virtue which makes a good man.

The same question may also be approached by another
road, from a consideration of the best constitution. If the
state cannot be entirely composed of good men, and yet
40 each citizen is expected to do his own business well, and
1277ª must therefore have virtue, still, inasmuch as all the citizens
cannot be alike, the virtue of the citizen and of the good
man cannot coincide. All must have the virtue of the good
citizen—thus, and thus only, can the state be perfect; but
they will not have the virtue of a good man, unless we assume that in the good state all the citizens must be good.

5 Again, the state, as composed of unlikes, may be compared to the living being: as the first elements into which a
living being is resolved are soul and body, as soul is made up
of rational principle and appetite, the family of husband
and wife, property of master and slave, so of all these, as
well as other dissimilar elements, the state is composed;
10 and, therefore, the virtue of all the citizens cannot possibly
be the same, any more than the excellence of the leader
of a chorus is the same as that of the performer who stands
by his side. I have said enough to show why the two kinds
of virtue cannot be absolutely and always the same.

But will there then be no case in which the virtue of the
15 good citizen and the virtue of the good man coincide? To
this we answer that the good ruler is a good and wise man,
and that he who would be a statesman must be a wise man.
And some persons say that even the education of the ruler
should be of a special kind; for are not the children of kings
instructed in riding and military exercises? As Euripides
says:

'No subtle arts for me, but what the state requires.'

As though there were a special education needed by a ruler.
If then the virtue of a good ruler is the same as that of a

good man, and we assume further that the subject is a [20] citizen as well as the ruler, the virtue of the good citizen and the virtue of the good man cannot be absolutely the same, although in some cases they may; for the virtue of a ruler differs from that of a citizen. It was the sense of this difference which made Jason say that 'he felt hungry when he was not a tyrant', meaning that he could not endure to live in a private station. But, on the other hand, it may be argued that men are praised for knowing both how to rule [25] and how to obey, and he is said to be a citizen of approved virtue who is able to do both. Now if we suppose the virtue of a good man to be that which rules, and the virtue of the citizen to include ruling and obeying, it cannot be said that they are equally worthy of praise. Since, then, it is sometimes thought that the ruler and the ruled must learn [30] different things and not the same, but that the citizen must know and share in them both, the inference is obvious. There is, indeed, the rule of a master, which is concerned with menial offices [12]—the master need not know how to perform these, but may employ others in the execution of them: the other would be degrading; and by the other I [35] mean the power actually to do menial duties, which vary much in character and are executed by various classes of slaves, such, for example, as handicraftsmen, who, as their name signifies, live by the labour of their hands:—under these the mechanic is included. Hence in ancient times, **1277**[1] and among some nations, the working classes had no share in the government—a privilege which they only acquired under the extreme democracy. Certainly the good man and the statesman and the good citizen ought not to learn the crafts of inferiors except for their own occasional use; [13] if they habitually practise them, there will cease to be a dis- [5] tinction between master and slave.

This is not the rule of which we are speaking; but there is

---

[12] Cp. i. 1255[b] 20–37.
[13] Cp. viii. 1337[b] 15.

a rule of another kind, which is exercised over freemen and
equals by birth—a constitutional rule, which the ruler must
10 learn by obeying, as he would learn the duties of a general
of cavalry by being under the orders of a general of cavalry,
or the duties of a general of infantry by being under the
orders of a general of infantry, and by having had the command of a regiment and of a company. It has been well said
that 'he who has never learned to obey cannot be a good
commander'. The two are not the same, but the good
citizen ought to be capable of both; he should know how
15 to govern like a freeman, and how to obey like a freeman—
these are the virtues of a citizen. And, although the temperance and justice of a ruler are distinct from those of a subject, the virtue of a good man will include both; for the
virtue of the good man who is free and also a subject,
e. g. his justice, will not be one but will comprise distinct
kinds, the one qualifying him to rule, the other to obey,
20 and differing as the temperance and courage of men and
women differ.[14] For a man would be thought a coward if
he had no more courage than a courageous woman, and a
woman would be thought loquacious if she imposed no
more restraint on her conversation than the good man; and
indeed their part in the management of the household is
25 different, for the duty of the one is to acquire, and of the
other to preserve. Practical wisdom only is characteristic of
the ruler: [15] it would seem that all other virtues must
equally belong to ruler and subject. The virtue of the subject is certainly not wisdom, but only true opinion; he may
be compared to the maker of the flute, while his master is
the flute-player or user of the flute.[16]

30   From these considerations may be gathered the answer
to the question, whether the virtue of the good man is the
same as that of the good citizen, or different, and how far
the same, and how far different.[17]

[14] Cp. i. 1260[a] 20.
[15] Cp. Rep. iv. 428.
[16] Cp. Rep. x. 601 D, E.
[17] Cp. 1278[a] 40, 1288[a] 39, iv. 1293[b] 5, vii. 1333[a] 11.

5   There still remains one more question about the citizen: Is he only a true citizen who has a share of office, 35 or is the mechanic to be included? If they who hold no office are to be deemed citizens, not every citizen can have this virtue of ruling and obeying; for this man is a citizen. And if none of the lower class are citizens, in which part of the state are they to be placed? For they are not resident aliens, and they are not foreigners. May we not reply, that **1278ª** as far as this objection goes there is no more absurdity in excluding them than in excluding slaves and freedmen from any of the above-mentioned classes? It must be admitted that we cannot consider all those to be citizens who are necessary to the existence of the state; for example, children are not citizens equally with grown-up men, who are citizens absolutely, but children, not being grown up, 5 are only citizens on a certain assumption.[18] Nay, in ancient times, and among some nations, the artisan class were slaves or foreigners, and therefore the majority of them are so now. The best form of state will not admit them to citizenship; but if they are admitted, then our definition of the virtue of a citizen will not apply to every citizen, nor to every free man as such, but only to those who are freed from necessary services. The necessary people are either 10 slaves who minister to the wants of individuals, or mechanics and labourers who are the servants of the community. These reflections carried a little further will explain their position; and indeed what has been said already [19] is of itself, when understood, explanation enough.

Since there are many forms of government there must be many varieties of citizens, and especially of citizens who are 15 subjects; so that under some governments the mechanic and the labourer will be citizens, but not in others, as, for example, in aristocracy or the so-called government of the best (if there be such an one), in which honours are given according to virtue and merit; for no man can practise 20

---

[18] sc. that they grow up to be men
[19] 1275ª 38 sqq.

virtue who is living the life of a mechanic or labourer. In oligarchies the qualification for office is high, and therefore no labourer can ever be a citizen; but a mechanic may, for an actual majority of them are rich. At Thebes [20] there was
25 a law that no man could hold office who had not retired from business for ten years. But in many states the law goes to the length of admitting aliens; for in some democracies a man is a citizen though his mother only be a citizen; and a similar principle is applied to illegitimate children; the law is relaxed when there is a dearth of population. But
30 when the number of citizens increases, first the children of a male or a female slave are excluded; then those whose mothers only are citizens; and at last the right of citizenship is confined to those whose fathers and mothers are both citizens.

(Hence, as is evident, there are different kinds of citizens;
35 and he is a citizen in the highest sense who shares in the honours of the state. Compare Homer's words 'like some dishonoured stranger'; [21] he who is excluded from the honours of the state is no better than an alien. But when this exclusion is concealed, then the object is that the privileged class may deceive their fellow inhabitants.

As to the question whether the virtue of the good man
40 is the same as that of the good citizen, the considerations
1278ᵇ already adduced prove that in some states the good man and the good citizen are the same, and in others different. When they are the same it is not every citizen who is a good
5 man, but only the statesman and those who have or may have, alone or in conjunction with others, the conduct of public affairs.

6   Having determined these questions, we have next to consider whether there is only one form of government or many, and if many, what they are, and how many, and what are the differences between them.

[20] Cp. vi. 1321ᵃ 28.
[21] Achilles complains of Agamemnon's so treating him, Il. ix. 648, xvi. 59.

A constitution is the arrangement of magistracies in a 10 state,[22] especially of the highest of all. The government is everywhere sovereign in the state, and the constitution is in fact the government. For example, in democracies the people are supreme, but in oligarchies, the few; and, therefore, we say that these two forms of government also are different: and so in other cases.

First, let us consider what is the purpose of a state, and 15 how many forms of government there are by which human society is regulated. We have already said, in the first part of this treatise,[23] when discussing household management and the rule of a master, that man is by nature a political 20 animal. And therefore, men, even when they do not require one another's help, desire to live together; not but that they are also brought together by their common interests in proportion as they severally attain to any measure of well-being. This is certainly the chief end, both of individuals and of states. And also for the sake of mere life 25 (in which there is possibly some noble element so long as the evils of existence do not greatly overbalance the good) mankind meet together and maintain the political community. And we all see that men cling to life even at the cost of enduring great misfortune, seeming to find in life a natural sweetness and happiness.

There is no difficulty in distinguishing the various kinds 30 of authority; they have been often defined already in discussions outside the school. The rule of a master, although the slave by nature and the master by nature have in reality the same interests, is nevertheless exercised primarily with a 35 view to the interest of the master, but accidentally considers the slave, since, if the slave perish, the rule of the master perishes with him. On the other hand, the government of a wife and children and of a household, which we have called household management, is exercised in the first instance for the good of the governed or for the common

22 Cp. 1274^b 38, iv. 1289^a 15.
23 Cp. i. 1253^a 2.

40 good of both parties, but essentially for the good of the
governed, as we see to be the case in medicine, gymnastic,
1279ᵃ and the arts in general, which are only accidentally concerned with the good of the artists themselves.[24] For there
is no reason why the trainer may not sometimes practise
gymnastics, and the helmsman is always one of the crew.
The trainer or the helmsman considers the good of those
committed to his care. But, when he is one of the persons
5 taken care of, he accidentally participates in the advantage,
for the helmsman is also a sailor, and the trainer becomes
one of those in training. And so in politics: when the state
is framed upon the principle of equality and likeness, the
citizens think that they ought to hold office by turns.
10 Formerly, as is natural, every one would take his turn of
service; and then again, somebody else would look after his
interest, just as he, while in office, had looked after theirs.[25]
But nowadays, for the sake of the advantage which is to be
gained from the public revenues and from office, men want
to be always in office. One might imagine that the rulers,
being sickly, were only kept in health while they continued
15 in office; in that case we may be sure that they would be
hunting after places. The conclusion is evident: that governments which have a regard to the common interest are
constituted in accordance with strict principles of justice,
and are therefore true forms; but those which regard only
20 the interest of the rulers are all defective and perverted
forms, for they are despotic, whereas a state is a community
of freemen.

7   Having determined these points, we have next to consider how many forms of government there are, and
what they are; and in the first place what are the true forms,
for when they are determined the perversions of them will
25 at once be apparent. The words constitution and government have the same meaning. and the government, which

[24] Cp. Pl. *Rep.* i. 341 D.
[25] Cp. ii. 1261ᵃ 37–ᵇ 6.

is the supreme authority in states, must be in the hands of one, or of a few, or of the many. The true forms of government, therefore, are those in which the one, or the few, or the many, govern with a view to the common interest; but governments which rule with a view to the private interest, 30 whether of the one, or of the few, or of the many, are perversions.[26] For the members of a state, if they are truly citizens, ought to participate in its advantages. Of forms of government in which one rules, we call that which regards the common interests, kingship or royalty; that in which more than one, but not many, rule, aristocracy; and it is so 35 called, either because the rulers are the best men, or because they have at heart the best interests of the state and of the citizens. But when the citizens at large administer the state for the common interest, the government is called by the generic name—a constitution. And there is a reason *constitutional* for this use of language. One man or a few may excel in 40 *gov't* virtue; but as the number increases it becomes more diffi- **1279**[b] cult for them to attain perfection in every kind of virtue, though they may in military virtue, for this is found in the masses. Hence in a constitutional government the fighting-men have the supreme power, and those who possess arms are the citizens.

Of the above-mentioned forms, the perversions are as follows:—of royalty, tyranny; of aristocracy, oligarchy; of 5 constitutional government, democracy. For tyranny is a kind of monarchy which has in view the interest of the monarch only; oligarchy has in view the interest of the wealthy; democracy, of the needy: none of them the com- 10 mon good of all.

8   But there are difficulties about these forms of government, and it will therefore be necessary to state a little more at length the nature of each of them. For he who would make a philosophical study of the various sciences,

[26] Cp. *N. Eth.* viii. 10.

15 and does not regard practice only, ought not to overlook or omit anything, but to set forth the truth in every particular. Tyranny, as I was saying, is monarchy exercising the rule of a master over the political society; oligarchy is when men of property have the government in their hands; democracy, the opposite, when the indigent, and not the men of property, are the rulers. And here arises the first of our .0 difficulties, and it relates to the distinction just drawn. For democracy is said to be the government of the many. But what if the many are men of property and have the power in their hands? In like manner oligarchy is said to be the government of the few; but what if the poor are fewer than 25 the rich, and have the power in their hands because they are stronger? In these cases the distinction which we have drawn between these different forms of government would no longer hold good.

Suppose, once more, that we add wealth to the few and poverty to the many, and name the governments accordingly—an oligarchy is said to be that in which the few and 30 the wealthy, and a democracy that in which the many and the poor are the rulers—there will still be a difficulty. For, if the only forms of government are the ones already mentioned, how shall we describe those other governments also just mentioned by us, in which the rich are the more numerous and the poor are the fewer, and both govern in their respective states?

35   The argument seems to show that, whether in oligarchies or in democracies, the number of the governing body, whether the greater number, as in a democracy, or the smaller number, as in an oligarchy, is an accident due to the fact that the rich everywhere are few, and the poor numerous. But if so, there is a misapprehension of the causes of the difference between them. For the real difference between democracy and oligarchy is poverty and wealth. 40 tween democracy and oligarchy is poverty and wealth. 1280ª Wherever men rule by reason of their wealth, whether they be few or many, that is an oligarchy, and where the poor rule, that is a democracy. But as a fact the rich are few

and the poor many; for few are well-to-do, whereas freedom
is enjoyed by all, and wealth and freedom are the grounds
on which the oligarchical and democratical parties respec- 5
tively claim power in the state.

9   Let us begin by considering the common definitions
of oligarchy and democracy, and what is justice oligarchical and democratical. For all men cling to justice
of some kind, but their conceptions are imperfect and they 10
do not express the whole idea. For example, justice is
thought by them to be, and is, equality, not, however, for
all, but only for equals. And inequality is thought to be,
and is, justice; neither is this for all, but only for unequals.
When the persons are omitted, then men judge errone-
ously. The reason is that they are passing judgement on
themselves, and most people are bad judges in their own 15
case. And whereas justice implies a relation to persons as
well as to things, and a just distribution, as I have already
said in the *Ethics*,[27] implies the same ratio between the persons and between the things, they agree about the equality
of the things, but dispute about the equality of the persons,
chiefly for the reason which I have just given—because they 20
are bad judges in their own affairs; and secondly, because
both the parties to the argument are speaking of a limited
and partial justice, but imagine themselves to be speaking of absolute justice. For the one party, if they are
unequal in one respect, for example wealth, consider
themselves to be unequal in all; and the other party, if
they are equal in one respect, for example free birth, consider themselves to be equal in all. But they leave out the 25
capital point. For if men met and associated out of regard
to wealth only, their share in the state would be proportioned to their property, and the oligarchical doctrine
would then seem to carry the day. It would not be just
that he who paid one mina should have the same share
of a hundred minae, whether of the principal or of the

[27] v. 1131ᵃ 15.

30 profits, as he who paid the remaining ninety-nine. But a
state exists for the sake of a good life, and not for the sake
of life only: if life only were the object, slaves and brute
animals might form a state, but they cannot, for they have
35 no share in happiness or in a life of free choice. Nor does
a state exist for the sake of alliance and security from injustice, nor yet for the sake of exchange and mutual intercourse; for then the Tyrrhenians and the Carthaginians, and
all who have commercial treaties with one another,[28] would
be the citizens of one state. True, they have agreements
40 about imports, and engagements that they will do no wrong
1280^b to one another, and written articles of alliance. But there
are no magistracies common to the contracting parties who
will enforce their engagements; different states have each
their own magistracies. Nor does one state take care that
the citizens of the other are such as they ought to be,
nor see that those who come under the terms of the treaty
do no wrong or wickedness at all, but only that they do no
5 injustice to one another. Whereas, those who care for good
government take into consideration virtue and vice in
states. Whence it may be further inferred that virtue must
be the care of a state which is truly so called, and not merely
enjoys the name: for without this end the community becomes a mere alliance which differs only in place from
alliances of which the members live apart; and law is
10 only a convention, 'a surety to one another of justice,' as
the sophist Lycophron says, and has no real power to make
the citizens good and just.

This is obvious; for suppose distinct places, such as
Corinth and Megara, to be brought together so that their
walls touched, still they would not be one city, not even if
15 the citizens had the right to intermarry, which is one of
the rights peculiarly characteristic of states. Again, if men
dwelt at a distance from one another, but not so far off as
to have no intercourse, and there were laws among them

[28] Cp. 1275^a 10.

that they should not wrong each other in their exchanges, neither would this be a state. Let us suppose that one man is a carpenter, another a husbandman, another a shoe-maker, and so on, and that their number is ten thousand: nevertheless, if they have nothing in common but exchange, alliance, and the like, that would not constitute a state. Why is this? Surely not because they are at a distance from one another: for even supposing that such a community were to meet in one place, but that each man had a house of his own, which was in a manner his state, and that they made alliance with one another, but only against evil-doers; still an accurate thinker would not deem this to be a state, if their intercourse with one another was of the same character after as before their union. It is clear then that a state is not a mere society, having a common place, established for the prevention of mutual crime and for the sake of exchange.[29] These are conditions without which a state cannot exist; but all of them together do not constitute a state, which is a community of families and aggregations of families in well-being, for the sake of a perfect and self-sufficing life. Such a community can only be established among those who live in the same place and inter-marry. Hence arise in cities family connexions, brother-hoods, common sacrifices, amusements which draw men together. But these are created by friendship, for the will to live together is friendship. The end of the state is the good life, and these are the means towards it. And the state is the union of families and villages in a perfect and self-sufficing life, by which we mean a happy and honourable life.[30]

Our conclusion, then, is that political society exists for the sake of noble actions, and not of mere companionship. Hence they who contribute most to such a society have a greater share in it than those who have the same

---

[29] Cp. Protag. 322 B.
[30] Cp. i. 1252[b] 27; N. Eth. i. 1097[b] 6.

or a greater freedom or nobility of birth but are inferior to
them in political virtue; or than those who exceed them in
wealth but are surpassed by them in virtue.

From what has been said it will be clearly seen that all
the partisans of different forms of government speak of a
10 part of justice only.

10 There is also a doubt as to what is to be the supreme
power in the state:—Is it the multitude? Or the
wealthy? Or the good? Or the one best man? Or a tyrant?
Any of these alternatives seems to involve disagreeable consequences. If the poor, for example, because they are more
in number, divide among themselves the property of the
rich—is not this unjust? No, by heaven (will be the reply),
15 for the supreme authority justly willed it. But if this is not
injustice, pray what is? Again, when in the first division all
has been taken, and the majority divide anew the property
of the minority, is it not evident, if this goes on, that they
will ruin the state? Yet surely, virtue is not the ruin of
those who possess her, nor is justice destructive of a state;
and therefore this law of confiscation clearly cannot be just.
20 If it were, all the acts of a tyrant must of necessity be just;
for he only coerces other men by superior power, just as
the multitude coerce the rich. But is it just then that the
25 few and the wealthy should be the rulers? And what if they,
in like manner, rob and plunder the people—is this just?
If so, the other case will likewise be just. But there can be
no doubt that all these things are wrong and unjust.

Then ought the good to rule and have supreme power?
30 But in that case everybody else, being excluded from power,
will be dishonoured. For the offices of a state are posts of
honour; and if one set of men always hold them, the rest
must be deprived of them. Then will it be well that the
one best man should rule? Nay, that is still more oligarchical, for the number of those who are dishonoured is
thereby increased. Some one may say that it is bad in any
35 case for a man, subject as he is to all the accidents of human

passion, to have the supreme power, rather than the law. But what if the law itself be democratical or oligarchical, how will that help us out of our difficulties? [31] Not at all; the same consequences [32] will follow.

11 Most of these questions may be reserved for another occasion.[33] The principle that the multitude ought to 40 be supreme rather than the few best is one that is maintained, and, though not free from difficulty, yet seems to contain an element of truth. For the many, of whom each **1281ᵇ** individual is but an ordinary person, when they meet together may very likely be better than the few good, if regarded not individually but collectively, just as a feast to which many contribute is better than a dinner provided out of a single purse. For each individual among the many has a share of virtue and prudence, and when they meet 5 together, they become in a manner one man, who has many feet, and hands, and senses; that is a figure of their mind and disposition. Hence the many are better judges than a single man of music and poetry; for some understand one part, and some another, and among them they understand 10 the whole. There is a similar combination of qualities in good men, who differ from any individual of the many, as the beautiful are said to differ from those who are not beautiful, and works of art from realities, because in them the scattered elements are combined, although, if taken separately, the eye of one person or some other feature in another person would be fairer than in the picture. 15 Whether this principle can apply to every democracy, and to all bodies of men, is not clear. Or rather, by heaven, in some cases it is impossible of application; for the argument would equally hold about brutes; and wherein, it will be asked, do some men differ from brutes? But there may 20 be bodies of men about whom our statement is nevertheless

[31] Cp. 1282ᵇ 6.
[32] Cp. ll. 11–34.
[33] cc. 12–17, iv. vi

true. And if so, the difficulty which has been already
raised, [34] and also another which is akin to it—viz. what
power should be assigned to the mass of freemen and
25 citizens, who are not rich and have no personal merit—
are both solved. There is still a danger in allowing them to
share the great offices of state, for their folly will lead them
into error, and their dishonesty into crime. But there is a
danger also in not letting them share, for a state in which
30 many poor men are excluded from office will necessarily be
full of enemies. The only way of escape is to assign to them
some deliberative and judicial functions. For this reason
Solon [35] and certain other legislators give them the power
of electing to offices, and of calling the magistrates to account, but they do not allow them to hold office singly.
When they meet together their perceptions are quite good
35 enough, and combined with the better class they are useful
to the state (just as impure food when mixed with what
is pure sometimes makes the entire mass more wholesome
than a small quantity of the pure would be), but each
individual, left to himself, forms an imperfect judgement.
On the other hand, the popular form of government involves certain difficulties. In the first place, it might be
40 objected that he who can judge of the healing of a sick
man would be one who could himself heal his disease, and
make him whole—that is, in other words, the physician;
1282ᵃ and so in all professions and arts. As, then, the physician
ought to be called to account by physicians, so ought men
in general to be called to account by their peers. But
physicians are of three kinds:—there is the ordinary practi-
tioner, and there is the physician of the higher class, and
thirdly the intelligent man who has studied the art: in all
arts there is such a class; and we attribute the power of
5 judging to them quite as much as to professors of the art.
Secondly, does not the same principle apply to elections?
For a right election can only be made by those who have

---

[34] c. 10.
[35] Cp. ii. 1274ᵃ 15.

knowledge; those who know geometry, for example, will choose a geometrician rightly, and those who know how to steer, a pilot; and, even if there be some occupations and arts in which private persons share in the ability to choose, they certainly cannot choose better than those who know. So that, according to this argument, neither the election of magistrates, nor the calling of them to account, should be entrusted to the many. Yet possibly these objections are to a great extent met by our old answer,[36] that if the people are not utterly degraded, although individually they may be worse judges than those who have special knowledge—as a body they are as good or better. Moreover, there are some arts whose products are not judged of solely, or best, by the artists themselves, namely those arts whose products are recognized even by those who do not possess the art; for example, the knowledge of the house is not limited to the builder only; the user, or, in other words, the master, of the house will even be a better judge than the builder, just as the pilot will judge better of a rudder than the carpenter, and the guest will judge better of a feast than the cook.

This difficulty seems now to be sufficiently answered, but there is another akin to it. That inferior persons should have authority in greater matters than the good would appear to be a strange thing, yet the election and calling to account of the magistrates is the greatest of all. And these, as I was saying,[37] are functions which in some states are assigned to the people, for the assembly is supreme in all such matters. Yet persons of any age, and having but a small property qualification, sit in the assembly and deliberate and judge, although for the great officers of state, such as treasurers and generals, a high qualification is required. This difficulty may be solved in the same manner as the preceding, and the present practice of democracies may be really defensible. For the power does not reside in the dicast, or senator, or ecclesiast, but in the court, and the

---

[36] 1281ᵃ 40–ᵇ 21.
[37] 1281ᵇ 32.

senate, and the assembly, of which individual senators, or ecclesiasts, or dicasts, are only parts or members. And for this reason the many may claim to have a higher authority than the few; for the people, and the senate, and the courts

40 consist of many persons, and their property collectively is greater than the property of one or of a few individuals holding great offices. But enough of this.

1282ᵇ   The discussion of the first question [38] shows nothing so clearly as that laws, when good, should be supreme; and that the magistrate or magistrates should regulate those

5 matters only on which the laws are unable to speak with precision owing to the difficulty of any general principle embracing all particulars.[39] But what are good laws has not yet been clearly explained; the old difficulty remains.[40] The goodness or badness, justice or injustice, of laws varies of

10 necessity with the constitutions of states. This, however, is clear, that the laws must be adapted to the constitutions. But if so, true forms of government will of necessity have just laws, and perverted forms of government will have unjust laws.

15 **12**   In all sciences and arts the end is a good, and the greatest good and in the highest degree a good in the most authoritative of all [41]—this is the political science of which the good is justice, in other words, the common interest. All men think justice to be a sort of equality; and to a certain extent [42] they agree in the philosophical distinc-

20 tions which have been laid down by us about Ethics.[43] For they admit that justice is a thing and has a relation to persons, and that equals ought to have equality. But there still remains a question: equality or inequality of what? here is a difficulty which calls for political speculation.

---

[38] c. 10.
[39] Cp. N. Eth. v. 1137ᵇ 19.
[40] Cp. 1281ᵃ 36.
[41] Cp. i. 1252ᵃ 2; N. Eth. i. 1094ᵃ 1.
[42] Cp. 1280ᵃ 9.
[43] Cp. N. Eth. v. 3.

For very likely some persons will say that offices of state ought to be unequally distributed according to superior excellence, in whatever respect, of the citizen, although there is no other difference between him and the rest of the 25 community; for that those who differ in any one respect have different rights and claims. But, surely, if this is true, the complexion or height of a man, or any other advantage, will be a reason for his obtaining a greater share of political 30 rights. The error here lies upon the surface, and may be illustrated from the other arts and sciences. When a number of flute-players are equal in their art, there is no reason why those of them who are better born should have better flutes given to them; for they will not play any better on the flute, and the superior instrument should be reserved for him who is the superior artist. If what I am saying is still obscure, it will be made clearer as we proceed. For if there were a superior flute-player who was far inferior in 35 birth and beauty, although either of these may be a greater good than the art of flute-playing, and may excel flute-playing in a greater ratio than he excels the others in his 40 art, still he ought to have the best flutes given to him, un-less the advantages of wealth and birth contribute to excel- **1283ᵇ** lence in flute-playing, which they do not. Moreover, upon this principle any good may be compared with any other. For if a given height may be measured against wealth and against freedom, height in general may be so measured. 5 Thus if A excels in height more than B in virtue, even if virtue in general excels height still more, all goods will be commensurable; for if a certain amount is better than some other, it is clear that some other will be equal. But since no such comparison can be made, it is evident that there is 10 good reason why in politics men do not ground their claim to office on every sort of inequality any more than in the rts. For if some be slow, and others swift, that is no reason why the one should have little and the others much; it is in gymnastic contests that such excellence is rewarded. Whereas the rival claims of candidates for office can only

15 be based on the possession of elements which enter into the composition of a state. And therefore the noble, or free-born, or rich, may with good reason claim office; for holders of offices must be freemen and tax-payers: a state can be no more composed entirely of poor men than entirely of slaves. But if wealth and freedom are necessary elements, justice and valour are equally so; [44] for without the former quali-
20 ties a state cannot exist at all, without the latter not well.

13 If the existence of the state is alone to be considered, then it would seem that all, or some at least, of these
25 claims are just; but, if we take into account a good life, then, as I have already said,[45] education and virtue have superior claims. As, however, those who are equal in one thing ought not to have an equal share in all, nor those who are unequal in one thing to have an unequal share in all, it is certain that all forms of government which rest on either of these principles are perversions. All men have
30 a claim in a certain sense, as I have already admitted,[46] but all have not an absolute claim. The rich claim because they have a greater share in the land, and land is the common element of the state; also they are generally more trust-worthy in contracts. The free claim under the same title as the noble; for they are nearly akin. For the noble are citizens in a truer sense than the ignoble, and good birth is
35 always valued in a man's own home and country.[47] Another reason is, that those who are sprung from better ancestors are likely to be better men, for nobility is excellence of race. (Virtue, too, may be truly said to have a claim, for justice has been acknowledged by us to be a social [48] virtue,
40 and it implies all others.[49] Again, the many may urge their claim against the few; for, when taken collectively, and

---

[44] Cp. iv. 1291ᵃ 19–33.
[45] Cp. 1281ᵃ 4.
[46] 1280ᵃ 9 sqq.
[47] Cp. i. 1255ᵃ 32.
[48] Cp. i. 1253ᵃ 37.
[49] Cp. N. Eth. v. 1129ᵇ 25.

compared with the few, they are stronger and richer and **1283**^{b}
better. But, what if the good, the rich, the noble, and the
other classes who make up a state, are all living together
in the same city, will there, or will there not, be any doubt
who shall rule?—No doubt at all in determining who
ought to rule in each of the above-mentioned forms of 5
government. For states are characterized by differences in
their governing bodies—one of them has a government of
the rich, another of the virtuous, and so on. But a difficulty
arises when all these elements coexist. How are we to decide? Suppose the virtuous to be very few in number: may 10
we consider their numbers in relation to their duties, and
ask whether they are enough to administer the state, or so
many as will make up a state? Objections may be urged
against all the aspirants to political power. For those who 15
found their claims on wealth or family might be thought
to have no basis of justice; on this principle, if any one
person were richer than all the rest, it is clear that he ought
to be ruler of them. In like manner he who is very distinguished by his birth ought to have the superiority over
all those who claim on the ground that they are freeborn.
In an aristocracy, or government of the best, a like difficulty 20
occurs about virtue; for if one citizen be better than the
other members of the government, however good they may
be, he too, upon the same principle of justice, should rule
over them. And if the people are to be supreme because
they are stronger than the few, then if one man, or more
than one, but not a majority, is stronger than the many, 25
they ought to rule, and not the many.

All these considerations appear to show that none of the
principles on which men claim to rule and to hold all
other men in subjection to them are strictly right. To those
who claim to be masters of the government on the ground 30
of their virtue or their wealth, the many might fairly answer
that they themselves are often better and richer than the
few—I do not say individually, but collectively. And another ingenious objection which is sometimes put forward

35 may be met in a similar manner. Some persons doubt
whether the legislator who desires to make the justest laws
ought to legislate with a view to the good of the higher
classes or of the many, when the case which we have
40 mentioned occurs.[50] Now what is just or right is to be inter-
preted in the sense of 'what is equal'; and that which is right
in the sense of being equal is to be considered with reference to the advantage of the state, and the common good
of the citizens. And a citizen is one who shares in governing
and being governed. He differs under different forms of
1284ᵃ government, but in the best state he is one who is able and
willing to be governed and to govern with a view to the life
of virtue.

If, however, there be some one person, or more than one,
although not enough to make up the full complement of a
state, whose virtue is so pre-eminent that the virtues or the
5 political capacity of all the rest admit of no comparison
with his or theirs, he or they can be no longer regarded as
part of a state; for justice will not be done to the superior,
if he is reckoned only as the equal of those who are so far
inferior to him in virtue and in political capacity. Such
10 an one may truly be deemed a God among men. Hence we
see that legislation is necessarily concerned only with those
who are equal in birth and in capacity; and that for men of
pre-eminent virtue there is no law—they are themselves a
law. Any one would be ridiculous who attempted to make
15 laws for them: they would probably retort what, in the
fable of Antisthenes, the lions said to the hares,[51] when in
the council of the beasts the latter began haranguing and
claiming equality for all. And for this reason democratic
20 states have instituted ostracism; equality is above all things
their aim, and therefore they ostracized and banished from
the city for a time those who seemed to predominate too
much through their wealth, or the number of their friends,
or through any other political influence. Mythology tells us

---

[50] i. e. when the many collectively are better than the few.
[51] i. e. 'where are your claws and teeth?'

that the Argonauts left Heracles behind for a similar reason; the ship Argo would not take him because she feared that 25 he would have been too much for the rest of the crew. Wherefore those who denounce tyranny and blame the counsel which Periander gave to Thrasybulus cannot be held altogether just in their censure. The story is that Periander, when the herald was sent to ask counsel of him, said nothing, but only cut off the tallest ears of corn till 30 he had brought the field to a level. The herald did not know the meaning of the action, but came and reported what he had seen to Thrasybulus, who understood that he was to cut off the principal men in the state; [52] and this is a 35 policy not only expedient for tyrants or in practice confined to them, but equally necessary in oligarchies and democracies. Ostracism [53] is a measure of the same kind, which acts by disabling and banishing the most prominent citizens. Great powers do the same to whole cities and nations, as the Athenians did to the Samians, Chians, and Lesbians; 40 no sooner had they obtained a firm grasp of the empire, 1284 than they humbled their allies contrary to treaty; and the Persian king has repeatedly crushed the Medes, Babylonians, and other nations, when their spirt has been stirred by the recollection of their former greatness.

The problem is a universal one, and equally concerns all forms of government, true as well as false; for, although perverted forms with a view to their own interests may 5 adopt this policy, those which seek the common interest do so likewise. The same thing may be observed in the arts and sciences; [54] for the painter will not allow the figure to have a foot which, however beautiful, is not in proportion, nor will the ship-builder allow the stern or any other part 10 of the vessel to be unduly large, any more than the chorus-master will allow any one who sings louder or better than all the rest to sing in the choir. Monarchs, too, may practise

[52] Cp. v. 1311[a] 20.
[53] Cp. v. 1302[b] 18.
[54] Cp. v. 1302[b] 34, 1309[b] 21; vii. 1326[a] 35; Rep. iv. 420.

15 compulsion and still live in harmony with their cities, if their own government is for the interest of the state. Hence where there is an acknowledged superiority the argument in favour of ostracism is based upon a kind of political justice. It would certainly be better that the legislator should from the first so order his state as to have no need of such a remedy. But if the need arises, the next best thing is that he should endeavour to correct the evil by this or 20 some similar measure. The principle, however, has not been fairly applied in states; for, instead of looking to the good of their own constitution, they have used ostracism for factious purposes. It is true that under perverted forms of government, and from their special point of view, such a measure is just and expedient, but it is also clear that it 25 is not absolutely just. In the perfect state there would be great doubts about the use of it, not when applied to excess in strength, wealth, popularity, or the like, but when used against some one who is pre-eminent in virtue—what is to be done with him? Mankind will not say that such an one is to be expelled and exiled; on the other hand, he 30 ought not to be a subject—that would be as if mankind should claim to rule over Zeus, dividing his offices among them. The only alternative is that all should joyfully obey such a ruler, according to what seems to be the order of nature, and that men like him should be kings in their state for life.

14   The preceding discussion, by a natural transition, leads 35   to the consideration of loyalty, which we admit to be __one of the true forms of government.__ Let us see whether in order to be well governed a state or country should be under the rule of a king or under some other form of government; and whether monarchy, although good for some, 40 may not be bad for others. But first we must determine whether there is one species of royalty or many. It is easy 1285ᵃ to see that there are many, and that the manner of government is not the same in all of them.

Of royalties according to law, (1) the Lacedaemonian is thought to answer best to the true pattern; but there the royal power is not absolute, except when the kings go on an expedition, and then they take the command. Matters of 5 religion are likewise committed to them. The kingly office is in truth a kind of generalship, irresponsible and perpetual. The king has not the power of life and death, except in a specified case, as for instance, in ancient times, he had it when upon a campaign, by right of force. This custom is described in Homer. For Agamemnon is patient when he 10 is attacked in the assembly, but when the army goes out to battle he has the power even of life and death. Does he not say?—'When I find a man skulking apart from the battle, nothing shall save him from the dogs and vultures, for in my hands is death.' [55]

This, then, is one form of royalty—a generalship for life: 15 and of such royalties some are hereditary and others elective.

(2) There is another sort of monarchy not uncommon among the barbarians, which nearly resembles tyranny. But this is both legal and hereditary. For barbarians, being 20 more servile in character than Hellenes, and Asiatics than Europeans, do not rebel against a despotic government. Such royalties have the nature of tyrannies because the people are by nature slaves; [56] but there is no danger of their being overthrown, for they are hereditary and legal. Wherefore also their guards are such as a king and not such 25 as a tyrant would employ, that is to say, they are composed of citizens, whereas the guards of tyrants are mercenaries.[57] For kings rule according to law over voluntary subjects, but tyrants over involuntary; and the one are guarded by their fellow-citizens, the others are guarded against them.

These are two forms of monarchy, and there was a third 30 (3) which existed in ancient Hellas, called an Aesymnetia

---

[55] *Il.* ii. 391–393. The last clause is not found in our Homer.
[56] Cp. i. 1252[b] 7.
[57] Cp. v. 1311[a] 7.

dictatorship (margin note)

or dictatorship. This may be defined generally as an elective tyranny, which, like the barbarian monarchy, is legal, but differs from it in not being hereditary. Sometimes the office 35 was held for life, sometimes for a term of years, or until certain duties had been performed. For example, the Mytilenaeans elected Pittacus leader against the exiles, who were headed by Antimenides and Alcaeus the poet. And Alcaeus himself shows in one of his banquet odes that they chose Pittacus tyrant, for he reproaches his fellow-citizens for 'having made the low-born Pittacus tyrant of 1285ᵇ the spiritless and ill-fated city, with one voice shouting his praises'.

These forms of government have always had the character of tyrannies, because they possess despotic power; but inasmuch as they are elective and acquiesced in by their subjects, they are kingly.

(4) There is a fourth species of kingly rule—that of the heroic times—which was hereditary and legal, and was 5 exercised over willing subjects. For the first chiefs were benefactors of the people [58] in arts or arms; they either gathered them into a community, or procured land for them; and thus they became kings of voluntary subjects, and their power was inherited by their descendants. They 10 took the command in war and presided over the sacrifices, except those which required a priest. They also decided causes either with or without an oath; and when they swore, the form of the oath was the stretching out of their sceptre. In ancient times their power extended continuously to 15 all things whatsoever, in city and country, as well as in foreign parts; but at a later date they relinquished several of these privileges, and others the people took from them, until in some states nothing was left to them but the sacrifices; and where they retained more of the reality they had only the right of leadership in war beyond the border.

These, then, are the four kinds of royalty. First the 20 monarchy of the heroic ages; this was exercised over volun-

Summary of kinds of royalty (margin note)

[58] Cp. v. 1310ᵇ 10.

tary subjects, but limited to certain functions; the king was a general and a judge, and had the control of religion. The second is that of the barbarians, which is an hereditary despotic government in accordance with law. A third is the power of the so-called Aesymnete or Dictator; this is an elective tyranny. The fourth is the Lacedaemonian, 25 which is in fact a generalship, hereditary and perpetual. These four forms differ from one another in the manner which I have described.

(5) There is a fifth form of kingly rule in which one has the disposal of all, just as each nation or each state has the disposal of public matters; this form corresponds to 30 the control of a household. For as household management is the kingly rule of a house, so kingly rule is the household management of a city, or of a nation, or of many nations.

15 (Of these forms we need only consider two, the Lace-
daemonian and the absolute royalty; for most of the others lie in a region between them, having less power than 35 the last, and more than the first. Thus the inquiry is reduced to two points: first, is it advantageous to the state that there should be a perpetual general, and if so, should the office be confined to one family, or open to the citizens in turn? Secondly, is it well that a single man should have 1286 the supreme power in all things? The first question falls under the head of laws rather than of constitutions; for perpetual generalship might equally exist under any form of government, so that this matter may be dismissed for the present.[59] The other kind of royalty is a sort of constitution; this we have now to consider, and briefly to run 5 over the difficulties involved in it. We will begin by inquiring whether it is more advantageous to be ruled by the best man or by the best laws.[60]

The advocates of royalty maintain that the laws speak only in general terms, and cannot provide for circum- 10

[59] It is not discussed later.
[60] Cp. Plato, *Polit.* 294 A–295 C.

stances; and that for any science to abide by written rules is absurd. In Egypt the physician is allowed to alter his treatment after the fourth day, but if sooner, he takes the
15 risk. Hence it is clear that a government acting according to written laws is plainly not the best. Yet surely the ruler cannot dispense with the general principle which exists in law; and that is a better ruler which is free from passion than that in which it is innate. Whereas the law is passion-
20 less, passion must ever sway the heart of man. Yes, it may be replied, but then on the other hand an individual will be better able to deliberate in particular cases.

The best man, then, must legislate, and laws must be passed, but these laws will have no authority when they
25 miss the mark, though in all other cases retaining their authority. But when the law cannot determine a point at all, or not well, should the one best man or should all decide? According to our present practice assemblies meet, sit in judgement, deliberate, and decide, and their judgements all relate to individual cases. Now any member of the assembly, taken separately, is certainly inferior to the wise man. But the state is made up of many individuals. And as a feast to which all the guests contribute is better than
30 a banquet furnished by a single man,[61] so a multitude is a better judge of many things than any individual.

Again, the many are more incorruptible than the few; they are like the greater quantity of water which is less easily corrupted than a little. The individual is liable to be
35 overcome by anger or by some other passion, and then his judgement is necessarily perverted; but it is hardly to be supposed that a great number of persons would all get into a passion and go wrong at the same moment. Let us assume that they are the freemen, and that they never act in violation of the law, but fill up the gaps which the law is obliged to leave. Or, if such virtue is scarcely attainable by the multitude, we need only suppose that the majority
40 are good men and good citizens, and ask which will be the

[61] Cp. 1281ª 42.

more incorruptible, the one good ruler, or the many who 1286^b
are all good? Will not the many? But, you will say, there
may be parties among them, whereas the one man is not
divided against himself. To which we may answer that
their character is as good as his. If we call the rule of many 5
men, who are all of them good, aristocracy, and the rule of
one man royalty, then aristocracy will be better for states
than royalty, whether the government is supported by force
or not,[62] provided only that a number of men equal in
virtue can be found.

The first governments were kingships, probably for this
reason, because of old, when cities were small, men of eminent virtue were few. Further, they were made kings be- 10
cause they were benefactors,[63] and benefits can only be
bestowed by good men. But when many persons equal in
merit arose, no longer enduring the pre-eminence of one,
they desired to have a commonwealth, and set up a constitution. The ruling class soon deteriorated and enriched
themselves out of the public treasury; riches became the
path to honour, and so oligarchies naturally grew up. These 15
passed into tyrannies and tyrannies into democracies; for
love of gain in the ruling classes was always tending to
diminish their number, and so to strengthen the masses,
who in the end set upon their masters and established democracies. Since cities have increased in size, no other form 20
of government appears to be any longer even easy to establish.[64]

Even supposing the principle to be maintained that
kingly power is the best thing for states, how about the
family of the king? Are his children to succeed him? If
they are no better than anybody else, that will be mis-
chievous. But, says the lover of royalty, the king, though 25
he might, will not hand on his power to his children.
That, however, is hardly to be expected, and is too much to

[62] Cp. 1. 27.
[63] Cp. 1285^b 6.
[64] Cp. iv. 1293^a 1, 1297^b 22.

ask of human nature. There is also a difficulty about the force which he is to employ; should a king have guards about him by whose aid he may be able to coerce the 30 refractory? if not, how will he administer his kingdom? Even if he be the lawful sovereign who does nothing arbitrarily or contrary to law, still he must have some force wherewith to maintain the law. In the case of a limited monarchy there is not much difficulty in answering this 35 question; the king must have such force as will be more than a match for one or more individuals, but not so great as that of the people. The ancients observe this principle when they have guards to any one whom they appointed dictator or tyrant. Thus, when Dionysius asked the Syracusans to allow him guards, somebody advised that 40 they should give him only such a number.

16 At this place in the discussion there impends the in-
1287ᵃ quiry respecting the king who acts solely according to his own will; he has now to be considered. The so-called limited monarchy, or kingship according to law, as I have already remarked,[65] is not a distinct form of government, 5 for under all governments, as, for example, in a democracy or aristocracy, there may be a general holding office for life, and one person is often made supreme over the administration of a state. A magistracy of this kind exists at Epidamnus,[66] and also at Opus, but in the latter city has a 10 more limited power. Now, absolute monarchy, or the arbitrary rule of a sovereign over all the citizens, in a city which consists of equals, is thought by some to be quite contrary to nature; it is argued that those who are by nature equals must have the same natural right and worth, and that for unequals to have an equal share, or for equals 15 to have an unequal share, in the offices of state, is as bad as for different bodily constitutions to have the same food and clothing. Wherefore it is thought to be just that

[65] 1286ᵃ 2.
[66] Cp. v. 1301ᵇ 21.

among equals every one be ruled as well as rule, and therefore that all should have their turn. We thus arrive at law; for an order of succession implies law. And the rule of the law, it is argued, is preferable to that of any indi- 20 vidual. On the same principle, even if it be better for certain individuals to govern, they should be made only guardians and ministers of the law. For magistrates there must be—this is admitted; but then men say that to give authority to any one man when all are equal is unjust. Nay, there may indeed be cases which the law seems un-able to determine, but in such cases can a man? Nay, it 25 will be replied, the law trains officers for this express pur-pose, and appoints them to determine matters which are left undecided by it, to the best of their judgement. Further, it permits them to make any amendment of the existing laws which experience suggests. Therefore he who bids the law rule may be deemed to bid God and Reason alone rule, but he who bids man rule adds an element of 30 the beast; for desire is a wild beast, and passion perverts the minds of rulers, even when they are the best of men. The law is reason unaffected by desire. We are told [67] that a patient should call in a physician; he will not get better if he is doctored out of a book. But the parallel of the arts is clearly not in point; for the physician does nothing con- 35 trary to rule from motives of friendship; he only cures a patient and takes a fee; whereas magistrates do many things from spite and partiality. And, indeed, if a man suspected the physician of being in league with his enemies to destroy him for a bribe, he would rather have recourse 40 to the book. But certainly physicians, when they are sick, call in other physicians, and training-masters, when they **1287** are in training, other training-masters, as if they could not judge truly about their own case and might be influenced by their feelings. Hence it is evident that in seeking for justice men seek for the mean or neutral, [68] for the law is 5

[67] Cp. 1286ᵃ 12–14, *Polit.* 296 B.
[68] Cp. N. *Eth.* v. 1132ᵃ 22.

the mean. Again, customary laws have more weight, and relate to more important matters, than written laws, and a
man may be a safer ruler than the written law, but not
safer than the customary law.)

Again, it is by no means easy for one man to superintend
many things; he will have to appoint a number of subordinates, and what difference does it make whether these
10 subordinates always existed or were appointed by him be
cause he needed them? If, as I said before,[69] the good man
has a right to rule because he is better, still two good men
are better than one: this is the old saying—

'two going together',[70]

and the prayer of Agamemnon—

'would that I had ten such counsellors!' [71]

And at this day there are magistrates, for example judges,
15 who have authority to decide some matters which the law
is unable to determine, since no one doubts that the law
would command and decide in the best manner whatever
it could. But some things can, and other things cannot, be
20 comprehended under the law, and this is the origin of the
vexed question whether the best law or the best man should
rule. For matters of detail about which men deliberate
cannot be included in legislation. Nor does any one deny
that the decision of such matters must be left to man, but
it is argued that there should be many judges, and not one
25 only. For every ruler who has been trained by the law
judges well; and it would surely seem strange that a person
should see better with two eyes, or hear better with two
ears, or act better with two hands or feet, than many with
many; indeed, it is already the practice of kings to make to
themselves many eyes and ears and hands and feet. For
30 they make colleagues of those who are the friends of them-

[69] 1283[b] 21, 1284[b] 32.
[70] Il. x. 224.
[71] Il. ii. 372.

selves and their governments. They must be friends of the
monarch and of his government; if not his friends, they
will not do what he wants; but friendship implies likeness
and equality; and, therefore, if he thinks that his friends
ought to rule, he must think that those who are equal to
himself and like himself ought to rule equally with him- 35
self. These are the principal controversies relating to monarchy.

17　But may not all this be true in some cases and not in
others? for there is by nature both a justice and an
advantage appropriate to the rule of a master, another to
kingly rule, another to constitutional rule; but there is
none naturally appropriate to tyranny, or to any other perverted form of government; for these come into being
contrary to nature. Now, to judge at least from what has
been said, it is manifest that, where men are alike and 40
equal, it is neither expedient nor just that one man should **1288ª**
be lord of all, whether there are laws, or whether there are
no laws, but he himself is in the place of law. Neither
should a good man be lord over good men, nor a bad man
over bad; nor, even if he excels in virtue, should he have a
right to rule, unless in a particular case, at which I have
already hinted, and to which I will once more recur.[72] But 5
first of all, I must determine what natures are suited for
government by a king, and what for an aristocracy, and
what for a constitutional government.

A people who are by nature capable of producing a race
superior in the virtue needed for political rule are fitted
for kingly government; and a people submitting to be ruled 10
as freemen by men whose virtue renders them capable of
political command are adapted for an aristocracy: while
the people who are suited for constitutional freedom are
those among whom there naturally exists a warlike multitude [73] able to rule and to obey in turn by a law which

[72] 1284ª 3, and 1288ª 15.
[73] Cp. 1279ᵇ 2.

15 gives office to the well-to-do according to their desert. But when a whole family, or some individual, happens to be so pre-eminent in virtue as to surpass all others, then it is just that they should be the royal family and supreme over all, or that this one citizen should be king of the whole 20 nation. For, as I said before,[74] to give them authority is not only agreeable to that ground of right which the founders of all states, whether aristocratical, or oligarchical, or again democratical, are accustomed to put forward (for these 25 all recognize the claim of excellence, although not the same excellence), but accords with the principle already laid down. For surely it would not be right to kill, or ostracize, or exile such a person, or require that he should take his turn in being governed. The whole is naturally superior to the part, and he who has this pre-eminence is in the relation of a whole to a part. But if so, the only alternative is that he should have the supreme power, and that 30 mankind should obey him, not in turn, but always. These are the conclusions at which we arrive respecting royalty and its various forms, and this is the answer to the question, whether it is or is not advantageous to states, and to which, and how.

18 We maintain [75] that the true forms of government 35 are three, and that the best must be that which is administered by the best, and in which there is one man, or a whole family, or many persons, excelling all the others together in virtue, and both rulers and subjects are fitted, the one to rule, the others to be ruled, in such a manner as to attain the most eligible life. We showed at the commencement of our inquiry [76] that the virtue of the good man is necessarily the same as the virtue of the citizen of the perfect state. Clearly then in the same manner, and by 40 the same means through which a man becomes truly

---

[74] 1283ᵇ 20, 1284ᵃ 3–17, ᵇ25.
[75] Cp. 1279ᵃ 22· ᵇ ·.
[76] cc. 4, 5.

good, he will frame a state that is to be ruled by an aristocracy or by a king, and the same education and the **1288**ᵇ
same habits will be found to make a good man and a man
fit to be a statesman or king.

Having arrived at these conclusions, we must proceed
to speak of the perfect state, and describe how it comes
into being and is established.   5

Rhetoric and Poetic

INTRODUCTION

Is dialectic not logic?

Rhetoric is closely allied to logic, for it is the counterpart of dialectic, in Aristotle's analysis, and it has not infrequently been used by his successors to suggest improvements or substitutions for logical devices. It has a moral and political dimension, and the Sophists, as Aristotle views their practices, confused it with the art of politics. It is finally a verbal art, the development of which, both before Aristotle's analyses and since, has been closely associated with the interpretation of poetry. Consistent with his differentiations among the arts and sciences, Aristotle separates the arts of rhetoric and poetic.

Rhetoric like dialectic is limited to no specific subject matter, but may be used in any consideration, and it is by that fact opposed to the method of science and limited to questions on which variation of opinion is possible. Aristotle emphasized the consideration of arguments, which are the form and essence of persuasion and which had been neglected by the previous writers on the art of rhetoric. There are three modes of persuasion available to a speaker: the use of his character to make his speech credible, the excitation of desired emotions in the audience, and proof or apparent proof. Rhetoric is therefore defined as the faculty or power of observing in any given case the available means of persuasion. It is the audience, however, which determines the means: the kinds of oratory—political or deliberative, forensic or legal, and epideictic or display—are determined by consideration of kinds of audience; the character which will be effective in the speaker depends on the susceptibility of audiences; and questions of rhetorical style and arrangement are in large part questions of appropriateness to the various kinds of oratory.

Poetic, too, treats of an art which employs words, and the end of that art is, as in all arts, the basic consideration; but the end is found, not in the peculiarities of audiences, but in the proper pleasure of the varieties of poetry. Poetry is defined in terms of imitation, not persuasion, and the consideration of the historical development of tragedy and the examination of particular tragedies elucidate the definition of tragedy in accordance with which the plot is the form or soul of tragedy. When, finally, tragedy is compared with other forms of poetry, and particularly with the epic, in the last four chapters of the Poetics as it has come to us, the kinds of poetry are not distinguished in terms of audiences but in terms of a comparison of values achieved and a distinction of devices employed.

Like other Greek philosophers, Aristotle was fond of comparing the arts and the sciences. Whereas Socrates used the likeness of the physician, the pilot, the shepherd, and the cobbler, to demonstrate that virtue is knowledge, that philosophers should be kings, and that statesmen are supreme poets, Aristotle used the analogy of the arts to distinguish them as poetic or productive sciences from the practical and theoretic sciences. Art is like virtue in its mode of acquisition and destruction, for both are produced by performing the same actions which they will in turn cause and both are destroyed by the same causes that produced them, but they differ from each other in that virtues are judged by the state of character from which the action is produced and arts are judged by the quality of the objects produced by the action. Art is like nature in its objects and the manner in which artificial and natural objects are produced, for Aristotle is fond of repeating the observation that the objects of art are produced as nature would have produced them, and that in the processes of production and the objects produced, art imitates nature. But nature is a cause of motion internal to the thing moved, while art is an external cause employed by the artist to impose on matter a form first conceived in his mind, and artificial objects are not natures or substances and therefore have no strict definitions comparable to those discovered in physics for natural objects.

DE POETICA

CONTENTS

(C) Rules for the construction of an epic.

  23. It must preserve unity of action.

  24. Points of resemblance and of difference between epic poetry and tragedy.

(D) 25. Possible criticisms of an epic or tragedy, and the answers to them.

(E) 26. Tragedy artistically superior to epic poetry.

De Poetica

Poetics

Translated by Ingram Bywater

⊓⊔⊓⊔

1 Our subject being Poetry, I propose to speak not only
of the art in general but also of its species and their
respective capacities; of the structure of plot required for a
good poem; of the number and nature of the constituent
parts of a poem; and likewise of any other matters in the
same line of inquiry. Let us follow the natural order and
begin with the primary facts.

Epic poetry and Tragedy, as also Comedy, Dithyrambic
poetry, and most flute-playing and lyre-playing, are all,
viewed as a whole, modes of imitation. But at the same
time they differ from one another in three ways, either by
a difference of kind in their means, or by differences in
the objects, or in the manner of their imitations.

I. Just as colour and form are used as means by some,
who (whether by art or constant practice) imitate and
portray many things by their aid, and the voice is used by
others; so also in the above-mentioned group of arts, the
means with them as a whole are rhythm, language, and
harmony—used, however, either singly or in certain combinations. A combination of harmony and rhythm alone is
the means in flute-playing and lyre-playing, and any other
arts there may be of the same description, e. g. imitative
piping. Rhythm alone, without harmony, is the means in
the dancer's imitations; for even he, by the rhythms of his

means of imitation

attitudes, may represent men's characters, as well as what
they do and suffer. There is further an art which imitates
by language alone, without harmony, in prose or in verse,
and if in verse, either in some one or in a plurality of
metres. This form of imitation is to this day without a 1447ᵛ
name. We have no common name for a mime of Sophron
or Xenarchus and a Socratic Conversation; and we should 10
still be without one even if the imitation in the two instances were in trimeters or elegiacs or some other kind of
verse—though it is the way with people to tack on 'poet'
to the name of a metre, and talk of elegiac-poets and epic-
poets, thinking that they call them poets not by reason of
the imitative nature of their work, but indiscriminately by 15
reason of the metre they write in. Even if a theory of
medicine or physical philosophy be put forth in a metrical
form, it is usual to describe the writer in this way; Homer
and Empedocles, however, have really nothing in common
apart from their metre; so that, if the one is to be called a
poet, the other should be termed a physicist rather than 20
a poet. We should be in the same position also, if the
imitation in these instances were in all the metres, like
the *Centaur* (a rhapsody in a medley of all metres) of
Chaeremon; and Chaeremon one has to recognize as a
poet. So much, then, as to these arts. There are, lastly,
certain other arts, which combine all the means enu- 25
merated, rhythm, melody, and verse, e. g. Dithyrambic
and Nomic poetry, Tragedy and Comedy; with this difference, however, that the three kinds of means are in some
of them all employed together, and in others brought in
separately, one after the other. These elements of difference in the above arts I term the means of their imitation.

2   II. The objects the imitator represents are actions, 1448ᵃ
with agents who are necessarily either good men or *objects*
bad—the diversities of human character being nearly al- *of*
ways derivative from this primary distinction, since the line *imitation*
between virtue and vice is one dividing the whole of man-

kind. It follows, therefore, that the agents represented
must be either above our own level of goodness, or be-
5 neath it, or just such as we are; in the same way as, with
the painters, the personages of Polygnotus are better than
we are, those of Pauson worse, and those of Dionysius just
like ourselves. It is clear that each of the above-mentioned
arts will admit of these differences, and that it will become
a separate art by representing objects with this point of difference. Even in dancing, flute-playing, and lyre-playing
10 such diversities are possible; and they are also possible in
the nameless art that uses language, prose or verse without
harmony, as its means; Homer's personages, for instance, are
better than we are; Cleophon's are on our own level; and
those of Hegemon of Thasos, the first writer of parodies,
15 and Nicochares, the author of the Diliad, are beneath it.
The same is true of the Dithyramb and the Nome: the personages may be presented in them with the difference exemplified in the . . . of . . . and Argas, and in the Cy-
clopses of Timotheus and Philoxenus. This difference it is
that distinguishes Tragedy and Comedy also; the one
would make its personages worse, and the other better,
than the men of the present day.

3   III. A third difference in these arts is in the manner in
20   which each kind of object is represented. Given both
the same means and the same kind of object for imitation,
one may either (1) speak at one moment in narrative and at
another in an assumed character, as Homer does; or (2)
one may remain the same throughout, without any such
change; or (3) the imitators may represent the whole story
dramatically, as though they were actually doing the
things described.

As we said at the beginning, therefore, the differences in
the imitation of these arts come under three heads, their
means, their objects, and their manner.

So that as an imitator Sophocles will be on one side
25 akin to Homer, both portraying good men; and on another

to Aristophanes, since both present their personages as
acting and doing. (This in fact, according to some, is the *play-drama*
reason for plays being termed dramas, because in a play the *because of acting*
personages act the story.) Hence too both Tragedy and
Comedy are claimed by the Dorians as their discoveries; 30
Comedy by the Megarians—by those in Greece as having
arisen when Megara became a democracy, and by the
Sicilian Megarians on the ground that the poet Epicharmus was of their country, and a good deal earlier than
Chionides and Magnes; even Tragedy also is claimed by
certain of the Peloponnesian Dorians. In support of this
claim they point to the words 'comedy' and 'drama'. Their
word for the outlying hamlets, they say, is *comae*, whereas 35
Athenians call them *demes*—thus assuming that comedians
got the name not from their *comoe* or revels, but from their
strolling from hamlet to hamlet, lack of appreciation keeping them out of the city. Their word also for 'to act', they 1448ᵇ
say, is *dran*, whereas Athenians use *prattein*.

  So much, then, as to the number and nature of the points
of difference in the imitation of these arts.

4   It is clear that the general origin of poetry was due to
      two causes, each of them part of human nature. Imita-
tion is natural to man from childhood, one of his ad- 5
vantages over the lower animals being this, that he is the
most imitative creature in the world, and learns at first by
imitation. And it is also natural for all to delight in works
of imitation. The truth of this second point is shown by
experience: though the objects themselves may be painful 10
to see, we delight to view the most realistic representations
of them in art, the forms for example of the lowest animals
and of dead bodies. The explanation is to be found in a
further fact: to be learning something is the greatest of
pleasures not only to the philosopher but also to the rest
of mankind, however small their capacity for it; the reason 11
of the delight in seeing the picture is that one is at the
same time learning—gathering the meaning of things, e. g.

that the man there is so-and-so; for if one has not seen the
thing before, one's pleasure will not be in the picture as an
20 imitation of it, but will be due to the execution or colour-
ing or some similar cause. Imitation, then, being natural
to us—as also the sense of harmony and rhythm, the metres
being obviously species of rhythms—it was through their
original aptitude, and by a series of improvements for the
most part gradual on their first efforts, that they created
poetry out of their improvisations.

Poetry, however, soon broke up into two kinds according
25 to the differences of character in the individual poets; for
the graver among them would represent noble actions, and
those of noble personages; and the meaner sort the actions
of the ignoble. The latter class produced invectives at first,
just as others did hymns and panegyrics. We know of no
such poem by any of the pre-Homeric poets, though there
were probably many such writers among them; instances,
however, may be found from Homer downwards, e. g. his
30 *Margites*, and the similar poems of others. In this poetry
of invective its natural fitness brought an iambic metre into
use; hence our present term 'iambic', because it was the
metre of their 'iambs' or invectives against one another.
The result was that the old poets became some of them
writers of heroic and others of iambic verse. Homer's position, however, is peculiar: just as he was in the serious style
35 the poet of poets, standing alone not only through the
literary excellence, but also through the dramatic character
of his imitations, so too he was the first to outline for us
the general forms of Comedy by producing not a dramatic
invective, but a dramatic picture of the Ridiculous; his
Margites in fact stands in the same relation to our come-
1449ᵃ dies as the *Iliad* and *Odyssey* to our tragedies. As soon, however, as Tragedy and Comedy appeared in the field, those
naturally drawn to the one line of poetry became writers
5 of comedies instead of iambs, and those naturally drawn
to the other, writers of tragedies instead of epics, because

[margin note:] on Homer & Comedy

these new modes of art were grander and of more esteem than the old.

If it be asked whether Tragedy is now all that it need be in its formative elements, to consider that, and decide it theoretically and in relation to the theatres, is a matter for another inquiry.

It certainly began in improvisations—as did also Com- 10 edy; the one originating with the authors of the Dithyramb, the other with those of the phallic songs, which still survive as institutions in many of our cities. And its advance after that was little by little, through their improving on whatever they had before them at each stage. It was in fact only after a long series of changes that the movement of Tragedy stopped on its attaining to its natural form. (1) 15 The number of actors was first increased to two by Aeschy-lus, who curtailed the business of the Chorus, and made the dialogue, or spoken portion, take the leading part in the play. (2) A third actor and scenery were due to Sophocles. (3) Tragedy acquired also its magnitude. Dis-carding short stories and a ludicrous diction, through its 20 passing out of its satyric stage, it assumed, though only at a late point in its progress, a tone of dignity; and its metre changed then from trochaic to iambic. The reason for their original use of the trochaic tetrameter was that their poetry was satyric and more connected with dancing than it now is. As soon, however, as a spoken part came in, nature herself found the appropriate metre. The iambic, we know, is the most speakable of metres, as is shown by the fact that we very often fall into it in conversation, 25 whereas we rarely talk hexameters, and only when we de-part from the speaking tone of voice. (4) Another change was a plurality of episodes or acts. As for the remaining matters, the superadded embellishments and the account of their introduction, these must be taken as said, as it would probably be a long piece of work to go through the details. 30

5   As for Comedy, it is (as has been observed [1] an imitation of men worse than the average; worse, however,
not as regards any and every sort of fault, but only as regards one particular kind, the Ridiculous, which is a species of the Ugly. The Ridiculous may be defined as a
35 mistake or deformity not productive of pain or harm to
others; the mask, for instance, that excites laughter, is something ugly and distorted without causing pain.

Though the successive changes in Tragedy and their authors are not unknown, we cannot say the same of Comedy;
its early stages passed unnoticed, because it was not as yet
1449^b taken up in a serious way. It was only at a late point in its
progress that a chorus of comedians was officially granted
by the archon; they used to be mere volunteers. It had also
already certain definite forms at the time when the record
of those termed comic poets begins. Who it was who supplied it with masks, or prologues, or a plurality of actors
and the like, has remained unknown. The invented Fable,
5 or Plot, however, originated in Sicily with Epicharmus
and Phormis; of Athenian poets Crates was the first to drop
the Comedy of invective and frame stories of a general and
non-personal nature, in other words, Fables or Plots.

Epic poetry, then, has been seen to agree with Tragedy
to this extent, that of being an imitation of serious subjects
10 in a grand kind of verse. It differs from it, however, (1) in
that it is in one kind of verse and in narrative form; and
(2) in its length—which is due to its action having no
fixed limit of time, whereas Tragedy endeavours to keep
as far as possible within a single circuit of the sun, or something near that. This, I say, is another point of difference
15 between them, though at first the practice in this respect
was just the same in tragedies as in epic poems. They differ
also (3) in their constituents, some being common to both
and others peculiar to Tragedy—hence a judge of good and
bad in Tragedy is a judge of that in epic poetry also. All the

[1] 1448^a 17; 1448^b 37.

parts of an epic are included in Tragedy; but those of
Tragedy are not all of them to be found in the Epic.

6   Reserving hexameter poetry and Comedy for con- 20
      sideration hereafter,[2] let us proceed now to the discus-
sion of Tragedy; before doing so, however, we must gather
up the definition resulting from what has been said. A
tragedy, then, is the imitation of an action that is serious 25
and also, as having magnitude, complete in itself; in language with pleasurable accessories, each kind brought in
separately in the parts of the work; in a dramatic, not in a
narrative form; with incidents arousing pity and fear, wherewith to accomplish its catharsis of such emotions. Here by
'language with pleasurable accessories' I mean that with
rhythm and harmony or song superadded; and by 'the kinds 30
separately' I mean that some portions are worked out with
verse only, and others in turn with song.

   I. As they act the stories, it follows that in the first
place the Spectacle (or stage-appearance of the actors)
must be some part of the whole; and in the second Melody
and Diction, these two being the means of their imitation.
Here by 'Diction' I mean merely this, the composition of 35
the verses; and by 'Melody', what is too completely understood to require explanation. But further: the subject represented also is an action; and the action involves agents, who
must necessarily have their distinctive qualities both of
character and thought, since it is from these that we ascribe 1450ᵛ
certain qualities to their actions. There are in the natural
order of things, therefore, two causes, Thought and Character, of their actions, and consequently of their success or
failure in their lives. Now the action (that which was done)
is represented in the play by the Fable or Plot. The Fable,
in our present sense of the term, is simply this, the combination of the incidents, or things done in the story;

   [2] For hexameter poetry cf. chap. 23 f.; comedy was treated of in
the lost Second Book.

5 whereas Character is what makes us ascribe certain moral
   qualities to the agents; and Thought is shown in all they
   say when proving a particular point or, it may be, enunciating a general truth. There are six parts consequently of
   every tragedy, as a whole (that is) of such or such quality,
   viz. a Fable or Plot, Characters, Diction, Thought, Spec-.
   tacle, and Melody; two of them arising from the means,
10 one from the manner, and three from the objects of the
   dramatic imitation; and there is nothing else besides these
   six. Of these, its formative elements, then, not a few of the
   dramatists have made due use, as every play, one may say,
   admits of Spectacle, Character, Fable, Diction, Melody,
   and Thought.

   II. The most important of the six is the combination of
15 the incidents of the story. Tragedy is essentially an imitation not of persons but of action and life, of happiness and
   misery. All human happiness or misery takes the form of
   action; the end for which we live is a certain kind of activity, not a quality. Character gives us qualities, but it is
   in our actions—what we do—that we are happy or the reverse. In a play accordingly they do not act in order to
20 portray the Characters; they include the Characters for the
   sake of the action. So that it is the action in it, i. e. its
   Fable or Plot, that is the end and purpose of the tragedy;
   and the end is everywhere the chief thing. Besides this, a
   tragedy is impossible without action, but there may be one
   without Character. The tragedies of most of the moderns
25 are characterless—a defect common among poets of all
   kinds, and with its counterpart in painting in Zeuxis as
   compared with Polygnotus; for whereas the latter is strong
   in character, the work of Zeuxis is devoid of it. And again:
   one may string together a series of characteristic speeches
   of the utmost finish as regards Diction and Thought, and
30 yet fail to produce the true tragic effect; but one will have
   much better success with a tragedy which, however inferior
   in these respects, has a Plot, a combination of incidents, in
   it. And again: the most powerful elements of attraction in

Tragedy, the Peripeties and Discoveries, are parts of the Plot. A further proof is in the fact that beginners succeed 35 earlier with the Diction and Characters than with the construction of a story; and the same may be said of nearly all the early dramatists. We maintain, therefore, that the first essential, the life and soul, so to speak, of Tragedy is the Plot; and that the Characters come second—compare the parallel in painting, where the most beautiful colours laid **1450ᵇ** on without order will not give one the same pleasure as a simple black-and-white sketch of a portrait. We maintain that Tragedy is primarily an imitation of action, and that it is mainly for the sake of the action that it imitates the personal agents. Third comes the element of Thought, i. e. the power of saying whatever can be said, or what is appropriate 5 to the occasion. This is what, in the speeches in Tragedy, falls under the arts of Politics and Rhetoric; for the older poets make their personages discourse like statesmen, and the modern like rhetoricians. One must not confuse it with Character. Character in a play is that which reveals the moral purpose of the agents, i. e. the sort of thing they seek or avoid, where that is not obvious—hence there is no room for Character in a speech on a purely indifferent subject. Thought, on the other hand, is shown in all they say when 10 proving or disproving some particular point, or enunciating some universal proposition. Fourth among the literary elements is the Diction of the personages, i. e., as before explained,[3] the expression of their thoughts in words, which is practically the same thing with verse as with prose. As 15 for the two remaining parts, the Melody is the greatest of the pleasurable accessories of Tragedy. The Spectacle, though an attraction, is the least artistic of all the parts, and has least to do with the art of poetry. The tragic effect is quite possible without a public performance and actors; and besides, the getting-up of the Spectacle is more a matter for the costumier than the poet. 20

[3] 1449ᵇ 34.

7   Having thus distinguished the parts, let us now consider the proper construction of the Fable or Plot, as
that is at once the first and the most important thing in
Tragedy. We have laid it down that a tragedy is an imitation of an action that is complete in itself, as a whole of
25 some magnitude; for a whole may be of no magnitude to
speak of. Now a whole is that which has beginning, middle, and end. A beginning is that which is not itself necessarily after anything else, and which has naturally some-
30 thing else after it; an end is that which is naturally after
something itself, either as its necessary or usual consequent,
and with nothing else after it; and a middle, that which is
by nature after one thing and has also another after it. A
well-constructed Plot, therefore, cannot either begin or end
at any point one likes; beginning and end in it must be of
the forms just described. Again: to be beautiful, a living
35 creature, and every whole made up of parts, must not only
present a certain order in its arrangement of parts, but also
be of a certain definite magnitude. Beauty is a matter of
size and order, and therefore impossible either (1) in a very
minute creature, since our perception becomes indistinct as
it approaches instantaneity; or (2) in a creature of vast size
—one, say, 1,000 miles long—as in that case, instead of the
1451ᵃ object being seen all at once, the unity and wholeness of
it is lost to the beholder. Just in the same way, then, as a
beautiful whole made up of parts, or a beautiful living
creature, must be of some size, but a size to be taken in by
5 the eye, so a story or Plot must be of some length, but of a
length to be taken in by the memory. As for the limit of its
length, so far as that is relative to public performances and
spectators, it does not fall within the theory of poetry. If
they had to perform a hundred tragedies, they would be
timed by water-clocks, as they are said to have been at one
period. The limit, however, set by the actual nature of the
10 thing is this: the longer the story, consistently with its
being comprehensible as a whole, the finer it is by reason
of its magnitude. As a rough general formula, 'a length
which allows of the hero passing by a series of probable or

necessary stages from misfortune to happiness, or from happiness to misfortune', may suffice as a limit for the magnitude of the story.   15

8   The Unity of a Plot does not consist, as some suppose,
         in its having one man as its subject. An infinity of
things befall that one man, some of which it is impossible
to reduce to unity; and in like manner there are many
actions of one man which cannot be made to form one action. One sees, therefore, the mistake of all the poets who
have written a *Heracleid*, a *Theseid*, or similar poems; they 20
suppose that, because Heracles was one man, the story also
of Heracles must be one story. Homer, however, evidently
understood this point quite well, whether by art or instinct,
just in the same way as he excels the rest in every other
respect. In writing an *Odyssey*, he did not make the poem
cover all that ever befell his hero—it befell him, for in- 25
stance, to get wounded on Parnassus and also to feign madness at the time of the call to arms, but the two incidents
had no necessary or probable connexion with one another
—instead of doing that, he took as the subject of the *Odyssey*, as also of the *Iliad*, an action with a Unity of the kind
we are describing. The truth is that, just as in the other 30
imitative arts one imitation is always of one thing, so in
poetry the story, as an imitation of action, must represent
one action, a complete whole, with its several incidents so
closely connected that the transposal or withdrawal of any
one of them will disjoin and dislocate the whole. For that
which makes no perceptible difference by its presence or
absence is no real part of the whole.   35

9   From what we have said it will be seen that the poet's
         function is to describe, not the thing that has happened, but a kind of thing that might happen, i. e. what is
possible as being probable or necessary. The distinction between historian and poet is not in the one writing prose 1451
and the other verse—you might put the work of Herodotus
into verse, and it would still be a species of history; it con-

sists really in this, that the one describes the thing that has
5 been, and the other a kind of thing that might be. Hence
poetry is something more philosophic and of graver import
than history, since its statements are of the nature rather of
universals, whereas those of history are singulars. By a universal statement I mean one as to what such or such a kind
of man will probably or necessarily say or do—which is the
10 aim of poetry, though it affixes proper names to the characters; by a singular statement, one as to what, say, Alcibiades
did or had done to him. In Comedy this has become clear
by this time; it is only when their plot is already made up
of probable incidents that they give it a basis of proper
names, choosing for the purpose any names that may occur
15 to them, instead of writing like the old iambic poets about
particular persons. In Tragedy, however, they still adhere to
the historic names; and for this reason: what convinces is
the possible; now whereas we are not yet sure as to the
possibility of that which has not happened, that which has
happened is manifestly possible, else it would not have
come to pass. Nevertheless even in Tragedy there are some
20 plays with but one or two known names in them, the rest
being inventions; and there are some without a single
known name, e. g. Agathon's *Antheus*, in which both incidents and names are of the poet's invention; and it is no
less delightful on that account. So that one must not aim
25 at a rigid adherence to the traditional stories on which
tragedies are based. It would be absurd, in fact, to do so, as
even the known stories are only known to a few, though
they are a delight none the less to all.

It is evident from the above that the poet must be more
the poet of his stories or Plots than of his verses, inasmuch
as he is a poet by virtue of the imitative element in his
work, and it is actions that he imitates. And if he should
30 come to take a subject from actual history, he is none the
less a poet for that; since some historic occurrences may
very well be in the probable and possible order of things;
and it is in that aspect of them that he is their poet.

Of simple Plots and actions the episodic are the worst.

Content more important than style [margin note]

I call a Plot episodic when there is neither probability nor
necessity in the sequence of its episodes. Actions of this sort
bad poets construct through their own fault, and good ones
on account of the players. His work being for public performance, a good poet often stretches out a Plot beyond
its capabilities, and is thus obliged to twist the sequence of
incident.

Tragedy, however, is an imitation not only of a complete **1452ᵃ**
action, but also of incidents arousing pity and fear. Such
incidents have the very greatest effect on the mind when
they occur unexpectedly and at the same time in consequence of one another; there is more of the marvellous in
them then than if they happened of themselves or by mere
chance. Even matters of chance seem most marvellous if
there is an appearance of design as it were in them; as for
instance the statue of Mitys at Argos killed the author of
Mitys' death by falling down on him when a looker-on at
a public spectacle; for incidents like that we think to be not
without a meaning. A Plot, therefore, of this sort is necessarily finer than others.

10   Plots are either simple or complex, since the actions
        they represent are naturally of this twofold description.
The action, proceeding in the way defined, as one continuous whole, I call simple, when the change in the hero's
fortunes takes place without Peripety or Discovery; and
complex, when it involves one or the other, or both. These
should each of them arise out of the structure of the Plot
itself, so as to be the consequence, necessary or probable,
of the antecedents. There is a great difference between a
thing happening *propter hoc* and *post hoc*.

11   A Peripety is the change of the kind described from
        one state of things within the play to its opposite,
and that too in the way we are saying, in the probable or
necessary sequence of events; as it is for instance in *Oedipus*: here the opposite state of things is produced by the
Messenger, who, coming to gladden Oedipus and to re-

move his fears as to his mother, reveals the secret of his birth.[4] And in *Lynceus:*[5] just as he is being led off for execution, with Danaus at his side to put him to death, the incidents preceding this bring it about that he is saved and
30 Danaus put to death. A Discovery is, as the very word implies, a change from ignorance to knowledge, and thus to either love or hate, in the personages marked for good or evil fortune. The finest form of Discovery is one attended by Peripeties, like that which goes with the Discovery in *Oedipus.* There are no doubt other forms of it; what we have said may happen in a way in reference to inanimate
35 things, even things of a very casual kind; and it is also possible to discover whether some one has done or not done something. But the form most directly connected with the Plot and the action of the piece is the first-mentioned.
1452[b] This, with a Peripety, will arouse either pity or fear—actions of that nature being what Tragedy is assumed to represent; and it will also serve to bring about the happy or unhappy ending. The Discovery, then, being of persons, it may be that of one party only to the other, the latter being
5 already known; or both the parties may have to discover themselves. Iphigenia, for instance, was discovered to Orestes by sending the letter;[6] and another Discovery was required to reveal him to Iphigenia.

Two parts of the Plot, then, Peripety and Discovery, are
10 on matters of this sort. A third part is Suffering; which we may define as an action of a destructive or painful nature, such as murders on the stage, tortures, woundings, and the like. The other two have been already explained.

12 The parts of Tragedy to be treated as formative ele-
15 ments in the whole were mentioned in a previous Chapter.[7] From the point of view, however, of its quantity, i e. the separate sections into which it is divided, a tragedy

[4] *O. T.* 911–1085.
[5] By Theodectes.
[6] *Iph. Taur.* 727 ff.
[7] Ch. 6.

has the following parts: Prologue, Episode, Exode, and a
choral portion, distinguished into Parode and Stasimon;
these two are common to all tragedies, whereas songs from
the stage and Commoe are only found in some. The Pro- 20
logue is all that precedes the Parode of the chorus; an Episode all that comes in between two whole choral songs;
the Exode all that follows after the last choral song. In the
choral portion the Parode is the whole first statement of the
chorus; a Stasimon, a song of the chorus without anapaests
or trochees; a Commos, a lamentation sung by chorus and
actor in concert. The parts of Tragedy to be used as forma- 25
tive elements in the whole we have already mentioned; the
above are its parts from the point of view of its quantity, or
the separate sections into which it is divided.

13   The next points after what we have said above will be
these: (1) What is the poet to aim at, and what is he
to avoid, in constructing his Plots? and (2) What are the
conditions on which the tragic effect depends?

We assume that, for the finest form of Tragedy, the Plot 30
must be not simple but complex; and further, that it must
imitate actions arousing fear and pity, since that is the distinctive function of this kind of imitation. It follows, therefore, that there are three forms of Plot to be avoided. (1) A
good man must not be seen passing from happiness to
misery, or (2) a bad man from misery to happiness. The 35
first situation is not fear-inspiring or piteous, but simply
odious to us. The second is the most untragic that can be;
it has no one of the requisites of Tragedy; it does not appeal
either to the human feeling in us, or to our pity, or to our
fears. Nor, on the other hand, should (3) an extremely **1453**
bad man be seen falling from happiness into misery. Such a
story may arouse the human feeling in us, but it will not
move us to either pity or fear; pity is occasioned by un- 5
deserved misfortune, and fear by that of one like ourselves;
so that there will be nothing either piteous or fear-inspiring
in the situation. There remains, then, the intermediate

kind of personage, a man not pre-eminently virtuous and just, whose misfortune, however, is brought upon him not by vice and depravity but by some error of judgement, of the number of those in the enjoyment of great reputation
10 and prosperity; e. g. Oedipus, Thyestes, and the men of note of similar families. The perfect Plot, accordingly, must have a single, and not (as some tell us) a double issue; the change in the hero's fortunes must be not from misery to happiness, but on the contrary from happiness to misery; and the cause of it must lie not in any depravity, but in
15 some great error on his part; the man himself being either such as we have described, or better, not worse, than that. Fact also confirms our theory. Though the poets began by accepting any tragic story that came to hand, in these days the finest tragedies are always on the story of some few
20 houses, on that of Alcmeon, Oedipus, Orestes, Meleager, Thyestes, Telephus, or any others that may have been involved, as either agents or sufferers, in some deed of horror. The theoretically best tragedy, then, has a Plot of this description. The critics, therefore, are wrong who blame Euripides for taking this line in his tragedies, and giving
25 many of them an unhappy ending. It is, as we have said, the right line to take. The best proof is this: on the stage, and in the public performances, such plays, properly worked out, are seen to be the most truly tragic; and Euripides, even if his execution be faulty in every other point, is seen to be nevertheless the most tragic certainly of the
30 dramatists. After this comes the construction of Plot which some rank first, one with a double story (like the Odyssey) and an opposite issue for the good and the bad personages. It is ranked as first only through the weakness of the audiences; the poets merely follow their public, writing as its
35 wishes dictate. But the pleasure here is not that of Tragedy. It belongs rather to Comedy, where the bitterest enemies in the piece (e. g. Orestes and Aegisthus) walk off good friends at the end, with no slaying of any one by any one.

14   The tragic fear and pity may be aroused by the Spectacle; but they may also be aroused by the very struc- 1453²
ture and incidents of the play—which is the better way and
shows the better poet. The Plot in fact should be so framed
that, even without seeing the things take place, he who 5
simply hears the account of them shall be filled with horror
and pity at the incidents; which is just the effect that the
mere recital of the story in *Oedipus* would have on one. To
produce this same effect by means of the Spectacle is less
artistic, and requires extraneous aid. Those, however, who
make use of the Spectacle to put before us that which is
merely monstrous and not productive of fear, are wholly 10
out of touch with Tragedy; not every kind of pleasure
should be required of a tragedy, but only its own proper
pleasure.

The tragic pleasure is that of pity and fear, and the poet
has to produce it by a work of imitation; it is clear, therefore, that the causes should be included in the incidents of
his story. Let us see, then, what kinds of incident strike 15
one as horrible, or rather as piteous. In a deed of this description the parties must necessarily be either friends, or
enemies, or indifferent to one another. Now when enemy
does it on enemy, there is nothing to move us to pity either
in his doing or in his meditating the deed, except so far as
the actual pain of the sufferer is concerned; and the same is
true when the parties are indifferent to one another. Whenever the tragic deed, however, is done within the family— 20
when murder or the like is done or meditated by brother on
brother, by son on father, by mother on son, or son on
mother—these are the situations the poet should seek after.
The traditional stories, accordingly, must be kept as they
are, e. g. the murder of Clytaemnestra by Orestes and of
Eriphyle by Alcmeon. At the same time even with these 25
there is something left to the poet himself; it is for him to
devise the right way of treating them. Let us explain more
clearly what we mean by 'the right way'. The deed of horror

may be done by the doer knowingly and consciously, as in
the old poets, and in Medea's murder of her children in
30 Euripides.[8] Or he may do it, but in ignorance of his relationship, and discover that afterwards, as does the Oedipus
in Sophocles. Here the deed is outside the play; but it may
be within it, like the act of the Alcmeon in Astydamas, or
that of the Telegonus in *Ulysses Wounded*.[9] A third pos-
35 sibility is for one meditating some deadly injury to another,
in ignorance of his relationship, to make the discovery in
time to draw back. These exhaust the possibilities, since the
deed must necessarily be either done or not done, and
either knowingly or unknowingly.

The worst situation is when the personage is with full
knowledge on the point of doing the deed, and leaves it
undone. It is odious and also (through the absence of suffering) untragic; hence it is that no one is made to act thus
1454ᵃ except in some few instances, e. g. Haemon and Creon in
Antigone.[10] Next after this comes the actual perpetration of
the deed meditated. A better situation than that, however,
is for the deed to be done in ignorance, and the relationship
discovered afterwards, since there is nothing odious in it,
and the Discovery will serve to astound us. But the best of
5 all is the last; what we have in *Cresphontes*,[11] for example,
where Merope, on the point of slaying her son, recognizes
him in time; in *Iphigenia*, where sister and brother are in a
like position; and in *Helle*,[12] where the son recognizes his
mother, when on the point of giving her up to her enemy.

This will explain why our tragedies are restricted (as we
said just now) [13] to such a small number of families. It was
10 accident rather than art that led the poets in quest of subjects to embody this kind of incident in their Plots. They

---

[8] *Med.* 1236.
[9] Perhaps by Sophocles.
[10] l. 1231.
[11] By Euripides.
[12] Authorship unknown.
[13] 1453ᵃ 19.

are still obliged, accordingly, to have recourse to the families in which such horrors have occurred.

On the construction of the Plot, and the kind of Plot
required for Tragedy, enough has now been said.   15

15 In the Characters there are four points to aim at. First
and foremost, that they shall be good. There will be an
element of character in the play, if (as has been observed) [14]
what a personage says or does reveals a certain moral purpose; and a good element of character, if the purpose so
revealed is good. Such goodness is possible in every type of
personage, even in a woman or a slave, though the one is 20
perhaps an inferior, and the other a wholly worthless being.
The second point is to make them appropriate. The Character before us may be, say, manly; but it is not appropriate
in a female Character to be manly, or clever. The third is to
make them like the reality, which is not the same as their
being good and appropriate, in our sense of the term. The 25
fourth is to make them consistent and the same throughout; even if inconsistency be part of the man before one for
imitation as presenting that form of character, he should
still be consistently inconsistent. We have an instance of
baseness of character, not required for the story, in the
Menelaus in *Orestes*; of the incongruous and unbefitting in
the lamentation of Ulysses in *Scylla*,[15] and in the (clever) 30
speech of Melanippe;[16] and of inconsistency in *Iphigenia
at Aulis*,[17] where Iphigenia the suppliant is utterly unlike
the later Iphigenia. The right thing, however, is in the
Characters just as in the incidents of the play to endeavour
always after the necessary or the probable; so that whenever 35
such-and-such a personage says or does such-and-such a
thing, it shall be the necessary or probable outcome of his

[14] 1450[b] 8.
[15] A dithyramb by Timotheus.
[16] (Euripides).
[17] ll. 1211 ff., 1368 ff.

character; and whenever this incident follows on that, it shall be either the necessary or the probable consequence of it. From this one sees (to digress for a moment) that the 1454ᵇ Dénouement also should arise out of the plot itself, and not depend on a stage-artifice, as in Medea,[18] or in the story of the (arrested) departure of the Greeks in the Iliad.[19] The artifice must be reserved for matters outside the play—for 5 past events beyond human knowledge, or events yet to come, which require to be foretold or announced; since it is the privilege of the Gods to know everything. There should be nothing improbable among the actual incidents. If it be unavoidable, however, it should be outside the tragedy, like the improbability in the Oedipus of Sophocles. But to return to the Characters. As Tragedy is an imitation of personages better than the ordinary man, we in our way 10 should follow the example of good portrait-painters, who reproduce the distinctive features of a man, and at the same time, without losing the likeness, make him handsomer than he is. The poet in like manner, in portraying men quick or slow to anger, or with similar infirmities of character, must know how to represent them as such, and at the same time as good men, as Agathon and Homer have represented Achilles.

15   All these rules one must keep in mind throughout, and, further, those also for such points of stage-effect as directly depend on the art of the poet, since in these too one may often make mistakes. Enough, however, has been said on the subject in one of our published writings.[20]

16 Discovery in general has been explained already.[21] As 20   for the species of Discovery, the first to be noted is (1) the least artistic form of it, of which the poets make most use through mere lack of invention, Discovery by signs or marks. Of these signs some are congenital, like the

---

[18] l. 1317.
[19] ii. 155.
[20] In the lost dialogue On Poets.
[21] 1452ᵃ 29.

'lance-head which the Earth-born have on them',[22] or 'stars', such as Carcinus brings in his Thyestes; others acquired after birth—these latter being either marks on the body, e. g. scars, or external tokens, like necklaces, or (to take another sort of instance) the ark in the Discovery in Tyro.[23] 25 Even these, however, admit of two uses, a better and a worse; the scar of Ulysses is an instance; the Discovery of him through it is made in one way by the nurse [24] and in another by the swineherds.[25] A Discovery using signs as a means of assurance is less artistic, as indeed are all such as imply reflection; whereas one bringing them in all of a sudden, as in the Bath-story,[26] is of a better order. Next 30 after these are (2) Discoveries made directly by the poet; which are inartistic for that very reason; e. g. Orestes' Discovery of himself in Iphigenia: whereas his sister reveals who she is by the letter,[27] Orestes is made to say himself what the poet rather than the story demands.[28] This, there- 35 fore, is not far removed from the first-mentioned fault, since he might have presented certain tokens as well. Another instance is the 'shuttle's voice' in the Tereus of Sophocles. (3) A third species is Discovery through memory, from a man's consciousness being awakened by something seen. Thus in The Cyprioe of Dicaeogenes, the sight 1455ᵃ of the picture makes the man burst into tears; and in the Tale of Alcinous,[29] hearing the harper Ulysses is reminded of the past and weeps; the Discovery of them being the result. (4) A fourth kind is Discovery through reasoning; e. g. in The Choephoroe; [30] 'One like me is here; there is no one like me but Orestes; he, therefore, must be here.' Or 5 that which Polyidus the Sophist suggested for Iphigenia;

[22] Authorship unknown.
[23] By Euripides.
[24] Od. xix. 386–475.
[25] Od. xxi. 205–25.
[26] Od. xix. 392.
[27] Iph. Taur. 727 ff.
[28] Ib., 800 ff.
[29] Od. viii. 521 ff. (Cf. viii, 83 ff.).
[30] ll. 168–234.

since it was natural for Orestes to reflect: 'My sister was
sacrificed, and I am to be sacrificed like her.' Or that in
the *Tydeus* of Theodectes: 'I came to find a son, and am to
10 die myself.' Or that in *The Phinidae*: [31] on seeing the place
the women inferred their fate, that they were to die there,
since they had also been exposed there. (5) There is, too,
a composite Discovery arising from bad reasoning on the
side of the other party. An instance of it is in *Ulysses the
False Messenger*: [31] he said he should know the bow—
15 which he had not seen; but to suppose from that that he
would know it again (as though he had once seen it) was
bad reasoning. (6) The best of all Discoveries, however, is
that arising from the incidents themselves, when the great
surprise comes about through a probable incident, like that
in the *Oedipus* of Sophocles; and also in *Iphigenia*; [32] for it
was not improbable that she should wish to have a letter
taken home. These last are the only Discoveries independ-
20 ent of the artifice of signs and necklaces. Next after them
come Discoveries through reasoning.

17   At the time when he is constructing his Plots, and
engaged on the Diction in which they are worked out,
the poet should remember (1) to put the actual scenes
25 as far as possible before his eyes. In this way, seeing everything with the vividness of an eye-witness as it were, he
will devise what is appropriate, and be least likely to overlook incongruities. This is shown by what was censured in
Carcinus, the return of Amphiaraus from the sanctuary; it
would have passed unnoticed, if it had not been actually
seen by the audience; but on the stage his play failed, the incongruity of the incident offending the spectators. (2) As
far as may be, too, the poet should even act his story with
30 the very gestures of his personages. Given the same natural
qualifications, he who feels the emotions to be described
will be the most convincing; distress and anger, for in-

---

[31] Authorship unknown.
[32] *Iph. Taur.* 582.

stance, are portrayed most truthfully by one who is feeling them at the moment. Hence it is that poetry demands a man with a special gift for it, or else one with a touch of madness in him; the former can easily assume the required mood, and the latter may be actually beside himself with emotion. (3) His story, again, whether already made or of his own making, he should first simplify and reduce to a **1455ᵇ** universal form, before proceeding to lengthen it out by the insertion of episodes. The following will show how the universal element in *Iphigenia*, for instance, may be viewed: A certain maiden having been offered in sacrifice, and spirited away from her sacrifices into another land, where the custom was to sacrifice all strangers to the 5 Goddess, she was made there the priestess of this rite. Long after that the brother of the priestess happened to come; the fact, however, of the oracle having for a certain reason bidden him go thither, and his object in going, are outside the Plot of the play. On his coming he was arrested, and about to be sacrificed, when he revealed who he was— either as Euripides puts it, or (as suggested by Polyidus) 10 by the not improbable exclamation, 'So I too am doomed to be sacrificed, as my sister was'; and the disclosure led to his salvation. This done, the next thing, after the proper names have been fixed as a basis for the story, is to work in episodes or accessory incidents. One must mind, however, that the episodes are appropriate, like the fit of madness [33] in Orestes, which led to his arrest, and the purify- 15 ing,[34] which brought about his salvation. In plays, then, the episodes are short; in epic poetry they serve to lengthen out the poem. The argument of the *Odyssey* is not a long one. A certain man has been abroad many years; Poseidon is ever on the watch for him, and he is all alone. Matters at home too have come to this, that his substance is being 20 wasted and his son's death plotted by suitors to his wife. Then he arrives there himself after his grievous sufferings;

[33] *Iph. Taur.* 281 ff.
[34] *Ib.,* 1163 ff.

reveals himself, and falls on his enemies; and the end is his salvation and their death. This being all that is proper to the Odyssey, everything else in it is episode.

18 (4) There is a further point to be borne in mind. Every tragedy is in part Complication and in part Dénouement; the incidents before the opening scene, and often certain also of those within the play, forming the 25 Complication; and the rest the Dénouement. By Complication I mean all from the beginning of the story to the point just before the change in the hero's fortunes; by Dénouement, all from the beginning of the change to the end. In the Lynceus of Theodectes, for instance, the Complication includes, together with the presupposed incidents, 30 the seizure of the child and that in turn of the parents; and 1456ᵃ7 the Dénouement all from the indictment for the murder to the end. Now it is right, when one speaks of a tragedy as the same or not the same as another, to do so on the ground before all else of their Plot, i. e. as having the same or not the same Complication and Dénouement. Yet there are many dramatists who, after a good Complication, fail in the Dénouement. But it is necessary for both points of construction to be always duly mastered. (5) There are 1455ᵇ32

four distinct species of Tragedy—that being the number of the constituents also that have been mentioned: [35] first, the complex Tragedy, which is all Peripety and Discovery: second, the Tragedy of suffering, e. g. the Ajaxes and Ixions; 1456ᵃ third, the Tragedy of character, e. g. The Phthiotides [36] and Peleus.[37] The fourth constituent is that of 'Spectacle', exemplified in The Phorcides,[38] in Prometheus,[39] and in all plays with the scene laid in the nether world. The poet's aim, then, should be to combine every element of interest,

---

[35] This does not agree with anything actually said before.
[36] By Sophocles.
[37] Probably Sophocles' Peleus is incorrect.
[38] By Aeschylus.
[39] Probably a satyric drama by Aeschylus.

if possible, or else the more important and the major part
of them. This is now especially necessary owing to the
unfair criticism to which the poet is subjected in these
days. Just because there have been poets before him strong 5
in the several species of tragedy, the critics now expect
the one man to surpass that which was the strong point
of each one of his predecessors. (6) One should also remember what has been said more than once,[40] and not 10
write a tragedy on an epic body of incident (i. e. one with a
plurality of stories in it), by attempting to dramatize, for
instance, the entire story of the *Iliad*. In the epic owing
to its scale every part is treated at proper length; with a
drama, however, on the same story the result is very dis-
appointing. This is shown by the fact that all who have 15
dramatized the fall of Ilium in its entirety, and not part by
part, like Euripides, of the whole of the Niobe story, instead of a portion, like Aeschylus, either fail utterly or
have but ill success on the stage; for that and that alone
was enough to ruin even a play by Agathon. Yet in their
Peripeties, as also in their simple plots, the poets I mean 20
show wonderful skill in aiming at the kind of effect they
desire—a tragic situation that arouses the human feeling in
one, like the clever villain (e. g. Sisyphus) deceived, or the
brave wrongdoer worsted. This is probable, however, only
in Agathon's sense, when he speaks of the probability of
even improbabilities coming to pass. (7) The Chorus too 25
should be regarded as one of the actors; it should be an
integral part of the whole, and take a share in the action—
that which it has in Sophocles, rather than in Euripides.
With the later poets, however, the songs in a play of theirs
have no more to do with the Plot of that than of any other
tragedy. Hence it is that they are now singing intercalary
pieces, a practice first introduced by Agathon. And yet 30
what real difference is there between singing such intercalary pieces, and attempting to fit in a speech, or even
a whole act, from one play into another?

[40] A loose reference to 1449^b 12, 1455^b 15.

19 The Plot and Characters having been discussed, it re-
       mains to consider the Diction and Thought. As for
35 the Thought, we may assume what is said of it in our Art
of Rhetoric,[41] as it belongs more properly to that department of inquiry. The Thought of the personages is shown
in everything to be effected by their language—in every
effort to prove or disprove, to arouse emotion (pity, fear,
1456ᵇ anger, and the like), or to maximize or minimize things.
It is clear, also, that their mental procedure must be on
the same lines in their actions likewise, whenever they wish
5 them to arouse pity or horror, or to have a look of importance or probability. The only difference is that with the
act the impression has to be made without explanation;
whereas with the spoken word it has to be produced by the
speaker, and result from his language. What, indeed, would
be the good of the speaker, if things appeared in the required light even apart from anything he says?

As regards the Diction, one subject for inquiry under this
head is the turns given to the language when spoken; e. g.
10 the difference between command and prayer, simple statement and threat, question and answer, and so forth. The
theory of such matters, however, belongs to Elocution and
the professors of that art. Whether the poet knows these
15 things or not, his art as a poet is never seriously criticized on
that account. What fault can one see in Homer's 'Sing of
the wrath, Goddess'?—which Protagoras has criticized as
being a command where a prayer was meant, since to bid
one do or not do, he tells us, is a command. Let us pass
over this, then, as appertaining to another art, and not to
that of poetry.

20 The Diction viewed as a whole is made up of the
10   following parts: the Letter (or ultimate element), the
Syllable, the Conjunction, the Article, the Noun, the Verb,
the Case, and the Speech. (1) The Letter is an indivisible
sound of a particular kind, one that may become a factor in

[41] Cf. especially Rhet. 1356ᵃ 1.

an intelligible sound. Indivisible sounds are uttered by the brutes also, but no one of these is a Letter in our sense of the term. These elementary sounds are either vowels, semi-vowels, or mutes. A vowel is a Letter having an audible 25 sound without the addition of another Letter. A semi-vowel, one having an audible sound by the addition of an-other Letter; e. g. S and R. A mute, one having no sound at all by itself, but becoming audible by an addition, that of one of the Letters which have a sound of some sort of their own; e. g. G and D. The Letters differ in various 30 ways: as produced by different conformations or in dif-ferent regions of the mouth; as aspirated, not aspirated, or sometimes one and sometimes the other; as long, short, or of variable quantity; and further as having an acute, grave, or intermediate accent. The details of these matters we must leave to the metricians. (2) A Syllable is a non-significant composite sound, made up of a mute and a 35 Letter having a sound (a vowel or semi-vowel); for GR, without an A, is just as much a Syllable as GRA, with an A. The various forms of the Syllable also belong to the theory of metre. (3) A Conjunction is (a) a non-significant sound which, when one significant sound is formable out of several, neither hinders nor aids the union, and which, if **1457ᵃ** the Speech thus formed stands by itself (apart from other Speeches), must not be inserted at the beginning of it; e. g. μέν, δή, τοι, δέ. Or (b) a non-significant sound capable of combining two or more significant sounds into one; e. g. 5 ἀμφί, περί &c. (4) An Article is a non-significant sound marking the beginning, end, or dividing-point of a Speech, its natural place being either at the extremities or in the middle. (5) A Noun or name is a composite significant 10 sound not involving the idea of time, with parts which have no significance by themselves in it. It is to be remembered that in a compound we do not think of the parts as having a significance also by themselves; in the name 'Theodorus', for instance, the δῶρον means nothing to us. (6) A Verb is a composite significant sound involving the idea of time,

with parts which (just as in the Noun) have no significance
15 by themselves in it. Whereas the word 'man' or 'white'
does not imply *when*, 'walks' and 'has walked,' involve in
addition to the idea of walking that of time present or time
past. (7) A Case of a Noun or Verb is when the word
20 means 'of' or 'to' a thing, and so forth, or for one or many
(e. g. 'man' and 'men'); or it may consist merely in the
mode of utterance, e. g. in question, command, &c.
'Walked?' and 'Walk!' are Cases of the verb 'to walk'
of this last kind. (8) A Speech is a composite significant
sound, some of the parts of which have a certain signifi-
25 cance by themselves. It may be observed that a Speech is
not always made up of Noun and Verb; it may be without
a Verb, like the definition of man; but it will always have
some part with a certain significance by itself. In the
Speech 'Cleon walks', 'Cleon' is an instance of such a part.
A Speech is said to be one in two ways, either as signifying
one thing, or as a union of several Speeches made into one
30 by conjunction. Thus the *Iliad* is one Speech by conjunction of several; and the definition of man is one through its
signifying one thing.

21 Nouns are of two kinds, either (1) simple, i. e. made
up of non-significant parts, like the word γῆ, or (2)
double; in the latter case the word may be made up either
of a significant and a non-significant part (a distinction
35 which disappears in the compound), or of two significant
parts. It is possible also to have triple, quadruple, or higher
compounds, like most of our amplified names; e. g. 'Hermo-
caïcoxanthus' and the like.

457ᵇ   Whatever its structure, a Noun must always be either
(1) the ordinary word for the thing, or (2) a strange word,
or (3) a metaphor, or (4) an ornamental word, or (5) a
coined word, or (6) a word lengthened out, or (7) curtailed, or (8) altered in form. By the ordinary word I mean
that in general use in a country; and by a strange word,
one in use elsewhere. So that the same word may obviously

be at once strange and ordinary, though not in reference to 5
the same people; σίγυνον, for instance, is an ordinary word
in Cyprus, and a strange word with us. Metaphor consists
in giving the thing a name that belongs to something else;
the transference being either from genus to species, or
from species to genus, or from species to species, or on
grounds of analogy. That from genus to species is ex- 10
emplified in 'Here stands my ship';[42] for lying at anchor
is the 'standing' of a particular kind of thing. That from
species to genus in 'Truly ten thousand good deeds has
Ulysses wrought',[43] where 'ten thousand', which is a particular large number, is put in place of the generic 'a large
number'. That from species to species in 'Drawing the life
with the bronze',[44] and in 'Severing with the enduring
bronze';[44] where the poet uses 'draw' in the sense of 15
'sever' and 'sever' in that of 'draw', both words meaning to 'take away' something. That from analogy is possible whenever there are four terms so related that the
second (B) is to the first (A), as the fourth (D) to
the third (C); for one may then metaphorically put D in
lieu of B, and B in lieu of D. Now and then, too, they
qualify the metaphor by adding on to it that to which the
word it supplants is relative. Thus a cup (B) is in relation 20
to Dionysus (A) what a shield (D) is to Ares (C). The
cup accordingly will be metaphorically described as the
'shield of Dionysus' (D + A), and the shield as the 'cup of
Ares'[45] (B + C). Or to take another instance: As old age
(D) is to life (C), so is evening (B) to day (A). One will
accordingly describe evening (B) as the 'old age of the day'
(D + A)—or by the Empedoclean equivalent; and old age
(D) as the 'evening'[46] or 'sunset of life'[47] (B + C). It may
be that some of the terms thus related have no special 25

---

[42] *Od.* i. 185, xxiv. 308.
[43] *Il.* ii. 272.
[44] Empedocles.
[45] Timotheus.
[46] Alexis.
[47] Pl., Laws 770 A.

name of their own, but for all that they will be metaphorically described in just the same way. Thus to cast forth seed-corn is called 'sowing'; but to cast forth its flame, as said of the sun, has no special name. This nameless act (B), however, stands in just the same relation to its object, sunlight (A), as sowing (D) to the seed-corn (C). Hence the expression in the poet, 'sowing around a god-created 30 flame' [48] (D + A). There is also another form of qualified metaphor. Having given the thing the alien name, one may by a negative addition deny of it one of the attributes naturally associated with its new name. An instance of this would be to call the shield not the 'cup of Ares', as in the former case, but a 'cup *that holds no wine*'. . . . A coined word is a name which, being quite unknown among a people, is given by the poet himself; e. g. (for there are some words that seem to be of this origin) ἔρνυγες for horns, and ἀρητήρ for priest.[49] A word is said to be lengthened 35 out, when it has a short vowel made long, or an extra 1458ª syllable inserted; e. g. πόληος for πόλεως, Πηληιάδεω for Πηλείδου. It is said to be curtailed, when it has lost a part; 5 e. g. κρῖ, δῶ, and ὄψ in μία γίνεται ἀμφοτέρων ὄψ.[50] It is an altered word, when part is left as it was and part is of the poet's making; e. g. δεξιτερόν for δεξιόν, in δεξιτερὸν κατὰ μαζόν.[51]

The Nouns themselves (to whatever class they may belong) are either masculines, feminines, or intermediates (neuter). All ending in N, P, Σ, or in the two compounds 10 of this last, Ψ and Ξ, are masculines. All ending in the invariably long vowels, H and Ω, and in A among the vowels that may be long, are feminines. So that there is an equal number of masculine and feminine terminations, as Ψ and Ξ are the same as Σ, and need not be counted. There is no 15 Noun, however, ending in a mute or in either of the two

[48] Authorship unknown.
[49] *Il.* i. 11.
[50] Empedocles.
[51] *Il.* v. 393.

short vowels, E and O. Only three (μέλι, κόμμι, πέπερι) end in I and five in Υ. The intermediates, or neuters, end in the variable vowels or in N, P, Σ.

22   The perfection of Diction is for it to be at once clear and not mean. The clearest indeed is that made up of the ordinary words for things, but it is mean, as is shown 20 by the poetry of Cleophon and Sthenelus. On the other hand the Diction becomes distinguished and non-prosaic by the use of unfamiliar terms, i. e. strange words, metaphors, lengthened forms, and everything that deviates from the ordinary modes of speech.—But a whole statement in such terms will be either a riddle or a barbarism, 25 a riddle, if made up of metaphors, a barbarism, if made up of strange words. The very nature indeed of a riddle is this, to describe a fact in an impossible combination of words (which cannot be done with the real names for things, but can be with their metaphorical substitutes); e. g. 'I saw a man glue brass on another with fire',[52] and the like. The 30 corresponding use of strange words results in a barbarism. —A certain admixture, accordingly, of unfamiliar terms is necessary. These, the strange word, the metaphor, the ornamental equivalent, &c., will save the language from seeming mean and prosaic, while the ordinary words in it will secure the requisite clearness. What helps most, however, to **1458ᵇ** render the Diction at once clear and non-prosaic is the use of the lengthened, curtailed, and altered forms of words. Their deviation from the ordinary words will, by making the language unlike that in general use, give it a non-prosaic appearance; and their having much in common with the words in general use will give it the quality of 5 clearness. It is not right, then, to condemn these modes of speech, and ridicule the poet for using them, as some have done; e. g. the elder Euclid, who said it was easy to make poetry if one were to be allowed to lengthen the words in the statement itself as much as one likes—a procedure

[52] Cleobulina.

10 he caricatured by reading Ἐπιχάρην εἶδον Μαραθῶνάδε βαδίζοντα, and οὐκ ἄν γ' ἐράμενος τὸν ἐκείνου ἐλλέβορον as verses. A too apparent use of these licences has certainly a ludicrous effect, but they are not alone in that; the rule of moderation applies to all the constituents of the poetic vocabulary; even with metaphors, strange words, and the rest, the effect will be the same, if one uses them improperly and with a view to provoking laughter. The proper

15 use of them is a very different thing. To realize the difference one should take an epic verse and see how it reads when the normal words are introduced. The same should be done too with the strange word, the metaphor, and the rest; for one has only to put the ordinary words in their place to see the truth of what we are saying. The same iambic, for instance, is found in Aeschylus and Euripides, and as it stands in the former it is a poor line; whereas

20 Euripides, by the change of a single word, the substitution of a strange for what is by usage the ordinary word, has made it seem a fine one. Aeschylus having said in his *Philoctetes*:

φαγέδαινα ἥ μου σάρκας ἐσθίει ποδός

Euripides has merely altered the ἐσθίει here into ϑοινᾶται. Or suppose

25   νῦν δέ μ' ἐὼν ὀλίγος τε καὶ οὐτιδανὸς καὶ ἀεικής [53]

to be altered, by the substitution of the ordinary words, into

νῦν δέ μ' ἐὼν μικρός τε καὶ ἀσθενικὸς καὶ ἀειδής.

Or the line

δίφρον ἀεικέλιον καταθεὶς ὀλίγην τε τράπεζαν [54]

into

30   δίφρον μοχθηρὸν καταθεὶς μικράν τε τράπεζαν.

[53] Od. ix. 515.
[54] Od. xx. 259.

Οι ἠιόνες βοόωσιν [55] into ἠιόνες κράζουσιν. Add to this
that Ariphrades used to ridicule the tragedians for intro-
ducing expressions unknown in the language of common
life, δωμάτων ἄπο (for ἀπὸ δωμάτων), σέθεν, ἐγὼ δέ νιν, [56]
Ἀχιλλέως πέρι (for περὶ Ἀχιλλέως), and the like. The
mere fact of their not being in ordinary speech gives the **1459ᵃ**
Diction a non-prosaic character; but Ariphrades was unaware of that. It is a great thing, indeed, to make a proper
use of these poetical forms, as also of compounds and
strange words. But the greatest thing by far is to be a master
of metaphor. It is the one thing that cannot be learnt from 5
others; and it is also a sign of genius, since a good metaphor implies an intuitive perception of the similarity in
dissimilars.

Of the kinds of words we have enumerated it may be observed that compounds are most in place in the dithyramb,
strange words in heroic, and metaphors in iambic poetry. 10
Heroic poetry, indeed, may avail itself of them all. But in
iambic verse, which models itself as far as possible on the
spoken language, only those kinds of words are in place
which are allowable also in an oration, i. e. the ordinary
word, the metaphor, and the ornamental equivalent.

Let this, then, suffice as an account of Tragedy, the art 15
imitating by means of action on the stage.

23 As for the poetry which merely narrates, or imitates
by means of versified language (without action), it is
evident that it has several points in common with Tragedy.

I. The construction of its stories should clearly be like
that in a drama; they should be based on a single action,
one that is a complete whole in itself, with a beginning,
middle, and end, so as to enable the work to produce its 20
own proper pleasure with all the organic unity of a living
creature. Nor should one suppose that there is anything
like them in our usual histories. A history has to deal not

[55] *Il.* xvii. 265.
[56] Soph., *O. C.*, 986

with one action, but with one period and all that happened in that to one or more persons, however discon-
25 nected the several events may have been. Just as two events may take place at the same time, e. g. the sea-fight off Salamis and the battle with the Carthaginians in Sicily, without converging to the same end, so too of two consecutive events one may sometimes come after the other with no one end as their common issue. Nevertheless most of our epic poets, one may say, ignore the distinction.

30   Herein, then, to repeat what we have said before,[57] we have a further proof of Homer's marvellous superiority to the rest. He did not attempt to deal even with the Trojan war in its entirety, though it was a whole with a definite beginning and end—through a feeling apparently that it
35 was too long a story to be taken in in one view, or if not that, too complicated from the variety of incident in it. As it is, he has singled out one section of the whole; many of the other incidents, however, he brings in as episodes, using the Catalogue of the Ships, for instance, and other episodes to relieve the uniformity of his narrative. As for the other epic poets, they treat of one man, or one period;
1459ᵇ or else of an action which, although one, has a multiplicity of parts in it. This last is what the authors of the Cypria [58] and Little Iliad [58] have done. And the result is that, whereas the Iliad or Odyssey supplies materials for only one, or at most two tragedies, the Cypria does that for several and the Little Iliad for more than eight: for an
5 Adjudgment of Arms, a Philoctetes, a Neoptolemus, a Eurypylus, a Ulysses as Beggar, a Laconian Women, a Fall of Ilium, and a Departure of the Fleet; as also a Sinon, and a Women of Troy.

24   II. Besides this, Epic poetry must divide into the same species as Tragedy; it must be either simple or complex, a story of character or one of suffering. Its parts, too, with the exception of Song and Spectacle, must be the same, as it requires Peripeties, Discoveries, and scenes of suffering just like Tragedy. Lastly, the Thought and Diction in it must be good in their way. All these elements appear in Homer first; and he has made due use of them. His two poems are each examples of construction, the *Iliad* simple and a story of suffering, the *Odyssey* complex (there is Discovery throughout it) and a story of character. And they are more than this, since in Diction and Thought too they surpass all other poems.

There is, however, a difference in the Epic as compared with Tragedy, (1) in its length, and (2) in its metre. (1) As to its length, the limit already suggested [59] will suffice: it must be possible for the beginning and end of the work to be taken in in one view—a condition which will be fulfilled if the poem be shorter than the old epics, and about as long as the series of tragedies offered for one hearing. For the extension of its length epic poetry has a special advantage, of which it makes large use. In a play one cannot represent an action with a number of parts going on simultaneously; one is limited to the part on the stage and connected with the actors. Whereas in epic poetry the narrative form makes it possible for one to describe a number of simultaneous incidents; and these, if germane to the subject, increase the body of the poem. This then is a gain to the Epic, tending to give it grandeur, and also variety of interest and room for episodes of diverse kinds. Uniformity of incident by the satiety it soon creates is apt to ruin tragedies on the stage. (2) As for its metre, the heroic has been assigned it from experience; were any one to attempt a narrative poem in some one, or in several, of the other metres, the incongruity of the thing would be apparent. The heroic in fact is the gravest and weightiest of metres —which is what makes it more tolerant than the rest of strange words and metaphors, that also being a point in which the narrative form of poetry goes beyond all others.

[59] 1451[a] 3.

The iambic and trochaic, on the other hand, are metres of
1460ª movement, the one representing that of life and action,
the other that of the dance. Still more unnatural would it
appear, if one were to write an epic in a medley of metres,
as Chaeremon did.[60] Hence it is that no one has ever
written a long story in any but heroic verse; nature herself,
as we have said,[61] teaches us to select the metre appropriate
to such a story.

5   Homer, admirable as he is in every other respect, is
especially so in this, that he alone among epic poets is not
unaware of the part to be played by the poet himself in
the poem. The poet should say very little *in propria per-
sona*, as he is no imitator when doing that. Whereas the
other poets are perpetually coming forward in person, and
say but little, and that only here and there, as imitators,
10 Homer after a brief preface brings in forthwith a man, a
a woman, or some other Character—no one of them
characterless, but each with distinctive characteristics.

The marvellous is certainly required in Tragedy. The
Epic, however, affords more opening for the improbable,
the chief factor in the marvellous, because in it the agents
15 are not visibly before one. The scene of the pursuit of
Hector would be ridiculous on the stage—the Greeks
halting instead of pursuing him, and Achilles shaking his
head to stop them;[62] but in the poem the absurdity is
overlooked. The marvellous, however, is a cause of pleasure,
as is shown by the fact that we all tell a story with additions,
in the belief that we are doing our hearers a pleasure.

Homer more than any other has taught the rest of us
20 the art of framing lies in the right way. I mean the use of
paralogism. Whenever, if A is or happens, a consequent,
B, is or happens, men's notion is that, if the B is, the A
also is—but that is a false conclusion. Accordingly, if A is
untrue, but there is something else, B, that on the assump-

[60] *Centaur*, cf. 1447ᵇ 21.
[61] 1449ª 24.
[62] *Il.* xxii. 205.

tion of its truth follows as its consequent, the right thing
then is to add on the B. Just because we know the truth
of the consequent, we are in our own minds led on to the
erroneous inference of the truth of the antecedent. Here is 25
an instance, from the Bath-story in the Odyssey.[63]

A likely impossibility is always preferable to an unconvincing possibility. The story should never be made up of
improbable incidents; there should be nothing of the sort
in it. If, however, such incidents are unavoidable, they
should be outside the piece, like the hero's ignorance in 30
Oedipus of the circumstances of Laius' death; not within it,
like the report of the Pythian games in Electra,[64] or the
man's having come to Mysia from Tegea without uttering
a word on the way, in The Mysians.[65] So that it is ridiculous to say that one's Plot would have been spoilt without them, since it is fundamentally wrong to make up such
Plots. If the poet has taken such a Plot, however, and one
sees that he might have put it in a more probable form,
he is guilty of absurdity as well as a fault of art. Even in 35
the Odyssey the improbabilities in the setting-ashore of
Ulysses [66] would be clearly intolerable in the hands of an
inferior poet. As it is, the poet conceals them, his other 1460
excellences veiling their absurdity. Elaborate Diction, however, is required only in places where there is no action, and
no Character or Thought to be revealed. Where there is
Character or Thought, on the other hand, an over-ornate 5
Diction tends to obscure them.

25 As regards Problems and their Solutions, one may see
the number and nature of the assumptions on which
they proceed by viewing the matter in the following way.
(1) The poet being an imitator just like the painter or
other maker of likenesses, he must necessarily in all instances represent things in one or other of three aspects,

---

[63] xix. 164–260.
[64] Soph. El. 660 ff.
[65] Probably by Aeschylus.
[66] xiii. 116 ff.

10 either as they were or are, or as they are said or thought to
be or to have been, or as they ought to be. (2) All this he
does in language, with an admixture, it may be, of strange
words and metaphors, as also of the various modified forms
of words, since the use of these is conceded in poetry.
(3) It is to be remembered, too, that there is not the same
kind of correctness in poetry as in politics, or indeed any
other art. There is, however, within the limits of poetry
15 itself a possibility of two kinds of error, the one directly,
the other only accidentally connected with the art. If the
poet meant to describe the thing correctly, and failed
through lack of power of expression, his art itself is at
fault. But if it was through his having meant to describe it
in some incorrect way (e. g. to make the horse in movement have both right legs thrown forward) that the
technical error (one in a matter of, say, medicine or some
20 other special science), or impossibilities of whatever kind
they may be, have got into his description, his error in that
case is not in the essentials of the poetic art. These, therefore, must be the premises of the Solutions in answer to
the criticisms involved in the Problems.

I. As to the criticisms relating to the poet's art itself. Any
impossibilities there may be in his descriptions of things
are faults. But from another point of view they are justi-
25 fiable, if they serve the end of poetry itself—if (to assume
what we have said of that end) [67] they make the effect of
either that very portion of the work or some other portion
more astounding. The Pursuit of Hector is an instance in
point. If, however, the poetic end might have been as well
or better attained without sacrifice of technical correctness
in such matters, the impossibility is not to be justified,
since the description should be, if it can, entirely free from
30 error. One may ask, too, whether the error is in a matter
directly or only accidentally connected with the poetic
art; since it is a lesser error in an artist not to know, for

[67] 1452ᵃ 4, 1454ᵃ 4, 1455ᵃ 17, 1460ᵃ 11.

instance, that the hind has no horns, than to produce an
unrecognizable picture of one.

II. If the poet's description be criticized as not true to
fact, one may urge perhaps that the object ought to be as
described—an answer like that of Sophocles, who said that
he drew men as they ought to be, and Euripides as they 35
were. If the description, however, be neither true nor of
the thing as it ought to be, the answer must be then, that it
is in accordance with opinion. The tales about Gods, for
instance, may be as wrong as Xenophanes thinks, neither
true nor the better thing to say; but they are certainly in
accordance with opinion. Of other statements in poetry 1461ᵃ
one may perhaps say, not that they are better than the
truth, but that the fact was so at the time; e. g. the description of the arms: 'their spears stood upright, butt-end upon
the ground'; ⁶⁸ for that was the usual way of fixing them
then, as it is still with the Illyrians. As for the question
whether something said or done in a poem is morally right
or not, in dealing with that one should consider not only 5
the intrinsic quality of the actual word or deed, but also
the person who says or does it, the person to whom he
says or does it, the time, the means, and the motive of
the agent—whether he does it to attain a greater good, or
to avoid a greater evil.

III. Other criticisms one must meet by considering a
language of the poet: (1) by the assumption of a strange 10
word in a passage like οὐρῆας μὲν πρῶτον,⁶⁹ where by
οὐρῆας Homer may perhaps mean not mules but sentinels.
And in saying of Dolon, ὅς ῥ' ἦ τοι εἶδος μὲν ἔην κακός,⁷⁰
his meaning may perhaps be, not that Dolon's body was de-
formed, but that his face was ugly, as εὐειδής is the Cretan
word for handsome-faced. So, too, ζωρότερον δὲ κέραιε⁷¹ 15

---

⁶⁸ Il. x. 152.
⁶⁹ Il. i. 50.
⁷⁰ Il. x. 316.
⁷¹ Il. ix. 202.

may mean not 'mix the wine stronger', as though for topers, but 'mix it quicker', (2) Other expressions in Homer may be explained as metaphorical; e. g. in ἄλλοι μέν ῥα θεοί τε καὶ ἀνέρες εὗδον <ἅπαντες> παννύχιοι,[72] as compared with what he tells us at the same time, ἦ τοι ὅτ' ἐς πεδίον τὸ Τρωικὸν ἀθρήσειεν, αὐλῶν συρίγγων †τε ὁμαδόν†,[73] the word ἅπαντες, 'all', is metaphorically put for 'many', since 'all' is a species of 'many'. So also his οἴη δ' ἄμμορος[74] is meta-
20 phorical, the best known standing 'alone'. (3) A change, : as Hippias of Thasos suggested, in the mode of reading a word will solve the difficulty in δίδομεν δέ οἱ,[75] and in τὸ μὲν οὗ καταπύθεται ὄμβρῳ[76] (4) Other difficulties may be solved by another punctuation; e. g. in Empedocles, αἶψα δὲ θνήτ'
25 ἐφύοντο, τὰ πρὶν μάθον ἀθάνατα ζωρά τε πρὶν κέκρητο. Or (5) by the assumption of an equivocal term, as in παρῴχηκεν δὲ πλέω νύξ,[77] where πλέω is equivocal. Or (6) by an appeal to the custom of language. Wine-and-water we call 'wine'; and it is on the same principle that Homer speaks of a κνημὶς νεοτεύκτου κασσιτέροιο[78] a 'greave of new-wrought tin'. A worker in iron we call a 'brazier'; and it is on the same principle that Ganymede is described as the 'wine-server' of Zeus,[79] though the Gods do not drink
30 wine. This latter, however, may be an instance of meta-phor. But whenever also a word seems to imply some con-tradiction, it is necessary to reflect how many ways there may be of understanding it in the passage in question, e. g. in Homer's τῇ ῥ' ἔσχετο χάλκεον ἔγχος[80] one should consider the possible senses of 'was stopped there'—whether by taking it in this sense or in that one will best

[72] Cf. Il. x. 1, ii. 1.
[73] Il. x. 11–13.
[74] Il. xviii. 489 = Od. v. 275.
[75] Cf. Soph. El. 166ᵇ 1; Il. ii. 15.
[76] Il. xxiii. 327.
[77] Il. x. 251.
[78] Il. xxi. 592.
[79] Il. xx. 234.
[80] Il. xx. 267.

avoid the fault of which Glaucon speaks: 'They start with 35
some improbable presumption; and having so decreed it 1461]
themselves, proceed to draw inferences, and censure the
poet as though he had actually said whatever they happen
to believe, if his statement conflicts with their own notion
of things.' This is how Homer's silence about Icarius has
been treated. Starting with the notion of his having been a
Lacedaemonian, the critics think it strange for Telemachus
not to have met him when he went to Lacedaemon. 5
Whereas the fact may have been as the Cephallenians say,
that the wife of Ulysses was of a Cephallenian family, and
that her father's name was Icadius, not Icarius. So that it
is probably a mistake of the critics that has given rise to the
Problem.

Speaking generally, one has to justify (1) the Impossible
by reference to the requirements of poetry, or to the better,
or to opinion. For the purposes of poetry a convincing im- 10
possibility is preferable to an unconvincing possibility; and
if men such as Zeuxis depicted be impossible, the answer
is that it is better they should be like that, as the artist
ought to improve on his model. (2) The Improbable one
has to justify either by showing it to be in accordance with
opinion, or by urging that at times it is not improbable; for
there is a probability of things happening also against 15
probability. (3) The contradictions found in the poet's
language one should first test as one does an opponent's
confutation in a dialectical argument, so as to see whether
he means the same thing, in the same relation, and in the
same sense, before admitting that he has contradicted
either something he has said himself or what a man of
sound sense assumes as true. But there is no possible apol-
ogy for improbability of Plot or depravity of character,
when they are not necessary and no use is made of them, 20
like the improbability in the appearance of Aegeus in
Medea [81] and the baseness of Menelaus in Orestes.

The objections, then, of critics start with faults of five

[81] l. 663.

objections others

kinds: the allegation is always that something is either (1)
impossible, (2) improbable, (3) corrupting, (4) contradictory, or (5) against technical correctness. The answers
25 to these objections must be sought under one or other of
the above-mentioned heads, which are twelve in number.

26 The question may be raised whether the epic or the
tragic is the higher form of imitation. It may be argued that, if the less vulgar is the higher, and the less
vulgar is always that which addresses the better public, an
art addressing any and every one is of a very vulgar order.
It is a belief that their public cannot see the meaning, un-
30 less they add something themselves, that causes the perpetual movements of the performers—bad flute-players,
for instance, rolling about, if quoit-throwing is to be represented, and pulling at the conductor, if Scylla is the subject
of the piece. Tragedy, then, is said to be an art of this order
—to be in fact just what the later actors were in the eyes of
their predecessors; for Mynniscus used to call Callippides
35 'the ape', because he thought he so overacted his parts;
1462ª and a similar view was taken of Pindarus also. All Tragedy,
however, is said to stand to the Epic as the newer to the
older school of actors. The one, accordingly, is said to address a cultivated audience, which does not need the ac-
companiment of gesture; the other, an uncultivated one.
5 If, therefore, Tragedy is a vulgar art, it must clearly be lower
than the Epic.

The answer to this is twofold. In the first place, one may
urge (1) that the censure does not touch the art of the
dramatic poet, but only that of his interpreter; for it is
quite possible to overdo the gesturing even in an epic
recital, as did Sosistratus, and in a singing contest, as
did Mnasitheus of Opus. (2) That one should not condemn all movement, unless one means to condemn even
the dance, but only that of ignoble people—which is the
point of the criticism passed on Callippides and in the
10 present day on others, that their women are not like
gentlewomen. (3) That Tragedy may produce its effect

even without movement or action in just the same way as Epic poetry; for from the mere reading of a play its quality may be seen. So that, if it be superior in all other respects, this element of inferiority is no necessary part of it.

In the second place, one must remember (1) that Tragedy has everything that the Epic has (even the epic metre being admissible), together with a not inconsiderable addition in the shape of the Music (a very real factor in the pleasure of the drama) and the Spectacle. (2) That its reality of presentation is felt in the play as read, as well as in the play as acted. (3) That the tragic imitation requires less space for the attainment of its end; which is a great advantage, since the more concentrated effect is more pleasurable than one with a large admixture of time to dilute it—consider the *Oedipus* of Sophocles, for instance, and the effect of expanding it into the number of lines of the *Iliad*. (4) That there is less unity in the imitation of the epic poets, as is proved by the fact that any one work of theirs supplies matter for several tragedies; the result being that, if they take what is really a single story, it seems curt when briefly told, and thin and waterish when on the scale of length usual with their verse. In saying that there is less unity in an epic, I mean an epic made up of a plurality of actions, in the same way as the *Iliad* and *Odyssey* have many such parts, each one of them in itself of some magnitude; yet the structure of the two Homeric poems is as perfect as can be, and the action in them is as nearly as possible one action. If, then, Tragedy is superior in these respects, and also, besides these, in its poetic effect (since the two forms of poetry should give us, not any or every pleasure, but the very special kind we have mentioned), it is clear that, as attaining the poetic effect better than the Epic, it will be the higher form of art.

So much for Tragedy and Epic poetry—for these two arts in general and their species; the number and nature of their constituent parts; the causes of success and failure in them; the Objections of the critics, and the Solutions in answer to them.

The Best of the World's Best Books
COMPLETE LIST OF TITLES IN
THE MODERN LIBRARY

MISCELLANEOUS